The
Princeton
Review®

GRE®

PREP

2021

The Staff of The Princeton Review

PrincetonReview.com

Penguin
Random
House

The Princeton Review
110 East 42nd St, 7th Floor
New York, NY 10017
E-mail: editorialsupport@review.com

Published in the United States by Penguin Random House LLC, New York,
and in Canada by Random House of Canada, a division of Penguin
Random House Ltd., Toronto.

Terms of Service: The Princeton Review Online Companion Tools
("Student Tools") for retail books are available for only the two most
recent editions of that book. Student Tools may be activated only twice
per eligible book purchased for two consecutive 12-month periods, for a
total of 24 months of access. Activation of Student Tools more than
twice per book is in direct violation of these Terms of Service and may
result in discontinuation of access to Student Tools Services.

ISBN: 978-0-525-56938-1
eBook ISBN: 978-0-525-56977-0
ISSN: 2688-0946

The $100 discount is valid only on new enrollments in The Princeton
Review's self-paced GRE course between May 19, 2020 and May 19, 2021.
Discount cannot be combined with any other offer (except referral
program) and is available to U.S., Puerto Rico, and Canada customers
only. For specific information on the course, visit Princetonreview.com/
grad/gre-selfguided-course.

GRE is a registered trademark of the Educational Testing
Service (ETS). This product is not endorsed or approved by ETS.

The Princeton Review is not affiliated with Princeton University.

The material in this book is up-to-date at the time of publication.
However, changes may have been instituted by the testing body in
the test after this book was published.

If there are any important late-breaking developments, changes, or
corrections to the materials in this book, we will post that information
online in the Student Tools. Register your book and check your Student
Tools to see if there are any updates posted there.

Editor: Selena Coppock
Prodution Editors: Emily Epstein White, Jim Melloan
Production Artist: Gabriel Berlin

Printed in the United States of America.

10 9 8 7 6 5 4 3 2 1

2021 Edition

Editorial
Rob Franek, Editor-in-Chief
David Soto, Director of Content Development
Stephen Koch, Student Survey Manager
Deborah Weber, Director of Production
Gabriel Berlin, Production Design Manager
Selena Coppock, Managing Editor
Aaron Riccio, Senior Editor
Meave Shelton, Senior Editor
Chris Chimera, Editor
Eleanor Green, Editor
Orion McBean, Editor
Brian Saladino, Editor
Patricia Murphy, Editorial Assistant

Penguin Random House Publishing Team
Tom Russell, VP, Publisher
Alison Stoltzfus, Publishing Director
Amanda Yee, Associate Managing Editor
Ellen Reed, Production Manager
Suzanne Lee, Designer

Acknowledgments

The following people deserve thanks for their help with this book:

Many thanks to John Fulmer, National Content Director for the GRE, Kyle Fox, Chris Benson, Brian Hong, Jim Havens, and Doug Scripture for their contributions to the 2021 edition of this title. Much appreciation as well to the stellar production team of Garbriel Berlin, Jim Melloan, and Emily Epstein White.

The Princeton Review would also like to give a special thank-you to Jim Havens for his dedication and leadership in coordinating this project, as well as the following top-notch contributors: Doug Scripture, Marty Cinke, Kevin Kelly, Sara Kuperstein, and Derek Smith.

Special thanks to Adam Robinson, who conceived of and perfected the Joe Bloggs approach to standardized tests, and many of the other successful techniques used by The Princeton Review.

Contents

(Free) Content

at **PrincetonReview.com/prep**

As easy as 1·2·3

1 Go to PrincetonReview.com/prep and enter the following ISBN for your book:
9780525569381

2 Answer a few simple questions to set up an exclusive Princeton Review account. *(If you already have one, you can just log in.)*

3 Enjoy access to your **FREE** content!

Once you've registered, you can...

- Take 2 full-length practice GRE exams

- Access crucial information and advice about the GRE, graduate schools, and the graduate school application process

- Get a code for $100 off The Princeton Review's self-paced GRE course (restrictions may apply)

- Check to see if there have been any corrections or updates to this edition

Need to report a potential **content** issue?

Contact **EditorialSupport@review.com** and include:

- full title of the book
- ISBN
- page number

Need to report a **technical** issue?

Contact **TPRStudentTech@review.com** and provide:

- your full name
- email address used to register the book
- full book title and ISBN
- Operating system (Mac/PC) and browser (Firefox, Safari, etc.)

Look For These Icons Throughout The Book

 PROVEN TECHNIQUES

 APPLIED STRATEGIES

 WATCH OUT

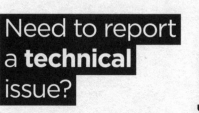 ANOTHER APPROACH

 GOING DEEPER

Chapter 1
Introduction

What is the GRE? Who makes the test? What's a good score? The answer to these questions and many others lie within this chapter. In the next few pages, we'll give you the lowdown on the things you need to know about the GRE.

CRACKING THE GRE

For a lot of people, taking a standardized test such as the GRE usually engenders a number of emotions—none of them positive. But here's the good news: The Princeton Review is going to make this whole ordeal a lot easier for you. We'll give you the information you will need to do well on the GRE, including our time-tested strategies and techniques.

Strategies Galore
In this book, you'll find The Princeton Review's trusted test-taking strategies to help you crack the GRE.

The GRE supposedly allows graduate schools to get a better sense of an applicant's ability to work in a post-graduate setting—a goal that is unrealistic indeed, considering that the people who take the GRE are applying to programs as diverse as physics and anthropology.

However, it's safe to say that the GRE is not a realistic measure of how well you'll do in grad school, or even how intelligent you are. In fact, the GRE provides a valid assessment of only one thing:

> The GRE assesses how well you take the GRE.

Got it? Even so, you still want to do well on the GRE, because you want grad schools to take you seriously when they consider your application. With this in mind, you should cultivate several very important skills when you're preparing for the test; each of them is attainable with the right guidance (which we'll give you), a strong work ethic (which you must provide), and a healthy dose of optimism. Who knows? Maybe after working through this book and learning how to crack the test, you'll actually look forward to taking the GRE.

So what exactly *is* this test you've heard so much about?

Fun fact: It's possible your GRE score could come in handy if you are interested in law school. Check a school's admissions page for more info, as some schools are (or are considering) accepting GRE scores in lieu of LSAT scores. Your grad school options may have opened up even further!

WHAT IS THE GRE?

The Graduate Record Examination (GRE) is a 3-hour, 45-minute exam that's used to rank applicants for graduate schools. The scored portion of the GRE consists of the following sections:

- One 30-minute Analysis of an Issue essay
- One 30-minute Analysis of an Argument essay
- Two 30-minute Verbal Reasoning sections
- Two 35-minute Quantitative Reasoning sections

The Verbal Reasoning sections test your skills on three different types of questions:

- Text Completion
- Sentence Equivalence
- Reading Comprehension

The Quantitative Reasoning sections measure your prowess in four areas:

- Arithmetic and Number Properties
- Algebra
- Geometry
- Data Analysis

WHY DO SCHOOLS REQUIRE IT?

Even though you will pay ETS $205 to take the GRE, it is important to note that you are not their primary customer. Their primary customers are the admissions offices at graduate programs across the United States. ETS provides admissions professionals with two important services. The first is a number, your GRE score. Everyone who takes the test gets a number. It is difficult for admissions committees to make a decision between a candidate with a 3.0 and a 3.2 GPA from drastically different schools and in two different majors. A GRE score, on the other hand, provides a quick and easy way for busy admissions offices to whittle a large applicant pool down to size.

Applicants could come from all over the world and will certainly have an enormous range in academic and professional experience. How does one compare a senior in college with a 32-year-old professional who has been out of college working in a different industry for the past 10 years? A GRE score is the only part of the application that allows for an apples-to-apples comparison among all applicants.

A few countries outside of the United States, such as Australia and China, charge slightly more than $205 for the administration of the GRE. You can find the most recent pricing at www.ets.org/gre/revised_general/about/fees.

The second service that ETS provides is mailing lists. That's right; they will sell your name. You can opt out, but when you sit down to take the test, ETS will ask you a whole bunch of questions about your educational experience, family background, race, and gender, as well as other biographical data. All of this information goes into their database. In fact, ETS is one of the most important sources of potential applicants that many graduate programs have.

Another reason schools require the GRE is that it ensures that most graduate school applicants are qualified. It helps to weed out the people who might be considering grad school, but who can't get their act together enough to fill out applications. When you ask a program how important the GRE score is to the application, they may say, "it depends" or "not very" and that may be true as long as your score is in the top half. If your score is in the bottom half, however, it may mean that your application never gets seen.

So the GRE may have little relevance to any particular field of study you might be pursuing, but as long as it helps graduate programs uncover potential candidates, and as long as it is the only tool available to compare a diverse candidate pool, the GRE is here to stay.

WHO IS ETS?

Like most standardized tests in this country, the GRE is created and administered by Educational Testing Service (ETS), a private company located in New Jersey. ETS publishes the GRE under the sponsorship of the Graduate Record Examinations Board, which is an organization affiliated with the Association of Graduate Schools and the Council of Graduate Schools in the United States.

ETS is also the organization that brings you the SAT, the Test of English as a Foreign Language (TOEFL), the Praxis, and licensing and certification exams in dozens of fields, including hair styling, plumbing, and golf.

TEST DAY

What to Take to the Test Center:
1. Your registration ticket
2. A photo ID and one other form of ID
3. A snack

The GRE is administered at Prometric testing centers. This company specializes in administering tests on computer. They administer citizenship exams, professional health certifications, dental exams, accounting exams, and hundreds of other exams on computer. When you arrive at the center, they will check your ID, give you a clipboard with a form to fill out, and hand you a locker key. Despite the fact that they already have your information, you will be asked to fill out a long form on paper. This form includes an entire paragraph that you have to copy over—in cursive (they specify this)—that states that you are who you say you are and that you are taking the test for admissions purposes. This process will take you about 10 minutes, and you can complete it while you wait for them to call you into the testing room. The locker is for all of your personal belongings, including books, bags, phones, bulky sweaters, and even watches. You are not allowed to take anything with you into the testing room.

When they call you into the testing room, they will first take a photo of you and, in some cases, fingerprint you before you go in. They will give you six sheets of scratch paper, stapled together to form a booklet, and two sharpened pencils with erasers. Then they lead you into the room where someone will start your test for you. The room itself will hold three or four rows of standard corporate cubicles, each with a monitor and keyboard. There will be other people in the room taking tests other than the GRE. Because people will be entering and exiting the room at different times, you will be provided with optional headphones.

Test Day Tips

- Dress in layers, so that you'll be comfortable regardless of whether the room is cool or warm.
- Don't bother to take a calculator; you're not allowed to use your own—just the one on the screen.
- Be sure to have breakfast, or lunch, depending on when your test is scheduled (but don't eat anything weird). Take it easy on the liquids and the caffeine.
- Do a few GRE practice problems beforehand to warm up your brain. Don't try to tackle difficult new questions, but go through a few questions that you've done before to help you review the problem-solving strategies for each section of the GRE. This will also help you put on your "game face" and get you into test mode.

- Make sure to take photo identification to the test center. Acceptable forms of identification include your driver's license, photo-bearing employee ID cards, and valid passports.
- If you registered by mail, you must also take the authorization voucher sent to you by ETS.
- Stretch, drink some water, go to the bathroom, and do whatever you need to do in order to be prepared to sit for this four-hour test.

TEST STRUCTURE

While your test structure may vary, you should expect to see something like this when you sit down to take the exam:

The first section of the test collects all of your biographical information. If you fill this out, you will start getting mail from programs that have bought your name from ETS. In general, this is not a bad thing. If you don't want them to sell your name, or you don't want to spend the time answering their questions, you can click on a box that tells ETS not to share your information.

Once all of that is done, you will begin your first scored section, the essays. The two essays will be back to back. You have 30 minutes for each essay. Immediately after your second essay, you will get your first multiple-choice section. It may be math or verbal. You will have a 1-minute break between sections. Here is the structure of the test:

More Online
For tons of information about the GRE, check out PrincetonReview.com/grad/gre-information

Section	Time	# of Questions
Biographical Information	+/– 10 minutes	–
Issue Essay	30 minutes	1
Argument Essay	30 minutes	1
Section 1	30 or 35 minutes	20
Section 2	30 or 35 minutes	20
Break	10 minutes	–
Section 3	30 or 35 minutes	20
Section 4	30 or 35 minutes	20
Section 5	30 or 35 minutes	20
Possible Research Section	Optional	Depends
Select Schools/Programs	5 minutes	Up to 4
Accept Scores	1 minute	–
Receive Scores	1 minute	–

Here are some things to keep in mind:

A Note on the Paper-Based GRE

The computer-delivered GRE is the standard format for test takers. The paper-based GRE is far more rare and offered up to only three times a year. But if you want to learn more about the paper-and-pencil test, visit ETS.org.

- You will see five multiple-choice sections, but only four will count. The fifth will either be mixed in with the other sections as an unidentified "experimental" section or as a final, identified "research" section.
- Math sections are 35 minutes. There are 20 math questions in each section. If your experimental section is math, your test will be five minutes longer than someone whose experimental section is verbal.
- Verbal sections are 30 minutes. There are 20 verbal questions in each section.
- For the computer-delivered test, the optional 10-minute break comes after the second multiple-choice section. For the paper-based test, the 10-minute break comes after the second Analytical Writing section.
- You may or may not get a research section. If you do, it will come last; it does not count toward your score, and it is optional.
- You must accept your scores and, if you choose, send your scores to selected programs prior to seeing your scores.
- If you choose not to accept your scores, neither you nor any program will ever see them.
- You may choose to send your scores to up to four graduate programs on the day of the test. This service is included in your testing fee.

The Experimental Section

ETS administers the experimental section to gather data on questions before they appear on real GREs. Because there are only two scored math sections and two scored verbal sections, you'll know by that last section whether the experimental section is math or verbal. However, you will have no way of knowing in advance which multiple-choice section is experimental, so you need to do your best on all of them. Don't waste time worrying about which sections count and which section does not.

Research Section

Instead of an experimental section, you may find that the last section of your test is marked as an unscored research section. This section is used only to help develop and test questions for the GRE and you have the option to skip it if you want. You may be offered some sort of prize to induce you to take it, but by that point in the test you will probably be exhausted. If you're offered a research section, you must choose your own ending: decline, get your scores, and go home, or forge ahead with the research section in the name of science, or something.

Practice Like You Play

When tackling practice tests during your test preparation, be sure to mimic the real GRE and give yourself these timed breaks.

The 10-Minute Break

You are given 1 minute between sections except for the second multiple-choice section, when you get a 10-minute break. Go to the bathroom, splash water on your face, wave your arms around. You want to re-oxygenate your brain. The goal, as much as it is possible, is to hit your brain's reset button. When you sit back down for the third multiple-choice section, you want to feel as if you are just sitting down at that computer for the first time that day. Your GRE test day is going to be a long and intense day, so be sure to take full advantage of break time.

Accepting Your Scores

Before you see your scores, you will be given the opportunity to cancel them. There are very few reasons to do so. First, if you cancel your scores, you will never see them and you will have to go through the whole experience again, including paying an additional $205 to take the test again. Second, GRE scores are curved. Most people believe that they are doing worse while taking the test than they actually are. Third, you can make use of the GRE *ScoreSelect*® service.

ScoreSelect®

ScoreSelect® allows you to select which scores get sent to which schools. Options for sending scores depend on whether you are sending scores on the day of your test or after your test day. On test day, you have the following options for sending scores:

- **Most recent.** This option sends the results of the test you just took.
- **All.** This option sends all your scores from the last five years.

If you send your scores to schools after test day, you have even more options. After test day, your options are:

- **Most recent.** This option sends the scores from the test you took most recently.
- **All.** As above, this option sends all your GRE scores from the last five years.
- **Any.** Send just the scores you want to send. You can send one score or multiple scores. For example, if you have taken the GRE three times and your second score is your best, you can send just that score.

When you use *ScoreSelect*® after your test day, the score report that is sent to schools shows only the scores that you choose to send. The report does not indicate how many times you have taken the GRE, nor does it indicate that you have sent, for example, your scores from the second time you took the test and you took the test a total of three times.

ScoreSelect® is another reason to think twice before cancelling your scores. Provided that you send your scores after your test date, your schools will never know that you didn't do as well as you would have liked or even that you took the test more than once if you don't want them to know.

Sending Additional Score Reports

On the day of your test, you can send your scores to up to four schools using the *ScoreSelect*® test day options. These score reports are included as part of the $205 fee that you pay to take the GRE. If you wish to send reports to additional schools, you'll need to request that these additional reports be sent after your test day. Each additional report costs $27. The fastest way to send additional score reports is to order them online using your *My GRE*® account that you create when you register to take the test.

WHAT DOES A GRE SCORE LOOK LIKE?

Every GRE score has two components: a scaled score and a percentile rank. GRE scores fall on a 130–170 point scale. However, your percentile rank is more important than your scaled score. Your percentile rank indicates how your GRE scores compare to those of other test takers. For example, a scaled score of 150 on the GRE translates to roughly the 43rd percentile, meaning that you scored better than 43 out of every 100 test takers—and worse than the other 57 percent of test takers. A score of 152 is about average, while scores of 163 and above are very competitive. Get the latest reported scores and percentiles at PrincetonReview.com and at www.ets.org/gre, the official ETS website for the GRE.

The Verbal Reasoning and Quantitative Reasoning sections are each reported on a scale of 130–170 in 1-point increments. For each section, a raw score is computed; this raw score is the number of questions you answered correctly. Each raw score is then converted to a scaled score through a process known as equating, which accounts for minor variations in difficulty between different test administrations as well as for differences in difficulty that occur as a result of the adaptivity of the test. These scaled scores are what are listed on your score report and lead to the percentile ranks referred to above.

The essays are scored a little differently than the Verbal and Quantitative sections. Each essay receives a scaled score of 0–6, in half-point increments, that is the average of two scores for that essay. The scores of the two essays are then averaged to produce a single score that is reported for the Analytical Writing section. The corresponding percentiles for this section are as follows:

Score	Analytical Writing Percentile
6.0	99
5.5	97
5.0	93
4.5	78
4.0	54
3.5	35
3.0	14
2.5	6
2.0	2
1.5	1
1.0	<1

In other words, a score of 5 on the essay portion of the GRE means you performed better than 93 percent of test takers.

Do Your Research

GRE scores are used in a number of different ways. The first step in figuring out how to prepare for the GRE is figuring out how your scores will be used. The only way to do that is to contact the programs to which you plan to apply. Larger programs may have many of these questions already spelled out on their websites. Smaller programs, on the other hand, may not want to be pinned down to specific answers, and the answers may change from year to year. If you are applying to a smaller program, you will have to dig a bit deeper to get answers to some of these questions. Here are some things you should be asking.

Grad School Info
Our Princeton Review homepage has tons of informational articles about graduate school. Head over to PrincetonReview.com/grad-school-advice and check them out! Also check out the GRE Insider at the end of this book for even more admissions guidance and need-to-know info.

1. **What scores do I need to be accepted?** The answer to this question is always "It depends." The GRE is not the only part of the application, and the quality of the applicant pool varies from year to year. Nevertheless, you need to have a target score so you can figure out how much work you need to put in between now and test day. If the school doesn't have or won't quote you a cutoff score, see if you can at least find out the average scores for last year's incoming class.

2. **Will you look at all parts of my score?** Some programs may care about your math score, but not your verbal score, and vice versa. Many programs don't use the essay scores at all. If a program doesn't care about your math or your essay score, then you know exactly where to put your prep time.

3. **Are scores used for anything else?** If your scores are to be used for placement or for scholarship, it would be good to know that now, while you still have time to prepare.

4. **How important are my scores?** In many ways, the importance of scores is a function of how competitive the program is. The scores may not matter much, but if it is a competitive program, every number will count. You might be confident that a master's program in English literature won't evaluate the GRE the same way as a PhD program in physics. But in a situation where most applicants may have high verbal scores, a strong math score might help you stand out.

5. **What do you do with multiple scores?** Depending upon your first scores, you may have to take the test a second time. It would be good to know, however, the importance of that first score. If a school is going to take the highest score, then you can relax a bit on test one, knowing that you can take it again if you need to.

If you plan your testing schedule well, you can send only your highest scores to the school using *ScoreSelect*®. Remember, however, that you must send your scores after your test day to use the *select any* option for *ScoreSelect*®.

In any case, remember that the GRE is only one part of an application to grad school. Admissions officers also consider many other factors, including:

- undergraduate transcripts (that is, your GPA, relevant courses, and the quality of the school you attended)
- work experience
- any research or work you've done in that academic field
- subject GREs (for certain programs)
- essays (Personal Statements or other essays)
- recommendations
- interviews

The GRE can be a significant part of your graduate school application (which is why you bought this book), but it certainly isn't the only part.

SCHEDULING A TEST

You can schedule a test session for the GRE by calling 800-GRE-CALL or by registering online at www.ets.org/gre. Registering online is the easiest way to register. As part of the registration process, you'll create a MyGRE® account. The account will also allow you to see your scores online and make use of the GRE Diagnostic Service, which will give you some insight into your performance. You can also register through a local testing center (the list of centers is available online). After you get the list of local testing centers from ETS, you can call the one nearest you and set up an appointment. You can also call ETS at 609-771-7670 or email them directly at their website to ask any general questions you have about the GRE.

Computer Testing Facts

- You can take the GRE almost any day—morning or afternoon, weekday or weekend. Appointments are scheduled on a first-come, first-served basis. You may take the test only once every 21 days. In addition, you cannot take the test more than five times in a continuous rolling 12-month period. Make sure to take your test early enough to book a second test date, if needed, before your applications are due.
- There's no real deadline for registering for the test (technically, you can register the day before). But there's a limited number of seats available on any given day and centers do fill up, sometimes weeks in advance. It's a good idea to register in advance, to give yourself at least a couple of weeks of lead time.
- The GRE is technically simple. Selecting an answer and moving to the next question involves three easy steps. All you need to do is point the mouse arrow at the answer and click, then click the "Next" button, and then click the "Answer Confirm" button to confirm your choice.

- Because the test is administered on a computer, it is impossible to write directly on the problems themselves (to underline text, cross out answer choices, and so on). Thus, all of your work must be done on scratch paper. Although the amount of scratch paper you may use is unlimited, requesting additional paper takes time. You should be efficient and organized in how you use it; learning to use your scratch paper effectively is one of the keys to scoring well on the GRE.

- When you've finished taking the test, you will be given the option to accept or cancel your scores. Of course, you have to make this decision before you learn what the scores are. If you choose to cancel your scores, they cannot be reinstated, and you will never learn what they were. No refunds are given for canceled scores, and your GRE report will reflect that you took the test on that day and canceled (though this shouldn't be held against you). If you choose to accept your scores, they cannot be canceled afterward. We suggest that unless you are absolutely certain you did poorly, you accept your score.

- You will receive your Verbal and Math scores the instant you finish the exam (provided that you choose not to cancel your score), but your Analytical Writing scores and "official" percentile scores for all three sections won't get to you until a few weeks later. If you registered for your test online, you'll be able to access your official scores through your *My GRE*® account.

- ETS offers the GRE® Diagnostic Service (grediagnostic.ets.org) as a free option for test takers to have a limited review of their tests. This service allows you to see the number of questions you missed and where they fell on the test, but you cannot review the actual questions. The diagnostic service also claims to let you know the difficulty of the questions you missed, but the scale used—a simple scale of 1 to 5— is not particularly useful.

Accommodated Testing

If you require accommodated testing, please see the Appendix at the end of this book. It contains information on the forms you must fill out and procedures you must follow to apply for accommodated testing. Be sure to start that application process well in advance of when you want to take your test, as it can take many weeks to complete.

HOW TO USE THIS BOOK

This book is chock full of our tried-and-true GRE test-taking techniques, some of which, at first, might seem to go against your gut instincts. In order to take full advantage of our methods, however, you'll have to trust them and use them consistently and faithfully.

Make sure to use the techniques on all of the practice problems you do and to thoroughly review the explanations for all of the questions—even the ones you get right. That way, the techniques will become second nature to you, and you'll have no problem using them on test day.

Trust in the Techniques

One thing that makes The Princeton Review's test prep so unique is our collection of powerful test-taking strategies. Trust them and use them faithfully, and you won't be disappointed!

Practice for Technique

There is a finite amount of GRE material available in the world. Once you have used it all up, that's it. You don't get any more. Many people will work through the books, doing problems, looking for answers. When they get a problem right, they are happy. When they get a problem wrong, they are frustrated, and then they go on to the next problem. The problem with this approach is that you can churn through lots and lots of questions without ever actually getting better at taking the GRE. The techniques you use and the way you solve a problem are what matters. The results just tell you how you did. When you are practicing, always focus on your approach. When you get good at the techniques, your score will take care of itself. If you focus on just the results, you do nothing more than reinforce the way you are taking the test right now.

Additional Resources

In addition to the material in the book, we offer a number of other resources to aid you during your GRE preparation.

With your purchase of this book, you gain access to many helpful tools in your Student Tools, which is the companion website that goes with this book. There you will find two full-length practice GRE exams, plus tons of useful articles, essays, and information. Go to PrincetonReview.com/prep to register. PrincetonReview.com/gre also contains a ton of useful information on graduate programs, financial aid, and everything else related to graduate school.

Real GREs

The practice problems in this book are designed to simulate the questions that appear on the real GRE. Part of your preparation, however, should involve working with real GRE problems. Working with real questions from past GRE exams is the best way to practice our techniques and prepare for the test. However, the only source of real GREs is the publisher of the test, ETS, which so far has refused to let anyone (including us) license actual questions from old tests.

Therefore, we strongly recommend that you obtain *POWERPREP® II* software for the computer-based GRE revised General Test. You can download the *POWERPREP® II* software directly from ETS's website. It contains two full-length adaptive General Tests. In addition, you can download the PDF *Practice Book for the Paper-delivered GRE® General Test.* While the format of the paper-based test is different from the computer-based test, the practice questions contained in the PDF are relevant and useful.

ETS also publishes *The Official Guide to the GRE® General Test.* This book can be found online or at most major book stores. Some of the practice questions in that book, however, are identical to the questions in the PDF, which is a free download.

Whatever you're using, always practice with scratch paper. As you prepare for the GRE, work through every question you do as if the question is being presented on a computer screen. This means not writing anything on the problems themselves. No crossing off answers, no circling, no underlining. Copy everything to scratch paper and do your work there. You shouldn't give yourself a crutch in your preparation that you won't have on the actual test.

About the Practice Tests in This Book

At the end of this book, you'll find two full-length practice tests. Please note that these paper-and-pencil tests do not adapt to your performance like the real GRE. The actual GRE and the online practice tests in your Student Tools are computer-adaptive; that is, the number of questions you answer correctly on your first scored Math or Verbal section determines whether you'll get an easy, medium, or hard second section of that topic later in the test. A paper-and-pencil test, of course, is not adaptive by section. Scoring a paper-based test like the computer-adaptive GRE would require you to stop and score each section during the test in order to determine the difficulty level of your second section. But even this would not truly get you closer to the computer-adaptive test experience, as you would be stopping to calculate scores—which, of course, is not something that happens during the real test. Much like the real exam, you won't know the difficulty level of the practice test questions. But you can still use the paper-and-pencil practice tests in this book as opportunities to practice with the question types and strategies, as well as work on your test-taking stamina.

MAKING A SCHEDULE

The GRE, like other standardized tests, is not a test for which you can cram. While you may have fond memories from your college days of spending the night before the midterm with a pot of coffee and a 500-page economics textbook, that strategy won't be as effective on the GRE. Why? Because, by and large, the GRE is a test of patterns, not of facts. This book does its best to reveal those patterns to you, but without sufficient time to practice and absorb the information in this book, your GRE score is not likely to improve. Thus, you should allow an adequate amount of time to fully prepare for the GRE.

You should allow yourself somewhere between 4 and 12 weeks to prepare for the GRE. Obviously we can't know exactly where you are in terms of your starting score, your target score, and the amount of time you can devote to studying, but in our experience, 4 weeks is about the minimum amount of time you should spend, while 12 weeks is about the maximum. There are a number of reasons for these suggested preparation times. Attempting to prepare in fewer than 4 weeks typically does not allow sufficient time to master the techniques presented in this book. As you'll see, some of our approaches are counterintuitive and take some getting used to. Without adequate practice time, you may not have full confidence in the techniques. Additionally, vocabulary is part of the Verbal section of the GRE, and it's difficult to substantially increase your vocabulary in a short period of time. Finally, as mentioned before, the GRE contains a number of patterns, and the more time you spend studying the test, the better you will be at recognizing these patterns.

On the other hand, spending an inordinate amount of time preparing for the GRE can have its downside as well. The first concern is a purely practical one: there is a finite amount of GRE practice material available. Budgeting six months of preparation time is unproductive because you'll run out of materials in less than half that time. Finally, spreading the material out over a long period of time may result in your forgetting some of the lessons from the beginning of your studies. It's better to work assiduously and consistently over a shorter time period than to dilute your efforts over a long time frame.

STAY UP TO DATE

We at The Princeton Review will continue to learn all about the GRE as it evolves. As you prepare for your GRE, make sure you periodically check both our website at PrincetonReview.com and the GRE website at www.ets.org/gre for the latest updates and information about the test.

Even More GRE Titles!
For extra practice, check out other GRE titles from The Princeton Review.

WANT EVEN MORE PREP?

The Princeton Review offers an assortment of test preparation options: classroom and online courses plus private and small group tutoring. We also have a bunch of other helpful GRE preparation books, including *Math Workout for the GRE, Verbal Workout for the GRE, 1,027 GRE Practice Questions,* and *Crash Course for the GRE.* When it comes to test preparation for the GRE, we've got you covered.

Now that we have that introduction out of the way, let's dive in and talk strategy.

Summary

- The GRE is a 3-hour, 45-minute exam broken down into six sections and used by graduate schools to rank applicants.

- The GRE tests your mathematical, verbal, and writing abilities.

- The importance of your GRE score varies from program to program. Schools also consider your undergraduate record, your personal essays, and your relevant experience.

- GRE tests can be scheduled online at <u>www.ets.org/gre</u>.

Chapter 2
General Strategy

This chapter contains some basic advice to get you into The Princeton Review mindset. You'll learn some core test-taking strategies to help you maximize your score. In addition, you'll see some of the different question formats you will probably encounter on test day.

CRACKING THE SYSTEM

Although ETS claims that the GRE measures "critical thinking, analytical writing, verbal reasoning, and quantitative reasoning skills that have been acquired over a long period of time," that isn't quite true. Again, what the GRE really measures is how well you take the GRE. The first step to bettering your GRE score is realizing that you can improve your score, in many cases substantially, by familiarizing yourself with the test and by practicing the techniques in this book.

Practice Your Way to Perfection
The GRE is not a test of intelligence. With practice, you can conquer the GRE.

I Thought the GRE Was Coach-Proof

ETS would have you believe that its tests are coach-proof, but that is simply untrue. In many ways, taking a standardized test is a skill and, as with any skill, you can become more proficient at it by both practicing and following the advice of a good teacher. Think of your GRE preparation as if you were practicing for a piano recital or a track meet; you wouldn't show up at the concert hall or track field without having put in hours of practice beforehand (at least we hope you wouldn't!). If you want to get a good score on the GRE, you'll have to put in the necessary preparation time.

Why Should I Listen to The Princeton Review?

Quite simply, because we monitor the GRE. Our teaching methods were developed through exhaustive analysis of all of the available GREs and careful research into the methods by which standardized tests are constructed. Our focus is on the basic concepts that will enable you to attack any problem, strip it down to its essential components, and solve it in as little time as possible.

Think like the Test Writers

You might be surprised to learn that the GRE isn't written by distinguished professors, renowned scholars, or graduate school admissions officers. For the most part, it's written by ordinary ETS employees, sometimes with freelance help from local graduate students. You have no reason to be intimidated.

As you become more familiar with the test, you will also develop a sense of "the ETS mentality." This is a predictable kind of thinking that influences nearly every part of nearly every ETS exam. By learning to recognize the ETS mentality, you'll earn points even when you aren't sure why an answer is correct. You'll inevitably do better on the test by learning to think like the people who wrote it.

Cracking the System

"Cracking the system" is our phrase for getting inside the minds of the people who write these tests. This emphasis on earning points rather than pinpointing the correct answer may strike you as somewhat cynical, but it is crucial to doing well on the GRE. After all, the GRE leaves you no room to make explanations or justifications for your responses.

You'll do better on the GRE by putting aside your feelings about real education and surrendering yourself to the strange logic of the standardized test.

COMPUTER-ADAPTIVE TEST

As discussed briefly in Chapter 1, the GRE is a computer-adaptive test, or CAT for short. During the test, you will see two scored Math and Verbal sections, and the difficulty of the second scored section of either subject is determined by your performance on the first scored section. Depending on your performance in the first scored section of a subject, you will receive an easy, medium, or hard second section. Obviously enough, to achieve a high score on the GRE you need to get as many questions correct as you can, which means that the highest scores will result from performing well on the first scored section and the hardest of the second sections. However, the difficulty of an individual question plays no role in determining your score; that is, your score is calculated by your performance on the entirety of the scored sections, not just a handful of the hardest questions on a given section.

GENERAL STRATEGIES

1: Take the Easy Test First

Within a section, each question counts equally toward your score. There will inevitably be questions you are great at and questions you don't like. The beauty of the GRE is that there is no need to bow to Phoenician numerical hegemony; you can answer questions in any order you like. The question you can nail in 25 seconds is worth just as much as the question that will torture you for minutes on end. To maximize your score, leave the questions you don't like for last. If you are going to run out of time anywhere—and unless you are shooting for a 160 or higher, you should be running out of time—make sure that the questions that get chopped off are the ones you didn't want to answer anyway.

This strategy is called Take the Easy Test First. Skip early and skip often. Doing so will result in two passes through an individual section. On the first pass, cherry pick. Answer the questions you like. Get all of those easy points in the bank before time starts running short. You know that the hard questions—or the ones that you don't like—are going to take more time. Also, although you should never rush, everyone starts to feel the pressure of the clock as time starts running low. This is often when mistakes happen. Leave those difficult, time-consuming questions for the end of the test. If you run out of time or make some mistakes at that point, it won't matter because these are questions that you are less likely to get right anyway, so don't sweat these too much. Focus your time where you feel confident you are likely to score points.

 **2. Mark and Move**

On your first pass through the questions, if you see a question you don't like, a question that looks hard, or a question that looks time consuming, you're going to walk on by and leave it for the end. Sometimes, however, a question that looks easy turns out to be more troublesome than you thought. The question may be trickier than it first appeared, or you may have simply misread it, and it seems hard only because you're working with the wrong information. From start to finish, the GRE is nearly a four-hour test. Over four hours your brain is going to get tired. When that happens, misreading a question is virtually inevitable. Once you read a question wrong, however, it is almost impossible to un-read that and see it right. As long as you are still immersed in the question, you could read it 10 times in a row and you will read it the same wrong way each time.

Whether a question is harder than it first appeared, or made harder by the fact that you missed a key phrase or piece of information, the approach you've taken is not working. This is where the Mark button comes in.

Reset your brain by walking away from the problem, but Mark the question before you do. Do two or three other questions, and then return to the marked problem. When you walk away, your brain doesn't just forget the problem, it keeps on processing in the background. The distraction of the other questions helps your brain to consider the question from other angles. When you return to the problem, you may find that the part that gave you so much trouble the first time is now magically clear. If the problem continues to give you trouble, walk away again.

Staying with a problem when you're stuck burns time but yields no points. You might spend two, three, five, or even six minutes on a problem but still be no closer to the answer. Spending five minutes to get one point will not get you enough points on a 30- or 35-minute section. In the five minutes you spend on a problem that you've misread, you could nail three or four easier questions. When you return to the question that gave you trouble, there is a good chance that you will spot your error, and the path to the correct answer will become clear. If it doesn't become clear, walk away again. Any time you encounter resistance on the test, do not keep pushing; bend like a reed and walk away. Use the Mark button to facilitate this key skill. Skip early and often so that you always have questions to distract your brain when you get stuck.

 **3. Use the Review Screen to Navigate**

Within a single section, you can mark an answered or unanswered question and return to it later. In fact you can skip any question you like and return to any question at any time you like. Navigating around a section is easy with the new Review Screen, which looks like this:

Question Number	Status	Marked
1	Not Answered	
2	Not Answered	✔
3	Not Answered	
4	Not Answered	
5	Not Answered	
6	Not Answered	
7	Answered	
8	Answered	
9	Answered	✔
10	Answered	✔
11	Answered	
12	Not Answered	

Simply click on a question and hit the button marked "Go To Question," and you will return directly to that question. This opens up a whole new realm of strategic opportunities for the savvy test taker.

4. There's No Penalty for Guessing

You should take the easy test first and you should spend most of your time on questions that you know how to answer, or are reasonably certain you can answer.

When you return for your second pass, you will be able to answer some of the questions that you marked during your first pass. A fresh set of eyes on a problem you've already seen is sometimes all it takes for a solution to present itself. But there may also be some questions that you do not know how to answer no matter how many times you look at them.

When you confront a question like this, try to eliminate any answer choice you can, but make sure to guess. There is no penalty for incorrect answers on the GRE. As a result, it's better to guess than it is to leave a question blank. At least by guessing, you stand a chance at getting lucky and guessing correctly.

5. Use Process of Elimination

Because there are many more wrong answers on the GRE than there are credited answers, on some of the more difficult questions (those you do on your second pass) you'll actually be better served not by trying to find the *correct* answer, but instead by finding the wrong answers and using POE, Process of Elimination.

ETS Doesn't Care How You Get the Correct Answer

Remember when you were in high school, and even if you got a question wrong on a test, your teacher gave you partial credit? For example, maybe you used the right formula on a math question, but miscalculated and got the wrong result, so your teacher gave you some credit because you understood the concept.

Well, those days are over. There is no partial credit on the GRE. On the other hand, ETS doesn't know or care how you get the right answer. A lucky guess is worth just as many points as a question that you solve completely and correctly.

There is one thing for which we must thank ETS. They have actually given us the answers! For most problems, there are five answer choices, and one of them is correct. It is important to remember that the answer choices are part of the problem. Many of them will be clearly wrong and can, therefore, be eliminated. In fact, sometimes it is easier to identify the wrong answers and eliminate them than it is to find the right ones, as we discussed on the previous page. As you know, this approach is called Process of Elimination, or POE.

POE will be crucial on the verbal side of the test. Vocabulary-based questions will include plenty of words you don't know. For such questions, you may not be able to identify the correct answer, but you will certainly be able to identify some wrong ones. Get rid of the wrong ones so that when you guess, you have a fifty-fifty shot and not a 20 percent chance. The same holds true for the reading comp questions, which will include plenty of answer choices that are clearly wrong.

On the math side of the test, ETS loves to sucker you into doing more math than is really necessary. You can often eliminate answer choices that are clearly too large or too small. Sometimes it is even more efficient to eliminate wrong answers than it is to do the math required to come up with the right one. We will discuss POE and its close cousin, Ballparking, in Part III.

The Importance of Distractors

On questions you find difficult, you should be able to improve your score on the GRE by using POE. Why? Because, once you've eliminated the wrong answers, picking the right one(s) can be a piece of cake.

Wrong answers on standardized multiple-choice tests are known in the testing industry as "distractors," or "trap answers." They are called distractors because their purpose is to distract test takers away from correct choices. Trap answers are specifically designed to appeal to test takers. Oftentimes, they're the answers that seem to scream out "pick me!" as you work through a question. However, these attractive answers are often incorrect.

Remembering this simple fact can be an enormous help to you as you sit down to take the test. By learning to recognize distractors, you will greatly improve your score.

Improve Your Odds Indirectly

Every time you're able to eliminate an incorrect choice on a GRE question, you improve your odds of finding the correct answer; the more incorrect choices you eliminate, the better your odds.

For this reason, some of our test-taking strategies are aimed at helping you arrive at ETS's answer indirectly. Doing this will make you much more successful at avoiding the traps laid in your path by the test writers. This is because most of the traps are designed to catch unwary test takers who try to approach the problems directly.

POE and Guessing

If you guessed blindly on a five-choice GRE problem, you would have a one-in-five chance of picking ETS's answer. Eliminate one incorrect choice, and your chances improve to one in four. Eliminate three, and you have a fifty-fifty chance of earning points by guessing. Get the picture?

> Guess, but guess intelligently.

6. Use Your Scratch Paper

STEP 6

ETS doesn't give you many useful tools on this test, so you have to make good use of the ones they do give you. You will get six sheets of scratch paper stapled into a booklet. You can get more by raising your hand during a section, but that takes time, so you will need an efficient system for using scratch paper.

Mistakes happen in your head, but good technique happens on scratch paper. When you do work in your head, you are really doing two things at once. The first is figuring out the answer at hand, and the second is keeping track of where you've been. Mistakes happen when you try to do two things in your head at once. It's better to park your thinking on your scratch paper. Get it out of your head and onto the page. Good things happen when you do.

On the math side, scratch paper is crucial. Not only is it important for performing complicated calculations, but when used properly, it can actually help to direct your thinking as you work through multistep problems. In the math sections of this book, we will give you graphic set-ups for each math concept that you will encounter. Use them consistently, and they will become good habits that will pay big dividends in accuracy, even over a four-hour exam.

On the verbal side, scratch paper is every bit as essential. It will help you to track your progress, to focus on only one answer choice at a time, and to work through a series of answer choices efficiently. In the verbal section of this book, we will give you a process for using scratch paper efficiently and effectively.

Remember
By crossing out a clearly incorrect choice, you permanently eliminate it from consideration.

7. Double-Check

STEP 7

Get into the habit of double-checking all of your answers before you click on your answer choice—or answer choices. Make sure that you reread the directions and have done everything they asked you to—don't get the answer wrong just because you chose only one answer for a question that required you to choose two or more.

The only way to reliably avoid careless errors is to adopt habits that make them less likely to occur. Always check to see that you've transcribed information correctly to your scratch paper. Always read the problem at least twice and note any important parts that you might forget later. Always check your calculations. And always read the question one last time before selecting your answer.

STEP 8 ≫ 8. Let It Go

Every time you begin a new section, focus on that section and put the last section you completed behind you. Don't think about that pesky synonym from an earlier section while a geometry question is on your screen. You can't go back, and besides, your impression of how you did on a section is probably much worse than reality.

STEP 9 ≫ 9. Don't Make Any Last-Minute Lifestyle Changes

The week before the test is not the time for any major life changes. This is NOT the week to quit smoking, start smoking, quit drinking coffee, start drinking coffee, start a relationship, end a relationship, or quit a job. Business as usual, okay?

YOUR STARTING POINT

Before you dive in, you might wish to take one of the practice tests in this book or online to get a sense of where you are starting from. It can be a good exercise to tackle a practice test before you know any strategies or have reviewed any content—while you have relatively fresh eyes to the test-taking experience. This will be a good initial impression and these first scores will show you what content areas need your focus. Of course, you'll review all necessary content for the GRE (won't you?), but this first test can serve as a helpful guide. Then, as you learn strategies and review math and verbal content, you'll have a genuine sense of accomplishment.

Now let's get cracking!

Summary

o   You can increase your score on the GRE through practice and successful application of test-taking strategies.

o   The GRE uses a variety of question formats throughout the test.

o   Accuracy is better than speed. Slow down and focus on accumulating as many points as possible. Forcing yourself to work faster results in careless errors and lower scores.

o   Process of Elimination is an extremely useful tool on the test. Use it to eliminate wrong answers and increase your odds of guessing correctly.

Part II
How to Crack the Verbal Section

Chapter 3
The Geography of the Verbal Section

The Verbal section of the GRE is designed to test your verbal reasoning abilities. This chapter will review the types of questions you will see, how to pace yourself, and the basic strategies that will best guide you through the Verbal section. Additionally, this chapter will cover the importance of vocabulary on the test, along with some useful tips on how to approach learning GRE vocabulary.

WHAT'S ON THE VERBAL SECTION

ETS claims that the Verbal section of the GRE accomplishes the following:

- places a greater emphasis on analytical skills and on understanding vocabulary in context rather than in isolation
- uses more text-based materials
- contains a broader range of reading selections
- tests skills that are more closely aligned with those used in graduate school
- expands the range of computer-enabled tasks

What does this mean for you?

- There won't be questions that involve analogies or antonyms on this test, as there were on the old version of the GRE.
- You'll see some wacky-looking question formats that you've probably never seen before.
- Though they say the new version of the test de-emphasizes vocabulary, there's no getting around the fact that the more vocabulary you know when you sit down to take the test, the better off you'll be. So vocabulary remains as important as it ever was. If you're especially eager to build your vocabulary, check out Chapter 8: Vocabulary for the GRE.

There are three types of questions on the Verbal section of the test:

- Text Completions
- Sentence Equivalence
- Reading Comprehension

Let's take a brief look at each question type.

Text Completions

Text Completion questions consist of short sections of text with one or more blanks; you are asked to choose the best word to place in each blank. You may see one blank in the text, in which case you will be offered five answer choices, or you may see two or three blanks, each of which will have three answer choices. No partial credit is given for getting some but not all blanks correct on a question, so be sure to read carefully.

Here is an example of a two-blank question:

Though Adam was incredulous upon hearing Madam
Sofia's psychic reading, after a few weeks had
passed, he was (i) _____ by how remarkably
(ii) _____ she had turned out to be.

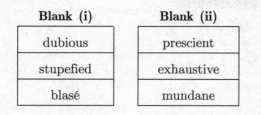

Blank (i)	Blank (ii)
dubious	prescient
stupefied	exhaustive
blasé	mundane

Sentence Equivalence

This is another vocabulary-oriented question type. Each question will consist of one sentence with six answer choices. Your job is to choose the two answer choices that logically complete the sentence. As with Text Completions, there is no partial credit, so you must select both correct answer choices to receive points.

Here's an example:

When Selena brought home the irascible puppy,
her more quiescent dogs were rattled by their new
_____ housemate.

- ☐ pugnacious
- ☐ languid
- ☐ bellicose
- ☑ juvenile
- ☐ diminutive
- ☐ phlegmatic

Reading Comprehension

Reading comprehension accounts for about half of the Verbal questions you will see. Passages range from one to five paragraphs, and each passage can consist of one to five questions. No matter the length, the passages offer some type of argument that the author is trying defend, even if it's just the author's opinion. Therefore, some of the questions in this section will ask you to identify an author's point of view or the assumptions and premises upon which that point of view rests. Other Reading Comprehension questions will ask about details of specific information in the passage or provable from the passage, the structure or tone of the text, how a word is used in context, or the main idea. Fortunately, these questions rarely test you on your prior vocabulary knowledge. Furthermore, Reading Comprehension questions are like an open-book test—everything you need is right there in the passage!

You will encounter three Reading Comprehension question formats:

Multiple Choice

Question 20 is based on this passage.

After examining the bodies of a dozen beached whales and finding evidence of bleeding around the animals' eyes and brains as well as lesions on their kidneys and livers, environmental groups fear that the Navy's use of sonar is causing serious harm to marine animals. A leading marine biologist reports that sonar induces whales to panic and surface too quickly, which causes nitrogen bubbles to form in their blood.

The argument above relies on which of the following assumptions?

○ Marine biologists have documented that other marine animals, including dolphins and sea turtles, have exhibited kidney and liver lesions.

○ No studies have been conducted on the possible detrimental effects of sonar on marine animals.

○ Whales in captivity panic only when exposed to man-made, rather than natural, sound waves.

○ The presence of nitrogen bubbles in the blood has been demonstrated to cause damage to various internal organs.

○ It is unlikely that the symptoms found in the beached whales could be caused by any known disease.

Select All That Apply

Questions 10 and 11 are based on this passage.

What was it about Oscar Wilde's only novel, *The Picture of Dorian Gray*, that caused it to create such an uproar when it was published in 1891? While critics attacked the quality of Wilde's formal elements, their denunciation merely masked the true concerns of many nineteenth-century critics. What these critics were actually railing against was the thematic content of Wilde's work, specifically his illustration of a lifestyle devoted to useless beauty. For many a nineteenth-century moralist, *The Picture of Dorian Gray* was nothing more than a primer for spiritual depravity. Wilde's ultimate sin was his leniency toward his protagonist, an unabashed hedonist. To the critics, allowing an evil character to escape his just desserts was an unforgivable sin. In their minds, Wilde's work was corrupting the genteel reading public by failing to show the proper consequences of immoral behavior.

Consider each of the choices separately and select all that apply.

The author of the passage would probably agree with which of the following statements?

☐ Most critics of Oscar Wilde's novel objected primarily to the lifestyle of its author.

☐ If *The Picture of Dorian Gray* were written in the twentieth century, the critical reaction would be less severe.

☐ Some critics of Wilde's *The Picture of Dorian Gray* believed that an author of a book had a moral responsibility to the book's audience.

Select a Sentence

Question 16 is based on this passage.

Called by some the "island that time forgot," Madagascar is home to a vast array of unique, exotic creatures. One such animal is the aye-aye. First described by western science in 1782, it was initially categorized as a member of the order Rodentia. Further research then revealed that it was more closely related to the lemur, a member of the primate order. Since the aye-aye is so different from its fellow primates, however, it was given its own family: *Daubentoniidae*. The aye-aye has been listed as an endangered species and, as a result, the government of Madagascar has designated an island off the northeastern coast of Madagascar as a protected reserve for aye-ayes and other wildlife.

Select the sentence in the passage that most seriously weakens the author's claim that "this practice may result in the loss of a superb example of life's variety."

When you see a Select-a-Sentence question like the one above, you need to click on the sentence in the passage that you think answers the question.

HOW IS THE GRE VERBAL SECTION STRUCTURED?

The GRE has two scored multiple-choice verbal sections. Each will be 30 minutes long with 20 questions per section. The way you perform on one Verbal section will affect the difficulty of the next Verbal section you are given. Verbal sections tend to follow the same order. Roughly the first six questions will be Text Completion, the next five or six will be Reading Comprehension, followed by about four Sentence Equivalence questions, and then another four or five Reading Comprehension questions. In profile, the two verbal sections will look something like this:

A better performance on the first scored Verbal section will yield more difficult questions on the second one!

Question	1	2	3	4	5	6	7	8	9	10	11	12	13	14	15	16	17	18	19	20
Section 3	Text Completion						Reading Comprehension					Sentence Equivalence				Reading Comprehension				
Section 5	Text Completion						Reading Comprehension						Sentence Equivalence			Reading Comprehension				

BEST STRATEGIES FOR THE GRE VERBAL SECTION

The basic test-taking strategies covered in Chapter 2 are effective for the entire test. They can be critical to your level of success on the GRE. They are time-tested and proven to be effective. You should always be mindful of them and take a few minutes to review them before working through the Verbal section.

Here are some strategies that will help you on the Verbal section, specifically. We'll show you how to use them as we go through specific question types in the chapters ahead, but for now read through the strategies and get a sense of what they are before moving on.

Accuracy vs. Speed

Any timed test will cause at least some level of stress. While it is important to mark an answer to every question on the Verbal section, nobody has ever won a medal for getting the most questions wrong in the shortest amount of time. The key is not speed, but rather efficiency. Answering correctly is not a matter of speed as much as it is a matter of applying the techniques that we will cover in the upcoming chapters. Don't let the clock force you to ignore good techniques and make silly mistakes.

Process of Elimination (POE) for Verbal

Determining correct answers on the Verbal section of the GRE can be tricky. For example, answer choices on Reading Comprehension questions are constructed with "clever" wordings that make correct answers seem wrong and incorrect answers seem right. This method of answer choice creation makes it difficult to find the correct answers.

So, reverse your approach. Instead of looking for the correct answer, look for the incorrect answers and eliminate them.

Using Process of Elimination (POE) is the most effective way to detect and avoid trap answer choices. Proper POE on the Verbal section abides by the following rules:

- Consider every answer choice, even if you think you know the answer.
- Eliminate any choice that contains something that you can point to and say, "Well, I *know* that's wrong." This is important and should be distinguished from "Well, I *think* that's wrong" or "Well, I'm *pretty sure* that's wrong." If you do not know for certain that an answer choice is wrong, do not eliminate it.
- If a choice seems weird or confusing, or just doesn't make sense the first time you read it, this is not cause to eliminate the answer. Instead, leave it as an option to come back to and evaluate later.
- Cycle through the answer choices until you're left with only the correct answer(s).

While your approach to POE may change slightly from one question type to another, the basic POE strategy is very effective. As Sherlock Holmes said, "When you have eliminated the impossible, whatever remains, however improbable, must be the truth." So, for questions that test your vocabulary, you might eliminate all answers you know cannot possibly be correct and be left with a word you have never seen before as the correct answer. For questions that require you to understand the premises, conclusions, and underlying assumptions of an argument, you might have to eliminate answers that obviously fall outside the scope of the question. POE techniques for each of the specific question types are addressed in later chapters.

Your first impression of POE might be that it is way too time-consuming, but don't knock it until you try it. Then try it again, and again. Most of the incorrect answer choices on the GRE Verbal sections can be quickly identified by spotting some minor detail that can't be supported by the question stem or passage. We'll discuss some of the ways to categorize these details in later chapters. For now, just realize that POE can actually be *faster* than trying to find the "correct" answer. And, before you pull out a stopwatch and time each method, remember that speed matters a lot less than accuracy.

Down to Two?

Let's say you've eliminated enough of the answer choices on a given question so that only two choices remain. You marked it and have come back to it. If you guess now, your chance of being correct is at 50%, which is pretty good! However, there is only one way to correctly answer every question on the GRE, so if you can't see why one of the remaining answer choices is wrong, you are missing something. Take a fresh look at the question and remind yourself what the answer should look like. Find it! If you are still stuck, Mark and Move.

Here's a GRE example:

Seven years ago, the state of Danrovia, in an attempt to promote the production of renewable energy, offered a flat tax credit to consumers who installed solar panels for the first time. In the years following the implementation of this tax credit, the annual government expenditures related to this tax credit have reduced steadily.

If the statements in this passage are true, then which of the following is most likely true based on the information in the passage?

○ The number of consumers who have installed solar panels for the first time on their property has gone down steadily.

○ The total amount of energy produced in Danrovia has increased annually.

○ The amount of non-renewable energy produced in Danrovia has decreased annually.

○ Consumers typically install solar panels after they take steps to introduce methods of creating renewable energy.

○ The amount of energy produced from renewable sources in Danrovia increased more relative to the amount of energy produced from unrenewable sources in Danrovia.

Here's How to Crack It

You know this is an inference question because of the phrase *which of the following is most likely true based on the information in the passage*. The premises are that Danrovia passed a tax credit for all consumers who installed solar panels for the first time, and that government expenditures based on the tax credit have steadily decreased. You have to decide which of the answers is a reasonable conclusion based on the premises.

Choice (A) is a possibility because if the number of consumers who have installed solar panels for the first time has decreased, it's reasonable to conclude that government expenditures based on the tax credit have also decreased, so keep (A). The total amount of energy produced in

Danrovia is beyond the scope of the question, so eliminate (B). The amount of non-renewable energy produced is also beyond the scope of the question, so eliminate (C). Choice (D) refers to consumers installing solar panels and could be a decent answer, so keep (D) as well. The amount of energy produced from renewable sources in Danrovia relative to the amount of energy produced from unrenewable sources in Danrovia is also beyond the scope of the question, so eliminate (E). You're down to (A) and (D). Reread the question. It asks what is most likely true based on the information in the passage. The passage states that Danrovia passed the tax credit for the installation of solar panels in an attempt to promote the production of renewable energy. While it may be true that consumers only install solar panels after they take other steps towards the production of renewable energy, (D) does not directly explain why the amount spent on the tax credit has decreased since the credit's implementation. That is, the information in choice (D) isn't necessarily true because of the information in the passage. Choice (D) is out of scope so eliminate it. The correct answer is (A).

It's also worth noting that (D) uses recycled language—*renewable energy*. This is a sign of a trap answer and frequently a good reason to be skeptical of an answer choice.

Stacking the Odds

There may be cases on the GRE when you are running out of time and you are going to have to guess on a question. POE can turn these questions into potential points. Before you guess on a question, quickly consider if some of the answer choices are clearly wrong. If you can eliminate a couple of choices, you've increased your chances of getting a free point!

Consider the following question:

When studying human history, one must be aware that the _____ between historical periods are arbitrary; certainly none of the people alive at the time were aware of a shift from one era to another.

judgments
ideologies
innovations
demarcations
episodes

Here's How to Crack It
If you encountered this question on the GRE, you might not know what the best answer is (you'll learn how to approach questions like this in Chapter 4). However, you might see that

some of the answer choices simply don't make sense. Choices (A), (B), and (C) don't seem to fit the sentence at all. By eliminating these wrong answers, you've suddenly given yourself a great chance of choosing the correct answer just by guessing, since only (D) and (E) are left. And if you realize that (E) doesn't make sense either, then you know the correct answer is (D).

POOD

Your Personal Order of Difficulty (POOD) should guide your approach on the Verbal section. Do you have a lot of success with Reading Comprehension and not much on Text Completion questions? Skip those six Text Completions for now and work your strengths. You do not want to be put in a situation in which you have to rush through the types of questions you would normally get correct simply because they show up later in the section.

With this in mind, think of the Verbal section as two tests—one easy and one difficult. Take the easy test first! Move briskly (without rushing) through the test, answering the questions that give you little trouble and skipping the questions that will bog you down. Do this all the way through question 20. Then go back and work those harder questions knowing that you will not have missed any easy points due to a lack of effective planning.

It's Your Test
You know what question types are a breeze and which are more challenging for you, so feel free to approach the test in the order that works for YOU.

Remember, there is no penalty for incorrect answers on the GRE. So, if time is running low, guess!

A Word on Vocabulary

While the GRE has scaled back on the sheer difficulty of vocabulary over the years, you still need to have a grasp on the words that are commonly used on the test if you want to see significant score improvements. In the coming chapters, we will go over strategies for answering Text Completion and Sentence Equivalence questions. However, there is no substitute for having a good understanding of the vocabulary that ETS tends to test. In Chapter 8, we offer the Key Terms List—a list of the most commonly used words tested on the GRE.

Effective ways to study vocabulary for the GRE may include the following:

- Prioritize words from the Key Terms List into three categories: Words I Know, Words I Sort of Know, and Words I Do Not Know. Spend most of your time studying the second group, followed by the final group.

- Read. You will absorb many of the words that will show up on the GRE by reading respected publications such as academic journals or some of the more highbrow newspapers and magazines.

- Keep a vocabulary list. When you come across new words on the practice tests or practice problems, add them to your list. They have been used before on the GRE and they may very well be used again.

Stressed About Vocab?
Check out The Princeton Review's flashcards, *Essential GRE Vocabulary*, which includes 500 essential vocabulary words plus 50 customizable cards!

Summary

o   The GRE Verbal section consists of two 30-minute sections, each containing 20 questions.

o   The Verbal section is made up of Text Completion, Sentence Equivalence, and Reading Comprehension questions.

o   Remember to utilize Process of Elimination (POE) to attack the wrong answers.

o   Use your Personal Order of Difficulty (POOD) to ensure that you take the easy test first. Skip questions that seem difficult, and Mark and Move when questions get tough.

o   Vocabulary is important. Prioritize the words from the Key Terms List into Words I Know, Words I Sort of Know, and Words I Do Not Know.

Chapter 4
Text Completions

If you took the SAT, you probably remember sentence completion questions. Well, they're back, retooled and renamed for the GRE. Text Completion questions test your ability to figure out which word or words best complete a given sentence or group of sentences. On the GRE, the sentence can have one, two, or even three blanks that you must fill. This chapter will show you The Princeton Review approach to Text Completions, a tried-and-true approach that will help you focus on exactly the parts of the sentences that you'll need to figure out the answer. Along the way, we'll provide you with some valuable tips on using Process of Elimination to help you when you don't know all the vocabulary on a question.

PART 1: TEXT COMPLETION BASICS

WHAT'S A TEXT COMPLETION?

On each Verbal section of the GRE you can expect to see about six Text Completion questions, or approximately 30% of the total questions. Each question is made up of a passage consisting of one or more sentences—sometimes up to five! The passage has blanks in place of key words. There can be one, two, or three blanks. One-blank questions have five answer choices per blank, while two- and three-blank questions have three answer choices per blank. Your job is to select the combination of answer choices—one choice per blank—that best completes the text. The completed sentence(s) must make sense as a whole. In multiple-blank questions, credit is given only if all blanks are answered correctly.

Therefore, the correct choice for each blank depends on the meaning of the sentence as a whole. While at first glance, Text Completions may seem to focus on vocabulary, these questions are not just a glorified vocab quiz. Even more important is a critical understanding of context and the ability to recognize the internal logic of the passage. You cannot rely on word power alone.

But you *will* need a strategy for approaching Text Completion questions. This strategy is where we will begin our discussion of how to successfully navigate Text Completions.

THE BASIC APPROACH FOR TEXT COMPLETION QUESTIONS

Using the basic approach for Text Completion questions, you will examine the sentence or sentences in the passage, which will include clues and transition words that indicate the intended meaning of the sentence. Examining these clues and transitions, you will aim to come up with your own word for each blank to compare against the answer choices.

STEPS FOR TEXT COMPLETION QUESTIONS

Follow these steps for each blank in turn. For now, we'll be working with only one-blank questions. Later, we'll tell you how to handle questions with two and three blanks.

1. **Find the clues and transition words.** Ask yourself these questions:
   - *Who or what* is the blank describing?
   - *What else* in the passage provides *insight* into that person or thing?
2. **Come up with your own word or phrase for the blank.** Write that word or phrase down on your scratch paper.
3. **Check each answer choice.**
   - ✓ an answer that sort of matches your word
   - ✗ an answer that does not at all match your word
   - ? any word you don't know

Before tackling the nuts and bolts of these steps, let's try an example to get started:

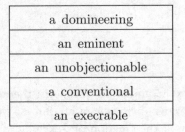

Robert Ingersoll, although virtually unknown today, was _____ orator of the nineteenth century; people traveled hundreds of miles to hear his eloquent speeches.

| a domineering |
| an eminent |
| an unobjectionable |
| a conventional |
| an execrable |

Here's How to Crack It

1. **Find the clues and transition words.** First ask, "*Who* or *what* is the blank describing?" Before you try to fill the blank, you must consider what the blank is talking about! In this sentence, the blank describes the kind of *orator* that *Robert Ingersoll* was.

   Next ask, "*What else* in the passage provides *insight* into that person or thing?" Find information in the surrounding text that provides insight into the kind of orator that Ingersoll was. The sentence tells us that *people traveled hundreds of miles to hear his… speeches.* So he was obviously a good orator. The sentence also tells us that Ingersoll is *virtually unknown today.* The transition word *although* puts this insight into opposition to the word in the blank describing the kind of orator Ingersoll was. Now you know that he wasn't just a good orator but a well-known one.

2. **Come up with your own word or phrase for the blank.** Use the insights you've gained to come up with your own word for the blank. You don't have to come up with the perfect word, and it doesn't have to be a single word. It's better to be as literal as possible in order to capture your insights. Feel free to recycle language in the sentence when coming up with your own word. From Step 1, you know that Ingersoll was a well-known orator—recycled from the word *unknown*—and also a good one. To capture all that, you could just call him "famously good."

3. **Check each answer choice.** Only now that you've come up with your own word (or phrase in this case) compare that word or phrase to the answer choices. Compare each of the answer choices in turn to your own phrase, "famously good."

   Choice (A), *domineering*, which means bossy, is not a match for "famously good." Eliminate (A). Choice (B), *eminent*, is a famous or respected person, so keep (B). The word *unobjectionable*, (C), means something that can't be objected to, so eliminate (C). Choice (D), *conventional*, is practically the opposite of "famously good," so eliminate it. Choice (E), *execrable*, might stump you, in which case you'd give it a question mark. *Execrable* means downright detestable. If you knew that, you'd eliminate the word. Either way, you'd go with the answer choice that you've assigned a checkmark, (B). Ingersoll was an *eminent* orator of the nineteenth century.

———————————◯———————————

Congratulations on completing your first Text Completion question!

GET A CLUE!

Here's the good news about Text Completion questions: there is only ever one answer choice that is correct. We know that seems obvious enough, but it's worth mentioning. It gives you a touch of insight into the reality of the creation of Text Completion questions. Somewhere in the question, the information to determine the correct answer is present. There are no alternative interpretations or Mad-Lib style games for Text Completion questions. The information to justify the answer is always right in front of you.

The trick, as always, is to determine where and what that information is. Step 1 in approaching Text Completions is to find clues in the passage about the word for the blank. The *text* of the passage provides the *context* for the correct answer. Your mission is to determine the intended meaning of the passage, based on the information in the passage. That's why it's very important to do Step 1 first. *Do not move on to Step 2 or look at the answer choices until you've identified the clues in the sentence!*

The clue is the information in the sentence that provides insight into the word or phrase that goes in the blank. But before you can even look for clues, you want a concrete idea of what exactly is missing. That's why, when you start on each Text Completion question, you need to find the clue. And, you begin finding the clue by first asking yourself this question:

- *Who or what* is the blank describing?

Take a moment to make sure you understand what's being talked about by the blank. If it's not crystal-clear, then determine what part of speech the blank should be. An adjective will be easiest to work with, because then the blank merely describes the noun next to the blank. If it's a verb that's missing, the blank describes some action or process. If it's noun that's missing, the blank represents a person, thing, or idea—or often some aspect of another noun in the passage. Once you know what the blank is describing, ask yourself this question:

- *What else* in the passage provides *insight* into that person or thing?

The next order of business is to find the information in the passage that tells you something about the person or thing described by the blank. ETS *never* gives you a passage in which the word that belongs in the blank is subject to opinion, debate, or poetic license. They always give you one or more pieces of information that offer insight into the topic of the blank. This information is the clue, and it's all there in the text.

To illustrate the importance of the clue, let's look at the following example:

Sophocles, who wrote the play *Oedipus Rex,* was one of the most _____ playwrights of ancient Greece.

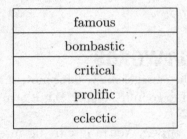

| famous |
| bombastic |
| critical |
| prolific |
| eclectic |

Who or what does the blank describe? It's an adjective describing the kind of playwright Sophocles was. What else in the sentence gives you insight into what kind of playwright Sophocles was? If you've come up empty-handed, that's because the sentence does not contain a clue. Based on what you may know about Sophocles, a few of the answer choices may work. To answer this question correctly, ETS would have to expect you to rely on outside knowledge about Sophocles. For fear of an army of angry lawyers knocking down their door, ETS will never produce a question that has a correct answer they cannot defend. The clue has to be there in the text. Let's try with another version of the same question:

Sophocles, who wrote the play *Oedipus Rex,* was one of the most _____ playwrights of ancient Greece, completing 123 plays in his lifetime—double that of any of his contemporaries.

| famous |
| bombastic |
| critical |
| prolific |
| eclectic |

Just as before, the blank should describe what kind of playwright Sophocles was. This time, however, you're given additional information: he completed *123 plays,* which was *double that of…his contemporaries.* Now you have something to work with in coming up with your own word. Sophocles wrote a lot of plays, so "productive" could be your word. You could even put down "adjective—wrote lots" on your scratch paper if you weren't able to come up with a single word that means "wrote lots." Remember that your job is to simply come up with a word or phrase that leads you to the correct answer. So, it's okay if your word is actually a phrase.

Now you're ready to take on the answer choices. The adjective *famous* is certainly tempting. Sophocles was unquestionably one of the most famous *playwrights of ancient Greece.* But this has no connection to the clue, which is all about the number of plays he wrote. This is a trap laid by ETS writers. ETS writers may not be able to use outside knowledge to create their correct answer choices, but they certainly can add in an incorrect answer choice relying on outside knowledge and hope the student does the rest. Assumptions and extrapolations are dangerous. One and only one of the answer choices matches the clue—(D), *prolific*. The other four words may indeed describe Sophocles and sound fine if inserted into the sentence. But only one answer choice will ever match the clue, and that's what counts.

A WORD ABOUT YOUR WORDS

Once you've found the clue in the passage, you've done most of the heavy lifting. Now it's time to come up with your own word to go in the blank. This is Step 2 of the basic approach.

This isn't about predicting the answer. You're just trying to come up with something that reflects the clues and will help you to identify the correct answer from among the choices. So don't waste time brainstorming the perfect GRE word to put in the blank. Think of your job as supplying the definition of what should go in the blank. To make your life easier, recycle! Just use a word or phrase recycled from the clues. What better way to capture the information you gleaned from the passage?

Practice: Finding the Clue

Underline the clue in each of the following sentences. Then, think of your own word for the blank and write it down. Answers can be found in Part V.

1 of 8

The _____ relationships in his life haunted Eugene O'Neill and are often reflected in the harrowing nature of many of his plays.

Be systematic! Ask yourself these questions. Who or what is the blank describing? What in the sentence gives insight into that?

2 of 8

Mount Godwin-Austen, more commonly known as K2, is the second highest mountain in the world, with its _____ peaks reaching more than 28,000 feet high.

3 of 8

A wind-chill warning is issued when the temperature is projected to reach minus 25 degrees Fahrenheit or lower, the point at which the cold has _____ effects on living creatures.

4 of 8

Divers still stumble across unexploded shells, 70-year-old _____ from World War II, in the waters outside Tokyo.

5 of 8

Although some people use the terms interchangeably, mastodons and mammoths were quite _____ ; mammoths were hairy with long tusks, while mastodons had low-slung bodies and flatter skulls.

6 of 8

The mayor was definitely _____ ; he crafted his policies not with an eye toward their political consequences but instead toward their practical effects.

7 of 8

The first-year law student was amazed at the sheer _____ of the material he had to read for his classes; he imagined that he would have to read for hours and hours each day to finish it all.

8 of 8

Our word "ghoul" is _____ from the Arabic word "Algol," the name for the Demon Star, a star in the constellation Perseus.

NEXT, TRANSITIONS

Let's take another look at the mastodon/mammoth question from the preceding Finding the Clue practice exercise:

Although some people use the terms interchangeably, mastodons and mammoths were quite _____ ; mammoths were hairy with long tusks, while mastodons had low-slung bodies and flatter skulls.

The first phrase of the sentence says that some people use the terms *mastodon* and *mammoth* interchangeably. However, the clause after the semicolon describes each animal, making it plain that they are very different in appearance. The clue to the word that goes in the blank is the word *interchangeably*, but context indicates that the word for the blank is the opposite of the clue. The reason you know this is because the phrase containing the clue begins with the transition word *[a]lthough*.

Transition words tell the reader how a clue relates to the blank—whether the clue has the same meaning as the blank or the opposite meaning. Consider the following two scenarios:

I won the lottery, *and*…
I won the lottery, *but*…

The first sentence is going to have a happy ending. The second one, not so much. Changing a single word sets up dramatically different outcomes. The same scenarios could also have been written with different transition words placed at the beginning:

Because I won the lottery, …
Although I won the lottery, …

Some transition words simply reinforce the clue. For these, you'd pick a word that agrees with the clue. Other transition words indicate that the word for the blank is the opposite of the clue. It's particularly important to take note of these contrast transitions.

Here are some of the most important transition words you'll encounter in Text Completion questions:

Same Meaning or Direction / Agreement		Opposite Meaning or Direction / Contrast	
accordingly	next	although	on the other hand
also	similarly	but	or
and	since	despite	previously
because	so	even though	rather than
consequently	therefore	however	still
for example	thus	in contrast	though
furthermore	too	instead	unfortunately
hence	; (semicolon)	nevertheless	whereas
in addition	: (colon)	nonetheless	while
moreover			yet

Two of the same-direction transition "words" are just punctuation marks. The semicolon is the equivalent of *and*, implying that the second clause follows logically from the first. The colon implies that the second clause is an explanation or illustration of the first. In either case, the clue for a blank in one part of the sentence will be found in the other part. Notice nuances in some of these transition words. Several of the same-direction words imply a cause-effect relationship: *accordingly*, *because*, *consequently*, *hence*, *so*, *therefore*, and *thus*. The word *previously* implies a change or contrast over time, and the word *unfortunately* implies a situation contrary to what was hoped for or expected.

Practice: Clues and Transitions

Underline the clues and circle the transition words in the following sentences; then come up with your own word for the blanks. Recycle the clues if possible. Answers can be found in Part V.

1 of 8

The star receiver is widely regarded as one of the top talents in the game, but his _____ performance as a rookie almost ended his career.

2 of 8

The prime minister received international _____ for her work; she brokered a diplomatic solution to a potential crisis.

3 of 8

While it is often assumed that drinking alcohol is detrimental to one's health, many studies have shown the _____ effects of having a glass or two of wine daily.

4 of 8

Despite the increasing technological connectivity of the modern world, many cultures still remain _____ from the global society.

5 of 8

Although many cultures view the toad as a symbol of ugliness and clumsiness, the Chinese revere the toad as a _____ symbol.

6 of 8

Stock analysts often use holiday sales to gauge future stock prices; thus, retail performance can be an important _____ of market trends.

7 of 8

It is somewhat ironic that while the population at large tends to have a negative view of the legal profession, individuals rarely display such _____ to their lawyers.

8 of 8

Methyl bromide is a pesticide that has devastating effects on insects; however, some believe it has the same _____ on humans.

PROCESS OF ELIMINATION STRATEGIES

After deciphering the clues in the passage and coming up with your own word for the blank, you arrive at the third and final step in Text Completion. In Step 3, you simply check each answer choice against the word you came up with. Use your scratch paper to mark any choice that's a match for your word with a ✓, any choice that's not a match with an ✗, and any word you don't know with a ?.

Ideally, your scratch paper will show one ✓, five ✗s, and no ?s. But life's not always that simple, and neither is the GRE. For those less-than-ideal situations, you'll need some POE skills and strategies to fall back on.

Here are some general points to keep in mind as you work through the answer choices.

- **Focus on the words you know.** Any answer choice that you know, you should be able to compare to your word and decisively mark with a ✓ or an ✗.
- **Never talk yourself into picking a word that you've eliminated**. Just because you know what it means does not mean the word is a better answer. If you are between choosing a word you've eliminated and choosing a word you don't know, pick the word you don't know.
- **Never eliminate a word you don't know.** If you have no good idea what an answer choice means, you can't rule it out as a match for your word.
- **Don't trust your ears.** If an answer choice matches your own word but doesn't sound quite right when inserted into the blank, it may still be correct. The question may be relying on a less common definition or usage of the word. Sometimes, too, the GRE will create a correct answer choice that's somewhat awkward while planting a trap answer that sounds better to the ear but has nothing to do with the clues.
- **Don't forget to Mark and Move.** There are certain situations in which Mark and Move makes sense on Text Completion questions. You might be having difficulty finding the clues. You might be daunted by a multi-blank question. The definition of a familiar word may have momentarily slipped your mind. You might have gone through POE and have two answer choices with checkmarks. In such cases, step away from the question, answer a few other questions and return to the one you've skipped. It's the best way to reset your brain and get a fresh start on a difficult question.

Take a look at the following example:

Years of confinement in a sunless cell had left the prisoner wan and weakened, with a shockingly _____ appearance.

sidereal
boisterous
etiolated
singular
circumscribed

Here's How to Crack It

Begin by asking "Who or what is the blank describing?" The blank is describing *the prisoner's... appearance*. Now ask "What else in the passage provides insight into the prisoner's appearance? The sentence describes this as *wan and weakened*. Therefore, recycle the words "wan and weakened" as the word for the blank. Now evaluate the answer choices one at a time.

Upon evaluating the answer choices, many will find that they are a total nightmare. Resolutely work through the answer choices one by one, comparing them to "wan and weakened." Choice (A) is tough. If you don't know this word, you can't eliminate it, so mark with a question mark and leave it for now. You may know that (B), *boisterous*, means noisy and rowdy. If so, you can eliminate (B). The next choice, (C), is *etiolated*—another difficult word, so mark it with a question mark and move on. Choice (D) is *singular*, which we usually think of as the opposite of *plural*. It can also mean one-of-a-kind or unique. In either sense, it's not a match for "wan and weakened," so eliminate (D). The final choice, (E), is *circumscribed*, which means to restrict something, or draw around, so eliminate (E).

At this point, you have three eliminated choices and two with question marks, so pick one of the two unknowns. The bottom line is that by using careful POE, you have increased your odds to one-in-two. By the way, the answer is (C), *etiolated*, which describes the pale appearance of plants grown with insufficient sunlight but by extension applies to anything feeble or sickly in appearance.

Positive and Negative Words

In some cases, your search for the clues will be less than conclusive. You might find the clues vague. You might be uncertain about the precise meaning of the word to go in the blank. Or, you may be faced with an intimidating lineup of answer choices. In situations such as these, try to simplify your POE. If you can determine whether the general sense of the word to go in the blank is positive or negative, you can separate the answer choices accordingly.

Look again at question 3 from the Finding the Clue practice exercise:

> A wind-chill warning is issued when the temperature is projected to reach minus 25 degrees Fahrenheit or lower, the point at which the cold has _____ effects on living creatures.

You might not be able to think of a good word to fit in the blank, but common sense (plus the clue that a *warning is issued*) tells you that *temperatures* of *minus 25 degrees...or lower* are bad for *living creatures*. So you can eliminate any answer choice that implies positive or beneficial—or even neutral!—effects on living creatures. This approach may not eliminate every answer choice (it may not eliminate any!), but every little bit helps. With a little thought, you might be able to take this positive/negative aspect of the passage a step further and eliminate any answer choice that doesn't reflect negative influences on *health* specifically.

It's important to remember that this strategy must not be your main approach to Text Completion questions. Your surest path to success remains the basic approach of finding clues and coming up with your own word to check the answer choices against. Positive/negative word associations can help you to leverage your vocabulary up to a point but should remain a tool of last resort.

THE FINAL WORD ON VOCABULARY

The strategies that we've been discussing emphasize critical assessment of the passage and smart POE. They're designed to make Text Completion questions as easy as possible and will get you far. Learning these strategies will also make you a better test taker overall.

But there's no getting around it. At the end of the day, Text Completions are about knowing words and their definitions. These questions are about vocabulary. You'll see this most clearly (and painfully) on the questions for which you successfully come up with a great word for the blank only to hit a slate of unfamiliar answer choices. Or the passage itself may be a minefield of verbiage, making it all but impossible to decipher the clues. The only solution for this predicament is to improve your vocabulary as much as possible, little by little, from now until test day.

Memorizing the Key Terms List of words in Chapter 9 is a good start. Try out the suggestions for Learning New Words at the beginning of that chapter (page 185). Deepen your vocabulary by exploring word roots as highlighted on page 70 of the Sentence Equivalence chapter. Bottom line: As you prepare for the GRE, keep learning new words every day, in whatever way works best for you. Make it fun!

PUTTING IT ALL TOGETHER

The following drill is your opportunity to apply all the skills and strategies you've learned so far. These are all one-blank Text Completion questions, each with five answer choices.

Remember how to go about it! Start by assessing the text to come up with your own word for the blank. Ignore the answer choices. Ask *who or what* the blank is describing—identifying the part of speech can clarify this. Then ask *what else* in the sentence gives insight into this person or thing. These are your clues, and you'll use transition words to determine whether the clues have the same or opposite meaning relative to the blank. Now, come up with a word or phrase for the blank. Use plain, descriptive, and literal language, recycling words from the clues if possible.

Compare each answer choice to your own word—eliminating words that don't match (✘), keeping the word that does (✔), and leaving any words you don't know (?). If it's not that straightforward, use your POE tools. Bear in mind that some words have figurative or uncommon usages that may sound awkward even if they are close to your own word and match the clues. If guessing, never choose a word you've eliminated over one you don't know.

Use the positive-and-negative approach to POE *only* if your understanding of the clues is vague or you're stumped by the majority of answer choices. If you wind up with two answer choices that work or find yourself paralyzed by a question for any other reason, use Mark and Move.

Good luck!

Text Completions Drill

Answers can be found in Part V.

1 of 6

Despite the smile that spread from ear to ear, her eyes relayed a certain _____ .

jubilance
sorrow
mischievousness
vision
liveliness

2 of 6

While grizzly bears have long, flat, and somewhat blunt claws, black bears have short, curved and_____ claws.

obtuse
abominable
barren
acute
fearful

3 of 6

One of social science's major themes is that of stability versus change; to what extent are individual personalities _____ or different over time?

transient
maladjusted
static
disturbed
discreet

4 of 6

The Erie Canal's completion caused _____ economic ripples; property values and industrial output along its route rose exponentially.

persistent
invaluable
incredulous
severe
prodigious

5 of 6

Voters have become so inured to the fickle nature of politicians that they responded to the levy of a new tax with _____ .

amazement
stolidity
exasperation
alarm
perplexity

6 of 6

It is desirable to expand the yield of a harvest only when _____ additions in time, exertion, and other variable factors of production are not also required.

predestined
commensurate
analogous
deliberate
indeterminate

PART 2: TEXT COMPLETION ADVANCED TOPICS

So far, we have been dealing with one-sentence, one-blank Text Completions with five answer choices. But not all Text Completion questions are created equal. Some are designed to be more challenging, but ETS has a specific repertoire of techniques it uses to make hard Text Completion questions. While it's true you will never see the same question twice, ETS does repeatedly pull from the same bag of tricks to make questions harder. No matter how tricky a question looks, however, the ground rules remain the same: the text contains the clues that tell you what goes in the blank(s).

Let's take a quick look at how ETS mixes things up in advanced Text Completion questions:

- **More Blanks.** Some passages have questions with two or three blanks. In such questions, each blank has three answer choices, not five as in one-blank questions.
- **More Sentences.** All Text Completion questions don't have just a single sentence. Some are passages of up to five sentences. That means more to read and more to keep track of, but also more information about the blanks.
- **More Complicated Sentences.** ETS will make the structure of the sentence more difficult to read. They will make the language thicker and harder to follow.
- **Difficult Transitions.** Transitions—agreement or contrast between parts of a passage—may not always be marked by obvious words like *and*, *but*, *since*, and *although*. And some sentences contain multiple transitions.
- **Vocabulary.** The words in the answer choices may be more difficult. However, it's more typical for ETS to make harder Text Completion questions by including more challenging vocabulary in the passage itself.

STEPS FOR TWO- AND THREE- BLANK TEXT COMPLETIONS

For two- and three- blank Text Completion questions, there are only three answer choices per blank. With just three answer choices per blank, multiple-blank questions have a simpler POE per blank than one-blank Text Completions. But that makes it even more important to analyze the text for clues about the word that goes in the blank. The strategies you've already learned in this chapter still apply, no matter how involved the question, but multiple blanks call for some slight modifications to the steps:

- **Start with the easiest blank.** This is not always the first blank. The easiest blank is the one with the most obvious clue. Read through the passage and determine the blank that has the most obvious clue and begin working there.
- **Answer each blank in turn.** Once you identify the blank with the strongest clue, work through the POE process for it first before moving on to another blank.
- **Reread the finished product.** Once you have selected answer choices for all the blanks, reread the entire passage with your choices. Make sure that it tells a consistent, logical story—the only possible story given the context of the passage.

You Can Do It
The Strategies that you learned for one-blank Text Completion questions apply to two- and three-blank questions. Flip back to one if you need a refresher and remember—you got this.

Let's apply this modified approach to the following example:

Federal efforts to regulate standards on educational achievements have been met by (i) _____ from the states; local governments feel that government imposition represents an undue infringement on their (ii) _____ .

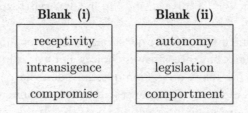

Blank (i)	Blank (ii)
receptivity	autonomy
intransigence	legislation
compromise	comportment

Here's How to Crack It

Without looking at any answer choices yet, scan the passage and determine which of the blanks has the more obvious clue. Because the second clause makes it clear that something bad is going on—*an undue infringement*, the first blank is easier to work with. The first blank is describing *the states'* reaction to *[f]ederal…standards on education achievements*. The sentence gives further insight into this by stating that *local governments* consider this *an…infringement*. The semicolon is a transition indicating agreement between the clauses. So, the word in the first blank describing the states' reaction will be something like "resistance." Now check the answer choices against "resistance." Choice (A) is the opposite of this, *receptivity*. Eliminate (A). If you don't know what *intransigence* means, then put a question mark next to (B). Choice (C), however, *compromise*, is not a match for "resistance." Even if you don't know what *intransigence* means, select (B) as it is the only non-eliminated answer. Now, work with the second blank.

The second blank describes something that *local governments* feel is negatively impacted by *government imposition*. The sentence provides insight into this by stating that *[f]ederal efforts to regulate standards on education achievements* have not been well-received by *the states*. A word or phrase for the second blank, then, could be a descriptive phrase like "freedom from interven-tion by the federal government," which you might simplify to "the right to govern themselves." Now check the answer choices. Choice (D), *autonomy*, means independence or self-government. This is a good match, so keep (D). Choice (E), *legislation*, is close but too neutral and broad given the clue. Eliminate (E). Choice (F), *comportment*, means demeanor or the way one carries oneself, so eliminate it.

The correct answer is *intransigence* and *autonomy*.

Let's try our hand at a three-blank question:

_____◯_____

Many popular musicians have (i) _____ new digital technologies that allow them unprecedented control over their music. These musicians use computers to (ii) _____ and modify their songs, resulting in a level of musical precision often unattainable naturally. Of course, though, as is often the case with new technologies, some traditionalists (iii) _____ these developments.

Blank (i)	Blank (ii)	Blank (iii)
incorporated	energize	balk at
synthesized	delineate	revel in
alleviated	recast	retaliate at

Here's How to Crack It

The second blank has the strongest clue, so begin there. The second blank is a verb that describes what *musicians* do to their songs using *computers*. The sentence gives further insight into how musicians use computers to impact songs by stating that computers result in a *precision…unattainable naturally*. The transition word *and* indicates that the word for the blank should be similar to the word *modify,* which the passage uses to describe the contents of the blank. So, recycle this language and use a word such as "modify." Choice (D), *energize,* is not a match for "modify," so eliminate it. Choice (E), *delineate,* means to outline or to define, which is also not a match for "modify," so eliminate (E). Although both these words describe something that musicians could do to their songs, neither is as close a match for the word "modify" as (F), *recast.* Keep (F) and move on to the blank with the next strongest clue.

The blank with the next strongest clue is the first blank. The first blank should be a verb describing what *[m]any popular musicians* have done with *new digital technologies.* The passage gives further insight into what musicians have done with new technologies by stating technologies gives them *control over their music* and that *[t]hese musicians use computers.* Therefore, the word for the first blank should be something close to "use," so let's reuse that fairly neutral word. The word for (A), *incorporated,* is a good fit, so keep (A). Choice (B), *synthesized,* is a trap answer. It may describe how musicians make their songs using digital technologies, but it doesn't describe what they do to these technologies. Eliminate (B). Choice (C), *alleviated,* means to make less severe, so also eliminate (C).

Now work with the third blank. The third blank is a verb describing the reaction of *traditionalists* to *these developments.* The passage provides further insight by stating that these are *new technologies* and the transition word *though* indicates that the reaction from *traditionalist* should be expected to be different than those of the musicians described earlier. Therefore, the traditionalists should have a negative reaction to new technologies, so a good phrase for the blank could simply be "don't like." Choice (G) is *balk at*, which matches "don't like," so keep (G). Choice (H), *revel in*, means celebrate, which is the opposite of "don't like," so eliminate (H). Choice (I) is *retaliate at*, certainly negative but this extreme reaction is not suggested by the text, so eliminate (I).

The correct answer is *incorporated*, *recast*, and *balk at*.

RELATIONSHIP BETWEEN THE BLANKS

Sometimes, there is no clear clue for the blank. On occasion (maybe once per test), there is no clear clue because the blanks are related to each other. If you're struggling to find a clear clue for either blank, look for how the transition words connect the two blanks. If you find a transition word that connects the two blanks, come up with a pair of words that work for the blanks. Or, all you may be able to determine is that the two words go in the same or opposite directions.

Once you have a pair of words that work for the blanks, work through the choices for the first blank. When you find a word that works with your word, put a checkmark next to it and begin evaluating the words for the second blank. If you find a word in the answers that works for the second blank that also pairs well with the first blank, put a check next to it. Continue that process until you have gone through all of the potential answer choices for the first blank. If you end up with more than one pair of words that work for the blanks, re-evaluate the sentence and work those blanks again.

Oftentimes, students will be scared off of their game by questions like this with no clear clue. The good news is these types of questions are relatively rare. Just stick to the process and keep your cool. But because these questions show up on average only once per test, you can always make a guess and devote your time to more customary questions.

Be Careful
Pay attention to tricky transitions.

TRICKY TRANSITIONS

Transitions indicate that two parts of the sentence are the same or opposite, similar or different, agreeing or contrasting. Not every transition is flagged by the obvious transition words that we highlighted in the earlier section: *and*, *but*, *so*, *however*, *because*, *despite*, *since*, *although*, *instead*, etc. Let's take a look at examples of more elusive transitions:

> They were twins in _____ only: their personalities could not have been more _____.

The word *twins* indicates that similarity is expected. The word *only*, however, suggests that their similarity is limited to one aspect, because (note the transitional colon) another aspect, *their personalities*, was not twin-like. The word in the first blank should match "appearance"; the word in the second blank should match "different."

Here the similarity was implied by the word *twins*. Similarity or difference could be implied by a mere description of two things:

> Among dog breeds, the endearingly diminutive Shih Tzu has _____ close kinship to its lupine ancestors.

The word *close kinship* implies similarity between *the…Shih Tzu* and the wolf (*lupine ancestors*). However, the description of the Shih Tzu as *endearingly diminutive* contradicts our typical image of the wolf. Therefore, the word in the blank describing the *close kinship* between the two would be something like "(an) unexpectedly."

Suffice it to say there are many ways to set up agreement or contrast between two parts of a sentence. The GRE will often use time transitions to indicate some sort of change or difference. The GRE will also unfurl words such as *unexpected*, *surprising*, *ironic*, or *unfortunate*. These words imply opposition or contrast to what was expected or hoped for. Things really get complicated when a sentence contains more than one transition. Read the following example and its variations:

1. It's ironic that the striking nurses' chief grievance is _____ health care.
2. It's ironic that, while content with their salaries and vacation packages, the striking nurses' chief grievance is _____ health care.
3. It's ironic that, while pressing for better salaries and vacation packages, the striking nurses' chief grievance is _____ health care.
4. It's ironic that, while content with their salaries and vacation packages, the striking nurses' chief objective is _____ health care.

In the first sentence, the word *ironic* indicates opposition between two things in the sentence, *the striking nurses* and their *chief grievance* or complaint. This complaint has to do with the kind of *health care* they are receiving. Since nurses work in the healthcare field, it would be ironic for them to have "poor" or "inadequate" health care, so that should be their complaint. The second and third sentences are the same except for two very different transitional clauses: the clause in the second sentence implying that the nurses are happy with their *salaries and vacation packages*, the clause in the third sentence implying that they are not. Even though these transitional clauses have opposite meanings, they have no impact on the word in the blank. In all three sentences, the word in the blank is driven by the *ironic* opposition of *striking nurses* and their complaint of "inadequate" *health care*. In the fourth sentence, we replace the word *grievance* in sentence 2 with *objective*. While the irony of the nurses and their inadequate health care remains the same, changing *grievance* to *objective* means that the word in the blank must change from the kind of health care the nurses are complaining about ("inadequate") to the kind of health care they are aiming for ("better").

Including multiple transitions in a passage is a predictable trick that ETS uses to complicate Text Completion questions. So get used to recognizing and deciphering them! It's impossible to establish set rules for how these compound transitions add up. You must pay close attention to how they are related logically.

Text Completions Practice Set

Answers can be found in Part V.

1 of 10

With global interconnectedness on the rise, the conviction of the United States to remain neutral in World War I seemed ever more _____ .

presumptuous
futile
contemptuous
pragmatic
admirable

2 of 10

Upon visiting the Middle East in 1850, Gustave Flaubert was so _____ belly dancing that he wrote, in a letter to his mother, that the dancers alone made his trip worthwhile.

overwhelmed by
enamored of
taken aback by
beseeched by
flustered by

3 of 10

The human race is a very (i)_____ species, as the facade of calm that covers our anxiety and (ii)_____ is flimsy and effortlessly ruptured.

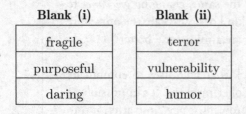

Blank (i)	Blank (ii)
fragile	terror
purposeful	vulnerability
daring	humor

4 of 10

The practice of purchasing books was primarily a (i)_____ of the well-to-do until the late 1800s, when the increased popularity of dime novels, the expansion in the number of bookstores, and the introduction of the paperback made books (ii)_____ the average man.

Blank (i)	Blank (ii)
conduit	dislikable to
prerogative	excitable to
plight	attainable by

5 of 10

Increasingly, the boundaries of congressional seats are drawn in order to protect incumbents, as legislators engineer the demographics of each district such that those already in office can coast to (i)_____ victory. Of course, there is always the possibility that the incumbent will face a challenge from within his or her own party. Nevertheless, once the primary is over, the general election is (ii)_____ .

Blank (i)	Blank (ii)
an ineluctable	seldom nugatory
an invidious	remarkably contentious
a plangent	merely denouement

While more (i)_____ professors continue to insist that video games will never be a proper object of study, the rising generation of more heterodox academics is inclined to view such talk as positively (ii)_____ .

Blank (i)	Blank (ii)
pedantic	antediluvian
progressive	pusillanimous
erudite	jejune

Political predictions generally prove fairly accurate when the presumption that the future will be similar to the past is (i)_____ . In periods with substantial (ii)_____ in the political world, however, predictions can be (iii)_____ wrong.

Blank (i)	Blank (ii)	Blank (iii)
disproved	upswings	thoughtfully
stipulated	insurgencies	perilously
fulfilled	changes	carelessly

Water is one of the few molecules that is less (i)_____ as a solid than as a (ii)_____ ; if you need (iii)_____ , just look at the floating ice in your water glass.

Blank (i)	Blank (ii)	Blank (iii)
intriguing	vapor	an illustration
dense	plasma	an imbibement
aqueous	liquid	a discordance

As Molly was (i)_____ Spanish with her friends before their trip to Chile, she discovered that although she could comprehend her friends, she could not (ii)_____ her thoughts in the (iii)_____ language.

Blank (i)	Blank (ii)	Blank (iii)
mastering	acknowledge	inherent
disregarding	articulate	objective
practicing	disencumber	unfamiliar

People accustomed to thinking that the human lifespan (i)_____ the outer bounds of animal longevity tend to dismiss tales of musket balls being found in the shells of living turtles. Samantha Romney, however, argues that while such stories may be (ii)_____ , some turtles do indeed exhibit a phenomenon known as "negligible (iii)_____ ," showing no signs of aging even as they pass the two-century mark.

Blank (i)	Blank (ii)	Blank (iii)
belies	apocryphal	rejuvenation
demarcates	authentic	superannuation
antedates	heresy	senescence

Summary

o   In Text Completion questions, ignore the answer choices and come up with your own word for the blank(s), using the clues and transition words in the passage.

o   To find the clue, ask these questions: "*Who or what* is the blank describing" and "*What else* in the passage gives insight into that?"

o   Transition words tell you whether the word in the blank should have the same sense as the clue or the opposite sense. Transitions are often marked by obvious words like *and, but, so, however, because, despite, since, although, instead,* etc.

o   When coming up with your own word for the blank, be as literal as possible. It's okay to use simple words, a descriptive phrase, or language recycled from the clue.

o   After coming up with your own word for the blank, use POE to eliminate words that aren't matches for your word. Focus on the words you know. Never eliminate a word that you don't know.

o   If the clue is hard to decipher, you can simplify POE by determining if the word to go in the blank should be positive or negative. Then narrow down the answer choices by eliminating those that don't match.

o   If the sentence has two or three blanks, do the blanks one at a time. Pick the easiest blank to start with, ask the questions, find the clue, come up with a word, and use POE. Then repeat for the remaining blanks. When done, plug in all answer choices to double-check the meaning of the passage.

o   Harder questions may have less obvious transitions or more than one transition. Look out for anything that sets up a similarity or difference between two elements of the sentence—things, ideas, actions, etc. Pay attention to how transitions are related and the overall logic of the passage.

o   Use Mark and Move if you need a fresh start on a question. Answer a few other questions and then come back to the marked question.

o   Keep working on vocabulary every day! Learn prefixes, suffixes, and other word roots. Learn not just the main definition of a new word but the secondary and figurative meanings.

Chapter 5
Sentence
Equivalence

This chapter details a variation on the Text Completions you learned about in the prior chapter. Sentence Equivalence questions require you to find the best word to complete a sentence. For these questions, however, you'll have to pick the two answers that best complete the sentence; this means the two correct answers will be synonyms. Because both words create sentences that are equivalent—both have the same meaning—we refer to these types of questions as Sentence Equivalence questions. This chapter shows you how to apply the strategies you learned last chapter and use Process of Elimination to answer these questions.

WHAT'S A SENTENCE EQUIVALENCE?

Sentence Equivalence questions make up approximately 20% of the questions in any individual Verbal section. There are usually four Sentence Equivalence questions in each Verbal section. These questions are similar to Text Completion questions, as both require test takers to select the answer choices that best complete the intended meaning of the given sentence. However, unlike Text Completion questions, Sentence Equivalence questions always have only one blank and six answer choices, and you must correctly select two answer choices to get credit for the question.

Sentence Equivalence questions look like this:

> Anthropologists contend that the ancient Mesopotamians switched from grain production to barley after excessive irrigation and salt accumulation made the soil _____ grains.

- ☐ indifferent to
- ☐ inhospitable to
- ☐ unsuitable for
- ☐ acrimonious to
- ☐ benignant to
- ☐ inured to

The goal of a Sentence Equivalence question is to choose the two answer choices that complete the sentence, fit the meaning of the sentence as a whole, and produce completed sentences that are alike in meaning.

A CAUTIONARY TALE ON SYNONYMS

A common mistake that test takers make is expecting answer choices that produce completed sentences that are alike in meaning to be synonyms. The test taker making this mistake believes when two synonyms are present in the answer choices, they must be the correct answer. The test writers know this is a commonly made assumption, so they use this information to trick test takers into selecting the wrong answer choices. But this question type is called Sentence Equivalence, not Word Equivalence!

The first way they trick test takers is by including a pair of synonyms in the answer choices that do not fit the meaning of the sentence as a whole. They are expecting a certain number of test takers to scan the answer choices, find two answer choices that are synonyms, and select them as their answer. These test takers will be sad to find that they have just been tricked by the test writers.

The second way the GRE writers trick test takers is by ensuring that the two correct answer choices are not synonyms at all. The correct choices for Sentence Equivalence questions do not need to be exact synonyms, as long as both words correspond to the clues and the meaning of the sentence remains consistent with both words.

Sometimes, the test writers combine these two tricks and include as answer choices synonyms that are incorrect and correct answer choices that are not synonyms.

Let's look at an example:

> Unconventional political ideology is considered _____ existing main stream political ideology until the new ideas gather enough evidence and support to be adopted by or replace existing ideologies.

- ☐ in juxtaposition to
- ☐ inconsequential to
- ☐ deviant from
- ☐ a threat to
- ☐ in light of
- ☐ foreboding to

The correct answer is (B) and (C), even though *inconsequential to* and *deviant from* are not even near-synonyms. Don't worry too much yet about the best strategy to answer a question like this—we'll go over that later on. For now, let's just look at the correct and incorrect answer choices. In this example, each of the two correct answer choices is supported by a different clue in the sentence. *Inconsequential to* is supported by the fact that that the *unconventional political ideology* has yet to *gather enough support to...replace existing ideologies*. *Deviant from* is supported by the fact that the new ideology has yet to be *adopted by...existing ideologies*. In this context, however, both words give the same general meaning to the completed sentence. Notice also the two synonyms, *a threat to* and *foreboding to*, lying in wait for the unwary test taker. These words may sound perfectly fine when plugged into the sentence, but they do not correspond to the clues in the sentence.

Of course, this doesn't mean that synonym pairs are always the wrong answer on Sentence Equivalence questions. In fact, the correct answers are often synonyms. But, answering a Sentence Equivalence question by picking any pair of synonyms is an unreliable strategy for conquering this portion of the GRE. At best, focusing on synonyms can be a last-resort approach for questions that you find difficult.

So, you ask, what is a good strategy?

Great question! We're glad you asked.

THE BASIC APPROACH FOR SENTENCE EQUIVALENCE QUESTIONS

The basic approach for Sentence Equivalence questions looks very similar to the basic approach for Text Completion questions. Much like Text Completion questions, Sentence Equivalence questions have clues and transition words built in, and you should come up with your own word or phrase for the blank before approaching the answer choices.

STEPS FOR SENTENCE EQUIVALENCE QUESTIONS

1. **Find the Clues and Transition words.**
2. **Come up with your own word or phrase for the blank.** Write that word or phrase down on your scratch paper.
3. **Check each answer choice and use your scratch paper.**
   - ✓ an answer that sort of matches your word
   - ✗ an answer that does not at all match your word
   - ? any word you don't know

CLUES AND TRANSITION WORDS

The first step in answering Sentence Equivalence questions is the same as that for Text Completions. You must find the clues and transition words in the sentence. *Do not move on to Step 2 or look at the answer choices until you've identified the clues and transition words in the sentence!* Consequently, as with Text Completion questions, much of your work for Sentence Equivalence questions happens by examining the sentence itself before considering the answer choices.

The clue is the words or phrases in the sentence that provide insight into the word or phrase that goes in the blank. When reading a Sentence Equivalence question and looking for the clue, ask yourself two questions:

- *Who or what* is the blank describing?
- *What else* in the sentence provides *insight* into that person or thing?

Transition words are words such as *and, but, so, however, because, despite, since, although, instead,* etc., that indicate how ideas in the sentence relate to each other. Thus, transition words convey important information about the intended meaning of a sentence. Some transition words, such as *but* and *however,* indicate that the portion of the sentence immediately following the transition word represents the opposite meaning to the other idea or action in the sentence. Here are some examples of sentences employing this sort of contrast transition words. The transition words are bolded.

I love coffee, **but** I cannot tolerate the caffeine.

> **Although** I love coffee, I cannot tolerate the caffeine.

Other transition words, such as *and, because,* and *since,* indicate that the portion of the sentence immediately following the transition word represents the same meaning as some other idea or action in the sentence. Here are some examples of sentences employing this sort of same direction transition words. The transition words are bolded.

> I cannot tolerate caffeine, **so** I take my coffee decaffeinated.
> **Because** I cannot tolerate caffeine, I take my coffee decaffeinated.

Try out the basic approach to Sentence Equivalence questions on the question we just saw:

Anthropologists contend that the ancient Mesopotamians switched from grain production to barley after excessive irrigation and salt accumulation made the soil _____ grains.

- [ ] indifferent to
- [ ] inhospitable to
- [ ] unsuitable for
- [ ] acrimonious to
- [ ] benignant to
- [ ] inured to

Here's How to Crack It

Begin working on this question by first looking for clues and transition words in the sentence. Ask yourself, *"Who or what is the blank describing?"* The blank describes what *the soil* was to *grains*—the relationship between the two. Now, ask yourself *"What else in the sentence provides insight into that person or thing?",* or in this case, what else in the sentence provides insight into the relationship of *the soil* to *grains*? The sentence states that *ancient Mesopotamians switched from grain production to barley* and that *excessive irrigation and salt accumulation* did something to *the soil.* These are the clues for the sentence.

Now that you've identified the clue, look for any transition words. In this sentence, the word *after* suggests that the switch from *grain production to barley* is the consequence of *irrigation and salt accumulation*'s impact on *the soil.* In other words, our two clues are in agreement and reflect the same meaning.

With all this in mind, now move on to Step 2. Come up with your own word or phrase for the blank that describes the effect on *the soil*'s relationship to *grains* brought about by *excessive irrigation and salt accumulation*—an effect that in turn would have caused *ancient Mesopotamians* to switch *from grain production to barley.* If ancient Mesopotamians had to switch from grain production to barley production, then excessive irrigation and salt accumulation must have made the soil bad for grains in some way. So, use the phrase "bad for" and move on to Step 3, checking the answer choices for any choice that indicates something "bad for."

Choice (A), *indifferent to*, does not mean something "bad for" so eliminate (A). Choice (B), *inhospitable to*, is a good match for "bad for" because if the soil was inhospitable to grain, it would explain why ancient Mesopotamians switched from grain production to barley production. Put a checkmark next to (B). Choice (C), *unsuitable for*, is also a good match for "bad for" as it would also explain why ancient Mesopotamians switched from grain production to barley production, so put another checkmark next to (C).

Don't stop evaluating the answer choices just because you found two that matched your word. Look at the remaining answer choices just in case another answer choice also matches. If that is the case, then you will need to reevaluate your interpretation of the sentence, or determine which words produce sentences that are closest in meaning. Choice (D), *acrimonious to*, may be a word you are unsure about, so put a question mark next to it. If you happen to know that *acrimonious* means angry or bitter, then you can eliminate this choice as not quite matching "bad for." Choice (E), *benignant to*, may also be a word you are unsure about, so put a question mark next to it as well. Choice (F), *inured to*, is not a good match for "bad" as inured means to grow accustomed to something, so eliminate (F).

You have two answer choices with checkmarks next to them, two choices with question marks next to them, and two choices that are eliminated. Select the two answer choices with checkmarks next to them, which is the correct answer.

Nice work.

Sentence Equivalence Drill

Work the following questions, using the same approach outlined in this chapter. Check your answers in Part V when you're done.

To any observer, ancient or _____ , the night sky appears as a hemisphere resting on the horizon.

☐ antiquated

☐ perceptive

☐ modern

☐ astute

☐ contemporary

☐ archaic

Researchers interested in the nature versus nurture debate use identical twins who were separated at birth to explore which personality characteristics are _____ and which arise through experience.

☐ intractable

☐ nascent

☐ erudite

☐ innate

☐ predilection

☐ inborn

The eccentric Canadian Prime Minister, Mackenzie King, often used séances to contact his dead pet dog for advice; despite this _____ behavior, the public had so much confidence in his ability as a leader that he was in power for 22 years.

☐ capricious

☐ lackluster

☐ poised

☐ unconventional

☐ repulsive

☐ decorous

The circulation of the blood makes human adaptability to the _____ conditions of life, such as fluctuating atmospheric pressure, level of physical activity, and diet, possible.

☐ inveterate

☐ dynamic

☐ timorous

☐ cowed

☐ turgid

☐ oscillating

Arriving in New Orleans days after Hurricane Zelda had passed and without an adequate number of vehicles of its own, the armed forces began to _____ any working form of transportation they could find, including a bus that had been chartered at great expense by a group of tourists.

☐ repatriate

☐ commandeer

☐ extradite

☐ interdict

☐ expurgate

☐ appropriate

LET'S TALK ABOUT VOCABULARY

The basic approach for Sentence Equivalence questions is going to be useful for each Sentence Equivalence question on the GRE. You're going to need to know how to proceed once you encounter a question. Knowing and believing in the basic approach is extremely valuable.

But, the basic approach can get you only so far. The truth is, for some Sentence Equivalence questions, if you do not know the meanings of the words in the answer choices, you'll likely end up guessing. There is only one, surefire defense against the possibility of guessing. That defense is having a robust vocabulary.

At the end of this section, we discuss in more detail vocabulary on the GRE. We have included the Key Terms List, which is a list of the words most commonly seen on the GRE. You should learn these words to stand the best chance of knowing many of the words you'll see on the GRE.

One of the best ways to help learn vocabulary, and to shed some light on unfamiliar words, is by understanding the roots of words.

Word Roots

Word roots are linguistic units that have distinct meanings. They're building blocks for words in modern English. Mastery of word roots can accelerate your vocabulary improvement. A knowledge of word roots can also sometimes help you infer enough about a mystery word to decide whether to keep or discard it as an answer choice. Here's a smattering of common word roots:

- *ben* or *bene*—good: *benefit, benefactor, benediction*
- *mal* or *male*—bad: *malign, malfeasance, malediction*
- *anthropo*—having to do with humankind: *anthropology, philanthropy, anthropocentric*
- *cise* or *cide*—strike, cut, or kill: *incisive, circumcise, homicide*
- *gen* or *gene*—origin, kind, or type: *genesis, generate, genus, homogenous*
- *morph* or *morpho*—form or shape: *morphology, amorphous, metamorphosis*
- *vol* or *voli*—will or intention: *volunteer, voluntary, volition*

Word roots are often combined. From the roots listed above you can now decipher several GRE-level words: *benevolence* (good intention), *malevolence* (bad intention), *anthropogenic* (caused by human activity), *anthropomorphic* (taking human form), *morphogenesis* (how something takes form), *genocide* (killing an entire group of people).

Prefixes and suffixes are especially common word roots. Just a handful of the prefixes you're sure to encounter: *ante* (before), *anti* (against), *circum* (around), *hyper* (over, above), *trans* (across). And here are some common suffixes: *able* (for adjectives indicating capability), *ism* (for nouns denoting a doctrine or belief), *less* (for adjectives indicating absence of something), *ly* (used to form adverbs from adjectives).

One good way to learn word roots is by noting the etymology (origin) of words that you look up in the dictionary. Look for word roots in your Key Terms List (in Chapter 8) and any other new words you learn.

But learning the entirety of the Key Terms List or memorizing a couple of word roots is in no way comprehensive. The GRE can test any word it wants, so unless you have a full working knowledge of the dictionary, it's likely you'll come across some words on test day that you are unfamiliar with. That's okay.

In the following section we're going to outline some strategies for you to fall back on in case you are unsure how to proceed with a particular question, and you don't know what the words mean.

It's worth repeating here that the top strategy for all Sentence Equivalence questions is first to determine whether you know the words. Test takers too often make the mistake of believing that the strategies suggested below are a cure-all (or, to use the GRE vocabulary, a nepenthe) for their Sentence Equivalence problems. We want to be very clear about this: there is no substitute for a killer vocabulary.

These strategies may not result in eliminating all the incorrect answer choices. But, if you can eliminate some, your chances of guessing correctly are certainly improved.

A PIECE OF ADVICE

When you come across a Sentence Equivalence question on test day, follow the basic approach. But, when you begin to evaluate the words in the answer choices, the best thing you can do is be honest with yourself. If you don't know any of the words, then start thinking about some of the Process of Elimination strategies below. When confronted with a word they do not know, many test takers will make the mistake of stubbornly staring at the word, convinced that if they continue to stare, the word's meaning will appear. This behavior wastes valuable time that could be spent dealing with other questions and words that they do know.

So, on test day, if you don't know a word, just admit it and move on to Process of Elimination strategies. Or, if you don't know the meanings of most or all of the words in the answer choices, make a guess and move on to the next question.

PROCESS OF ELIMINATION STRATEGIES

Ideally, when you encounter a Sentence Equivalence question, you are able to discern the clues in the sentence clearly and come up with a spot-on word for the blank. Ideally, too, you will know the meaning of every answer choice.

Needless to say, this ideal scenario isn't the only situation you will come up against when working through the Sentence Equivalence questions in the verbal sections of the GRE. The precise nuance of the clues may elude you, making it hard to come up with a word for the blank. Or you may find yourself fuzzy, or even downright clueless, about the definition of some of the answer choices. Fret not. This happens to everyone!

Luckily, with two correct answer choices and four wrong ones, there are many opportunities for effective use of Process of Elimination. Let's look at a few of the POE strategies and considerations available to you.

Positive and Negative Words

One way to slice quickly through the lineup of answer choices is to decide whether the word in the blank should have a positive or negative connotation and then separate the answer choices into positive ones and negative ones. You don't need to know the exact dictionary definition of every answer choice if you can somewhat confidently identify it as positive or negative. However, note that with the exception of words such as "sizzle" words do NOT have meanings that relate to their sounds. So, don't fall for the trap of saying something like "Oh, that word sounds ugly so it must be a negative word." After all, pulchritude isn't a particularly nice sounding word, but it means beauty. So, you can't separate words that you've never encountered before into positive or negative. But, you may remember that a word you've studied has a negative meaning even though you can't remember the precise meaning of that word.

Let's practice using this approach on the following question:

Despite the implications of their noble status, many aristocrats were virtually penniless and lived in a state of _____ .

- [ ] indigence
- [ ] opulence
- [ ] eminence
- [ ] penury
- [ ] depravity
- [ ] complacency

> Can you identify any of the words as positive or negative?

Here's How to Crack It

The transition word that begins this sentence, *Despite*, tells us that the *state* in which *many aristocrats…lived* is the opposite of *their noble status*. Because noble status is a positive idea, the word in the blank should be negative. This is reinforced by the additional clue that *many aristocrats were virtually penniless*. Evaluate the answer choices one at a time, eliminating positive words and holding onto negative words.

Choice (A), *indigence*, is an uncommon word. Instead of spending time trying to decipher whether it's positive or negative, just mark it with a question mark and move on. Choice (B) is another uncommon word, *opulence*, so give that one a question mark as well. Choice (C), *eminence*, is a positive word—think of someone described as *an eminent doctor* or as *an eminent author*. Therefore, eliminate (C) because the word in the blank has to be negative. Choice (D), *penury*, is another uncommon word, so mark it with a question mark. Choice (E), *depravity*, means moral corruption. This is certainly a negative word, but would you describe a penniless person as depraved? Not likely, so eliminate (E) as well. The final word, (F), is *complacency*, which means a feeling of self-satisfaction, so eliminate (F).

After all that, you have three answer choices remaining—(A) *indigence*, (B) *opulence*, and (D) *penury*. This is a much better situation than guessing from among all six. And if you happen to know that the word *opulence* is a positive word suggesting luxury, you've got the answer—it has to be (A) and (D).

Let's move on to another strategy.

Synonym / No Synonym

One strategy is to look over the answer choices for synonym pairs and choose one of these pairs for the answer. However, the warning given earlier in the chapter still holds: it is sometimes the case that the correct answer choices will not be strict synonyms while synonym pairs can be found among the incorrect answer choices! Therefore, this strategy must be used with caution and considered a last resort. It's best reserved for times when you are pretty familiar with the words in the answer choices but having difficulty with the clue.

Consider this example:

Because mercury has a variety of innocuous uses, including in thermometers and dental fillings, few people realize that it is one of the most _____ substances on the planet.

- ☐ acidic
- ☐ irritating
- ☐ mundane
- ☐ deleterious
- ☐ disagreeable
- ☐ pernicious

Here's How to Crack It

The clue here may be confusing, making it hard to come up with a word for the blank. So work with the answer choices to pair those that are synonyms and eliminate those with no synonyms. Evaluate the answer choices one at a time.

Start by eliminating (A), which has no synonyms among the other answer choices. Choice (B) is *irritating*. Scanning the other answer choices for a synonym, you'll find (E), *disagreeable*.

If one of these is correct, the other is likely to be as well, so make them a pair. Choice (C) is *mundane*, which can mean either worldly or unexciting. This has no synonym among the other answer choices, so eliminate (C). Choice (D) is *deleterious*, a word similar in meaning to (F), *pernicious*, the only word remaining. Make these another pair.

This process eliminates two choices and leaves you with two pairs of synonyms. Guessing at this point will give you a 50/50 chance of getting the correct answer. If you've searched for the clue and come up empty-handed, those are not bad odds.

Here's how to choose between the answer choices. The blank should describe what kind of substance mercury is. The sentence gives the insight that *mercury has a variety of innocuous* or harmless *uses*. The transition word *because* suggests agreement between this clue and the blank. However, the sentence contains another transition in the phrase *few people*, which indicates that the word in the blank should actually be the opposite of *innocuous*. This insight makes the correct answer (D) and (F).

ADVANCED SENTENCE EQUIVALENCE QUESTIONS AND HOW TO CONQUER THEM

With Text Completion questions, we saw that GRE ups the difficulty by creating questions with multiple blanks. Some of these questions might even have two or more sentences! Neither of these complications occurs in Sentence Equivalence questions—they are always a single sentence containing a single blank. For Sentence Equivalence questions, the writers have some other tools to make questions difficult.

Difficult Transitions. When we introduced the topic of transitions, we focused on words such as *and, but, so, however, because, despite, since, although, instead,* etc. But not all transitions are marked by the obvious words that typically serve this function. Be on the lookout for less-than-obvious transitions. A transition can be any language indicating that two parts, ideas, or actions in the sentence are the same or opposite in sense. Let's consider these examples:

> Being a confirmed coffee snob, Boris reluctantly _____ the foul gas-station brew.
> Being a confirmed coffee snob, Boris surprised me by _____ the foul gas-station brew.

The clue in both sentences is that Boris is a coffee snob. In the first sentence, the adverb *reluctantly* implies that whatever he did with the gas-station brew was the opposite of his inclination. In the second sentence, the fact that Boris's actions were surprising again implies an action that is the opposite of the clue. In both cases, Boris has acted against his nature as a coffee snob. Therefore, the word in the blank should suggest that Boris was willing to drink the *foul gas-station brew.*

For another example, consider the use of *few people* in the mercury example used in the previous section, on page 73. There are many ways for a sentence to present things as the same or opposite, as agreeing or contrasting, as similar or different. Read carefully and critically!

Secondary Definitions. Sometimes the folks at ETS will make a question harder the old-fashioned way: with harder vocabulary.

There's no getting around it—your best defense against a lineup of scary answer choices is a formidable vocabulary. But it's not just about learning those polysyllabic, arcane, and unusual words. Many common words have less-common meanings or nuances that may be exploited on the test. The verb *apprehend*, for example, usually means to catch or arrest a wrongdoer. But it may also simply mean to perceive or to understand. While the verb *realize* commonly means to become fully aware of something, it can also mean to make something a reality. The adjective *fast* may describe something speedy or something fixed securely in place. And, as a verb, *flag* can mean to mark with a flag or to become droopy or tired. Here's the moral of the story: when you learn a new word, take the time to learn the secondary and tertiary definitions as well.

Tips for Advanced Sentence Equivalence. Our tips for conquering the most difficult Sentence Equivalence questions fit within the three steps of the basic approach:

1. **Find the clues and transition words**.
   - Begin by asking "Who or what is the blank describing?" and "What else in the sentence gives insight into that person or thing?"
   - For Sentence Equivalence questions it may be difficult to identify the clue using the questions above. If that is the case, then start by determining the part of speech needed in the blank. This helps you to more concretely and efficiently answer the question "Who or what is the blank describing?"
   - Transitions are not always clearly marked with words such as *and, but, so, however, because, despite, since, although, instead*, etc. Be alert to other ways that a sentence can make two parts the same or opposite, agreeing or contrasting.
2. **Come up with your own word or phrase for the blank.**
   - The more thoroughly you've done Step 1, the easier it will be to come up with a word for Step 2, and the better that word will predict the correct answer choices.
   - Do not be preoccupied with coming up with the perfect, most GRE-worthy word. Feel free to recycle from the clues in the sentence. Use a phrase instead of a single word. You do want a word or phrase that accurately reflects the clues. But your goal is not to have a scratch pad full of elegant words; it's to answer the questions quickly and correctly.
3. **Check each answer choice and use your scratch paper.**
   - Stick with the clues and the word you come up with. In reviewing the answer choices, if you have to choose between words you know that don't match and words you don't know, pick from the words you don't know! For example, if you have eliminated three answer choices and put question marks next to the other three, pick two from the ones that you've marked with question marks.
   - What makes a Sentence Equivalence question harder is often just the difficulty of the words in the answer choices. Your best defense is to build a strong vocabulary. Learn your word lists, and learn the range of meanings for each word.
   - The correct answer will not always be a pair of synonyms, and synonym pairs in the answer choices are not necessarily the correct answer. See the Cautionary Tale on Synonyms at the beginning of this chapter (page 64).

Let's put these advanced skills together in working through some more difficult questions.

Despite their outward negativity, many a cynic harbors an inner faith in the _____ of humankind.

- ☐ benevolence
- ☐ precocity
- ☐ parsimony
- ☐ ignobility
- ☐ antipathy
- ☐ probity

Here's How to Crack It

Find the clue for this Sentence Equivalence question by asking, "Who or what is the blank describing?" If the answer to that question is unclear, then determine the part of speech to more easily answer the question. In this case, the blank is a noun describing some aspect *of humankind* that *cynics* have *faith in*. Now ask, "What else in the sentence gives insight into that person or thing?" This clue comes from the introductory phrase, *[d]espite their outward negativity*. *Despite* is a transition word suggesting that *their outward negativity* is the opposite of their *inner faith in* some aspect *of humankind*. Therefore, the blank must refer to some positive aspect of humankind. Pick an appropriate word such as the "good" of humankind for the blank, or focus on positive words in the answer choices. Evaluate the answer choices individually.

Choice (A), *benevolence,* is a positive word so keep (A). Choice (B), *precocity,* is an uncommon word, so put a question mark next to this one. The same can be done for (C), *parsimony*. Choice (D) has the root word *noble* in it, which is certainly positive, but the prefix *ig-* makes it a bad thing—think of the word *ignorant*. Eliminate this choice. Choice (E) has the prefix *anti-*, meaning against. This generally implies something negative, so eliminate (E). Choice (F), *probity,* is another tough word, so put a question mark next to it.

At this point, select (A), as it is the only choice with a checkmark next to it. Choices (B), (C), and (F) all have question marks, so if there is no way to further parse out what those words mean, pick one of them to go with (A) and move on. At the worst, you have a 1-in-3 chance of guessing correctly. Taking the POE a little further, you should also be able to eliminate (B). The word *precocity* is related to *precocious*. It also begins with the prefix *pre-*, meaning before—an idea that's neither positive nor negative. Choice (C), *parsimony,* means frugality, and (F), *probity*, means honesty and integrity. Thus, the correct answer is (A) and (F).

Let's try one more:

Formerly seen only on sailors and bikers, tattoos in the United States have become so _____ in urban culture as to lose any rebel cachet.

- ☐ prepossessing
- ☐ fascinating
- ☐ pedestrian
- ☐ peripheral
- ☐ marginal
- ☐ pervasive

Here's How to Crack It

Find the clue by asking first, "Who or what is the blank describing?" If the answer to that question is unclear, then determine the part of speech to more easily answer the question. In this case, the blank is an adjective describing what *tattoos have become...in urban culture*. Now ask, "What else in the sentence gives insight into that person or thing?" Clues here are that they were *[f]ormerly seen only on sailors and bikers* and that, as a consequence of what they've become, they have lost *any rebel cachet*. The word *formerly* is a transition word suggesting that tattoos— or specifically their cultural significance—have changed in some way. Therefore, the blank should suggest the opposite of being *seen only on sailors and bikers*. A good word might simply be "common," so use that for evaluating the answer choices. Evaluate the answer choices individually, looking for reasons to eliminate each.

Choice (A), *prepossessing*, might be unfamiliar. Trying to determine the meaning from its parts, you'd come up with something like "owning before." It's hard to see how this matches "common," so eliminate (A). Choice (B) is *fascinating*. While modern culture may be fascinated with tattoos, it doesn't match the word "common," so eliminate (B). Choice (C) is *pedestrian*. As an adjective, *pedestrian* can mean either walking on foot or ordinary. In the sense of ordinary, this is a good match for "common," so put a checkmark next to (C). Choice (D), *peripheral*, means at the edge of something—not a match for "common." Eliminate (D). Choice (E), *marginal*, means the same thing as *peripheral*, so eliminate it as well. The final choice is (F), *pervasive*, which describes something that is found everywhere. This could be another way of saying "common," so (F) earns a checkmark. The answer is (C) and (F).

Notice some pitfalls that we've avoided in this question. Two of the answer choices, *peripheral* and *marginal*, are synonyms but don't match "common." They'd be tempting if you missed the time transition implying that tattoos have changed from being something unusual. The words *prepossessing*, meaning impressive or pleasing, and *fascinating* are another decoy synonym pair. The correct answer choices, *pedestrian* and *pervasive*, aren't strict synonyms. Furthermore, recognizing *pedestrian* as a correct choice depends on knowing its secondary definition. These are all traps that might have tripped you up before, so you've learned a lot!

Sentence Equivalence Practice Set

Work the following questions, using all the techniques you've learned for Sentence Equivalence. Check your answers in Part V when you're done.

1 of 5

Possessed of an insatiable sweet tooth, Jim enjoyed all kinds of candy, but he had a special _____ for gumdrops, his absolute favorite.

- ☐ container
- ☐ affinity
- ☐ odium
- ☐ nature
- ☐ disregard
- ☐ predilection

2 of 5

Although the Wright brothers' first attempted flight in 1901 was a _____ and subsequent efforts similarly ended in failure, they persisted and ultimately made the first successful airplane flight in 1903.

- ☐ fiasco
- ☐ debacle
- ☐ hindrance
- ☐ feat
- ☐ triumph
- ☐ precedent

3 of 5

The fuel efficiency of most vehicles traveling at speeds greater than 50 miles per hour _____ as the vehicle's speed increases, due to the increased aerodynamic drag placed on the vehicle.

- ☐ equalizes
- ☐ adapts
- ☐ stabilizes
- ☐ diminishes
- ☐ increases
- ☐ wanes

4 of 5

Despite the vast amount of time Francis dedicated to learning six different languages, he was _____ communicator; his mastery of vocabulary and grammar failed to redress his inability to construct cogent prose.

- ☐ a florid
- ☐ an inept
- ☐ a prolific
- ☐ an astute
- ☐ a morose
- ☐ a maladroit

5 of 5

The twins' heredity and upbringing were identical in nearly every respect, yet one child remained unfailingly sanguine even in times of stress while her sister was prone to angry outbursts that indicated an exceptionally choleric _____ .

- ☐ genotype
- ☐ environment
- ☐ physiognomy
- ☐ incarnation
- ☐ temperament
- ☐ humor

Summary

o The approach for Sentence Equivalence questions is the same as that for Text Completions. Ignore the answer choices, ask who or what the blank is describing, look for clues and transition words, fill in your own word for the blank, and check the answer choices against your word using POE. You must pick two answer choices.

o Identifying the part of speech that should go in the blank will help answer who or what the blank is describing.

o Pay close attention to transitions. Transitions indicate two parts of the sentence are the same or opposite in meaning. They are often marked by obvious words like *and, but, so, however, because, despite, since, although, instead,* etc. Other transitions are not as obvious but still important.

o If the clue is hard to decipher, you can simplify POE by determining if the word to go in the blank should be positive or negative. Then narrow down the answer choices by eliminating those that don't match.

o The two correct answer choices may not be strict synonyms.

o Sentence Equivalence questions can be made harder simply by having more difficult words in the answer choices. Keep working on vocabulary every day! Learn prefixes, suffixes, and other word roots.

Chapter 6
Reading Comprehension

Reading Comprehension questions on the GRE can be quite deceptive. On the one hand, the answer to each question is somewhere in the passage. On the other hand, ETS is really good at crafting answers that seem right but are, in fact, wrong. This chapter will teach you the best way to approach the reading passages on the test and how to attack the questions. Furthermore, you'll learn how to use Process of Elimination to eliminate wrong answers and maximize your score.

READING COMPREHENSION OVERVIEW

Reading Comprehension questions make up approximately one-half of the questions in the Verbal section. Recall that the reading passages will appear after the Text Completion questions, and then again at the end of the section after the Sentence Equivalence questions. All questions related to the passages will be presented together.

The passages you will see will vary in length from one paragraph for the shortest passages to five paragraphs for the longest passages. For short passages, you will be asked to answer 3 questions. For long passages, you will be asked to answer 4 questions.

Reading Comprehension passages can be intimidating to test takers, as there is a sudden influx of information on the screen and the test taker prepares for the task of reading and answering questions about a passage that is often dense, wordy, and boring. During Reading Comprehension passages, it is not uncommon for test takers to feel rushed, which makes it hard to pay attention to a passage that covers a topic area that most find dry. However, contrary to popular belief, everything you need to know to crack Reading Comprehension questions can be found in the text. This chapter is going to teach you how to crack the passages and questions, leading you to the correct answers.

More Information on Reading Comprehension Passages

GRE passages cover a variety of topics, but will typically come from the physical sciences, biological sciences, social sciences, business, arts and humanities, as well as everyday topics and are based on material found in books and periodicals, both academic and nonacademic.

Reading Comprehension questions are presented on a split screen. The passage is on the left-hand side and stays there while you work on the questions; you may have to use the scroll bar to read the whole passage. The questions appear one at a time on the right-hand side. After you answer the first question, another appears in its place. The passage remains unchanged and in place so you can always refer to it. As with any other type of question on the GRE, Reading Comprehension questions can be answered in any order you wish by using the skip function on the test. Just make sure you answer all the questions!

Since the passage will appear only on the screen, it's very important to practice reading comprehension without underlining words or bracketing text directly in the passage. Every time you practice reading comprehension on paper, anything you write must be written on scratch paper. In your preparation for the GRE, never give yourself a crutch you won't have when you take the real test.

THE PRINCETON REVIEW APPROACH

The Basic Approach to Cracking GRE Reading Comprehension

Before we begin to crack the Reading Comprehension passages and questions, it is important to establish The Basic Approach. The Basic Approach allows you to:

- actively read the passages and seek out the most important information
- understand the different types of questions and what they require you to do
- quickly find the credited response by eliminating incorrect answers

Don't Be Predictable

The typical test taker is predictable and approaches questions on the test in a certain way. The people who write the GRE create questions and passages that are designed with those people in mind. They will make questions that trick and confuse test takers who follow the typical approach. However, if you approach the test in a better way, you improve your chances of getting a better score. One hard-and-fast rule of test-taking is that whenever you do what the test writers expect, you don't get the best score possible. When you do things in a different way, you increase your chances of getting a better score. So, our approach to reading needs to be that "different way." The different ways you are going to learn are the Basics of Cracking the Passage, The Basics of Cracking the Questions, and The Basics of Cracking the Answer Choices. These combine to form the foundation that is used for The Basic Approach to Cracking Reading Comprehension.

The Basics of Cracking the Passage

The typical test taker reads the passage without a plan. So, to crack the passage, you need to have a plan for reading the passage. The typical test taker concentrates on the facts in the passage rather than why those facts are there. So, to crack the passage, you also need to focus on how facts relate to the main idea of the passage.

The Basics of Cracking the Questions

The typical test taker reads the question but doesn't identify the question task. To crack the questions, you must learn to locate both the subject and the task of the question. The **subject** of the question is what you need to find in the passage. The **question task** tells you what type of information you need to find about the subject of the question. For example, do you need to locate what the author said about the subject or do you need to find out why the author mentioned the subject?

The Basics of Cracking the Answer Choices

The typical test taker is focused on simply finding the correct answer. While that may seem like a reasonable goal, it's more effective to utilize Process of Elimination (POE) and eliminate wrong answers. Cracking the Answer Choices is all about understanding how ETS constructs incorrect answer choices. If you can learn to identify common trap answer choices, you can often eliminate them with confidence.

Additionally, the typical test taker relies a lot on memory and reads only those parts of sentences that are referenced by the question or answer choices. Reading only parts of sentences makes it easy to misconstrue the context of the sentence. Flipping this behavior around by not only reading full sentences but also reading sentences before and after it is crucial to cracking both the question and the answer choices. Remember, the correct answer is always found in the text. Always refer to the passage and always read full sentences when you do so.

THE STEPS OF THE BASIC APPROACH TO CRACKING GRE READING COMPREHENSION

Here are the steps of the Basic Approach:

1. **Work the Passage**

   This is where you apply **The Basics of Cracking the Passage.** You must have a plan for reading the passage and you must learn to read actively. As you read, always be on the lookout for how each element of the passage relates to the main idea of the passage. To find the main idea, ask yourself questions such as: What does the author want me to remember or believe about the topic under discussion? What's the author's conclusion? How is that conclusion supported?

2. **Understand the Question**

   This is where you apply **The Basics of Cracking the Questions.** Try to break the question down. First, look for the subject of the question. Then, find the words that indicate the task.

3. **Find the Information in the Passage that Addresses the Task of the Question**

   Refer back to the passage. ETS needs to be able to justify its credited responses by referring to specific information mentioned in the passage. When you understand the task of the question, it becomes easier to find this information. Once you locate the information in the passage that addresses the question task, you're ready to look at the answer choices.

4. **Use Process of Elimination**

   This is where you use **The Basics of Cracking the Answer Choices.** Approach each answer choice with a healthy level of suspicion. Since there are more incorrect answers than correct answers for most questions, you are more likely to be reading a wrong answer than a right answer. Look for signs that are more likely to make an answer wrong, the most common of which are the signs outlined later in this chapter as tools for POE. Don't be afraid to just pick the answer that remains if you can find good reasons to eliminate the other answer choices. An overview of common trap answer choices can be found later in this chapter.

Now, let's dive in deeper.

THE BASIC APPROACH TO CRACKING THE GRE READING COMPREHENSION

STEP 1 >> Step 1: Work the Passage

Overview

Working the passage is the first step of **The Basic Approach to Cracking GRE Reading Comprehension Passages**. By following the recommendations here on how to Work the Passage, you will be able to follow a strategic plan for reading the passage, avoid wasting time by actively reading the passage, and map the passage to glean all the relevant information from the passage, which enables you to answer the questions later on. All in all, you will know what it takes to Crack the Passage. From there, it's time to practice!

How Do You Plan to Read?

Before we talk about how to Crack the Passage, let's explore how the typical test taker handles the passage. The typical test taker approaches Reading Comprehension passages in the same way they would approach any reading assignment. They read as quickly as possible while barely scratching the surface of the major points of the passage that the author was trying to express. Often about halfway through the passage, the typical test taker realizes they have not retained a single major point of the passage. The test taker is now forced to either re-read the entire passage or move on to the answer choices without a full comprehension of the material. This strategy is ineffective and worse, wastes a lot of time!

A better way to approach the passage is to have a plan before you read! Central to the plan is the test taker's ability to comprehend the passage through Active Reading. Active Reading keeps you engaged with the passage, fights off the tendency to let your mind wander away from the task at hand, and leaves you with a better understanding of the author's main point once you are finished. But what is Active Reading and how do you do it?

The Basics of Cracking the Passage

Active Reading

The easiest way to define "Active Reading" is to define the opposite, or "Passive Reading." During passive reading, you look at the words, but the content just isn't registering. You may remember some of the details from the passage, but you probably missed *why* the author told you about those details. This is common on GRE passages, as the content is often dense and boring.

Active Reading, on the other hand, means that you follow the author's argument. Put another way, you try to separate the author's claims from the facts and other evidence used to back up those claims. This is an essential ingredient for Cracking the Passage.

Effective Active Reading involves the following elements:

- *Asking questions as you read:* Asking questions helps to engage your mind. For example, ask yourself key questions about the passage and its author. Why did the author provide the information in the sentence I just read? What is the author's purpose for writing the passage? What kind of tone is the author adopting (scholarly, friendly, critical, objective, biased)? At the end of a paragraph, try to predict where the author takes the argument next. Applying this kind of thinking will help you develop a full understanding of the passage.
- *Claims versus evidence*: As you ask questions about what you are reading, your overall objective is to understand why the author included the information you read. While GRE Reading Comprehension passages can cover myriad topics, what they have in common is that they typically involve the author attempting to convince you of his/her point of view regarding the topic of the passage. To construct a convincing argument, the author must present his/her opinion and then provide evidence to back it up. So, as you read GRE Reading Comprehension passages, ask yourself if what you just read could be considered a claim or evidence. Claims are opinions expressed by the author or by a third-party cited by the author. Evidence is information used to support a claim. A good way to distinguish between claims and evidence is to apply the "Why" Test. If the information you read can be used to answer *why* the author believes his/her claim, then that information is evidence. If the information you read tells you *what* the author believes, then the information is a claim. By asking yourself what the function is of each sentence you read, you'll become more effective at determining the main point of the passage.
- *Identifying the structure of the passage*: The structure of a passage is an undervalued hint to deciphering the intentions of the author and the main point of the passage. Passages written in a conventional manner usually proceed from the general to the specific and then return to the general. Individual paragraphs are also usually written that way. Be on the lookout for pivotal words or phrases in the middle of a paragraph (*however, on the contrary, on the other hand*). These words are indicators of the author's perspective on the topic of the passage. Often, the author follows up one of these pivotal words with the perspective he/she is trying to convince you to adopt.

The Main Idea

One of the central goals of Active Reading is to determine the main idea. The main idea of the passage is what the author wants you to believe about the issue being presented in the passage.

Note how the main idea is distinct from the topic of the passage. The topic of the passage is what the passage is about. The main idea is what the author wants YOU to believe about the topic. So, if you find yourself agreeing or disagreeing with the author, or noticing the author pushing an opinion or arguing a point, chances are that is the main idea of the passage.

By identifying the main idea of the passage, you can quickly and easily determine the purpose of the passage, which is one of the key components of successfully Cracking the Passage.

Mapping the Passage

Mapping the Passage is the final tool in learning how to Crack the Passage. By Mapping the Passage, you can easily identify the main idea of the passage, the structure of the passage, and the author's side on the various claims presented in the passage. But, to successfully map the passage, you must do something that a typical test taker never does. You must write things down. Just because you reach a Reading Comprehension passage does not give you an excuse to stop writing things down. In fact, as a time-saving tactic alone, writing things down while working on a Reading Comprehension passage is worth the effort. Writing things down also helps you get a better understanding on the topic being presented, which yields a more complete appreciation for the passage and makes answering the questions a lot more manageable!

The idea behind Mapping the Passage is to separate each sentence into one of three categories: claim, evidence/objection, and background. Recall that a *claim* is an opinion expressed in the passage, either the author's or a third-party's. *Evidence* is information presented to support a claim, while an *objection* is information presented to call a claim into question. *Background* is any information that is generally accepted as fact. Read the passage one sentence at a time. At the end of each sentence, stop and try to identify the function of the sentence as either a claim, evidence/objection, or background. Also, write a short summary of that sentence down. You don't need to write the entire sentence, but you do want to write more than one or two words. If the sentence provides any insight into what the author believes about a claim stated in the passage, note that on your scratch paper, as well.

The idea behind mapping the passage is to uncover the author's original outline for the passage. When you are finished mapping the passage, you should be able to see how the sentences link together to construct the author's argument.

For longer passages (which can run up to 100 lines), scrutinizing each sentence in detail is far less practical. Instead, think of each paragraph as a series of short passages that make up a long passage. For each paragraph, determine the function of each sentence to then determine the overall function of the paragraph itself. Your approach to Cracking the Passage for long passages shouldn't change in any significant way. Because long passages are simply longer, there is more space for the author to include background information.

STEP 2 » Step 2: Understand the Question

Overview

Understanding the task of the question is important to Cracking GRE Reading Comprehension and it is largely overlooked by the average test taker. The Basics of Cracking the Questions can be broken down into two parts: identifying the subject and understanding the task.

The Basics of Cracking the Questions

Part 1: Identifying the Subject

When cracking GRE Reading Comprehension questions, it's crucial to identify the subject of the question. For example, in the question "The author mentions land management policy in order to," the subject of the question is *land management policy*. The subject helps you locate what you need to read *about* to answer the question.

By identifying the subject, you will know what the question writer is testing you on. This is important for two reasons. First, by knowing the content that the question writer is testing you on, you will be able to locate that information in the passage more easily. This is outlined in Step 3 of The Basic Approach. Secondly, without identifying the subject, you may struggle to eventually answer the question and will be susceptible to some of the common trap incorrect answer choices. Identifying the subject is critical to Cracking the Questions, but equally as important is understanding the task of the question.

Part 2: Understanding the Task

If you have been actively reading this chapter thus far, you may have been able to predict that the second part of Cracking the Questions is understanding the task of the question. The task of the question is what you need to find out about the subject. For example, is the question asking for a detail from the passage, or is it asking why that detail is in the passage? Are you required merely to describe something, or does the question expect you to analyze it? Meanwhile, you should also be on the lookout for words such as EXCEPT, LEAST, and NOT.

In the example question given earlier, "The author mentions land management policy in order to," the task words are *in order to*. The tasks that questions can ask about are diverse and can be categorized as *general*, *specific*, or *complex* tasks.

General tasks ask about the passage as a whole. General questions can take a few different forms: primary purpose, main idea, structure, and tone.

- **Primary Purpose** questions ask *why* the author wrote the passage. The answers to these are tied closely to the main idea of the passage. The subject of primary purpose questions is usually the whole passage. These questions can be identified by the phrase *"primary purpose,"* and *"primarily concerned with."* Not to be confused with purpose questions, primary purpose questions test very broad ideas. If you have carefully Cracked the Passage, you should be able to answer these questions easily.
- The task of **Main Idea** questions is to figure out what the author wants you to believe. The main idea is the overall claim, supported by the evidence contained in the rest of the text; in other words, what does the author want you to accept as true? Main idea questions differ from primary purpose questions in that the former deal with *what* the passage is about rather than *why* the author wrote it. However, much like primary purpose questions, these questions are easily answerable if you have successfully Cracked the Passage.

- **Structure** questions ask about the overall sequence of the passage, while others ask about a smaller piece of it, such as a single paragraph. Either way, these questions test the general flow of the passage. If you can describe the flow of ideas—a task made easier by Mapping the Passage on your scratch paper—you'll be able to narrow down the answer choices, crossing off answers that describe things that didn't happen in the passage.
- **Tone** questions ask you to evaluate how strongly or negatively the author feels about the subject of the question. Find the subject in the passage and look for words that reveal the author's feelings. Examples of such words and phrases include *misrepresenting, unlikely, considerable importance, unfortunately,* and *a poor grasp,* among many others. Questions that ask about the author's tone generally use the words *"tone"* or *"attitude."*

Specific tasks reference a small part of the passage. There are four different specific question tasks: Vocabulary-in-Context, Retrieval, Inference, and Specific Purpose.

- **Vocabulary-in-Context** questions ask you to state what the author means by a certain word or phrase. These questions will typically contain the task words *most nearly means.* The correct answer must fit the context of the sentence that contains the word or phrase as well as the paragraph containing that sentence.
- **Retrieval** questions ask you to find information in the passage and may make reference to a detail or fact (a person's name, a theory, a time period, etc.). The answer is typically just a paraphrase of this information in the passage. Retrieval questions do not contain standard wording that will help you identify this question type. If the task words in the question require you to find a detail in the passage, then you are dealing with a Retrieval question.
- **Inference** questions make test takers nervous because they appear to suggest that the answer has to be figured out using knowledge about the author. However, it is important to remember that, on the GRE, the word *infer* means only one thing: "what must be true." In other words, you do not need to draw a conclusion based on information in the passage, nor do you need to read between the lines. The answer to an Inference question will just be a paraphrase of information in the passage. Thus, Inference questions are essentially the same as retrieval tasks. There is no need for interpretation. Inference questions can be identified by phrases such as *infer, imply, suggest,* or ask with what *the author would most likely agree/disagree.*
- **Specific Purpose** questions ask *why* the author included the subject or a particular piece of information. In general, the subject of a Specific Purpose question is evidence used by the author to support or object to a claim in the passage. Therefore, the task of the question is to find the claim that the author supports or objects to. In many cases, this claim is in the sentence just before where the subject appears in the passage. These questions can be identified by phrases such as *purpose, in order to, role,* or *function.*

Complex tasks require a good understanding of the main idea, so Cracking the Passage is essential. Complex questions usually appear as Weaken or Strengthen questions. With either type of complex question, it is crucial to take an extra second and consider the author's point carefully.

- **Weaken** questions ask the test taker to *weaken* a claim presented in the passage. The task is to identify the answer choice that makes the claim *less believable*. When claims are introduced in GRE passages, they are usually followed by evidence that supports the claim. So, typical correct answers to Weaken questions will call the evidence used to support the claim into question.
- **Strengthen** questions ask the test taker to *strengthen* a claim in the passage. In other words, you must find the answer choice that makes the claim *more believable*. In contrast with Weaken questions, correct answers to Strengthen questions will tend to further support the evidence associated with the claim referenced in the question stem.

Step 3: Find the Information in the Passage that Addresses the Task of the Question

Overview

Step 3 of the Basic Approach to Cracking the GRE Reading Comprehension is finding the information in the passage that addresses the question task. After you have Cracked the Question by identifying the subject and the task, look for the subject in the passage. Once you locate the subject, find the information about the subject that addresses the task of the question. You will always be able to prove the correct answer with something in the passage. If you cannot put your finger on a specific word, phrase, or sentence that proves your answer choice, don't pick it.

This is when Cracking the Passage from Step 1 of the Basic Approach is invaluable. Use your map of the passage to find the appropriate place in the text that addresses the subject and start reading. Try to read a few lines before and after where the subject appears. Then, make sure you understand what you have read. Your goal is to find the information from the passage that addresses the task of the question. And, as always, the answers to the questions can always be found in the passage. You may need to state how ideas in the passage are connected, as authors do not always explicitly make these connections. However, it is important for you not to add your own ideas or assumptions into the passage, so as you spell out what the correct answer needs to do, stick closely to the content of the passage.

Remember to use the **Active Reading** strategies from Step 1. After you have found the appropriate place to begin reading, keep the task of the question in the back of your mind and be on constant lookout for any information that addresses the task of the question. After you have found this information, and have taken measures to ensure you truly understand the information, you are ready to move on to Step 4 of the Basic Approach to Cracking GRE Reading Comprehension—examining and eliminating answer choices.

STEP 4 » Step 4: Use Process of Elimination

Overview

The final step of The Basic Approach to Cracking GRE Reading Comprehension is using Process of Elimination (POE) to find the answer. If you have followed all the steps up to this point, then you have worked the passage and have a thorough understanding of it through Active Reading, analyzed and achieved understanding of the question subject and task, and located and read the information about the question subject and task in the passage. Now, it's time to look at the answer choices and find the correct answer by using POE.

As discussed throughout this entire book thus far, POE is one of the most powerful tools at your disposal on test day. This holds true for Reading Comprehension as well, as POE is the best tool to help you find the correct answer by eliminating the incorrect ones. Once you understand the task of the question and have been able to locate its information in the passage, eliminating wrong answer choices is the most effective way to answer the question correctly.

Many test takers do exactly what the writers of the test want them to do—they answer questions based on memory or what sounds correct. However, if you learn how ETS creates incorrect answer choices, you can eliminate answers quickly and give yourself the best chance at achieving the highest score possible for you.

In light of that, the final step to Cracking the GRE Reading Comprehension is learning about the different ways that the test writers create wrong answer choices, learning how to spot wrong answers, and then confidently eliminating the offending answer choices. A savvy test taker learns to stop considering which choice is "better." The incorrect answers are wrong, not just "worse," so when multiple choices remain, the key is to identify why all but the correct answer are 100% wrong for some reason.

The Basics of Cracking the Answer Choices

Knowing the types of answer choices that test writers use to create wrong answers is the key to applying POE effectively on test day. Test writers use certain kinds of answer choices to make an answer choice look attractive. The problem is, even if you have read the passage and followed the steps, a lot of times the incorrect answer choices still look correct! The test writers have to write hard answer choices like this or else the questions would be too easy. Your job is to become familiar with the ways in which they create these wrong answers so that when you read an answer choice constructed in a certain way, it raises suspicion. The more suspicious you are of the answer choices, the more likely you are to be able to eliminate them.

The following are the ways in which test writers create wrong answers:

- *Recycled Language*
- *Extreme Language*
- *No Such Comparison*
- *Reversals*
- *Outside Knowledge*
- *Emotional Appeals*

Become familiar with these and you are one step closer to Cracking GRE Reading Comprehension.

Recycled Language

One of the easiest and most common ways that test writers create wrong answer choices is by repeating memorable words or phrases from the passage. The correct answers for GRE Reading Comprehension questions are generally paraphrases of the passage. So, the presence of words or phrases that are very reminiscent of the passage is a reason to be skeptical of the answer choice.

Recycled language in an answer choice is easily identified because recycled language is words or phrases that are direct quotes from the text. There's a really good chance that the recycled language comes from the wrong part of the passage or that the answer says something a little different from what the passage says. If you see words or phrases that fit the description of recycled language, you should be very suspicious of the answer choice. Did the passage say exactly what the answer choice says regarding the recycled language? If it doesn't, the answer choice is incorrect.

Extreme Language

Another common way to create wrong answer choices is by using language that is too strong or too broad. Common ways to do that are by using words such as *must, always, never, only, best,* and other very strong words, or by answers that use verbs that are overly strong, such as *prove* or *fail*. These types of answers will make claims that are much stronger than can be reasonably drawn from the information in the passage.

For instance, a primary purpose question may have answer choices that use a powerful verb such as *defend* or *criticize*. If the passage does not explicitly defend or criticize the main idea, this answer choice is incorrect because it contains extreme language. Below is a chart of common words that should raise suspicion as extreme language.

Common Extreme Words			
Never	Not	Defend	Contradict
Always	No	Attack	Failure
Only	Must	Denounce	
None	Prove	Counter	

Once you identify extreme language in an answer choice, consider what the author stated about that topic and compare it to the extreme language. If the author's claim is not as strong as the extreme language, eliminate the answer choice.

No Such Comparison

Comparison words such as *better, more than,* or *less than* are used by test writers to make answer choices more appealing by drawing a comparison between two items referenced in the passage. If you see comparison words in an answer choice, you should be suspicious of that answer choice. As with every answer choice, make sure to reference the information in the answer choice against the information in the passage. Often, the ideas being compared in the answer choices were discussed in the passage but not explicitly compared.

Reversals

Reversal answer choices seek to confuse the test taker by stating a contradiction of the main idea or a fact from the passage. These answer choices are more difficult to spot because there isn't a list of common words. However, if you have successfully Cracked the Passage and found the information in the passage that references the task of the question, then identifying reversal answer choices becomes a lot more manageable. These choices can be tricky to spot because they often sound appealing, and then include a contradictory detail. Analyze every word of the answer choices. If a choice is perfect, except for a contradictory detail, eliminate it as a reversal.

Outside Knowledge

This answer choice type is fairly rare on the GRE. However, it is still worth mentioning. Correct answer choices on the GRE contain information that is found only in the passage. However, an outside knowledge answer choice can be very tempting because you may know a piece of information that is not mentioned in the passage but is reflected in an answer choice. Remember, you must rely only on the information in the passage to answer questions on the GRE. An outside knowledge answer choice is likely to include a commonly known detail about a topic, but that detail will not be present in the passage.

Emotional Appeals

Much like outside knowledge answer choices, emotional appeals are also fairly rare on the GRE. These types of answer choices state positions that you believe, but are not discussed in the passage. For instance, a political passage may contain an answer choice that values one political stance over another even if the passage made no such claim. If you have successfully followed the steps to Crack the Passage and identified the main idea and the task of the question, these answer choices are easily eliminated.

Down to 2?

Let's suppose you've used POE to Crack the Answer Choices. You were able to eliminate answers using the POE tools mentioned above, but two answer choices remain and you're having trouble eliminating that last answer choice. This is a pretty common situation that can occur in the GRE Reading Comprehension. So how do you choose between the two? First, remember that this situation means you are probably missing why one of the answer choices is wrong, and should look carefully at each word in the remaining choices. At some point, however, you may need to simply make a decision. Well, the same POE tools can be used to play the odds when guessing by asking yourself the following questions:

1. ***Which answer uses more words or phrases from the passage?*** If one answer uses recycled language and the other doesn't, choose the one that doesn't, as answers with recycled language often turn out to be wrong.
2. ***Which answer uses stronger language or makes a stronger claim?*** Eliminate the answer that uses more extreme language and choose the other.
3. ***Which answer makes a comparison?*** Always be on the lookout for answers that make comparisons, as they are often incorrect.

If you're still struggling, don't linger on the question. Just mark it, move on, and come back to it later.

Reading Comprehension Practice Set

Answers can be found in Part V.

Questions 1 through 4 are based on the following reading passage.

Called by some the "island that time forgot," Madagascar is home to a vast array of unique, exotic creatures. One such animal is the aye-aye. First described by western science in 1782, it was initially categorized as a member of the order Rodentia. Further research then revealed that it was more closely related to the lemur, a member of the primate order. Since the aye-aye is so different from its fellow primates, however, it was given its own family: *Daubentoniidae*. The aye-aye has been listed as an endangered species and, as a result, the government of Madagascar has designated an island off the northeastern coast of Madagascar as a protected reserve for aye-ayes and other wildlife.

Long before Western science became enthralled with this nocturnal denizen of Madagascar's jungles, the aye-aye had its own reputation with the local people. The aye-aye is perhaps best known for its large, round eyes and long, extremely thin middle finger. These adaptations are quite sensible, allowing the aye-aye to see well at night and retrieve grubs, which are one of its primary food sources, from deep within hollow branches. However, the aye-aye's striking appearance may end up causing its extinction. The people of Madagascar believe that the aye-aye is a type of spirit animal, and that its appearance is an omen of death. Whenever one is sighted, it is immediately killed. When combined with the loss of large swaths of jungle habitat, this practice may result in the loss of a superb example of life's variety.

Based on the information given in the passage, the intended audience would most likely be

○ visitors to a natural science museum

○ professors of evolutionary science

○ a third-grade science class

○ students of comparative religions

○ attendees at a world culture symposium

The author's attitude toward the aye-aye, as represented in the highlighted text, could best be described as

○ admiring

○ mystified

○ reverent

○ appalled

○ lachrymose

Select the sentence in the first paragraph that suggests the author's claim that "this practice may result in the loss of a superb example of life's variety" is unlikely to happen.

For the following question, consider each of the choices separately and select all that apply.

Which of the following statements can be logically inferred from the passage about the aye-aye?

☐ The aye-aye currently lives only on a protected reserve off the northeastern coast of Madagascar.

☐ The aye-aye is a nocturnal animal.

☐ The aye-aye is a prominent part of the religion practiced by the people of Madagascar.

Questions 5 through 6 are based on the following reading passage.

A novel that is a bestseller is often, because of its popularity, not taken seriously as literature. Critics seem to presuppose that great literature must be somehow burdensome to the reader; it must be difficult for the uninitiated to understand. It is precisely this inverted snobbery that has hindered Isabel Allende's *The House of the Spirits* from gaining the critical attention it deserves.

Published in 1982, the novel draws deeply on the author's own family history. Allende is the first cousin once removed of former Chilean president Salvador Allende, who was murdered during a right-wing military coup in 1973. Yet rather than the to-be-expected socialist harangue, Allende subtly works her political message within the fabric of the compelling narrative she weaves. While Allende borrows a bit too freely from Gabriel García Márquez's work, she nevertheless has a powerful and original voice within the construct of magical realism.

The author of the passage would probably consider which of the following situations to be most analogous to the critics' viewpoint as it is described in the highlighted sentence?

○ Avant-garde movies with complicated storylines are deemed cinematically superior works to Hollywood blockbusters with straightforward narratives.

○ Scientific journals are thought of as providing coverage of natural events that is inferior to that provided by nature documentaries.

○ Poetry is considered superior literature to prose because it is shorter, and therefore the message it conveys is more easily understood.

○ Political diatribes are viewed as falling outside the accepted literary canon because they are too controversial.

○ A movie version of a popular novel is considered artistically superior to the original.

It can be inferred from the passage that

○ Allende's novel is a retelling of her family's political struggles

○ Allende's novel would have received more favorable reviews if critics had believed it to be great literature

○ Allende learned about magical realism from Gabriel García Márquez

○ Allende's novel could have been more compelling if she had included a stronger political message

○ readers might have expected Allende's work to be more political than it actually was

Questions 7 through 8 are based on the following reading passage.

Bronson Alcott is perhaps best known not for who he was, but for whom he knew. Indeed, Alcott's connections were impressive by any standards: He was a close confidante of such luminaries as Margaret Fuller, Ralph Waldo Emerson, and Henry David Thoreau. Yet, to remember the man solely by his associations is to miss his importance to nineteenth-century American philosophy as a whole and to the Transcendental Movement in particular. Admittedly, Alcott's gift was not as a writer. His philosophical treatises have rightly been criticized by many as being ponderous, esoteric, and lacking focus.

However, Alcott was an erudite orator, and it is in the text of his orations that one begins to appreciate him as a visionary. Most notably, Alcott advocated what were at the time polemical ideas on education. He believed that good teaching should be Socratic in nature and that a student's intellectual growth was concomitant with his or her spiritual growth.

It can be inferred from the passage that the author would agree with all of the following statements EXCEPT

○ Alcott should be remembered for his contributions to Transcendentalism

○ Alcott's ideas were ahead of those of many of his contemporaries

○ Alcott believed that learning should not neglect a student's spiritual education

○ Alcott's ideas about education were not always accepted by his compatriots

○ Alcott should not be regarded as a particularly gifted orator

It can be inferred that the author would agree with which of the following statements?

○ Transcendentalism was an esoteric field of inquiry promulgated by a select group of visionaries.

○ Alcott's prose style is not always easily understood.

○ A Socratic pedagogical style is difficult to align with spiritual teaching.

○ Alcott should be chiefly appreciated for the strengths of his association.

○ The text of Alcott's orations were widely accepted by his peers.

Questions 9 through 10 are based on the following reading passage.

Consider each of the choices separately and select all that apply.

    Echinosorex gymnura, known colloquially as the moonrat or gymnure, is one of the many fascinating creatures that inhabit the jungles of Southeast Asia. A close relative of the hedgehog, the moonrat likewise belongs to the order *Insectivora* and the family *Erinaceidae.* However, the family then splits into the sub-family *Hylomyinae,* which contains three separate genera and eight distinct species. The appearance and habitat of the moonrat are actually far more similar to those of various members of the order *Rodentia,* though its eating habits are more in line with its fellow insectivores. Ultimately, the taxonomic classification of this animal is useful only when considered along with other information regarding the animal's ecological niche.

Which of the following scenarios demonstrates the idea put forth by the author of this passage regarding animal classification?

- ☐ While studying a population of bears, scientists rely solely on the traditional taxonomic designations to identify likely hunting grounds.

- ☐ A team of medical researchers closely monitors the actions of the animals involved in a study and compares its findings with prevailing beliefs about those animals.

- ☐ A zookeeper designs a habitat for a new acquisition, disregards taxonomic classifications and instead focuses on observational data.

The author's tone could best be described as

- ○ exasperated
- ○ didactic
- ○ ambivalent
- ○ morose
- ○ laudatory

Summary

- Before answering the questions, attack the passage. Read the passages looking for the main idea, structure, and tone. Remember to read actively.

- Make sure you identify the question subject and task.

- Return to the passage to find the answer to the question. Don't answer from memory! Go back to the text and find the answer.

- Use POE aggressively, being on the lookout for common trap answers left by the test writers.

Chapter 7
Critical Reasoning

While ETS considers Critical Reasoning questions to fall within the category of Reading Comprehension questions, the questions are different enough to merit a separate discussion. Let's jump in!

CRITICAL REASONING

Critical Reasoning questions are composed of short reading passages, typically just one paragraph long, followed by a series of questions about the author's argument. You should expect to see anywhere from two to four Critical Reasoning questions within the two GRE Verbal sections.

Each Critical Reasoning question contains a passage, the question, and 5 answer choices.

The Passage

Critical Reasoning passages tend to be short (usually 20–100 words) and often take the form of an argument. The subjects they consider rarely fall into neat categories, and generally reference hypothetical scenarios. Read your passages carefully, pay attention to the language employed, and interpret that language literally. It is important to be precise when reading the passage for Critical Reasoning questions. As you'll see in the pages to come, the difference between getting a Critical Reasoning question correct and falling for a trap answer often lies in the particulars of the passage's wording.

Know the Questions
We'll go into these in more detail later on in this chapter, but the main question types are *assumption, weaken, strengthen,* and *inference*, and the secondary ones are *resolve/explain, evaluate, identify the reasoning,* and *flaw*.

The Question

There are 8 types of Critical Reasoning questions, each of which involves a different task with respect to the passage. Most questions test your ability to evaluate the reasoning employed in an argument, but some test your ability to reason on the basis of information. This chapter will outline the different types of questions you will see, how to identify them, and what to look for in the passage based on the type of question. So much of your evaluation of the passage depends on what the question is asking you to identify in the passage. Because of this, you should read the question first, and then read the passage.

The Answer Choices

All things verbal come down to Process of Elimination, and Critical Reasoning is no exception. Each question type for Critical Reasoning questions has its own set of POE tools. These tools are based off the common trap answers constructed by the test makers. Because the question types all vary, the common trap answers and POE tools to employ also vary based on question type. After mastering the different types of questions, you'll learn how answer choices for those question types are constructed and, with enough practice, you'll be able to spot a bad answer choice with confidence.

HOW GRE ARGUMENTS ARE CONSTRUCTED

Most Critical Reasoning passages take the form of *arguments* in which the writer tries to convince the reader of something. GRE arguments consist of three connected parts:

- Conclusion: what the author tries to persuade the reader to accept.
- Premise: evidence provided in support of a conclusion.
- Assumption: unstated ideas upon which an argument's validity rests.

Conclusions

A conclusion is the primary claim made in an argument. The easiest way to identify the conclusion is to ask yourself what its author wants you to believe. Here's an example:

> During the past 10 years, advertising revenues for the magazine *True Investor* have fallen by thirty-percent. The magazine has failed to attract new subscribers, and newsstand sales are at an all-time low. Thus, sweeping changes to the editorial board will be necessary for the magazine to survive.

In the argument above, the conclusion is found in the last sentence, where the author attempts to persuade the reader that *sweeping changes to the editorial board will be necessary for the magazine to survive.*

> Remember: The conclusion is often the author's opinion about what *might* happen.

In some cases, indicator words can help you to find the conclusion. These include:

- Therefore
- Clearly
- Thus
- Hence
- Consequently
- So

Indicator words can help you to identify the parts of an argument, but not every argument uses them. However, almost every argument has a conclusion of some kind. A conclusion can be a plan or course of action, an argument, a statement of supposed truth, or any number of resolutions to the contents of the passage.

Learning to identify the conclusion is the first important step in evaluating the passage. Once you've identified the conclusion, the remaining information in the passage should reveal evidence that is used in support of the conclusion.

Practice: Identifying Conclusions

Underline the conclusions of the arguments in the following Critical Reasoning passages. Answers can be found in Part V.

1 of 5

Despite the support of the president, it is unlikely that the new defense bill will pass. A bipartisan group of 15 senators has announced that it does not support the legislation.

2 of 5

The earliest known grass fossils date from approximately 55 million years ago. Dinosaurs most likely disappeared from the earth around 60 million years ago. Based on this evidence, as well as fossilized remains of dinosaur teeth that indicate the creatures were more suited to eating ferns and palms, scientists have concluded that grass was not a significant part of the dinosaur diet.

3 of 5

Automaker X has lost over 2 billion dollars this year due to rising costs, declining automobile sales, and new governmental regulations. Because of the company's poor financial situation, it has asked its employees to pay more for health care and to accept a pay cut. However, the workers at automaker X are threatening to go on strike. If that happens, automaker X will have no choice but to file for bankruptcy.

4 of 5

The rise of obesity among citizens of country Y has been linked to a variety of health problems. In response to this situation, the country's largest health organization has called for food manufacturers to help combat the problem. Since the leading members of the nation's food industry have agreed to provide healthier alternatives, reduce sugar and fat content, and reduce advertisements for unhealthy foods, it is likely that country Y will experience a decrease in obesity-related health problems.

5 of 5

Recent advances in technology have led to a new wave of "smart" appliances, including refrigerators that note when food supplies are low and place an order at the grocery store, washing machines that automatically adjust the wash cycle and temperature based upon the clothes in the machine, and doorknobs that can identify the house owner and automatically open the door. A technology expert predicts that, due to these new innovations, machines will soon outnumber humans as the number-one users of the Internet.

Premises

The premises of an argument include any reasons, statistics, or other evidence provided in support of the conclusion. In the case of GRE arguments, you must accept the truth of the premises, whether you agree with them or not. The easiest way to identify the premises is to ask what information the author has provided to justify the truth of the conclusion.

> During the past 10 years, <u>advertising revenues for the magazine *True Investor* have fallen by thirty-percent</u>. <u>The magazine has failed to attract new subscribers, and newsstand sales are at an all-time low</u>. Thus, sweeping changes to the editorial board will be necessary for the magazine to survive.

In the argument above, the premises can be found in the first two sentences, where the author provides three pieces of evidence in support of the conclusion: *advertising revenues for the magazine* True Investor *have fallen by thirty-percent*, *the magazine has failed to attract new subscribers*, and *newsstand sales are at an all-time low*.

Sometimes you'll see indicator words that can help you to find the premises. These include:

- Because
- Given that
- As a result of
- In view of
- Since
- Supposing that

Practice: Finding the Premise

For each of the following arguments, identify the premise or premises that support the conclusion. (Remember, you already found the conclusions in the exercise on page 104.) Answers can be found in Part V.

1 of 5

Despite the support of the president, it is unlikely that the new defense bill will pass. A bipartisan group of 15 senators has announced that it does not support the legislation.

Conclusion: _____

Why?

Premise: _____

2 of 5

The earliest known grass fossils date from approximately 55 million years ago. Dinosaurs most likely disappeared from the Earth around 60 million years ago. Based on this evidence, as well as fossilized remains of dinosaur teeth that indicate the creatures were more suited to eating ferns and palms, scientists have concluded that grass was not a significant part of the dinosaur diet.

Conclusion: _____

Why?

Premise: _____

3 of 5

Automaker *X* has lost over 2 billion dollars this year due to rising costs, declining automobile sales, and new governmental regulations. Because of the company's poor financial situation, it has asked its employees to pay more for health care and to accept a pay cut. However, the workers at automaker *X* are threatening to go on strike. If that happens, automaker *X* will have no choice but to file for bankruptcy.

Conclusion: _____

Why?

Premise: _____

4 of 5

The rise of obesity among citizens of country *Y* has been linked to a variety of health problems. In response to this situation, the country's largest health organization has called for food manufacturers to help combat the problem. Since the leading members of the nation's food industry have agreed to provide healthier alternatives, reduce sugar and fat content, and reduce advertisements for unhealthy foods, it is likely that country *Y* will experience a decrease in obesity-related health problems.

Conclusion: _____

Why?

Premise: _____

5 of 5

Recent advances in technology have led to a new wave of "smart" appliances, including refrigerators that note when food supplies are low and place an order at the grocery store, washing machines that automatically adjust the wash cycle and temperature based upon the clothes in the machine, and doorknobs that can identify the house owner and automatically open the door. A technology expert predicts that, due to these new innovations, machines will soon outnumber humans as the number-one users of the Internet.

Conclusion: _____

Why?

Premise: _____

Assumptions

Assumptions are unstated premises on which the author relies to prove his or her conclusion. Even well-reasoned arguments rest on assumptions; because it's impossible to say everything, some things must go unsaid. Therefore, assumptions play a crucial role in the structure of an argument, bridging gaps in reasoning from the premises to the conclusion.

> During the past 10 years, advertising revenues for the magazine *True Investor* have fallen by thirty-percent. The magazine has failed to attract new subscribers, and newsstand sales are at an all-time low. Thus, sweeping changes to the editorial board will be necessary for the magazine to survive.

The argument above assumes that the editorial board *caused* the problems now attributed to the magazine. If something other than the editorial board were responsible—had the local population declined by thirty percent, for example—then sweeping changes to the board might do little to improve the magazine's financial situation. In that case, the connection between the premises (the magazine's problems) and the conclusion (changes to the editorial board) would fall apart. The reader would no longer be persuaded that *changes to the editorial board will be necessary for the magazine to survive.* The argument would collapse.

The easiest way to identify an assumption is to distinguish an argument's conclusion from its premises. Then, ask what additional information is required to link the conclusion to the premises.

Practice: Locating Assumptions

For each of the following Critical Reasoning questions, identify the conclusion and the premise. Then note what assumption is required to make the argument work. Answers can be found in Part V.

1 of 4

City University recently announced the retirement of Professor Jones. Professor Jones is a leading biologist and widely published author and her presence was a major factor in many students' decisions to attend City University. The University predicts no decline in enrollment, however, because it plans to hire two highly credentialed biology professors to replace Professor Jones.

Conclusion: _____

Premise: _____

Assumption: _____

2 of 4

It is unjust to charge customers under the age of 25 more to rent a car than those over the age of 25. After all, most states allow people as young as 16 to have a driver's license and all states allow 18-year-olds the right to vote.

Conclusion: _____

Premise: _____

Assumption: _____

3 of 4

It is easy to demonstrate that extraterrestrial life exists by simply looking at our own solar system. In our solar system, there are eight planets and at least one of them obviously has life on it. Thus, roughly 12.5% of planets in the universe should have life on them.

Conclusion: _____

Premise: _____

Assumption: _____

4 of 4

State A is facing a serious budget shortfall for the upcoming year. Recent polls indicate that 58% of voters in Township B approve of a proposed 2-cent gasoline tax in order to make up the deficit. It is clear, therefore, that the leaders of State A should institute the gas tax.

Conclusion: _____

Premise: _____

Assumption: _____

Gaps

One common way to identify assumptions is to look for gaps in the reasoning. In many cases, gaps in reasoning are indicated by gaps in language. Look for words or phrases in the conclusion that do not come from the premises. Identify an assumption in the following example:

> Cream cheese contains half as many calories per tablespoon as does butter or margarine. Therefore, a bagel with cream cheese is more healthful than is a bagel with butter.

First, find the conclusion. The word "therefore" gives the conclusion away: *a bagel with cream cheese is more healthful than is a bagel with butter.*

Second, find the premises. What information does the author provide to support the conclusion? The premise states that *cream cheese contains half as many calories per tablespoon.*

Third, look for shifts in language between the premise and conclusion. The premise compares the calorie content of a tablespoon of cream cheese to that of a tablespoon of butter or margarine. The conclusion introduces the word "healthful," which does not appear in the premise. This shift in the argument's language is indicative of a gap in reasoning—the argument leaps from a thing that *has fewer calories per tablespoon* to a thing that *is more healthful.* Therefore, this argument rests on the assumption that a food with *fewer calories* is a food that is *more healthful.*

Although most Critical Reasoning passages consist of three basic parts—conclusions, premises, and assumptions—some passages also include extraneous ideas, background information, or opposing points of view. The efficiency with which you identify assumptions depends in large part on the accuracy with which you identify conclusions and premises, so don't be distracted by non-essential information.

COMMON REASONING PATTERNS

Like the other question formats on the GRE, Critical Reasoning questions tend to be predictable. While you'll never see the same question twice, many Critical Reasoning passages employ similar patterns of reasoning. Learning to recognize these patterns provides you with another means of identifying assumptions.

Not every GRE argument models one of the common reasoning patterns, so you'll sometimes still need to look for shifts in language. However, when one of the common reasoning patterns is present, it can help you to locate information needed to strengthen or weaken an argument. Each of the five common patterns involves its own standard assumption or assumptions. Learning to recognize these patterns, and the assumptions they incorporate, will help you to identify unstated presuppositions and pinpoint an argument's flaws.

Know the Test
On the Verbal section, the best way to save time is to know exactly what you're looking for, and familiarizing yourself with the types of questions and patterns can help you more quickly pinpoint this.

Causal Reasoning Patterns

Causal reasoning is the most common type of reasoning you'll encounter in GRE arguments. Test writers are fond of causal arguments, and you're likely to see several of them on the GRE. In a causal argument, the premises usually state that two things happened, from which the author concludes that one thing caused the other. Consider the following simple example:

> A study indicated that adults who listen to classical music regularly are less likely to have anxiety disorders. Clearly, classical music calms the nerves and reduces anxiety.

The author of this argument concludes that *classical music calms the nerves and reduces anxiety*. This conclusion is based on a study indicating that *adults who listen to classical music regularly are less likely to have anxiety disorders*. Thus, the premise posits a correlation between two things —exposure to classical music and reduced likelihood of anxiety disorders—and the conclusion makes a leap from correlation to causation.

Every causal argument involves two standard assumptions:

- **There's no other cause.**
- **It's not a coincidence.**

The argument assumes that there is nothing other than classical music that caused study participants to experience fewer anxiety disorders and that it is not a coincidence that adults who listened to classical music were less likely to have anxiety disorders.

Don't Assume Assumptions Are the Same

This causal argument should remind you of the earlier example we used when discussing assumptions. Pay close attention to the approach for this example—which specifically follows a causal reasoning pattern—and the remaining patterns. You have to note the difference!

The first standard assumption suggests that classical music, and only classical music, caused participants in the study to experience fewer anxiety disorders. But what if something else was responsible? The passage doesn't rule out the possibility that study participants used anxiety reducing medication, or that they simply happened to be calm people to begin with. In neither of these cases would it follow that *classical music calms the nerves and reduces anxiety*. Thus, the argument must assume that a causal relationship exists.

The second standard assumption denies that the correlation between classical music and anxiety is a coincidence. But what if a different study indicated that adults who listen to classical music regularly were more likely to have anxiety disorders? In that case, it no longer follows that classical music calms the nerves and reduces anxiety—on the contrary, the counter-example suggests that the first study's results were coincidental. Thus, the argument must assume that the correlation between classical music and lower anxiety is not a coincidence.

When you spot an argument that employs a causal reasoning pattern, remember that the argument relies on two assumptions: first, there's no other cause; and second, it's not a coincidence.

Planning Patterns

Many GRE arguments introduce plans that are designed to solve problems: a municipal government's plan to improve water quality, a transit authority's plan to reduce traffic congestion, or a town board's plan to increase voter turnout. The premises of planning arguments describe what the plan is supposed to accomplish and how it is supposed to work. For example:

> During the past 5 years, Meridian Township has seen a dramatic rise in crime. As a result, Meridian's police force plans to install video surveillance cameras at major intersections in neighborhoods that suffer the worst crime rates. Clearly, the crime rate in Meridian Township will drop.

Consider this argument in terms of its parts. Meridian Township has a problem: *a dramatic rise in crime*. To address this problem, the police force plans to *install video surveillance cameras*. These are the premises of the argument because they outline the plan for addressing the problem. The argument concludes that, as a result of instituting the plan, the crime rate will drop. In general, the conclusion of an argument that employs the planning pattern can simply be expressed: *do the plan*.

Every planning argument involves one standard assumption:

- **There's no problem with the plan.**

Evaluating an argument with a planning reasoning pattern will revolve around the plan itself. For instance, what if there *is* a problem with the plan to reduce crime by installing video cameras at major intersections? After all, crime is not limited to major intersections. Perhaps the cameras will malfunction or produce poor quality images. Perhaps criminals will simply relocate to neighborhoods without cameras. In these cases, our confidence in the conclusion is shaken. On the basis of the premises alone, it no longer seems to follow that *the crime rate will drop*. Thus, in order for the argument to "work," its author must assume that installing the cameras reduces crime. In other words, there's no problem with the plan. A question could ask to identify a potential problem with the plan, or to strengthen the plan with the addition of some other fact.

No matter what the question asks, when you encounter an argument that employs a planning pattern, remember the standard assumption at play: there's no problem with the plan.

Sampling Patterns

Arguments that exhibit a sampling pattern are less common than causal or planning arguments. In a sampling argument, the author reaches a general conclusion about a population based on evidence about some members of the population. Sampling arguments assume that a smaller group is typical of a larger group and accurately reflects the relevant characteristics or feelings of the larger group.

Here is an example:

> Contrary to popular belief, football fans overwhelmingly approve of the decisions made by the administrative staffs of their local teams. We know this to be true because a large group of fans leaving a stadium expressed admiration for their teams' coaches and coordinators in an interview last week.

The author of this argument concludes that *football fans overwhelmingly approve of the decisions made by the administrative staffs of their local teams.* This conclusion is based on the premise that *a large group of fans leaving a stadium expressed admiration for their teams' coaches and coordinators in an interview last week.* Thus, the conclusion makes a leap from the opinion of one group of fans at a particular moment to the opinion of football fans in general.

Every sampling argument involves one standard assumption:

- **The sample is representative.**

When you encounter a sampling reasoning pattern, look for reasons why the sample itself is either representative or not. What if the opinion of the interviewed group of football fans isn't representative of the opinions of football fans in general? Perhaps the interviewed fans attended a game their team won, and perhaps their local team has long enjoyed a winning record. It does not follow from this that fans of every team approve of the decisions made by their team's administrative staff. To properly link the argument's conclusion to its premise, the author must assume that the opinions of interviewed fans accurately reflect those of football fans in general.

When you run into an argument that employs a sampling pattern, remember that the argument relies on the assumption that a sample is representative of a larger population.

Interpretation of Evidence Patterns

In some GRE arguments, the author understands the conclusion to be synonymous with one or more of the premises. In other words, information in the premises is interpreted to mean information in the conclusion. These arguments exhibit the interpretation of evidence pattern.

One particularly common instance of this pattern involves the misinterpretation of statistical data. Not every argument that incorporates statistics is an interpretation of evidence argument, but arguments that exhibit this pattern frequently involve statistics. Most often, the argument confuses percentages with actual values.

Consider the following example:

> Local grocer: Ninety percent of customers bought store brand soup last winter, but only eighty percent bought store brand soup this winter. Obviously, more customers bought store brand soup last winter.

The author concludes that *more customers bought store brand soup last winter*. This conclusion is based on the premise that *ninety percent of customers bought store brand soup last winter, but only eighty percent bought store brand soup this winter*. The premise describes a change in the percentage of customers who bought store brand soup, and the conclusion leaps from percentages to actual numbers.

Every interpretation of evidence argument involves one standard assumption:

- **There's no other way to interpret the evidence.**

What if there's another way to interpret the data? If 100 customers visited the grocer last winter, and ninety percent bought soup, then 90 bought soup last winter. But if 200 customers visited the grocer this winter, and eighty percent bought soup, then 160 bought soup this winter. In this case, it no longer follows that more people bought soup last winter—the author misinterprets the statistical data.

When you come across an interpretation of evidence pattern, the argument most likely relies on the standard assumption that there's no other way to interpret the evidence.

Analogy Patterns

Reasoning by analogy is relatively rare on the GRE, but that doesn't mean you won't see arguments by analogy. These arguments characteristically assume that what is appropriate in one case is also appropriate in another. They typically rely on the assumption that two things are similar enough to sustain a comparison. Here is a simple example:

> Using this line of products has been shown to cause
> cancer in laboratory animals. Therefore, you should
> stop using this line of products.

The author concludes that *you should stop using this line of products*. This conclusion is based on the premise that *this line of products has been shown to cause cancer in laboratory animals*. The premise concerns lab animals, and the conclusion leaps to humans. Thus, the argument relies on the assumption that humans and lab animals are similar: what causes cancer in laboratory animals also causes cancer in humans.

Arguments by analogy involve one standard assumption:

- **One thing is similar to another.**

What if humans are significantly different from laboratory animals? For example, if a feature of human physiology not shared by lab animals prevented the growth of cancers in humans who used the products, it no longer follows that you should stop using the products.

When you encounter an argument that employs an analogy pattern, it probably relies on the assumption that one thing is similar to another in some relevant way.

THE BASIC APPROACH TO CRITICAL REASONING QUESTIONS

Critical Reasoning questions come in eight flavors. The majority of the questions are *assumption*, *weaken*, *strengthen*, or *inference* questions. However, there are some minor question types, such as *resolve/explain*, *evaluate*, *ID the reasoning*, or *flaw* questions, of which you should be aware. Each of these question types has its own unique task and common trap answers.

Most Critical Reasoning questions present you with an argument, but not all questions involve arguments. In fact, some Critical Reasoning passages don't look like arguments at all. In order to master the Critical Reasoning format, you need a basic approach that can be applied to any Critical Reasoning question you encounter, no matter what kind of question it is.

The Basic Approach: Critical Reasoning Questions

Step 1: Identify the Question

Look for words or phrases in the question stem that can be used to identify the question type. Your knowledge of the question type informs your approach to the passage, so always read the question stem before you read the passage.

Step 2: Work the Argument

For most question types, begin working an argument by distinguishing its conclusion from its premises. Then, look for shifts in language or reasoning patterns that can help you to identify the argument's assumption.

Step 3: Predict What the Answer Should Do

It can be difficult to outright predict the answer, but you may be able to predict what the answer should do. Before turning to the answer choices, use your knowledge of the question and the information in the passage to determine what the correct answer needs to accomplish.

Step 4: Use POE to Find the Answer

It's often easier to identify incorrect answers than it is to identify correct answers, so use POE aggressively. The POE tools changed based on the question type, which is why it is critically important for you to become familiar with the different types of questions and how answer choices are constructed for them.

Step 1: Identify the Question

The surest way to improve performance and boost confidence in your Critical Reasoning ability is to take control of your approach to Critical Reasoning questions. Every question includes a word or phrase that can help you to identify what kind of question it is, and each question type involves a unique task with respect to the passage. Not all tasks are created equally, so it's important to know what's required of you.

Your knowledge of the question type should inform your approach, suggesting what kind of information to look for in the passage and what kind of answers to avoid. For now, we'll introduce the different question types, saving a more detailed discussion for later in the chapter.

Assumption Questions

Assumptions are necessary but invisible parts of a passage that bridge gaps in reasoning between an argument's premises and conclusion. Here's where all that practice identifying the parts of an argument really begins to pay off. Simply put, assumption questions ask you to identify an unstated premise on which an argument depends.

Assumption questions typically ask:

- The argument above assumes which of the following?
- The author of the argument above presupposes which of the following to be true?
- Which of the following is an assumption on which the truth of the author's conclusion depends?

Forms of indicator words such as *presupposition*, *expectation*, and *assumption* can alert you to the fact that you've encountered an assumption question.

Weaken Questions

Weaken questions ask you to find a reason why the information in the passage could be wrong, or is incomplete. The vast majority of weaken questions require you to undermine the conclusion by attacking one of the argument's assumptions. Most commonly, the real job when answering weaken questions is not to attack the conclusion, but to attack *the way the conclusion follows from the premises*.

Weaken questions typically ask:

- Which of the following, if true, most seriously weakens the argument above?
- Which of the following casts the most doubt on the author's conclusion?
- Which of the following calls into question the reasoning above?

Forms of indicator words and phrases such as *weaken*, *undermine*, and *cast doubt* can help you to spot a weaken question.

Warning Signs
Our book presents a wide range of typical questions and common indicator words and phrases—but it doesn't contain a comprehensive list of every possible usage. Train yourself with these examples, but don't be so rigid in your studying that you're unable to quickly categorize other words.

Strengthen Questions

Strengthen questions require you to reinforce an argument's conclusion. This is usually accomplished by strengthening one of the argument's assumptions. In order to answer a strengthen question with confidence, therefore, you must first identify an assumption. Once the pivotal assumption has been found, your job is to strengthen it—support the conclusion by strengthening the assumption.

Strengthen questions typically ask:

- Which of the following provides the best support for the claims made above?
- Which of the following statements, if true, most strengthens the argument's conclusion?
- Which of the following, if true, increases the likelihood that the author's claim is true?

Forms of indicator words such as *strengthen*, *support*, and *justify* can help you to recognize a strengthen question.

Inference Questions

Inference questions are the most commonly confusing type of critical reasoning question. The question appears to be asking for you to determine what the author of the argument is thinking or, as the name of the question type suggests, what can be *inferred* from the information in the passage.

Remember that the GRE cannot ask you for information that is not provided. Therefore, inference questions are typically just a test of reasoning and reading comprehension. The correct answer must be definitively provable based on the information provided in the passage. When presented with an inference question, you need to determine what it is that you know, without ambiguity, based on the information in the passage.

Inference questions typically ask:

- Which of the following can be inferred from the information above?
- The passage suggests that which of the following must be true?
- The information in the passage implies that the author would be most likely to agree with which of the following?

Forms of indicator words such as *inference*, *suggest*, and *imply* can help you spot an inference question.

Resolve/Explain Questions

Some Critical Reasoning questions ask you to resolve an apparent discrepancy or explain a paradoxical situation. The passages that accompany these questions almost never resemble arguments. Like inference passages, they merely present you with information. Resolve/explain questions ask how two seemingly incongruous statements can be true

Just the Passage, and Nothing but the Passage
This is a critical concept worth reiterating. If you can't point to evidence for your answer in the passage, then you may have fallen for a trap answer. Always make sure you can prove the truth of the answer based on the evidence in the passage.

at the same time. Clearly state the two ideas that seem to be opposed, and then select the answer that allows both ideas to be true.

Resolve/Explain questions typically ask:

- Which of the following, if true, resolves the paradox outlined above?
- Which of the following best explains the apparent contradiction?
- Which of the following statements goes farthest in explaining the situation above?

Resolve/Explain questions can be easier to recognize because they include forms of the word *resolve* or *explain*. Forms of indicator words such as *paradox* and *discrepancy* can also help you identify resolve/explain questions.

Evaluate Questions

Evaluate questions target your ability to spot a question (or test) that could be answered (or performed) to *evaluate* or *assess* an argument. Your job is to identify the question that, if answered, would allow you to test the argument's key assumption. Thus, evaluate questions are similar to strengthen and weaken questions in that they first require you to identify an unstated premise. However, once the key assumption has been found, your task is not to weaken or strengthen it, but to identify the test that could help determine whether the argument is weak or strong.

Evaluate questions typically ask:

- The answer to which of the following questions would most likely yield information that could be used to assess the author's claim?
- Which of the following experiments would be most useful in evaluating the argument above?
- Which of the following tests could be performed to determine the truth of the argument's conclusion?

Forms of indicator words such as *evaluate* and *assess* can help you to recognize an evaluate question.

Identify the Reasoning Questions

Occasionally, a Critical Reasoning question will ask you to identify the method, technique, or strategy used by the author of an argument, or to describe the roles played by bolded phrases in an argument. ID the reasoning questions concern the relationships that exist between an argument's parts. Before you can answer a question about that relationship, you must first identify those parts. Distinguish the argument's conclusion from its premises, and then select the answer that accurately describes the structure of the argument.

Identify the reasoning questions typically state or ask:

- The author provides support for the argument above by
- Which of the following methods of reasoning does the argument above exhibit?
- The bolded phrases play which of the following roles in the argument above?

Forms of indicator words such as *technique*, *strategy*, *method*, and *by* can help you to spot an ID the reasoning question.

Flaw Questions

Flaw questions ask you to describe what went wrong in an argument. The question stem already acknowledges that you're dealing with a bad argument. Your job is to identify its vulnerability. Flaw questions tend to resemble a blend of the ID the reasoning and weaken question types. Select the answer that accurately describes a vulnerability in the argument's reasoning.

Flaw questions typically ask:

- Which of the following statements describes a flaw in the argument above?
- The argument above is vulnerable to criticism for which of the following reasons?
- Which of the following criticisms most directly addresses a flaw in the argument above?

To identify a flaw question, look for the words *vulnerable*, *criticism*, and *flaw*.

STEP 2 Step 2: Work the Argument

After you've read a Critical Reasoning question, read the accompanying passage. Allow your knowledge of the question type to guide you to relevant information.

- **Assumption:** The correct answer will bridge a gap in the argument's reasoning between its premise and conclusion, so begin by distinguishing the conclusion from the premises that support it. Use shifts in language and reasoning patterns to help you spot the assumption that links the conclusion to the premises.

- **Weaken:** Because the correct answer will likely attack one of the argument's key assumptions, approach this like an assumption question: by identifying the premises and the conclusion. Use these to identify the unstated information on which the argument depends.

- **Strengthen:** Because the correct answer will reinforce one of the argument's key assumptions, treat this like an assumption question: by identifying the argument's premises and conclusion, as well as any gaps in reasoning between them. Once you've found the pivotal assumption, choose the answer that suggests it's true.

- **Evaluate:** The correct answer is the one that would allow you to determine whether you're looking at a weak or strong argument. What differentiates this from those types of questions is that here, you need to select a test you could perform or a question you could answer to determine the truth or falsity of an assumption.

- **Identify the Reasoning:** If there are bolded phrases, begin by assessing those, as they pertain to the correct answer. If not, look to the argument itself. In either case, determine which part of the argument functions as its claim and which parts function as evidence, and then choose the answer that accurately describes this structure. (There's no need to worry about assumptions.)

- **Flaw:** Because the correct answer describes a weakness in the structure of the argument, use the techniques from ID the reasoning and weaken questions. Begin by distinguishing the argument's conclusion from its premises and use shifts in language or reasoning patterns to identify the faulty assumption.

- **Inference:** The correct answer is essentially the conclusion to the evidence given by the question, so begin by familiarizing yourself with the information provided. (If it helps, use your whiteboard to create a list of facts.) Then, choose the answer that must be true on the basis of the facts.

- **Resolve/Explain:** The correct answer isn't based on an argument, but rather on a resolution between two opposing ideas. Rather than looking for premises and conclusions, begin by using your whiteboard to clarify the apparent conflict: "On the one hand, *X*, but on the other, *Y*." Indicator words such as *but*, *yet*, and *however* can draw your attention to opposing ideas and help you to articulate the apparent conflict. Choose the answer that explains how *X* and *Y* might both be true at the same time.

Step 3: Predict What the Answer Should Do

≪STEP3

Just as your knowledge of the question type can help you to identify relevant information in a Critical Reasoning passage, your knowledge of the question type can help you to recognize the characteristics of the answer you're looking for.

Predicting the answer to a Critical Reasoning question is often quite difficult. Predicting what the answer should do is usually easier. Before turning to the answers, think about what the correct answer needs to accomplish based on the question type and information in the argument. In this way, you continue to exercise control over a question as you move from information gathering to answer selection.

- **Assumption Questions:** good answers to assumption questions bridge a gap in reasoning between the premises of an argument and its conclusion. For this reason, they often employ words or phrases that appear in the premises, as well as language from the conclusion. A good answer links the author's claim to evidence that supports it, or rules out obstacles to that link.

- **Weaken Questions:** good answers to weaken questions widen a gap in reasoning between the premises of an argument and its conclusion. In order to do so, they often introduce new information that attacks one of the argument's assumptions. A good answer makes the truth of an author's claim seem less likely by disrupting the link between that claim and the evidence that supports it.

- **Strengthen Questions:** good answers to strengthen questions are very similar to those for assumption questions. That's because both question types require you to find an assumption that supports the argument's conclusion. A good answer will confirm the pivotal assumption or introduce new information that rules out obstacles to it.

- **Inference Questions:** inference questions in the Critical Reasoning format don't really ask you to make an inference beyond the scope of the information provided. It can be difficult to come up with your own answer to an inference question, so let the test writers worry about the phrasing. Simply keep in mind that you want the answer best supported by the facts. An answer that paraphrases a fact from the passage is often the credited response.

- **Resolve/Explain Questions:** passages that accompany resolve/explain questions introduce a pair of facts or ideas that seem to oppose each other. Once you've clarified the apparent conflict, look for answer choices that allow both facts to be true simultaneously. Good answers address both sides of the issue, rather than ignoring one side or the other.

- **Evaluate Questions:** evaluate questions require you to select a test you could perform, or a question you could ask, to assess the validity of an argument. If the answer choices are phrased as questions, try answering each question "Yes" and "No" to see whether different answers change your belief in the argument's conclusion. If so, you're probably dealing with the credited response. Good answers make it possible to determine the truth or falsity of an assumption made in the argument.

- **Identify the Reasoning Questions:** once you've identified the premises and conclusion of an ID the reasoning passage, look for answer choices that accurately describe the relationships between an argument's parts. There's no reason to look for gaps or assumptions; the task is purely descriptive. Keep an eye out for answers that focus on the structure of the argument rather than its content. Good answer choices accurately mirror the argument's structure.

- **Flaw Questions:** good answers to flaw questions accurately reflect the structure of the argument. They describe flaws in reasoning and the correct answer most often articulates a faulty assumption.

STEP 4 ≫ Step 4: Use POE to Find the Answer

This is the last step in the basic approach to Critical Reasoning questions. You've done most of the work required to answer the question. All that remains is to select and confirm your answer. You're already armed with a sense of what the correct answer needs to accomplish. Now, supplement that understanding with an efficient, effective process for weeding out bad answers and avoiding traps—tempting answers that are nevertheless incorrect.

Just as your knowledge of question types can help you find relevant information in a passage and predict what the correct answer should do, it can also help you to narrow your search for the correct answer by enabling you to quickly eliminate answers that are flawed. You've read about the characteristics of good answers. It's time to consider the characteristics of poor answers. Each Critical Reasoning question type has its own set of attractor answers that you will learn to anticipate. GRE arguments are often quite specific, so read them carefully and interpret them literally. Pay close attention to the language used in arguments and answer choices.

Assumption questions ask you for the unstated premise in the argument. Correct answers link conclusions to the premises that support them, so ask how each answer affects the author's claim. When you think you've found the correct answer, apply the **Negation Test**. Negate your preferred answer, and if your belief in the argument's conclusion isn't affected, the answer is incorrect. Avoid answers that:

- Are out of scope
- Use extreme language

Weaken questions ask you to select the answer that disrupts the link between the premises and the conclusion. Ask yourself how each choice affects the author's claim. Eliminate answers that:

- Are out of scope
- Use extreme language
- Strengthen the argument

Strengthen questions ask you to select the answer that reinforces the link between the premises and the conclusion. Ask yourself how each choice affects the author's claim. Eliminate answers that:

- Are out of scope
- Use extreme language
- Weaken the argument

Inference questions ask for the answer choice that follows necessarily from the facts in the passage. The answers to inference questions generally don't stray far from the information provided, so look to eliminate answers that require additional assumptions. Avoid answers that:

- Are out of scope
- Use extreme language

Resolve/Explain questions ask for the answer that resolves an apparent conflict between two ideas, or that explains the conflict away. When you consider the answer choices, adhere closely to the opposing ideas. Avoid answers that:

- Are out of scope
- Make the conflict worse
- Address only one side of the conflict

Evaluate questions ask you to select the answer that allows the strength or weakness of an argument to be determined. Incorrect answers offer new information that does not connect the argument's conclusion to its premises in a meaningful way. Eliminate answers that:

- Are out of scope

Time Enough At Last
These strategies may at first take a lot of time, but if you continue to practice them, you'll get faster. Also remember that taking your time isn't a bad thing: working more slowly increases your accuracy, which increases your GRE score!

Identify the reasoning questions ask you to find the answer that accurately describes the structure of an argument. Avoid answers that:

- Do not match the structure of the argument
- Only partially match the structure

Flaw questions ask you to choose the answer that accurately describes a flaw in the structure of an argument. Watch out for answers that describe the argument faithfully, but neglect to mention a flaw. Eliminate answers that:

- Are out of scope
- Cannot be matched to the argument or are only partial matches

CRITICAL REASONING PRACTICE QUESTIONS

Now that you've been introduced to the parts of a GRE argument, the reasoning patterns typical of GRE arguments, and the basic approach to Critical Reasoning questions, it's time to work through some guided example questions and bolster your understanding of the Critical Reasoning question format.

Assumption Question

Take a look at the following example:

For the following explanation, we've modeled the proper use of Steps 1, 2, 3, and 4. As you do the following questions, do your best to identify and apply each step of the process.

Most people believe that gold and platinum are the most valuable commodities. To the true entrepreneur, however, gold and platinum are less valuable than is the knowledge of opportunities. Thus, in the world of high finance, information is the most valuable commodity.

The author of the passage above makes which of the following assumptions?

○ Gold and platinum are not the most valuable commodities.

○ Entrepreneurs are not like most people.

○ The value of information is incalculably high.

○ Information about business opportunities is accurate and leads to increased wealth.

○ Only entrepreneurs feel that information is the most valuable commodity.

Here's How to Crack It

The question asks for the *assumption* made by the author, so this is an assumption question.

An assumption supports the conclusion of an argument, so when you read the passage, look for the conclusion. The word "thus" in the passage's final sentence gives it away: *in the world of high finance, information is the most valuable commodity.*

Now determine what information in the passage is in support of the conclusion. Two pieces of information are provided in support of the conclusion. One group of people—*most people*—*believe that gold and platinum are the most valuable commodities.* Another group—*true entrepreneurs*—believe that *gold and platinum are less valuable than is the knowledge of opportunities.*

From the opinions of two groups of people, the author concludes that the opinion of one group is to be preferred, but the passage doesn't say why. Therefore, it's likely that the correct answer will explain why the opinion of *the true entrepreneur* is to be preferred. With that in mind, you're ready to attack the answer choices:

○ Gold and platinum are not the most valuable commodities.

This answer appears to support the conclusion. If *gold and platinum are not the most valuable commodities*, there's a chance that *information is.* By itself, however, the idea that gold and platinum *are not* the most valuable commodities doesn't mean information *is* the most valuable commodity. This assumption provides no reason why the author should agree with *the true entrepreneur*; it doesn't link the argument's premises to its conclusion. Eliminate (A).

○ Entrepreneurs are not like most people in other careers.

This answer choice doesn't tell you anything you don't already know: if the true entrepreneur doesn't share the opinion of most people, then entrepreneurs aren't like most people (at least not in the way they value commodities). In any case, this answer doesn't provide a reason to favor the opinion of the true entrepreneur. Eliminate (B).

○ The value of information is incalculably high.

Be wary of the extreme language in this answer choice. The author needn't assume the value of information is incalculable in order to believe that it's the most valuable commodity. Moreover, while the value of many commodities might be incalculable, it doesn't follow from this that information is most valuable. Eliminate (C).

○ Information about business opportunities is accurate and leads to increased wealth.

This answer links the argument's conclusion to its premises by providing a reason to side with the true entrepreneur. To check whether this assumption is required by the argument, apply the Negation Test. If information *isn't* accurate and *doesn't* lead to increased wealth, it's unclear why the author believes it to be most valuable. Negating this answer disrupts the argument, so keep (D).

○ Only entrepreneurs feel that information is the most valuable commodity.

This answer is out of scope. It doesn't matter *who* believes information to be most valuable. What matters is *why* the author believes it to be most valuable. Eliminate (E).

The correct answer is (D).

Weaken Question

Take a look at the following example:

Given the current economic climate, universal healthcare is an impossibility in the United States. More than half of all U.S. households report feeling overwhelmed by expenses, and many people are struggling to find additional sources of income. Funding such a massive program would require significant tax increases, adding to the financial burden of many individuals. The employer-sponsored healthcare system currently in place keeps taxes low, protecting our nation's economy.

Which of the following, if true, would most weaken the argument above?

○ Many U.S. citizens enjoy sizeable tax breaks for medical expenses.

○ Universal healthcare would reduce the financial burden on employers, resulting in significant job growth and wage increases.

○ A majority of profitable, private health insurers have indicated that they expect to increase their payrolls in the coming quarter.

○ Pharmaceutical companies have fewer incentives to innovate new drugs in a universal healthcare system.

○ Most U.S. citizens depend on their employers for health coverage and could not afford comparable coverage under the current system.

Here's How to Crack It

The question asks you to *weaken* the argument, so this is a weaken question.

Let's break this argument down into its core components. The author concludes that *universal healthcare is an impossibility in the United States.* Why? Because *Funding such a massive program would require significant tax increases,* and *more than half of all US households already report feeling overwhelmed by expenses....*

Did you spot the gap in the argument's reasoning? The premises refer to the financial burden faced by Americans and to the costs associated with universal healthcare. The conclusion leaps from the cost of such a system to its impossibility. This shift in language exposes a gap in the author's reasoning. Bridging this gap requires an assumption that links the cost of universal healthcare to its impossibility. We know what the correct answer needs to do, and we have a good idea how it might get done. Let's turn to the answer choices.

○ Many US citizens enjoy sizeable tax breaks for medical expenses.

Under the current healthcare system, many people are compensated for medical expenses via tax breaks. However, there's no information about what will happen to these tax breaks under a universal healthcare system. This answer touches on the financial problem mentioned in the premises, but because it doesn't link this problem to the impossibility of instituting universal healthcare, it can't be used to weaken the argument. This choice is out of scope, so eliminate (A).

○ Universal healthcare would reduce the financial burden on employers, resulting in significant job growth and wage increases.

This answer suggests that universal healthcare might lead to positive financial outcomes. If the benefits of universal healthcare outweigh its costs, then those costs don't contribute to the impossibility of universal healthcare. This choice breaks the link between the cost of universal healthcare and its impossibility, so keep (B).

○ A majority of profitable, private health insurers have indicated that they expect to increase their payrolls in the coming quarter.

Are the plans of private health insurers to increase their payrolls relevant to the argument we identified? No, what private insurers do with their payrolls has no bearing on the argument that universal healthcare is impossible because it's expensive. Choice (C) is out of scope. Eliminate it.

○ Pharmaceutical companies have fewer incentives to innovate in a universal healthcare system.

If drug companies have fewer incentives to innovate, then there's evidence to suggest universal healthcare might be a bad idea. This answer addresses the impossibility of universal healthcare by introducing another reason not to pursue it, but that reason doesn't link the impossibility of universal healthcare to its cost. Eliminate (D).

○ Most US citizens depend on their employers for health coverage and could not afford comparable coverage under the current system.

This answer acknowledges the high cost of healthcare under the current system. However, the argument concerns the cost of instituting a universal healthcare system, not the cost of the current system, which is out of scope. Eliminate (E).

The correct answer is (B).

Try another weaken question:

Psychologists have just completed an extensive study of recently divorced parents in order to determine which factors contributed most to the dissolution of the marriage. The researchers found that in a great majority of the cases of failed marriages, the couples ate, on average, fewer than 10 meals per week with each other. From this data, the psychologists have determined that a failure to spend time together during meal times is a major factor leading to divorce.

Which of the following, if true, would cast the most doubt on the researchers' hypothesis?

○ Many couples who have long and successful marriages eat together fewer than ten times per week.

○ Most of the couples in the study who were unable to share meals with each other worked outside of the home.

○ People who lack a regular dining schedule tend to have more disorders and illnesses of the digestive system.

○ Couples in the study who reported that they ate together more than ten times per week also indicated that they tended to perceive their relationships with their spouses as healthy.

○ In many cases, people in unhappy marriages tend to express their displeasure by avoiding contact with their partners when possible.

Here's How to Crack It

The question asks you to identify which answer choice *casts the most doubt* on the researchers' hypothesis, so this is a weaken question.

Begin by identifying the conclusion and premise. The conclusion of the argument is *the psychologists have determined that a failure to spend time together during meal times is a major factor leading to divorce.* The premise of the argument is that *researchers found that in a great majority of the cases of failed marriages, the couples ate, on average, fewer than 10 meals per week with each other.*

This argument exhibits a causal reasoning pattern. The standard assumptions of causal reasoning patterns are that there is no other cause and its not a coincidence. In this case, there is no other cause that links not spending time together during meal times and divorce, and it's not a coincidence that couples who get divorced eat fewer than 10 meals per week with each other. Because this is a weaken question, the correct answer will likely provide evidence that there is another cause for the relationship between not eating together and divorce or that the relationship is a coincidence.

○ Many couples who have long and successful marriages eat together fewer than ten times per week.

This answer choice is out of scope. The argument is concerned with divorced couples. This answer choice focuses on married couples. This does not weaken the argument because it could be true that couples in successful marriages and unsuccessful marriages eat together fewer than ten times per week. Eliminate (A).

○ Most of the couples in the study who were unable to share meals with each other worked outside of the home.

This choice is out of scope. Where the couples *worked* does not weaken the argument, as the argument is concerned with how many times the couples ate together and divorce rates. Eliminate (B).

○ People who lack a regular dining schedule tend to have more disorders and illnesses of the digestive system.

The relative health of people's digestive system's is not the focus of the argument, so this answer choice is out of scope. Eliminate (C).

○ Couples in the study who reported that they ate together more than ten times per week also indicated that they tended to perceive their relationships with their spouses as healthy.

This choice concerns *couples…who reported that they ate together more than ten times per week.* This group of people is not the focus of the argument, so this answer choice is out of scope. Eliminate (D).

○ In many cases, people in unhappy marriages tend to express their displeasure by avoiding contact with their partners when possible.

This choice provides an alternative reason why divorced couples infrequently are meals together. If the couples are intentionally avoiding contact with each other because they are unhappy, then they'll end up eating fewer meals together. This casts doubt on the claim that there is a causal relationship between the number of times couples eat together and their likelihood of divorce.

The correct answer (E).

Strengthen Question

Take a look at the following example:

Many countries have recently proposed adopting an all-volunteer army. This policy was tried on a limited basis in a handful of countries several years ago and was a miserable failure. The level of education of the volunteers was unacceptably low, while levels of drug use and crime soared among army personnel. Should these nations trust their national defense to a volunteer army? The answer is clearly "No."

Which of the following statements, if true, provides the most support for the claim that an all-volunteer army should not be implemented?

○ The population's level of education has risen since the first time an all-volunteer army was tried.

○ The proposal was made by an organization called Citizens for Peace.

○ The first attempt to create a volunteer army was carried out according to the same plan now under proposal and under the same conditions as those that exist today.

○ A volunteer army would be less expensive than an army that relies on the draft.

○ Armies are smaller today than they were when a volunteer army was last proposed.

Here's How to Crack It

The question asks for the statement that *provides the most support for the claim*, so this is a strengthen question. Begin by distinguishing the argument's conclusion from its premises, and then find the assumption.

The conclusion of the argument is easy to identify because it's stated in the question stem: *an all-volunteer army should not be implemented*. As you read the passage, be on the lookout for premises that support the author's claim.

The author provides only one piece of evidence to suggest that an all-volunteer army shouldn't be implemented: it was *tried on a limited basis several years ago and was a miserable failure*. According to the argument, we shouldn't implement an all-volunteer army now because it didn't work out then. This argument exhibits the analogy pattern; it assumes that the current attempt to institute an all-volunteer army will be like the previous attempt.

Because this is a strengthen question, look for answer choices that suggest the two attempts are similar. The more similar they are, the more likely the current attempt will end in failure, and the easier it is to conclude that we shouldn't implement an all-volunteer army.

   ○ The population's level of education has risen since the first time an all-volunteer army was tried.

This answer choice introduces a difference between the current attempt to implement an all-volunteer army and the past attempt. If the education level of the population increased, there's reason to expect a different result this time around. Rather than strengthen the argument against an all-volunteer army, this answer weakens it. Eliminate (A).

   ○ The proposal was made by an organization called Citizens for Peace.

The identity of the group that made the proposal is out of scope. The relevant question asks whether there's good reason to believe that acting on the proposal will end in failure. Eliminate (B).

   ○ The first attempt to create a volunteer army was carried out according to the same plan now under proposal and under the same conditions as those that exist today.

Eureka! This answer introduces a relevant similarity between the two attempts to institute an all-volunteer army. If the last attempt ended in disaster, and the current attempt follows the same plan under the same conditions, there's reason to believe the outcome will be similar. Choice (C) strengthens the argument against an all-volunteer army, so keep it.

   ○ A volunteer army would be less expensive than an army that relies on the draft.

The cost of a volunteer army is out of scope. The argument concerns the trustworthiness of such an army, not its cost. Eliminate (D).

   ○ Armies are smaller today than they were when a volunteer army was last proposed.

Like (A), (E) introduces a dissimilarity between the two attempts to institute a volunteer army. For that reason, it's unlikely to be the correct answer. More importantly, like (B) and (D), it's out of scope. It doesn't matter how big the army is or was, but whether it's staffed by trustworthy people or criminals. Eliminate (E).

The correct answer is (C).

———————○———————

Try another strengthen question:

———————○———————

> Several book publishing companies have recently switched at least partially from distributing hard copy, paper page proofs (shared with book development team members such as editor, copyeditor, etc.) to digital page proofs (PDFS) shared and marked-up electronically with no use of paper at all. Therefore, less printer paper will be used as a result of these changes than would have been used if these companies had continued to use hard copy pages.
>
> Which of the following, if true, most strengthens the argument above?
>
> ○ Many of the companies that have switched to electronic page proofs have increased the number of page proofs sent.
>
> ○ More printer paper was used to create guidelines for the use of electronic, PDF page proofs than was used to simply share hard copy page proofs.
>
> ○ Companies that used more printer paper were more likely to switch to electronic, PDF page proofs than companies that used less printer paper.
>
> ○ Some of the industries that have switched at least partially to digital page proofs still primarily use printer paper for other operations.
>
> ○ The amount of printer paper needed to explain the digital, PDF page proofing system is less than the amount that would have been used for hard copy page proofs.

Here's How to Crack It

The question asks which of the answer choices *most strengthens the argument*, so this is a strengthen question. Begin by distinguishing the argument's conclusion from its premises, and then find the assumption.

The conclusion of the argument is that *less printer paper will be used as a result of these changes than would have been used if these companies had continued to distribute hard copy page proofs.* The changes referenced by the conclusion are defined in the premise of the argument that companies *switched…from distributing hard copy, paper page proofs… to digital page proofs (PDFs) shared and marked-up electronically with no use of paper at all.* The argument concludes that because of these changes, less printer paper will be used. The assumption of this argument is that the introduction of the new process does not result in increased use of paper for any other reason. Put another way, there are no unintended consequences of the decision.

Because this is a strengthen question, look for an answer choice that eliminates a possible reason the electronic memo system does not result in less printer paper being used.

○ Many of the companies that have switched to electronic page proofs have increased the number of page proofs sent.

The number of pages sent electronically is out of scope. The number of pages or chapters sent by companies that have switched to the electronic system does not address a reason that less printer paper is being used. Eliminate (A).

○ More printer paper was used to create guidelines for the use of electronic, PDF page proofs than was used to simply share hard copy page proofs.

If more printer paper was used to create manuals to explain how to use the digital page proofs (PDFs) than would have been used to proof hard copy, printed pages, then the changes did not have the intended effect. This weakens the argument. Eliminate (B).

○ Companies that used more printer paper were more likely to switch to electronic, PDF page proofs than companies that used less printer paper.

At first glance, this appears to be a good answer, but this choice does not address whether the digital page proofs caused less printer paper to be used. Therefore, this choice is out of scope. Eliminate (C).

○ Some of the industries that have switched at least partially to digital page proofs still primarily use printer paper for other operations.

This choice does not impact the argument because the use of printer paper for other operations does not give any information regarding whether the use of digital page proofs decreased the amount of printer paper used. Eliminate (D).

○ The amount of printer paper needed to explain the digital, PDF page proofing system is less than the amount that would have been used for hard copy page proofs.

This choice provides information to suggest that less printer paper is used to create the electronic system than would have been used to create page proofs, so a company that adopts the electronic digital, page proof system uses less printer paper. This choice strengthens the argument. Keep (E).

The correct answer is (E).

Inference Question

Take a look at the following example:

In film and television, it's possible to induce viewers to project their feelings onto characters on the screen. In one study, a camera shot of a woman's face was preceded by images of a baby. The audience thought the woman's face registered contentment. When the same woman's face was preceded by images of a shark attack, the audience thought the woman's face registered fear. Television news teams must be careful to avoid such manipulation of their viewers.

Which of the following is best supported by the information in the passage?

○ Television news teams have abused their position of trust in the past.

○ The expression on the woman's face was, in actuality, blank.

○ Images of a baby engendered feelings of happiness in the audience.

○ Audiences should strive to be less gullible.

○ The technique for manipulating audiences described in the passage would also work in a radio program that played dramatic music.

Here's How to Crack It

The question asks for the answer *best supported by the information in the passage*. The direction of support is from the passage to the answer choices, so this is an inference question. Begin by getting clear on the facts.

Fact 1: *In film and television, it's possible to induce viewers to project their feelings onto characters on the screen.*

Fact 2: *In one study, a camera shot of a woman's face was preceded by images of a baby. The audience thought the woman's face registered contentment.*

Fact 3: *When the same woman's face was preceded by images of a shark attack, the audience thought the woman's face registered fear.*

Once you're clear on the facts, look for the answer that must be true on their basis. Be wary of extreme language and eliminate answers that are beyond the scope of the information provided. The correct answer is likely to paraphrase information in the passage.

○ Television news teams have abused their position of trust in the past.

This answer goes well beyond the scope of the passage. We have no idea what news teams did in the past based on the information provided. Eliminate (A).

○ The expression on the woman's face was, in actuality, blank.

Like the previous choice, this answer is out of scope. Based on the information provided, we simply don't know whether the woman's face was expressionless. Eliminate (B).

○ Images of a baby engendered feelings of happiness in the audience.

Images of a baby led the audience to believe the woman's face registered contentment. If audience members projected their feelings onto the woman, then audience members must have experienced contentment, and it's likely the images of a baby were responsible. Keep (C).

○ Audiences should strive to be less gullible.

Of course, we should all strive to be less gullible, but we know that simply because we know what "gullible" means, not because of the information provided. Nothing in the passage suggests that audience members were gullible. Eliminate (D).

○ The technique for manipulating audiences described in the passage would also work in a radio program that played dramatic music.

It's possible that the information in this answer choice is true, but possible isn't good enough. We need an answer that *must be* true, and the passage provides no information about the projection of emotion in the medium of sound. Eliminate (E).

The correct answer is (C).

───────────○───────────

Try another inference question:

The Mayville Fire Department always fills its employment vacancies "in-house"—when a firefighter retires or leaves the force, his or her position is filled by interviewing all qualified members of the Mayville Department who are interested in the position. Only if this process fails to produce a qualified candidate does the department begin interviewing potential employees from outside the department. This year, the Mayville Fire Department has hired three new firefighters from outside the department.

If the statements above are true, which of the following must also be true?

○ For the coming year, the Mayville Fire Department will be understaffed unless it hires three additional firefighters.

○ Firefighters hired from outside the Mayville Fire Department take longer to properly train for the job.

○ At the time of the vacancies in the Mayville Fire Department, either there were no qualified in-house candidates or no qualified in-house candidates were interested in the open positions.

○ The three firefighters who left the department had jobs for which no other members of the Mayville Fire Department were qualified to fill.

○ The three new firefighters are the first new employees hired by the Mayville Fire Department.

Here's How to Crack It

This question asks which of the answer choices *must be true*, so this is an inference question.

For inference questions, there is no need to identify the conclusion and premise of the argument. Instead, be sure to understand what the argument states. The argument states that *when a firefighter retires or leaves the force* [from the Mayville Fire Department], *his or her position is filled by interviewing all qualified members of the Mayville Department who are interested in the position.* The argument then goes on to state that if the process of interviewing internal candidates fails *does the department begin interviewing potential employees from outside the department.* Finally, the argument reveals that *the Mayville Fire Department has hired three new firefighters from outside the department.*

Evaluate the answer choices, looking for one that must be true based on the facts in the argument.

○ For the coming year, the Mayville Fire Department will be understaffed unless it hires three additional firefighters.

This is out of scope. The passage provides no information to suggest that the department needs to hire three additional firefighters. The passage only states that the department has hired three new firefighters from outside the department. Eliminate (A).

○ Firefighters hired from outside the Mayville Fire Department take longer to properly train for the job.

This is out of scope. The passage provides no information about the amount of time it takes to train a firefighter for the Mayville Fire Department. Eliminate (B).

○ At the time of the vacancies in the Mayville Fire Department, either there were no qualified in-house candidates or no qualified in-house candidates were interested in the open positions.

This answer can be properly inferred based on the information in the passage. Because the department hired three candidates from outside the department, and they only hire candidates from outside the department if there are no qualified people inside the department who are interested in the position, then there must have been no qualified people from the Mayville department who wanted the job. Keep (C).

○ The three firefighters who left the department had jobs for which no other members of the Mayville Fire Department were qualified to fill.

The reason the firefighters left the Mayville department is out of scope. The passage is not concerned with why the firefighters left the department, only with the process to replace the ones that do leave. Eliminate (D).

○ The three new firefighters are the first new employees hired by the Mayville Fire Department.

This choice is out of scope. There is no way to determine if the three new firefighters are the first new employees hired by the Mayville Fire Department from the information in the argument. Eliminate (E).

The correct answer is (C).

Resolve/Explain Question

Take a look at the following example:

---○---

In 2008, the world's airlines reported an increase in the total number of passengers carried, but a decrease in total revenues, even though prices for airline tickets on all routes remained unchanged from the year before.

Which of the following resolves the paradox described above?

○ The airline industry was a victim of the recession in 2008.

○ Total passenger miles were up in 2008.

○ Fuel costs remained constant from 2007 to 2008.

○ Passengers traveled shorter distances on less expensive flights in 2008.

○ No new aircraft were purchased by any carrier in 2008.

Here's How to Crack It

The question asks for the answer that *resolves the paradox*, so this is a resolve/explain question. Your knowledge of question types suggests that the accompanying passage will present two pieces of information that seem to be in conflict. State that opposition as clearly as possible.

Fact 1: *On the one hand, more passengers traveled by air.*

Fact 2: *On the other, airline revenues decreased, even though ticket prices remained unchanged.*

The correct answer to a resolve/explain question will allow both pieces of information to be true simultaneously. Eliminate answers that are out of scope, address only one side of the conflict, or make the conflict worse.

○ The airline industry was a victim of the recession in 2008.

A recession might account for the decrease in revenue, but if ticket prices remained the same, it's unclear how the number of passengers could have increased. Choice (A) addresses only one side of the conflict, so eliminate it.

○ Total passenger miles were up in 2008.

If passengers flew farther in 2008 and ticket prices remained the same, it's unclear how revenues could have decreased. Like (A), this answer addresses only one side of the conflict. Eliminate (B).

○ Fuel costs remained constant from 2007 to 2008.

Fuel costs are out of scope. An increase in fuel costs might have affected airline profits, but profits are not revenues. This answer has no bearing on either side of the conflict. Eliminate (C).

○ Passengers traveled shorter distances on less expensive flights in 2008.

This answer looks promising. If the increase in passengers was offset by passengers taking cheaper flights, then revenues could have decreased even as the number of passengers increased. Keep (D).

○ No new aircraft were purchased by any carrier in 2008.

New aircraft are out of scope. The purchase of new aircraft might have affected airline profits, but if no new aircraft were purchased, then new aircraft affected neither profits nor revenues, and this answer has no relevance at all. Eliminate (E).

The correct answer is (D).

Try another resolve/explain question:

Over the past few decades, how music lovers access their music has changed dramatically. Digital file sharing technology such as iTunes, Spotify, and the like, have threatened the traditional market for entire music albums. In the case of iTunes, specifically, users are now able to download single songs from their favorite artists, enabling them to acquire the songs they desire without having to purchase the entire album. Some music industry leaders contend that this practice causes untold financial losses, as the cost of individual songs is not enough to offset the money lost producing the songs that were not purchased from the rest of the album. However, consumer groups report that there has been an increase in the sales of entire music albums.

Which of the following, if true, would best explain the situation above?

○ Some consumers who have illegally downloaded songs from the Internet have been sued by major record companies.

○ Research indicates that persons who engage in file-sharing or song-downloading are usually only casual music fans.

○ The music industry is developing new technology to help prevent users from illegally downloading songs.

○ Music artists tend to release more material today, on average, than they did a few decades ago.

○ Entire music albums released now often include bonus features that are appealing to fans, such as hidden tracks, interviews with the band, and music videos, that are not available unless the entire album is purchased.

Here's How to Crack It

The question asks which of the answer choices *best explains the situation above,* so this is a resolve/explain passage.

For resolve/explain passages, look for two facts presented in the passage that are in conflict.

> **Fact 1:** *Users who purchase music through iTunes are now able to download single songs from their favorite artists, enabling them to acquire the songs they desire without having to purchase the entire album.*

Fact 2: *consumer groups report that there has been an increase in the sales of entire music albums.*

The correct answer will explain the apparent discrepancy between these two facts.

      ○ Some consumers who have illegally downloaded songs from the Internet have been sued by major record companies.

This choice is out of scope. Major record companies suing consumers who have illegally downloaded songs does not explain the discrepancy between the ability to download single songs and the increase in sales of entire music albums. Eliminate (A).

      ○ Research indicates that persons who engage in file-sharing or song-downloading are usually only casual music fans.

This is out of scope. The degree of a downloader's fandom does nothing to explain the discrepancy in the argument. Eliminate (B).

      ○ The music industry is developing new technology to help prevent users from illegally downloading songs.

Choice (C) does not explain the increase in entire album sales, so this addresses only one side of the conflict. Eliminate (C).

      ○ Music artists tend to release more material today, on average, than they did a few decades ago.

This choice adequately addresses one side of the conflict, as artists releasing more material could explain the increase in album sales. However, this does not address the paradox in the argument, so eliminate (D).

      ○ Entire music albums released now often include bonus features that are appealing to fans, such as hidden tracks, interviews with the band, and music videos, that are not available unless the entire album is purchased.

This choice states that entire music albums feature bonus material that is not available unless the entire album is purchased. This could explain both the fact that people are downloading individual songs and that entire music album sales are increasing.

The correct answer is (E).

———————————○———————————

Evaluate Question

Take a look at the following example:

During a period of low growth after a recent and remarkable boom in the solar energy sector, Company X, a major manufacturer of solar-powered generators, attributed its success during the boom to the sale of excess inventory it had discovered in one of its warehouses.

Which of the following tests would most help to evaluate the company's hypothesis as to the cause of its success?

○ Comparing the length of the low-growth period to the length of the preceding boom

○ Comparing the boom experienced by Company X to those experienced by similarly sized manufacturers of solar-powered generators that did not have inventory on hand

○ Calculating average sales increases within the individual divisions of Company X

○ Comparing the total number of generators sold by Company X during the boom to the total number sold by Company X during the period of low growth

○ Using economic theory to predict the next economic boom for Company X

Here's How to Crack It

The question asks for the test that would most help to *evaluate* the company's hypothesis, so this is an evaluate question. According to the question stem, the hypothesis concerns the cause of Company X's success. As you begin to work the argument, look for claims that provide a reason Company X succeeded.

The passage's final sentence states that Company X *attributed its success during the boom to the sale of excess inventory*, but how does Company X come to believe that? The only other piece of information we get from the passage is that there was a *boom in the solar energy sector*, followed by a *period of low growth*.

Without additional information, it's unclear how changes in the solar energy sector relate to the company's claim about its own success. However, if you noticed the word *cause* in the question stem, then you probably recognized that Company X makes a causal argument.

Take advantage of the causal reasoning pattern by recalling its standard assumptions: there's no other cause, and it's not a coincidence. The former assumption seems more relevant here, because Company X assumes the sale of excess inventory alone was responsible for its success.

Evaluate the answer choices one at a time, looking for the test that would allow you to determine whether there isn't another reason for Company X's success.

○ Comparing the length of the low-growth period to the length of the preceding boom

Executing this comparison would tell us how long each of the periods lasted, but connecting that information to the sale of excess inventory would require inferences beyond the scope of the information provided. Eliminate (A).

○ Comparing the boom experienced by Company X to those experienced by similarly-sized manufacturers of solar-powered generators that did not have inventory on hand

This answer choice is tempting. We're looking for a way to determine whether something other than the sale of excess inventory might have caused Company X's success. If competitors without excess inventory to sell experienced booms comparable to that of Company X, then the company's claim might be incorrect. On the other hand, if competitors didn't experience as big a boom, it appears more likely that the sale of excess inventory was responsible for Company X's success. Keep (B).

○ Calculating average sales increases within the individual divisions of Company X

Individual divisions of Company X are out of scope. We already know that the company sold excess inventory; which divisions saw sales increases is irrelevant. Eliminate (C).

○ Comparing the total number of generators sold by Company X during the boom to the total number sold by Company X during the period of low growth

At first glance, this answer choice looks appealing. The comparison described here would allow us to determine how many generators were sold during each period. If more generators were sold during the boom than during the low-growth period, it might seem as though Company X's success during the boom resulted from the sale of excess inventory. However, the passage states that the period of low growth *followed* the boom. If more generators were sold during the boom, then at best, we could infer that a *decline* in sales led to *decreased* success. To determine whether the sale of excess inventory *caused* Company X's success during the boom, we'd need sales numbers from the period *before* the boom, not the period *after* it. Eliminate (D).

○ Using economic theory to predict when the next economic boom for Company X will occur

Of the five answer choices, this one is most obviously out of scope. An estimate of the time that will elapse before the next boom needn't have any relevance to the cause of the last boom. Eliminate (E).

The correct answer is (B).

Identify the Reasoning Question

Take a look at the following example:

Although measuring the productivity of outside consultants is a complex endeavor, **Company K, which relies heavily on consultants, must find ways to assess the performance of these workers.** The risks to a company that does not review the productivity of its human resources are simply too great. **Last year, Company L was forced into receivership after its productivity declined for three consecutive quarters.**

The bolded clauses play which of the following roles in the argument above?

○ The first bolded clause states the author's conclusion, and the second introduces unrelated information.

○ The first bolded clause provides background information, and the second offers evidence to contradict that information.

○ The first bolded clause states one of the author's premises, while the second states the author's conclusion.

○ The first bolded clause expresses a position, and the second warns against the adoption of that position.

○ The first bolded clause represents the author's conclusion, and the second supports the conclusion with an analogy.

Here's How to Crack It

The bolded clauses in the passage immediately indicate that this is an ID the reasoning question, so begin by distinguishing the argument's conclusion from the premises that support it. Don't worry about finding assumptions.

The phrase *must find ways to assess* is strong language, making the first bolded phrase a good candidate for the argument's conclusion. Why must Company K find ways to assess the performance of its outside consultants? Because companies that don't review the productivity of human resources face risks—just look at Company L! Both of the passage's remaining sentences operate in support of the first bolded phrase. The second bolded clause supports the conclusion by offering the example of a company that was *forced into receivership after its productivity declined.*

Now that you've got a good sense of the argument's structure, look for the answer that correctly mirrors it.

    ○ The first bolded clause states the author's conclusion, and the second introduces unrelated information.

The first part of this answer looks good, because the first bolded clause *does* state the author's conclusion. However, the second bolded clause supports the conclusion; it does not introduce unrelated information. Choice (A) only partially matches the argument's structure, so eliminate it.

    ○ The first bolded clause provides background information, and the second offers evidence to contradict that information.

Part of the first bolded clause states that Company K *relies heavily on consultants*, which does resemble background information. However, nothing in the second bolded clause contradicts that information. Choice (B) is a partial match. Eliminate it.

    ○ The first bolded clause states one of the author's premises, while the second states the author's conclusion.

This answer choice reverses the roles played by the bolded clauses. Since it doesn't match the structure of the argument, eliminate (C).

    ○ The first bolded clause expresses a position, and the second warns against the adoption of that position.

Like (A) and (B), (D) is a partial match. The first bolded clause expresses a position, but the second doesn't warn against the adoption of that position. Eliminate (D).

○ The first bolded clause represents the author's conclusion, and the second supports the conclusion with an analogy.

This answer accurately reflects the relationship between the bolded clauses: the first is the author's conclusion, and the second supports the conclusion by offering the example of analogous Company L. Keep (E).

The correct answer is (E).

_____ ○ _____

Flaw Question
Take a look at the following example:

_____ ○ _____

A telephone poll conducted in two states asked respondents whether their homes were cold during the winter months. Ninety-nine percent of respondents said their houses were always warm during the winter. The pollsters published their findings, concluding that ninety-nine percent of all homes in the United States have adequate heating.

Which of the following most accurately describes a questionable technique employed by the pollsters in drawing their conclusion?

○ The poll wrongly ascribes the underlying causes of the problem.

○ The poll assumes conditions in the two states are representative of the entire country.

○ The pollsters conducted the poll by telephone, thereby relying on the veracity of respondents.

○ The pollsters didn't visit respondents' houses in person, so no measure of the temperature in a subject's home was actually made.

○ The pollsters never defined the term "cold" in terms of a specific temperature.

Here's How to Crack It
The question asks for a *questionable technique* used by the pollsters, so this is a flaw question.

You already know from the question stem that the argument has a serious problem. Your job is to figure out what that problem is. Begin by identifying the argument's premises and conclusion.

Then, use a gap in the reasoning to hone in on the assumption. Because this is a flaw question, be on the lookout for common reasoning patterns.

The word *concluding* in the last sentence of the passage gives away the conclusion: *ninety-nine percent of all homes in the United States have adequate heating*. Why did the pollsters conclude this? Their findings were based on the results of *a telephone poll conducted in two states*, in which *ninety-nine percent of respondents said their houses were always warm during the winter*.

Did you recognize the pattern of reasoning in this argument? Information about one group of people (the poll was conducted in two states) is used to make a claim about a much larger group (all households in the United States). This argument employs the sampling pattern. The standard assumption involved in the sampling pattern is that the sample is representative of the larger population. Look for answers that call attention to this assumption.

○ The poll wrongly ascribes the underlying causes of a problem.

Underlying causes are out of scope. The pollsters ask whether people's homes are cold. The reason they might be cold is irrelevant. Eliminate (A).

○ The poll assumes conditions in the two states are representative of the entire country.

This answer expresses the standard assumption involved in the sampling pattern. Nothing in the passage suggests that the households surveyed are representative of U.S. householders in general. Keep (B).

○ The pollsters conducted the poll by telephone, thereby relying on the veracity of respondents.

The information in this answer might betray a weakness in the pollsters' methodology, but it isn't a weakness in the pollsters' reasoning. Eliminate (C).

○ The pollsters didn't visit respondents' houses in person, so no measurement of the temperature in a subject's home was actually made.

Like (C), this answer describes a problem with the poll, not with the argument. Eliminate (D).

○ The pollsters never defined the term "cold" in terms of a specific temperature.

It's true that the pollsters never defined the term "cold," but does that represent a flaw in the pollsters' reasoning? The flaw identified here concerns the poll itself, not the argument. Eliminate (E).

The correct answer is (B).

Now that you know how to identify and approach each of the eight Critical Reasoning question types, the best way to proceed is to practice. The more you experience through preparation, the less likely you are to be surprised on test day.

As you complete Critical Reasoning drills and exercises, force yourself to follow the basic approach. Your knowledge of the question type informs every step of the basic approach to Critical Reasoning questions, from reading the passage to eliminating incorrect answers, so always read the question first. Memorize the common reasoning patterns and the assumptions that go with them, develop a familiarity with the characteristics of good and bad answers, and you'll be well on your way to mastering the Critical Reasoning format.

Critical Reasoning Practice Set

In this practice set, follow the steps exactly as we have presented them. Answers can be found in Part V.

In 1989, corporate tax rates in some regions of the United States fell to their lowest level in 15 years, while the rates in other regions reached new highs. In 1974, similar conditions led to a large flight of companies from regions with unfavorable corporate tax policies to regions with favorable policies. There was, however, considerably less corporate flight in 1989.

Which of the following, if true about 1989, most plausibly accounts for the finding that there was less corporate flight in 1989 ?

○ The regions with the most favorable corporate tax policies had many of the same types of corporations as did those with unfavorable tax policies, but this was not true in 1974.

○ In contrast to 1974, office rental costs in the regions with the most favorable corporate tax policies were significantly higher than rental costs in other areas of the country.

○ In contrast to 1974, in 1989, the areas with the most favorable corporate tax policies reaped the most benefit from tax incentives, although the tax codes were particularly difficult to decipher.

○ Tax incentives offered by foreign countries were higher in 1989 than in 1974.

○ Individual tax incentives in the areas with favorable corporate tax policies were slightly lower than they were 15 years earlier in areas with favorable corporate tax policies.

Aramayo: Our federal government seems to function most efficiently when decision-making responsibilities are handled by only a few individuals. Therefore, our government should consolidate its leadership and move away from a decentralized representative democracy.

Tello: But moving our government in this direction could violate our constitutional mission to provide government of, for, and by the people.

Which of the following statements describes Tello's response to Aramayo?

○ Tello contradicts the reasoning used by Aramayo.

○ Tello uncovers an assumption used in Aramayo's reasoning.

○ Tello brings up a possible negative consequence of accepting Aramayo's argument.

○ Tello reveals the circular reasoning used by Aramayo.

○ Tello shows that Aramayo overgeneralizes a very special situation.

Business computer systems are designed to make workers more productive by automating a portion of the work that must be completed in a business process. As a result, the employee is free to perform more tasks that require human attention. Although productivity may be lost during a learning period, many businesses experience dramatic gains in productivity after installing a new computer system. While discussing the connection between productivity gains and computer systems, a well-respected business journal recently stated that the person who serves as the Chief Information Officer is the consummate business computer system.

By comparing a Chief Information Officer to business computer systems, the journal implicitly argues that

○ Chief Information Officers should always communicate the value of computer systems to their companies

○ the productivity of a company can be increased through the hiring of a Chief Information Officer

○ many companies have not improved their productivity with new computer systems

○ Chief Information Officers are more effective than are new computer systems

○ the impact of a Chief Information Officer on a company's productivity is difficult to measure

Whenever Joe does his laundry at the Main Street Laundromat, the loads turn out cleaner than they do when he does his laundry at the Elm Street Laundromat. Laundry done at the Main Street Laundromat is cleaner because the machines at the Main Street Laundromat use more water per load than do those at the Elm Street Laundromat.

Which of the following statements, if true, helps support the conclusion above?

○ The clothes washed at the Elm Street Laundromat were, overall, less clean than those washed at the Main Street Laundromat.

○ Joe uses the same detergent at both laundromats.

○ The machines at the Oak Street Laundromat use twice as much water as do those at the Main Street Laundromat.

○ Joe does three times as much laundry at the Main Street Laundromat as he does at the Elm Street Laundromat.

○ Joe tends to do his dirtier laundry at the Elm Street Laundromat.

According to the United States Postal Service bureau of information, the rate of complaints concerning late delivery was 30 times higher in 1991 than in 1964. Because the United States Postal Service changed neighborhood routes from a multiple-truck delivery system to a single-truck delivery system between 1964 and 1991, the enormous increase in complaints must be a result of this systematic change.

Which of the following, if true, weakens the conclusion drawn above?

○ In 1991, most late-mail complaints were reported, whereas in 1964 most were not.

○ Even in a multiple-truck delivery system, certain letters will arrive late.

○ According to the United States Postal Service bureau of information, most of the complaints concerning late delivery in 1991 were about registered mail.

○ The bulk amount of mail processed by the United States Postal Service was not much larger in 1991 than it was in 1964, before the systemic change occurred.

○ The change in neighborhood routes from a multiple-truck to a single-truck delivery system sometimes causes enormous increase in the price of stamps.

Summary

o Most Critical Reasoning questions require you to break down an argument. The conclusion is the main point of an argument. The premise is the fact cited in support of the conclusion.

o The assumption is used to link the premise and the conclusion with each other. Without an assumption, an argument breaks down.

o To crack a Critical Reasoning question, make sure to follow the steps of the basic approach:
   • Identify the Question
   • Work the Argument
   • Predict What the Answer Should Do
   • POE to Find the Answer

o After reading the question, break down the argument into its premise and conclusion and, if necessary, the assumption.

o Keep an eye out for common reasoning patterns and the standard assumptions of each.

Chapter 8
Vocabulary Basics

This chapter is all about vocabulary. While vocabulary is not directly tested on the GRE, recognizing words, or being able to parse out the meaning of unfamiliar words, can sometimes be the difference between a correct and incorrect answer. So let's go back to basics.

WHAT'S IN THIS CHAPTER?

This chapter is divided into two sections. The first section contains some basic information on the English language including its history and origins. The evolution of the English language is a fascinating tale and knowing some of its history helps lend context to the second section of the chapter.

The second section lists common roots, prefixes, and suffixes from the most prominent languages that influence English. These lists are broken down by language of origin and separated into two groups: roots and prefixes, and suffixes.

Why Roots, Prefixes, and Suffixes?

As of January 1, 2019, there were 1,052,010 words in the English language.

Your Vocabulary Can Never Been Too Extensive
This is especially true of the GRE. You can use all the strategies you want, but there is just no substitute for a killer vocabulary.

For additional information about vocabulary, English, and words check out www.language monitor.com, www.ecomomist.com, or www.sohopress.com.

Estimates of the average person's vocabulary vary between 20,000 to 35,000 words. There is a distinction between words people use in everyday conversation and words people just simply know and/or recognize. In any event, your vocabulary can never be too extensive.

In other words, if you were to memorize a list of 10,000 brand-new words you've never seen before, you'd still only have a 0.9% chance of seeing one of those words on test day.

There are ample resources available to you to find a list of new words to memorize. Instead of adding to that list of resources, we've provided you with something we consider more valuable. By providing you with a list of common roots, prefixes, and suffixes, we've given you the ability to determine an approximate definition for many different words. For example, suppose the word "prescient" was one of the answer choices in a fill-in-the-blank question. The Latin prefix *pre-* means "earlier, in front of" and the Latin root *sci* means "know." So "prescient" is "having knowledge of events before they take place." Because you know the prefix *pre-* you know that any word that contains that prefix has something to do with an earlier time. Similarly, because you know the root *sci* you know that any words that contains that root has something to do with knowing something.

Why is English So Complex and Difficult to Learn?

English is arguably one of the most complex languages in the world. Why is it you *caught* a cold, but you *thought* of a good idea? Why does the vowel *i* precede the vowel *e* in the words *siege* and *sieve*, but *i* follows *e* in the word *seize*? While it may be unrealistic to expect to know everything about the English language, learning some of the basic roots and affixes of words can significantly improve your understanding of some of the more obscure words found on the GRE.

A BRIEF HISTORY OF ENGLISH

Up until the 5th century, Celtic was spoken in what is now the British Isles. The Anglos, Saxons, and Jutes were three Germanic tribes that invaded England in the 5th century. Accordingly, England became known as Anglo-Saxon England.

Towards the end of the 9th century, the Viking raiders ("Norsemen") invaded northern France. In 1066, William the Conqueror invaded England and brought along Norman French. Hence, many words in the English lexicon are derived from Germanic (from the Anglos and the Saxons), French (derived from Latin), Latin, and Greek (which found its way into Latin).

Where Did All the English Words Come From?

The origins of English are numerous and exploring them in depth is beyond the scope of this chapter. However, approximately 29% of English words are derived from Latin, another 29% from French, 26% from Germanic, and 6% from Greek.

Virtually all English can ultimately be traced back to a hypothetical language, Proto-Indo-European, which is no longer spoken. Proto-Indo-European begat Germanic, Balto-Slavic, Italic, Celtic, Hellenic, and Indo-Iranian. English gets most of its words from the Italic (Latin), French (derived from Latin), Germanic, and Greek languages.

The English language is primarily comprised of two main groups of words: 1) Anglo-Saxon words are the oldest and form many of basic English words, and 2) Greek and Latin, which also largely contributed to the literature and speech of cultured people. In addition, the English language is comprised of many words borrowed from other languages. For example, *cot* and *loot* are derived from Hindu, *cotton* from Arabic, *candy* and *lilac* from Persian, *tea* from Chinese, and *paprika* from Hungarian.

Words About Words

> For more information, see https://www. etymonline.com

Any study of words will inevitably involve the use of words that directly relate to said study. Here are a few key words you might run across:

Cognate–1640s, connected or descended from a common ancestor, from Latin *cognatus* "of common descent." In other words, cognates are words that came from the same root. Many words in the Romance languages (French, Spanish, Portuguese, Romanian, and Italian) have cognates in Latin. Similarly, words in North German, Old Norse, Swedish, Norwegian, and Icelandic have cognates in Germanic.

Many English words have cognates in Germanic, Greek, Latin, and French (and some others), and can, in most cases, be traced back to their origins. For example, the English word "cold" is a cognate of the German word "kalt," and the English words "fragile" and "frail" are cognates of the Latin word "fragilis."

Etymology–Late 14th Century, "facts of the origin and development of a word," from Old French *etimlogie, ethimologie* (14th Century, Modern French *étymologie*), from Latin *etymologia,* from Greek *etymologia* "analysis of a word to find its true origin," properly "study of the true sense (of a word)," with *logia* study of, a speaking of + *etymon* "true sense, original meaning."

Lexicon–c. 1600, "a dictionary, a word-book," from Middle French *lexicon,* from Greek *lexicon (biblion)* "word (book)," from neuter of *lexikos* "pertaining to words," from *lexis* "a word, a phrase; reason; way of speech, diction, style," from *legein* "to say." A lexicon is basically a dictionary of the words of a language.

Lexicography–"the writing of dictionaries," 1670s, from *lexico-* + *-graphy.*

Prefixes and Suffixes–Prefixes and suffixes are both affixes. Prefixes are the common beginning and ending of words. Since so many English words have Greek or Latin roots and affixes, it makes sense to know as many as you can.

> **Affix** (noun)– "that which is joined or attached," 1610s, from *affix* or from French *affixe,* noun used in French.
>
> **Affix** (verb)– "fasten, join, attach," 1530s from Medieval Latin *affixare,* from ad "to" + *figere* "to fasten" (from Proto-Indo-European root dheigw- "to stick, fix")

GREEK AND LATIN ORIGINS

The Greek and Latin languages are the oldest languages that influenced English. Let's explore these in more detail.

What Came First, Greek, or Latin?

It's not quite that simple. Latin and Greek both developed from Proto-Indo-European. While written Greek pre-dates written Latin, the same is not true of spoken Greek and spoken Latin. As spoken languages go, they are both about the same age. However, there are over 5,100 Latin words that were derived from Ancient Greek.

Is All Latin the Same?

Actually, no. Classical Latin was essentially the language of literature and politics, whereas Vulgar Latin, also known as Late Latin (*Sermo Vulgaris* "common speech") was the non-classical Latin spoken by ordinary Roman citizens and soldiers during the late Roman Empire. The Romance languages–French, Italian, Spanish, Portuguese, etc.) developed from Vulgar Latin.

Let's Take a Closer Look at Seize, Siege, and Sieve

> *Seize*–mid 13c., from Old French *seisir* to take possession by force; from Late Latin *sacire.*
>
> *Siege*–early 13c., from Old French *sege* "seat, throne"; from Vulgar Latin *sedicum.*
>
> *Sieve*–from Old English *sife,* from Proto-Germanic *sib.*

In short, the spellings of words are dependent on their origins, which is another reason English can be confusing.

ROOTS, PREFIXES, AND SUFFIXES

Greek

Only about 6% of English words are directly of Greek origin. However, one estimate puts the number of English words derived, directly or indirectly, from Greek at more than 150,000.

The Greek language is derived from Indo-European, spoken primarily in Greece. In addition, Greek words have cognates in Sanskrit, Latin, Armenian, and others. The Romans used Greek scribes, and this ultimately contributed to the number of English and Greek cognates.

The following is a list of common Greek roots and prefixes, followed by a list of common Greek suffixes. While both lists are not comprehensive, they provide a solid basis for getting at the meanings of some of the words found on the GRE.

Root/prefix	Meaning	Examples
a-	not, without	abyss - without bottom; achromatic - without color
acro-	top, height, tip	acrobat - "high" walker; acrophobia - fear of heights
an-	not, without	anhydrous - without water
aer-	air	aerate - to let air reach something; aerial - relating to the air
aero-	air	aerospace - the air space
agr-	farming	agrarian - relating to the management of land
agri-	farming	agriculture - management of the land
ana-	up, back, against	analysis - a close examination of something
andr	man, male	misandry - hatred toward men
andro-	man, male	androgynous - being both male and female; android - resembling a human
anthro	human	philanthropy -the love to mankind (through good deeds)
anthro-	human	anthropomorphism - giving human form to non-living things
anti-	against, opposite of	antiseptic - preventing infection; antisocial - against social norms
apo-	away, off, separate	apology - an explicit expression of regret
arch	chief, most important	matriarch - a female who rules a group; monarch - king or queen
arch-	chief, most important	archbishop - highest ranking bishop; archenemy - worst enemy
arch-	primitive, ancient	archaeology - the study of ancient cultures; archaic - belonging to an earlier period

Root/ prefix	Meaning	Examples
aster-	space	asterisk - a star shaped sign used as a reference tool
arthri-	joint, jointed	arthritis - inflammation of a joint; arthroscope - a tool to see inside
astro-	star, stars, outer space	astronomer - someone who studies the stars; astronaut - someone who travels to the stars
auto-	self	autocrat - a person who governs with absolute power; automatic - moving by itself
bar-	pressure, weight	baric - pertaining to pressure; baryon - heavy elementary particle
biblio-	book	bibliophile - a person who loves books; bibliography - a list of books used as sources
bio-	life, living, matter	biology - science of life; biography - a life story written by another person
blast	cell, primitive, immature cell	fibroblast - a cell that forms connective tissue
blast-	cell, primitive, immature cell	blastula - an early stage of embryonic development
cardi-	heart	cardiac - relating to the heart; cardiologist - heart doctor
cata-	completely, intensive, according to	cataclysm - a flood or other disaster; catalog - complete listing; catastrophe - disaster
caut	to burn	holocaust - total devastation, especially by fire
caut-	to burn	cauterize - to burn with a hot instrument; caustic - capable of burning or eating away
centr	center	egocentric - self-centered; eccentric - not having a common center
centr-	center	centrifugal - moving outward from a center
cephal	head	encephalitis - inflammation of the brain
cephal-	head	cephalopod - marine mollusks with tentacles growing from their head; cephalic - pertaining to the head
chrom	color, pigment	achromatic - without color
chrom-	color, pigment	chromium - a blue-white element; chromatics - the study of color
chrono	time	synchronize - happening at the same time
chrono-	time	chronic - lasting for a long time; chronological - arranging events in time order
chrys-	gold, yellow	chrysanthemum - golden/yellow flowers
cosm	universe	microcosm - a miniature universe
cosm-	universe	cosmonaut - a Russian astronaut; cosmos - the universe

Root/ prefix	Meaning	Examples
crani-	skull	cranium - skull of vertebrates; cranial - pertaining to the skull; craniology - the study of skull characteristics
crypto-	hidden, secret	cryptography - science of secret codes; cryptic - of hidden meaning
cycl	circle, ring	bicycle - a vehicle with two wheels
cycl-	circle, ring	cycle - a sequence that is repeated; cyclone - a storm with whirling winds
dec-	ten	decade - 10 years; December - formerly the 10th month of the Roman calendar
dem	people	spreading among people in a region
demo-	people	democracy - government of the people; demographic - the study of people
dendr	tree	philodendron - a climbing plant that grows on trees
dendr-	tree	dendrochronology - dating events by studying growth in tree rings
derm	skin	pachyderm - a class of animals with very thick skin
derm-	skin	dermatologist - a doctor for the skin; dermatitis - inflammation of the skin
di-	two, twice	dichromatic - displaying two colors; dilemma - a situation that requires a choice between two alternatives
dia-	through, between, apart, across	diagnosis - understanding a condition by going through a detailed review; dialog - conversation between two people
dyn-	power, energy, strength	dynamo - generator of energy; dynamite - powerful explosive; dynamic - having great physical energy/power
dys-	abnormal, bad	dyspepsia - abnormal digestion; dystopia - an imaginary place of misery
ego	self	alter ego - a higher aspect of oneself
ego-	self	egoistic - self-centered; egomania - excessive preoccupation with oneself
endo-	within, inside	endotherm - a creature that can keep its inside temperature fairly constant; endogamy - the custom to marry within one's clan, tribe, etc.
epi-	on, upon, over, among, at, after, to, outside	epidemic - the rapid spread of something negative; epilogue - a short speech delivered after a play
erg	work	energy - the power to accomplish work; energetics - the science that looks at energy and its transformation
erg-	work	ergonomics - the study of a working environment
ethn-	race, people	ethnic - pertaining to a defined group of people; ethnocentric - focusing on the ethnicity of people

Root/ prefix	Meaning	Examples
eu-	good, well	euphemism - replacing an offensive word with an inoffensive one; euphoria - feeling of well-being
gastr-	stomach	gastric - pertaining to the stomach; gastritis - inflammation of the stomach
gen-	birth, production	genealogy - the study of the history of a family; generation - all the people born at approximately the same time
geo-	earth, soil, global	geography - study of the earth's surface; geology - study of the structure of the earth
ger-	old age	geriatrics - medicine pertaining to the elderly; gerontology - the study of aging
giga-	a billion	gigabyte -unit of computer storage space; gigawatt - a billion watts
gon	angle	decagon - a polygon with 10 angles; octagon - a geometrical figure with 8 angles
gram	letter, written	diagram - a simple drawing; telegram - a message sent by telegraph
gram-	letter, written	grammar - rules of how to write words in sentences
graph	writing, recording, written	autograph - written by one's own hand; seismograph - a machine noting strength and duration of earthquakes
graph-	writing, recording, written	graphology - the study of handwriting
gyn-	woman, female	gynecology - the science of female reproductive health; gynecoid - resembling a woman
hect-	hundred	hectoliter - 100 meters; hectare - 100 acres
helic-	spiral, circular	helicopter - an aircraft with horizontal rotating wings; helix - a spiral form
helio-	sun	heliograph - apparatus used to send message with help of sunlight;
hemi-	half, partial	hemicycle - a semicircular structure; hemisphere - one half of the earth
hem-	blood	hemorrhage - clotting of the blood; hemoglobin - red blood particle
hept-	seven	heptagon - a shape with 7 angles; heptameter - a line of verse containing 7 metrical feet
hetero-	different, other	heterogeneous - made up of unrelated parts; heteronyms - words with same spelling but different meanings
hex-	six	hexagon - shape with 6 angles; hexapod - having 6 legs
histo-	tissue	histology - study of the microscopic structure of tissues
homo-	like, alike, same	homogeneous - of the same nature or kind; homonym - something alike

Root/prefix	Meaning	Examples
hydr-	water, liquid	hydrate - to add water to; hydrophobia - intense fear of water; hydraulic - operated by force of a liquid
hygr-	moisture, humidity	hygrometer - tool used to measure humidity
hyper-	too much, over, excessive	hyperactive - very restless; hypercritical - too critical; hypertension - above normal pressure
hyp-	under	hypothermia - abnormally low body temperature
iatr	medical care	geriatrics - medical care of the elderly; pediatrician - doctor who treats children
icon-	image	icon - an (often religious) image; iconoclast - someone who destroys religious images and religious beliefs
idio-	peculiar, personal, distinct	idiomatic - peculiar to a particular language, idiosyncrasy - a physical or mental characteristic
kilo-	thousand	kilobyte - 1,000 bytes; kilometer - 1,000 meters
kine	motion	telekinesis - the ability to move object with your mind
leuk-	white, colorless	leukemia - abnormal increase in white blood cells; leukocyte - a mature white blood cell
lex	word, law, reading	alexia - loss of the ability to read
lex-	word, law, reading	lexicology - the study and history of words
lip-	fat	liposuction - the mechanical removal of fat; lipoid - resembling fat
lite	mineral, rock, fossil	apatite - a group of common minerals
lith	mineral, rock, fossil	monolith - a single great stone often in the form of an obelisk or column
log	word, doctrine, discourse	monologue - a long speech; analogy - similarity, especially between things otherwise dissimilar
log-	word, doctrine, discourse	logic - correct reasoning
macro-	large, great	macroevolution - large scale evolution; macroeconomics - study of overall forces of economy
mania	madness, insanity, excessive desire	maniac - an insane person
mania-	madness, insanity, excessive desire	bibliomania - a crazy love of books; egomania - a mad love of oneself
mega-	great, large, million	megalopolis - an area with many, nearby cities; melanoma - malignant, dark tumor of the skin
meso-	middle	Mesoamerica - Middle America; meson - elementary particle with a mass between an electron and a proton
meta-	change, after, beyond, between	metaphysics - study of nature and reality; metastasis - the transmission of disease to other parts of the body

Root/ prefix	Meaning	Examples
meter	measure	audiometer - an instrument that measures hearing acuteness; chronometer - an instrument that measures time
micro-	very small, short, minute	microbe - a very small living thing; microscope - a device to see very small things
mid-	middle	midriff - that area between the chest and the waist; midterm = middle of a term in school
mis-	bad, badly, wrong, wrongly, to hate	misbehave - to behave badly; misprint - an error in printing
mon-	one, single, alone	monochromat - having one color; monologue - a speech given by one person
morph	form	metamorphosis - complete change in form; amorphous - without distinct shape or form
necr-	dead, death	necrophile - loving death; necrosis - the death of tissue due to disease or injury
nephro-	kidney	nephritis - inflammation of the kidneys; nephrostomy - surgical incision of the kidney
neur-	nerve	neuralgia - pain along a nerve; neurologist - doctor specializing in the nerves
oct-	eight	octagon - a figure with 8 angles; octopus - sea animal with 8 arms
od	path, way	diode - an electron tube having 2 electrodes, a cathode and an anode
od-	path, way	odometer - an instrument attached to a vehicle to measure distance
op-	eye, visual condition, sight	optic - relating to the eyes; optician - a person who fits eyeglasses
ortho-	straight	orthodontist - a dentist that straightens teeth; orthopedic - doctor who is concerned with proper alignment of bones
osteo-	goes beyond, surpasses	osteoarthritis - inflammation caused by degeneration of the joints; osteology - the study of bones
oxi-, oxy-	sharp	oxymoron - combining two ideas that sharply contradict each other; oxidize - corrode a surface
pale-	ancient	paleontology - study of ancient fossils; Paleolithic - period of the Stone Age
pan-	all, any, everyone	panacea - a cure for all diseases or problems; panorama - an all-around view; pandemic - affecting all
para-	beside, beyond, abnormal	parasite - an organism that lives on and off another living being; parallel - alongside and always an equal distance apart

Root/ prefix	Meaning	Examples
pater-, patr-	father	paternal - relating to fathers; patriarch - a man who rules a group
pent-	five	pentagon - having 5 angles and sides; pentagram - a 5-pointed star, especially in magic
pept, peps	digestion	dyspepsia - abnormal digestion; peptic - aiding digestion
peri-	around, enclosing	periodontal - pertaining to bone and tissue around a tooth; perimeter - the outer boundary of an area
phag	to eat	esophagus - muscular tube that carries food to the stomach
phil-	love, friend	philanthropist - one who loves humanity
phon	sound	cacophony - loud unpleasant sound; microphone - a device that records and amplifies sound
phot-	light	photogenic - caused by light; photograph - image made on light-sensitive film
phyll	leaf	chlorophyll - a group of green pigments found in leaves
phyll-	leaf	phyllite - a rock that forms sheets, similar to slate
phys-	nature, medicine, the body	physical - relating to the body; physician - doctor
phyt	plant, to grow	epiphyte - a plant growing independently on the surface of another; neophyte - a beginner
plas	to form, development	protoplasm - something that is first made or formed
plas-	to form, development	plastic - able to be formed
pneum-	breathing, lung, air, spirit	pneumonia - inflammation of the lungs; pneumatic - using the force of air
pod-	foot	podiatrist - a doctor of the feet; podium - a small platform to stand upon
poli	city	metropolis - a large city
poli-	city	police - people who work for the government in order to enforce laws; politics - actions of a government or political party
poly-	many, more than one	polychrome - with many colors; polyglot - a person fluent in many languages
pro-	before, in front of, for, forward	prognosis - a prediction of what will happen; prologue - a passage before the main part
prot-	primitive, first, chief	prototype - the first of a kind; proton - one of the very basic parts of an atom
pseud-	wrong, false	pseudonym - a fictitious name; pseudoscience - theories presumed without proof of a scientific nature

Root/ prefix	Meaning	Examples
psych-	mind, mental	psyche - the human spirit or soul; psychic - relating to the human mind or someone who has supernatural mental abilities
pyr-	fire, heat	pyrometer - a thermometer for measuring high temperature; pyrotechnics - the art of making fireworks
rhin-	nose	rhinoceros - a species of animals with a big horn on the snout; rhinoplasty - surgery of the nose
rhod-	red	rhododendron - a flower with red/pink flowers
rrh	flow, discharge	hemorrhage - heavy blood flow
scler-	hard	multiple sclerosis - disease which causes the tissue of the brain and spinal cord to harden
scop	see, examine, observe	microscope - a device used to see tiny places; periscope - a seeing instrument on a submarine
soph	wise	philosopher - a wise person
soph-	wise	sophisticated - wise about the ways of the world; sophism - a clever but misleading argument
sphere	ball	biosphere - the whole round surface of the earth; hemisphere - half the earth spherically shaped like a ball
sym-, syn-	together, with, same	symmetry - similarity in size, form, or arrangement; synergy - the combined effect
tax	arrangement	syntax - the systematic arrangement of words
tax-	arrangement	taxonomy - the science of classification
techno-	technique, skill	technology - the practical application of knowledge
tel-	far, distant, complete	telescope - a device to view distant objects; telephone - a device to talk with a distant person
the-	put	theme - a proposition for discussion or argument
therm-	heat	thermal - relating to heat; thermos - an insulated jar that keeps heat in
tri-	three, once in every three, third	triangle - a figure with 3 sides and 3 angles; tricycle - a 3-wheel vehicle with pedals
xen-	foreign	xenophobic - afraid of foreigners; xenophile - attracted to foreigners
xer-	dry	xerophyte - a plant that grows in a dry climate; xeric - requiring small amounts of moisture
xyl-	wood	xyloid - resembling wood
zo-	animal life	zoology - study of animals; zooid - resembling an animal
zyg	pair	zygomorphic - pertaining to organisms that can be divided into symmetrical halves along one axis only

List of Common Greek Suffixes

Suffix	Meaning	Examples
-biosis	mode of living, way of life	symbiosis - the living together of two dissimilar organisms
-blast	formative, embryonic	mesoblast - the mesoderm
-chrome	color	Mercurochrome - a brand of merbromin
-cocci	round, seed, kernel	streptococcus - any of several spherical or oval bacteria which are pathogenic for humans
-cyst	pouch, sac	trichocyst - an organ of offense and defense embedded in certain protozoans
-dactyl	finger	pentadactyl - having five digits on each hand or foot
-derm, -dermis	skin, layer	epidermis - the outer layer of the skin
-emia	blood disease	anemia - a quantitative deficiency of the hemoglobin
-gamous, -gamy	marriage, sexual fusion	polygamy - the practice of having more than one spouse
-gen, -geny	origin, production	progeny - a descendent or offspring; hydrogen - colorless, odorless, flammable gas
-graph	drawing, writing	chromatograph - a piece of equipment used to produce a chromatogram
-hedral, -hedron	side	polyhedral - of, relating to, or having the shape of a polyhedron
-hydrate	compound formed by union of water with other substances	carbohydrate - any of a class of organic compounds that are polyhydroxy aldehydes
-ism	act, practice, or result of	terrorism - the use of violence or threats to intimidate or coerce
-itis	inflammation or infection	appendicitis - inflammation of the appendix
-logy	science or study of	biology - the science of life or living matter
-lysis	loosening, separation	photolysis - the chemical decomposition of materials under the influence of light
-mer	a part, piece	polymer - a compound formed from two or more polymeric compounds
-meter	a measurement	diameter - straight line passing through the center of a circle or sphere and meeting the circumference at each end
-morph	form	endomorph - a mineral enclosed within another mineral
-nomy	systematized knowledge of	astronomy - the science that deals with the material universe beyond the earth's atmosphere

Suffix	Meaning	Examples
-oma	tumorous	carcinoma - malignant tumor, cancer
-osis, -otic	abnormal condition, disease	neurosis - a relatively mild personality disorder typified by excessive anxiety
-phase	a stage or condition	metaphase - a stage of mitosis or meiosis
-phil, -phile	fear, fearing	hydrophobia - abnormal fear of water
-phyll	leaf	chlorophyll - the green coloring matter of leaves and plants
-phyta, phyte	plant	epiphyte - a plant that grows above the ground
-plasm	formative substance	cytoplasm - the cell substance between the cell membrane and the nucleus
-pod, -poda	foot	arthropod - any invertebrate of the phylum Arthropoda
-some	body	chromosome - any of several threadlike bodies that carry genes in a linear order
-stasis	a stationary position	homeostasis - the tendency of a system to maintain internal stability
-stat, -static	stationary, still	hemostat - an instrument or agent used to treat bleeding vessels in order to arrest hemorrhage
-stomy	opening into	colostomy - the construction of an opening from the colon through the abdominal wall
-therm	heat	homeotherm - An organism, such as a mammal or bird, having a body temperature that is constant and largely independent of the temperature of its surroundings.
-thes, thesis	arrangement, in order	hypothesis - a proposition assumed as a premise or argument
-tom, -tomy	dividing, surgery	lobotomy - the operation of cutting into a lobe, as of the brain or the lung
-trope, -tropic	turning	phototropic - growing toward or away from the light
-zoa, -zoan, -zoic	animal, life	protozoa - a major grouping or the kingdom Protista, comprising the protozoans

Latin

The Latin language was originally derived from the Indo-European language.

As Rome grew in power and influence, first throughout Italy, and then throughout most of western and southern Europe and the central and western Mediterranean coastal regions of Africa, so did the Latin language. Latin was widely used in the Middle Ages, and has, until relatively recent times, been used for scholarly and literary purposes. The Roman Catholic Church spoke Latin in the liturgy until the latter part of the 20th Century.

During the Classical period there were at least three types of Latin: Classical Latin, Classical oratorical Latin, and the ordinary colloquial Latin. After the 3rd century CE, many texts were written in Vulgar Latin, and in the 4th and 5th centuries, writers wrote in Late Latin.

Because of Latin's heavy influence on the Romance languages, of particular note Norman French, many Latin roots and affixes have found their way into the English language.

What follows is a list of common Latin roots and prefixes, followed by a list of common Latin suffixes. Again, neither list is comprehensive, but by knowing these, you may be able to determine the meanings of some of the words found on the GRE.

List of Common Latin Roots and Prefixes

Root/ prefix	Meaning	Examples
a-	on	afire - on fire; ashore - on the shore
ab-	from, away, off	abduct - carry away from; abnormal - away from normal; aside - on the side
a-	to, toward, near	accelerate - to increase the speed of; accessible - easily entered, approached, or obtained
act	do	interaction - communication between two or more things
act-	do	activity - something that a person does
agr-	farming	agriculture - management of the land
alg	pain	neuralgia - pain caused by a nerve; nostalgia - aching for the familiar; analgesic - drug that relieves pain
ambi-, amphi	both, on both sides	ambiguous - having more than one meaning; ambivalence - conflicting or opposite feelings toward a person or thing
ambul-	walk, move	ambulance - a vehicle that moves a patient; ambulant - walking or moving around
ami-, amo-	love	amiable - friendly; amorous - showing romantic love
anim	life, spirit	equanimity - of balanced spirit

Root/prefix	Meaning	Examples
anim-	life, spirit	animal - a living organism; animate - to make alive
ann-	year	anniversary - a date observed once a year
ante-	before, in front	anteroom - a small room before the main room
aqu-	water	aquarium - a water container for fish; aqueduct - a pipeline for water
arbor-	tree	arborist - someone working with trees; arbor - a shady area formed by trees
art-	skill	artifact - object made by a person's skill; artisan - a person skilled in a craft
aud-	hear	audible - loud enough to be heard; audience - people who listen to a program
avi-	bird	aviary - a large enclosure for birds; aviatrix - a female pilot
bel	war	rebel - person who opposes or fights
bell-	war	bellicose - warlike; belligerent - hostile
bene-	good, well	beneficial - producing a good effect; benevolent - showing kindness or goodwill
bi	two, twice, once every two	biannual - happening every 2 years; bilateral - of or involving 2 sides
burs	pouch, purse	disburse - to expend especially from a public fund
burs-	pouch, purse	bursar - an administrative officer in charge of funds
calc-	stone	calcification - impregnation with calcareous matter
cand	glowing, incandescent	incandescent - white, glowing, or luminous
cand-	glowing, incandescent	candid - free from bias; candle - something that gives light
capt-	take, hold	captivating - taking hold of
carn-	flesh, meat	carnivorous - flesh eating animal; carnal - pertaining to the body or flesh
cede, ceed, cess	go, yield	exceed - to go beyond the limits; recede - to go back
celer	fast	accelerate - to increase the speed of
cent-	hundred, hundredth	centennial - the 100th anniversary; centimeter - 1/100th of a meter
cept, ceive	take, hold	intercept - to stop or intercept; perceive - to take notice of something
cerebr-	brain	cerebral - pertaining to the brain
cert	sure	ascertain - to find out something with certainty

Root/ prefix	Meaning	Examples
cert-	sure	certain - being absolutely sure; certify - to state that something is true
cide, cise	cut, kill	homicide - murder; incisor - a sharp tooth for cutting food
circum-, circle-	around, about	circumnavigate - to sail around; circumspect - looking around
claim, clam	shout, speak out	exclaim - to cry out loudly; proclamation - announce something in public
claim-, clam-	shout, speak out	clamor - to shout and make noise
clar	clear	declare - to state something clearly
clar-	clear	clarification - an explanation; clarify - to make something clear
clud, clus	close	conclusion - the end or last part; exclusion - shutting out
cline	lean	recline - to lean back and relax
co-	with, together, joint	coauthor - writer who collaborates with another author; coeducation - educating males and females together
col-	together, jointly	collaborate - to work together; collision - smashing together
com-	together, common	commemorate - to memorize together; commune - living together while owning things in common
cogn	know	incognito - disguised so no one knows you; recognize - to discover that one knows
cogn-	know	cognition - process of acquiring knowledge
con-	with, jointly	concur - to agree with someone; contemporary - of the same time period as others
contra-, contro-	against, opposite	contradict - to argue against
corp-	body	corporation - a company recognized by law as a single body; corporal - pertaining to the body
dent-, dont-	tooth	dental - pertaining to the teeth; dentist - doctor for the teeth
di-	apart, away, not, to the opposite	digression - departure from the main issue; disappear - to move out of sight
dict	speak	contradict - to express the opposite of; prediction - a statement foretelling the future
dict-	speak	dictate - to speak out loud for another person to write own
domin	master	predominate - to have more power than others

Root/prefix	Meaning	Examples
domin-	master	dominate - to be the master of
don	give	pardon - to give forgiveness
don-	give	donation - a contribution or gift; donor - someone who gives
duc	lead	conduct - to lead musicians; educate - to lead to knowledge
du-	two, twice	duplicate - make an identical copy; duo - a pair normally thought of as being together
dur	enduring	able to last
dur-	harden, to last, lasting	durable - having the quality of lasting
e-	out, away	eloquent - speaking beautifully; eject - throw out forcefully
ego-	self	egoistic - self-centered
enn, anni	years	bicentennial - of or relating to a period of 200 years; perennial - lasting through many years
en-, in-	inside, inward	envision - to picture in the mind; enclose - lock inside
equ-, equi-	equal, equally	equidistant - equal distance between 2 points; equation - a statement of equality
esth, aesth	feeling, sensation, beauty	kinesthesia - the sensation of bodily movement
esth-, aesth-	feeling, sensation, beauty	esthetician - someone who beautifies; aesthetic - pertaining to a sense of beauty
ex-	from, out	excavate - do dig out; exhale - to breath out
extra-, extro-	outside, beyond	extraordinary - beyond ordinary; extrovert - an outgoing person
fac, fact	make, do	artifact - object made by a person; malefactor - a person who does wrong
fac-, fact-	make, do	factory - a place where things are made
fer	bear, bring, carry	confer - to bring honor to someone; transfer - to move to another place
fer-	bear, bring, carry	ferry - a boat that carries passengers
fid	faith	confide - place trust in someone
fid-	faith	fiduciary - a trustee; fidelity - faithfulness
flect	bend	flexible - easily bending
flect-	bend	deflect - to bend course because of hitting something; inflection - a bending in the voice's tone or pitch
flor-, flora-, fleur-	flower	florist - someone who works with flowers; floral - flowerlike

Root/ prefix	Meaning	Examples
form	shape	conformity - correspondence in form; reformatory - intended for reformation
form-	shape	formation - something that is formed
fract-, frag-	break	fragile - easy to break; fracture - a break
fug	flee, run away, escape	refuge - a sheltered place to flee to; refugee - a person seeking protection
fug-	flee, run away, escape	fugitive - a person who is running away
funct	perform, work	defunct - no longer working or alive; malfunction - to fail to work correctly
funct-	perform, work	function - to work normally
fus	pour	confusion - being flooded with too much information that is hard to make sense of; infuse - to put into
fus-	pour	fuse - to melt by heating
gon	angle	decagon - a polygon with 10 angles
grad-	to step, to go	gradual - step by step
gran-	grain	granary - a storehouse or repository for grain; granola - a mixture of rolled oats and other ingredients
grat-	pleasing	gratify - to please someone; grateful - feeling thankful
gress	to step, to go	digression - departure from the main issue; progress - movement forward or onward
hem-	blood	hemoglobin - red blood particle
hepa-	liver	hepatitis - inflammation of the liver; hepatoma - a tumor of the liver
herbi-	plant, grass	herbicide - any chemical used to kill unwanted plants; herbal - relating to plants
homo-	like, alike, same	homogeneous - of the same nature or kind
hyper-	too much, over, excessive, beyond	hyperactive - very restless
icon-	image	iconology - science of symbols and icons
il-, in-	in, into	illuminate - to give light to; innovation - a new ideal, method, or device
ig-, il-, im-, in-, ir-	not, without	illegal - not legal; impossible - not possible; inappropriate - not appropriate
imag-	likeness	image - a likeness of someone; imagine - to form a picture or likeness in the mind
infra-	beneath, below	infrastructure - underlying framework of a system; infrared - below the regular light spectrum

Root/ prefix	Meaning	Examples
inter-	between, among, jointly	to stop or interrupt the course of
intra-, intro-	within, inside	intrastate - existing in one state; introvert - shy person who keeps within him/herself
ir-	not	irredeemable - not redeemable; irrational - not rational
ject	throw	eject - to throw someone/thing out; interject - to throw a remark into a discussion
jud-	law	judgment - a decision of a court of law; judicial - having to do with judges or courts of law
junct	join	conjunction - a word that joins parts of sentences; disjunction - a disconnection
junct-	join	junction - a place where 2 things join
juven	young	rejuvenate - to bring back to youthful experience
juven-	young	juvenile - youthful or childish
lab	work	collaborate - to work with a person; elaborate - to work out the details
lab-	work	laborious - requiring a lot of work
lact-	milk	lactate - to give milk, nurse; lactose - the sugar contained in mild
later	side	bilateral - of or involving 2 sides; unilateral - affecting one side of something
liber-	free	liberate - to set free; liberty - freedom
lingu	language, tongue	multilingual - able to communicate in more than 1 language
lingu-	language, tongue	linguist - one who studies languages
loc	place	dislocate - to put something out of its usual place
loc-	place	location - a place
loqu, locu	speak	eloquent - speaking beautifully
loqu-, locu-	speak	loquacious - very talkative
luc	light	elucidate - to explain, to throw light on; translucent - allowing light to pass through
luc-	light	easily understood
lud, lus	to play	prelude - introduction to the major performance; illusion - misleading optical image or impression
lumin	light	illuminate - to fill with light
lumin-	light	lumen - unit measuring light

Root/ prefix	Meaning	Examples
lun-	moon	lunar - relating to the moon; lunarscape - the surface of the moon
magn-	great, large	magnify - make larger - magnificent - grand
mal-	bad, ill, wrong	malcontent - wrong content; malicious- showing strong ill will
man-	hand	maneuver - to move by hand; manual - done by hand
mand	to order	command - an order of instruction; demand - a hard-to-ignore order
mand-	to order	mandate - an official order
mar	sea	submarine - an undersea boat; aquamarine - color of sea water
mar-	sea	marina - a harbor for pleasure boats
mater-, matr-	mother	maternal - relating to motherhood; maternity - the state of being a mother
max-	greatest	maximal - the best or greatest possible; maximize - the make as great as possible
medi-	middle	medium - in the middle; mediocre - only of medium quality
memor	remember	commemorate - to honor the memory of
memor-	remember	memorial - related remembering a person or event; memory - ability to retain knowledge
merge, mers	dip, dive	immerge or immerse - to put or dip something into a liquid
mid-	middle	midterm - middle of a term in school
migr	move	immigrant - a person who moves to a new country
migr-	move	migrant - person who moves from place to place
milli-	one thousandth	milliliter—one thousandth of a meter
min-	small, less	mini - something that is very small
miss, mit	send, let go	dismiss - to send someone away; emit - to send something out
miss-, mit-	send, let go	missile - a weapon sent into the air
mob	move	immobilize - to stop from moving
mob-	move	mobility - the quality of being able to move
mot, mov	move	promote - to move someone forward
mot-, mov-	move	motion - the act of moving; motivate - to move someone into action
mort	death	immortal - living forever

Root/prefix	Meaning	Examples
mort-	death	mortal - certain to die; mortician - an undertaker
multi-	many, more than one or two	multicolored - having many colors; multitasking - doing many things at once
mut	change	immutable - not changing
mut-	change	mutant - an organism that has undergone change
my-, myo	muscle	myocardium - the middle muscle of the heart
narr-	tell	narrate - to tell a story; narrator - a person who tells a story
nat	born	innate - included since birth
nat-	born	natal - relating to birth; natural - gotten at birth
nav	ship	circumnavigate - to sail around a place
nav-	ship	relating to a navy or ships; navigate - to sail a ship throughout a place
neg	no	renege - to go back on a promise
neg-	no	negate - to say it didn't happen; negative - meaning "no"
nom	name	misnomer - an error in naming a person or thing
nom-	name	nominal - being something in name only; nominate—to name for election or appointment
non-	no, not, without	nondescript - with no special characteristics; nonfiction - true, real
noun, nunc	declare	announce - to declare in public; denounce - to proclaim harsh criticism
nov	new	innovate - to introduce a new way; renovate - to make something like new again
nov-	new	novice - someone who is new at something
numer	number	enumerate - to name a number of items on a list
numer-	number	numerology - the study of magical uses of numbers; numerous - a large number
ob-, op-	in the way, against	object - to be against something; obscure - hard to understand; opposition - the act of resistance
ocu	eye	binoculars - lens device for seeing distances; monocular - relating to the eye
ocu-	eye	oculist - an eye doctor
odor	smell, scent	deodorant - a substance that helps prevent body odor; malodorous - having a terribly bad smell
odor-	smell, scent	odoriferous - something that bears or diffuses a scent

Root/prefix	Meaning	Examples
omni-	all	omnipotent - all powerful; omniscient - knowing all things
opt-	best	optimal - the best; optimize - to make the best of
pater-, patr-	father	paternal - relating to fathers
ped-	foot, feet	pedal - a lever pushed by the feet; pedestrian - a person who walks
pel	drive, force	compel - to force someone to act; expel - to drive someone out of place
per-	through, throughout	permanent - lasting throughout all time; permeate - to spread throughout
plaud, plod, plaus, plos	approve, clap	applaud - to show approval of especially by clapping the hands
plaus-	approve, clap	plausible - worthy of being applauded
pon	place, put	opponent - a person who places him/herself against an action, idea, etc., postpone - to put off doing something
pop-	people	popular - appealing to a lot of people; populist - a supporter of the rights of people
port	carry	export - to carry goods out of a place to another
port-	carry	portable - able to be carried; porter - a person who carries luggage
pos	place, put	deposit - to place or drop something; expose - to place out in the open for all to see
pos-	place, put	position - the place where someone is
post-	after, behind	posthumous - after someone's death; postscript - an addition to an already completed document
pre-	earlier, before, in front of	preamble - a part in front of a formal document; prepare - to get ready in advance
pro-	before, in front of, for, forward	prognosis - a prediction of what will happen; prophet - a person who foretells the future
pugn, pung	to fight	repugnant - distasteful, offensive, or revolting
pugn-, pung-	to fight	pugnacious - having a quarrelsome or aggressive nature; pungent - piercing
purg	clean	expurgate - remove objectionable passages from publication
purg-	clean	purge - remove anything undesirable
put	think	computer - an electronic thinking device; dispute - to disagree with what another person thinks

Root/ prefix	Meaning	Examples
quad-	four	quadrant - open space with buildings on 4 sides; quadruped - a 4-footed animal
quart-	fourth	quarter - one fourth; quart - one fourth of a gallon
quin-	five, fifth	quintet - a composition for 5 voices or instruments; quintuple - fivefold
radic, radix	root	eradicate - pull out at the roots
radic-, radix-	root	radical - fundamental, looking at things from a drastic point of view
ram-	branch	ramification - the resulting consequence of a decision; ramus - a branchlike part
re-	again, back, backward	rebound - to spring back again; rewind - to wind something backward
reg-	guide, rule	regent - a person who rules on behalf of a king or queen; regime - a government that rules
retro-	backward, back	retroactive - relating to something in the past; retrospect - the remembering of past events
rid	laugh	deride - to make fun of someone
rid-	laugh	ridicule - to make fun of or mock; ridiculous - silly, causing laughter
rrh, ea, oca, ag	flow, discharge	hemorrhage - heavy blood flow
rub	red	bilirubin - reddish pigment in bile
rub-	red	ruby - deep red color and a precious stone; rubella - measles
rupt	break, burst	bankrupt - unable to pay because you're "broke"; interrupt - to break into a conversation
rupt-	break, burst	rupture - a break in something
san-	health	sane - mentally healthy; sanitary - relating to cleanliness and health
scend	climb, go	ascend - to climb upward; crescendo - a climbing up of volume
sci	know	conscience - sense of knowing right from wrong; conscious - knowing what is happening
scrib, script	write, written	inscribe - to write letters or words on a surface; describe - to represent with words or pictures
scrib-, script-	write, written	scribe - a person who writes out documents
se-	apart	secede - to formally break away from; seclude - to keep away from

Root/ prefix	Meaning	Examples
sect	cut	dissect - to cut apart piece by piece; intersection - the place where two things cross each other
sed, sid, sess	sit	reside - be stationed; sediment - the matter that settles to the bottom of a liquid
sess-	sit	session - an actual or constructive sitting of a body
semi-	half, partial	semiannual - every half year; semicircle - half a circle
sept-	seven	September - used to be the seventh month in the Roman calendar; septet - a group of 7 musicians
serv	save, keep	conserve - to save or keep something safe; preserve - to save something; reservation - a place kept for a person
sex-	six	sextet or sextette - a composition or group of 6; sextuple - six-fold
sol	sun	parasol - umbrella protecting from the sun
sol-	sun	solar - solitary - done alone; solarium - a room where one is exposed to sunlight
somn	sleep	insomnia - inability to fall asleep
somn-	sleep	somniloquy - talking in your sleep; somnolent - feeling sleepy
son	sound	consonant - a speech sound; unison - as one voice
son-	sound	sonorous - producing loud, full, rich sounds; supersonic - faster than sound
spec	see, look	circumspect - cautious, looking all around; retrospective - a looking back on things
spec-	see, look	spectator - a person who sees an event
spir	breathe	inspire - to stimulate or animate; perspire - to give of vapor with waste product through the skin
spir-	breathe	spirit - invisible life force
sta-	stand	stable - standing steady and firm; stagnant - standing still, not moving
stell	star	constellation - a group of stars that forms a pattern; interstellar - between the stars
stell-	star	stellar - relating to stars
struct	build	construct - to build; destruction - the act of destroying something that was built
struct-	build	structure - something built
sub-	under, lower than, inferior to	submarine - an underwater boat; substandard - inferior to accepted standards
sum-	highest	sum - the combined total of everything; summit - the highest point or top

Root/ prefix	Meaning	Examples
super-	higher in quality or quantity	Superbowl - the final annual football game; supersonic - faster than the speed of sound
tact, tang	touch	contact - a state in which two things touch; intact - with nothing missing
tact-, tang-	touch	tangible - able to be touched; tactile - relating to the sense of touch
temp, tempor	time	contemporary - existing at the same time
temp-, tempor-	time	temporal - relating to time; temporary - lasting for a limited time
ten, tin, tent	hold	continent - serving to restrain or limit; detention - the act or fact of detaining
ten-	hold	tenacious - having parts or elements strongly adhering to each other
ter, trit	rub	attrition - the act of rubbing together or wearing down
trit-	rub	trite - used or occurring so often as to have lost interest, freshness, or force
term, termina	end, limit	determine - to find something out at the end of an investigation; exterminate - to destroy or get rid of
term-, termina-	end, limit	terminate - to end
terr-, terra-, terri-	land, earth	territory - an area of land; terrain - ground or land
tetra-	four	tetrapod - having 4 legs; tetrarchy - government by 4 rulers
tort	twist	contortion - a twisted shape or position; distort - to alter the shape or condition of
tox	poison	the process of removing poisons
tox-	poison	toxic - poisonous; toxicology - the study of poisons
tract	pull, drag	attract - to pull objects nearer; distract - to drag attention away from
tract-	pull, drag	tractor - a motor vehicle that pulls things
trans-	across, beyond, through	transcontinental - across the continent; transfer - to move from one place to another
tri-	three, once every three, third	triangle - a figure with 3 sides and 3 angles; triathlon - an athletic contest with 3 events
ultra-	beyond, extreme, more than	ultrahigh - extremely high; ultramodern - more modern than anything else
un-	not, opposite of, lacking	unabridged - not shortened; unfair - opposite of fair

Root/ prefix	Meaning	Examples
uni-	one, single	unicycle - a vehicle with 1 wheel; unilateral - decided by only one person or nation
urb	city	suburb - residential area on the edge of a city
urb-	city	urban - relating to a city; urbanology - the study of city life
vac	empty	evacuate - to empty a dangerous place
vac-	empty	vacant - empty, not occupied; vacation - a time without work
ven, vent	come	circumvent - to find a way around, get past; connivent - coming into contact
ver-	truth	veracious - truthful, honest; veracity - the truth
verb	word	adverb - a word relating to a verb; proverb - a short saying that expresses a well-known truth
verb-	word	verbalize - to put into words
vers, vert	turn	reverse - to turn around; introvert - being turned towards the inside
vers-, vert-	turn	version - a variation of the original
vice-	acting in place of	vice-president - the person next in rank to the president
vince, vic	conquer	convince - to win someone over; invincible - not able to be conquered
vince-, vic-	conquer	victory - the conquest of an enemy
vis, vid	see	envision - to picture in the mind; evident - clearly visible
vis-, vid-	see	vision - the ability to see
viv, viva, vit	live, life	revival - the act of bringing back to life
viv-, viva-, vit-	live, life	vivacious - high-spirited and full of life; vital - pertaining to life
voc, voci	voice, call	advocate - to speak in favor of; equivocate - to use misleading language that could be interpreted 2 different ways
voc-, voci-	voice, call	vocalize - to produce with your voice
vol, voli, volu	wish, will	benevolent - showing good will and kindness
vol-, voli-, volu-	wish, will	volition - the act of making a choice or decision; voluntary - resulting from your own free will

Root/ prefix	Meaning	Examples
vor, vour	eat	carnivorous - meat - eating; devour - to eat quickly
vor-, vour-	eat	voracious - desiring or eating food in great quantities
xanth-	yellow	xanthium - a genus of coarse and rough or spiny herbs; xanthochromia - yellowish discoloration (as of the skin)

List of Common Latin Suffixes

Suffix	Meaning	Examples
-cidal, -cide	killer, a killing	insecticide - a substance or preparation used for killing insects
-elle, -ule, -la, -le, -let, -ole	small, diminutive endings	globule - a small spherical body; piglet - a little pig
-fer	bearer, producer, carry	conifer - any of numerous, chiefly evergreen trees or shrubs; transfer - to convey or move from place to place
-genesis	origin, development of	embryogenesis - the formation and development of the embryo
-gony	something produced	cosmogony - the study of the origin and development of the universe
-ite	a division or part	somite - any of the longitudinal series of segments or parts into which the body of certain animals is divided
-jugal, -jugate	to yoke, join together	conjugate - to join together, especially in marriage
-vor, -vore	feeding	carnivore - an animal that eats flesh

FRENCH

French is one of a family of Romance languages ultimately derived from Vulgar Latin. Other Romance languages are Portuguese, Italian, Romanian, and Spanish. They are called Romance languages because they originated from a language spoken by the Romans.

Old French was spoken in Northern France from the 8th Century to the 14th Century. These dialects ultimately became spoken in all of France and became known simply as French.

In 1066, the Normans, led by William the Conqueror, conquered England. As a direct result, French was spoken by the elite class, and subsequently evolved to the point where it was spoken in mainland France as well.

In addition, France had a significant influence on all of Europe from the Renaissance to the end of the 19th Century. This, combined with the proximity of France to England, contributed to the large percentage of English words that have distinctly French origins.

What follows is a list (by no means comprehensive) of some common English words that have French origins. While these are not listed in terms of roots and affixes, just knowing where these words originated may come in handy on the GRE.

List of Common English Words with French Origin

Government, Law, and Warfare	
Word	**Meaning/Origin**
attorney	from the Old French *atourné*
fee	from the original French word *fie*, 14th Century
finance	from the finer to end or settle by payment
guard	from *garde*, 15th Century
inherit	from Old French *enheriter*, 14th Century
jail	from Old French *jaiole* (meaning cage), 13th Century
jury	from Old French *juree*, originally from *jurer* (meaning to swear) 13th Century
lieutenant	from Old French *literally* (meaning place-holding), 14th Century
march	from Old French, from *Latin Martius* (month) of Mars
medal	from French *médaille*, probably from Italian *medaglia*, ultimately from Latin *metallum* (meaning metal), 16th Century
mutiny	from Old French *mutin* (meaning rebellious), ultimately from Latin *movēre* (meaning to move), 16th Century
parliament	from Old French *parlement, from parler* to speak, 13th Century
soldier	from Old French *soudier*, from *soude* (army) pay, from Late Latin *solidus* (a gold coin), 13th Century
treaty	from Old French *traité*, from Medieval Latin *tractātus* (meaning treaty), 14th Century

Cooking and Cuisine

Word	Meaning/Origin
apertif	from French, from Medieval Latin *aperitīvus*, from Latin *aperīre* (meaning to open), 19th Century
bacon	from Old French *bacon*, from Old High German *bahho*, 12th Century
beef	from Old French *boef*, 13th Century
café	from French: *coffee*, 19th Century
courgette	from French, diminutive of *courge*
grape	from Old French *grape*, 13th Century
juice	from Old French *jus*, 13th Century
larder	from Old French *lardier*, 14th Century
mackerel	from Anglo-French, from Old French *maquerel*, 13th Century
menu	from French *menu*, meaning small, 19th Century
nutmeg	from Old French *nois muguede*, 13th Century
omelette	from French *omelette*, changed from *alumette*, from *alumelle* (meaning sword blade), changed by mistaken division from *la lemelle*, from Latin; apparently from the flat shape of the omelette
picnic	from French *piquenique*, 18th Century
poultry	from Old French *pouletrie*, from *pouletier* (meaning poultry-dealer), 14th Century
quiche	from French, from German K*uchen* (meaning cake)
restaurant	from French, from *restaurer* (meaning to restore), 19th Century
salad	from Old French *salade*, from Latin *sal* (meaning salt), 15th Century
sausage	from Old Norman French *saussiche*, from Late Latin *salsīcia*, from Latin *salsus* (meaning salted), 15th Century
soup	from Old French *soupe*, from Late Latin *suppa*, 17th Century
spice	from Old French *espice*, from Late Latin *speciēs* (plural) (meaning spices, 13th Century

GERMANIC

The Germanic languages can be divided into three groups—West Germanic, which includes English, German, and Dutch; North Germanic, which includes Danish, Swedish, Icelandic, and Norwegian; and East Germanic, which is now extinct.

The English spoken in early medieval England is a Germanic language. English itself is named after the Anglos, one of three Germanic tribes that invaded England during the 5th Century. At that time, the people of Britain spoke a Celtic language. Most of those were pushed west and north by the invaders—into what is now Wales, Scotland, and Ireland. The Angles spoke "Englisc," from which both England and English were derived.

What follows is a list of common English words of Germanic origin.

List of Common English Words with Germanic Origins

Word	Meaning
abseil	descend by rope
angst	fear, depression, anger
ansatz	mathematical approach
anschlsuss	connection, union
autobahn	an expressway
automat	machine
bagel	a type of food
bratwurst	a type of food
pretzel	a crisp biscuit baked in the form of a knot or stick and flavored with salt (soft or hard)
cobalt	a color
cringle	a part of a sail on a boat
dachshund	breed of dog
delicatessen	proper name for a deli
doppelgänger	someone's double, often used in literature
echt	true, genuine
edelweiss	type of flower
eiderdown	a type of down
einkorn	an ancient type of wheat
feldspar	specific types of minerals
fest	feast, celebration, party
fife	a small type of flute

Word	Meaning
gestalt	a psychological term
gestapo	police force
gesundheit	bless you
graupel	snowflakes coated with ice
hamster	a small animal
haversack	a bag worn over the shoulder
hinterland	backwoods
homburg	a felt hat, generally for a man
kaput	not working, broken
kindergarden	grade before first grade
kitsch	fake art, art mocking something else
knapsack	a backpack or book pack
kohlrabi	a type of cabbage
kraut	herb, cabbage
kuchen	coffee cakes
langlauf	cross country running or skiing
lederhosen	leather shorts
leitmotif	theme, often used in literature
liverwurst	type of food
noodle	a type of pasta, a pool tool
nosh	a small amount of food, or to eat a small amount of food
panzer	a type of German tank
pitchblende	a mineral
poltergeist	ghost
prattle	utter sounds
pumpernickel	a type of bread
realpolitik	political practice
rucksack	backpack
sauerbraten	a type of food
schnauzer	a breed of dog
seltzer	a type of soda
spare rib	a type of meat cut from the ribs of a pig
spritz	a small amount of something, usually a liquid
stollen	sweet yeast bread

Word	Meaning
streusel	a dessert type of food
plunder	taking goods by force
ubermensch	superhuman
umlaut	two dots placed over a vowel that change its pronunciation
verboten	forbidden
vorlage	a skiing position
Wagnerian	suggestive of the music of composer Richard Wagner
waltz	a formal dance
wanderlust	pleasure, desire, wanting
wunderkind	child prodigy

Chapter 9
Vocabulary
for the GRE

Words, words, words. That's what you'll find in this chapter. The following pages contain the Key Terms List, a list of some of the most common words that appear on the GRE. There are also some handy tips on studying and learning new vocabulary words and exercises to test your progress. Be advised, though, that the words in the chapter ahead are just a starting point. As you prepare for your GRE, keep your eyes open for words you don't know and look them up!

VOCAB, VOCAB, VOCAB

As much as ETS would like to claim that the GRE doesn't rely much on vocabulary, the simple fact remains that many of the questions, answer choices, and reading passages contain some difficult vocabulary. You can't improve your score substantially without increasing your vocabulary. You might think that studying vocabulary is the most boring part of preparing for the GRE, but it's one of the most important, and it's also the one part of GRE preparation that's actually useful to you beyond the confines of the test itself. And the more words that you recognize (and know the meaning of) on the test, the easier it will be. So there's no avoiding the importance of vocabulary to your success on the GRE. Unfortunately, it is virtually impossible to fairly test someone's vocabulary on a standardized test. If you memorize 1,000 words and on test day none of those words appear, does that mean you have a bad vocabulary? Of course not—it just means that you've been victimized by the limitations of standardized testing.

> Improving your vocabulary is one of the most important things you can do to improve your Verbal score.

This doesn't mean that you should take a defeatist attitude toward learning vocabulary! Even if you have only a few weeks before your test, you can still expand your vocabulary and increase your prospects of doing better on the GRE. One thing you have working in your favor is the fact that ETS loves to do the same things over and over. The words we've collected for you in this chapter are the words that appear most frequently on the GRE. So let's get started learning some new words!

LEARN TO LOVE THE DICTIONARY

Get used to looking up words. ETS uses words that it believes the average college-educated adult should know. These words show up in newspaper and magazine articles, in books, and in textbooks. If you see a word you don't know while studying for the GRE or elsewhere, it's probably a good GRE word. Look it up and make a flash card. Dictionaries will give you the pronunciation, while digital apps can provide quick, handy look-ups for new words. Looking up words is a habit. You may have to force yourself to do it in the beginning, but it becomes more natural over time. Many of the techniques in this book will help you on the GRE but don't have much relevance in day-to-day life, but a great vocabulary and good vocabulary habits will add a tremendous amount of value to your graduate school career and beyond.

> **Flashcards from Us**
> You can make your own flashcards or you can buy Essential GRE Vocabulary flashcards from us!

Learning New Words

How will you remember all the new words you should learn for the test? By developing a routine for learning new words. Here are some tips.

- To learn words that you find on your own, get into the habit of reading good books, magazines, and newspapers. Start paying attention to words you come across for which you don't know the definition. You might be tempted to just skip these, as usual, but train yourself to write them down and look them up.
- When you look up the word, say it out loud, being careful to pronounce it correctly. This will help you remember it.

- When you look up a word in the dictionary or, let's be real, type it into Google or Dictionary.com, don't assume that the first definition is the only one you need to know. The first definition may be an archaic one, or one that applies only in a particular context, so scan through all the definitions.

- Now that you've learned the dictionary's definition of a new word, restate it in your own words. You'll find it much easier to remember a word's meaning if you make it your own.

- Mnemonics—Use your imagination to create a mental image to fix the new word in your mind. For example, if you're trying to remember the word *voracious*, which means having an insatiable appetite for an activity or pursuit, picture an incredibly hungry boar, eating huge piles of food. The voracious boar will help you to recall the meaning of the word. The crazier the image, the better.

- Keep a vocabulary notebook, or make a file with a list of new vocabulary words and put it on your desktop. Simply having a notebook with you will remind you to be on the lookout for new words, and using it will help you to remember the ones you encounter. Writing something down also makes it easier to memorize. Jot down the word when you find it, note its pronunciation and definition (in your own words) when you look it up, and jot down your mnemonic or mental image. You might also copy the sentence in which you originally found the word, to remind yourself of how the word looks in context.

- Do the same thing with flash cards. Write the word on one side and the pronunciation, the meaning, and perhaps a mental image on the other. Stick five or six of your flash cards in your pocket every morning and use them whenever you can. Stuck on a delayed subway train? Look at your flashcards. Standing in a long line at the bank? Look at your flashcards. Sick of engaging in small talk with boring acquaintances? Look at your flashcards. (Only kidding about that last one.)

- Use your new word every chance you get. Make it part of your life. Insert it into your speech at every opportunity. Developing a powerful vocabulary requires lots of exercise.

- Learn word roots. Many words share similar origins. By learning these common roots, you'll be better able to work with words you've never seen before. A good dictionary should list the origin and roots of the words in it.

> Learn new words little by little; don't try to learn a ton at once!

THE KEY TERMS LIST

You should start your vocabulary work by studying the Key Terms List, a list we've compiled of some of the most frequently tested words on the GRE. We put together this list by analyzing released GREs and keeping tabs on the test to make sure that these words are still popular with ETS. At the very least, answer choices that contain Key Terms make very good guesses on questions for which you don't know the answer. Each word on the Key Terms List is followed by the part of speech and a brief definition for the word. Some of the words on this list may have other definitions as well, but the definitions we have given are the ones most likely to appear on the GRE.

We've broken the Key Terms List down into four groups of about 75 words each. Don't try to learn all four groups of words at once—work with one list at a time. Write the words and their definitions down in a notebook or on flash cards. It is very important to write them down yourself, because this will help you remember them. Just glancing through the lists printed in this book won't be nearly as effective. Before doing the exercises for each group, spend some time studying and learning the words first. Then use the exercises as a way to test yourself. Answers for the matching exercises appear in Part V of this book.

Key Terms Group 1

aberrant (adj.)	deviating from the norm (noun form: *aberration*)
abscond (verb)	to depart clandestinely; to steal off and hide
alacrity (noun)	eager and enthusiastic willingness
anomaly (noun)	deviation from the normal order, form, or rule; abnormality (adj. form: *anomalous*)
approbation (noun)	an expression of approval or praise
arduous (adj.)	strenuous, taxing; requiring significant effort
assuage (verb)	to ease or lessen; to appease or pacify
audacious (adj.)	daring and fearless; recklessly bold (noun form: *audacity*)
austere (adj.)	without adornment; bare; severely simple; ascetic (noun form: *austerity*)
axiomatic (adj.)	taken as a given; possessing self-evident truth (noun form: *axiom*)
canonical (adj.)	following or in agreement with accepted, traditional standards (noun form: *canon*)
capricious (adj.)	inclined to change one's mind impulsively; erratic, unpredictable
censure (verb)	to criticize severely; to officially rebuke
chicanery (noun)	trickery or subterfuge
connoisseur (noun)	an informed and astute judge in matters of taste; expert
convoluted (adj.)	complex or complicated
disabuse (verb)	to undeceive; to set right
discordant (adj.)	conflicting; dissonant or harsh in sound
disparate (adj.)	fundamentally distinct or dissimilar
effrontery (noun)	extreme boldness; presumptuousness
eloquent (adj.)	well-spoken, expressive, articulate (noun form: *eloquence*)
enervate (verb)	to weaken; to reduce in vitality
ennui (noun)	dissatisfaction and restlessness resulting from boredom or apathy
equivocate (verb)	to use ambiguous language with a deceptive intent (adj. form: *equivocal*)
erudite (adj.)	very learned; scholarly (noun form: *erudition*)

exculpate (verb)   to exonerate; to clear of blame

exigent (adj.)   urgent, pressing; requiring immediate action or attention

extemporaneous (adj.)   improvised; done without preparation

filibuster (noun)   intentional obstruction, especially using prolonged speechmaking to delay legislative action

fulminate (verb)   to loudly attack or denounce

ingenuous (adj.)   artless; frank and candid; lacking in sophistication

inured (adj.)   accustomed to accepting something undesirable

irascible (adj.)   easily angered; prone to temperamental outbursts

laud (verb)   to praise highly (adj. form: *laudatory*)

lucid (adj.)   clear; easily understood

magnanimity (noun)   the quality of being generously noble in mind and heart, especially in forgiving (adj. form: *magnanimous*)

martial (adj.)   associated with war and the armed forces

mundane (adj.)   of the world; typical of or concerned with the ordinary

nascent (adj.)   coming into being; in early developmental stages

nebulous (adj.)   vague; cloudy; lacking clearly defined form

neologism (noun)   a new word, expression, or usage; the creation or use of new words or senses

noxious (adj.)   harmful, injurious

obtuse (adj.)   lacking sharpness of intellect; not clear or precise in thought or expression

obviate (verb)   to anticipate and make unnecessary

onerous (adj.)   troubling; burdensome

paean (noun)   a song or hymn of praise and thanksgiving

parody (noun)   a humorous imitation intended for ridicule or comic effect, especially in literature and art

perennial (adj.)   recurrent through the year or many years; happening repeatedly

perfidy (noun)   intentional breach of faith; treachery (adj. form: *perfidious*)

perfunctory (adj.)   cursory; done without care or interest

perspicacious (adj.)   acutely perceptive; having keen discernment (noun form: *perspicacity*)

prattle (verb)   to babble meaninglessly; to talk in an empty and idle manner

precipitate (adj.)   acting with excessive haste or impulse

precipitate (verb)   to cause or happen before anticipated or required

predilection (noun)   a disposition in favor of something; preference

prescience (noun)   foreknowledge of events; knowing of events prior to their occurring (adj. form: *prescient*)

prevaricate (verb)   to deliberately avoid the truth; to mislead

qualms (noun)		misgivings; reservations; causes for hesitancy
recant (verb)		to retract, especially a previously held belief
refute (verb)		to disprove; to successfully argue against
relegate (verb)		to forcibly assign, especially to a lower place or position
reticent (adj.)		quiet; reserved; reluctant to express thoughts and feelings
solicitous (adj.)		concerned and attentive; eager
sordid (adj.)		characterized by filth, grime, or squalor; foul
sporadic (adj.)		occurring only occasionally, or in scattered instances
squander (verb)		to waste by spending or using irresponsibly
static (adj.)		not moving, active, or in motion; at rest
stupefy (verb)		to stun, baffle, or amaze
stymie (verb)		to block; to thwart
synthesis (noun)		the combination of parts to make a whole (verb form: *synthesize*)
torque (noun)		a force that causes rotation
tortuous (adj.)		winding, twisting; excessively complicated
truculent (adj.)		fierce and cruel; eager to fight
veracity (noun)		truthfulness, honesty
virulent (adj.)		extremely harmful or poisonous; bitterly hostile or antagonistic
voracious (adj.)		having an insatiable appetite for an activity or pursuit; ravenous
waver (verb)		to move to and fro; to sway; to be unsettled in opinion

Group 1 Exercises

Match the following words to their definitions. Answers can be found in Part V.

1.	improvised; without preparation	A.	veracity
2.	a newly coined word or expression	B.	recant
3.	a song of joy and praise	C.	extemporaneous
4.	to praise highly	D.	stymie
5.	truthfulness; honesty	E.	paean
6.	artless; frank and candid	F.	lucid
7.	associated with war and the military	G.	laud
8.	to retract a belief or statement	H.	onerous
9.	cursory; done without care or interest	I.	tortuous
10.	troubling; burdensome	J.	neologism
11.	to criticize; to officially rebuke	K.	martial
12.	winding; twisting; complicated	L.	ingenuous
13.	to block; to thwart	M.	censure
14.	clear; easily understood	N.	perfunctory

Key Terms Group 2

abate (verb)	to lessen in intensity or degree
accolade (noun)	an expression of praise
adulation (noun)	excessive praise; intense adoration
aesthetic (adj.)	dealing with, appreciative of, or responsive to art or the beautiful
ameliorate (verb)	to make better or more tolerable
ascetic (noun)	one who practices rigid self-denial, especially as an act of religious devotion
avarice (noun)	greed, especially for wealth (adj. form: *avaricious*)
burgeon (verb)	to grow rapidly or flourish
bucolic (adj.)	rustic and pastoral; characteristic of rural areas and their inhabitants
cacophony (noun)	harsh, jarring, discordant sound; dissonance (adj. form: *cacophonous*)
canon (noun)	an established set of principles or code of laws, often religious in nature (adj. form: *canonical*)
castigation (noun)	severe criticism or punishment (verb form: *castigate*)
catalyst (noun)	a substance that accelerates the rate of a chemical reaction without itself changing; a person or thing that causes change
caustic (adj.)	burning or stinging; causing corrosion
chary (adj.)	wary; cautious; sparing
cogent (adj.)	appealing forcibly to the mind or reason; convincing
complaisance (noun)	the willingness to comply with the wishes of others (adj. form: *complaisant*)
contentious (adj.)	argumentative; quarrelsome; causing controversy or disagreement
contrite (adj.)	regretful; penitent; seeking forgiveness (noun form: *contrition*)
culpable (adj.)	deserving blame (noun form: *culpability*)
dearth (noun)	smallness of quantity or number; scarcity; a lack
demur (verb)	to question or oppose
didactic (adj.)	intended to teach or instruct
discretion (noun)	cautious reserve in speech; ability to make responsible decisions (adj. form: *discreet*)
disinterested (adj.)	free of bias or self-interest; impartial
dogmatic (adj.)	expressing a rigid opinion based on unproved or improvable principles (noun form: *dogma*)

Hold Up and Break
Did you just tackle Key Terms Group 1? Before you jump into Group 2, give yourself a break. Take a walk, get some air, eat a snack. Let the Group 1 words sink in before you dive into Group 2.

ebullience (noun)	the quality of lively or enthusiastic expression of thoughts and feelings (adj. form: *ebullient*)
eclectic (adj.)	composed of elements drawn from various sources
elegy (noun)	a mournful poem, especially one lamenting the dead (adj. form: *elegiac*)
emollient (adj.)/ (noun)	soothing, especially to the skin; making less harsh; mollifying; an agent that softens or smoothes the skin
empirical (adj.)	based on observation or experiment
enigmatic (adj.)	mysterious; obscure; difficult to understand (noun form: *enigma*)
ephemeral (adj.)	brief; fleeting
esoteric (adj.)	intended for or understood by a small, specific group
eulogy (noun)	a speech honoring the dead (verb form: *eulogize*)
exonerate (verb)	to remove blame
facetious (adj.)	playful; humorous
fallacy (noun)	an invalid or incorrect notion; a mistaken belief (adj. form: *fallacious*)
furtive (adj.)	marked by stealth; covert; surreptitious
gregarious (adj.)	sociable; outgoing; enjoying the company of other people
harangue (verb)/ (noun)	to deliver a forceful or angry speech; ranting speech or writing.
heretical (adj.)	violating accepted dogma or convention (noun form: *heresy*)
hyperbole (noun)	an exaggerated statement, often used as a figure of speech (adj. form: *hyperbolic*)
impecunious (adj.)	lacking funds; without money
incipient (adj.)	beginning to come into being or to become apparent
inert (adj.)	unmoving; lethargic; sluggish
innocuous (adj.)	harmless; causing no damage
intransigent (adj.)	refusing to compromise (noun form: *intransigence*)
inveigle (verb)	to obtain by deception or flattery
morose (adj.)	sad; sullen; melancholy
odious (adj.)	evoking intense aversion or dislike
opaque (adj.)	impenetrable by light; not reflecting light
oscillation (noun)	the act or state of swinging back and forth with a steady, uninterrupted rhythm (verb form: *oscillate*)
penurious (adj.)	penny-pinching; excessively thrifty; ungenerous
pernicious (adj.)	extremely harmful in a way that is not easily seen or noticed
peruse (verb)	to examine with great care (noun form: *perusal*)
pious (adj.)	extremely reverent or devout; showing strong religious devotion (noun form: *piety*)
precursor (noun)	one that precedes and indicates or announces another

preen (verb)	to dress up; to primp; to groom oneself with elaborate care
prodigious (adj.)	abundant in size, force, or extent; extraordinary
prolific (adj.)	producing large volumes or amounts; productive
putrefy (verb)	to rot; to decay and give off a foul odor (adj. form: *putrid*)
quaff (verb)	to drink deeply
quiescence (noun)	stillness; motionlessness; quality of being at rest (adj. form: *quiescent*)
redoubtable (adj.)	awe-inspiring; worthy of honor
sanction (noun)/ (verb)	authoritative permission or approval; a penalty intended to enforce compliance; to give permission or authority
satire (noun)	a literary work that ridicules or criticizes a human vice through humor or derision (adj. form: *satirical*)
squalid (adj.)	sordid; wretched and dirty as from neglect (noun form: *squalor*)
stoic (adj.)	indifferent to or unaffected by pleasure or pain; steadfast (noun form: *stoicism*)
supplant (verb)	to take the place of; to supersede
torpid (adj.)	lethargic; sluggish; dormant (noun form: *torpor*)
ubiquitous (adj.)	existing everywhere at the same time; constantly encountered; widespread
urbane (adj.)	sophisticated; refined; elegant (noun form: *urbanity*)
vilify (verb)	to defame; to characterize harshly
viscous (adj.)	thick; sticky (noun form: *viscosity*)

Group 2 Exercises

Match the following words to their definitions. Answers can be found in Part V.

1. brief; fleeting
2. a forceful or angry speech
3. arousing strong dislike or aversion
4. to free from blame or responsibility
5. arousing fear or awe; worthy of honor; formidable
6. unexpectedly harmful
7. to drink deeply
8. stinging; corrosive; sarcastic; biting
9. impressively great in size, force, or extent; enormous
10. greed; hunger for money
11. unmoving; lethargic
12. impartial; unbiased
13. lack; scarcity
14. to win over by deception, coaxing or flattery

A. pernicious
B. ephemeral
C. avarice
D. quaff
E. caustic
F. odious
G. dearth
H. inert
I. disinterested
J. exonerate
K. inveigle
L. prodigious
M. harangue
N. redoubtable

Break Time!
How did you do in Group 2? Take a moment to relax and let your mind rest before diving into Group 3. Remember to do this between each group of words so you don't overload your brain!

Key Terms Group 3

acumen (noun)	keen, accurate judgment or insight
adulterate (verb)	to reduce purity by combining with inferior ingredients
amalgamate (verb)	to combine several elements into a whole (noun form: *amalgamation*)
archaic (adj.)	outdated; associated with an earlier, perhaps more primitive, time
aver (verb)	to state as a fact; to declare or assert
bolster (verb)	to provide support or reinforcement
bombastic (adj.)	pompous; grandiloquent (noun form: *bombast*)
diatribe (noun)	a harsh denunciation
dissemble (verb)	to disguise or conceal; to mislead
eccentric (adj.)	departing from norms or conventions
endemic (adj.)	characteristic of or often found in a particular locality, region, or people
evanescent (adj.)	tending to disappear like vapor; vanishing
exacerbate (verb)	to make worse or more severe
fervent (adj.)	greatly emotional or zealous (noun form: *fervor*)
fortuitous (adj.)	happening by accident or chance
germane (adj.)	relevant to the subject at hand; appropriate in subject matter
grandiloquence (noun)	pompous speech or expression (adj. form: *grandiloquent*)
hackneyed (adj.)	rendered trite or commonplace by frequent usage
halcyon (adj.)	calm and peaceful
hedonism (noun)	devotion to pleasurable pursuits, especially to the pleasures of the senses (a *hedonist* is someone who pursues pleasure)
hegemony (noun)	the consistent dominance of one state or group over others
iconoclast (noun)	one who attacks or undermines traditional conventions or institutions
idolatrous (adj.)	given to intense or excessive devotion to something (noun form: *idolatry*)
impassive (adj.)	revealing no emotion
imperturbable (adj.)	marked by extreme calm, impassivity, and steadiness
implacable (adj.)	not capable of being appeased or significantly changed
impunity (noun)	immunity from punishment or penalty
inchoate (adj.)	in an initial stage; not fully formed
infelicitous (adj.)	unfortunate; inappropriate
insipid (adj.)	lacking in qualities that interest, stimulate, or challenge
loquacious (adj.)	extremely talkative (noun form: *loquacity*)
luminous (adj.)	characterized by brightness and the emission of light
malevolent (adj.)	having or showing often vicious ill will, spite, or hatred (noun form: *malevolence*)

malleable (adj.)	capable of being shaped or formed; tractable; pliable
mendacity (noun)	the condition of being untruthful; dishonesty (adj. form: *mendacious*)
meticulous (adj.)	characterized by extreme care and precision; attentive to detail
misanthrope (noun)	one who hates all other humans (adj. form: *misanthropic*)
mitigate (verb)	to make or become less severe or intense; to moderate
obdurate (adj.)	unyielding; hardhearted; intractable
obsequious (adj.)	exhibiting a fawning attentiveness
occlude (verb)	to obstruct or block
opprobrium (noun)	disgrace; contempt; scorn
pedagogy (noun)	the profession or principles of teaching or instructing
pedantic (adj.)	overly concerned with the trivial details of learning or education; show-offish about one's knowledge
penury (noun)	poverty; destitution
pervasive (adj.)	having the tendency to permeate or spread throughout
pine (verb)	to yearn intensely; to languish; to lose vigor
pirate (verb)	to illegally use or reproduce
pith (noun)	the essential or central part
pithy (adj.)	precise and brief
placate (verb)	to appease; to calm by making concessions
platitude (noun)	a superficial remark, especially one offered as meaningful
plummet (verb)	to plunge or drop straight down
polemical (adj.)	controversial; argumentative
prodigal (adj.)	recklessly wasteful; extravagant; profuse; lavish
profuse (adj.)	given or coming forth abundantly; extravagant
proliferate (verb)	to grow or increase swiftly and abundantly
queries (noun)	questions; inquiries; doubts in the mind; reservations
querulous (adj.)	prone to complaining or grumbling; peevish
rancorous (adj.)	characterized by bitter, long-lasting resentment (noun form: *rancor*)
recalcitrant (adj.)	obstinately defiant of authority; difficult to manage
repudiate (verb)	to refuse to have anything to do with; to disown
rescind (verb)	to invalidate; to repeal; to retract
reverent (adj.)	marked by, feeling, or expressing a feeling of profound awe and respect (noun form: *reverence*)
rhetoric (noun)	the art or study of effective use of language for communication and persuasion
salubrious (adj.)	promoting health or well-being
solvent (adj.)	able to meet financial obligations; able to dissolve another substance
specious (adj.)	seeming true, but actually being fallacious; misleadingly attractive; plausible but false

spurious (adj.)	lacking authenticity or validity; false; counterfeit
subpoena (noun)	a court order requiring appearance and/or testimony
succinct (adj.)	brief; concise
superfluous (adj.)	exceeding what is sufficient or necessary
surfeit (verb)/(noun)	an overabundant supply; excess; to feed or supply to excess
tenacity (noun)	the quality of adherence or persistence to something valued; persistent determination (adj. form: *tenacious*)
tenuous (adj.)	having little substance or strength; flimsy; weak
tirade (noun)	a long and extremely critical speech; a harsh denunciation
transient (adj.)	fleeting; passing quickly; brief
zealous (adj.)	fervent; ardent; impassioned, devoted to a cause (a *zealot* is a zealous person)

Group 3 Exercises

Match the following words to their definitions. Answers can be found in Part V.

1. brief; concise; tersely cogent
2. prone to complaining; whining
3. fawning; ingratiating
4. marked by bitter, deep-seated resentment
5. controversial; argumentative
6. dominance of one state or group over others
7. uninteresting; tasteless; flat; dull
8. thin; flimsy; of little substance
9. excess; overindulgence
10. wasteful; recklessly extravagant
11. to appease; to pacify with concessions
12. to assert; to declare; to allege; to state as fact
13. pompous; grandiloquent
14. tending to vanish like vapor

A. hegemony
B. aver
C. insipid
D. pithy
E. placate
F. prodigal
G. querulous
H. surfeit
I. rancorous
J. bombastic
K. obsequious
L. evanescent
M. polemical
N. tenuous

Key Terms Group 4

acerbic (adj.)	having a sour or bitter taste or character; sharp; biting
aggrandize (verb)	to increase in intensity, power, influence, or prestige
alchemy (noun)	a medieval science aimed at the transmutation of metals, especially base metals into gold (an *alchemist* is one who practices alchemy)
amenable (adj.)	agreeable; responsive to suggestion
anachronism (noun)	something or someone out of place in terms of historical or chronological context
astringent (noun)/ (adj.)	having a tightening effect on living tissue; harsh; severe; something with a tightening effect on tissue
contiguous (adj.)	sharing a border; touching; adjacent
convention (noun)	a generally agreed-upon practice or attitude
credulous (adj.)	tending to believe too readily; gullible (noun form: *credulity*)
cynicism (noun)	an attitude or quality of belief that all people are motivated by selfishness (adj. form: *cynical*)
decorum (noun)	polite or appropriate conduct or behavior (adj. form: *decorous*)
derision (noun)	scorn, ridicule, contemptuous treatment (adj. form: *derisive*; verb form: *deride*)
desiccate (verb)	to dry out or dehydrate; to make dry or dull
dilettante (noun)	one with an amateurish or superficial interest in the arts or a branch of knowledge
disparage (verb)	to slight or belittle
divulge (verb)	to disclose something secret
fawn (verb)	to flatter or praise excessively
flout (verb)	to show contempt for, as in a rule or convention
garrulous (adj.)	pointlessly talkative; talking too much
glib (adj.)	marked by ease or informality; nonchalant; lacking in depth; superficial
hubris (noun)	overbearing presumption or pride; arrogance
imminent (adj.)	about to happen; impending
immutable (adj.)	not capable of change
impetuous (adj.)	hastily or rashly energetic; impulsive and vehement
indifferent (adj.)	having no interest or concern; showing no bias or prejudice
inimical (adj.)	damaging; harmful; injurious
intractable (adj.)	not easily managed or directed; stubborn; obstinate
intrepid (adj.)	steadfast and courageous
laconic (adj.)	using few words; terse

What's Your Strategy?
Do you find flash cards helpful? Or do you prefer word lists? Or smartphone apps? Figure out the strategy that works best for you when it comes to learning vocabulary and stick to it!

maverick (noun)	an independent individual who does not go along with a group or party
mercurial (adj.)	characterized by rapid and unpredictable change in mood
mollify (verb)	to calm or soothe; to reduce in emotional intensity
neophyte (noun)	a recent convert; a beginner; a novice
obfuscate (verb)	to deliberately obscure; to make confusing
obstinate (adj.)	stubborn; hard-headed; uncompromising
ostentatious (adj.)	characterized by or given to pretentious display; showy
pervade (verb)	to permeate throughout (adj. form: *pervasive*)
phlegmatic (adj.)	calm; sluggish; unemotional
plethora (noun)	an overabundance; a surplus
pragmatic (adj.)	practical rather than idealistic
presumptuous (adj.)	overstepping due bounds (as of propriety or courtesy); taking liberties
pristine (adj.)	pure; uncorrupted; clean
probity (noun)	adherence to highest principles; complete and confirmed integrity; uprightness
proclivity (noun)	a natural predisposition or inclination
profligate (adj.)	excessively wasteful; recklessly extravagant (noun form: *profligacy*)
propensity (noun)	a natural inclination or tendency; penchant
prosaic (adj.)	dull; lacking in spirit or imagination
pungent (adj.)	characterized by a strong, sharp smell or taste
quixotic (adj.)	foolishly impractical; marked by lofty romantic ideals
quotidian (adj.)	occurring or recurring daily; commonplace
rarefy (verb)	to make or become thin, less dense; to refine
recondite (adj.)	hidden; concealed; difficult to understand; obscure
refulgent (adj.)	radiant; shiny; brilliant
renege (verb)	to fail to honor a commitment; to go back on a promise
sedulous (adj.)	diligent; persistent; hard-working
shard (noun)	a piece of broken pottery or glass
soporific (adj.)	causing drowsiness; tending to induce sleep
sparse (adj.)	thin; not dense; arranged at widely spaced intervals
spendthrift (noun)	one who spends money wastefully
subtle (adj.)	not obvious; elusive; difficult to discern
tacit (adj.)	implied; not explicitly stated
terse (adj.)	brief and concise in wording
tout (verb)	to publicly praise or promote
trenchant (adj.)	sharply perceptive; keen; penetrating
unfeigned (adj.)	genuine; not false or hypocritical

untenable (adj.)	indefensible; not viable; uninhabitable
vacillate (verb)	to waver indecisively between one course of action or opinion and another
variegated (adj.)	multicolored; characterized by a variety of patches of different color
vexation (noun)	annoyance; irritation (verb form: *vex*)
vigilant (adj.)	alertly watchful (noun form: *vigilance*)
vituperate (verb)	to use harsh condemnatory language; to abuse or censure severely or abusively; to berate
volatile (adj.)	readily changing to a vapor; changeable; fickle; explosive (noun form: *volatility*)

Group 4 Exercises

Match the following words to their definitions. Answers can be found in Part V.

1. acidic or biting; bitter in taste or tone   A. anachronism
2. sleep-inducing; causing drowsiness   B. contiguous
3. a surplus; an overabundance   C. dilettante
4. one with superficial interest in a subject   D. intractable
5. arrogance; overbearing pride   E. prosaic
6. sharing a border; touching; adjacent   F. quixotic
7. talking too much; rambling   G. recondite
8. something out of place in history   H. vituperate
   or chronology
9. difficult to understand; obscure; hidden   I. acerbic
10. dull; unimaginative; ordinary   J. garrulous
11. unemotional; calm   K. hubris
12. stubborn; obstinate; difficult to manage   L. soporific
    or govern
13. condemn with harsh, abusive words;   M. phlegmatic
    berate
14. foolishly impractical; marked by lofty   N. plethora
    ideals

BEYOND THE KEY TERMS LIST

So you've finished the Key Terms List and you're now the master of many more words than you were before. What to do next? Why, go *beyond the Key Terms List* of course! The Key Terms List was just the beginning. To maximize your score on the GRE you must be relentless in increasing your vocabulary. Don't let up. Keep learning words until the day you sit down for the exam. The following lists of extra words don't have exercises, so just keep working with your notebook or flash cards and get your friends to quiz you. You are a vocabulary machine!

Beyond the Key Terms Group 1

The following list contains some of those simple-sounding words with less common secondary meanings that ETS likes to test on the GRE.

alloy (verb)	to commingle; to debase by mixing with something inferior; *unalloyed* means pure
appropriate (verb)	to take for one's own use; to confiscate
arrest, arresting (verb)/(adj.)	to suspend; to engage; holding one's attention: as in an arresting portrait
august (adj.)	majestic, venerable
bent (noun)	leaning, inclination, proclivity, tendency
broach (verb)	to bring up; to announce; to begin to talk about
brook (verb)	to tolerate; to endure; to countenance
cardinal (adj.)	major, as in cardinal sin
chauvinist (noun)	a blindly devoted patriot
color (verb)	to change as if by dyeing, i.e., to distort, gloss, or affect (usually the first)
consequential (adj.)	pompous, self-important (primary definitions are logically following; important)
damp (verb)	to diminish the intensity or check the vibration of a sound
die (noun)	a tool used for shaping, as in a tool-and-die shop
essay (verb)	to test or try; to attempt; to experiment
exact (verb)	to demand; to call for; to require; to take
fell (verb)	to cause to fall by striking
fell (adj.)	inhumanly cruel
flag (verb)	to sag or droop; to become spiritless; to decline
flip (adj.)	sarcastic, impertinent, as in flippant: a flip remark
ford (verb)	to wade across the shallow part of a river or stream
grouse (verb)	to complain or grumble
guy (noun)/(verb)	a rope, cord, or cable attached to something as a brace or guide; to steady or reinforce using a guy: think *guide*. (verb form: *guyed, guying*)
intimate (verb)	to imply, suggest, or insinuate
list (verb)	to tilt or lean to one side
lumber (verb)	to move heavily and clumsily
meet (adj.)	fitting, proper
milk (verb)	to exploit; to squeeze every last ounce of
mince (verb)	to pronounce or speak affectedly; to euphemize, to speak too carefully. Also, to take tiny steps; to tiptoe
nice (adj.)	exacting, fastidious, extremely precise

occult (adj.)	hidden, concealed, beyond comprehension
pedestrian (adj.)	commonplace, trite, unremarkable, quotidian
pied (adj.)	multicolored, usually in blotches
pine (verb)	to lose vigor (as through grief); to yearn
plastic (adj.)	moldable, pliable, not rigid
pluck (noun)	courage, spunk, fortitude
prize (verb)	to pry, to press or force with a lever; something taken by force, spoils
rail (verb)	to complain about bitterly
rent (verb)/(noun)	torn (past tense of *rend*); an opening or tear caused by such
quail (verb)	to lose courage; to turn frightened
qualify (verb)	to limit
sap (verb)	to enervate or weaken the vitality of
sap (noun)	a fool or nitwit
scurvy (adj.)	contemptible, despicable
singular (adj.)	exceptional, unusual, odd
stand (noun)	a group of trees
steep (verb)	to saturate or completely soak, as in to let a tea bag steep
strut (noun)	the supporting structural cross-part of a wing
table (verb)	to remove (as a parliamentary motion) from consideration
tender (verb)	to proffer or offer
waffle (verb)	to equivocate; to change one's position
wag (noun)	wit, joker

Beyond the Key Terms Group 2

abjure (verb)	to renounce or reject solemnly; to recant; to avoid
adumbrate (verb)	to foreshadow vaguely or intimate; to suggest or outline sketchily; to obscure or overshadow
anathema (noun)	a solemn or ecclesiastical (religious) curse; accursed or thoroughly loathed person or thing
anodyne (adj.)/(noun)	soothing; something that assuages or allays pain or comforts
apogee (noun)	farthest or highest point; culmination; zenith
apostate (noun)	one who abandons long-held religious or political convictions
apotheosis (noun)	deification; glorification to godliness; an exalted example; a model of excellence or perfection
asperity (noun)	severity, rigor; roughness, harshness; acrimony, irritability
asseverate (verb)	to aver, allege, or assert

assiduous (adj.)	diligent, hard-working, sedulous
augury (noun)	omen, portent
bellicose (adj.)	belligerent, pugnacious, warlike
calumniate (verb)	to slander, to make a false accusation; *calumny* means slander, aspersion
captious (adj.)	disposed to point out trivial faults; calculated to confuse or entrap in argument
cavil (verb)	to find fault without good reason
celerity (noun)	speed, alacrity; think *accelerate*
chimera (noun)	an illusion; originally, an imaginary fire-breathing she-monster
contumacious (adj.)	insubordinate, rebellious; *contumely* means insult, scorn, aspersion
debacle (noun)	rout, fiasco, complete failure
denouement (noun)	an outcome or solution; the unraveling of a plot
descry (verb)	to catch sight of
desuetude (noun)	disuse
desultory (adj.)	random; aimless; marked by a lack of plan or purpose
diaphanous (adj.)	transparent, gauzy
diffident (adj.)	reserved, shy, unassuming; lacking in self-confidence
dirge (noun)	a song of grief or lamentation
encomium (noun)	glowing and enthusiastic praise; panegyric, tribute, eulogy
eschew (verb)	to shun or avoid
excoriate (verb)	to censure scathingly, to upbraid
execrate (verb)	to denounce, to feel loathing for, to curse, to declare to be evil
exegesis (noun)	critical examination, explication
expiate (verb)	to atone or make amends for
extirpate (verb)	to destroy, to exterminate, to cut out, to exscind
fatuous (adj.)	silly, inanely foolish
fractious (adj.)	quarrelsome, rebellious, unruly, refractory, irritable
gainsay (verb)	to deny, to dispute, to contradict, to oppose
heterodox (adj.)	unorthodox, heretical, iconoclastic
imbroglio (noun)	difficult or embarrassing situation
indefatigable (adj.)	not easily exhaustible; tireless, dogged
ineluctable (adj.)	certain, inevitable
inimitable (adj.)	one of a kind, peerless
insouciant (adj.)	unconcerned, carefree, heedless
inveterate (adj.)	deep rooted, ingrained, habitual
jejune (adj.)	vapid, uninteresting, nugatory; childish, immature, puerile
lubricious (adj.)	lewd, wanton, greasy, slippery

mendicant (noun)	a beggar, supplicant
meretricious (adj.)	cheap, gaudy, tawdry, flashy, showy; attracting by false show
minatory (adj.)	menacing, threatening (reminds you of the Minotaur, a threatening creature indeed)
nadir (noun)	low point, perigee
nonplussed (adj.)	baffled, bewildered, at a loss for what to do or think
obstreperous (adj.)	noisily and stubbornly defiant, aggressively boisterous
ossified (adj.)	tending to become more rigid, conventional, sterile, and reactionary with age; literally, turned into bone
palliate (verb)	to make something seem less serious, to gloss over, to make less severe or intense
panegyric (noun)	formal praise, eulogy, encomium; *panegyrical* means expressing elaborate praise
parsimonious (adj.)	cheap, miserly
pellucid (adj.)	transparent, easy to understand, limpid
peroration (noun)	the concluding part of a speech; flowery, rhetorical speech
plangent (adj.)	pounding, thundering, resounding
prolix (adj.)	long-winded, verbose; *prolixity* means verbosity
propitiate (verb)	to appease; to conciliate; *propitious* means auspicious, favorable
puerile (adj.)	childish, immature, jejune, nugatory
puissance (noun)	power, strength; *puissant* means powerful, strong
pusillanimous (adj.)	cowardly, craven
remonstrate (verb)	to protest, to object
sagacious (adj.)	having sound judgment; perceptive, wise; like a sage
salacious (adj.)	lustful, lascivious, bawdy
salutary (adj.)	remedial, wholesome, causing improvement
sanguine (adj.)	cheerful, confident, optimistic
saturnine (adj.)	gloomy, dark, sullen, morose
sententious (adj.)	aphoristic or moralistic; epigrammatic; tending to moralize excessively
stentorian (adj.)	extremely loud and powerful
stygian (adj.)	gloomy, dark
sycophant (noun)	toady; servile, self-seeking flatterer; parasite
tendentious (adj.)	biased; showing marked tendencies
timorous (adj.)	timid, fearful, diffident
tyro (noun)	novice, greenhorn, rank amateur
vitiate (verb)	to corrupt, to debase, to spoil, to make ineffective
voluble (adj.)	fluent, verbal, having easy use of spoken language

Watch Out For Burnout
Now that you've slogged through so much Verbal review, take a moment and give yourself a break before you dive into the Math section. Slow and steady wins the race!

Part III
How to Crack the Math Section

Chapter 10
The Geography of the Math Section

This chapter contains an overview of the content and structure you'll see on the Math section of the GRE. It provides valuable information on pacing strategies and the various question formats you'll encounter on the GRE. It also goes over how to use basic test-taking techniques such as Process of Elimination and Ballparking as they relate to math questions. After finishing this chapter, you'll have a good idea of what the Math section of the GRE looks like and some basic approaches to help you navigate it.

WHAT'S IN THE MATH SECTION

The GRE Math section primarily tests math concepts you learned in seventh through tenth grades, including arithmetic, algebra, and geometry. ETS alleges that the Math section tests the reasoning skills that you'll use in graduate school, but what the Math section primarily tests is your comfort level with some basic math topics and your ability to take a test with strange-looking questions under timed conditions.

The Math section of the exam consists of two 35-minute sections, each of which will consist of 20 questions. The first 7 or 8 questions of each section will be *quantitative comparisons* (quant comp, for short). The remainder will consist of multiple-choice or numeric-entry questions.

Junior High School?

The Math section of the GRE mostly tests how much you remember from the math courses you took in seventh, eighth, ninth, and tenth grades. But here's some good news: GRE math is easier than SAT math. Why? Because many people study little or no math in college. If the GRE tested college-level math, everyone but math majors would bomb the test.

If you're willing to do a little work, this is good news for you. By brushing up on the modest amount of math you need to know for the test, you can significantly increase your GRE Math score. All you have to do is shake off the dust.

Predictable Questions

The beauty of a standardized test is that it is, well, standardized. Standardized means predictable. We know exactly what ETS is going to test and how they're going to test it. The math side of the test consists of a series of utterly predictable questions, to which we have designed a series of highly scripted responses. ETS wants you to see each problem as a new challenge to solve. What you will find, however, is that there are only about 20 math concepts that are being tested. All of the questions you will see are just different ways of asking about these different concepts. Most of these concepts you already know. Once you recognize what's being tested, even the trickiest questions become familiar and easy to solve.

It's Really a Reading Test

In constructing the Math section, ETS is limited to the math that nearly everyone has studied: arithmetic, basic algebra, basic geometry, and elementary statistics. There's no calculus (or even precalculus), no trigonometry, and no major-league algebra or geometry. Because of these limitations, ETS has to resort to traps in order to create hard problems. Even the most commonly missed GRE math problems are typically based on relatively simple principles. What makes the problems difficult is that these simple principles are disguised.

Your Student Tools contain tons of informational videos, practice tests, helpful articles, and more to help with your GRE preparation. Head over there and take advantage of this fantastic resource!

Many test takers have no problem doing the actual calculations involved in the math questions on the GRE; in fact, you'll even be allowed to use a calculator (more on that soon). However, on this test, your ability to carefully read the problems and figure out how to set them up is more important than your ability to make calculations.

As you work through this section, don't worry about how quickly you're doing the problems. Instead, take the time to really understand what the questions are asking; pay close attention to the wording of the problems. Most math errors are the result of careless mistakes caused by not reading the problem carefully enough!

Read and Copy Carefully

You can do all the calculations right and still get a question wrong. How? What if you solve for x but the question asked for the value of $x + 4$? Ugh. Always reread the question before you choose an answer. Take your time and don't be careless. The problem will stay on the screen as long as you want it to, so reread the question and double-check your work before answering it.

Or how about this? The radius of the circle is 5, but when you copied the picture onto your scratch paper, you accidentally made it 6. Ugh! If you make a mistake copying down information from the screen, you'll get the question wrong no matter how perfect your calculations are. You have to be extra careful when copying down information.

THE CALCULATOR

As we mentioned before, on the GRE you'll be given an on-screen calculator. The calculator program on the GRE is a rudimentary one that gives you the five basic operations: addition, subtraction, multiplication, division, and square root, plus a decimal function and a positive/negative feature. It follows the order of operations, or PEMDAS (more on this topic in Chapter 10). The calculator also has the ability to transfer the answer you've calculated directly into the answer box for certain questions. The on-screen calculator can be a huge advantage—if it's used correctly!

As you might have realized by this point, ETS is not exactly looking out for your best interests. Giving you a calculator might seem like an altruistic act, but rest assured that ETS knows that there are certain ways in which calculator use can be exploited. Keep in mind the following:

1. **Calculators Can't Think.** Calculators are good for one thing and one thing only: calculation. You still have to figure out how to set up the problem correctly. If you're not sure what to calculate, then a calculator isn't helpful. For example, if you do a percent calculation on your calculator and then hit "Transfer Display," you will have to remember to move the decimal point accordingly, depending on whether the question asks for a percent or a decimal.

2. **The Calculator Can Be a Liability.** ETS will give you questions that you can solve with a calculator, but the calculator can actually be a liability. You will be tempted to use it. For example, students who are uncomfortable adding, subtracting, multiplying, or dividing fractions may be tempted to convert all fractions to decimals using the calculator. Don't do it. You are better off mastering fractions than avoiding them. Working with exponents and square roots is another way in which the calculator will be tempting but may yield really big and awkward numbers or long decimals. You are much better off learning the rules of manipulating exponents and square roots. Most of these problems will be faster and cleaner to solve with rules than with a calculator. The questions may also use numbers that are too big for the calculator. Time spent trying to get an answer out of a calculator for problems involving really big numbers will be time wasted. Find another way around.

3. **A Calculator Won't Make You Faster.** Having a calculator should make you more accurate, but not necessarily faster. You still need to take time to read each problem carefully and set it up. Don't expect to blast through problems just because you have a calculator.

4. **The Calculator Is No Excuse for Not Using Scratch Paper.** Scratch paper is where good technique happens. Working problems by hand on scratch paper will help to avoid careless errors or skipped steps. Just because you can do multiple functions in a row on your calculator does not mean that you should be solving problems on your calculator. Use the calculator to do simple calculations that would otherwise take you time to solve. Make sure you are still writing steps out on your scratch paper, labeling results, and using setups. Accuracy is more important than speed!

Of course, you should not fear the calculator; by all means, use it and be grateful for it. Having a calculator should help you eliminate all those careless math mistakes.

GEOGRAPHY OF A MATH SECTION

Each of the two Math sections contains 20 questions. Test takers are allowed 35 minutes per section. The first 7 or 8 questions of each Math section are quantitative comparisons, while the remainder are a mixed bag of problem solving, all that apply, numeric entry, and charts and graphs. Each section covers a mixture of algebra, arithmetic, quantitative reasoning, geometry, and real-world math.

QUESTION FORMATS

Much like the Verbal section, the Math portion of the GRE contains a variety of different question formats. Let's go through each type of question and discuss how to crack it.

Standard Multiple Choice

These questions are the basic five-answer multiple-choice questions. These are great candidates for POE (Process of Elimination) strategies we will discuss later in this chapter.

Multiple Choice, Multiple Answer

These questions appear similar to the standard multiple-choice questions; however, on these you will have the opportunity to pick more than one answer. There can be anywhere from three to eight answer choices. Here's an example of what these will look like:

If $\frac{1}{12} < x < \frac{1}{6}$, then which of the following could be the value of x?

Indicate <u>all</u> such values.

☐ $\frac{2}{9}$

☐ $\frac{1}{5}$

☐ $\frac{2}{15}$

☐ $\frac{1}{10}$

☐ $\frac{2}{25}$

Your approach on these questions won't be radically different from the approach you use on standard multiple-choice questions. But obviously, you'll have to consider all of the answers—make sure you read each question carefully and remember that more than one answer can be correct. For example, for this question, you'd click on (C) and (D). You must select *every* correct choice to get credit for the problem.

Quantitative Comparison Questions

Quantitative comparison questions, hereafter affectionately known as "quant comp" questions, ask you to compare Quantity A to Quantity B. These questions have four answer choices instead of five, and all quant comp answer choices are the same. Here they are:

○ Quantity A is greater.

○ Quantity B is greater.

○ The two quantities are equal.

○ The relationship cannot be determined from the information given.

Your job is to compare the two quantities and choose one of these answers.

Quant comp problems test the same basic arithmetic, algebra, and geometry concepts as do the other GRE math problems. So, to solve these problems, you'll apply the same techniques you use on the other GRE math questions. But quant comps also have a few special rules you need to remember.

There Is No "(E)"

Because there are only four choices on quant comp questions, after you use POE to eliminate all of the answer choices you can, your odds of guessing correctly are even better. Think about it this way: eliminating even one answer on a quant comp question will give you a one-in-three chance of guessing correctly.

If a Quant Comp Question Contains Only Numbers, the Answer Can't Be (D)

Any quant comp problem that contains only numbers and no variables must have a single solution. Therefore, on these problems, you can eliminate (D) immediately because the larger quantity can be determined. For example, if you're asked to compare $\frac{3}{2}$ and $\frac{3}{4}$, you can determine which fraction is larger, so the answer cannot be (D).

Compare, Don't Calculate

> Do only as much work as you need to.

You don't always have to calculate the exact value of each quantity before you compare them. After all, your mission is simply to compare the two quantities. It's often helpful to treat the two quantities as though they were two sides of an equation. Anything you can do to both sides of an equation, you can also do to both quantities. You can add the same number to both sides, you can multiply both sides by the same positive number, and you can simplify a single side by multiplying it by one.

If you can simplify the terms of a quant comp, you should always do so.

Here's a quick example:

Quantity A	Quantity B
$\frac{1}{16} + \frac{1}{7} + \frac{1}{4}$	$\frac{1}{4} + \frac{1}{16} + \frac{1}{6}$

○ Quantity A is greater.

○ Quantity B is greater.

○ The two quantities are equal.

○ The relationship cannot be determined from the information given.

Here's How to Crack It

Don't do any calculating! Remember: Do only as much work as you need to in order to answer the question! The first thing you should do is eliminate (D). After all, there are only numbers here. After that, get rid of numbers that are common to both columns (think of this as simplifying). Both columns contain a $\frac{1}{16}$ and a $\frac{1}{4}$, so because we're talking about addition, they can't make a difference to the outcome. With them gone, you're merely comparing the $\frac{1}{7}$ in column A to the $\frac{1}{6}$ in column B. Now we can eliminate (C) as well—after all, there is no way that $\frac{1}{7}$ is equal to $\frac{1}{6}$. So, we're down to two choices, (A) and (B). If you don't remember how to compare fractions, don't worry—it's covered in Chapter 10 (Math Fundamentals). The answer to this question is (B).

Okay, let's talk about another wacky question type you'll see in the Math section.

Numeric Entry

Some questions on the GRE won't even have answer choices, and you'll have to generate your own answer. Here's an example:

Each month, Renaldo earns a commission of 10.5% of his total sales for the month, plus a salary of $2,500. If Renaldo earns $3,025 in a certain month, what were his total sales?

$

Click on the answer box and type in a number.
Backspace to erase.

Here's How to Crack It

On this type of question, POE is not going to help you! That means if you're not sure how to do one of these questions, you should immediately move on. Leave it blank and come back to it in your second pass through the test.

If Renaldo earned \$3,025, then his earnings from the commission on his sales are \$3,025 – \$2,500 = \$525. So, \$525 is 10.5% of his sales. Set up an equation to find the total sales: $525 = \frac{10.5}{100}x$, where x is the amount of the sales. Solving this equation, $x = 5,000$. (We'll review how to set up and solve equations like this in later chapters.)

To answer this question, you'd enter 5000 into the box. Alternately, you could transfer your work directly from the on-screen calculator to the text box.

Best Strategies for the GRE Math Section

The basic test-taking strategies covered in Chapter 2 are effective for the entire test. They can be critical to your level of success on the GRE. They are time-tested and proven to be effective. You should always be mindful of them and take a few minutes to review them before working through the Math section.

A Little Something Extra

This book's primary goal is to provide appropriate time management skills, strong study habits, and content practice and expertise for everything that may be tested. But it doesn't hurt to prepare for a situation in which you still end up needing an extra edge.

Here are some strategies that will help you on the Math section, specifically. We'll show you how to use them as we go through specific question types in the chapters ahead, but for now, read through the strategies and get a sense of what they are before moving on.

It's extremely important to be mindful that the strategies that follow are secondary to actually solving the problem. There is no ambiguity when it comes to the correct answer on a problem in the Math section, and actually solving the problem should be your primary goal. However, there are times when you may encounter a problem that seems overly difficult or complicated, or you are running out of time on a section. In those cases, these strategies may be helpful.

Process of Elimination (POE) for Math

Use POE whenever you can on questions that are in standard multiple-choice format. It's good practice to always read the answer choices before you start to solve a math problem because often they will help guide you—you might even be able to eliminate a couple of answer choices before you begin to calculate the answer.

Say you were asked to find 30 percent of 50. Wait—don't do any math yet. Let's say you glanced at the answer choices and you see these:

○ 5

○ 15

○ 30

○ 80

○ 150

Think about it. Whatever 30 percent of 50 is, it must be less than 50, right? So any answer choice that's greater than 50 can't be right. That means that you should eliminate both (D) and (E) before you do any calculations! Thirty percent is less than half, so you can eliminate anything greater than 25, which means that (C) is gone too. What is 10 percent of 50? Eliminate (A). You're done. The only answer left is (B).

This process is known as Ballparking. Remember that the answers are part of the question, and there are four times as many wrong answers as there are right answers. In the example above, the correct answer is fairly easy to calculate. This question is not representative of the difficulty of a GRE problem. While Ballparking is not a substitute for actually solving the problem, and should only be used as a last resort, it can help you to eliminate wrong answer choices that are clearly "out of the ballpark" and increase your odds of zeroing in on the correct answer.

Trap Answers

ETS likes to include "trap answers" in the answer choices to their math problems. Trap answers are answer choices that appear correct upon first glance. These answers often look so tempting that you'll choose them without actually bothering to complete the necessary calculations. Watch out for this! If a problem seems way too easy, be careful and double-check your work.

Here's a GRE example:

The price of a jacket is reduced by 10%. During a special sale, the price is discounted by another 10%. The special sale price is what percent less than the original price of the jacket?

○ 15%

○ 19%

○ 20%

○ 21%

○ 25%

Here's How to Crack It

The answer might seem like it should be 20 percent. But wait a minute! Is it likely that the GRE is going to give you a problem that you can solve just by adding 10 + 10? Probably not. Choice (C) is a trap answer.

To solve this problem, imagine that the original price of the jacket is $100. After a 10 percent discount, the new price is $90. But now when you take another 10 percent discount, we're taking it from $90, not $100. Ten percent of 90 is 9, so the final price is $90 − $9 = $81. That represents a 19 percent total discount from the original price of $100. The correct answer is (B).

Down to Two?

Suppose you've eliminated three of the five answers you know are wrong and you're down to two. You marked it and have come back to it. At this point, you can just guess—not bad considering your chances of being right have gone from twenty percent to fifty percent. However, there is only one way to correctly answer every question on the GRE, so if you can't see why one of the remaining answer choices is wrong, you are missing something. Take a fresh look at the question and remind yourself what the answer should look like. Find it! If you are still stuck, Mark and Move.

Here's a GRE example:

At a certain factory, each employee either drives to work or takes the bus. The ratio of employees who take the bus to work to those who drive to work is 2 : 5. If 120 employees drive to work, how many employees work at the factory?

○ 240

○ 168

○ 110

○ 48

○ 24

Here's How to Crack It

If 120 workers drive to work, there must be at least that many who work in the factory, so you can eliminate (C), (D), and (E) immediately. You marked it and now you've come back to the question to choose between (A) and (B). The ratio is 2 : 5, which means that for every 2 workers who take the bus to work, there are 5 workers who drive to work. So the total number of workers must be a multiple of 2 + 5 = 7. 168 is a multiple of 7, but 240 is not a multiple of 7, so the answer is (B).

Stacking the Odds

There may be cases on the GRE when you are running out of time and you are going to have to guess on a question. POE can turn these questions into potential points. Before you just guess on a question, quickly consider if some of the answer choices are clearly wrong. If you can eliminate a couple of choices, you've increased your chances of getting a free point!

Consider this GRE example:

A 100-foot rope is cut so that the shorter piece is $\dfrac{2}{3}$ the length of the longer piece. What is the length of the shorter piece in feet?

○ 75

○ $66\dfrac{2}{3}$

○ 50

○ 40

○ $33\dfrac{1}{3}$

Here's How to Crack It

Before we dive into the calculations, let's use a little common sense. The rope is 100 feet long. If we cut the rope in half, each part would be 50 feet. However, the rope was cut into two unequal pieces—a shorter piece and a longer piece. The shorter piece must be less than 50 feet, so you can eliminate (A), (B), and (C) immediately. By the way, the correct answer is (D), but solving this problem was not the point of the exercise. The point here to show you that we can quickly eliminate answer choices to improve the odds of guessing correctly, if guessing is necessary.

HOW TO STUDY

Make sure you learn the content of each of the following chapters before you go on to the next one. Don't try to cram everything in all at once. It's much better to do a small amount of studying each day over a longer period; you will master both the math concepts and the techniques if you focus on the material a little bit at a time. Just as we have been telling you in earlier chapters, let the content sink in by taking short study breaks between study sessions and giving yourself plenty of time to prepare for the GRE. Slow and steady wins the race!

Practice, Practice, Practice

Practice may not make perfect, but it sure will help. Use everyday math calculations as practice opportunities. Balance your checkbook without a calculator! Make sure your check has been added correctly at a restaurant, and figure out the exact percentage you want to leave for a tip. The more you practice simple adding, subtracting, multiplying, and dividing on a day-to-day basis, the more your arithmetic skills will improve for the GRE.

After you work through this book, be sure to practice doing questions on our online tests and on real GREs. There are always sample questions at www.ets.org/gre, and practice will rapidly sharpen your test-taking skills.

Finally, unless you trust our techniques, you may be reluctant to use them fully and automatically on the real GRE. The best way to develop that trust is to practice before you get to the real test.

Online Practice Tests
Take advantage of all of the online practice tests that come with this book! Head over to your Student Tools and get practicing!

Summary

o   The GRE contains two 35-minute Math sections. Each section has 20 questions.

o   The GRE tests math concepts up to about the tenth-grade level of difficulty.

o   You will be allowed to use a calculator on the GRE. The calculator is part of the on-screen display.

o   The Math section employs a number of different question formats, including multiple-choice, numeric entry, and quantitative comparison questions.

o   Use the Two-Pass system on the Math section. Find the easier questions and do them first. Use your remaining time to work some of the more difficult questions.

o   When you get stuck on a problem, walk away. Do a few other problems to distract your brain, and then return to the question that was giving you problems.

o   Ballpark or estimate the answers to math questions, eliminating answers that don't make sense.

o   Watch out for trap answers. If an answer seems too easy or obvious, it's probably a trap.

o   Always do your work on your scratch paper, not in your head. Even when you are Ballparking, make sure that you are eliminating answer choices on your scratch paper. If your hand isn't moving, you're stuck and you need to walk away, or you're doing work in your head, which leads to errors.

Chapter 11
Math Fundamentals

Numbers and equations form the basis of all the math questions on the GRE. Simply put, the more comfortable you are working with numbers and equations, the easier the math portion of the exam will be. This chapter gives you a review of all the basic mathematical concepts including properties of numbers, factors and multiples, fractions and decimals, math vocabulary, and some basic rules of math.

GET FAMILIAR

To do well on the GRE Math section, you'll have to be comfortable working with numbers. The concepts tested on the GRE are not exceptionally difficult, but if you are even the least bit skittish about numbers, you'll have a harder time working the problems.

> You may be a little rusty when it comes to working with numbers, but with a little practice, you'll be surprised at how quickly you'll become comfortable again.

This chapter will familiarize you with all the basics you need to know about numbers and how to work with them. If you're an arithmophobe or haven't used math in a while, take it slowly and make sure you're comfortable with this chapter before moving onto the succeeding ones.

GRE MATH VOCABULARY

Quick—what's an integer? Is 0 even or odd? How many even prime numbers are there?

Before we go through our techniques for specific types of math problems, we'll acquaint ourselves with some basic vocabulary and properties of numbers. The GRE loves to test your knowledge of integers, fractions, decimals, and all those other concepts you probably learned years ago. Make sure you're comfortable with the topics in this chapter before moving on. Even if you feel fairly at ease with number concepts, you should still work through this chapter. ETS is very good at coming up with questions that require you to know ideas forward and backward.

> Learn your math vocabulary!

The math terms we will review in this section are very simple, but that doesn't mean they're not important. Every GRE math question uses simple terms, rules, and definitions. You absolutely need to know this math "vocabulary." Don't worry; we will cover only the math terms that you *must* know for the GRE.

Digits

Digit refers to the numbers that make up other numbers. There are 10 digits: 0, 1, 2, 3, 4, 5, 6, 7, 8, 9, and every number is made up of one or more digits. For example, the number 10,897 has five digits: 1, 0, 8, 9, and 7. Each of the digits in a number has its own name, which is designated by a place value. In the number 10,897

- 7 is the ones, or units, digit.
- 9 is the tens digit.
- 8 is the hundreds digit.
- 0 is the thousands digit.
- 1 is the ten-thousands digit.

Numbers

A **number** is made up of either a digit or a collection of digits. There are, of course, an infinite number of numbers. Basically, any combination of digits you can imagine is a number, which includes 0, negative numbers, fractions and decimals, and even weird numbers such as $\sqrt{2}$.

> GRE problems like to try to trip you up on the difference between a number and an integer.

Integers

Integers are numbers that have no fractional or decimal part, such as –6, –5, –4, –3, –2, –1, 0, 1, 2, 3, 4, 5, 6, and so on.

Notice that fractions, such as $\frac{1}{2}$, are not integers.

> Remember: Fractions are NOT integers.

Remember that the number zero is an integer! The values of positive integers increase as they move away from 0 (6 is greater than 5); the values of negative integers decrease as they move away from zero (–6 is less than –5).

PROPERTIES OF NUMBERS AND INTEGERS

Now that you've learned the proper names for various types of numbers, let's look at properties of numbers and integers.

Positive or Negative

Numbers can be positive or negative. Negative numbers are less than zero, while positive numbers are greater than zero. Zero itself is neither positive nor negative—all other numbers are either positive or negative.

Even or Odd

Only integers possess the property of being even or odd. Fractions, decimals, and other non-integers cannot be described as even or odd. Integers that are even are those that are divisible by 2; odd integers are those integers that are not divisible by 2. Put another way, even integers have a remainder of 0 when divided by 2, while odd integers have a remainder of 1 when divided by 2.

- Here are some even integers: –4, –2, 0, 2, 4, 6, 8, 10.
- Here are some odd integers: –3, –1, 1, 3, 5, 7, 9, 11.

Zero has a number of special properties that are tested frequently on the GRE. Technically, zero is a multiple of every number, but this fact is rarely tested on the GRE.

Zero

Zero is a special little number. It is an integer, but it is neither positive nor negative. However, try to remember these facts about zero:

- 0 is even.
- 0 plus any other number is equal to that other number.
- 0 multiplied by any other number is equal to 0.
- You cannot divide by 0.

Keep in Mind

- Fractions are neither even nor odd.
- Any integer is even if its units digit is even; any integer is odd if its units digit is odd.
- The results of adding and multiplying odd and even integers are as follows:
  - even + even = even
  - odd + odd = even
  - even + odd = odd
  - even × even = even
  - odd × odd = odd
  - even × odd = even

Be careful: Don't confuse odd and even with positive and negative!

If you have trouble remembering some of these rules for odd and even, don't worry. As long as you remember that there are rules, you can always figure them out by plugging in numbers. Let's say you forget what happens when an odd number is multiplied by an odd number. Just pick two odd numbers, say 3 and 5, and multiply them. 3 × 5 = 15. Now you know: odd × odd = odd.

Consecutive Integers

Consecutive integers are integers listed in order of value without any integers missing in between them. Here are some examples:

- 0, 1, 2, 3, 4, 5
- −6, −5, −4, −3, −2, −1, 0
- −3, −2, −1, 0, 1, 2, 3

By the way, fractions and decimals cannot be consecutive; only integers can be consecutive. However, you can have different types of consecutive integers. For example consecutive even integers could be 2, 4, 6, 8, 10. Consecutive multiples of four could be 4, 8, 12, 16.

Absolute Value

The **absolute value** of a number is equal to its distance from 0 on the number line, which means that the absolute value of any number is always positive, whether the number itself is positive or negative. The symbol for absolute value is a set of double lines: $|\ \ |$. Thus $|{-5}| = 5$, and $|5| = 5$ because both −5 and 5 are a distance of 5 from 0 on the number line.

FACTORS, MULTIPLES, AND DIVISIBILITY

Now let's look at some ways that integers are related to each other.

Factors

A **factor** of a particular integer is a number that will divide evenly into the integer in question. For example, 1, 2, 3, 4, 6, and 12 are all factors of 12 because each number divides evenly into 12. In order to find all the factors of a particular integer, write down the factors systematically in pairs of integers that, when multiplied together, make 12, starting with 1 and the integer itself:

- 1 and 12
- 2 and 6
- 3 and 4

If you always start with 1 and the integer itself and work your way up, you'll make sure you get them all.

Multiples

The **multiples** of an integer are all the integers for which the original integer is a factor. For example, the multiples of 8 are all the integers of which 8 is a factor: 8, 16, 24, 32, 40, and so on. Note that there are an infinite number of multiples for any given number. Also, zero is a multiple of every number, although this concept is rarely tested on the GRE.

> There are only a few factors of any number; there are many multiples of any number.

Prime Numbers

A **prime number** is an integer that has only two factors: itself and 1. Thus, 37 is prime because the only integers that divide evenly into it are 1 and 37, while 10 is not prime because its factors are 1, 2, 5, and 10.

Here is a list of all the prime numbers that are less than 30: 2, 3, 5, 7, 11, 13, 17, 19, 23, 29.

Here are some other facts about primes that are important to remember:

- 0 is not a prime number.
- 1 is not a prime number.
- 2 is the only even prime number.
- Prime numbers are positive integers. There's no such thing as a negative prime number or a prime fraction.

> 1 is not prime!

Divisibility

An integer is always divisible by its factors. If you're not sure if one integer is divisible by another, a surefire way to find out is to use the calculator. However, there are also certain rules you can use to determine whether one integer is a factor of another.

- An integer is divisible by 2 if its units digit is divisible by 2. For example, we know just by glancing at it that 598,447,896 is divisible by 2, because the units digit, 6, is divisible by 2.
- An integer is divisible by 3 if the sum of its digits is divisible by 3. For example, we know that 2,145 is divisible by 3 because 2 + 1 + 4 + 5 = 12, and 12 is divisible by 3.
- An integer is divisible by 4 if its last two digits form a number that's divisible by 4. For example, 712 is divisible by 4 because 12 is divisible by 4.
- An integer is divisible by 5 if its units digit is either 0 or 5. For example, 23,645 is divisible by 5 because its units digit is 5.
- An integer is divisible by 6 if it's divisible by both 2 and 3. For example, 4,290 is divisible by 6 because it is divisible by 2 (it's even) and by 3 (4 + 2 + 9 = 15, which is divisible by 3).
- An integer is divisible by 8 if its last three digits form a number that's divisible by 8. For example, 11,640 is divisible by 8 because 640 is divisible by 8.
- An integer is divisible by 9 if the sum of its digits is divisible by 9. For example, 1,881 is divisible by 9 because 1 + 8 + 8 + 1 = 18, which is divisible by 9.
- An integer is divisible by 10 if its units digit is 0. For example, 1,590 is divisible by 10 because its units digit is 0.

Remainders

If one integer is not divisible by another—meaning that the second integer is not a factor of the first number—you'll have an integer left over when you divide. This leftover integer is called a **remainder**; you probably remember working with remainders in grade school.

> If a question asks about a remainder, don't use the calculator. Use long division.

For example, when 4 is divided by 2, there's nothing left over, so there's no remainder. In other words, 4 is divisible by 2. You could also say that the remainder is 0.

On the other hand, 5 divided by 2 is 2, with 1 left over; 1 is the remainder. Also, 13 divided by 8 is 1, with 5 left over as the remainder.

Note that remainders are always less than the number that you are dividing by. For example, the remainder when 13 is divided by 7 is 6. What happens if you divide 14, the next integer, by 7? The remainder is 0.

Here's one more thing to know about remainders. What's the remainder when 5 is divided by 6? The remainder is 5 because 5 can be divided by 6 zero times and the amount that remains is 5. When the positive integer you are dividing by is greater than the integer being divided, the remainder will always be the number being divided.

MORE MATH VOCABULARY

In a way, the Math section is almost as much of a vocabulary test as the Verbal section. Below, you'll find some more standard terms that you should commit to memory before you do any practice problems.

Term	Meaning
sum	the result of addition
difference	the result of subtraction
product	the result of multiplication
quotient	the result of division
divisor	the number you divide by
numerator	the top number in a fraction
denominator	the bottom number in a fraction
consecutive	in order from least to greatest
terms	the numbers and expressions used in an equation

BASIC OPERATIONS WITH NUMBERS

Now that you've learned about numbers and their properties, you're ready to begin working with them. As we mentioned above, there are four basic operations you can perform on a number: addition, subtraction, multiplication, and division.

Order of Operations

When you work with numbers, you can't just perform the four operations in any way you please. Instead, there are some very specific rules to follow, which are commonly referred to as the **order of operations.**

It is absolutely necessary that you perform these operations in exactly the right order. In many cases, the correct order will be apparent from the way the problem is written. In cases in which the correct order is not apparent, you need to remember the following mnemonic.

> Please Excuse My Dear Aunt Sally, or **PEMDAS**.

What does PEMDAS stand for?

$$P \mid E \mid MD \mid AS$$
$$\rightarrow \quad \rightarrow$$

P stands for "parentheses." Solve anything in parentheses first.

E stands for "exponents." Solve exponents next. (We'll review exponents soon.)

M stands for "multiplication" and **D** stands for "division." The arrow indicates that you do all the multiplication and division together in the same step, going from left to right.

A stands for "addition" and **S** stands for "subtraction." Again, the arrow indicates that you do all the addition and subtraction together in one step, from left to right.

Let's look at an example:

$$12 + 4(2 + 1)^2 \div 6 - 7 =$$

Here's How to Crack It

Start by doing all the math inside the parentheses: $2 + 1 = 3$. Now the problem looks like this:

$$12 + 4(3)^2 \div 6 - 7 =$$

Next we have to apply the exponent: $3^2 = 9$. Now this is what we have:

$$12 + 4(9) \div 6 - 7 =$$

Now we do multiplication and division from left to right: $4 \times 9 = 36$, and $36 \div 6 = 6$, which gives us

$$12 + 6 - 7 =$$

Finally, we do the addition and subtraction from left to right: $12 + 6 = 18$, and $18 - 7 = 11$. Therefore,

$$12 + 4(2 + 1)^2 \div 6 - 7 = 11$$

Multiplication and Division

When multiplying or dividing, keep the following rules in mind:

- positive × positive = positive $2 \times 2 = 4$
- negative × negative = positive $-2 \times -2 = 4$
- positive × negative = negative $2 \times -2 = -4$
- positive ÷ positive = positive $8 \div 2 = 4$
- negative ÷ negative = positive $-8 \div -2 = 4$
- positive ÷ negative = negative $8 \div -2 = -4$

Before taking the GRE, you should have your times tables memorized from 1 through 15. It will be a tremendous advantage if you can quickly and confidently recall that $7 \times 12 = 84$, for example.

> It seems like a small thing, but memorizing your times tables will really help you on test day.

FRACTIONS, DECIMALS, AND PERCENTAGES

One of the ways ETS tests your fundamental math abilities is through fractions, decimals, and percents. So let's expand our conversation on math fundamentals to include these concepts.

Fractions

A **fraction** expresses the number of parts out of a whole. In the fraction $\frac{2}{3}$, for instance, the top part, or **numerator**, tells us that we have 2 parts, while the bottom part of the fraction, the **denominator**, indicates that the whole, or total, consists of 3 parts. We use fractions whenever we're dealing with a quantity that's between two whole numbers.

Notice that the fraction bar is simply another way of expressing division. Thus, the fraction $\frac{2}{3}$ is just expressing the idea of "2 divided by 3."

> Fractions are important on the GRE. Make sure you're comfortable with them.

Reducing and Expanding Fractions

Fractions express a relationship between numbers, not actual amounts. For example, saying that you did $\frac{1}{2}$ of your homework expresses the same idea whether you had 10 pages of homework to do and you've done 5 pages, or you had 50 pages to do and you've done 25 pages. This concept is important because on the GRE you'll frequently have to reduce or expand fractions.

To reduce a fraction, express the numerator and denominator as the products of their factors. Then cross out, or "cancel," factors that are common to both the numerator and denominator. Here's an example:

$$\frac{16}{20} = \frac{2 \times 2 \times 2 \times 2}{2 \times 2 \times 5} = \frac{\cancel{2} \times \cancel{2} \times 2 \times 2}{\cancel{2} \times \cancel{2} \times 5} = \frac{2 \times 2}{5} = \frac{4}{5}$$

You can achieve the same result by dividing the numerator and denominator by the factors that are common to both. In the example you just saw, you might realize that 4 is a factor of both the numerator and the denominator. That is, both the numerator and the denominator can be divided evenly (without a remainder) by 4. Doing this yields the much more manageable fraction $\frac{4}{5}$.

When you confront GRE math problems that involve fractions with great numbers, always reduce them before doing anything else.

Look at each of the following fractions:

$$\frac{1}{4} \qquad \frac{2}{8} \qquad \frac{6}{24} \qquad \frac{18}{72} \qquad \frac{90}{360} \qquad \frac{236}{944}$$

What do you notice about each of these fractions? They all express the same information! Each of these fractions expresses the relationship of "1 part out of 4 total parts."

Adding and Subtracting Fractions

Adding and subtracting fractions that have a common denominator is easy—you just add the numerators and put the sum over the common denominator. Here's an example:

$$\frac{1}{10} + \frac{2}{10} + \frac{4}{10} =$$

$$\frac{1+2+4}{10} = \frac{7}{10}$$

In order to add or subtract fractions that have different denominators, you need to start by finding a common denominator. You may remember your teachers from grade school imploring you to find the "lowest common denominator." Actually, any common denominator will do, so find whichever one you find most comfortable working with.

$$\frac{7}{8} - \frac{5}{12} = \frac{21}{24} - \frac{10}{24} = \frac{11}{24}$$

Here, we expanded the fraction $\frac{7}{8}$ into the equivalent fraction $\frac{21}{24}$ by multiplying both the numerator and denominator by 3. Similarly, we converted $\frac{5}{12}$ to $\frac{10}{24}$ by multiplying both denominator and numerator by 2. This left us with two fractions with the same denominator, which meant that we could simply subtract their numerators.

Why Bother?

You may be wondering why, if the GRE allows the use of a calculator, you should bother learning how to add or subtract fractions or to reduce them or even know any of the topics covered in the next few pages. While it's true that you can use a calculator for these tasks, for many problems it's actually slower to do the math with the calculator than without. Scoring well on the GRE Math section requires a fairly strong grasp of the basic relationships among numbers, fractions, percents, and so on, so it's in your best interest to really understand these concepts rather than to rely on your calculator to get you through the question. In fact, if you put in the work now, you'll be surprised at how easy some of the problems become, especially when you don't have to refer constantly to the calculator to perform basic operations.

When adding and subtracting fractions, you can also use a technique we call the Bowtie. The Bowtie method accomplishes exactly what we just did in one fell swoop. To use the Bowtie, first multiply the denominators of each fraction. This gives you a common denominator. Then multiply the denominator of each fraction by the numerator of the other fraction. Take these numbers and add or subtract them—depending on what the question asks you to do—to get the numerator of the answer. Then reduce if necessary.

$$\frac{2}{3} + \frac{3}{4} =$$

$$\overset{8}{\underset{3}{\frac{2}{3}}} \times \overset{9}{\underset{4}{\frac{3}{4}}} = \frac{8}{12} + \frac{9}{12} = \frac{17}{12}$$

The Bowtie method is a convenient shortcut to use when you're adding and subtracting fractions.

and

$$\frac{2}{3} - \frac{3}{4} =$$

$$\overset{8}{\underset{3}{\frac{2}{3}}} \times \overset{9}{\underset{4}{\frac{3}{4}}} = \frac{8}{12} - \frac{9}{12} = -\frac{1}{12}$$

Multiplying Fractions

Multiplying fractions is relatively straightforward when compared to addition or subtraction. To successfully multiply fractions, multiply the first numerator by the second numerator and the first denominator by the second denominator. Here's an example:

$$\frac{4}{5} \times \frac{10}{12} = \frac{40}{60} = \frac{2}{3}$$

When multiplying fractions, you can make your life easier by reducing before you multiply. Do this once again by dividing out common factors.

Multiplying fractions is a snap. Just multiply straight across, numerator times numerator and denominator times denominator.

$$\frac{4}{5} \times \frac{10}{12} = \frac{4}{5} \times \frac{5}{6} = \frac{20}{30} = \frac{2}{3}$$

Also remember that when you're multiplying fractions, you can even reduce diagonally; as long as you're working with a numerator and a denominator of opposite fractions, they don't have to be in the same fraction. So you end up with

$$\overset{2}{\underset{1}{\frac{\cancel{4}}{\cancel{5}}}} \times \overset{1}{\underset{3}{\frac{\cancel{5}}{\cancel{6}}}} = \frac{2}{1} \times \frac{1}{3} = \frac{2}{3}$$

Of course, you get the same answer no matter what method you use, so attack fractions in whatever fashion you find easiest. Or better yet, use one method to check your work on the other method.

Dividing Fractions

Dividing fractions is just like multiplying fractions, with one crucial difference: before you multiply, you have to find the reciprocal of the second fraction. To do this, all you need to do is flip the fraction upside down! Put the denominator on top of the numerator and then multiply just like before. In some cases, you can also reduce before you multiply. Here's an example:

$$\frac{2}{3} \div \frac{4}{5} = \frac{2}{3} \times \frac{5}{4} = \frac{1}{3} \times \frac{5}{2} = \frac{5}{6}$$

ETS tests problems that involve fractions in which the numerators or denominators are themselves fractions. These problems might look intimidating, but if you're careful, you won't have any trouble with them. All you have to do is remember what we said about a fraction being shorthand for division. Always rewrite the expression horizontally. Here's an example:

$$\frac{7}{\frac{1}{4}} = 7 \div \frac{1}{4} = \frac{7}{1} \times \frac{4}{1} = \frac{28}{1} = 28$$

Comparing Fractions

Sometimes ETS will test your ability to compare two fractions to decide which is greater. These are typically found on quant comp questions. There are a couple of ways to accomplish this. One is to find equivalent fractions that have a common denominator. If the fraction is fairly simple, this is a good strategy, but oftentimes the common denominator may be hard to find or work with.

If the denominator is hard to find or work with, you can use a variant of the Bowtie technique. In this variant, you don't have to multiply the denominators together; instead, just multiply the denominators and the numerators. The fraction with the greater product in its numerator is the greater fraction. Let's say we had to compare the following fractions:

$$\frac{3}{7} \qquad \frac{7}{12}$$

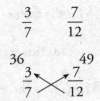

You can also use the calculator feature to change the fractions into decimals.

Multiplying the first denominator by the second numerator yields 49. This means the numerator of the second fraction $\left(\dfrac{7}{12}\right)$ is 49. Multiplying the second denominator by the first numerator gives you 36, which means the first fraction has a numerator of 36. Since 49 is greater than 36, $\dfrac{7}{12}$ is greater than $\dfrac{3}{7}$.

Comparing More Than Two Fractions

You may also be asked to compare more than two fractions. On these types of problems, don't waste time trying to find a common denominator for all of them. Simply use the Bowtie to compare two of the fractions at a time.

Here's an example:

Which of the following statements is true?

○ $\dfrac{3}{8} < \dfrac{2}{9} < \dfrac{4}{11}$

○ $\dfrac{2}{5} < \dfrac{3}{7} < \dfrac{4}{13}$

○ $\dfrac{4}{13} < \dfrac{2}{5} < \dfrac{3}{7}$

○ $\dfrac{3}{7} < \dfrac{3}{8} < \dfrac{2}{5}$

○ $\dfrac{2}{9} < \dfrac{3}{7} < \dfrac{3}{8}$

Here's How to Crack It

As you can see, it would be a nightmare to try to find common denominators for all these fractions, so instead we'll use the Bowtie method. Simply multiply the denominators and numerators of a pair of fractions and note the results. For example, to check (A), we first multiply 8 and 2, which gives us a numerator of 16 for the fraction $\dfrac{2}{9}$. But multiplying 9 and 3 gives us a numerator of 27 for the first fraction. This means that $\dfrac{3}{8}$ is greater than $\dfrac{2}{9}$, and we can eliminate (A), because the first part of it is wrong. Here's how the rest of the choices shape up:

○ $\dfrac{2}{5} < \dfrac{3}{7} < \dfrac{4}{13}$ Compare $\dfrac{3}{7}$ and $\dfrac{4}{13}$; $\dfrac{3}{7}$ is greater. Eliminate (B).

○ $\dfrac{4}{13} < \dfrac{2}{5} < \dfrac{3}{7}$ These fractions are in order.

○ $\dfrac{3}{7} < \dfrac{3}{8} < \dfrac{2}{5}$ $\dfrac{3}{7}$ is greater than $\dfrac{3}{8}$. Eliminate (D).

○ $\dfrac{2}{9} < \dfrac{3}{7} < \dfrac{3}{8}$ $\dfrac{3}{7}$ is greater than $\dfrac{3}{8}$. Eliminate (E).

The answer is (C).

Converting Mixed Numbers into Fractions

A **mixed number** is a number that is represented as an integer and a fraction, such as $2\dfrac{2}{3}$. In most cases on the GRE, you should get rid of mixed fractions by converting them to improper fractions. How do you do this? By multiplying the denominator of the fraction by the integer, then adding that result to the numerator, and then putting the whole thing over the denominator. In other words, for the fraction above, we would get $\dfrac{3 \times 2 + 2}{3}$, or $\dfrac{8}{3}$.

> Improper fractions have a numerator that is greater than the denominator. When you convert mixed numbers, you'll get an improper fraction as the result.

The result, $\dfrac{8}{3}$, is equivalent to $2\dfrac{2}{3}$. The only difference is that $\dfrac{8}{3}$ is easier to work with in math problems. Also, answer choices are usually not given in the form of mixed numbers.

Decimals

Decimals are just fractions in disguise. Basically, decimals and fractions are two different ways of expressing the same thing. Every decimal can be written as a fraction, and every fraction can be written as a decimal. For example, the decimal 0.35 can be written as the fraction $\dfrac{35}{100}$. Therefore, these two numbers, 0.35 and $\dfrac{35}{100}$, have the same value.

To turn a fraction into its decimal equivalent, all you have to do is divide the numerator by the denominator. Here, for example, is how you would find the decimal equivalent of $\dfrac{3}{4}$:

$$\frac{3}{4} = 3 \div 4 = 4\overline{)3.00}\,^{0.75}$$

Try this problem:

$$\frac{1}{3} + \frac{2}{5} = x$$

$$y = 3$$

Quantity A	Quantity B
$\dfrac{y}{x}$	4

○ Quantity A is greater.

○ Quantity B is greater.

○ The two quantities are equal.

○ The relationship cannot be determined from the information given.

Here's How to Crack It

Begin this quant comp question by solving for *x*. The common denominator is easy to find, as it is 15, so adjust the fractions to have the denominator of 15.

$$\frac{1}{3} + \frac{2}{5} = \frac{5}{15} + \frac{6}{15} = \frac{11}{15}$$

The problem gives the value of *y*, so now solve for Quantity A. Quantity A is $\left(\frac{3}{\frac{11}{15}}\right)$, which equals $3 \times \frac{15}{11} = \frac{45}{11}$. Now compare this to Quantity B. Dividing 45 by 11 yields a result slightly greater than 4, which means that Quantity A is greater than Quantity B and the correct answer is (A).

Comparing Decimals

Which is greater: 0.00099 or 0.001? ETS loves this sort of problem. You'll never go wrong, though, if you follow these easy steps.

- Line up the numbers by their decimal points.
- Fill in the missing zeros.

Here's how to answer the question we just asked. First, line up the two numbers by their decimal points.

$$0.00099$$
$$0.001$$

Now fill in the missing zeros.

$$0.00099$$
$$0.00100$$

Can you tell which number is greater? Of course you can. 0.00100 is greater than 0.00099, because 100 is greater than 99.

Digits and Decimals

Sometimes ETS will ask you questions about digits that fall after the decimal point as well. Suppose you have the number 0.584.

- 0 is the units digit.
- 5 is the tenths digit.
- 8 is the hundredths digit.
- 4 is the thousandths digit.

Percentages

A **percentage** is just a special type of fraction, one that always has 100 as the denominator. Percent literally means "per 100" or "out of 100" or "divided by 100." If your best friend finds a dollar and gives you 50¢, your friend has given you 50¢ out of 100¢, or $\frac{50}{100}$ of a dollar, or 50 percent of the dollar. To convert fractions to percentages, just expand the fraction so it has a denominator of 100:

$$\frac{3}{5} = \frac{60}{100} = 60\%$$

Another way to convert a fraction into a percentage is to divide the numerator by the denominator and multiply the result by 100.
So, $\frac{3}{5} = 3 \div 5 =$ 0.6 x 100 = 60%.

For the GRE, you should memorize the following percentage-decimal-fraction equivalents. Use these friendly fractions and percentages to eliminate answer choices.

$$0.01 = \frac{1}{100} = 1\%$$

$$0.333... = \frac{1}{3} = 33\frac{1}{3}\%$$

$$0.1 = \frac{1}{10} = 10\%$$

$$0.4 = \frac{2}{5} = 40\%$$

$$0.2 = \frac{1}{5} = 20\%$$

$$0.5 = \frac{1}{2} = 50\%$$

$$0.25 = \frac{1}{4} = 25\%$$

$$0.6 = \frac{3}{5} = 60\%$$

Converting Decimals to Percentages

To convert decimals to percentages, just move the decimal point two places to the right. For example, 0.8 turns into 80 percent, 0.25 into 25 percent, 0.5 into 50 percent, and 1 into 100 percent.

Translation

One of the best ways to handle percentages in word problems is to know how to translate them into an equation that you can manipulate. Use the following table to help you translate percentage word problems into equations you can work with.

These translations apply to any word problem, not just percent problems.

Word	Equivalent Symbol
percent	$\overline{100}$
is	=
of, times, product	×
what (or any unknown value)	any variable (x, k, b)

Here's an example:

---○---

56 is what percent of 80 ?

○   66%

○   70%

○   75%

○   80%

○   142%

Here's How to Crack It

To solve this problem, let's translate the question and then solve for the variable. So, "56 is what percent of 80," in math speak, is equal to

$$56 = \frac{x}{100}(80)$$

$$56 = \frac{80x}{100}$$

Don't forget to reduce the fraction: $56 = \frac{4}{5}x$.

Now multiply both sides of the equation by the reciprocal, $\frac{5}{4}$.

$$\frac{5}{4}(56) = x$$

$$\frac{56 \times 5}{4} = x$$

$$\frac{280}{4} = x = 70$$

The correct answer is (B), 70%.

---○---

Let's try a quant comp example.

―――――――――――○―――――――――――

5 is r percent of 25.

s is 25 percent of 60.

Quantity A   **Quantity B**

r s

○ Quantity A is greater.

○ Quantity B is greater.

○ The two quantities are equal.

○ The relationship cannot be determined from the information given.

Here's How to Crack It

First translate the first statement.

$$5 = \frac{r}{100}(25)$$

$$5 = \frac{25r}{100}$$

$$5 = \frac{r}{4}$$

$$(4)(5) = \left(\frac{r}{4}\right)(4)$$

$$20 = r$$

That takes care of Quantity A. Now translate the second statement.

$$s = \frac{25}{100}(60)$$

$$s = \frac{1}{4}(60)$$

$$s = 15$$

So Quantity A is greater than Quantity B. The answer is (A).

―――――――――――○―――――――――――

Percentage Increase/Decrease

Rather than asking for percents, ETS typically will test your knowledge by asking for percent change. Percent change is the percentage by which something has increased or decreased. To find percent change, use the following formula.

$$\text{Percent Change} = \frac{\text{Difference}}{\text{Original}} \times 100$$

> On percent increase problems, the original is always the smaller number. On percent decrease problems, the original is the larger number.

When presented with a percent change problem, you will typically be given two numbers. The "difference" is the result when the lesser number is subtracted from the greater number. The "original" is whichever number you started with. If the question asks you to find a **percent increase**, then the original number is the **lesser number**. If the question asks you to find a **percent decrease**, then the original number is the **greater number**.

On the GRE, a percent change will not be stated as a negative number. Instead, the problem will ask for a percent decrease. So, if something declined by 50%, the problem will ask for a percent decrease and the answer will be stated as 50%. Note that when you use the percent change formula, you always subtract the lesser number from the greater number to find the difference. Doing so ensures that you get a positive result.

Here's an example.

During a certain three-month period, Vandelay Industries reported a $3,500 profit. If, over the next three-month period, Vandelay Industries reported $6,000 profit for those months, by approximately what percent did Vandelay Industries' profit increase?

○ 25%

○ 32%

○ 42%

○ 55%

○ 70%

Here's How to Crack It

Let's use the percent change formula we just learned. The first step is to find the difference between the two numbers. The initial profit was $3,500 and the final profit is $6,000. The difference between these two numbers is $6,000 - 3,500 = 2,500$. Next, we need to divide this number by the original, or starting, value.

One way to help you figure out what value to use as the original value is to check to see whether you're dealing with a percent increase or a percent decrease question. Remember that on a percent increase question, you should always use the lesser of the two numbers as the denominator and on a percent decrease question, you need to use the greater of the two numbers as the denominator. Because the question asks to find the percent increase, the number we want to use for our denominator is 3,500. The percent increase fraction looks like this: $\frac{2,500}{3,500}$. This can be reduced to $\frac{25}{35}$ by dividing by 100, and reduced even further by dividing by 5. The reduced fraction is $\frac{5}{7}$, which is approximately 70% (remember that the fraction bar means divide, so if you divide 5 by 7, you'll get 0.71). Thus, (E) is the correct answer.

Here's another question.

Model	Original Price	Sale Price
A	$12,000	$9,500
B	$16,000	$13,000
C	$10,000	$7,500
D	$17,500	$13,000
E	$20,000	$15,500
F	$22,000	$16,000

The table above shows the original price and the sale price for six different models of cars. For which car models is the percent decrease at least 25% ?

Indicate all such models.

☐ A

☐ B

☐ C

☐ D

☐ E

☐ F

Here's How to Crack It

The task of this question is to identify a 25% or greater percent decrease between the two prices for the different car models. Use the percent change formula for all of the models to solve this question. Start with model A. Using the calculator, subtract 9,500 from 12,000 to get 2,500. This is the difference. Divide it by the original, 12,000, to get about 0.2, which when multiplied by 100 is 20%. Since 20% is less than 25%, eliminate (A). Try the next one. 16,000 − 13,000 = 3,000. Divide 3,000 by 16,000. The result is less than 25%, so eliminate (B). Repeat this process for each of the answer choices. Choices (C), (D), and (F) are the correct answers.

A FEW LAWS

These two basic laws are not necessary for success on the GRE, so if you have trouble with them, don't worry too much. However, ETS likes to use these laws to make certain math problems more difficult. If you're comfortable with these two laws, you'll be able to simplify problems using them, so it's definitely worth it to use them.

Associative Laws

There are two associative laws—one for addition and one for multiplication. For the sake of simplicity, we've lumped them together.

Here's what you need to know:

> When you are adding or multiplying a series of numbers, you can regroup the numbers in any way you'd like.

Here are some examples:

$$4 + (5 + 8) = (4 + 5) + 8 = (4 + 8) + 5$$
$$(a + b) + (c + d) = a + (b + c + d)$$
$$4 \times (5 \times 8) = (4 \times 5) \times 8 = (4 \times 8) \times 5$$
$$(ab)(cd) = a(bcd)$$

Distributive Law

This is often tested on the GRE. Here's what it looks like:

> $$a(b + c) = ab + ac$$
> $$a(b - c) = ab - ac$$

Here's an example:

$$12(66) + 12(24) = ?$$

Here's How to Crack It

This is in the same form as $ab + ac$. Using the distributive law, this must equal $12(66 + 24)$, or $12(90) = 1,080$.

Math Fundamentals Drill

Test your new skills and check your answers in Part V.

If a prime number, p, is squared and the result is added to the next prime number greater than p, which of the following integers could be the resulting sum?

Indicate all such integers.

☐ 3
☐ 4
☐ 7
☐ 14
☐ 58
☐ 60
☐ 65
☐ 69

A bookstore will only order books that come in complete cases. Each case has 150 books and costs $1,757.

Quantity A	Quantity B
The number of books that can be ordered for $10,550	The number of books that can be ordered for $12,290

○ Quantity A is greater.

○ Quantity B is greater.

○ The two quantities are equal.

○ The relationship cannot be determined from the information given.

If the product of two distinct integers is 91, then which of the following could be the sum of the two integers?

Indicate all such sums.

☐ −92
☐ −91
☐ 7
☐ 13
☐ 20

Which of the following is the units digit for the sum of all of the distinct prime integers less than 20?

○ 4

○ 5

○ 6

○ 7

○ 8

During a sale, a store decreases the prices on all of its scarves by 25 to 50 percent. If all of the scarves in the store were originally priced at $20, which of the following prices could be the sale price of a scarf?

Indicate all such prices.

☐ $8
☐ $10
☐ $12
☐ $14
☐ $16

$$-2, 3, -5, -2, 3, -5, -2, 3, -5,\ldots$$

In the sequence above, the first 3 terms repeat without end. What is the product of the 81st term through the 85th term?

Quantity A	Quantity B
$4\left(\dfrac{1}{2}x + 2y\right)$	$2x + 8y$

○ Quantity A is greater.

○ Quantity B is greater.

○ The two quantities are equal.

○ The relationship cannot be determined from the information given.

Quantity A	Quantity B
The greatest number of consecutive nonnegative integers which have a sum less than 22	6

○ Quantity A is greater.

○ Quantity B is greater.

○ The two quantities are equal.

○ The relationship cannot be determined from the information given.

If x is the remainder when a multiple of 4 is divided by 6, and y is the remainder when a multiple of 2 is divided by 3, what is the greatest possible value of $x + y$?

○ 2

○ 3

○ 5

○ 6

○ 9

$$12 - \left(\frac{6}{3} - 4 \times 3\right) - 8 \times 3 =$$

○ −46

○ −30

○ −18

○ −6

○ −2

Summary

- Familiarity with the basic math concepts on the GRE is essential to achieving a great score.

- Digits are the numbers that make up other numbers, which are collections of digits, and those other numbers are determined by the place value of the digits.

- Integers are numbers with no fractional part (such as −6, −1, 1, 10, etc.) and can be positive or negative, and even or odd.

- Zero is an integer that is neither positive nor negative.

- Consecutive integers are integers listed from least to greatest.

- The absolute value of a number is that number's distance away from zero on a number line.

- A factor of a particular integer is an integer that divides evenly into that integer.

- A multiple of a number is a number that has the original number as a factor.

- Prime numbers have only two factors: 1 and the number itself.

- Divisibility is the ability for one number to be divided into another number with a result that is an integer. If a number divided by another number and the result is not an integer, the amount that is leftover is called the remainder.

- Always follow the order of operations when working a math problem.

- Fractions, decimals, and percents are all ways of expressing parts of integers and can be manipulated and compared.

- The associative and distributive laws are useful ways to group and regroup numbers.

Chapter 12
Algebra
(And When to Use It)

The basics for math on the GRE are often used in the context of algebra. While comfort with algebraic operations is a good skill to have, plugging in numbers in lieu of doing the algebra is often a much faster way of getting the correct answer. This chapter provides an introduction to the strategies we call Plugging In and Plugging In the Answers. It also explains how to deal with exponents and square roots and how to manipulate equations, inequalities, quadratic equations, and simultaneous equations.

Why Plug In?

Plugging In is a powerful tool that can greatly enhance your math score, but you may be wondering why you should Plug In when algebra works just fine. Here's why:

Plugging In converts algebra problems into arithmetic problems. No matter how good you are at algebra, you're better at arithmetic. Why? Because you use arithmetic every day, every time you go to a store, balance your checkbook, or tip a waiter. Chances are you rarely use algebra in your day-to-day activities.

Plugging In is oftentimes more accurate than algebra. When you Plug In real numbers, you make the problems concrete rather than abstract. Once you're working with real numbers, it's easier to notice when and where you've messed up a calculation. It's much harder to see where you went wrong (or to even know you've done something wrong) when you're staring at a bunch of x's and y's.

The GRE allows the use of a calculator. A calculator can do arithmetic but it can't do algebra, so Plugging In allows you to take advantage of the calculator function.

ETS expects its students to attack the problems algebraically and many of the tricks and the traps built into the problem are designed to catch students who use algebra. By Plugging In, you'll avoid these pitfalls.

As you can see, there are a number of excellent reasons for Plugging In. Mastering this technique can have a significant impact on your score.

PLUGGING IN

Many of the hardest questions you might encounter on the GRE involve algebra. Algebra questions are generally difficult for two reasons. First, they are often complicated, multistep problems. Second, ETS studies the types of mistakes that people make when they solve questions using algebra. They generate wrong answers for the questions based on these common algebraic errors. So, if you aren't careful, you can make an algebraic mistake and still find your answer among the choices.

If you are one of the many students who take the GRE and struggle with algebra, you're in luck. Plugging In is a strategy that will turn even the hardest, messiest GRE algebra problem into an arithmetic problem.

Let's look at an example of how Plugging In can make a seemingly messy algebra problem much easier to work with.

Dale gives Miranda x bottles of water. He gives Marcella two fewer bottles of water than he gives to Miranda and he gives Mary three more bottles of water than he gives to Marcella. How many bottles of water did Dale give to Miranda, Marcella, and Mary, in terms of x ?

○ $3x - 1$

○ $3x$

○ $3x + 1$

○ $3x + 2$

○ $x - 2$

Here's How to Crack It

This problem can definitely be solved using algebra. However, the use of Plugging In makes this problem much easier to solve. The problem has one variable in it, x, so start plugging in by picking a number for x. An easy number to use would be 10, so use your scratch paper and write down $x = 10$. Now read the problem again and follow the directions, only this time do the arithmetic instead of the algebra on the scratch paper. So, Miranda gets 10 bottles of water. The problem then states that Marcella gets two fewer bottles of water than Miranda, so Marcella gets 8 bottles. Next, Mary gets three more bottles than Marcella, so Mary gets 11 bottles. That's a total of 10 + 8 + 11 = 29 bottles of water. The problem asks how many bottles of water Dale gave to Miranda, Marcella, and Mary, so the answer to the question is 29 bottles of water.

This is the target answer, which should always be circled on the scratch paper so you don't forget it. Now Plug In 10 for the variable x in all the answer choices and see which answer choice equals 29. Be sure to check all five answer choices.

(A)	$3(10) - 1 = 29$	Looks good!
(B)	$3(10) = 30$	Nope
(C)	$3(10) + 1 = 31$	Nope
(D)	$3(10) + 2 = 32$	Nope
(E)	$10 - 2 = 8$	Nope

The correct answer to this question is (A), and if you successfully completed the algebra you would have gotten the same answer. Pretty easy compared to the algebra, huh?

———————————○———————————

As you can see, Plugging In turned this algebra problem into an arithmetic problem. The best news is that you can solve any problem with variables by using Plugging In.

Here are the steps:

Step 1: **Recognize the opportunity.** See variables in the problem and answer choices? Get ready to Plug In. The minute you see variables in a question or answer choices, you should start thinking about opportunities to Plug In.

Step 2: **Set up the scratch paper.** Plugging In is designed to make your life easier. Why make it harder again by trying to solve problems in your head? You are not saving any notable amount of time by trying to work out all the math without writing it down, so use the scratch paper. Even if it seems like an easy question of translating a word problem into an algebraic equation, remember that there are trap answer choices. Whenever you recognize the opportunity to Plug In, set up the scratch paper by writing (A) through (E) down before you start to solve.

Plugging In
This technique can be achieved by following these five simple steps. Plugging in numbers in place of variables can make algebra problems much easier to solve.

Step 3: **Plug In.** If the question asks for "x apples," come up with a number for x. The goal here is to make your life easier, so plugging in numbers such as 2, 3, 5, 10, 100 are all good strategies. However, for the first attempt at Plugging In on any given problem, avoid the numbers 1 or 0. These numbers can oftentimes create a situation in which more than one answer choice produces the target answer. If you Plug In a number and the math starts getting difficult (for example, you start getting fractions or negative numbers), don't be afraid to just change the number you Plug In.

Step 4: **Solve for the Target.** The Target is the value the problem asks you to solve for. Remember to always circle the Target so you don't forget what it is you are solving for.

Step 5: **Check all of the answer choices.** Anywhere you see a variable, Plug In the number you have written down for that variable and do the arithmetic. The correct answer is the one that matches the Target. If more than one answer matches the Target, just Plug In a different number for the variables and test the answer choice you were unable to eliminate with the original number.

Can I Just Plug In Anything?

You can Plug In any numbers you like, as long as they're consistent with any restrictions stated in the problem, but it's more effective if you use easy numbers. What makes a number easy? That depends on the problem, but in most cases, lesser numbers are easier to work with than greater numbers. Usually, it's best to start with a lesser number, such as 2 for example. Avoid the numbers 0 and 1; both 0 and 1 have special properties, which you'll hear more about later. You want to avoid these numbers because they will often make more than one answer choice match the target. For example, if we Plug In 0 for a variable such as x, then the answers 2x, 3x, and 5x would all equal 0. Also, try to avoid plugging in any numbers that are repeats of numbers that show up a lot in the question or answer choices. If you can avoid plugging in 0, 1, or repeat numbers, you can oftentimes avoid situations that may make you have to Plug In again.

> Plug In numbers that make the calculations EASY.

Good Numbers Make Life Easier

However, numbers of lesser value aren't always the best choices for Plugging In. What makes a number good to work with depends on the context of the problem, so be on the lookout for clues to help choose the numbers you are going to use to Plug In. For instance, in a problem involving percentages the numbers 10 and 100 are good numbers to use. In a problem that involves minutes or seconds any multiple or factor of 60, such as 30 or 120 are often good choices.

Let's use the Plugging In steps from above to work through the following problem.

Mara has six more than twice as many apples as Robert and half as many apples as Sheila. If Robert has x apples, then, in terms of x, how many apples do Mara, Robert, and Sheila have combined?

○ $2x + 6$

○ $2x + 9$

○ $3x + 12$

○ $4x + 9$

○ $7x + 18$

Here's How to Crack It

Step 1: **Recognize the opportunity.** Look at the question. There is the variable x in the question stem and the answer choices. This is a clear indication to start thinking about Plugging In.

Step 2: **Set up the scratch paper.** Keep yourself organized by listing (A) through (E) on the scratch paper. Leave some space to work the problem.

Step 3: **Plug In.** Plug In a good number. The problem states that Robert has x apples, and doesn't indicate that the number of apples needs to be anything specific, so choose an easy number such as $x = 4$.

Step 4: **Solve for the Target.** Now use $x = 4$ to read the problem again and solve for the target. The problem states that "Mara has six more than twice as many apples as Robert." If Robert has 4 apples, then Mara must have 14. Next, the problem states that Mara has "half as many apples as Sheila." That means that Sheila must have 28 apples. The question asks for the number of apples that Robert, Sheila, and Mara have combined so add 4 + 14 + 28 = 46 apples. This is the target number, so circle it.

> Always be on the lookout for variables, and if you see them, get ready to Plug In!

Step 5: **Check all of the answer choices.** Plug In $x = 4$ for all of the variables in the answer choices and use the scratch paper to solve them, eliminating any answer choice that does not equal 46.

    (A) $2(4) + 6 = 14$—This is not 46, so eliminate it.

    (B) $2(4) + 9 = 17$—Eliminate this too.

    (C) $3(4) + 12 = 24$—Also not 46, so eliminate this.

    (D) $4(4) + 9 = 25$—This is still not 46, so eliminate this as well.

    (E) $7(4) + 18 = 46$—Bingo! This is the correct answer.

On the GRE, Plug In for variables in the question and answer choices. Remember to Plug In numbers that will be easy to work with based on the problem, as some numbers can end up causing more trouble than they are worth.

When Plugging In within the Math section of the GRE, follow these general rules (we'll get more specific later on):

1. Avoid plugging in 0 or 1. These numbers, while easy to work with, have special properties.
2. Avoid plugging in numbers that are already in the problem; this often leads to more than one answer matching your target.
3. Avoid plugging in the same number for multiple variables. For example, if a problem has x, y, and z in it, pick three different numbers to Plug In for the three variables.
4. Avoid plugging in conversion numbers. For example, don't use 60 for a problem involving hours, minutes, or seconds.

Finally, Plugging In is a powerful tool, but you **must remember to always check all five answer choices when you Plug In.** In certain cases, two answer choices can yield the same target. This doesn't necessarily mean you did anything wrong; you just hit some bad luck. When this happens, just Plug In different numbers, solve for a new target, and recheck the answer choices that worked the first time.

Strategy!
At the right is a tried-and-true Princeton Review strategy, PITA (which has nothing to do with the delicious type of bread).

PLUGGING IN THE ANSWERS (PITA)

Some questions may not have variables in them but will try to tempt you into using algebra to solve them. We call these Plugging In the Answers questions, or PITA for short. These are almost always difficult problems but once you recognize the opportunity to PITA, these questions turn into simple arithmetic questions. In fact, the hardest part of these problems is often identifying them as opportunities for PITA. The beauty of these questions is that they take advantage of one of the inherent limitations of a multiple-choice test: the answers are given to you. ETS has actually given you the answers, and only one of them is correct. The essence of this technique is to systematically Plug In the Answers to see which answer choice works given the information in the problem.

Let's look at an example of a Plugging In the Answers question.

Are you tempted to try to set up an algebraic equation? Are there no quickly identifiable variables? Are the answer choices real numbers? Try Plugging In the Answers!

An office supply store sells binder clips that cost 14 cents each and binder clips that cost 16 cents each. If a customer purchases 85 binder clips from this store at a total cost of $13.10, how many 14-cent binder clips does the customer purchase?

○   16

○   25

○   30

○   35

○   65

Here's How to Crack It

ETS would like you to solve this problem using algebra, and there is a good chance that you started to think about the variables you could use to set up some equations to solve this problem. That urge to do algebra is actually the first sign that you can solve this problem using Plugging In the Answers. Other signs that you can Plug In the Answers to solve this problem are that the question asks for a specific amount and that the numbers in the answer choices reflect that specific amount. With all these signs, it's definitely time to Plug In the Answers!

Start by setting up your scratch paper. To do so, just list the five answer choices in a column, with the actual numbers included. Since the problem is asking for the number of 14-cent binder clips purchased, these answer choices have to represent the number of 14-cent binder clips purchased. Label this column 14¢.

The answer choices will always be listed in either ascending or descending numerical order, so when you Plug In the Answers, start with (C). By determining whether or not (C) works, you can eliminate the other answer choices that are either greater or less than (C), based on the result of this answer choice. This effectively cuts the amount of work you need to do in half. So, start with the idea that the customer purchased 30 binder clips that cost 14 cents each. What can you figure out with this information? You'd know that the total spent on these binder clips is 30 × $0.14 = $4.20. So, make a column with the heading "amount spent" and write $4.20 next to (C). Now, look for the next thing you'd know from this problem. If the customer purchased a total of 85 binder clips and 30 of them cost 14 cents each, that means that the customer purchased 55 binder clips at 16¢ each. Make another column with the heading "16¢" and write 55 in the row for (C). Next, make another column for the amount spent on 16-cent binder clips, label it "amount spent," and write 55 × $0.16 = $8.80 under this column in the row for (C). The next piece of information in the problem is that the customer spends a total of $13.10 on the binder clips. This information allows you to determine if (C) is correct. All Plugging In the Answers questions contain a condition like this that lets you decide if the answer is correct. In this case, $4.20 + $8.80 = $13.00, which is less than $13.10, so eliminate (C). Since the total was not great enough, you can determine that to increase the total, the customer must have purchased more 16-cent binder clips. Since (D) and (E) would increase the number of 14-cent binder clips purchased, they cannot be correct. Eliminate (D) and (E) as well.

Now, do the same steps starting with (B). If the customer purchased 25 of the 14-cent binder clips, they cost $3.50. The customer also purchased 60 of the 16-cent binder clips at a cost of $9.60. The total amount spent is $3.50 + $9.60 = $13.10. Since this matches the amount spent in the problem, (B) is correct.

Here's what your scratch paper should look like after this problem:

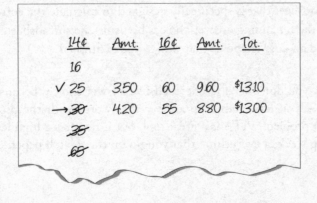

When you want to Plug In the Answers, here are the steps that you should follow.

Step 1:   **Recognize the opportunity.** There are three ways to do this. The first indications are the phrases "how much…," "how many…," or "what is the value of…." When you see one of these phrases in a question, it's a good indicator that you may be able to Plug In the Answers. The second tip-off is specific numbers in the answer choices in ascending or descending order. The last tip-off is your own inclination. If you find yourself tempted to write your own algebraic formulas and to invent your own variables to solve the problem, it's a good sign that you can Plug In the Answers.

Step 2:   **Set up the scratch paper.** The minute you recognize the opportunity, list the numbers in the answer choices in a column on the scratch paper.

Step 3:   **Label the first column.** The question asks you to find a specific number of something so the answer choices must be options for that number. At the top of the column above the answer choices, write down what the numbers represent.

Step 4:   **Start with (C).** Choice (C) will always be the number in the middle. This is the most efficient place to start because it will allow you to eliminate as many as three answer choices if it is wrong.

Step 5:   **Create your spreadsheet.** Use (C) to work through the problem. It is always easier to understand the problem using a specific number. Work through the problem one step at a time, and every time you have to do something with the number, make a new column. Each column is a step in solving the problem that you may need to use again with a different answer choice, so don't leave anything out.

Step 6:   **Repeat with the other answer choices.** On single-answer multiple-choice questions, only one answer choice can work. If (C) is correct, you are finished with the problem. If it is not correct, you may be able to determine if the value of the number is too great or too small. If it is too great, you can eliminate it and every answer choice that is greater. The same thing can be done if the value of the resulting answer is less than the value indicated by the problem. At this point, you have basically created your own little spreadsheet that is specifically designed to calculate the correct answer. Check the remaining answer choices by using the spreadsheet. As soon as you find an answer choice that works, you're finished.

On PITA questions, you don't need to check all five answer choices because only one of them can be correct. Once you have found an answer that works with the problem, select it and move on to the next problem. PITA is a great tool, but it requires a high level of organization, so make sure to keep track of everything that you do on the scratch paper.

PLUGGING IN ON QUANTITATIVE COMPARISON QUESTIONS

Quantitative comparison, or quant comp, questions with variables can be extremely tricky because the obvious answer is often wrong, whereas finding the correct answer may involve a scenario that is not commonly thought of. On the other hand, there is a simple setup and approach that you can use to help find the correct answers. As always, whenever you see variables, replace them with real numbers. On quant comp questions, however, it is crucial that you Plug In more than once and specifically that you Plug In different kinds of numbers that may not occur to you to think of initially. A good way to help you think of this is to always keep the nature of the answer choices in mind. Picking (A) means that you believe that the quantity in column A will *always* be greater than Quantity B—*no matter what number you Plug In.* Choice (B) means that the quantity in column B will *always* be greater than Quantity A—*no matter what number you Plug In,* and so forth. To prove that one of these statements is true you have to Plug In every possible number that could change the outcome. Don't worry. We have a simple process to help figure out what to Plug In and how to track your progress as you do.

> Quantitative comparison questions often test your knowledge of the properties of fractions, zero, one, negatives, and other weird numbers.

Here are the steps:

Step 1: **Recognize the opportunity.** The first seven or eight questions of any Math section will be quant comp. When a quant comp question appears and you see variables, you know that you can Plug In.

Step 2: **Set up the scratch paper.** The minute you see quant comp and variables, set up the scratch paper. The recommended setup should look something like the diagram below. Place Quantity A and B on either side. Quant comp questions have only four potential answer choices, so write (A), (B), (C), and (D) down as well, so you can eliminate answers as you go. Finally, leave space to write down the numbers that you Plug In for the variables in between the Quantities, so you can stay organized.

$$\underline{A} \quad a\,b\,c\,d \quad \underline{B}$$
$$y =$$
$$y =$$
$$y =$$

Step 3: **Plug In and eliminate.** Start with an easy number, just like outlined in the earlier Plugging In section, but make sure that you also follow any conditions in the problem. With the number you plugged in for the variable, solve for Quantity A and Quantity B and write the solutions down. If Quantity A is greater than Quantity B, eliminate (B) and (C). If Quantity B is greater than Quantity A, eliminate (A) and (C). If both quantities are the same, eliminate (A) and (B).

Step 4:   **Plug In again using FROZEN numbers.** On quant comp questions with variables, you always need to Plug In more than once and the second time you do it, you need to use FROZEN numbers. FROZEN is an acronym that will be explained in the next section, as well the entire concept behind why to Plug In more than once, so keep reading!

On quant comp questions, Plug In easy numbers such as 2 or 5, and eliminate two choices. Then Plug In FROZEN numbers (Fractions, Repeats, One, Zero, Extremes, Negatives) to try to disprove your first answer. If different numbers give you different answers, you've proved that the answer is (D).

Always Plug In More Than Once on Quant Comp Questions

Quant comp questions only have four options for answer choices but one of those options, (D), can be selected if the relationship between Quantity A and Quantity B cannot be determined based on the information given. After you Plug In the first time, you need to Plug In again, but this time you need to try to choose a number that will produce a different outcome for the question. While the first time you Plug In you can usually reliably eliminate two of answer choices (A), (B), or (C), you Plug In again to try to make sure that you can eliminate (D). Choice (D) can be eliminated only when you have a high level of confidence that no matter what number you Plug In, the answer will always remain the same. If even one of the numbers you choose creates a different answer, (D) should be selected.

So, to eliminate (D), you need to choose a different number. But what makes a number different and what makes for a good number to choose that might create a different outcome for the problem? When you Plug In for the second (or sometimes third or fourth) time in a quant comp question, you should pick a FROZEN number. FROZEN is an acronym that highlights different types of numbers and it stands for

Fractions
Repeats
One
Zero
Extremes
Negatives

Pay Attention!
Note that on general GRE Math questions, conversion numbers (60 if a question is about minutes, hours, seconds) are a bad idea, but for quant comp questions, specifically, they are a great idea. This is because for quant comp Qs, we are seeking a number that will produce a different outcome for Quantity A and Quantity B, so Plugging In a repeat is great.

Fractions are numbers such as $\frac{1}{2}$ or $\frac{1}{4}$ that are great to use if the problem contains exponents or roots, as fractions respond to these two stimuli in a different way from whole numbers. Repeats are numbers that are found in the question stem, can be used in both Quantities, or numbers that are implied by the question stem (such as using the number 60 if the question is about seconds, minutes, or hours). The numbers 1 and 0 are special because they can result in two quantities being equal to each other, and each has a unique effect on other numbers. Extreme numbers are numbers such as 10 or 100 that should be used to see if the relationship between the quantities changes for numbers that are greater than the one that was initially chosen. Negative numbers, such as –2 or –3, are numbers that create different outcomes when plugged in for variables, as they can make Quantities negative or positive, which can alter the outcome.

FROZEN numbers can also be combined to create different numbers, such as -100, $-\frac{1}{2}$, or -1. ETS will often create a quant comp question that has a correct answer that depends on using these types of numbers. They do that because they know that most people will not think of these numbers, which is why it is important to Plug In more than once and, when you do, use FROZEN numbers.

Let's look at an example problem:

Quantity A	Quantity B
$2x^3$	$4x^2$

○ Quantity A is greater.

○ Quantity B is greater.

○ The two quantities are equal.

○ The relationship cannot be determined from the information given.

Here's How to Crack It

Step 1: **Recognize the opportunity.** This is a quant comp question with variables in the quantities, so this is a Plug In problem.

Step 2: **Set up the scratch paper.** Get yourself organized and ready to answer the problem by setting up the scratch paper.

Step 3: **Plug In.** Let's start with an easy number such as 2. Plug in 2 for x. When $x = 2$, Quantity A is $2 \times 2^3 = 16$, and Quantity B is $4 \times 2^2 = 16$ as well. Since both quantities are equal in this case, neither Quantity A nor Quantity B is always greater than the other, so eliminate (A) and (B).

Step 4: **Plug In again using FROZEN numbers.** Now look at the problem and try to decide on a FROZEN number for x that may create a different answer. Try One. If $x = 1$, then Quantity A is $2 \times 1^3 = 2$ and Quantity B is $4 \times 1^2 = 4$. Quantity B is now greater than Quantity A, which means that (C) is incorrect. Eliminate (C) and select (D), which is the correct answer.

If you chose to follow the recommended setup for the scratch paper, it should look like this:

You might also have noticed that choosing different FROZEN numbers, such as Fractions or Zero, would also yield a different result that would have allowed you to eliminate (C). This is not uncommon, as ETS is hoping you forget to use these FROZEN numbers when Plugging In. Make sure you use these numbers aggressively on quant comp problems because they can radically affect the relationship between the two Quantities.

PLUGGING IN ON FRACTION AND PERCENT PROBLEMS

Plugging In on fraction and percent problems is a great way to make these problems much easier.

Now that you've become familiar with fractions and percents, we'll show you a great method for solving many of these problems. When you come to regular multiple-choice questions, or multiple-choice, multiple-answer questions, that involve fractions or percents, you can simply Plug In a number and work through the problem using that number. This approach works even when the problem doesn't have variables in it. Why? Because, as you know, fractions and percents express only a relationship between numbers—the actual numbers don't matter. For example, look at the following problem:

A recent survey of registered voters in City X found that $\frac{1}{3}$ of the respondents support the mayor's property tax plan. Of those who did not support the mayor's plan, $\frac{1}{8}$ indicated they would not vote to reelect the mayor if the plan were implemented. Of all the respondents, what fraction indicated that they would not vote for the mayor if the plan were enacted?

○ $\frac{1}{16}$

○ $\frac{1}{12}$

○ $\frac{1}{6}$

○ $\frac{1}{3}$

○ $\frac{2}{3}$

> What important information is missing from the problem?

Here's How to Crack It

Even though there are no variables in this problem, we can still Plug In. On fraction and percent problems, ETS will often leave out one key piece of information: the total. Plugging In for that missing value will make your life much easier. What crucial information did ETS leave out of this problem? The total number of respondents. So let's Plug In a value for it. Let's say that there were 24 respondents to the survey. 24 is a good number to use because we'll have to work with $\frac{1}{3}$ and $\frac{1}{8}$, so we want a number that's divisible by both those fractions. Working through the problem with our number, we see that $\frac{1}{3}$ of the respondents support the plan. $\frac{1}{3}$ of 24 is 8, so that means 16 people do not support the plan. Next, the problem says that $\frac{1}{8}$ of those who do not support the plan will not vote for the mayor. $\frac{1}{8}$ of 16 is 2, so 2 people won't vote for the mayor. Now we just have to answer the question: Of all respondents, what fraction will not vote for the mayor? Well, there were 24 total respondents and we figured out that 2 aren't voting. So that's $\frac{2}{24}$, or $\frac{1}{12}$. Choice (B) is the one we want.

ALGEBRA: OPERATIONS WITH VARIABLES

While Plugging In is a great strategy to make algebra problems easy on the GRE by turning them into arithmetic, in many cases being comfortable manipulating variables in an equation is necessary to answering a question. Plugging In will help you solve for a variable in a question, but sometimes the question requires only that you manipulate an equation to get the correct answer.

Dealing with Variables

The previous chapter familiarized you with number concepts and the previous section showed you how to turn algebra into arithmetic by using Plugging In. However, it's time to learn the basics of dealing with variables and manipulating equations to help make problems easier to work with and give you the best opportunity to optimize your score.

Manipulating Equations

When working with equations, you can do pretty much anything you want to them as long as you follow the golden rule:

> Whatever you do on one side of the equals sign you must also do on the other side.

Solving for One Variable

> Don't assume you'll always need to solve for the variable on the GRE; sometimes you'll simply have to manipulate the equation to get the answer.

Let's begin the discussion of manipulating equations with one variable by solving for one variable. When presented with an equation with one variable, start by isolating the variable on one side of the equation and the numbers on the other side. You can do this by adding, subtracting, multiplying, or dividing both sides of the equation by the same number. Just remember that anything you do to one side of an equation, you must do to the other side. Let's look at a simple example:

$$3x - 4 = 5$$

Here's How to Crack It

When presented with a problem like this, your goal is to isolate the variable on one side of the equation with all the real numbers, or constants, on the other. In the example above, begin manipulating this question by adding 4 to both sides of the equation. In general, you can eliminate negative numbers by adding them to both sides of the equation, just as you can eliminate positives by subtracting them from both sides of the equation.

$$3x - 4 = 5$$
$$\underline{+\ 4 = +\ 4}$$
$$3x = 9$$

The variable is not quite isolated yet, as it is still being multiplied by 3. In the same way that you manipulated the equation earlier by moving the 4 to the other side of the equation, you must move the 3. Since the 3 is being multiplied to the variable, move it by doing the opposite operation, in this case division. This allows you to solve for x and finish the problem.

$$\frac{3x}{3} = \frac{9}{3}$$

$$x = 3$$

Let's try another one:

$$5x - 13 = 12 - 20x$$

Here's How to Crack It

Again, we want to get all the x values on the same side of the equation. This time, however, there is more than one instance of x so begin the question by combining the x values.

$$5x - 13 = 12 - 20x$$
$$\underline{+\ 20x \qquad\qquad +\ 20x}$$
$$25x - 13 = 12$$

As the problems get more involved, make sure to keep yourself organized by utilizing the scratch paper given to you.

Now that the values of x are combined, isolate the x by moving the negative 13 to the other side of the question.

$$25x - 13 = 12$$
$$\underline{+\ 13 + 13}$$
$$25x = 25$$

Solve for x by finishing the isolation by moving the 25 that it is being multiplied by.

$$25x = 25$$
$$\frac{25x}{25} = \frac{25}{25}$$
$$x = 1$$

Let's try one more that is slightly more complicated.

$$5x + \frac{3}{2} = 7x$$

You must always do the same thing to both sides of an equation.

Here's How to Crack It

The first thing you probably notice here is the fraction. Whenever you see an equation like this that contains a fraction, begin by "clearing" the fraction. To clear the fraction, multiply all the terms in the equation by the denominator of the fraction. In this case, multiply all the terms by 2.

$$10x + 3 = 14x$$

Notice how all the terms have by multiplied by 2! This is very important, so don't forget to do it! Now, manipulate the equation to collect all the x's on the same side of the equation.

$$
\begin{array}{r}
10x + 3 = 14x \\
-10x \quad\ \ -10x \\
\hline
3 = 4x
\end{array}
$$

Now finish isolating the x by moving the 4.

$$3 = 4x$$

$$\frac{3}{4} = \frac{4x}{4}$$

$$\frac{3}{4} = x$$

WORKING WITH TWO VARIABLES

Many times, however, an equation on the GRE will involve two variables. An example of an equation with two variables looks like this:

$$3x + 10y = 64$$

Here's How to Crack It

The important thing to note about this situation is that we cannot solve this equation. Why, you ask? The problem is that since there are two variables, there are many possible solutions to this equation, all of which are equally valid. For example, plugging in the values $x = 8$ and $y = 4$ would satisfy the equation. But the equation would also be satisfied if you plugged in the values $x = 10$ and $y = 3.4$. Therefore, the GRE cannot test an equation with two variables without either providing a definitive way to solve for one of the variables, or providing a second equation. By giving two equations, you are able to find definitive values for the variables. So a more likely problem would look something like this:

You can't solve an equation with two variables unless you have a second equation.

$$3x + 10y = 64$$
$$6x - 10y = 8$$

Now there are 2 variables and 2 equations, which means we can solve for the variables. When two equations are given, look to combine them by adding or subtracting the entire equations. We do this so that we can cancel out one of the variables, leaving us with a simple equation with one variable. In this case, it's easier to add the two equations together, which will eliminate the y variable as seen below.

$$
\begin{array}{rl}
3x + 10y & = 64 \\
+6x - 10y & = 8 \\
\hline
9x \quad\quad & = 72
\end{array}
$$

Add these two equations to get $9x = 72$. This is a simple equation, just like the ones discussed in the previous section, which we can solve to find $x = 8$. Once we've done that, we can solve for the other variable by inserting the value of x into one of the original equations. For example, if we substitute $x = 8$ into the first equation, we get $3(8) + 10y = 64$, and we can solve to find that $y = 4$.

The GRE will rarely give you two equations that line up as nicely as the above example does, though. You are more likely to find two equations with two variables and, while the variables match, the numbers associated with the variables are not equal. In this case, you will need to manipulate one equation so the numbers associated with a variable are equal. Doing this will allow the elimination of a variable when the two equations are added or subtracted. Try the next problem as an example.

$$4x + 7y = 41$$
$$2x + 3y = 19$$

Here's How to Crack It

Notice here that the numbers associated with the variables are not equal, which means that you cannot eliminate a variable. Adding the two equations yields $6x + 10y = 60$. That doesn't help; it's a single equation with two variables, which is impossible to solve. Subtracting the equations leaves $2x + 4y = 22$, which is also a single equation with two variables. To solve this system of equations, we need to make the coefficient for one of the variables in the first equation equal to the coefficient for that same variable in the second equation. In this case, try multiplying the second equation by 2.

$$2(2x + 3y) = 2(19)$$

This gives us the following:

$$4x + 6y = 38$$

Now we can subtract this equation from the first equation. Doing this operation yields $y = 3$. Now we can substitute $y = 3$ into either one of the original equations to find that $x = 5$.

Simultaneous Equations

Thus far, we have learned how to manipulate equations with one variable and two equations with two variables in order to solve for the variables. However, it is not uncommon for ETS to give you two equations and ask you to use them to find the value of a given expression. Much like manipulating two equations with two variables, all you need to do is add or subtract the two equations! The only difference is this time you won't end up solving for an individual variable.

Here's an example:

If $5x + 4y = 6$ and $4x + 3y = 5$, then what does $x + y$ equal?

Here's How to Crack It

Remember that the problem is asking you to solve for $x + y$. This may appear like you need to solve for the variables individually, but try to add or subtract the equations first to see what they yield. First, try adding the two equations together.

$$5x + 4y = 6$$
$$+ \ 4x + 3y = 5$$
$$\overline{9x + 7y = 11}$$

Since the problem wants the value of $x + y$ and this gives us the value of $9x + 7y$, this is not useful. So try subtracting the two equations.

$$5x + 4y = 6$$
$$- \ (4x + 3y = 5)$$
$$\overline{x + \ \ y = 1}$$

Bingo. The value of the expression $(x + y)$ is exactly what we're looking for. You could have tried to solve for each variable individually and solved the problem that way, but since the question is asking for the value of an expression, it was easier to manipulate the equations like this. So remember, on the GRE, you may see two equations written horizontally. Now you know that you don't need complicated math to solve them! Just rewrite the two equations, putting one on top of the other, and simply add or subtract them.

INEQUALITIES

The difference between an equation and an inequality is that in an equation one side always equals the other and in an inequality one side does *not* equal the other. Equations contain equal signs, while inequalities contain one of the following symbols:

$\neq$	is not equal to
$>$	is greater than
$<$	is less than
$\geq$	is greater than or equal to
$\leq$	is less than or equal to

The point of the inequality sign always points to the lesser value.

The good news is that inequalities are manipulated in the same way that you manipulated any of the equations in the previous sections of this chapter. However, there is one critical difference. When you multiply or divide both sides of an inequality by a negative number, the direction of the inequality symbol must change. So, if the inequality $x > y$ is multiplied by -1, the resulting inequality is $-x < -y$.

To see this rule in action, take a look at the following inequality:

$$12 - 6x > 0$$

Here's How to Crack It

There are two ways to solve this inequality. You could manipulate this inequality without ever multiplying or dividing by a negative number by just adding $6x$ to both sides and then dividing both sides of the inequality by the positive 6. In this case, the sign would not change, as seen below.

$$
\begin{array}{r}
12 - 6x > 0 \\
\underline{+\ 6x > +\ 6x} \\
12 > 6x
\end{array}
$$

$$\frac{12}{6} > \frac{6x}{6}$$

$$2 > x$$

The other way to solve this inequality is to subtract 12 from both sides first. This will create a situation in which you need to divide both sides of the equation by -6, as shown below.

$$
\begin{array}{r}
12 - 6x > 0 \\
\underline{-12 \qquad > -12} \\
-6x > -12
\end{array}
$$

$$\frac{-6x}{-6} < \frac{-12}{-6}$$

$$x < 2$$

> Flip the sign! When you multiply or divide both sides of an inequality by a negative number, the greater than/less than sign points the opposite way.

Notice that the sign flipped because you divided both sides by a negative number, but the answer for both methods of solving this inequality is the same thing. The first answer says that the number 2 is greater than x, and the second says that x is less than the number 2!

Inequalities show up on the GRE in a variety of ways. For instance, ETS may give you a range for two variables and then ask you to combine them in some way. This type of problem looks like the following question:

If $0 \le x \le 10$ and $-10 \le y \le -1$, then what is the range for $x - y$?

Here's How to Crack It

First, determine what the question is asking you to do. The question is asking you to solve for the range for the expressions $x - y$. To determine this, you need to consider all possible combinations of $x - y$. Since the inequalities are ranges themselves, find the greatest and least possible values of $x - y$ by calculating the largest x minus the largest y, the largest x minus the least y, the least x minus the largest y, and the least x minus the least y. The greatest value of x is 10 and the least value of x is 0. The greatest value of y is −1 and the least value is −10. Calculate these values and keep yourself organized by writing this all down on the scratch paper.

The calculations look as follows:

$$10 - (-1) = 11$$
$$10 - (-10) = 20$$
$$0 - (-1) = 1$$
$$0 - (-10) = 10$$

Since the least possible value of $x - y$ is $0 - (-1) = 1$ and the greatest possible value of $x - y$ is $10 - (-10) = 20$, the range is $1 \le x - y \le 20$.

QUADRATIC EQUATIONS

A quadratic equation is a special type of equation that generally shows up on the GRE in two forms. There is more to say about quadratic equations than simply stating that they are special types of equations, but that conversation is beyond the scope of this book. Instead, let's cover the two primary forms that quadratic equations take on the GRE and discuss how to respond to each of them.

On the GRE, quadratic equations are typically found as either full, expanded equations or fully factored equations.

Expanded Quadratic Equations

An expanded quadratic equation looks like this:

$$x^2 + 10x + 24 = 0$$

The hallmarks of this questions is a variable that is squared, a variable that multiplied by some coefficient, and then a coefficient. The operations in the equation are either addition or subtraction.

Occasionally, the GRE will try to disguise a fully expanded quadratic equation by moving terms around or including additional terms. But, if you can recognize the potential to create the more standard expanded quadratic, then you can treat these equations like any other expanded quadratic. For example, the GRE may try to disguise a standard expanded quadratic by writing it like this:

$$x^3 + 10x^2 + 24x = 0$$

While this may look similar to the previous instance of the equation, the exponents in the second instance of the equation are greater. But, this equation can be manipulated to look more like the standard quadratic by factoring out a value of x.

$$x(x^2 + 10x + 24) = 0$$

Now the information inside the parentheses looks exactly like the standard quadratic, and it can be manipulated by factoring the entire equation.

Factoring An Expanded Quadratic

The goal of factoring an expanded quadratic is to break the equation apart into values that would make the equation true. In the case of quadratics on the GRE, the way to make the equation true is to find the values of the variable that make the expression equal to 0. These are referred to as the roots of the equation. So, the roots of a quadratic equation are the values of the variable that make the expression equal to 0. For a standard expanded quadratic on the GRE, there are two correct roots for the equation.

To find these roots, you will need to factor the equation. Let's look at how to factor a quadratic and the steps that should be used to find the roots of the equation.

$$x^2 + 10x + 24 = 0$$

1. Begin by separating the x^2 into two values of x and placing them each inside of their own parentheses.

$$x^2 + 10x + 24 = 0$$
$$(x\quad)(x\quad) = 0$$

2. Find the factors of the third term that, when added or subtracted, yield the second term. In this case, the third term is 24 and the second term is 10. The factors of 24 are: 1×24, 2×12, 3×8, and 4×6. There are two pairs of factors that can be added or subtracted to produce a value of 10. Those factors are 2×12 and 4×6. So, you may need to try both pairs. Begin with 4 and 6 and place them inside the parentheses.

$$x^2 + 10x + 24 = 0$$
$$(x\quad 4)(x\quad 6) = 0$$

3. Determine the operations that correspond to each term. The combination of the signs and the term have to yield the second term of the original equation when added and the third term of the original equation when multiplied. In case this, because the second term of the original equation is 10 and the third term is 24, and both are positive, both operations are addition.

$$x^2 + 10x + 24 = 0$$
$$(x + 4)(x + 6) = 0$$

4. Finally, solve for the roots of the equation. Remember that the roots of the equation are the values of x that yield a value of 0 in the original equation. Therefore, to solve for the roots, take each element of the factored equation, set it equal to 0, and solve for x.

$$x^2 + 10x + 24 = 0$$
$$(x + 4)(x + 6) = 0$$
$$(x + 4) = 0 \text{ and } (x + 6) = 0$$
$$x = -4 \text{ and } x = -6$$

Therefore, the roots of the equation are −4 and −6. If these values are substituted for x in the equation, the equation is true.

Here's an example:

$$x^2 + 2x - 15 = 0$$

Quantity A   **Quantity B**

2   x

○ Quantity A is greater.

○ Quantity B is greater.

○ The two quantities are equal.

○ The relationship cannot be determined from the information given.

Here's How to Crack It

There is a fully expanded quadratic in the stem of the question, and Quantity B is the value of the variable in the quadratic, so solve for the roots of the equation. Do this by factoring the quadratic. First, set up the quadratic by placing the variables inside adjacent parentheses, $(x \quad)(x \quad)$. Next, determine the factors of −15 that, when added together, produce a sum of 2. The only factor pair of −15 that sums to 2 is 5 and −3, so place these values into the newly formed quadratic. This yields $(x + 5)(x - 3) = 0$. Now, solve for the roots of the equation, which are $x + 5 = 0$ and $x - 3 = 0$, so the roots are $x = -5$ and $x = 3$. Evaluate the quantities. If $x = 3$, then Quantity B is greater, so eliminate (A) and (C). However, if $x = -5$, then Quantity A is greater, so eliminate (B). The correct answer is (D).

Let's try another one:

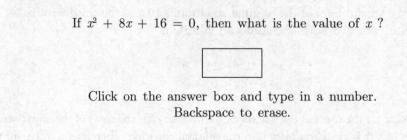

Click on the answer box and type in a number.
Backspace to erase.

Here's How to Crack It

Let's factor the equation. Start with $(x \quad)(x \quad)$. Next, find the factors of 16 that have a sum of 8. Of the factors of 16, only 4 and 4 have a sum of 8. Thus, we end up with $(x + 4)(x + 4) = 0$. Now, we need to solve the equation. If $x + 4 = 0$, then $x = -4$.

Fully Factored Quadratic Equations

The fully factored quadratic equation is the other form that quadratics typically take on the GRE. You have already seen what this fully factored form looks like near the end of the previous section. The fully factored form of a quadratic equation looks like this:

$$(x + 4)(x - 7) = 0$$

In this form, the roots of the equation can be easily found by solving for each value of x, as done in the previous section. When working with full factored quadratics, usually the goal is to expand the quadratic back to the standard form. The completed standard form of the equation above is:

$$x^2 - 3x - 28 = 0$$

The goal of working with a fully factored quadratic will be to manipulate it into its expanded form. To do this, it's necessary to employ the FOIL tactic.

FOIL

FOIL stands for *First*, *Outside*, *Inside*, and *Last*. This acronym represents the order by which the elements of the factored quadratic will need to be multiplied by one another to manipulate a fully factored quadratic equation into its expanded form. The end result is to multiply each term in the first set of parentheses by each term in the second set of parentheses and then add the results.

The *First* step indicates to multiply the first term in the first set of parentheses by the first term in the second set of parentheses. In the fully factored equation provided above, the first term in each of the sets of parentheses is x, which produces a product of x^2.

$$(x + 4)(x - 7) = 0$$
$$x^2 = 0$$

The *Outside* step indicates to multiply the terms that are on the "outside" of the terms inside the parentheses. The terms that are on the outside of the terms inside the parentheses are the first term of the first set of parentheses and the second term of the second set of parentheses. In this case, those terms are x and -7, respectively, to produce a product of -7.

$$(x + 4)(x - 7) = 0$$
$$x^2 - 7x = 0$$

The Inside step indicates to multiply the terms that are on the "inside" of the terms inside the parentheses. The terms that are on the inside of the terms inside the parentheses are the second term of the first set of parentheses and the first term of the second set of parentheses. In this case, these terms are 4 and x, respectively, to product a product of $4x$.

$$(x + 4)(x - 7) = 0$$
$$x^2 - 7x + 4x = 0$$

Finally, the *Last* step indicates to multiply the terms that are "last" of the terms inside the parentheses. The terms that are last are the second term of the first set of parentheses and the second term of the second set of parentheses. In this case, those terms are 4 and -7, which produces a product of -28.

$$(x + 4)(x - 7) = 0$$
$$x^2 - 7x + 4x - 28 = 0$$

Combine the terms in the equation to reveal the expanded form of the quadratic, $x^2 - 3x - 28 = 0$.

Let's look at a question that uses quadratics that you may see on the GRE.

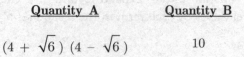

Quantity A	Quantity B
$(4 + \sqrt{6})(4 - \sqrt{6})$	10

○ Quantity A is greater.

○ Quantity B is greater.

○ The two quantities are equal.

○ The relationship cannot be determined
from the information given.

Here's How to Crack It

First, eliminate (D) because there are only numbers in this question, so the answer can be determined. Quantity A is in the format to be solved for using FOIL. Begin by multiplying the first terms, $4 \times 4 = 16$. Next, multiply the outer terms to yield $-4\sqrt{6}$. Multiply the inner terms to get $4\sqrt{6}$. Multiply the last terms to get -6. So, Quantity A is now $16 - 4\sqrt{6} + 4\sqrt{6} - 6$. The two inner terms cancel each other out and all that remains is $16 - 6$, or 10. Since Quantity B is also equal to 10, the two answer choices are equal and the correct answer is (C).

Common Quadratics

There are three types of quadratics that are considered common quadratics. They are considered common quadratics, because if you see a quadratic written in this exact form, it can always be factored out in the same way. Knowing these equations both in their factored and expanded forms may drastically save you time on these questions. These common quadratics are:

1. $x^2 - y^2 = (x + y)(x - y)$—this is sometimes referred to as the difference of squares.
2. $(x + y)^2 = x^2 + 2xy + y^2$
3. $(x - y)^2 = x^2 - 2xy + y^2$

You should devote some time to committing these common quadratics to memory.

Let's look at one more example.

⎯⎯⎯⎯⎯⎯⎯⎯⎯⎯⎯⎯○⎯⎯⎯⎯⎯⎯⎯⎯⎯⎯⎯⎯

If x and y are positive integers, and if $x^2 + 2xy + y^2 = 25$, then what is the value of $(x + y)^3$?

○   5

○   15

○   50

○   75

○   125

Here's How to Crack It

While this problem may look like a lot of work, if you have committed the common quadratic equations from earlier in this section to memory, then the answer is easier to come by. The equation in this question is reflective of the common quadratic: $x^2 + 2xy + y^2 = (x + y)^2$. The question tells us that $x^2 + 2xy + y^2$ is equal to 25, which means that $(x + y)^2$ is also equal to 25. Think of $x + y$ as one unit that, when squared, is equal to 25. Since this question specifies that x and y are positive integers, what positive integer squared equals 25? The number 5 does, so $x + y = 5$. The question is asking for $(x + y)^3$. In other words, what's 5 cubed, or $5 \times 5 \times 5$? The answer is (E), 125.

⎯⎯⎯⎯⎯⎯⎯⎯⎯⎯⎯⎯○⎯⎯⎯⎯⎯⎯⎯⎯⎯⎯⎯⎯

EXPONENTS AND SQUARE ROOTS

Finally, the last section of this chapter is going to deal with exponents and square roots. Questions with exponents and square roots are common on the GRE and solving these questions often requires manipulating the exponents or roots. Here's the information you need to know in order to work with them.

What Are Exponents?

Exponents are a sort of mathematical shorthand for repeated multiplication. Instead of writing $(2)(2)(2)(2)$, you can use an exponent and write 2^4. The little 4 is the **power** and the 2 is called the **base**. The power tells you how many times to multiply the base by itself. Knowing this terminology will be helpful in following the discussion in this section.

The Five Rules of Working with Exponents

For the GRE there are five major rules that apply when you work with exponents. The more comfortable you are with these rules, the more likely you will be to approach an exponent question with confidence and get the answer correct!

The first three rules deal with the combination and manipulation of exponents. Those three rules are represented by the acronym **MADSPM**, which stands for the following:

Multiply
Add

Divide
Subtract

Power
Multiply

These three rules will be explained in more detail shortly, but for now just remember the following conditions:

- When you see exponents with equal bases which are being **multiplied**, **add** the powers.
- When equal bases are **divided**, **subtract** the exponents.
- When an exponent is raised to a **power**, **multiply** the powers.

The fourth rule is the definition of a **negative exponent**. The fifth and final rule is the definition of a **zero exponent**.

The Multiply-Add Rule of Exponents

When two exponents with equal bases are multiplied, you must add the exponents. Consider the following example:

$$3^2 \times 3^3$$

As defined earlier, a power just tells you how many times to multiply a base by itself. So another way to write this expression is as follows:

$$3^2 \times 3^3 = (3 \times 3)(3 \times 3 \times 3) = 3^5$$

As you can see, the number of bases, which in this case is the integer 3, that are actually being multiplied together is five, as there are two 3's that are represented by 3^2 and three 3's that are represented by 3^3.

Now solve this question more quickly by using the multiply-add rule.

$$3^2 \times 3^3 = 3^{2+3} = 3^5$$

The Divide-Subtract Rule of Exponents

When two exponents with equal bases are divided, you must subtract the exponents. Consider the following example and expand the exponents to make it clear.

$$\frac{5^3}{5^2} = \frac{5 \times 5 \times 5}{5 \times 5} = \frac{5}{1} = 5$$

Now, instead of expanding the exponents, just apply the divide-subtract rule for the same problem.

$$\frac{5^3}{5^2} = 5^{3-2} = 5^1 = 5$$

The Power-Multiply Rule of Exponents

When an expression with an exponent is raised to another power, multiply the powers together. Consider the following example and expand the exponents to make it clear.

$$(6^2)^3 = (6^2)\,(6^2)\,(6^2) = (6 \times 6)\,(6 \times 6)\,(6 \times 6) = 6^6$$

Now, apply the power-multiply rule to solve the same problem.

$$(6^2)^3 = 6^{2 \times 3} = 6^6$$

For all of these rules, the bases must be the same. So, for example, you could not divide-subtract the expression $\frac{3^3}{2^2}$ because the bases are not the same.

Negative Exponents

A negative exponent is another way ETS uses exponents on the GRE. Consider the following example.

$$\frac{8^3}{8^5} = 8^{3-5} = 8^{-2} = \frac{1}{8^2} = \frac{1}{64}$$

So when you have a negative exponent, all that needs to be done is to put the entire expression in a fraction, with 1 in the numerator and the exponent in the denominator, and change the negative exponent to a positive. A term raised to a negative power is the reciprocal of that term raised to the positive power.

Zero Exponents

Sometimes ETS will give you an exponent question that, after you have successfully manipulated it, results in a base number raised to a power of 0. Any nonzero number raised to a power of 0 is equal to 1. Consider the following example.

$$4^3 \times 4^{-3} = 4^{3-3} = 4^0 = 1$$

Exponent Tips Beyond the Five Rules

Sometimes you will have an exponent problem for which none of the five rules discussed apply. If you reach this point, there are two tips to keep you moving forward.

Tip 1: Rewrite Terms Using Common Bases

ETS will always write questions that work out nicely, so if none of the bases in an exponent question seem to match up, see if you can find a way to rewrite the bases so that they match, and you will be able to use one of the five rules.

Tip 2: Look for a Way to Factor the Expression

Factoring the expression is often a way to reveal something about the exponent expression that you may not have noticed before. If you get stuck with an exponent question, try to factor the expression and see if there is a way to use one of the five rules.

It will be uncommon for ETS to test just one or two of these concepts on a GRE problem. Most times, two or more of these concepts will be combined to create a problem. Let's look at a couple of examples.

If $y \neq 0$, which of the following is equivalent to $\dfrac{y^9}{y\left(y^2\right)^3}$?

- ○ y
- ○ y^2
- ○ y^3
- ○ y^4
- ○ y^5

Here's How to Crack It

Begin by simplifying the denominator of the fraction. Use the power-multiply rule to combine $(y^2)^3$ into y^6. Since a number, or in this case a variable, by itself is the same thing as having that number or variable raised to a power of 1, use the add-multiply rule to combine $y(y^6)$ into y^7. Now use the divide-subtract rule to solve the problem; the correct answer is (B).

Let's look at another problem.

Quantity A	Quantity B
$15^{15} - 15^{14}$	$15^{14}(14) - 1$

○ Quantity A is greater.

○ Quantity B is greater.

○ The two quantities are equal.

○ The relationship cannot be determined from the information given.

Here's How to Crack It

The question wants you to compare the two quantities, but since none of the rules for exponents apply here, see if there is something else you can do to this problem. The expression in Quantity A can be factored, so begin there. Quantity A is now $15^{15} - 15^{14} = 15^{14}(15 - 1)$, which is the same thing as $15^{14}(14)$. Notice how this is the same as Quantity B, except Quantity B is 1 less than $15^{14}(14)$. Therefore, Quantity A is greater and the correct answer is (A).

Take a look at one more exponent problem.

If $x \neq 0$ and $64^3 = 8^x$, then what is the value of x^2 ?

○ 5

○ 6

○ 25

○ 36

○ 64

Here's How to Crack It

Solve this question by determining the value for x. To solve for x in this equation, start by rewriting the exponent expressions using a common base. Since 64 can be written as 8^2, the equation can be rewritten as $(8^2)^3 = 8^x$. Since the bases are the same, for the equation to be equal the powers have to be the same as well. $(8^2)^3$ can be rewritten as 8^6 because of the power-multiply rule, so if $8^6 = 8^x$ then $x = 6$. Now plug that number into the value for x^2. This is now 6^2 which equals 36, so the correct answer is (D).

The Peculiar Behavior of Exponents

- Raising a number greater than 1 to a power greater than 1 results in a greater number. For example, $2^2 = 4$.

- Raising a fraction that's between 0 and 1 to a power greater than 1 results in a lesser number. For example, $\left(\frac{1}{2}\right)^2 = \frac{1}{4}$.

- A negative number raised to an even power results in a positive number. For example, $(-2)^2 = 4$, because $(-2)(-2) = 4$.

- A negative number raised to an odd power results in a negative number. For example, $(-2)^3 = -8$, because $(-2)(-2)(-2) = -8$.

- A number raised to the first power ALWAYS results in the number itself. For example, $1{,}000^1 = 1{,}000$.

What Is a Square Root?

The radical sign $\sqrt{}$ indicates the **square root** of a number. For example, $\sqrt{4}$ means that some number times itself is equal to 4. In this case, since $2^2 = 4$, it can be determined that $\sqrt{4} = 2$. Think of square roots as the opposite of exponents. If you want to eliminate a square root in an equation, all you need to do is raise that square root to a power of 2. Just remember to do that for all of the elements in the equation!

Square roots can exist only on the GRE with nonnegative numbers. If the problem states that $x^2 = 16$, then $x = \pm 4$ as both a positive and a negative 4, when multiplied by itself, yields 16. However, when you find the square root of any number, the result will always be positive.

> You can multiply and divide any square roots, but you can add or subtract roots only when the number under the radical sign is the same.

Rules for Square Roots

There are rules that dictate what you can and cannot do with square roots, just like there are rules about exponents.

Adding and Subtracting Square Roots

You can add or subtract square roots only if the values under the radical sign are equal. So, for example, the expression $2\sqrt{5} + 4\sqrt{5}$ can be simplified to $6\sqrt{5}$ because the value under the radical sign is equal. Conversely, the expression $3 + 2\sqrt{5}$ cannot be reduced any further because the values of the roots are not the same.

Rules for Adding and Subtracting Square Roots

$$a\sqrt{r} + b\sqrt{r} = (a+b)\sqrt{r}$$
$$a\sqrt{r} - b\sqrt{r} = (a-b)\sqrt{r}$$

Multiplying and Dividing Square Roots

Any square roots can be multiplied or divided. There aren't any restrictions on this, so keep an eye out for opportunities to combine roots by multiplying or dividing that could make a root easier to work with. For example, $\sqrt{3} \times \sqrt{12} = \sqrt{36} = 6$. Roots can be divided as well; for example, $\sqrt{\dfrac{12}{3}} = \dfrac{\sqrt{12}}{\sqrt{3}} = \sqrt{4} = 2$.

Rules for Multiplying and Dividing Square Roots

$$a\sqrt{r} \times b\sqrt{s} = (a \times b)\sqrt{rs}$$
$$\sqrt{\frac{a}{b}} = \frac{\sqrt{a}}{\sqrt{b}}$$

Simplifying Square Roots

Oftentimes when you multiply square roots on the GRE, you will not get numbers under the radical sign that work out perfectly. When this happens, you will need to simplify the square root. You simplify a square root by looking for ways to factor the number under the root that results in at least one perfect square. A perfect square is an integer that when the square root of that integer is taken, the result is another integer. For example, 4 is a perfect square because $\sqrt{4} = 2$. Similarly, 9 and 25 are perfect squares because $\sqrt{9} = 3$ and $\sqrt{25} = 5$, respectively. Look at the following expression and try to simplify it.

$$\sqrt{2} \times \sqrt{10}$$

You can combine this expression to result in $\sqrt{20}$. However, this is not in the most simplified form. Look for ways to factor 20 in which one of the pairs of numbers is a perfect square. The factors of 20 are 1 and 20, 2 and 10, and 4 and 5. Since 4 is a perfect square, this can now be simplified even further.

$$\sqrt{2} \times \sqrt{10} = \sqrt{20} = \sqrt{4 \times 5} = \sqrt{4} \times \sqrt{5} = 2\sqrt{5}$$

Now let's take a look at some examples of how ETS might test roots on the GRE.

What is the value of the expression $3\sqrt{80} - 2\sqrt{5}$?

- ◯ $4\sqrt{5}$
- ◯ $5\sqrt{3}$
- ◯ $10\sqrt{5}$
- ◯ $12\sqrt{3}$
- ◯ $20\sqrt{5}$

Here's How to Crack It

The problem is subtracting roots. Since roots cannot be subtracted unless the numbers under the radical sign are equal, look for a way to simplify the roots. Since 5 cannot be simplified any further, work with 80. The factors of 80 are 1 and 80, 2 and 40, 4 and 20, 5 and 16, and 8 and 10. Two of these pairs of factors contain a perfect square, but one contains a perfect square and a prime number. This is a good thing. This means that it could be reduced no further, so choose 5 and 16 and simplify to read $3\sqrt{80} = 3\sqrt{5 \times 16} = (3 \times 4)\sqrt{5} = 12\sqrt{5}$. Now that the bases are equal, subtract the expression to find that $12\sqrt{5} - 2\sqrt{5} = 10\sqrt{5}$, which is (C). The same answer would have been found if the numbers 4 and 20 had been chosen as the factors of 80, but there would have been another round of simplifying the root, as 20 would have needed to be reduced to 4 and 5 as factors.

Here's another problem.

$$z^2 = 144$$

Quantity A	**Quantity B**
z	$\sqrt{144}$

- ◯ Quantity A is greater.
- ◯ Quantity B is greater.
- ◯ The two quantities are equal.
- ◯ The relationship cannot be determined from the information given.

Here's How to Crack It

The trap answer here is (C). Remember that if $z^2 = 144$, then the value of z is either 12 or –12. However, when a value is under a radical sign—that is, when you're looking for the square root—it can only be positive. Therefore, Quantity A could be 12 or –12 and Quantity B can only be 12. Since there is no way to ensure that one is always greater than the other, the correct answer is (D).

○

Try one more problem:

○

What is the value of $\dfrac{\sqrt{75}}{\sqrt{27}}$?

○ $\dfrac{5}{3}$

○ $\dfrac{25}{9}$

○ 3

○ $3\sqrt{3}$

○ $3\sqrt{5}$

To Simplify Roots
1. Rewrite the number as the product of two factors, one of which is a perfect square.
2. Use the multiplication rule for roots.

Here's How to Crack It

First, simplify each of these roots. $\sqrt{75}$ has a factor that is a perfect square—25, so it can be rewritten as $\sqrt{25 \times 3}$ and simplified to $5\sqrt{3}$. $\sqrt{27}$ has the perfect square 9 as a factor, so it can be written as $\sqrt{9 \times 3}$ and then simplified to $3\sqrt{3}$. This means that $\dfrac{\sqrt{75}}{\sqrt{27}}$ is equal to $\dfrac{5\sqrt{3}}{3\sqrt{3}}$; the $\sqrt{3}$ in the numerator and denominator cancel, leaving $\dfrac{5}{3}$. The correct answer is (A).

○

Algebra (And When to Use It) Drill

Now it's time to try out what you have learned on some practice questions. Try the following problems and then check your answers in Part V.

1 of 10

The original selling price of an item at a store is 40 percent more than the cost of the item to the retailer. If the retailer reduces the price of the item by 15 percent of the original selling price, then the difference between the reduced price and the cost of the item to the retailer is what percent of the cost of the item to the retailer?

Percent

Click on the answer box and type in a number. Backspace to erase.

2 of 10

$$x^2 + 8x = -7$$

Quantity A	**Quantity B**
x	0

○ Quantity A is greater.

○ Quantity B is greater.

○ The two quantities are equal.

○ The relationship cannot be determined from the information given.

3 of 10

If $3^3 \times 9^{12} = 3^x$, what is the value of x ?

Click on the answer box and type in a number. Backspace to erase.

4 of 10

If $A = 2x - (y - 2c)$ and $B = (2x - y) - 2c$, then
$A - B =$

○ $-2y$

○ $-4c$

○ 0

○ $2y$

○ $4c$

5 of 10

A merchant sells three different sizes of canned tomatoes. A large can costs the same as 5 medium cans or 7 small cans. If a customer purchases an equal number of small and large cans of tomatoes for the same amount of money needed to buy 200 medium cans, how many small cans does she purchase?

○ 35

○ 45

○ 72

○ 199

○ 208

6 of 10

If $6k - 5l = 27$ and $3l - 2k = -13$ and $5k - 5l = j$, what is the value of j ?

Click on the answer box and type in a number. Backspace to erase.

If a is multiplied by 3 and the result is 4 less than 6 times b, what is the value of $a - 2b$?

○ -12

○ $-\dfrac{4}{3}$

○ $-\dfrac{3}{4}$

○ $\dfrac{4}{3}$

○ 12

Quantity A	Quantity B
$\dfrac{2^{-4}}{4^{-2}}$	$\dfrac{\sqrt{64}}{-2^3}$

○ Quantity A is greater.

○ Quantity B is greater.

○ The two quantities are equal.

○ The relationship cannot be determined from the information given.

$$11x + 14y = 30 \text{ and } 3x + 4y = 12$$

Quantity A	Quantity B
$x + y$	$(x + y)^{-2}$

○ Quantity A is greater.

○ Quantity B is greater.

○ The two quantities are equal.

○ The relationship cannot be determined from the information given.

If $x = 3a$ and $y = 9b$, then all of the following are equal to $2(x + y)$ EXCEPT

○ $3(2a + 6b)$

○ $6(a + 3b)$

○ $24(\dfrac{1}{4}a + \dfrac{3}{4}b)$

○ $\dfrac{1}{3}(18a + 54b)$

○ $12(\dfrac{1}{2}a + \dfrac{3}{4}b)$

Summary

- Plugging In converts algebra problems to arithmetic problems. Plug In by replacing variables in the question with real numbers or by working backward from the answer choices provided.

- Use easy numbers first when Plugging In for variables. If the need arises to Plug In again, use the FROZEN numbers to help eliminate tricky answer choices on math problems.

- The golden rule of equations: whatever you do to one side of the equation, you must do to the other.

- In order to solve an equation with two variables, you need two equations. Stack them up and add or subtract to cancel out one of the variables.

- Inequalities are manipulated the same way that equations are, with one notable difference: always remember to flip the sign when you multiply or divide by a negative number.

- Use the FOIL process to expand quadratics. To solve a quadratic equation, set it equal to zero, and factor.

- An exponent is shorthand for repeated multiplication. When in doubt on exponent problems, look to find common bases or ways to factor the expressions.

- Think of a square root as the opposite of an exponent. Square roots are always positive.

Chapter 13
Real-World Math

Real-world math is our title for the grab bag of math topics that will be heavily tested on the GRE. This chapter details a number of important math concepts, many of which you've probably used at one point or another in your daily adventures, even if you didn't recognize them. After completing this chapter, you'll have brushed up on important topics such as ratios, proportions, and averages. You'll also learn some important Princeton Review methods for organizing your work and efficiently and accurately answering questions on these topics.

EVERYDAY MATH

A few years ago when ETS reconfigured the GRE, they wanted the Math section to test more of what they call "real life" scenarios that a typical graduate student might see. You can therefore expect the math questions on the GRE to heavily test topics such as proportions, averages, and ratios—mathematical concepts that are theoretically part of your everyday life. Regardless of whether that's true of your daily life or not, you'll have to master these concepts in order to do well on the GRE Math section.

RATIOS AND PROPORTIONS

If you're comfortable working with fractions and percentages, you'll be comfortable working with ratios and proportions, because ratios and proportions are simply special types of fractions. Don't let them make you nervous. Let's look at ratios first and then we'll deal with proportions.

What Is a Ratio?

Recall that a fraction expresses the relationship of a part to the whole. A **ratio** expresses a different relationship: part to part. Imagine yourself at a party with 8 women and 10 men in attendance. Remembering that a fraction expresses a part-to-whole relationship, what fraction of the partygoers are female? $\frac{8}{18}$, or 8 women out of a total of 18 people at the party. But what's the ratio, which expresses a part to part relationship, of women to men? $\frac{8}{10}$, or as ratios are more commonly expressed, 8:10. You can reduce this ratio to 4:5, just like you would a fraction.

On the GRE, you may see ratios expressed in several different ways:

$$x : y$$
$$\text{the ratio of } x \text{ to } y$$
$$x \text{ is to } y$$

In each case, the ratio is telling us the relationship between parts of a whole.

Every Fraction Can Be a Ratio, and Vice Versa

Every ratio can be expressed as a fraction. A ratio of 1:2 means that the total of all the parts is either 3 or a multiple of 3. So, the ratio 1:2 can be expressed as the fraction $\frac{1}{2}$, or the *parts* of the ratio can be expressed as fractions *of the whole* as $\frac{1}{3}$ and $\frac{2}{3}$. Likewise, the fraction $\frac{1}{3}$ expresses the ratio 1:3. So if a question says "the ratio of x to $2y$ is $\frac{1}{3}$," then that would be expressed as $\frac{x}{2y} = \frac{1}{3}$.

Treat a Ratio Like a Fraction

Anything you can do to a fraction you can also do to a ratio. You can cross multiply, find common denominators, reduce, and so on.

Find the Total

The key to dealing with ratio questions is to find the whole, or the total. Remember, a ratio tells us only about the parts, not the total. In order to find the total, add the numbers in the ratio. A ratio of 2:1 means that there are three total parts. A ratio of 2:5 means that we're talking about a total of 7 parts. And a ratio of 2:5:7 means there are 14 total parts. Once you have a total you can start to do some fun things with ratios.

For example, let's say you have a handful of pennies and nickels. If you have 30 total coins and the pennies and nickels are in a 2:1 ratio, how many pennies do you have?

The total for our ratio is 3, meaning that out of every 3 coins, there are 2 pennies and 1 nickel. So if there are 30 total coins, there must be 20 pennies and 10 nickels. Notice that $\frac{20}{10}$ is the same as $\frac{2}{1}$, is the same as 2:1!

> Like a fraction, a ratio expresses a relationship between numbers.

When you are working with ratios, there's an easy way not only to keep track of the numbers in the problem but also to quickly figure out the values in the problem. It's called a ratio box. Let's try the same question, but with some different numbers; if you have 24 coins in your pocket and the ratio of pennies to nickels is 2:1, how many pennies and nickels are there? The ratio box for this question is below, with all of the information we're given already filled in.

> The minute you see the word "ratio," draw a Ratio Box on your scratch paper.

	Pennies	Nickels	Total
ratio	2	1	**3**
multiply by			
actual numbers			**24**

Remember that ratios are relationships between numbers, not actual numbers, so the real total is 24; that is, you have 24 actual coins in your pocket. The ratio total (the number you get when you add the number of parts in the ratio) is 3.

The middle row of the table is for the multiplier. How do you get from 3 to 24? You multiply by 8. Remember when we talked about finding equivalent fractions? All we did was multiply the numerator and denominator by the same value. That's exactly what we're going to do with ratios. This is what the ratio box looks like now:

> The multiplier is the key concept in working with ratios. Just remember that whatever you multiply one part by, you must multiply *every* part by.

	Pennies	Nickels	Total
ratio	2	1	**3**
multiply by	8	8	**8**
actual numbers			**24**

Now let's finish filling in the box by multiplying everything else.

	Pennies	Nickels	Total
ratio	2	1	**3**
multiply by	8	8	**8**
actual numbers	16	8	**24**

Therefore, of the 24 coins, 16 are pennies and 8 are nickels.

Let's try a GRE example.

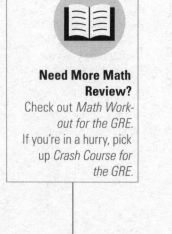

Need More Math Review?
Check out *Math Workout for the GRE*. If you're in a hurry, pick up *Crash Course for the GRE*.

Flour, eggs, yeast, and salt are mixed by weight in the ratio of 11 : 9 : 3 : 2, respectively. How many pounds of yeast are there in 20 pounds of the mixture?

○ $1\frac{3}{5}$

○ $1\frac{4}{5}$

○ 2

○ $2\frac{2}{5}$

○ $8\frac{4}{5}$

Here's How to Crack It

The minute you see the word *ratio*, draw a ratio box on your scratch paper and fill in what you know.

	Flour	Eggs	Yeast	Salt	Total
ratio	11	9	3	2	
multiply by					
actual numbers					**20**

First, add all of the numbers in the ratio to get the ratio total.

	Flour	Eggs	Yeast	Salt	Total
ratio	11	9	3	2	**25**
multiply by					
actual numbers					**20**

Now, what do we multiply 25 by to get 20?

$$25x = 20$$

$$\frac{25x}{25} = \frac{20}{25}$$

$$x = \frac{20}{25}$$

$$x = \frac{4}{5}$$

So $\frac{4}{5}$ is our "multiply by" number. Let's fill it in.

	Flour	Eggs	Yeast	Salt	Total
ratio	11	9	3	2	**25**
multiply by	$\frac{4}{5}$	$\frac{4}{5}$	$\frac{4}{5}$	$\frac{4}{5}$	$\frac{4}{5}$
actual numbers					**20**

The question asks for the amount of yeast, so we don't have to worry about the other ingredients. Just look at the yeast column. All we have to do is multiply 3 by $\frac{4}{5}$ to get the answer: $3 \times \frac{4}{5} = \frac{12}{5} = 2\frac{2}{5}$, which is (D).

What Is a Proportion?

So you know that a fraction is a relationship between part and whole, and that a ratio is a relationship between part and part. A **proportion** is an equivalent relationship between two fractions or ratios. Thus, $\frac{1}{2}$ and $\frac{4}{8}$ are proportionate because they are equivalent fractions. But $\frac{1}{2}$ and $\frac{2}{3}$ are not in proportion because they are not equal ratios.

The GRE often contains problems in which you are given two proportional, or equal, ratios from which one piece of information is missing. These questions take a relationship or ratio, and project it onto a larger or smaller scale. Proportion problems are recognizable because they always give you three values and ask for a fourth value. Here's an example:

If the cost of a one-hour telephone call is $7.20, what would be the cost in dollars of a 10-minute telephone call at the same rate?

[ ] dollars

Click on the answer box and type in a number.
Backspace to erase.

Here's How to Crack It

It's very important to set up proportion problems correctly. That means placing your information on your scratch paper. Be especially careful to label *everything*. It takes only an extra two or three seconds, but doing this will help you catch lots of errors.

For this question, let's express the ratios as dollars over minutes, because we're being asked to find the cost of a 10-minute call. That means that we have to convert 1 hour to 60 minutes (otherwise it wouldn't be a proportion).

$$\frac{\$}{\min} = \frac{\$7.20}{60} = \frac{x}{10}$$

Now cross multiply.

$$60x = (7.20)(10)$$
$$60x = 72$$
$$\frac{60x}{60} = \frac{72}{60}$$
$$x = \frac{6}{5}$$

Now we can enter 1.20 into the box.

Relationship Review

You may have noticed a trend in the preceding pages. Each of the major topics covered—fractions, percents, ratios, and proportions—described a particular relationship between numbers. Let's review:

- A fraction expresses the relationship between a part and the whole.
- A percent is a special type of fraction, one that expresses the relationship of part to whole as a fraction with the number 100 in the denominator.
- A ratio expresses the relationship between part and part. Adding the parts of a ratio gives you the whole.
- A proportion expresses the relationship between equal fractions, percents, or ratios.
- Each of these relationships shares all the characteristics of a fraction. You can reduce them, expand them, multiply them, and divide them using the exact same rules you used for working with fractions.

AVERAGES

The **average** (arithmetic mean) of a list of numbers is the sum, or total value, of all the numbers in the list divided by the number of numbers in the list. The average of the list 1, 2, 3, 4, 5 is equal to the total of the numbers (1 + 2 + 3 + 4 + 5, or 15) divided by the number of numbers in the list (which is 5). Dividing 15 by 5 gives us 3, so 3 is the average of the list.

ETS always refers to an average as an "average (arithmetic mean)." This confusing parenthetical remark is meant to keep you from being confused by other more obscure kinds of averages, such as geometric and harmonic means. You'll be less confused if you simply ignore the parenthetical remark and know that average means total of the elements divided by the number of elements.

GRE average problems always give you two of the three numbers needed.

Think Total

Don't try to solve average problems all at once. Do them piece by piece. The key formula to keep in mind when doing problems that involve averages is

$$\text{Average} = \frac{\text{Total}}{\text{\# of things}}$$

Drawing an Average Pie will help you organize your information.

> The minute you see the word *average*, draw an Average Pie on your scratch paper.

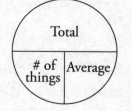

Here's how the Average Pie works. The *total* is the sum of the numbers being averaged. The *number of things* is the number of different elements that you are averaging. And the *average* is, naturally, the average.

Say you wanted to find the average of 4, 7, and 13. You would add those numbers to get the total and divide that total by three.

$$4 + 7 + 13 = 24$$

$$\frac{24}{3} = 8$$

> Which two pieces of the pie do you have?

Mathematically, the Average Pie works like this:

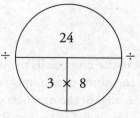

The horizontal bar is a division bar. If you divide the *total* by the *number of things,* you get the *average.* If you divide the total by the *average,* you get the *number of things.* If you have the *number of things* and the *average,* you can simply multiply them together to find the *total.* This is one of the most important things you need to be able to do to solve GRE average problems.

Using the Average Pie has several benefits. First, it's an easy way to organize information.

Furthermore, the Average Pie makes it clear that if you have two of the three pieces, you can always find the third. This makes it easier to figure out how to approach the problem. If you fill in the number of things, for example, and the question wants to know the average, the Average Pie shows you that the key to unlocking that problem is finding the total.

Try this one.

The average (arithmetic mean) of seven numbers is 9 and the average of three of these numbers is 5. What is the average of the other four numbers?

○ 4

○ 5

○ 7

○ 10

○ 12

> Draw a new Average
> Pie each time you
> encounter the word
> *average* in a question.

Here's How to Crack It

Let's take the first sentence. You have the word *average*, so draw an Average Pie and fill in what you know. We have seven numbers with an average of 9, so plug those values into the Average Pie and multiply to find the total.

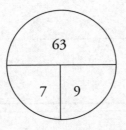

Now we also know that three of the numbers have an average of 5, so draw another Average Pie, plug those values into their places, and multiply to find the total of those three numbers.

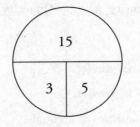

The question is asking for the average of the four remaining numbers. Draw one more Average Pie and Plug In 4 for the number of things.

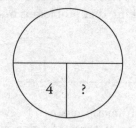

In order to solve for the average, we need to know the total of those four numbers. How do we find this? From our first Average Pie we know that the total of all seven numbers is 63. The second Average Pie tells us that the total of three of those numbers was 15. Thus, the total of the remaining four has to be 63 – 15, which is 48. Plug 48 into the last Average Pie, and divide by 4 to get the average of the four numbers.

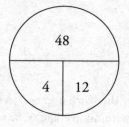

The average is 12, which is (E).

Let's try one more.

The average (arithmetic mean) of a set of 6 numbers is 28. If a certain number, y, is removed from the set, the average of the remaining numbers in the set is 24.

Quantity A	Quantity B
y	48

○ Quantity A is greater.

○ Quantity B is greater.

○ The two quantities are equal.

○ The relationship cannot be determined from the information given.

Here's How to Crack It

All right, let's attack this one. The problem says that the average of a set of six numbers is 28, so let's immediately draw an Average Pie and calculate the total.

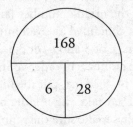

If a certain number, *y*, is removed from the set, there are now five numbers left. We already know that the new average is 24, so draw another Average Pie.

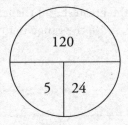

The difference between the totals must be equal to *y*: 168 − 120 = 48. Thus, the two quantities are equal, and the answer is (C).

Up and Down

Averages are very predictable. You should make sure you automatically know what happens to them in certain situations. For example, suppose you take three tests and earn an average score of 90. Now you take a fourth test. What do you know?

If your average goes up as a result of the fourth score, then you know that your fourth score was higher than 90. If your average stays the same as a result of the fourth score, then you know that your fourth score was exactly 90. If your average goes down as a result of the fourth score, then you know that your fourth score was less than 90.

MEDIAN, MODE, AND RANGE

The **median** is the middle value in a list of numbers; above and below the median lie an equal number of values. For example, in the list of numbers (1, 2, 3, 4, 5, 6, 7), the median is 4, because it's the middle number (and there are an odd number of numbers in the list). If the list contained an even number of integers such as (1, 2, 3, 4, 5, 6), the median is the average of 3 and 4, or 3.5. When looking for the median, sometimes you have to put the numbers in order yourself. What is the median of the list of numbers (13, 5, 6, 3, 19, 14, 8)? First, put the numbers in order from least to greatest, (3, 5, 6, 8, 13, 14, 19). Then take the middle number. The median is 8. Just think *median = middle* and always make sure the numbers are in order.

The **mode** is the number in a list of numbers that occurs most frequently. For example, in the list (2, 3, 4, 5, 3, 8, 6, 9, 3, 9, 3), the mode is 3, because 3 shows up the most. Just think *mode = most*.

The **range** is the difference between the greatest and the least numbers in a list of numbers. So, in the list of numbers (2, 6, 13, 3, 15, 4, 9), the range is 15 (the greatest number in the list) − 2 (the least number in the list), or 13.

Here's an example:

Set $F = \{4, 2, 7, 11, 8, 9\}$

Quantity A	Quantity B
The range of Set F	The median of Set F

○ Quantity A is greater.

○ Quantity B is greater.

○ The two quantities are equal.

○ The relationship cannot be determined from the information given.

Here's How to Crack It

Let's put the numbers in order first, so it'll be easier to see what we have: {2, 4, 7, 8, 9, 11}. First, let's look at Quantity A. The range is the greatest number, or 11, minus the least number, or 2. That's 9. Now let's look at Quantity B. The minute you see the word *median*, be sure to put the numbers in order. The median is the middle number of the set, but because there are two middle numbers, 7 and 8, we have to find the average. Or do we? Isn't the average of 7 and 8 clearly going to be smaller than the number in Quantity A, which is 9? Yes, in quant comp questions, we compare, not calculate. The answer is (A).

STANDARD DEVIATION

Standard deviation is one of those phrases that people uncomfortable with math shy away from. In truth, standard deviation is fairly straightforward and with some understanding and a little practice, you can conquer standard deviation on the GRE. The prevalence of standard deviation questions on the GRE is small, and though the GRE might ask you questions about standard deviation, you'll never have to actually calculate it; instead, you'll just need a basic understanding of what standard deviation is and how it's tested on the GRE. Generally, the GRE treats standard deviation as a measure of spread.

A QUESTION OF SPREAD

The first thing to know is what is meant by standard deviation on the GRE. Standard deviation is a measure of the amount of spread, or variation, of a set of data values. A low standard deviation indicates that the data values tend to be close to the mean (thus, to have little spread), while a high standard deviation indicates that the values are spread out over a wider range. So, the further the distance between the members of a set and the set's average, the greater the standard deviation of the set.

Consider two sets of numbers, {4, 4, 4} and {3, 4, 5}. The first set, {4, 4, 4}, has a mean value of 4, as $\left(\dfrac{4+4+4}{3}\right)$ is equal to 4. However, since each member of the set is equal to the mean (and thus to each other member of the set), there is no distance between the members of the set and the mean of the set, so there is no spread amongst the numbers. Now look at the second set, {3, 4, 5}. This set also has a mean of 4, as $\left(\dfrac{3+4+5}{3}\right)$ is equal to 4. However, in this group, instead of all numbers being equal to the mean, two members of the set have some distance from the mean (3 and 5 are not equal to the mean of 4). Therefore, since the second set has more spread (the members of the set have more distance from the mean), the second set has a greater standard deviation.

Here's an example of how ETS might test standard deviation:

---○---

Quantity A

The standard deviation of a list of data consisting of 10 integers ranging from –20 to –5

Quantity B

The standard deviation of a list of data consisting of 10 integers ranging from 5 to 20

○ Quantity A is greater.

○ Quantity B is greater.

○ The two quantities are equal.

○ The relationship cannot be determined from the information given.

Here's How to Crack It

ETS is hoping you'll make a couple of wrong turns on this problem. The first trap they set is that one of the list of numbers contains negative integers while the other doesn't—but this doesn't mean that one list has a negative standard deviation. Standard deviation is defined as the distance a point is from the mean, so it can never be negative. The second trap is that ETS hopes you'll waste a lot of time trying to calculate standard deviation based on the information given. But you know better than to try to do that. Remember that ETS won't ask you to calculate standard deviation; it's a complex calculation. Plus, as you know, you need to know the mean in order to calculate the standard deviation and there's no way we can find it based on the information here. Thus, we have no way of comparing these two quantities, so the answer is (D).

---○---

Now, let's try a question that deals with standard deviation differently.

---○---

For a certain distribution, the value 12.0 is one standard deviation above the mean and the value 15.0 is three standard deviations above the mean. What is the mean of the data set?

○ 9.0

○ 9.5

○ 10.0

○ 10.5

○ 11.0

Here's How to Crack It

This one's a little tougher than the earlier standard deviation questions. The question provides neither the individual data points nor the mean, and ETS is hoping that this will throw you off. But remember that standard deviation deals with the distance from the mean. Start by determining the size of one standard deviation. Since 12.0 is one standard deviation above the mean and 15.0 is three standard deviations above the mean, the difference between the data values represents the difference in the number of standard deviations. Therefore,

$$15.0 - 12.0 = 3.0 \text{ st dev} - 1.0 \text{ st dev, so } 3.0 = 2.0 \text{ st dev}$$

Now set up a proportion to find the size of one standard deviation:

$$\frac{3.0}{2.0 \, st \, dev} = \frac{x}{1 \, st \, dev}$$

Solve to find that $x = 1.5$, which means that one standard deviation for this data set is equal to 1.5. Since 12.0 is one standard deviation above the mean, the mean of the data set is 12.0 − 1.5 = 10.5, so the answer is (D).

RATE

Rate problems are similar to average problems. A rate problem might ask for an average speed, distance, or the length of a trip, or how long a trip (or a job) takes. To solve rate problems, use the Rate Pie.

> A rate problem is really just an average problem.

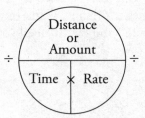

The Rate Pie works exactly the same way as the Average Pie. If you divide the *distance* or *amount* by the *rate*, you get the *time*. If you divide the *distance* or *amount* by the *time*, you get the *rate*. If you multiply the *rate* by the *time*, you get the *distance* or *amount*.

Let's take a look.

───────────────────◯───────────────────

It takes Carla three hours to drive to her brother's house at an average speed of 50 miles per hour. If she takes the same route home, but her average speed is 60 miles per hour, what is the time, in hours, that it takes her to drive home?

○ 2 hours

○ 2 hours and 14 minutes

○ 2 hours and 30 minutes

○ 2 hours and 45 minutes

○ 3 hours

Here's How to Crack It

The trip to her brother's house takes three hours, and the rate is 50 miles per hour. Plug those numbers into a Rate Pie and multiply to find the distance.

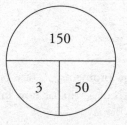

So the distance is 150 miles. On her trip home, Carla travels at a rate of 60 miles per hour. Draw another Rate Pie and Plug In 150 and 60. Then all you have to do is divide 150 by 60 to find the time.

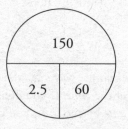

So it takes Carla two and a half hours to get home. That's (C).

───────────────────◯───────────────────

Try another one.

⎯⎯⎯⎯⎯⎯⎯⎯○⎯⎯⎯⎯⎯⎯⎯⎯

A machine can stamp 20 envelopes in 4 minutes. How many of these machines, working simultaneously, are needed to stamp 60 envelopes per minute?

○ 5

○ 10

○ 12

○ 20

○ 24

Here's How to Crack It

First, we have to find the rate per minute of one machine. Plug 20 and 4 into a Rate Pie and divide to find the rate.

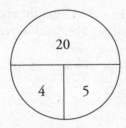

The rate is 5. If one machine can stamp 5 envelopes per minute, how many machines do you need to stamp 60 per minute? 60 ÷ 5 = 12, or (C).

⎯⎯⎯⎯⎯⎯⎯⎯○⎯⎯⎯⎯⎯⎯⎯⎯

CHARTS

Every GRE Math section has a few questions that are based on a chart or graph (or on a group of charts or graphs). But don't worry; the most important thing that chart questions test is your ability to interpret the information provided in the chart. Remember, the information is already there for you! You just need to go find it.

Chart Questions

There are usually two or three questions per chart or per set of charts. Chart questions appear on split screens. Be sure to click on the scroll bar and scroll down as far as you can; there may be additional charts underneath the top one, and you want to make sure you've seen all of them.

Chart problems mostly recycle the basic arithmetic concepts we've already covered: fractions, percentages, and so on. This means you can use the techniques we've discussed for each type of question, but there are two additional techniques that are especially important to use when doing chart questions.

Get Your Bearings
Before you start the questions, spend a few seconds looking over the charts.

- Scroll down to find any data or notes that aren't visible.
- Read titles and legends.
- Check units.

Work the Questions
1. Read the questions and determine
   - Which chart the question deals with
   - What information you need to find
   - What calculations you need to perform
2. Work the chart(s)
   - Get the information you need from the chart(s).
   - Write down what you found on your scratch paper.
3. Approximate or calculate
   - Are the numbers in the answers far apart? If so, you can probably estimate the answer.
   - Use the calculator!

Notice that, when working the questions, the final step is to determine whether to approximate or to calculate the answer. While the calculator is available to you, it's important to remember that the calculator is only a tool and is only as smart as you are. Additionally, you can save yourself precious seconds by knowing the "friendly" percentages and their fractions (from back in Chapter 10) by heart.

Nonetheless, with chart questions it is occasionally easier to estimate percentages and round to whole numbers. This is most effective when the numbers in the answers are far apart and the values in the chart are difficult to work with. By estimating and rounding numbers under these conditions, often you can determine the correct answer based on the proximity of the answer to your estimated values.

Chart Problems

Make sure you've read everything on the chart carefully before you try the first question.

Chart questions frequently test percents, percent change, ratios, proportions, and averages.

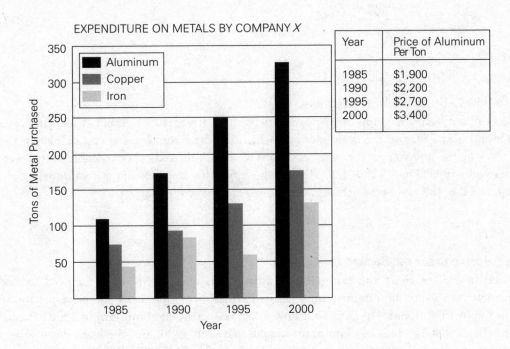

EXPENDITURE ON METALS BY COMPANY X

Year	Price of Aluminum Per Ton
1985	$1,900
1990	$2,200
1995	$2,700
2000	$3,400

Approximately how many tons of aluminum and copper combined were purchased in 1995 ?

- ○ 125
- ○ 255
- ○ 325
- ○ 375
- ○ 515

How much did Company X spend on aluminum in 1990 ?

- ○ $675,000
- ○ $385,000
- ○ $333,000
- ○ $165,000
- ○ $139,000

Approximately what was the percent increase in the price of aluminum from 1985 to 1995 ?

- ○ 8%
- ○ 16%
- ○ 23%
- ○ 30%
- ○ 42%

Here's How to Crack the First Question

As you can see from the graph on the previous page, in 1995, the black bar (which indicates aluminum) is at 250, and the dark gray bar (which indicates copper) is at approximately 125. Add those figures and you get the number of tons of aluminum and copper combined that were purchased in 1995: 250 + 125 = 375. That's (D). Notice that the question says "approximately." Also notice that the numbers in the answer choices are pretty far apart.

Here's How to Crack the Second Question

We need to use the chart and the graph to answer this question, because we need to find the number of tons of aluminum purchased in 1990 and multiply it by the price per ton of aluminum in 1990 in order to figure out how much was spent on aluminum in 1990. The bar graph tells us that 175 tons of aluminum was purchased in 1990, and the little chart tells us that aluminum was $2,200 per ton in 1990: 175 × $2,200 = $385,000. That's (B).

Here's How to Crack the Third Question

Remember that percent increase formula from Chapter 10, Math Fundamentals?

$$\text{Percent change} = \frac{\text{Difference}}{\text{Original}} \times 100$$

We'll need to use the little chart for this one. In 1985, the price of aluminum was $1,900 per ton. In 1995, the price of aluminum was $2,700 per ton. Now let's use the formula: 2,700 − 1,900 = 800, so that's the difference. This is a percent increase problem, so the original number is the smaller one. Thus, the original is 1,900, and our formula looks like this: Percent change $= \frac{800}{1,900} \times 100$. By canceling the 0's in the fraction, you get $\frac{8}{19} \times 100$, and multiplying gives you $\dfrac{800}{19}$. At this point you could divide 800 by 19 to get the exact answer, but because they're looking for an approximation, let's round 19 to 20. What's $800 \div 20$? That's 40, and (E) is the only one that's close.

Real-World Math Drill

Now it's time to try out what you have learned on some practice questions. Try the following problems and then check your answers in Part V.

1 of 12

Sadie sells half the paintings in her collection, gives one-third of her paintings to friends, and keeps the remaining paintings for herself. What fraction of her collection does Sadie keep?

Click on each box and type in a number.
Backspace to erase.

2 of 12

$$5x - 2y = 2y - 3x$$

Quantity A	**Quantity B**
x	y

○ Quantity A is greater.

○ Quantity B is greater.

○ The two quantities are equal.

○ The relationship cannot be determined from the information given.

Questions 3 through 5 refer to the following graph.

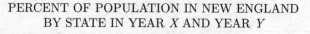

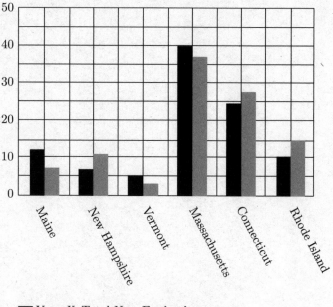

■ Year X: Total New England population= 15 million
▪ Year Y: Total New England population= 25 million

3 of 12

If the six New England states are ranked by population in Year X and Year Y, how many states would have a different ranking from Year X to Year Y?

○ None

○ One

○ Two

○ Three

○ Four

In Year X, the population of Massachusetts was approximately what percent of the population of Vermont?

- ○ 50%
- ○ 120%
- ○ 300%
- ○ 800%
- ○ 1,200%

By approximately how much did the population of Rhode Island increase from Year X to Year Y?

- ○ 750,000
- ○ 1,250,000
- ○ 1,500,000
- ○ 2,250,000
- ○ 3,375,000

A water jug with a capacity of 20 gallons is 20 percent full. At the end of every third day, water is added to the jug. If the amount of water added is equal to 50 percent of the water in the jug at the beginning of that day, how many days does it take for the jug to be at least 85% full?

- ○ 4
- ○ 6
- ○ 12
- ○ 15
- ○ 20

Towns A, B, C, and D are all in the same voting district. Towns A and B have 3,000 people each who support referendum R and the referendum has an average (arithmetic mean) of 3,500 supporters in towns B and D and an average of 5,000 supporters in Towns A and C.

Quantity A	**Quantity B**
The average number of supporters of Referendum R in Towns C and D	The average number of supporters of Referendum R in Towns B and C

- ○ Quantity A is greater.
- ○ Quantity B is greater.
- ○ The two quantities are equal.
- ○ The relationship cannot be determined from the information given.

A company paid $500,000 in merit raises to employees whose performances were rated A, B, or C. Each employee rated A received twice the amount of the raise that was paid to each employee rated C; and each employee rated B received one-and-a-half times the amount of the raise that was paid to each employee rated C. If 50 workers were rated A, 100 were rated B, and 150 were rated C, how much was the raise paid to each employee rated A?

- ○ $370
- ○ $625
- ○ $740
- ○ $1,250
- ○ $2,500

Questions 9 through 11 refer to the following graphs.

NUMBER OF STUDENTS IN GRADES
9 THROUGH 12 FOR SCHOOL DISTRICT
X IN 1995 AND 2013

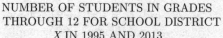
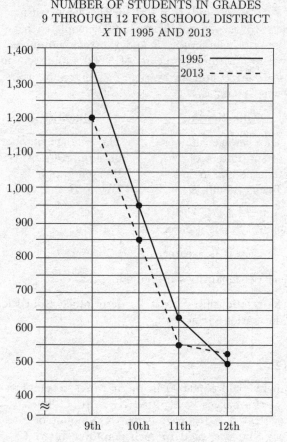

Grade

DISTRIBUTION OF READING TEST
SCORES* FOR SCHOOL DISTRICT *X*
STUDENTS IN 2013
(*Reading Test scores can range from
0–100 points)

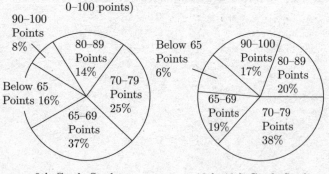

9th Grade Students   10th–12th Grade Students

In 2013, the median reading test score for ninth-grade students was in which score range?

○ Below 65 points

○ 65–69 points

○ 70–79 points

○ 80–89 points

○ 90–100 points

If the number of students in grades 9 through 12 in School District *X* in 1995 comprised 35 percent of the number of students in City *Y* in 1995, then approximately how many students were in City *Y* in 1995 ?

○ 9,700

○ 8,700

○ 3,400

○ 3,000

○ 1,200

Assume that all students in School District *X* took the reading test each year. In 2013, approximately how many more ninth-grade students had reading test scores in the 70–79 point range than in the 80–89 point range?

○ 470

○ 300

○ 240

○ 170

○ 130

One ounce of Solution X contains only ingredients a and b in a ratio of $2 : 3$. One ounce of Solution Y contains only ingredients a and b in a ratio of $1 : 2$. If Solution Z is created by mixing solutions X and Y in a ratio of $3 : 11$, then 630 ounces of Solution Z contains how many ounces of a ?

○ 68

○ 73

○ 89

○ 219

○ 236

Summary

o   A ratio expresses a part-to-part relationship. The key to ratio problems is finding the total. Use the ratio box to organize ratio questions.

o   A proportion expresses the relationship between equal fractions, percents, or ratios. A proportion problem always provides you with three pieces of information and asks you for a fourth.

o   Use the Average Pie to organize and crack average problems.

o   The median is the middle number in a set of values. The mode is the value that appears most frequently in a set. The range of a set is the difference between the largest and smallest values in the set.

o   You will never have to calculate standard deviation on the GRE.

o   Standard deviation problems are really average and percent problems. Make sure you know the percentages associated with the bell curve: 34%, 14%, 2%.

o   Use the Rate Pie for rate questions.

o   On chart questions, make sure you take a moment to understand what information the chart is providing. Estimate answers to chart questions whenever possible.

Chapter 14
Geometry Basics

Chances are you probably haven't used the Pythagorean Theorem recently or had to find the area of a circle in quite a while. However, you'll be expected to know geometry concepts such as these on the GRE. This chapter reviews all the important rules and formulas you'll need to crack the geometry problems on the GRE.

WHAT TO EXPECT

On the math section of the GRE, about 25% of the questions you will encounter are geometry questions. Geometry questions come in all shapes and sizes–literally and figuratively. The GRE can ask you about a variety of geometric shapes of any possible size. GRE geometry questions are asked in all question types–Quant Comp, multiple choice, numeric entry, all that apply–and span all difficulties.

Luckily, the GRE typically only asks about a handful of shapes and concepts. If the GRE did not have any limitations on what concepts or figures could be tested, the scope of the geometry section would be enormous.

This chapter is going to re-introduce you to the basics of each shape and the types of information the GRE could ask about in general. The next chapter focuses on how the GRE takes this information and tests it.

It is worth repeating that this chapter does not contain GRE-specific questions. This chapter presents the foundational knowledge needed to tackle GRE geometry questions. In this chapter, you'll learn about figure types, equations necessary to solve for certain aspects of figures, and basic relationships between figures. The next chapter presents questions that are specific to the GRE but does not cover any of these introductory concepts.

Unsure whether you should tackle this chapter or skip straight to the next chapter?

Take this short quiz to find out!

"Should I Do This Chapter?" Quiz

1. What is the formula for the volume of a rectangular solid? _____

2. If the radius of a circle is 4, what is its area? _____

3. What is the equation of a line? _____

4. How many degrees are there in a line? _____

5. What is the sum of the interior angle measurements of a figure with 6 sides? _____

6. What is the formula for the perimeter of a rectangle? _____

7. The side lengths of what kind of triangle can be found using the Pythagorean Theorem?
   _____

8. What is the equation for the slope of a line? _____

9. How many degrees are in a circle? _____

10. What is the formula for the area of a triangle? _____

The answers to these questions are at the back of this chapter.

So, how'd you do? If you got more than two questions wrong, you should start with this chapter. Lucky for you, we can dive in right now.

What to Know

The following tables show a list of shape types, what can be asked about them, and geometry vocabulary the writers of the GRE can use. Once you're confident in your ability to maneuver through all these topics, move onto the next chapter. That chapter contains more explicit information about geometry on the GRE, including questions that mimic the types of questions that you'll see on test day. When scanning the table below, if you see only a couple of items that you are unsure of feel free to flip to those sections and ignore the rest. If nothing on this table looks familiar to you, then prepare to spend time in this chapter before moving on to the next.

Figure	What to Know
3D Figures	• Cylinder • Diagonals in Rectangular Solids • Rectangular Solid • Surface Area • Volume
Circles	• Arc • Area • Central Angle • Chord • Circumference • Degrees • Diameter • Radius
Coordinate Plane	• Equation of a line • Parallel Lines • Perpendicular Lines • Points on a line • Quadrants • Slope • x- and y-intercept
Degrees, Lines, and Angles	• Degrees • Vertical Angles
Other Figures	• Polygons • Parallelograms • Trapezoids
Rectangles	• Area • Perimeter
Right Triangles	• Area • Angles • Pythagorean Theorem • Side and angle relationships of special right triangles
Squares	• Area • Perimeter • Relationship to triangles
Triangles	• Angles • Area • Equilateral • Isosceles • Perimeter • Third-Side Rule

This list is not totally comprehensive. The chapter covers the most likely scenarios. The GRE can use these shapes, or variations of them, in any combination they please.

The chapter is organized by progressing complexity. We'll start by looking at the most straight-forward topics and gradually move into the more complex.

Degrees, Lines, and Angles

For the GRE, you will need to know that:

- A line is a 180-degree angle. In other words, a line is a perfectly flat angle.

- When two lines intersect, four angles are formed; the sum of these angles is 360 degrees.

- When two lines are perpendicular to each other, their intersection forms four 90-degree angles. Here is the symbol ETS uses to indicate perpendicular lines: ⊥.

- Ninety-degree angles are also called *right angles*. A right angle on the GRE is identified by a little box at the intersection of the angle's arms.

90°

There are two important concepts that you need to understand regarding degrees, lines, and angles. These are vertical angles and parallel lines.

Vertical Angles

Vertical angles are the angles that are across from each other when two lines intersect. Vertical angles are always equal. In the drawing below, angle x is equal to angle y (they are vertical angles) and angle a is equal to angle b (they are also vertical angles).

On the GRE, the measure of only one of the vertical angles is typically shown. But usually you'll need to use the other angle to solve the problem.

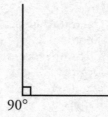

Parallel Lines

Parallel lines are lines that never intersect (they have the same slope). When a pair of parallel lines is intersected by a third line, two types of angles are formed: big angles and small angles. Any big angle is equal to any big angle, and any small angle is equal to any small angle. The sum of any big angle and any small angle is 180°. When ETS says that two lines are parallel, this is what is being tested. The symbol for parallel lines (‖) and the word *parallel* are both clues that tell you what to look for in the problem.

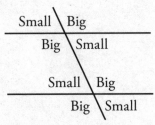

Degrees, Lines, and Angles Drill

Look at the following exercise and answer the questions about degrees, lines, and angles. Answers can be found in Part V.

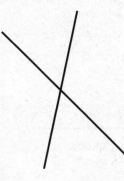

Circle Yes or No if the groups of angle measurements below could be the measurements of the figure above. The measurements in each group are listed in no particular order.

1. Yes   No   30°-30°-200°-100°

2. Yes   No   90°-90°-90°-90°

3. Yes   No   60°-40°-80°-80°

4. Yes   No   80°-100°-80°-100°

5. Yes   No   5°-5°-175°-175°

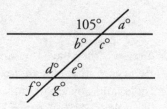

6. Label the correct measure of each of the angles.

    a. _____   d. _____   g. _____

    b. _____   e. _____

    c. _____   f. _____

Triangles

Each triangle contains three angles that add up to 180 degrees. The angles can be any positive number so long as they sum to 180 degrees. An **equilateral triangle** is a triangle in which all three sides are equal and each angle is 60 degrees. An **isosceles triangle** is a triangle in which two of the three sides are equal and two of the angles are also equal.

> An equilateral triangle has to have angles that measure 60 degrees each. An isosceles triangle can have angles that have any measure so long as the two of the angles are equal and all three angles have a sum of 180 degrees.

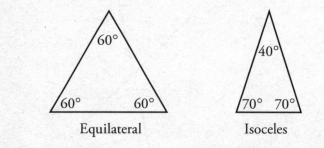

Equilateral   Isoceles

In any triangle, the longest side is opposite the largest interior angle; the shortest side is opposite the smallest interior angle. Furthermore, equal sides are opposite equal angles.

Perimeter

The perimeter of a triangle is a measure of the distance around it. All you must do to find the perimeter of a triangle is add up the lengths of the sides.

Third Side Rule

Why is it impossible for the following triangle to exist?

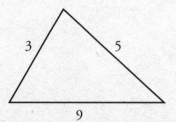

This triangle could not exist because the length of any one side of a triangle is limited by the lengths of the other two sides. This can be summarized by the **third side rule**:

> The length of any one side of a triangle must be less than the sum of the other two sides and greater than the difference between the other two sides.

This rule is not tested frequently on the GRE, but when it is, it's usually the key to solving the problem. Here's what the rule means in application: take the lengths of any two sides of a triangle. Add them together, then subtract one from the other. The length of the third side must lie between those two numbers.

Take the sides 3 and 5 from the triangle above. What's the longest the third side could measure? Just add and subtract. The third side must be shorter than 5 + 3 = 8 but longer than 5 – 3 = 2.

Therefore, the third side must lie between 2 and 8. It's important to remember that the third side cannot be equal to either 2 or 8. It must be greater than 2 and less than 8.

For the GRE, knowing two sides of a right triangle is enough to find the third side using the Pythagorean Theorem. If the problem doesn't indicate that the triangle is a right triangle, it's not possible to find the third side—only a range of possible values.

For geometry outside of the GRE, you could use trigonometry to find the length of the missing side of a non-right triangle. But, the GRE does not test this.

Area of a Triangle

The area of any triangle is equal to its height (or altitude) multiplied by its base divided by 2.

$$Area = \frac{1}{2} \left(base \right) \left(height \right)$$

The height of a triangle is defined as the length of a perpendicular line drawn from the point of the triangle to its base.

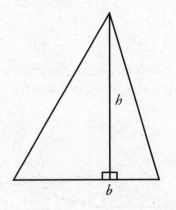

This area formula works on any triangle.

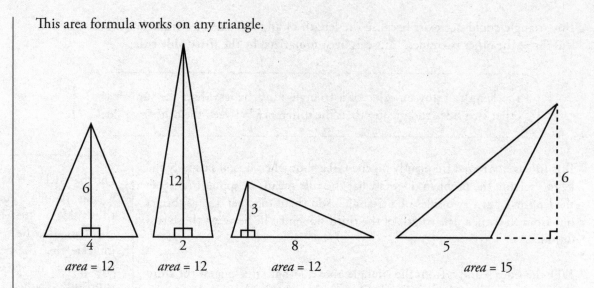

area = 12   area = 12   area = 12   area = 15

Triangles Drill

Consider the following statements about different triangles and fill in the blanks. Answers can be found in Part V.

1. A triangle with two equal sides also has two equal _____ and is called an _____ triangle.

2. The height of a triangle with a base of 3 and an area of 18 is _____.

3. A triangle with side lengths 2 and 6 has a third side length of between _____ and _____.

4. A certain isoceles triangle has angle measurements of 20, 20, and _____.

5. The perimeter of a triangle with a single side length of 5 and two angles of 60 degrees is _____.

Right Triangles

Right triangles are triangles in which one interior angle measures 90 degrees. Right triangles are easily identifiable due to the presence of the indicator for right angles.

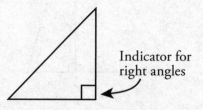

Indicator for right angles

Like all triangles, right triangles have interior angles that total 180 degrees. One of the angles is 90 degrees, so the other two angles have a sum of 90 degrees.

Area of a Triangle

Calculating the area of a right triangle is no different from calculating the area of any other triangle. The equation is the same.

$$Area = \frac{1}{2}\left(base\right)\left(height\right)$$

The base and the height of the triangle are the legs of the triangle. The legs are the two shortest sides. The longest side is called the hypotenuse. In order to calculate the area of a right triangle, it's necessary to know how to calculate the lengths of the three sides of a right triangle.

Pythagorean Theorem

The lengths of the three sides of a right triangle can be found using the Pythagorean Theorem, which is the equation:

$$a^2 + b^2 = c^2$$

This theorem states that in a right triangle, the square of the length of the hypotenuse, which is the longest side, is equal to the sum of the squares of the lengths of the two other sides. In the equation above, c is the length of the hypotenuse and a and b are the lengths of the legs (short sides) of the triangle.

Pythagorean Theorem and Area of a Triangle Drill

Try out calculating the area and the length of the missing side for the following right triangles. Answers can be found in Part V.

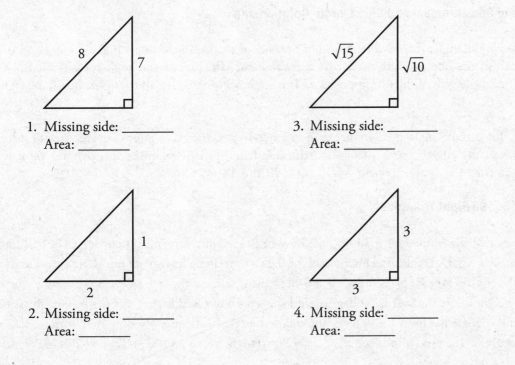

1. Missing side: _____
   Area: _____

2. Missing side: _____
   Area: _____

3. Missing side: _____
   Area: _____

4. Missing side: _____
   Area: _____

Pythagorean Triples

Certain right triangles have properties that make them "special." These properties allow you to quickly identify any missing side or angle measurements of the right triangle. They are called Pythagorean Triples.

Missing Sides

The two most common Pythagorean Triples are **3 : 4 : 5** and **5 : 12 : 13**.

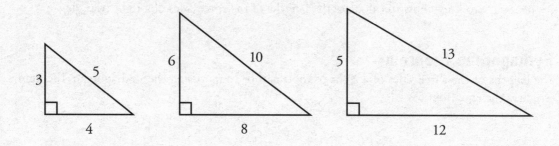

Note that a triangle could have sides with actual lengths of 3, 4, and 5, or 3 : 4 : 5 could just be the ratio of the sides. If you double the ratio, you get a triangle with sides equal to 6, 8, and 10. If you triple it, you get a triangle with sides equal to 9, 12, and 15.

These special right triangle side measurements allow you to easily determine the value of any missing side. If you know these ratios, you may be able to save yourself the time of working with the Pythagorean Theorem. But, don't worry–if you are unsure whether the relationship of the side lengths is a special right triangle, you can always use the Pythagorean Theorem.

Angle Measurement and Side Length Relationship

For every triangle, there is a relationship between the value of the angle measurement and the length of the side opposite that angle measurement. The greater the angle measurement, the greater the length of the side opposite it. This statement is true for all triangles, including right triangles.

But, for certain angle measurements in right triangles, there is a more concrete relationship between the angle measurements and the side lengths. This relationship exists for right triangles with angle measurements of 30 : 60 : 90 and 45 : 45 : 90.

30 : 60 : 90 Right Triangles

If you take an equilateral triangle and draw in the height, you end up cutting it in half and creating a right triangle. The hypotenuse of the right triangle has not changed; it's just one side of the equilateral triangle. One of the 60-degree angles stays the same as well. The angle where the height meets the base is 90 degrees and the length of the side that was the base of the equilateral triangle has been cut in half. The smallest angle, at the top, opposite the shortest side, is 30 degrees. The ratio of sides on a 30 : 60 : 90 triangle is $x : x\sqrt{3} : 2x$. Here's what it looks like:

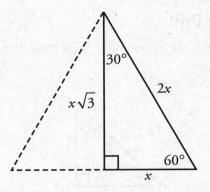

This is significant for two reasons. The first is that if you see a problem with a right triangle and the hypotenuse is double one of the legs or there is a $\sqrt{3}$ anywhere in the problem, you know what to look for. The second is that you always know the area of an equilateral triangle because you always know the height. The height is one half of one side of the equilateral triangle times the square root of 3.

45 : 45 : 90 Right Triangles

If you take a square and cut it in half along its diagonal, you create an isosceles right triangle. The two sides of the square stay the same. The 90-degree angle stays the same, and the other two angles that were 90 degrees each get cut in half and are now 45 degrees. The ratio of sides in a right isosceles triangle is $x : x : x\sqrt{2}$. Here's what it looks like:

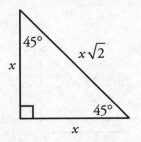

This is significant for two reasons. First, if you see a problem with a right triangle and there is a $\sqrt{2}$ or two sides that are equal anywhere in the figure, you know what to look for. Second, you always know the length of the diagonal of a square because it is the length of one side times the square root of 2.

Special Right Triangle Drill

In the following exercise, match the figure on the right with the value of *x* on the left. Answers can be found in Part V.

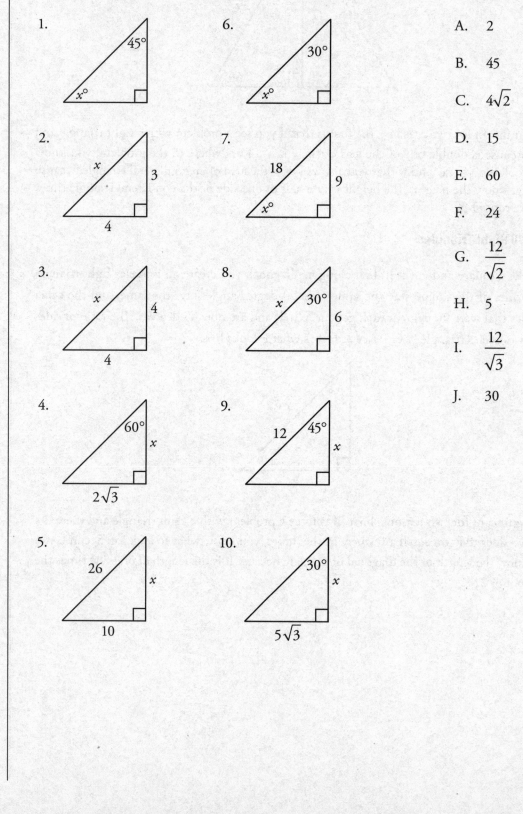

1.

6.

A. 2

B. 45

C. $4\sqrt{2}$

2.

7.

D. 15

E. 60

F. 24

3.

8.

G. $\dfrac{12}{\sqrt{2}}$

H. 5

I. $\dfrac{12}{\sqrt{3}}$

4.

9.

J. 30

5.

10.

Rectangles

This chapter covers the perimeter and area of rectangles, as well as a rectangle's relationship to a triangle. While it is true that parallelograms and squares are related to rectangles, these each have their contents in their own sections. This section deals specifically with rectangles.

Perimeter of a Rectangle

The perimeter of a rectangle is the sum of the lengths of its four sides.

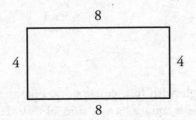

perimeter = 4 + 8 + 4 + 8 = 24

Area of a Rectangle

The area of a rectangle is equal to its length times its width. For example, the area of the rectangle above is 8 × 4 = 32.

Each corner of a rectangle is a 90-degree angle, which means that the total interior angles of a rectangle is 360 degrees.

Rectangles Drill

Work through the following exercises on rectangles to determine the area and perimeter. Answers can be found in Part V.

1. How many possible integer perimeters are there for a rectangle with an area of 24?

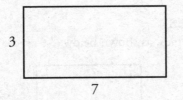

2. What are the perimeter and area of the rectangle shown above?

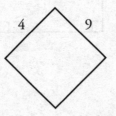

3. What are the perimeter and area of the rectangle shown above?

4. What is the sum of the interior angles of a rectangle with an area of 108?

5. For each of the following base-height combinations, indicate whether the area or perimeter of the corresponding rectangle is greater.

    a. Base = 6, Height = 6

    b. Base = 12, Height = 2

    c. Base = 3, Height = 4

    d. Base = 1, Height = 1

> All squares are rectangles, but not all rectangles are squares.

Squares

A square is a rectangle with four equal sides. Like the interior angles of a rectangle, the interior angles of a square have a sum of 360 degrees. The three primary concepts tested about squares on the GRE are perimeter, area, and the relationship to triangles.

Perimeter

Because the sides of a square are equal, the perimeter of a square can be found by either adding the sides together or multiplying one of the side lengths by 4. This creates the equation:

$$Perimeter = 4(side)$$

Area

The area of a square is equal to the length of any side times itself. In other words, the area of a square can be represented by the equation:

$$Area = side^2$$

Relationship to Triangles

A square has four 90-degree angles, as shown below:

Placing a diagonal line that extends from one corner to the other of a square bisects the corners and splits the 90-degree angle into two 45-degree angles.

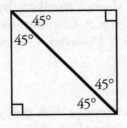

The diagonal line splits the square into two 45:45:90-degree right triangles. The sides of a 45:45:90-degree right triangle are in a relationship of $x : x : x\sqrt{2}$. Therefore, if you know the side length of one of the sides of the square, you know the length of the diagonal. Similarly, if you know the length of the diagonal, you can determine the length of the sides.

> This is true for squares only. The corners of rectangles that are not squares are not split evenly by the diagonal line extending from one corner to the other.

Squares Drill

Determine whether the following statements regarding different squares are True or False. Answers can be found in Part V.

1. True   False   The perimeter of a square with side length 2 is 4.

2. True   False   The area and perimeter of a square with side length 4 are equal.

3. True   False   The diagonal of a square with side length 3 is 6.

4. True   False   The side length of a square with a diagonal of 7 is $\dfrac{7}{\sqrt{2}}$.

5. True   False   The interior angles of a square have a sum of 180 degrees.

Circles

There are myriad topics about circles that are tested on the GRE, but some are more common than others. This section covers these topics—from the obscure to the typical—and groups them into three primary categories: Radius & Diameter, Circumference, and Area.

Radius & Diameter

The **radius** of a circle is any line that extends from the center of the circle to a point on the circumference of the circle. The **diameter** of a circle is a line that connects two points on the circumference of the circle through the center of the circle. Therefore, the diameter of a circle is twice the length of the radius.

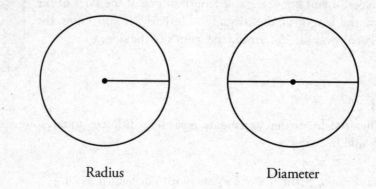

Radius   Diameter

Solving geometry problems on the GRE typically involves finding the radius of the circle. The radius of the circle is central to finding the circumference and the area of a circle.

Circumference

The circumference of a circle is the distance around the outside of the circle, as shown below.

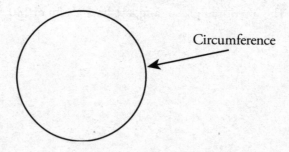

Circumference

The circumference of a circle is found by the equation:

$$circumference = 2\pi r \text{ or } \pi d$$

The value of π can be approximated as a little over 3. If the diameter of a circle is 4, then its circumference is 4π, or a little over 12. If the diameter of a circle is 10 then its circumference is 10π, or a little more than 30.

When solving for the area or circumference of a circle, it's typically best to leave π as a symbol, instead of converting it to a number. It is easier to recognize opportunities to cancel out π when it is in symbol form.

Radii is the plural form of radius

Understanding what the circumference of a circle is and how to derive it is essential to understanding several other elements of a circle, such as chords, arcs, and central angles. A **chord** is a line that connects two points on the circumference of a circle. The diameter of a circle is the longest chord in the circle. However, keep in mind that the radius is not a chord because it only touches one point on the circumference. An **arc** is a section of the outside, or circumference, of a circle. Any angle formed by two radii is called a **central angle**. There are 360 degrees in a circle, so if there is an arc formed by a 60-degree central angle, and 60 is $\frac{1}{6}$ of 360, then the arc formed by this 60-degree central angle is $\frac{1}{6}$ of the circumference of the circle. Chords, arcs, and central angles are typically represented as shown below:

> There are 360 degrees in every circle. This is important to know, as the GRE likes to carve up circles into smaller wedges and ask you questions about the size of those wedges. If you can determine the central angle of those wedges, you are usually on your way to the correct answer.

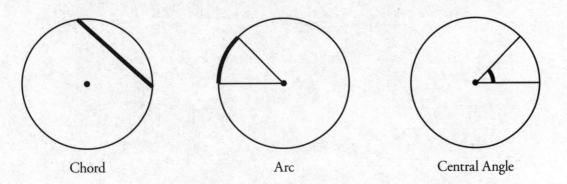

| Chord | Arc | Central Angle |

Area

The area of a circle is the amount of space inside the circle. The equation for the area of the circle is:

$$area = \pi r^2$$

The area of a circle is represented by the shaded area inside the circle below:

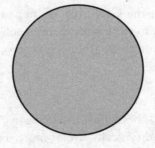

Circles Drill

Now it's time to practice. Use the information provided in the table below to determine the missing information. Answers can be found in Part V.

Radius	Diameter	Circumference	Area
4			
		16π	
	2		
			49π
	12		
		8	
$\sqrt{3}$			
			9
		$\dfrac{6}{\pi}$	
			$\dfrac{64}{\pi}$

Other Figures

There are several figures tested on the GRE that are not easily categorized. This section covers some of those figures and how to work with them to solve for degrees, area, and perimeter. These other figures are separated into three groups—polygons, parallelograms, and trapezoids.

Polygons

Polygons are figures like pentagons, hexagons, and octagons. A polygon is a figure with at least three straight sides and angles, and typically five or more. For the purposes of this discussion, we are going to focus on polygons with more than four sides. The GRE sometimes refers to these figures by name, such as labeling a figure a hexagon. Other times, the GRE mentions the number of sides of the figure, instead of the name of the figure. Typically, if the GRE references the name of the figure, the name is accompanied by a figure. However, if the GRE refers the figure by the number of sides, they do not always show a figure.

Sometimes the GRE refers to a polygon as a *regular* figure. For instance, they may reference a *regular pentagon* or a *regular five-sided figure.* The word *regular* means the figure has equal sides and angles. If the figure is not regular, than the lengths of the sides and the angles are not necessarily equal.

One kind of problem asked about polygons involves determining the degree measure of the angles inside the figure. The equation for determining the measure of the total angles in a polygon is:

$$180(n-2)$$

where *n* is the number of sides in the figure. By extension, if you want to find out the measure of a single interior angle in a regular polygon, the equation is:

$$\frac{180\left(n-2\right)}{n}$$

Once the measures of interior angles are found, it's possible to determine several different measures of the figure such as the area of the whole figure or the area of a section.

> This equation actually works for any polygon, including triangles, rectangles, and squares. However, it is best to commit to memory the total angle measure for triangles, rectangles, and squares.

> Polygons that are not regular polygons cannot use this equation. A regular polygon has an even distribution of the total angle of the figure between all of its sides because all side lengths and angles are equal.

Area of Figures With More Than Four Sides

Solving for the area of a figure with more than four sides can be tricky. Take a look at the following regular six-sided figure:

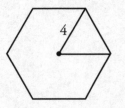

How would you go about solving for the area of the entire figure?

This process begins by realizing that the straight-line distance between the center of the figure and each of the corners of the figure is the same. This is true of all regular polygons. A triangle with two equal sides can be created using this piece of knowledge.

Because the two lengths inside the figure are equal, the angles opposite both lengths are equal.

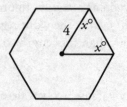

The central angle created by the intersection of the two lengths inside the figure is a portion of the entire area of the figure. There are 6 sides to the figure, so the entire area is $180(6 - 2) = 180(4) = 720$. The degree measure of the interior angle is $\frac{720}{6} = 120$. If the figure is split up into 6 equal triangles, a total of 12 angles are created. Each 120-degree angle is split in half. Therefore, each interior angle is 60 degrees, which means the third angle is also 60 degrees since a triangle has a total of 180 degrees. If the triangle has three equal angles, it is equilateral and also has three equal sides, so all sides are 4.

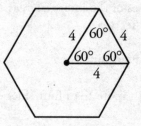

Draw in the height of the triangle that splits the base in half and this creates a 30:60:90-degree right triangle with side lengths $2 : 2\sqrt{3} : 4$. The area of this triangle is $\frac{1}{2}(4)(2\sqrt{3}) = 4\sqrt{3}$. Since there are six equal triangles in all, multiply the area of this triangle by 6. So, the area of the whole figure is $24\sqrt{3}$.

Other Figures—Polygons Drill

Determine the total interior angles and a single interior angle for each of the following regular polygons. Answers can be found in Part V.

1.

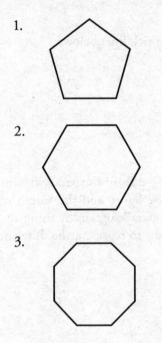

2.

3.

Parallelograms

Parallelograms on the GRE often look like this:

The sides of a parallelogram that are opposite each other are parallel. Finding the perimeter and area of a parallelogram requires the height of the figure. The height of the figure is used to determine the area of the figure or the length of the slanted side of the figure.

To find the area of a parallelogram, it is necessary to determine the height by dropping a line from one of the corners straight down, as shown by the dotted line below:

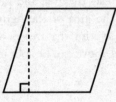

The dotted line in the figure above is the height of the figure. Where the dotted line intersects with the base is a right angle. To find the area of the parallelogram, multiply the height by the length of one of the bases. The equation for the area of a parallelogram is:

$$Area = base \times height$$

The base is the top or the bottom of the figure, as indicated by the thick lines below:

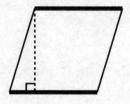

The height of a parallelogram creates a right triangle with one of the sides of the parallelogram. If the parallelogram provides the length of the slanted side of the figure and the length of the base of the right triangle, you can solve for the height of the parallelogram by using the Pythagorean Theorem. The figure below has sides labeled *a*, *b*, and *c* to represent the different variables of the Pythagorean Theorem.

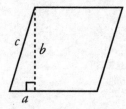

Solving for the perimeter of a parallelogram follows a similar pattern. You can use the height of the figure and the base of the triangle created by the height to solve for the length of the slanted edge.

Trapezoids

A trapezoid is a quadrilateral with only one set of parallel sides. A trapezoid could look like this:

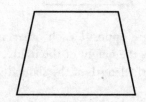

In the case of the figure above, the parallel sides are the top and the bottom of the figure. The GRE tests the area and perimeter of trapezoids. The most effective way to solve for the area of the figure is to split the trapezoid into more familiar shapes and solve for the area of each of those shapes individually. For instance, the trapezoid above can be split into two right triangles and a rectangle:

Anytime there is an unfamiliar figure, look for ways to split that figure up into more familiar shapes.

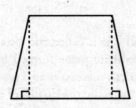

You can then solve for the area of each of these familiar shapes individually and add them together to get the area of the trapezoid.

Finding the perimeter of a trapezoid follows a similar pattern to finding that of a parallelogram. Finding the lengths of the sides typically involves using the Pythagorean Theorem.

Parallelograms and Trapezoids Drill

Now work on solving for the area of the parallelogram and trapezoid below. Answers can be found in Part V.

1.

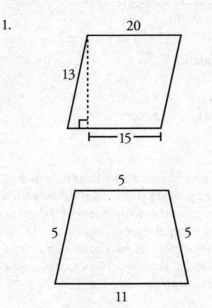

Coordinate Plane

In a coordinate system, the horizontal line is called the **x-axis** and the vertical line is called the **y-axis**. The four sections of the coordinate plane formed by the intersection of these axes are called **quadrants**. While it is not strictly necessary to know the ordering of the quadrants for most coordinate plane problems, occasionally the quadrant numbers are asked about directly or mentioned as a compass on a question. So being familiar with them is a good idea. The point where the axes intersect is called the **origin** and its coordinates are (0, 0). This is what it looks like:

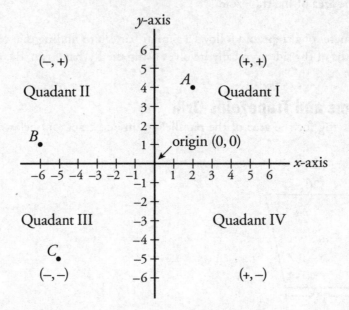

To express any point in the coordinate system, you first give the horizontal value, which is the value of the point associated with the x-axis. Next, you provide the vertical value, which is the value of the point associated with the y-axis. This creates the coordinates of the point, or (x, y). In the diagram above, point A can be described by the coordinates (2, 4). That is, the point is two spaces to the right of the origin and four spaces above the origin. Point B is described by the coordinates (–6, 1). That is, it is six spaces to the left and one space above the origin. What are the coordinates of point C?

> The coordinates of point C are (–5, –5).

The coordinate plane is often used to test shapes drawn onto the plane, such as circles, triangles, or rectangles. However, information about lines found on the plane, such as intercepts, the equation of a line, slope, points on a line, and perpendicular and parallel lines is also fair game for the GRE.

Intercepts

The **x-intercept** and **y-intercept** are the points at which a line on the coordinate plane crosses the x-axis or y-axis, respectively. The point at which a line crosses the x-axis happens when the coordinate of the point has a y-value of 0. The point at which a line crosses the y-axis happens when the coordinate of the point has an x-value of 0. Therefore, in order to determine the x-intercept or y-intercept, find the value of the x- or y-coordinate when the y or x coordinate is equal to 0.

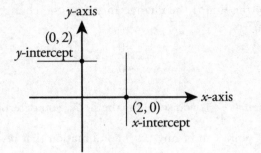

The Equation of a Line & Slope

Trickier questions involving the coordinate system might give you the equation for a line on the coordinate plane. The **equation of a line** is:

$$y = mx + b$$

In this equation x and y are both points on the line, b stands for the y-intercept, and m is the slope of the line. **Slope** is defined as the vertical change divided by the horizontal change, often called "rise over the run" or "the change in y over the change in x."

$$Slope = \frac{rise}{run} = \frac{y_2 - y_1}{x_2 - x_1}$$

Slope can be any number, positive or negative, and this designation dictates how a line appears on the coordinate plane. A line with a positive slope trends upward from Quadrant III to Quadrant I and a line with a negative slope trends downward from Quadrant II to Quadrant IV.

> Sometimes on the GRE, m is written instead as a, as in $y = ax + b$. If you see this, don't worry. Nothing has changed about the equation for the line or the slope if m is written as a.

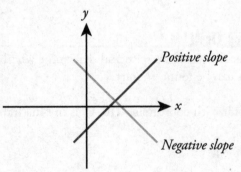

Points On A Line

If the problem provides 2 points on a line, or one point on a line and the slope, it is possible to determine the location of other points on the line. The equation of a line can be used, in combination with the information provided, to determine missing points. Typically, the GRE provides one of the points on the line and then ask to determine either the x- or y-coordinate of a missing point.

For instance, if a question provided the information that a line passes through the origin and has a slope of 3, you could determine that the line also passes through the point (1, 3). You can do this by setting up a proportion. If the slope of the line is 3, the line passes through the origin, and the slope of the line is the change in y over the change in x, then the following equation can be written:

$$\frac{y_2 - 0}{x_2 - 0} = 3$$

The slope can be rewritten as $\frac{3}{1}$. If you solve for the slope, you determine that $y_2 = 3$ and $x_2 = 1$. The value of the missing point can be any (x, y) combination that results in a value of 3 for the expression $\frac{y}{x}$. Alternatively, if a problem provides to you two points on a line, it is possible to find a third point. Use the two points to determine the slope and then use one of the points and the slope in the same manner shown above.

Perpendicular and Parallel Lines

Perpendicular lines are lines with slopes that are negative reciprocals of each other. These lines intersect at a right angle. **Parallel lines** are lines with the same slope. Parallel lines will never intersect.

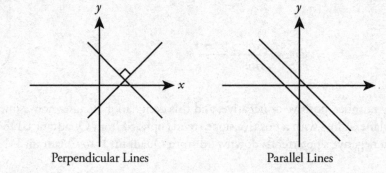

Perpendicular Lines   Parallel Lines

Coordinate Geometry Drill

Work your way through the following exercise and determine whether the statements provided are True or False. Answers can be found in Part V.

1.   True   False   A point with coordinates (10, 6) is in Quadrant II.

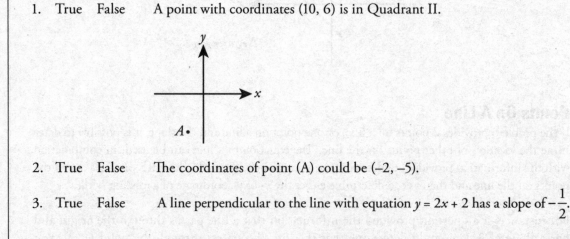

2.   True   False   The coordinates of point (A) could be (–2, –5).

3.   True   False   A line perpendicular to the line with equation $y = 2x + 2$ has a slope of $-\frac{1}{2}$.

4. True   False   A line that passes through the origin and point (–2, –1) also passes through the point (–1, 2).

5. True   False   The slope of a line that passes through points (1, 2) and (–1, 6) is 2.

6. True   False   A line with equation $3x + 2y = 6$ has a positive slope.

7. True   False   The equation of a line that passes through the origin and point (2, 6) is $y = 3x$.

8. True   False   The x- and y-intercepts of a line that passes through points (3, 1) and

(–1, 9) are $\dfrac{7}{2}$ and 7, respectively.

3D Figures

3D figures on the GRE typically come in one of two forms: cylinders or rectangular solids. In order to answer most questions regarding 3D figures, you'll need to know how to calculate the surface area and volume of each figure, and how to find the length of the diagonal of a rectangular solid or cube.

Cylinder

When represented visually, cylinders look like some variation of the following:

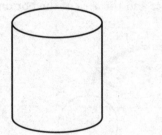 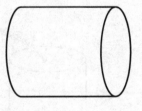

A cylinder may also be described as a *right circular cylinder*. No matter how a cylinder is represented, the most common concepts to test about this figure are surface area and volume.

Surface area is the area of the outer part of a figure. For example, the surface area of a can of soup is the area of the top and bottom of the can plus the area of the curved sides of the can.

Volume is the amount of space that a substance could occupy. The volume of a can of soup is the amount of soup that can fit inside the can.

The GRE can also use the concept of circular cylinder in word problems and refer to them as a word that describes a cylinder, such as "tanks," "circular cylindrical tanks," "tubes," and "pipes."

Surface Area

The surface area of a cylinder is calculated by the equation:

$$Surface\ Area = 2\pi r(height) + 2(\pi r^2)$$

This equation looks like a lot. But, let's break it down into its individual components.

The surface area of a cylinder is the sum of the area of the top of the cylinder, the area of the bottom of the cylinder, and the area of the curved side of the cylinder. The curved side of the cylinder is actually a rectangle that has been curved. Imagine taking a rectangular piece of paper and rolling it so two opposing edges now touch. Alternatively, imagine what would result if you removed the top and bottom from a can of soup, cut the resulting piece straight down just one side, and flattened it out. The height of the resulting rectangle is the same as the height of the can. However, the length of the rectangle is equal to the circumference of the top or bottom of the can. The circumference of a circle is found by the expression $2\pi r$. Visually, the length and height of a cylinder can be represented by something like this:

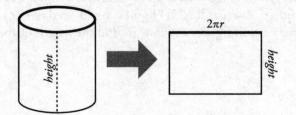

On the GRE, the area of the top of the cylinder and the area of the bottom of the cylinder are equivalent circles.

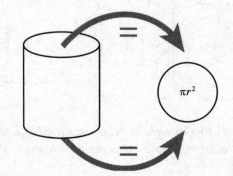

The equation for surface area given above is just the sum of the areas of all these individual components. This can be represented graphically as:

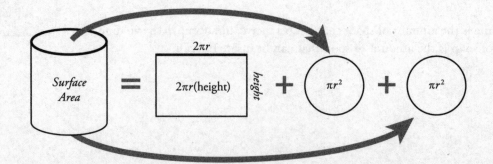

In order to solve for the surface area of a circular cylinder, it is necessary to have, or be able to derive, a value for the radius of the top or bottom of the cylinder as well as the height of the cylinder.

Volume

The volume of a cylinder is calculated by the equation:

$$Volume = \pi r^2 (height)$$

The volume of a cylinder is the value of all the space inside the cylinder.

In the cylinder above, the volume is represented by the shaded area. Consider volume as the amount of water it would take to fill the cylinder. If water were to be poured into the cylinder, the water would first fill up the area of the bottom of the cylinder and then fill that area for the entirety of the height of the cylinder. This is the information that the equation for the volume of a cylinder is asking for—solve first for the area of the base of the cylinder and then multiply it by the height.

3D Figures–Cylinders Drill

Now that you're equipped with some knowledge about finding surface area and volume for a cylinder, fill in the blanks in the following exercises. Answers can be found in Part V.

1.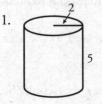

   Area of the curved side of the figure: _____

   Area of the top of the figure: _____

   Surface area: _____

2. A cylinder with a volume of 18π and a radius of 3 has a height of _____.

3. What is the volume of a cylinder with a height of 4 and the following measurements:

    a. a radius of 3 ? _____

    b. a base with an area of 4π ? _____

    c. a diameter of 8 ? _____

4. Determine the surface area of cylinders with the following measurements:

    a. Height 2; Radius 3

    b. Height 3; Radius 2

    c. Height 5; Radius 1

    d. Height 1; Radius 3

Rectangular Solids

When represented visually, rectangular solids or cubes look like this:

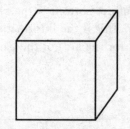

The most commonly tested concepts with rectangular solids are volume and surface area. However, occasionally the GRE tests the length of the diagonal of the rectangular solid or cube.

Surface area is the area of the outer part of the rectangular solid. This is represented by the area of the top and bottom, front and back, and both sides of the figure.

Volume is the amount of space inside the figure. This is the amount of space that could be occupied by a substance placed inside the rectangular solid.

> Don't be afraid to draw in these dotted lines on your own figure during the test if it makes the figure easier to look at.

It is easier to visualize the items required to calculate the surface area and volume by placing dotted lines in the figure to represent the missing edges. This makes it clear that there are 6 faces (flat sides) that create the outside of the figure. The sum of the areas of each of these six sides is the surface area.

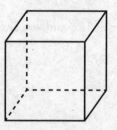

The diagonal of the rectangular solid or cube is the longest distance between two corners. This is represented by the xxx dotted line below.

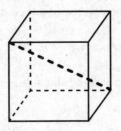

Surface Area

The surface area of a rectangular solid is calculated via the equation:

$$Surface\ Area = 2(length \times width) + 2(length \times height) + 2(width \times height)$$

For a regular rectangular solid, the side lengths are labeled as follows:

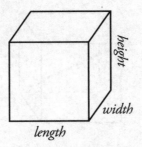

Let's look at each of the components of the equation for surface area independently.

The expression *length* × *width* produces the area for the top or the bottom of the figure. The equation for surface area multiplies this by 2 to represent the area of both the top and bottom of the figure. The expression *length* × *height* represents the area of the front or back of the rectangular solid and this is also multiplied by 2 to represent the front and the back. Finally, the expression *width* × *height* represents the area of one of the sides of the rectangular solid. The product is multiplied by 2 to account for both faces on the sides.

Ultimately, the surface area of a rectangular solid or cube is the sum of the areas of the faces. For a cube, this equation is greatly simplified. A cube is a rectangular solid that has equal length, width, and height. To find the surface area of a cube, the expression is $6(s^2)$, where s is the length of one of the edges of the cube.

The formula for the surface area of a cube is just the formula for the area of a square multiplied by 6.

Volume

The equation for the volume of a rectangular solid is simpler than that of the surface area of the rectangular solid. The equation for the volume of a rectangular solid is:

$$Volume = length \times width \times height$$

Therefore, calculating the volume of a rectangular solid only involves figuring out the values of the length, width, and height.

The volume of a cube is found by the expression s^3, where s is the value for either the length, width, or height of the cube.

Diagonal

In the figure below, the diagonal of a rectangular solid is depicted by the dotted line. The diagonal of a rectangular solid is the straight-line distance between points A and B. This is the longest length inside of a rectangular solid.

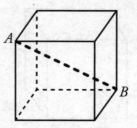

Solving for the distance between A and B requires only one equation. The equation is:

$$a^2 + b^2 + c^2 = d^2$$

In the equation, d is the value of the diagonal distance while a, b, and c are the dimensions of the rectangular solid. If you're familiar with right triangles, this equation will remind you a lot of the Pythagorean Theorem. In fact, this equation is called the Super Pythagorean Theorem.

Great work!

3D Figures—Rectangular Solids Drill

Now work with the following rectangular solids and determine their surface area, volume, and diagonal length. Answers can be found in Part V.

1.

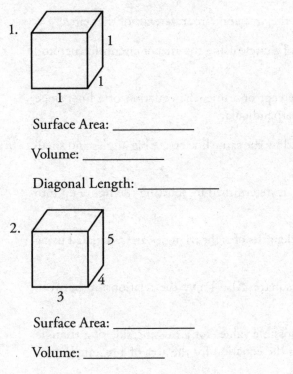

Surface Area: _____

Volume: _____

Diagonal Length: _____

2.

Surface Area: _____

Volume: _____

Diagonal Length: _____

3.

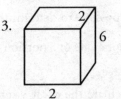

Surface Area: _____

Volume: _____

Diagonal Length: _____

4.

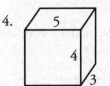

Surface Area: _____

Volume: _____

Diagonal Length: _____

> Notice any similarities between the rectangular solids in questions 2 and 4? That's right—their values are the same. When calculating the surface area, volume, and diagonal of a rectangular solid, it typically does not matter what edge receives what length or label. The only time it does matter is if another figure shares one of the edges.

ANSWERS TO THE "SHOULD I DO THIS CHAPTER?" QUIZ

1. $V = Length \times width \times height$

2. 16π

3. $y = mx + b$

4. 180

5. 720

6. $P = 2(length) + 2(width)$

7. Right triangle

8. $\frac{rise}{run}$ or $\frac{y_2 - y_1}{x_2 - x_1}$

9. 360

10. $A = \frac{1}{2}\left(base\right)\left(height\right)$

Summary

o   Cylinders and rectangular solids are the most common types of 3D figures on the GRE. Know how to find the surface area and volume of each.

o   Using the radius of a circle, it is possible to determine the area and circumference of that circle.

o   Calculate the arc length or interior angle of a portion of a circle using the area or circumference and a proportion.

o   Use coordinate geometry to calculate the *x*- or *y*-intercept of a line, the equation of a line, slope, points on a line, or whether two lines are parallel or perpendicular.

o   There are 180 degrees in a line. Parallel lines intersected by the same line create big angles and small angles. Vertical angles are equal.

o   The area of polygons, such as hexagons and octagons, is determined by splitting the figure up into familiar shapes.

o   Right triangles are a special kind of triangle. The side lengths of right triangles are calculated using the Pythagorean Theorem.

o   Know how to calculate the perimeter and area of a square. Also know the relationship between squares and right triangles.

o   The Third Side Rule can be used to find a range of possible values for a missing side of a triangle. The equation for the area of a triangle is exactly half of the equation for the area of a rectangle.

Chapter 15
GRE Geometry

Now that you know the basics of geometry on the GRE, it's time to put those skills to the test. This chapter contains practice problems and solutions, actionable advice on how to crack certain problem types, and information about specific types of questions you may encounter on test day.

WHAT'S INSIDE?

The previous chapter explored the basics of geometry on the GRE. It covered the types of figures you can expect to see, what you might be expected to calculate, and the calculations necessary to get to the correct answers. While the previous chapter focuses mostly on **what** geometry concepts the GRE tests, this chapter focuses on **how** those geometry concepts are tested on the GRE.

This chapter <u>does not</u> discuss, in any detail, what figures look like, their specific properties, or the equations needed to solve for specific measurements. This chapter assumes a basic working knowledge of geometry rules and formulas. We covered all the rules and formulas that you need to know in the previous chapter.

Unsure whether you should tackle this chapter or start with the previous chapter?

Take this short quiz to find out!

"Should I Do This Chapter?" Quiz

1. What is the formula for the volume of a rectangular solid? _____

2. If the radius of a circle is 4, what is its area? _____

3. What is the equation of a line? _____

4. How many degrees are there in a line? _____

5. What is the sum of the interior angle measurements of a figure with 6 sides? _____

6. What is the formula for the perimeter of a rectangle? _____

7. The side lengths of what kind of triangle can be found using the Pythagorean Theorem? _____

8. What is the equation for the slope of a line? _____

9. How many degrees are in a circle? _____

10. What is the formula for the area of a triangle? _____

The answers to these questions are at the back of this chapter.

So, how'd you do? If you got more than two questions wrong, you might want to consider starting with the previous chapter.

For those of you who are continuing forward with this chapter (or for those of you who rejoined us after a sojourn with the previous chapter), welcome! This chapter shows you how the GRE typically tests geometry concepts. It is filled with sample GRE problems to test your skills. We will be with you the whole time to walk you through how to answer these sample problems. Along the way, we'll reveal to you some important tips and tricks for how to increase your odds of getting the question correct, and trends for how the GRE likes to test geometry concepts.

There is also a 15-question drill at the end of this chapter. Answer the questions in that drill when you feel confident in the material contained within the chapter. This is the most obvious place to test yourself in this chapter. Meanwhile, the questions contained in the body of the chapter are explained immediately following each question. When possible, we'd recommend that you try to answer each question before reading the explanation. Don't be bothered if you get the question wrong—that's how you learn!

We'll start by looking at the most straightforward topics and gradually move into the more complex. The questions each try to outline a common way the GRE tests a specific topic.

Without any further preamble, let's get started.

A Couple Important Tips to Remember

While every geometry question on the GRE is unique and requires a unique combination of equations, there are a couple of universal tips that can be applied across all problems.

1. Draw the figure and label any information from the problem on the figure.

Oftentimes, GRE geometry problems provide or describe a figure. Occasionally, problems describe a relationship among data points that create a common figure when drawn. Even if a figure is provided for a given question, that figure appears on a computer screen. Avoid trying to do calculations in your head by first drawing or redrawing the figure from the problem on your scratch paper and labeling any information from the problem on the figure.

2. Figures are not necessarily drawn to scale.

Figures provided to you on the GRE may not be drawn to scale, so be skeptical of them. Always make sure to draw and label figures based on the information provided in the problem.

Degrees, Lines, and Angles

Consider the following question, which asks about angles and lines:

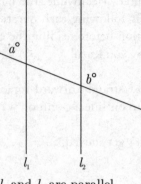

> Degrees, lines, and angles are asked about in conjunction with other basic shapes to make these questions more difficult.

l_1 and l_2 are parallel.

Quantity A	Quantity B
$a + b$	180

○ Quantity A is greater.

○ Quantity B is greater.

○ The two quantities are equal.

○ The relationship cannot be determined from the information given.

Here's How to Crack It:

This is a Quant Comp question with geometry, so begin by drawing the figure and labeling any information from the problem on the figure. The question only states that lines l_1 and l_2 are parallel. Now work with the quantities. Quantity A is the value of $a + b$. The parallel lines in the figure are intersected by the same line, which creates big angles and small angles at each intersection. The rule of parallel lines dictates that when two parallel lines are crossed by a third line, the big angles are equal and the small angles are equal. Additionally, the sum of any big angle and any small angle is 180 degrees, as there are 180 degrees in a line. Angle a is a small angle and angle b is a large angle, so the value of $a + b$ is 180. Quantity B is also 180. The quantities are equal. The correct answer is choice (C).

Knowing the properties of parallel lines helps answer the previous question. Occasionally, the GRE asks about lines or angles independently of any other figure or concept, such as in the previous question. However, most of the time the GRE asks about degrees, lines, and angles in relationship to other figures. How could knowing the properties of parallel lines, plus a little knowledge about parallelograms, help to answer this more complex question?

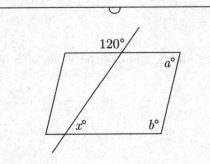

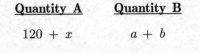

	Quantity A	Quantity B

$120 + x$ $a + b$

○ Quantity A is greater.

○ Quantity B is greater.

○ The two quantities are equal.

○ The relationship cannot be determined from the information given.

Here's How to Crack It:

This is a Quant Comp question with geometry, so begin by drawing the figure and labeling any information from the problem on the figure. The problem states that the figure is a parallelogram, so the sides opposite each other are parallel. There is no additional information in the problem, so begin working with the quantities. Quantity A is $120 + x$. The angle marked as 120 is the large angle created by a line intersecting two parallel sides. The angle marked x is the small angle created by the same line. When two parallel lines are intersected by the same line, the large and small angles that are formed have a sum of 180. Therefore, $x = 180 - 120 = 60$ and Quantity A is $120 + 60 = 180$. Now work with Quantity B. Quantity B is $a + b$. For any parallelogram, angles on the same side add up to 180°. Therefore, Quantity B is 180. The quantities are equal. The correct answer is choice (C).

The previous example shows how the GRE combines concepts from two different knowledge bases to make a more difficult problem. In that example, if you do not know about the big and small angles of parallel lines or about parallelograms you may struggle to determine the correct answer.

Let's try another example of how the GRE could test degrees. But, this time let's consider an example that only involves vertical angles and lines.

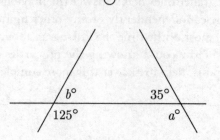

In the figure above, what is the value of $a + b$?

- ○ 145
- ○ 155
- ○ 180
- ○ 200
- ○ 225

Here's How to Crack It:

This is a geometry question, so begin by drawing the figure and labeling any information from the problem on the figure. The question stem provides no additional information, so work the problem. The question asks for the value of $a + b$. Determine the value of these variables independently. Angle a is adjacent to a 35-degree angle that is created by the intersection of two lines. Therefore, angle a is the difference between the degrees in the line and 35, which is $180 - 35 = 145$. Angle b is adjacent to a 125-degree angle that is created by a different intersection of two lines. So, angle b is the difference between the degrees in the line and 125, which is $180 - 125 = 55$. The value of $a + b$ is $145 + 55 = 200$. The correct answer is choice (D).

On the GRE, the measure of only one of the vertical angles is typically shown. But usually you'll need to use the other angle to solve the problem.

There were several ways to solve the problem above. For instance, you could have noticed that the two lines are each 180 degrees, so the total degrees for both lines is 360 degrees. Then, it would have been reasonable to write the equation $a + b + 35 + 125 = 360$ and solve to find that $a + b = 200$.

Much like with parallel lines, vertical angles are often paired with another domain of knowledge. Take, for example, the following question that works with circles.

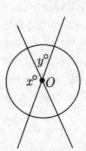

In the figure above, the circle has center O and the two lines intersect at point O. If the length of the arc of the circle opposite angle y is $\frac{1}{6}$ the total circumference of the circle, then what is the measure of angle x ?

○ 45

○ 90

○ 120

○ 135

○ 150

Here's How to Crack It:

While this problem appears to be predominantly about circles, it is primarily about vertical angles with only a little circle knowledge required. This is a geometry question, so begin by drawing the figure and labeling any information from the problem on the figure. The question states that the arc opposite angle y is $\frac{1}{6}$ the total circumference of the circle. Because the length of an arc is proportional to its corresponding angle, angle y is $\frac{1}{6}$ the total angle of the circle. A circle has 360 degrees, so angle y is $360 \times \frac{1}{6} = 60$ degrees. Because angle y was created by two intersecting lines, angle y has a vertical angle pair with the angle directly below it. Therefore, the angle directly below angle y is also 60 degrees. The total value of these two angles is 120 degrees. Angle x and the angle opposite angle x are also vertical angles, so they are also equal. Because the vertical pair with angle y makes up 120 of the 360 degrees in a circle, the vertical angle pair with angle x makes up $360 - 120 = 240$ degrees. Because the angles are equal, both angle x and the angle opposite it are $240 \div 2 = 120$ degrees. The correct answer is choice (C).

LIFE IS BETTER WITH FRIENDS

Beginning this chapter's specific discussions with degrees, lines, and angles serves a few valuable purposes. First, the line is the simplest form of a geometric figure. Maybe more critically, this topic illustrates how the GRE often pairs more than one concept together. If you had an in-depth understanding of lines and angles, but only a cursory understanding of circles or parallelograms, you may have missed one of these questions.

> The most common way the GRE increases the difficulty of a question is by pairing it with another figure. This allows them to test domain knowledge from two shapes instead of one.

The GRE does not stop pairing concepts with degrees, lines, and angles. They pair all sort of figures together—circles, squares, triangles, coordinate planes, polygons, etc. Always keep your eye open for figures or descriptions that indicate more than one shape. If you see these types of figures, take the problem one shape at a time. Typically, something about one of the shapes leads to opportunities to uncover missing information about the other.

Triangles

The GRE often tries to ask for the area of a triangle, or the length of one of the sides of a triangle, by hiding the fact that it is asking about a triangle at all. Don't be fooled! Take the following problem, for example:

Adam's house is 3 kilometers due west of the local high school and 7 kilometers due north of the local grocery store.

Quantity A	Quantity B
The straight-line distance, in kilometers, between the local high school and the local grocery store.	8 kilometers

○ Quantity A is greater.

○ Quantity B is greater.

○ The two quantities are equal.

○ The relationship cannot be determined from the information given.

Here's How to Crack It:

The question begins by describing the location of three places: Adam's house, the local high school, and the local grocery store. Draw each of these places and label any information. Place a point and label it *A* for Adam's house. Draw a line from point *A* directly to the right to another point labeled *H*, for the local high school. Label the length of that line 3 kilometers. Draw another line directly down from point A to another point labeled *G*, for the local grocery store. Label the length of this line 7 kilometers. This is all the information in the problem, so now work with the quantities. Quantity A is the straight-line distance, in kilometers, between the local high school and the local grocery store. Draw the line between points G and H and label it x. This creates triangle AGH. Because point A is directly to the right of point H and directly north of point G, this creates a right angle. So, triangle AGH is a right triangle. Determine the length of the missing side by using the Pythagorean Theorem. The length of the missing side is between $3^2 + 7^2 = 58$, so $c^2 = 58$ and $c = \sqrt{58}$. Quantity B is 8 kilometers. Because $\sqrt{64} = 8$, Quantity B is greater than Quantity A. The correct answer is choice (B).

Do you notice anything interesting about the previous triangle question? How about the fact that at no point during the question stem or the quantities did the word "triangle" ever appear? The only reasonable way we know this is a triangle question is if we draw the figure described, label the information in the problem, and recognize the presence of the triangle.

Now work with the following question:

A right triangle has legs of length x and y such that $3 \leq x \leq 5$ and $4 \leq y \leq 8$. Which of the following could be the length of the hypotenuse?

Indicate <u>all</u> such lengths.

- ◯ 5
- ◯ 6
- ◯ 7
- ◯ 8
- ◯ 9

Here's How to Crack It:

This is an All that Apply question, so make sure to evaluate each answer choice. The question describes a right triangle with leg lengths $3 \leq x \leq 5$ and $4 \leq y \leq 8$ and asks for the length of the hypotenuse. The hypotenuse of a right triangle is found using the Pythagorean Theorem, so find the range of possible values of the hypotenuse. The least possible length of the hypotenuse is when $x = 3$ and $y = 4$, so use the Pythagorean Theorem to find that the hypotenuse is $9 + 16 = c^2$ and $c^2 = 25$. Therefore, $c = 5$ and the least length of the hypotenuse is 5. The greatest possible length of the hypotenuse is when $x = 5$ and $y = 8$, so that length is $25 + 64 = c^2$ and $c^2 = 89$. So, $c = \sqrt{89}$. While it may not be apparent what $\sqrt{89}$ is as a decimal or fraction, it can be determined that it is greater than 9 but less than 10 because $\sqrt{81} = 9$ and $\sqrt{100} = 10$. All the answer choices are integer lengths, so the range for the length of the hypotenuse is $5 \leq hypotenuse < 10$. All of the answer choices fall within this range, so the correct answer is choices (A), (B), (C), (D), and (E).

The preceding question is an example of combining two concepts into one question using geometry and one of the other GRE math topics. In the case above, we needed to use knowledge of triangles and knowledge of working with inequalities to find a range in order to answer the question.

Which leads us to another important point for how GRE geometry questions are made more difficult—they are not always paired with another figure. They are occasionally paired with a concept from another discipline. This means that GRE geometry questions are more chameleon-like than algebra and arithmetic—they can take on different styles.

Nonetheless, the difficulty of a GRE geometry question is usually increased by pairing two figures. This is especially true of triangles. The hypotenuse of a triangle is a natural pair for the diameter of a circle of the diagonal length of a rectangle. Take the following question for example:

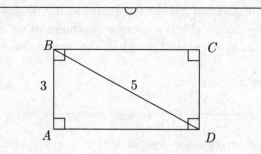

In the rectangle above, what is the area of triangle *ABD* ?

Click on the answer box and type in a number.
Backspace to erase.

Here's How to Crack It:

This is a geometry question, so redraw the figure and label any information from the problem.

The problem states that figure *ABCD* is a rectangle. This was apparent from the presence of the small squares at the corners of the rectangle, which indicate a right angle. The question asks for the area of triangle *ABD*, which can be found by the expression $\frac{1}{2}(base)(height)$. The figure provides the height, which is 3. The figure also provides the length of the hypotenuse, 5, so solve for the length of the base using the Pythagorean Theorem. Alternatively, recognize that 3 and 5 are both members of a 3:4:5 special right triangle. Either way, the length of the base is 4. Therefore, the area of triangle *ABD* is $\frac{1}{2}(4)(3) = 6$. The correct answer is 6.

The previous question makes it apparent that *ABD* is a triangle and that *BD* is both the hypotenuse of the triangle and the diagonal of the rectangle. The same is true about the hypotenuse of the triangle and the side of the square in the following figure. For practice, try to use the information provided to determine the area of square *ABDE*.

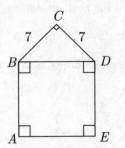

While the previous two figures made it obvious what role the sides of the triangle play in the relationship to the other figure, oftentimes the GRE does not provide for you all the necessary lines. Instead, they may expect you to draw them in yourself. An example of this is in the next question, which tests another special right triangle.

Because the legs of the triangle are both 7 and the angle opposite the hypotenuse is a right angle, this is a 45:45:90 triangle. The sides of a 45:45:90 triangle have a relationship of $x : x : x\sqrt{2}$ so the hypotenuse, which is also a side of the square, is $7\sqrt{2}$. The area of the square is $(7\sqrt{2})^2 = 49 \times 2 = 98$.

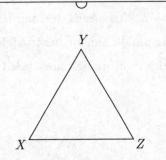

Triangle *XYZ* in the figure above is an equilateral triangle. If the perimeter of the triangle is 12, what is its area?

○ $2\sqrt{3}$

○ $4\sqrt{3}$

○   8

○   12

○ $8\sqrt{3}$

Here's How to Crack It:

This is a geometry question, so begin by drawing the figure and labeling any information from the problem on the figure. The question states that triangle *XYZ* is an equilateral triangle, so each of the angles is 60 degrees. The question also states that the perimeter of the triangle is 12, so the length of each side of the triangle is 4. The question asks for the area of the triangle, which is found by the equation $area = \frac{1}{2}(base)(height)$. The base of the triangle is the length of one of the sides, so the base is 4. However, to determine the height, it is necessary to drop a line from one of the points straight down to intersect the opposite side. Because the triangle is equilateral, this line bisects the angle it originated from, creating two 30-degree angles, as shown below:

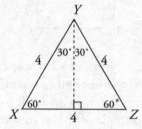

This creates two 30:60:90-degree special right triangles, each with a side relationship of $x : x\sqrt{3} : 2x$, respectively. The length of the hypotenuse of the triangle is 4 and that corresponds to the side of $2x$, so $2x = 4$ and $x = 2$. This means the short leg of the triangle (the one opposite the 30-degree angle) is 2 and the middle side of the triangle, which is also the height of the triangle, is $2\sqrt{3}$. The lengths of this right triangle are labeled in the figure below:

If you see square root 2 or square root 3 in the answer choices, it's a tip off that the problem is testing special right triangles.

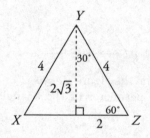

The height of the triangle is $2\sqrt{3}$, so the area of the triangle is $\frac{1}{2}(4)(2\sqrt{3}) = 4\sqrt{3}$. The correct answer is choice (B).

Knowing the relationships between the sides and angle measurements of right triangles is essential to answering some GRE questions, so make sure to know these cold.

The previous question did not make it explicit that it was testing 30:60:90 triangles. Instead, getting the question correct relied on you to draw the height, recognize that the height creates two 30:60:90 triangles, and know the relationship between the sides and angles of a 30:60:90 triangle. While that question only tested one figure—a single triangle—the most difficult triangle questions include a relationship between a triangle and another figure while concealing the presence of the relationship. This requires that you be capable of parsing out the missing information. And here's the real kicker—the question may not even appear to include a triangle at all!

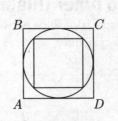

In the figure above, a circle is inscribed in a square and another square is inscribed in the circle. If the area of the smaller square is 36, what is the straight-line distance between points A and C ?

○ $6\sqrt{2}$

○ 12

○ 24

○ $36\sqrt{2}$

○ 72

Here's How to Crack It:

This is a geometry question, so begin by drawing the figure and labeling any information from the problem on the figure. The problem states that a circle is inscribed in a square and a square is inscribed in that circle. The area of the smaller square is 36, which means that the length of the sides of the smaller square is 6. If the length of each of the sides is 6, then the smaller square is made up of two 45:45:90-degree triangles that have legs of length 6. The side relationship of a 45:45:90 triangle is $x : x : x\sqrt{2}$, so the length of the hypotenuse is $6\sqrt{2}$. The hypotenuse of the smaller square is the same length as the diameter of the circle. Because a circle's diameter is constant for all lines that pass through the center of the circle, this figure could be redrawn as follows:

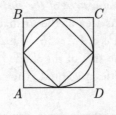

Considering this, the diameter of the circle is the same length as the sides of the larger square. This is also described by the word *inscribed* in the question stem, which means that the circle touches the square at the ends of the diameter. The question asks about the distance between points A and C. Square $ABCD$ is also made up of two 45:45:90 triangles with legs of length $6\sqrt{2}$. Therefore, the length of the diagonal of the larger square is $6\sqrt{2}\left(\sqrt{2}\right) = 12$. The correct answer is choice (B).

Rectangles, Squares, and other Quadrilaterals

One common way for the GRE to test relationships between figures is by shading portions of a figure, such as can be seen in the next question:

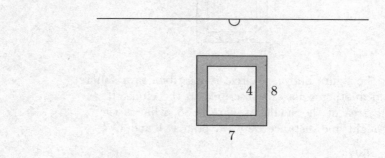

In the figure above, a square is placed inside of a rectangle.

Quantity A	Quantity B
The area of the shaded region	40

○ Quantity A is greater.

○ Quantity B is greater.

○ The two quantities are equal.

○ The relationship cannot be determined from the information given.

Here's How to Crack It:

This is a Quant Comp question with geometry, so begin by drawing the figure and labeling any information from the problem on the figure. The problem states that a square is placed inside a rectangle, so the larger quadrilateral is a rectangle and the smaller quadrilateral is a square. Now work with the quantities. Quantity A is the area of the shaded region. The area of the shaded region is found by the expression *area of the entire figure – area of the unshaded region* (that is, area of the entire figure minus area of the unshaded region). The area of the entire figure is the area of the rectangle, which is 8 × 7 = 56. The area of the unshaded region is the area of the square, which is 4^2 = 16. So, the area of the shaded region is 56 – 16 = 40. Quantity A is 40. Quantity B is also 40. The quantities are equal. The correct answer is choice (C).

If you look closely, there is something curious about the figure in the previous problem. The larger quadrilateral certainly *looks* like a square, but the problem states it's a rectangle and the lengths of the sides are not the same, which means it is not a square. What gives?

The GRE is under no obligation to draw figures to scale. The GRE occasionally uses this fact to trip students up. Consider the following problem:

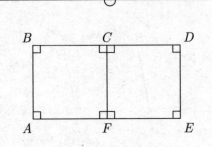

In the figure above, $BC = CF$.

Quantity A	**Quantity B**
The area of	The area of
ABCF	*FCDE*

○ Quantity A is greater.

○ Quantity B is greater.

○ The two quantities are equal.

○ The relationship cannot be determined from the information given.

Here's How to Crack It:

This is a Quant Comp question with geometry, so begin by drawing the figure and labeling any information from the problem on the figure. The figure states that $BC = CF$, so mark both BC and CF as x. Now there is a variable in the question, so be prepared to Plug In more than once. There is no further information in the problem, so work with the quantities. Quantity A is the area of *ABCF*. Because $BC = CF$ and the angles of *ABCF* are right angles, *ABCF* is a square. The area of a square is found by the expression $side^2$. The side of *ABCF* is x, so Plug In. If $x = 2$, then the area of *ABCF* is 4. Now work with Quantity B. Quantity B is the area of *FCDE*. The length of side *CF* is $x = 2$. If the length of side *CD* equals the length of side *BC*, then *CD* is also 2 and the area of *FCDE* is 4. In this case, the quantities are equal and choices (A) and (B) can be eliminated. However, the problem gives no indication that $BC = CD$ or that $CF = CD$. Therefore, it is possible that the length of *CD* is 3, for example. If that is the case, then *FCDE* is a rectangle with area $3 \times 2 = 6$. Quantity B is now greater than Quantity A. Eliminate choice (C). The correct answer is choice (D).

When the GRE asks about quadrilaterals, it tends to test the area or the perimeter. Much like it does for every other topic, the GRE increases the difficulty of questions that involve common concepts by obscuring the fact that they are testing something basic by cloaking it with other concepts.

The area of quadrilaterals is one of the knowledge bases the GRE likes to ask about unfamiliar contexts. Check out the following problem:

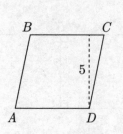

If $AD = 6$, what is the area of parallelogram $ABCD$?

Click on the answer box and type in a number.
Backspace to erase.

Here's How to Crack It:

This is a geometry question, so begin by drawing the figure and labeling any information from the problem on the figure. The problem states that $AD = 6$, so write that on the figure. The question asks for the area of parallelogram $ABCD$. The area of a parallelogram is found by the expression *base* × *height*. The height of the parallelogram is 5 and the base is 6, so the area is 6 × 5 = 30.

The last question is a straightforward area question, so long as you know the formula for the area of a parallelogram. If you don't know the formula for the area of a parallelogram, you may be at a loss for how to find an answer to the question. Next, let's look at an example of how the GRE may obfuscate the concept of quadrilaterals.

A rectangular patio is 6 feet wide by 15 feet long. The rectangular bricks used to make the patio are 6 inches by 12 inches. How many bricks were used to make this patio? (Note: 1 foot = 12 inches)

○ 45

○ 90

○ 120

○ 180

○ 200

Here's How to Crack It:

Start by converting the dimensions of the patio into inches so that both the patio and the bricks are measured using the same units. Because 1 foot is equivalent to 12 inches, the dimensions of the patio are 72 inches wide (6 x 12) by 180 inches long (15 x 12). The area of the patio, in square inches, is A = lw = (72)(180) = 12,960. The area of each brick, in square inches, is A = lw = 6 x 12 = 72. To find the number of bricks needed for the patio, divide the area of the patio by the area of one brick: 12,960/72 = 180. The correct answer is choice (D).

───────────────○───────────────

There are many ways the GRE can test the area or perimeter of quadrilaterals. The best way to prepare for this figure type is to know the equations, be familiar with the different types of quadrilaterals, and understand the relationship between the dimensions that make up the area and the dimensions that make up the perimeter. The area and the perimeter of quadrilaterals are derived from the same dimensions (length and width). If you have the necessary information to solve for one of either the area or perimeter of a quadrilateral, it's often the case that you have the necessary information to solve for both. This tactic can often be combined with less familiar quadrilaterals to really up the difficulty of a problem.

> Unsure of all these formulas and relationships? Check out the previous chapter.

───────────────○───────────────

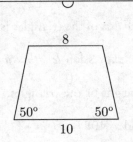

If the area of the trapezoid above is 108, what is the perimeter?

○ $9 + \sqrt{145}$

○ $18 + 2\sqrt{145}$

○ $9 + \sqrt{290}$

○ $18 + 2\sqrt{290}$

○ $27 + \sqrt{145}$

Here's How to Crack It:

This is a geometry question, so begin by drawing the figure and labeling any information from the problem on the figure. The problem states that the area of the trapezoid is 108. The area of the trapezoid can be found by splitting the trapezoid into 3 familiar figures—a rectangle and two right triangles, as shown below.

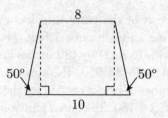

By splitting this figure, it's easier to recognize the right triangles that are created by the heights. Because each right triangle has a right angle and an angle of 50 degrees, the right triangles are identical. Therefore, the length of the base of each triangle is half the difference between the length of the top and the bottom of the trapezoid. The difference between the top and the bottom is $10 - 8 = 2$, so the length of the base for each triangle is 1. There are two identical right triangles, and the area of each is found by the expression $\frac{1}{2}(base)(height)$. Because the triangles are identical, the combined area of the triangles is $2\left(\frac{1}{2}\right)(base)(height) = base \times height$. The base of the triangles is 1, so the combined area of the triangles is equal to whatever the height is. The area of the rectangle is found by the expression *length* × *width*. The width of the rectangle is 8 and the length is the same as the height of the triangles. Therefore, it is possible to write the equation for the area of the trapezoid as $108 = height + 8(height) = 9(height)$ and *height* = 12.

The question asks for the perimeter of the figure. The perimeter of the figure is the sum of the top of the trapezoid, the bottom of the trapezoid, and the hypotenuse of each of the triangles created above. The top and bottom of the trapezoid are given by the problem. The triangles are right triangles and the legs of the triangles are known, so use the Pythagorean Theorem. The hypotenuse is $1^2 + 12^2 = c^2$ and $c^2 = 145$. Thus, $c = \sqrt{145}$. So, the perimeter of the trapezoid is $8 + 10 + \sqrt{145} + \sqrt{145} = 18 + 2\sqrt{145}$. The correct answer is choice (B).

Circles

The GRE asks about a multitude of characteristics of circle—area, circumference, central angles, sectors, arcs, diameter, radius, etc. Finding the correct answer for difficult circle questions on the GRE is often about understanding the relationship between these different characteristics. For instance, it's important to know that if you're given the radius of a circle, you can calculate the area or circumference. Similarly, if you know radius and the length of an arc, you can calculate the central angle or sector area. Take a look at the following problems that illustrate some of the common ways that the GRE tests circles.

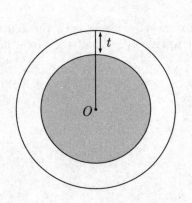

In the wheel above, with center O, the area of the entire wheel is 169π. If the area of the shaded hubcap is 144π, then $t =$

Click on the answer box and type in a number.
Backspace to erase.

Here's How to Crack It:

This is a geometry question, so begin by drawing the figure and labeling any information from the problem on the figure. The problem states that the area of the entire wheel is 169π. The area of a circle is found by the expression πr^2, so $\pi r^2 = 169\pi$. This means $r^2 = 169$ and $r = 13$. The radius of the entire circle with center O is 13. The problem then states that the area of the shaded hubcap is 144π. The radius of the shaded area is found by the equation $\pi r^2 = 144\pi$, which means $r^2 = 144$ and $r = 12$. The problem asks for the value of t, which is the difference between the radius of the circle with center O and the radius of the shaded area, which is $13 - 12 = 1$. The correct answer is 1.

Let's try another one:

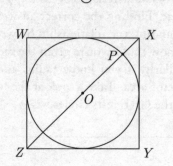

In the figure above, a circle with the center O is inscribed in square $WXYZ$. If the circle has radius 3, then $PZ =$

○ 6

○ $3\sqrt{2}$

○ $6 + \sqrt{2}$

○ $3 + \sqrt{3}$

○ $3\sqrt{2} + 3$

Here's How to Crack It:

This is a geometry question, so begin by drawing the figure and labeling any information from the problem on the figure. The problem states that the circle is inscribed in the square and the circle has a radius of 3. Because the circle is inscribed in the square, the diameter of the circle is the same length as a side of the square. The radius of the circle is 3, so the diameter of the circle is 6, which means that each of the sides of the square are also 6. The question asks for the value of PZ. The length of PZ is the diameter of the circle plus the distance between the end of the circle and the corner of the square. The value for the distance between the edge of the circle and the corner of the square is the difference between the diameter of the circle and the diagonal of the square divided by two. The difference is divided by two because both PX and the distance between Z and the perimeter of the circle are equal. Begin by solving for the value of the diagonal of the square. The diagonal of the square splits the square in half, forming two 45:45:90-degree right triangles. The lengths of the sides of a 45:45:90-degree right triangle are is $x : x : x\sqrt{2}$, respectively. If two sides of the square are 6, then the diagonal is $6\sqrt{2}$. The diameter of the circle is 6. Therefore, the distance between the edge of the circle and the corner of the square is $\frac{6\sqrt{2}-6}{2} = 3\sqrt{2} - 3$. Add this distance to the diameter of the circle to find that the length of PZ is $3\sqrt{2} - 3 + 6 = 3\sqrt{2} + 3$. The correct answer is choice (E).

———————————————○———————————————

Solving the previous two questions involves using the diameter and radius of a circle to yield other information about the circle, such as the area. This diameter and radius of a circle can also be used to determine information about other figures, such as a triangle or a square. But there is more about circles that the GRE can test besides area, diameter, and radius. The following question is a good example of two other measures of circles that are related: arc length and central angle.

———————————————○———————————————

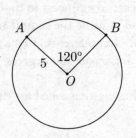

In the circle with center O shown above, what is the length of minor arc AB ?

- $\frac{3}{10\pi}$

- $\frac{10}{3\pi}$

- 3π

- $\frac{10\pi}{3}$

- 10π

Here's How to Crack It:

This is a geometry question, so begin by drawing the figure and labeling any information from the problem on the figure. The problem states that angle AOB is 120 degrees. The question asks about the length of arc AB, which is a portion of the circumference of the circle. Begin by determining the circumference of the circle. The circumference of a circle is found by the expression $2\pi r$. The radius of the circle is 5, so the circumference is 10π. The length of an arc of the circle is proportional to the degree measure of the angle with which it is associated. In this case, arc *AB* is associated with angle *AOB*, which is 120 degrees. The circumference of the circle is associated with the degree measure of the entire circle, so the circumference is related to all 360 degrees in the circle. In order to find the length of the arc, set up a proportion that states $\frac{120 \text{ degrees}}{360 \text{ degrees}} = \frac{x}{10\pi}$. Cross-multiply and divide to find that $1200\pi = 360x$ and $\frac{1200\pi}{360} = \frac{10\pi}{3}$. The correct answer is choice (E).

The previous problem provided the radius and a central angle and asked to solve for the length of an arc. However, the problem could have given the radius and the length of the arc and asked for the central angle. In that case, the process to find the central angle is the same as the process to find the arc length. Instead of using the central angle to find the proportion, find the relationship between the arc and the circumference. Once that fraction is determined, set that equal to the fraction of the missing angle and 360 degrees.

A similar process could be used if the question asked for the area of a shaded segment, such as seen in the figure below.

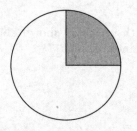

The shaded area of the circle (called a sector) can be calculated if you can determine the area of the entire circle and the central angle that is associated with the shaded region.

Let's try a version of this kind of problem:

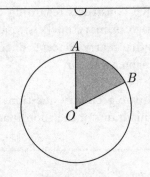

In the circle with center O shown above, if the shaded region has an area of 8ϖ and the measure of angle AOB is 60 degrees, what is the radius of the circle?

○ $2\sqrt{3}$

○ $4\sqrt{3}$

○ $6\sqrt{3}$

○ $8\sqrt{3}$

○ $10\sqrt{3}$

Here's How to Crack It:

This is a geometry question, so begin by drawing the figure and labeling any information from the problem on the figure. The problem states that the area of the shaded region is 8π and the measure of angle AOB is 60 degrees, so set up a proportion to find the area of the entire circle.

That proportion is $\dfrac{60}{360} = \dfrac{8\pi}{x}$. Cross-multiply and divide to find that $60x = 2{,}880\pi$ and $x = 48\pi$. The area of the circle is 48π, so use this and the equation for the area of a circle to calculate the radius as $\pi r^2 = 48\pi$ and $r = \sqrt{48} = 4\sqrt{3}$. The correct answer is choice (B).

There are many iterations of how circles can be tested on the GRE. Circles can be tested alone or with other figures. Covering all these iterations is beyond the scope of this chapter. But, if you take the practice tests and drills, you'll see a good sampling of the different ways the GRE can ask about this versatile shape.

COORDINATE GEOMETRY

The types of questions that the GRE constructs regarding coordinate geometry may be best thought of as falling into one of two primary buckets: questions about concepts specific to coordinate geometry and questions that marry concepts of coordinate geometry with the other types of figures we've seen in this chapter thus far.

Let's begin our discussion of coordinate geometry questions on the GRE with the first group, starting with a question about the quadrants of the coordinate system.

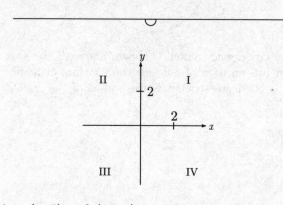

Points $(x, 5)$ and $(-6, y)$, not shown in the figure above, are in Quadrants I and III, respectively. If $xy \neq 0$, in which quadrant is point (x, y) ?

○ IV

○ III

○ II

○ I

○ It cannot be determined from the information given.

Here's How to Crack It:

If point $(x, 5)$ is in Quadrant I, that means x is positive. If point $(-6, y)$ is in Quadrant III, then y is negative. The quadrant that contains coordinate points that have a positive x and a negative y is Quadrant IV. The correct answer is choice (A).

Another basic concept that is specific to coordinate geometry is the slope of a line. Occasionally the GRE asks about the slope of a given line directly. More commonly, the GRE asks about slope as part of the equation of a line. The equation of a line is sometimes provided by the problem. However, the GRE can also ask that the equation be derived by using a line drawn on the coordinate plane that has clearly defined points. An example of this can be seen in the following problem:

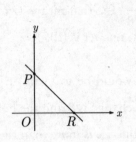

The line $y = -\dfrac{8}{7}x + 1$ is graphed on the rectangular

coordinate axes.

Quantity A	**Quantity B**
OR	OP

○ Quantity A is greater.

○ Quantity B is greater.

○ The two quantities are equal.

○ The relationship cannot be determined from the information given.

Here's How to Crack It:

This is a Quant Comp question with coordinate geometry. The question stem provides a figure and the equation of the line on the figure. Determine the different elements of the equation of the line. The y-intercept, or b, is 1. That means the line crosses the y-axis at 1. So, the coordinates of point P are (0, 1). Now determine the coordinates of point R. We know the y-coordinate is 0 because point R is on the x-axis. Let's use that information along with the equation of the line in the question stem to determine the x-coordinate value of R.

$$y = mx + b$$

$$0 = -\frac{8}{7}x + 1$$

Now let's solve for x.

$$0 = -\frac{8}{7}x + 1$$

$$0 - 1 = -\frac{8}{7}x + 1 - 1$$

$$-1 = -\frac{8}{7}x$$

$$\left(-\frac{7}{8}\right)(-1) = \left(-\frac{7}{8}\right)\left(-\frac{8}{7}\right)x$$

$$\frac{7}{8} = x$$

So the coordinates of point R are $(\frac{7}{8}, 0)$. That means OR, in Quantity A, is equal to $\frac{7}{8}$, and OP, in Quantity B, is equal to 1. The answer is (B).

Another approach to this question would be to focus on the meaning of slope. Because the slope is $-\frac{8}{7}$, that means the vertical change is 8 and the horizontal change is 7. In other words, you count up 8 and over 7. Clearly the rise is more than the run; thus OP is more than OR.

Another way the coordinate plane is tested on the GRE is a question that asks to find a point on a line. Knowing the rise over run equation for computing the slope can help solve these problems.

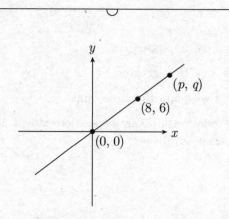

In the rectangular coordinate system above, $q = 9$. If the line passes through the origin, what is the value of p ?

○ 6

○ 8

○ 9

○ 12

○ 13

Here's How to Crack It:

The question states the line passes through the origin and the figure shows that the line passes through point (8, 6). Therefore, the slope of the line is $\frac{6 - 0}{8 - 0} = \frac{3}{4}$. Now that the slope of the line is known, use this information to determine the value of p when $q = 9$ by pairing these points with one of the other points on the line and setting it equal to the slope. The equation is $\frac{9 - 0}{p - 0} = \frac{3}{4}$ and $3p = 36$, so $p = 12$. The correct answer is choice (D).

Coordinate system questions may also ask you to solve for the intercept of a line. The intercept of a line is the point at which the line crosses another. Typically, on the GRE, the intercept is where the line crosses the *x*- or *y*-axis.

Knowing the slope-intercept form of a linear equation can help to solve these types of questions.

Take a look at a question that involves solving for the intercepts:

What is the *x*-intercept of the line defined by the equation $y = 2x + 3$?

○ $\left(\dfrac{2}{3}, \dfrac{2}{3}\right)$

○ $\left(2, -\dfrac{3}{2}\right)$

○ $\left(-\dfrac{3}{2}, 0\right)$

○ $\left(-2, 0\right)$

○ $\left(0, -3\right)$

Here's How to Crack It:

The *x*-intercept is the point at which the line crosses the *x*-axis. The line crosses the *x*-axis when $y = 0$. To solve for the *x*-intercept, set $y = 0$ in the equation and solve for *x*: $0 = 2x + 3$ and $x = -\dfrac{3}{2}$. The answer choices are shown as the points of the *x*-intercept, so find the one where $x = -\dfrac{3}{2}$ and $y = 0$. The correct answer is choice (C).

Coordinate systems sometimes have more than two lines on a single plot. The GRE may ask you to determine the relationship between the two lines.

Many times, the relationship is determined by the slope of the lines. Parallel lines have the same slope. Perpendicular lines have slopes that are negative reciprocals of each other. In other words, if the slope of one line is 2, then the slope of a line perpendicular to it is $-\dfrac{1}{2}$.

Points C and D are located at $(-3, 4)$ and $(5, -12)$, respectively. Line m passes through points C and D. What is the slope of a line that is perpendicular to line m ?

○ -4

○ -2

○ $-\dfrac{1}{2}$

○ $\dfrac{1}{2}$

○ 2

Here's How to Crack It

The slope of line m is equal to $\dfrac{(y_2 - y_1)}{(x_2 - x_1)} = \dfrac{(-12 - 4)}{(5 - (-3))} = \dfrac{-16}{8} = -2$. The negative reciprocal of -2 is $\dfrac{1}{2}$, so the correct answer is (D). Another way to solve this would be to plot line m using points C and D.

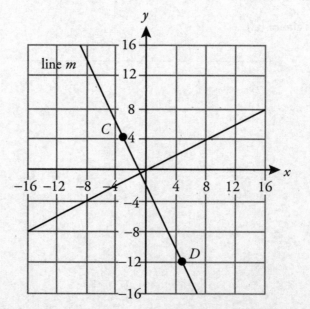

Line *m* slopes rather sharply down from left to right, so it has a negative slope. A line perpendicular to line m would have a positive slope, so (A), (B), and (C) can be eliminated. Finally, a line perpendicular to line m would have a rather gradual positive slope, so eliminate (E).

To recap, the types of coordinate geometry questions that are specific to coordinate geometry involve quadrants, slopes, points on a line, intercepts, and parallel and perpendicular lines.

But, one of the primary ways to ramp up the difficulty of coordinate geometry questions is to involve other figures. The next question is an example of this, which pairs circles and coordinate geometry concepts.

> **Coordinate geometry questions on the GRE test:**
>
> Quadrants
>
> Slope
>
> Points on a line
>
> Intercepts of a line
>
> Parallel or Perpendicular lines

A circle with center (2, 5) and a radius of 4 sits on the coordinate plane. Which of the following points are inside the circle?

Indicate <u>all</u> such points.

○ (5, 6)

○ (6, 9)

○ (−1, 5)

○ (0, 3)

Here's How to Crack It:

In order to determine if a point is inside the circle, it's necessary to determine the number of units that the point is away from the center of the circle. If the number of units is less than the radius of the circle then the point sits inside the circle. The distance between the center of the circle and a point can be considered the hypotenuse of a right triangle that is created by the intersection between the extension of the center and the point. Consider the following example:

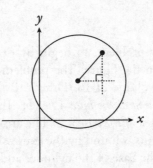

So, for each answer choice, find the intersection of the point from the answer choice and the center of the circle extended and apply the Pythagorean Theorem to determine the length of the hypotenuse.

For choice (A), the distance along the *x*-axis is $5 - 2 = 3$ and the distance along the *y*-axis is $6 - 5 = 1$. Therefore, the hypotenuse is $3^2 + 1^2 = c^2$ and $c^2 = 10$, so $c = \sqrt{10}$. Because $4 = \sqrt{16}$, the distance from the center of the circle to the point is less than the radius. Therefore, this point lies within the circle. Keep choice (A). Apply this to each of the remaining points. The hypotenuse of choice (B) is $4^2 + 4^2 = c^2$ and $c = \sqrt{32}$, which is greater than the radius, so eliminate choice (B). Choice (C) is a straight horizontal line that has a length of 3. This is less than the radius, so keep choice (C). The hypotenuse of choice (D) is $2^2 + 2^2 = c^2$ and $c = \sqrt{8}$, which is less than the radius, so keep choice (D). The correct answer is choices (A), (C), and (D).

○

The GRE could pair any figure along with the coordinate plane—triangles, squares, rectangles, etc. The key to these questions is to look for common relationships between the concepts of coordinate geometry and the dimensions of the figures.

○

VOLUME, SURFACE AREA, AND POLYGONS

The final section of this chapter on GRE geometry focuses on 3D figures and polygons. The GRE asks about these types of questions in only a handful of ways. We'll discuss each below, starting with basic questions about volume and surface area.

○

A right circular cylinder with height 2 inches has volume 16 cubic inches.

Quantity A	**Quantity B**
The radius of the base of the cylinder, in inches	4 inches

Here's How to Crack It:

This is a Quant Comp geometry problem, so begin by drawing the figure and labeling any information from the problem on the figure. The problem describes a right circular cylinder with a height of 2 inches and a volume of 16. Draw this figure. The volume of a cylinder is found by the equation *volume = area of the base × height*. The height is 2 and the volume is 16, so rewrite this equation as 16 = *area of the base* × 2. The area of the base is the area of the circle at the bottom of the cylinder, so this is found by the expression πr^2. Now work with the quantities. Quantity A is the radius of the base of the cylinder and Quantity B is 4 inches. Instead of solving for the radius, use the value in Quantity B as the radius and compare the result to the volume provided by the problem. In this case $4^2(\pi)(2) = 32\pi$ and $32\pi > 16$, so the radius of the cylinder is less than 4. Quantity B is greater. The correct answer is choice (B).

○

Here's another example:

---○---

What is the volume of a rectangular box, expressed in terms of its length, *l*, that is four times as long as it is high, and twice as wide as it is long?

○ l^3

○ $\dfrac{l^3}{2}$

○ $\dfrac{l^3}{4}$

○ $\dfrac{l^3}{8}$

○ $\dfrac{l^3}{16}$

Here's How to Crack It:

This is a geometry problem, so begin by drawing the figure and labeling any information from

the problem on the figure. The question describes a rectangular box. The volume of a rectan-

gular box is from by the expression *length × width × height*. The problem provides information

about the height and width in terms of the length, so rewrite these. The problem says the box is

four times as long as it is high, so *height* = $\dfrac{length}{4}$. The problem states that the box is *twice as wide*

as it is long, so *width* = 2(*length*). Now rewrite the equation for volume in terms of length, so

volume = *length* × 2(*length*) × $\dfrac{length}{4}$ = $\dfrac{l^3}{2}$. The correct answer is choice (B).

---○---

Sometimes, the GRE can combine the concepts of surface area and volume into the same question, as shown below:

———————————◯———————————

What is the volume of a cube with a surface area of 96 inches² ?

◯ 64 inches³

◯ 70 inches³

◯ 74 inches³

◯ 78 inches³

◯ 82 inches³

Here's How to Crack It:

This is a geometry problem, so begin by drawing the figure and labeling any information from the problem on the figure. The problem gives the surface area of a cube. The surface area of a cube is found by the expression $6(s^2)$, where s is the length of one of the sides. This is true because a cube is a three-dimensional square and the surface area is the sum of the areas of each of the faces of the cube. Therefore, $96 = 6(s^2)$ and $s^2 = 16$. Thus, $s = 4$. The volume of a cube is found by the expressions s^3, so the volume of this cube is $4^3 = 64$. The correct answer is choice (A).

———————————◯———————————

One of the ways in which the GRE makes these types of problems more difficult is by adding an additional element to the description of the figure, such as shown below:

———————————◯———————————

A right circular tank with a height of 6 is halfway filled with water. If the volume of water in the tank is 27π, then what is the radius of the base of the tank?

┌─────────┐
│   │
└─────────┘

Click on the answer box and type in a number. Backspace to erase.

Here's How to Crack It:

The problem states that the tank is halfway filled with water. The volume of water in the tank is 27π, so the total volume of the tank is 54π. The volume of a cylinder is found by the expression $\pi r^2(height)$. The height is 6, so solve for the radius: $54\pi = \pi r^2(6)$ and $r^2 = 9$. Therefore, $r = 3$. The correct answer is 3.

———————————◯———————————

There's a special formula that you can use if you are ever asked to find the length of a diagonal (the longest distance between any two corners) inside a three-dimensional rectangular box. It is $a^2 + b^2 + c^2 = d^2$, where a, b, and c are the dimensions of the figure.

Take a look:

What is the length, in inches, of the longest distance between any two corners in a rectangular box with dimensions 3 inches by 4 inches by 5 inches?

○ 5

○ $5\sqrt{2}$

○ 12

○ $12\sqrt{2}$

○ 50

Questions that ask about the length of the diagonal of a rectangular box sometimes ask about the longest length of an object that could be placed inside the box. These questions are solved in the same way–the GRE is just trying to mask what it is asking about!

Here's How to Crack It:

Let's use our formula, $a^2 + b^2 = c^2$. The dimensions of the box are 3, 4, and 5.

$$3^2 + 4^2 + 5^2 = d^2$$
$$9 + 16 + 25 = d^2$$
$$50 = d^2$$
$$\sqrt{50} = d$$
$$\sqrt{25 \times 2} = d$$
$$\sqrt{25} \times \sqrt{2} = d$$
$$5\sqrt{2} = d$$

The correct answer is choice (B).

The GRE also asks about figures with more than four sides. For the purpose of this chapter, we are going to refer to these as polygons. These questions can come in all shapes and sizes, but they mostly boil down to one of two calculations: the degree measure of the angles or the area of the figure. Take a look at the following question that tests both concepts.

A polygon is technically a figure with at least three straight sides and angles, and typically five or more. A triangle is a polygon, as well as a rectangle and square.

If the length of one side of a regular hexagon is 8, what is the area of the hexagon?

○ $24\sqrt{3}$

○ $36\sqrt{3}$

○ $48\sqrt{3}$

○ $64\sqrt{3}$

○ $96\sqrt{3}$

Here's How to Crack It:

This is geometry problem, so begin by drawing the figure and labeling any information from the problem on the figure. The problem describes a hexagon with the length of one side equal to 8. Because the problem describes the hexagon as a *regular hexagon,* all the sides are the same length. Draw this figure and label one of the sides as 8. The problem asks for the area of the hexagon. When solving for the area of an unfamiliar figure, begin by breaking the figure down into recognizable figures. In this case, a straight line drawn from the center of the hexagon to two adjacent corners on the perimeter of the hexagon creates a triangle with two sides of equal length. The angles opposite those sides are also equal. Determine the value of these angles by finding the value of the central angle created by the two lines from the center. This is the value of x in the figure below.

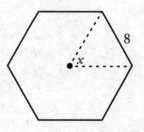

The central angle of the figure is found by dividing 360 degrees by the number of sides. In this case, there are 6 sides, so the interior angle is $360 \div 6 = 60$ degrees. Because there are 180 degrees in a triangle, the remaining two angles have a sum of $180 - 60 = 120$ degrees. Because this is a regular hexagon, the distances between the center of the figure and the corners are equal. Therefore, each of the angles opposite the lengths are also equal. So, each additional angle in the triangle is 60 degrees. All the angles are equal, so this is an equilateral triangle and the length of all the sides is 8. Now solve for the area of the triangle. The area is $\frac{1}{2}(base)(height)$ and $base = 8$. When drawn in, the height bisects one of the 60 degree angles and cuts the base in half. This creates two 30:60:90 right triangles. The side relationship of a 30:60:90 is $x : x\sqrt{3} : 2x$. The value of x is half of the base, so $x = 4$. The height is the side opposite the

60-degree angle, so the height of the triangle is $4\sqrt{3}$. Therefore, the area of the triangle is $\frac{1}{2}(4)(4\sqrt{3}) = 8\sqrt{3}$. There are six such triangles that make up the area of the hexagon, so the area of the hexagon is $6 \times 8\sqrt{3} = 48\sqrt{3}$. The correct answer is choice (C).

———————○———————

In the problem above, you had to solve for the area of a hexagon by using the length of a side, the central angle, the length from the center of the figure to the corners, the properties of equilateral triangles, the side relationships of a 30:60:90 triangle, and the area of a triangle. That's a lot to cover in one problem!

However, consider how different drawing the figure for the problem above would have been if the problem read:

If the length of one side of a hexagon is 8, what is the area of the hexagon?

This new question stem removes the word "regular." The word "regular" indicates that the sides and angles are all equal length. Without that word, it is impossible to accurately draw this figure, let alone solve for the area.

This is an example of how the GRE uses precise wording to create questions. While the GRE may occasionally include information that is unnecessary to answer the question, it will never leave anything out.

There is one additional aspect of working with polygons that was not covered in the previous problem. When asked about these types of figures, you may be asked to find the measure of the interior angles, or the sum of certain interior angles. For instance, consider the following problem, which is a derivative of the problem you just worked through.

———————○———————

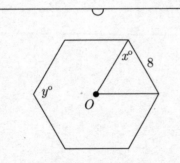

In the regular hexagon with center O shown above, what is the value of $x + y$?

○ 60

○ 120

○ 150

○ 180

○ 240

Here's How to Crack It:

This is geometry problem, so begin by drawing the figure and labeling any information from the problem on the figure. You know from the previous problem that the measure of x is 60. The process to find this degree measure is the same no matter what the problem is ultimately asking for, so we are not going to run through that explanation again. If you are unsure, check out the previous problem. However, this problem introduces another variable, y, which is the measure of the interior angle of the hexagon. The formula to solve for the interior angle of a hexagon is $\frac{180\,(n-2)}{n}$, where n is the number of sides in the figure. In this case, there are 6 sides in the figure, so the interior angle of a single corner is $\frac{180\,(6-2)}{6} = \frac{180(4)}{6} = \frac{720}{6} = 120$ degrees. The question asks for the value of $x + y$, which is $60 + 120 = 180$. The correct answer is choice (D).

PLUGGING IN ON GEOMETRY PROBLEMS

Remember, whenever you have a question that has answer choices, like a regular multiple-choice question or a multiple-choice, multiple-answer question that has variables in the answer choices, Plug In. On geometry problems, you can Plug In values for angles or lengths as long as the values you plug in don't contradict either the wording of the problem or the laws of geometry (you can't have the interior angles of a triangle add up to anything but 180, for instance).

Here's an example:

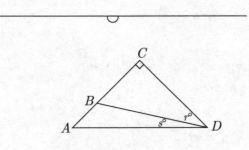

In the drawing above, if $AC = CD$, then $r =$

- ◯ $45 - s$
- ◯ $90 - s$
- ◯ s
- ◯ $45 + s$
- ◯ $60 + s$

Here's How to Crack It

See the variables in the answer choices? Let's Plug In. First of all, we're told that AC and CD are equal, which means that ACD is an isosceles right triangle. So both angles A and D have to be 45 degrees. Now it's Plugging In time. The smaller angles, r and s, must add up to 45 degrees, so let's make $r = 40$ degrees and $s = 5$ degrees. The question asks for the value of r, which is 40, so that's our target answer. Now eliminate answer choices by plugging in 5 for s.

(A) $45 - 5 = 40$. Bingo! Check the other choices to be sure.

(B) $90 - 5 = 85$. Nope.

(C) 5. Nope.

(D) $45 + 5 = 50$. Eliminate it.

(E) $60 + 5 = 65$. No way.

Key Formulas and Rules

Here is a review of the key rules and formulas to know for the GRE Math section.

Lines and angles

- All straight lines have 180 degrees.
- A right angle measures 90 degrees.
- Vertical angles are equal.
- Parallel lines cut by a third line have two kinds of angles: big angles and small angles. All of the big angles are equal and all of the small angles are equal. The sum of a big angle and a small angle is 180 degrees.

Triangles

- All triangles have 180 degrees.
- The angles and sides of a triangle are in proportion—the largest angle is opposite the largest side and the smallest side is opposite the smallest angle.
- The Pythagorean Theorem is $c^2 = a^2 + b^2$, where c is the length of the hypotenuse.
- The area formula for a triangle is $A = \dfrac{bh}{2}$.

Quadrilaterals

- All quadrilaterals have 360 degrees.
- The area formula for squares and rectangles is bh.

Circles

- All circles have 360 degrees.
- The radius is the distance from the center of the circle to any point on the edge.
- The area of a circle is πr^2.
- The circumference of a circle is $2\pi r$.

Don't forget to Plug In on geometry questions. Just pick numbers according to the rules of geometry.

By the way, we knew that the correct answer couldn't be greater than 45 degrees, because that's the measure of the entire angle *D*, so you could have eliminated (D) and (E) right away.

DRAW IT YOURSELF

When ETS doesn't include a drawing with a geometry problem, it usually means that the drawing, if supplied, would make ETS's answer obvious. In cases like this, you should just draw it yourself. Here's an example of a time when ETS doesn't provide a drawing because it would make the correct answer too obvious—so go ahead and draw one yourself!

Quantity A	**Quantity B**
The diameter of a circle with area 49π	14

○ Quantity A is greater.

○ Quantity B is greater.

○ The two quantities are equal.

○ The relationship cannot be determined from the information given.

Here's How to Crack It

Visualize the figure. If the area is 49π, what's the radius? Right: 7. And if the radius is 7, what's the diameter? Right: 14. The answer is (C).

Redraw

On tricky quant comp questions, you may need to draw the figure once, eliminate two answer choices, and then draw it another way to try to disprove your first answer and to see if the answer is (D). Here's an example of a problem that might require you to do this:

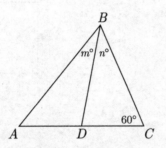

D is the midpoint of AC.

Quantity A	Quantity B
m	n

○ Quantity A is greater.

○ Quantity B is greater.

○ The two quantities are equal.

○ The relationship cannot be determined from the information given.

> For quant comp geometry questions, draw, eliminate, and REDRAW; it's like Plugging In twice.

Here's How to Crack It

Are you sure that the triangle looks exactly like this? Nope. We know only what we are told—that the lengths of AD and DC are equal; from this figure, it looks like angles m and n are also equal. Because this means that it's possible for them to be, we can eliminate (A) and (B). But let's redraw the figure to try to disprove our first answer.

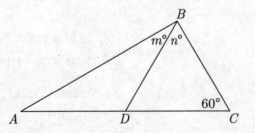

Try drawing the triangle as stretched out as possible. Notice that n is now clearly greater than m, so you can eliminate (C), and the answer is (D).

Geometry Drill

Think you have mastered these concepts? Try your hand at the following problems and check your work after you have finished. You can find the answers in Part V.

Which of the following could be the degree measures of two angles in a right triangle?

Indicate <u>all</u> such angles.

☐ 20° and 70°

☐ 30° and 60°

☐ 45° and 45°

☐ 55° and 55°

☐ 75° and 75°

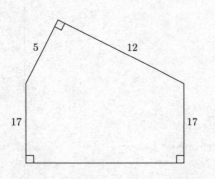

What is the perimeter of the figure above?

○   51

○   64

○   68

○   77

○   91

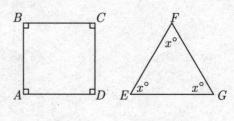

$$AB = BC = EG$$
$$FG = 8$$

Quantity A	**Quantity B**
The area of square $ABCD$	32

○ Quantity A is greater.

○ Quantity B is greater.

○ The two quantities are equal.

○ The relationship cannot be determined from the information given.

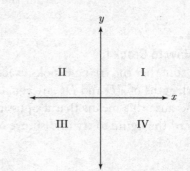

$(a, 6)$ is a point (not shown) in Quadrant I.

$(-6, b)$ is a point (not shown) in Quadrant II.

Quantity A	**Quantity B**
a	b

○ Quantity A is greater.

○ Quantity B is greater.

○ The two quantities are equal.

○ The relationship cannot be determined from the information given.

A piece of twine with length of t is cut into two pieces. The length of the longer piece is 2 yards greater than 3 times the length of the shorter piece. Which of the following is the length, in yards, of the longer piece?

○ $\dfrac{t+3}{3}$

○ $\dfrac{3t+2}{3}$

○ $\dfrac{t-2}{4}$

○ $\dfrac{3t+4}{4}$

○ $\dfrac{3t+2}{4}$

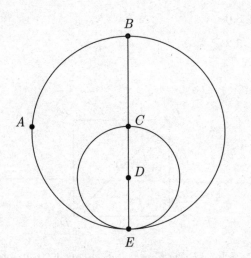

The circle with center D is drawn inside the circle with center C, as shown in the figure above. If $CD = 3$, what is the area of semicircle EAB?

○ $\dfrac{9}{2}\pi$

○ 9π

○ 12π

○ 18π

○ 36π

For the final exam in a scuba diving certification course, Karl navigates from one point in a lake to another. Karl begins the test x meters directly beneath the boat and swims straight down toward the bottom of the lake for 8 meters. He then turns to his right and swims in a straight line parallel to the surface of the lake and swims 24 meters, at which point he swims directly from his location, in a straight line, back to the boat. If the distance that Karl swims back to the boat is 26 meters, what is the value of x?

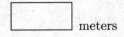 meters

Click on the answer box and type in a number. Backspace to erase.

Quantity A	**Quantity B**
The circumference of a circular region with radius r	The perimeter of a square with side r

○ Quantity A is greater.

○ Quantity B is greater.

○ The two quantities are equal.

○ The relationship cannot be determined from the information given.

Triangle ABC is contained within a circle with center C. Points A and B lie on the circle. If the area of circle C is 25π, and the measure of angle ACB is $60°$, which of the following are possible lengths for side AB of triangle ABC?

Indicate all such lengths.

☐ 3

☐ 4

☐ 5

☐ 6

☐ 7

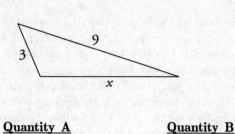

Quantity A	**Quantity B**
x	5.9

○ Quantity A is greater.

○ Quantity B is greater.

○ The two quantities are equal.

○ The relationship cannot be determined from the information given.

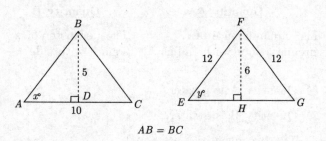

$$AB = BC$$

Quantity A	**Quantity B**
x	y

○ Quantity A is greater.

○ Quantity B is greater.

○ The two quantities are equal.

○ The relationship cannot be determined from the information given.

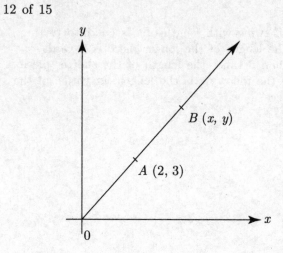

Given points $A(2, 3)$ and $B(x, y)$ in the rectangular coordinate system above, if $y = 4.2$, then $x =$

○ 2.6

○ 2.8

○ 2.9

○ 3.0

○ 3.2

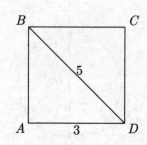

In rectangle $ABCD$ above, which of the following is the area of the triangle ABD ?

○ 6

○ 7.5

○ 10

○ 12

○ 15

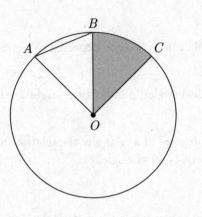

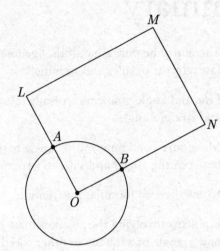

The circle above has a center O.

$$\angle AOB = \angle BOC$$

Quantity A	Quantity B
The area of triangle AOB	The area of the shaded region

○ Quantity A is greater.

○ Quantity B is greater.

○ The two quantities are equal.

○ The relationship cannot be determined from the information given.

The circumference of the circle with center O shown above is 15π. $LMNO$ is a parallelogram and $\angle OLM = 108°$. What is the length of minor arc AB ?

○　15π

○　9π

○　3π

○　2π

○　π

ANSWERS TO THE "SHOULD I DO THIS CHAPTER?" QUIZ

1.　$V = Length \times width \times height$

2.　16π

3.　$y = mx + b$

4.　180

5.　720

6.　$P = 2(length) + 2(width)$

7.　Right triangle

8.　$\dfrac{rise}{run}$ or $\dfrac{y_2 - y_1}{x_2 - x_1}$

9.　360

10.　$A = \dfrac{1}{2}\left(base\right)\left(height\right)$

Summary

o   There may be only a handful of geometry questions on the GRE, but you'll be expected to know a fair number of rules and formulas.

o   Line and angle problems typically test your knowledge of vertical angles, parallel lines, right angles, and straight angles.

o   Make sure you know your triangle basics, including the total degrees of a triangle, the relationship between the angles and sides of a triangle, the third side rule, and right triangles.

o   Know the area formulas for triangles, rectangles, and circles.

o   Problems involving the *xy*-coordinate plane can test common geometry concepts, such as the area of a triangle or a square, or other coordinate geometry concepts, such as slope and the equation of a line.

o   Understand how to solve for the volume and surface area of 3D figures and the interior angle and area of figures with more than four sides.

o   Don't forget to Plug In on geometry problems!

Chapter 16
Math Et Cetera

There are a few more math topics that may appear on the GRE that don't fit nicely into the preceding chapters. This chapter looks at some of these leftover topics, including probability, permutations and combinations, and factorials. The topics in this chapter are not essential to your GRE Math score, because these areas are not tested as frequently as the topics detailed earlier. However, if you feel confident with the previous math topics, and you're looking to maximize your GRE Math score, this chapter will show you all you need to know to tackle these more obscure GRE problems.

OTHER MATH TOPICS

The bulk of the GRE Math section tests your knowledge of fundamentals, basic algebra, and geometry. However, there are a few other topics that may appear. These "et cetera" concepts usually show up only once or twice per test (although at higher scoring levels they may appear more frequently) and often cause anxiety among test takers. Many test takers worry excessively about probability problems, for example, even though knowledge of more familiar topics such as fractions and percents will be far more important in determining your GRE math score. So tackle these problems only after you've mastered the rest. If you find these concepts more difficult, don't worry—they won't make or break your GRE score.

> These topics show up rarely on the GRE, but if you're going for a very high score, they are useful to know.

PROBABILITY

If you flip a coin, what's the probability that it will land heads up? The probability is equal to one out of two, or $\frac{1}{2}$. What is the probability that it won't land heads up? Again, one out of two, or $\frac{1}{2}$. If you flip a coin nine times, what's the probability that the coin will land on heads on the tenth flip? Still 1 out of 2, or $\frac{1}{2}$. Previous flips do not affect the outcome of the current coin flip.

> Since probability is expressed as a fraction, it can also be expressed as a decimal or a percentage. A probability of one-half is equivalent to a probability of 0.5, or 50%.

You can think of probability as just another type of fraction. **Probabilities** express a special relationship, namely the chance of a certain outcome occurring. In a probability fraction, the denominator is the total number of possible outcomes that may occur, while the numerator is the number of outcomes that would satisfy the criteria. For example, if you have 10 shirts and 3 of them are black, the probability of selecting a black shirt from your closet without looking is $\frac{3}{10}$.

Think of probability in terms of fractions:

- If it is impossible for something to happen—if no outcomes satisfy the criteria— then the numerator of the probability fraction is 0 and the probability is equal to 0.
- If something is certain to happen—if all possible outcomes satisfy the criteria— then the numerator and denominator of the fraction are equal and the probability is equal to 1.
- If it is possible for something to occur, but it will not definitely occur, then the probability of it occurring is between 0 and 1.

$$\text{probablity} = \frac{\text{number of possible outcomes that satisfy the condition}}{\text{number of total possible outcomes}}$$

Let's see how it works.

At a meeting of 375 members of a neighborhood association, $\frac{1}{5}$ of the participants have lived in the community for less than 5 years and $\frac{2}{3}$ of the attendees have lived in the neighborhood for at least 10 years. If a member of the meeting is selected at random, what is the probability that the person has lived in the neighborhood for at least 5 years but less than 10 years?

○ $\frac{2}{15}$

○ $\frac{4}{15}$

○ $\frac{3}{10}$

○ $\frac{1}{2}$

○ $\frac{8}{15}$

Here's How to Crack It

In order to solve this problem, we need to put together our probability fraction. The denominator of our fraction is going to be 375, the total number of people from which we are selecting. Next we need to figure out how many attendees satisfy the criteria of having lived in the neighborhood for more than 5 years but fewer than 10 years.

> What number goes on the bottom of the probability fraction?

First, we know that $\frac{1}{5}$ of the participants have lived in the neighborhood for less than 5 years. $\frac{1}{5}$ of 375 is 75 people, so we can take them out of the running. Also, $\frac{2}{3}$ of the attendees have lived in the neighborhood for at least 10 years. $\frac{2}{3}$ of 375 (be careful not to use 300 as the total!) is 250, so we can also remove them from consideration. Thus, if 75 people have lived in the neighborhood for less than 5 years and 250 have lived for at least 10, the remaining people are the ones we want. 250 + 75 is 325, so that leaves us with 50 people who satisfy the criteria. We need to make 50 the numerator of our fraction, which gives us $\frac{50}{375}$. This reduces to $\frac{2}{15}$, so (A) is the answer.

Two Important Laws of Probability

Probability of A and B
= Probability of A
× Probability of B

When you want to find the probability of a series of events in a row, you multiply the probabilities of the individual events. What is the probability of getting two heads in a row if you flip a coin twice? The probability of getting a head on the first flip is $\frac{1}{2}$. The probability is also $\frac{1}{2}$ that you'll get a head on the second flip, so the combined probability of two heads is $\frac{1}{2} \times \frac{1}{2}$, which equals $\frac{1}{4}$. Another way to look at it is that there are four possible outcomes: HH, TT, HT, TH. Only one of those outcomes consists of two heads in a row. Thus, $\frac{1}{4}$ of the outcomes consist of two heads in a row. Sometimes the number of outcomes is small enough that you can list them and calculate the probability that way.

Probability of A or B
= Probability of A
+ Probability of B

(The full formula for the Probability of A or B includes subtracting the Probability of *both* A and B, but the GRE uses only mutually exclusive events, so both A and B can't happen, and you don't need to worry about it!)

Occasionally, instead of finding the probability of one event AND another event happening, you'll be asked to find the probability of either one event OR another event happening. In this situation, instead of multiplying the probabilities, you add them. Let's say you have a normal deck of 52 cards. If you select a card at random, what's the probability that you select a 7 or a 4? The probability of selecting a 7 is $\frac{4}{52}$, which reduces to $\frac{1}{13}$. The probability of selecting a 4 is the same; $\frac{1}{13}$. Therefore, the probability of selecting a 7 or a 4 is $\frac{1}{13} + \frac{1}{13} = \frac{2}{13}$.

Let's look at a problem:

When a pair of six-sided dice, each with faces numbered 1 to 6, is rolled once, what is the probability that the result is either a 3 and a 4 or a 5 and a prime number?

Give your answer as a fraction.

Click on each box and type in a number.
Backspace to erase.

Here's How to Crack It

Probability is fundamentally about counting. You need to be able to count all the things that can happen and count all the situations that meet the conditions of the problem. Sometimes, the easiest way to count both everything that can happen and the situations that meet the condition is to write everything out. In this case, let's use a table:

What number goes on the bottom of the probability fraction?

	1	2	3	4	5	6
1	✘	✘	✘	✘	✘	✘
2	✘	✘	✘	✘	✓	✘
3	✘	✘	✘	✓	✓	✘
4	✘	✘	✓	✘	✘	✘
5	✘	✓	✓	✘	✓	✘
6	✘	✘	✘	✘	✘	✘

Each cell of this table represents a result when the dice are rolled. For example, the cell at the intersection of the row shown as 1 and the column shown as 1 would represent that 1 was showing on each of the two die. This cell has been marked with an ✘ because it does not meet either condition of the problem.

The cells marked with a ✓ are the only dice rolls that meet one of the conditions of the problem. To finish, just count the ✓ marks—there are 7. (Remember that 1 is not prime. That's why combinations such as 5 and 1 are not checked.) Next, count the total possibilities—there are 36. So, the probability of rolling either a 3 and a 4 or a 5 and prime number is $\frac{7}{36}$.

One last important thing you should know about probabilities is that the probability of an event happening and the probability of an event not happening must add up to 1. For example, if the probability of snow falling on one night is $\frac{2}{3}$, then the probability of no snow falling must be $\frac{1}{3}$. If the probability that it will rain is 80%, then the probability that it won't rain must be 20%. The reason this is useful is that, on some GRE probability problems, it will be easier to find the probability that an event doesn't occur; once you have that, just subtract from 1 to find the answer.

Let's look at the following example.

Dipak has a 25% chance of winning each hand of blackjack he plays. If he has $150 and bets $50 a hand, what is the probability that he will still have money after the third hand?

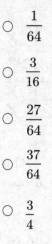

○ $\frac{1}{64}$

○ $\frac{3}{16}$

○ $\frac{27}{64}$

○ $\frac{37}{64}$

○ $\frac{3}{4}$

Here's How to Crack It

If Dipak still has money after the third hand, then he must have won at least one of the hands, and possibly more than one. However, directly calculating the probability that he wins at least one hand is tricky because there are so many ways it could happen (for example, he could lose-lose-win, or W-W-L or W-L-W or L-W-L, and so on). So think about it this way: the question asks for the probability that he will win at least one hand. What if he doesn't? That would mean that he doesn't win any hands at all. If we calculate the probability that he loses every hand, we can then subtract that from 1 and find the corresponding probability that he wins at least one hand. Since Dipak has a 25% chance of winning each hand, this means that he has a 75% chance of losing it, or $\frac{3}{4}$ (the answers are in fractions, so it's best to work with fractions). To find the probability that he loses all three hands, simply multiply the probabilities of his losing each individual hand. $\frac{3}{4} \times \frac{3}{4} \times \frac{3}{4} = \frac{27}{64}$, so there is a $\frac{27}{64}$ probability that he will lose all three hands. Subtracting this from 1 gives you the answer you're looking for: $1 - \frac{27}{64} = \frac{37}{64}$. The answer is (D).

Given events A and B, the probability of
- A and B = (Probability of A) × (Probability of B)
- A or B = Probability of A + Probability of B

Given event A
- Probability of A + Probability of Not A = 1

FACTORIALS

The **factorial** of a number is equal to that number times every positive whole number smaller than that number, down to 1. For example, the factorial of 6 is equal to 6 × 5 × 4 × 3 × 2 × 1, which equals 720. The symbol for a factorial is !, so 4! doesn't mean we're really excited about the number 4: it means 4 × 3 × 2 × 1, which is equal to 24. (0! is equal to 1, by the way.) When factorials show up in GRE problems, always look for a shortcut like canceling or factoring. The point of a factorial problem is not to make you do a lot of multiplication. Let's try one.

Quantity A	Quantity B
$\dfrac{12!}{11!}$	$\dfrac{4!}{2!}$

- ○ Quantity A is greater.

- ○ Quantity B is greater.

- ○ The two quantities are equal.

- ○ The relationship cannot be determined from the information given.

Here's How to Crack It

Let's tackle Quantity A. We definitely don't want to multiply out the factorials since that would be pretty time-consuming: 12! and 11! are both huge numbers. Instead let's look at what they have in common. What we're really talking about here is $\dfrac{12 \times 11 \times 10 \times 9 \times 8 \times 7 \times 6 \times 5 \times 4 \times 3 \times 2 \times 1}{11 \times 10 \times 9 \times 8 \times 7 \times 6 \times 5 \times 4 \times 3 \times 2 \times 1}$. Now it's clear that both factorials share everything from 11 on down to 1. The entire bottom of the fraction will cancel and the only thing left on top will be 12, so the value of Quantity A is

12. For Quantity B, we can also write out the factorials and get $\dfrac{4 \times 3 \times 2 \times 1}{2 \times 1}$. The 2 and the 1 in the bottom cancel, and the only thing left on top will be 4×3, which is equal to 12. The two quantities are equal, so the answer is (C).

PERMUTATIONS AND COMBINATIONS

The basic definition of a **permutation** is an arrangement of things in a particular order. Suppose you were asked to figure out how many different ways you could arrange five statues on a shelf. All you have to do is multiply $5 \times 4 \times 3 \times 2 \times 1$, or 120. (Yes, this is another application of factorials.) You have five possible statues that could fill the first slot on the shelf; then, once the first slot is filled, there are four remaining statues that could fill the second slot, three that could fill the third slot, and so on, down to one.

> Permutation problems often ask for arrangements, orders, schedules, or lists.

Now suppose that there are five people running in a race. The winner of the race will get a gold medal, the person who comes in second will get a silver medal, and the person who comes in third will get a bronze medal. You're asked to figure out how many different orders of gold-silver-bronze winners there can be. (Notice that this is a permutation because the order definitely matters.)

First, ask yourself how many of these runners can come in first? Five. Once one of them comes in first, she's out of the picture, so how many can then come in second? Four. Once one of them comes in second, she's out of the picture, so how many of them can come in third? Three. And now you're done because all three slots have been filled. The answer is $5 \times 4 \times 3$, which is 60.

To solve a permutation
- Figure out how many slots you have.
- Write down the number of options for each slot.
- Multiply them.

> Combination problems usually ask for groups, teams, or committees.

The difference between a permutation and a combination is that in a combination, the order is irrelevant. A **combination** is just a group, and the order of elements within the group doesn't matter. For example, suppose you were asked to go to the store and bring home three different types of ice cream. Now suppose that when you got to the store, there were five flavors in the freezer—chocolate, vanilla, strawberry, butter pecan, and mocha. How many combinations of three ice cream flavors could you bring home? Notice that the order doesn't matter, because bringing home chocolate, strawberry, and vanilla is the same thing as bringing home strawberry, vanilla, and chocolate. One way to solve this is the brute force method; in other words, write out every combination.

VCS VCB VCM VSB VSM VBM CSB CSM CBM SBM

That's 10 combinations, but there's a quicker way to do it. Start by filling in the three slots as you would with a permutation (there are three slots because you're supposed to bring home three different types of ice cream). Five flavors could be in the first slot, four could be in the second, and three could be in the third. So far, that's 5 × 4 × 3. But remember, this takes into account all the different orders that three flavors can be arranged in. We don't want that, because the order doesn't matter in a combination. So we have to divide 5 × 4 × 3 by the number of ways of arranging three things. In how many ways can three things be arranged? That's 3!, 3 × 2 × 1, which is 6. Thus we end up with $\dfrac{5 \times 4 \times 3}{3 \times 2 \times 1}$. Cancel the denominators, to find that all that remains is 5 × 2 = 10. Bingo.

> Does the order matter?

To solve a combination

- Figure out how many slots you have.
- Fill in the slots as you would a permutation.
- Divide by the factorial of the number of slots.

The denominator of the fraction will always cancel out completely, so it's best to cancel first before you multiply.

Here's an example:

> Always cross off wrong answer choices on your scratch paper.

---⟲---

Brooke wants to hang three paintings in a row on her wall. She has six paintings to choose from. How many arrangements of paintings on the wall can she create?

- ○ 6
- ○ 30
- ○ 90
- ○ 120
- ○ 720

Here's How to Crack It

The first thing you need to do is determine whether the order matters. In this case it does, because we're arranging the paintings on the wall. Putting the Monet on the left and the Van Gogh in the middle isn't the same arrangement as putting the Van Gogh on the left and the Monet in the middle. This is a permutation question. We have three slots to fill because we're arranging three paintings. There are 6 paintings that could fill the first slot, 5 paintings that could fill the second slot, and 4 paintings that could fill the third slot. So we have 6 × 5 × 4, which equals 120. Thus, the correct answer is (D).

———————○———————

Here's another example:

———————○———————

A pizza may be ordered with any of eight possible toppings.

<u>Quantity A</u>	<u>Quantity B</u>
The number of different ways to order a pizza with three different toppings	The number of different ways to order a pizza with five different toppings

○ Quantity A is greater.

○ Quantity B is greater.

○ The two quantities are equal.

○ The relationship cannot be determined from the information given.

Here's How to Crack It

First, note that for both quantities we're dealing with a combination, because the order of toppings doesn't matter. A pizza with mushrooms and pepperoni is the same thing as a pizza with pepperoni and mushrooms. Let's figure out Quantity A first.

We have eight toppings and we're picking three of them. That means we have three slots to fill. There are 8 toppings that could fill the first slot, 7 that could fill the second slot, and 6 that could fill the third, so we have 8 × 7 × 6. Since this is a combination, we have to divide by the factorial of the number of slots. In this case we have three slots, so we have to divide by 3!, or 3 × 2 × 1. So our problem looks like this: $\frac{8 \times 7 \times 6}{3 \times 2 \times 1}$. To make the multiplication easier, let's cancel first. The 6 on top will cancel with the 3 × 2 on the bottom, leaving us with $\frac{8 \times 7}{1}$, which is 56. Thus, there are 56 ways to order a three-topping pizza with eight toppings to choose from.

Now let's look at Quantity B.

We still have eight toppings, but this time we're picking five of them so we have five slots to fill. There are 8 toppings that could fill the first slot, 7 that could fill the second slot, 6 that could fill the third, 5 that could fill the fourth, and 4 that could fill the fifth. That's $8 \times 7 \times 6 \times 5 \times 4$, but we still have to divide by the factorial of the number of slots. We have five slots, so that means we need to divide by 5!, or $5 \times 4 \times 3 \times 2 \times 1$. Thus we have $\frac{8 \times 7 \times 6 \times 5 \times 4}{5 \times 4 \times 3 \times 2 \times 1}$. We definitely want to cancel first here, rather than doing all that multiplication. The 5 on top will cancel with the 5 on the bottom. Likewise, the 4 on top will cancel with the 4 on the bottom. The 6 on top will cancel with the 3×2 on the bottom, leaving us again with $\frac{8 \times 7}{1}$, which is 56. Therefore, there are also 56 ways to order a five-topping pizza with eight toppings to choose from. The two quantities are equal, so the answer is (C).

Let's try one more:

Nicole needs to form a committee of 3 from a group of 8 research attorneys to study possible changes to the Superior Court. If two of the attorneys are too inexperienced to serve together on the committee, how many different arrangements of committees can Nicole form?

○   20

○   30

○   50

○   56

○   336

Here's How to Crack It

This problem is a little more complicated than an ordinary combination problem, because an extra condition has been placed on the committee. Without that condition, this would be a fairly ordinary combination problem, and we'd simply calculate how many groups of three can be created with eight people to choose from.

There's more than one way to approach this problem. First, you should realize that there are two ways that we could form this committee. We could have three experienced attorneys, or we could have two experienced attorneys and one inexperienced attorney. If we find the number of ways to create each of those two possibilities, we can add them together to get the answer. It's fairly straightforward to calculate the number of ways to have three experienced attorneys on a committee. There are three slots to fill, and we have 6 options for the first slot, 5 for the second, and 4 for the third. Here the order doesn't matter, so we divide by 3! to get $\frac{6 \times 5 \times 4}{3 \times 2 \times 1} = 20$. Thus, there are 20 ways to create the committee using three experienced attorneys. What about creating a committee that has two experienced attorneys and one inexperienced attorney? We have 6 options for the first experienced attorney and 5 options for the second. Order doesn't matter so we divide by 2!. So far we have $\frac{6 \times 5}{2 \times 1}$. Next we have 2 options for the inexperienced attorney, so now we have to multiply by 2, and our calculation is $\frac{6 \times 5}{2 \times 1} \times \frac{2}{1} = 30$. As you can see, there are 30 ways to create the committee using two experienced attorneys and one inexperienced attorney. Adding 20 and 30 gives us 50 total committees, so the answer is (C).

Here's another way that you could solve the problem. If there were no conditions placed on the committee, we could just calculate $\frac{8 \times 7 \times 6}{3 \times 2 \times 1}$, which would give us 56 committees. But we know some of those committees are not allowed; any committee that has the two inexperienced attorneys on it isn't allowed. How many of these types of committees are there? Let's call the inexperienced attorneys A and B. An unacceptable committee would be A B __, in which the last slot could be filled by any of the experienced attorneys. Since there are 6 experienced attorneys, there are 6 unacceptable committees. Subtracting them from 56 gives us 50 acceptable committees. Hey, the answer's still (C)!

FUNCTIONS AND THE GRE

f(*x*) Notation

ETS often employs the use of function notation to create difficult problems. Generally speaking, the function notation is a style of math problem that causes test takers to be nervous. The function notation, $f(x)$, is unfamiliar to look at, seems difficult and involved, and evokes memories of graphs and charting lines that you may have learned in high school geometry.

The good news is that pure function problems on the GRE are much more straightforward than that and become very manageable if you utilize Plugging In strategies.

The easiest way to think about a function question is to look at an example. Take $f(x) = x + 2$, for instance. All this problem is stating is that for any value of x, the function $f(x)$ is that value plus 2. Let's say that $x = 3$; therefore, to solve this problem, take the value of x and plug it into the given equation. So if $x = 3$, the equation now reads $f(3) = 3 + 2$, or $f(3) = 5$. To solve function notation problems, all you need to do is read the instructions carefully and fill in the values for the variables where appropriate. If you used the same equation, but the value of x is 10, then the function is now $f(10) = 10 + 2$, so $f(10) = 12$.

Sometimes a function problem gives a restriction such as $x \neq 0$. If this is the case, you know that x could be equal to any value but 0, and this is generally for a good reason. If $f(x) = \dfrac{2}{x}$, then x cannot equal 0 because a number cannot be divided by 0.

Try this example of a function question on the GRE.

If $-3 \leq g \leq 2$ and $f(g) = -2g$ and g is an integer, then which of the following integers could be a value of $f(g)$?

Indicate all such integers.

- ☐   −6
- ☐   −5
- ☐   −2
- ☐   0
- ☐   2
- ☐   4
- ☐   6

Here's How to Crack It

This is a function problem with restrictions, so find all the different values that can be plugged in for g. Since g is an integer that is equal to or between −3 and 2, then there is a range for its values. Therefore, $f(g)$ (which equals $-2g$) is all the integer values between the high and low end of the range of g multiplied by 2. In other words, Plug In 2 and −3 for g in the function and figure out what the range is. If $g = -3$, then $f(g)$ is $f(-3) = -2(-3) = 6$. And if $g = 2$, then $f(g)$ is $f(2) = -2(2) = -4$. So the range of $f(g)$ is $-4 \leq f(g) \leq 6$. Choices (A) and (B) are less than −4 and fall out of the range. The rest of the integers fall in the range, so they are possible values of $f(g)$. Therefore, the correct answer is (C), (D), (E), (F), and (G).

Evaluating functions is all about following the directions. Just Plug In the values for the variable and solve.

Functions with Uncommon Symbols: #*μ°ⵝ

The GRE also tries to scare students using functions in another way: picking strange symbols and putting them in a problem. When you see a funny symbol that you have never seen before, don't stress out! It's just a function problem in disguise. Follow the directions to find the correct answer.

A problem with funny symbols may look something like the following.

If the operation ⵝ is defined for all integers x and y as x ⵝ $y = x^2 + y - 2$, then which of the following is equal to 4 ⵝ −3 ?

- ○ 21
- ○ 17
- ○ 15
- ○ 11
- ○ 10

Here's How to Crack It

Remember, this is a function problem, so just follow the directions. The problem wants to know the value of 4 ⵝ −3, and it states that x ⵝ $y = x^2 + y - 2$. To solve this problem, Plug In $x = 4$ and $y = -3$. So 4 ⵝ −3 $= 4^2 + (-3) - 2$. Now, solve: 4 ⵝ −3 $= 16 - 3 - 2 = 11$. The correct answer is (D).

You may get a different symbol when you get another problem like this, but the process is still the same. Just Plug In the values given for the variables and solve the problem. If you have worked your way through this book and mastered the content, then there won't be any actual mathematical symbols on the GRE that are unfamiliar to you. If you see a symbol like that, it's a function problem!

Let's look at one more example.

For any nonnegative integer x, let $x^* = x - 1$.

Quantity A	Quantity B
$\dfrac{15*}{3*}$	$\left(\dfrac{15}{3}\right)^*$

- ○ Quantity A is greater.
- ○ Quantity B is greater.
- ○ The two quantities are equal.
- ○ The relationship cannot be determined from the information given.

Here's How to Crack It

Just follow the directions: 15* = 15 − 1, or 14, and 3* = 3 − 1, or 2. So Quantity A is $\frac{14}{2}$, or 7. Don't forget PEMDAS for Quantity B. First, $\frac{15}{3}$ is 5. Then, 5* = 5 − 1, or 4. So because Quantity A is 7 and Quantity B is 4, the correct answer is (A).

GROUPS

Group problems, although not too common on the GRE, can be troublesome if you don't know how to set them up. When confronted by a group problem, use the group equation:

$$T = G_1 + G_2 - B + N$$

You might see one group problem on the GRE.

In the equation, T represents the Total, G_1 is one group, G_2 is the second group, B is for the members in both groups and N is for the members in neither group. Here's an example of a typical group problem.

A biologist studying breeding groups noted that of 225 birds tagged for the study, 85 birds made nests in pine trees, 175 made nests in oak trees, and 40 birds did not build nests in either type of tree. How many birds built nests in both types of trees?

- ○ 45
- ○ 60
- ○ 75
- ○ 80
- ○ 125

Here's How to Crack It

Let's use the group equation. The total is 225, one group consists of 85 birds, the other group has 175 birds in it, and we know that 40 birds built nests in neither type of tree. Our equation would look like this:

$$225 = 85 + 175 - B + 40$$

All we have to do is solve for B. Simplifying the equation gives us $225 = 300 - B$, so B must equal 75. Choice (C) is our answer.

Wrapping Up Math
You're almost done with the Math section. Tackle the Math Drills on the following pages. Then, give yourself a break. Take a walk, eat a snack, or meet up with a pal and give yourself some downtime before you dive into Part IV, the Analytical Writing Section.

Et Cetera Drill

Here are some math questions to practice on. Remember to check your answers when you finish. You can find the answers in Part V.

1 of 10

A bowl contains 15 marbles, all of which are either red or blue. If the number of red marbles is one more than the number of blue marbles, what is the probability that a marble selected at random is blue?

○ $\dfrac{1}{15}$

○ $\dfrac{2}{15}$

○ $\dfrac{7}{15}$

○ $\dfrac{1}{2}$

○ $\dfrac{8}{15}$

2 of 10

If $¥(x) = 10x - 1$, what is $¥(5) - ¥(3)$?

○   15

○   18

○   19

○   20

○   46

3 of 10

For all positive integer values of x, $\#x = 2^{-x}$.

Quantity A	Quantity B
#8	#4

○ Quantity A is greater.

○ Quantity B is greater.

○ The two quantities are equal.

○ The relationship cannot be determined from the information given.

4 of 10

At a recent dog show, there were 5 finalists. One of the finalists was awarded "Best in Show" and another finalist was awarded "Honorable Mention." In how many ways could the two awards be given out?

☐

Click on the answer box and type in a number.
Backspace to erase.

5 of 10

Company X budgets \$90,000 total on advertising for all of its products per year. Company X budgets \$40,000 for all advertising for product A and \$30,000 for all advertising for product B. From the budgets for products A and B, \$15,000 is budgeted for advertisements that feature both products used as a system.

Quantity A	Quantity B
The total amount Company X budgets for advertising products other than products A and B	\$20,000

○ Quantity A is greater.

○ Quantity B is greater.

○ The two quantities are equal.

○ The relationship cannot be determined from the information given.

Lee randomly selects a 2-digit prime number less than 50. What is the probability that the tens digit is greater than the units digit?

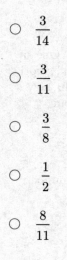

○ $\dfrac{3}{14}$

○ $\dfrac{3}{11}$

○ $\dfrac{3}{8}$

○ $\dfrac{1}{2}$

○ $\dfrac{8}{11}$

An elected official wants to take five members of his staff to an undisclosed secure location. What is the minimum number of staff members the elected official must employ in order to have at least 20 different groups that could be taken to the location?

○   7

○   8

○   9

○   10

○   11

For all real numbers x and y, if $x \# y = x(x - y)$, then $x \# (x \# y) =$

○ $x^2 - xy$

○ $x^2 - 2xy$

○ $x^3 - x^2 - xy$

○ $x^3 - (xy)^2$

○ $x^2 - x^3 + x^2 y$

A jar contains 12 marbles. Each is either yellow or green and there are twice as many yellow marbles as green marbles. If two marbles are to be selected from the jar at random, what is the probability that exactly one of each color is selected?

○ $\dfrac{8}{33}$

○ $\dfrac{16}{33}$

○ $\dfrac{1}{2}$

○ $\dfrac{17}{33}$

○ $\dfrac{25}{33}$

A set of 10 points lies in a plane such that no three points are collinear.

<u>Quantity A</u>	<u>Quantity B</u>
The number of distinct triangles that can be created from the set	The number of distinct quadrilaterals that can be created from the set

○ Quantity A is greater.

○ Quantity B is greater.

○ The two quantities are equal.

○ The relationship cannot be determined from the information given.

Comprehensive Math Drill

Let's do a drill involving all of the math topics we have covered throughout the book. Remember to check your answers when you finish. You can find the answers in Part V.

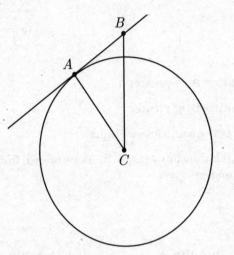

Line AB is tangent to the circle C at point A.

The radius of the circle with center C is 5 and $BC = \dfrac{10\sqrt{3}}{3}$.

Quantity A	**Quantity B**
The length of line segment AB	The length of line segment AC

○ Quantity A is greater.

○ Quantity B is greater.

○ The two quantities are equal.

○ The relationship cannot be determined from the information given.

$$x \neq 0$$

Quantity A	**Quantity B**
$\dfrac{x}{10}$	$\dfrac{\frac{x}{5}}{2}$

○ Quantity A is greater.

○ Quantity B is greater.

○ The two quantities are equal.

○ The relationship cannot be determined from the information given.

Quantity A	**Quantity B**
The standard deviation of the set $\{1,3,5\}$	The standard deviation of the set $\{8,10,12\}$

○ Quantity A is greater.

○ Quantity B is greater.

○ The two quantities are equal.

○ The relationship cannot be determined from the information given.

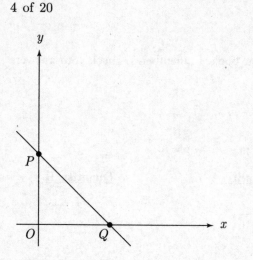

The line $y = -\dfrac{5}{6}x + 1$ is graphed on the rectangular coordinate axes.

Quantity A	**Quantity B**
OQ	OP

○ Quantity A is greater.

○ Quantity B is greater.

○ The two quantities are equal.

○ The relationship cannot be determined from the information given.

5 of 20

At a dog show, there are 20 judges and 10 dogs in the final round.

Quantity A	**Quantity B**
The number of distinct pairs of judges	The number of possible rankings of dogs from first to third place

○ Quantity A is greater.

○ Quantity B is greater.

○ The two quantities are equal.

○ The relationship cannot be determined from the information given.

$$k > 0$$
$$l > 1$$

Quantity A	**Quantity B**
$\dfrac{1}{\dfrac{1}{k} + \dfrac{1}{l}}$	$\dfrac{kl}{\dfrac{1}{k} + \dfrac{1}{l}}$

○ Quantity A is greater.

○ Quantity B is greater.

○ The two quantities are equal.

○ The relationship cannot be determined from the information given.

7 of 20

Quantity A	**Quantity B**
The greatest odd factor of 78	The greatest prime factor of 78

○ Quantity A is greater.

○ Quantity B is greater.

○ The two quantities are equal.

○ The relationship cannot be determined from the information given.

Joe has $200. If he buys a DVD player for $150, what is the greatest number of DVDs he can buy with the remaining money if DVDs cost $12 each?

Click on the answer box and type in a number. Backspace to erase.

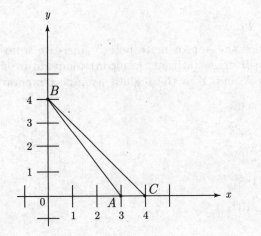

What is the area of triangle ABC in the figure above?

- ○ 2
- ○ 4
- ○ $4\sqrt{2}$
- ○ 7
- ○ 8

By which of the following could $10(9^6)$ be divided by to produce an integer result?

Indicate <u>all</u> such values.

- ☐ 90
- ☐ 100
- ☐ 330
- ☐ 540
- ☐ 720

Roberta drove 50 miles in 2 hours. Her rate in miles per hour is equivalent to which of the following proportions?

Indicate <u>all</u> such proportions.

- ☐ 5 to 20
- ☐ 100 to 4
- ☐ 400 to 16
- ☐ 20 to 500
- ☐ 520 to 20

Questions 12 through 14 refer to the following graph.

TEMPERATURES OF U.S. CITIES IN YEARS X AND Y

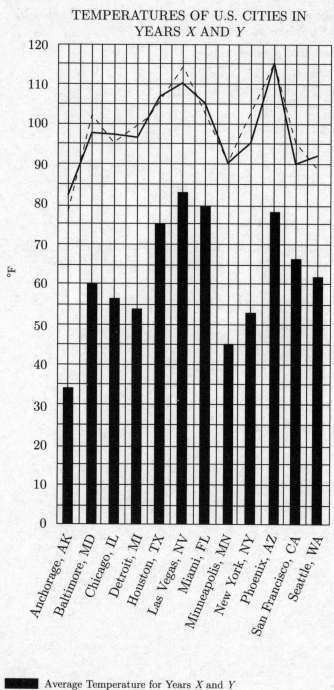

■ Average Temperature for Years X and Y

- - - - High for Year Y

———— High for Year X

For how many of the cities shown was the highest temperature in Year Y greater than or equal to the highest temperature in Year X ?

○   4

○   5

○   7

○   8

○   12

What is the approximate percent increase from the lowest average (arithmetic mean) temperature for Years X and Y to the highest average temperature?

○   60%

○   82%

○   140%

○   188%

○   213%

The average (arithmetic mean) temperature for any city in Years X and Y is the average of the high and low temperatures for those years. What is the average of the low temperatures for Baltimore for Years X and Y ?

○   –9° F

○   11° F

○   20° F

○   44° F

○   It cannot be determined from the information given.

If $|2x - 3| + 2 > 7$, which of the following could be the value of x ?

Indicate all such values.

- ☐ −4
- ☐ −3
- ☐ −2
- ☐ −1
- ☐ 0
- ☐ 1
- ☐ 2
- ☐ 3

If x, y, and z are consecutive odd integers where $x < y < z$ and $x + y + z < z$, then which of the following could be the value of x ?

Indicate all such values.

- ☐ −3
- ☐ −1
- ☐ 0
- ☐ 1
- ☐ 3

If $4^x = 1,024$, then $(4^{x+1})(5^{x-1}) =$

- ○ 10^6
- ○ $(5^4)(10^5)$
- ○ $(4^4)(10^5)$
- ○ $(5^4)(10^4)$
- ○ $(4^4)(10^4)$

What is the greatest distance between two vertices of a rectangular solid with a height of 5, a length of 12, and a volume of 780 ?

- ○ 12
- ○ $12\sqrt{2}$
- ○ 13
- ○ $13\sqrt{2}$
- ○ $13\sqrt{3}$

If three boys and three girls sit in a row on a park bench, and no boy can sit on either end of the bench, how many arrangements of the children on the bench are possible?

- ○ 46,656
- ○ 38,880
- ○ 1,256
- ○ 144
- ○ 38

If 16 is the average (arithmetic mean) of p, 24, and q, what is $16(p + q)$?

- ○ 180
- ○ 192
- ○ 384
- ○ 524
- ○ 768

Summary

o   Topics such as probability, permutations and combinations, factorials, and functions represent only a small percentage of the math topics tested on the GRE. Make sure you've mastered all the more important topics before attempting these.

o   Probability is expressed as a fraction. The denominator of the fraction represents the total number of possible outcomes, while the numerator stands for the desired outcomes.

o   If a probability question asks for the chance of event A or event B, find the probability of each event and add them together. If the question asks for the probability of event A and event B, multiply the individual probabilities.

o   The key to factorial problems is to look for ways to cancel or factor out terms.

o   Permutations and combinations are related concepts. A permutation tells you how many arrangements or orderings of things are possible. A combination tells you how many groupings of things are possible.

o   Function problems use funny-looking symbols as shorthand for the operations to perform on a certain number.

o   The group equation is Total = Group 1 + Group 2 – Members of Both Groups + Members of Neither Group.

Part IV
How to Crack the Analytical Writing Section

Chapter 17
The Geography
of the Analytical
Writing Section

This chapter clues you in on everything you've ever wanted to know about the Analytical Writing section of the GRE. It contains important information on how the essays are used by graduate schools, the scoring system ETS graders use to evaluate your essays, and the crucial distinctions between the issue essay and the argument essay. This chapter also looks at the basic word-processing program used by ETS.

ESSAYS AND THE GRE

The Analytical Writing section of the GRE requires you to write two essays—one will be an analysis of an issue and the other will be an analysis of an argument. You will have 30 minutes for each essay.

In the past, ETS has had problems with test takers relying on preplanned essays. The essay questions have been reformulated to reduce the possibility of testers preparing their essays in advance. However, while you may not be able to plan your entire essay in advance, you can still go into your test session having a good idea of what type of essay you're going to write.

> Even if your program doesn't care much about the essay, a poor score might still raise a red flag.

How Do Schools Use the Writing Assessment?

First, the essays are probably more important for international students and those for whom English is not a first language. If you are not a native English speaker, expect your essay score and the essays you wrote to receive more attention. (ETS also makes the essays available to schools, which may choose to read them or not.) Second, and not surprisingly, the essays will probably be weighted more heavily by programs for which writing is a frequent and necessary task. A master's program in applied mathematics might not care so much about your 30-minute written opinion about whether or not it's necessary for a person to read imaginative literature, but a program in creative writing probably would.

More Online!
Head over to PrincetonReview.com/grad-school-advice for useful information and helpful articles about graduate school.

Ultimately, though, here's the most honest answer to this question: it depends. Some schools will not care at all about the Analytical Writing score, while others will say that they want only applicants who scored a 5 or higher on this section. Call the schools you're interested in and talk to people in the department. By finding out how important your target schools consider the Analytical Writing section, you'll be able to determine the appropriate amount of effort to devote to it.

Regardless of your target score on this section, you should at least read through these chapters to get a better sense of what ETS is looking for. You'll have to write these essays, so no matter what, you want to do a decent job. You'll find that writing high-scoring essays is not as hard as it may seem once you've been shown how to do it.

> *What* you write—the content—will be weighted more than *how* you write.

How Will the Essays Be Scored?

Your essays will be read by two graders, and each will assign a score from 1 to 6, based on how well you do the following:

- follow the instructions of the prompt
- consider the complexities of the issue or argument
- effectively organize and develop your ideas
- support your position with relevant examples
- control the elements of written English

The grades you receive for each essay will be totaled and averaged. For example, if you receive a 4 and a 5 on your issue essay and a 3 and a 4 on your argument essay, your Analytical Writing score will be a 4.0; 16 total points divided by 4 scores. If the graders' scores for your essays differ by more than one point, a third person will be brought in to read the essay. The graders use a holistic grading system; they're trained to look at the big picture, not to focus on minor details. Your essay is not expected to be perfect, so the graders will overlook minor errors in spelling, punctuation, and grammar. However, pervasive or egregious errors will affect your score.

Here are ETS's descriptions of the scoring levels:

Issue Essay		Argument Essay	
6	An essay that scores a 6 presents a cogent, well-articulated critique of the issue and conveys meaning skillfully.	6	An essay that scores a 6 presents a cogent, well-articulated critique of the argument and conveys meaning skillfully.
5	An essay that scores a 5 presents a generally thoughtful, well-developed analysis of the complexities of the issue and conveys meaning clearly.	5	An essay that scores a 5 presents a generally thoughtful, well-developed critique of the argument and conveys meaning clearly.
4	An essay that scores a 4 presents a competent analysis of the issue and conveys meaning adequately.	4	An essay that scores a 4 presents a competent critique of the argument and conveys meaning adequately.
3	An essay that scores a 3 demonstrates some competence in its analysis of the issue and in conveying meaning but is obviously flawed.	3	An essay that scores a 3 demonstrates some competence in its critique of the argument and in conveying meaning but is obviously flawed.
2	An essay that scores a 2 demonstrates serious weaknesses in analytical writing.	2	An essay that scores a 2 demonstrates serious weaknesses in analytical writing.
1	An essay that scores a 1 demonstrates fundamental deficiencies in analytical writing skills.	1	An essay that scores a 1 demonstrates fundamental deficiencies in both analysis and writing.

An essay written on a topic other than the one provided will receive a score of 0.

Who Are These Readers Anyway?

We'll put this in the form of a multiple-choice question:

Your essays will initially be read by

(A)   captains of industry

(B)   leading professors

(C)   college TAs working part time

If you guessed (C), you're correct. Each essay will be read by part-time employees of ETS, mostly culled from graduate school programs.

How Much Time Do They Devote to Each Essay?

> ETS graders spend less than two minutes grading your essay.

The short answer is this: not much. It is unusual for a grader to spend more than two minutes grading an essay, and some essays are graded in less than a minute. The graders are reading many, many GRE essays and they aren't going to spend time admiring that clever turn of phrase you came up with. So don't sweat the small stuff—it probably won't even be noticed. Focus on the big picture—that's what the graders will be focusing on.

So How Do You Score High on the Analytical Writing Essays?

> Make the graders' jobs easy. Give them exactly what they're looking for.

On the face of it, you might think it would be pretty difficult to impress these jaded readers, but it turns out that there are some very specific ways to persuade them of your superior writing skills.

What ETS Doesn't Want You to Know

In a recent analysis of a group of essays written by actual test takers, and the grades that those essays received, ETS researchers noticed that the most successful essays had one thing in common. Which of the following characteristics do you think it was?

*   Good organization
*   Proper diction
*   Noteworthy ideas
*   Good vocabulary
*   Sentence variety
*   Length

What Your Essay Needs in Order to Look Like a Successful Essay

The ETS researchers discovered that the essays that received the highest grades from ETS essay graders had one single factor in common: length.

To ace the Analytical Writing section, you need to take one simple step: write as much as you possibly can. Each essay should include *at least* four indented paragraphs. Your Issue essay should be 400 to 750 words in length, and your Argument essay should be 350 to 600 words.

So All I Have to Do Is Type "I Hate the GRE" Over and Over Again?

Well, no. The length issue isn't that easy. The ETS researchers also noted that, not surprisingly, the high-scoring essays all made reasonably good points addressing the topic. So you have to actually write something that covers the essay topic. And in your quest for length, it's more important that you add depth than breadth. What this means is that it's better to have a few good examples that are thoroughly and deeply explored than it is to add length by tacking more and more examples and paragraphs onto your essay until it starts to feel like a superficial list of bulleted points rather than a thoughtful piece of writing.

Read the Directions Every Time

You should read the directions for each essay prompt. The instructions we provide here for each essay task are not necessarily the ones you will see on the GRE. Directions can vary in focus, so you shouldn't memorize any particular set of instructions. Visit the ETS website at www.ets.org/gre for a complete list of all the potential essay topics and direction variants. (Yes, you really get to see this information in advance of the test!) Practice responding to the different instructions, combined with a variety of issue and argument prompts. Be sure to mix it up; the prompt/directions pairings you see on the ETS website are not necessarily the duos you will see on the real test. Practicing with a variety of these essays will prepare you for whatever comes your way on test day.

Oh, Yes, You Can Plan Your Essays in Advance

In fact, there are some very specific ways to prepare for the essays that go beyond length and good typing skills. So how can you prepare ahead of time?

Creating a Template

When a builder builds a house, the first thing he does is construct a frame. The frame supports the entire house. After the frame is completed, he can nail the walls and windows to the frame. We're going to show you how to build the frame for the perfect GRE essay. Of course, you won't know the exact topic of the essay until you get there (just as the builder may not know what color his client is going to paint the living room), but you will have an all-purpose frame on which to construct a great essay no matter what the topic is. We call this frame the template.

Preconstruction

Just as a builder can construct the windows of a house in his workshop weeks before he arrives to install them, so can you pre-build certain elements of your essay. We call this "preconstruction."

In the next two chapters, we'll show you how to prepare ahead of time to write essays on two topics that you won't see until they appear on your screen.

ISSUE VERSUS ARGUMENT ESSAY

It is worth noting at this time that the essay section gives you two very distinct writing tasks, and that a failure to appropriately address these tasks will severely reduce your score.

The Issue Essay

The Issue essay asks for your opinion; you're expected to present your viewpoint on a particular topic and support that viewpoint with various examples. The following is one example of the instructions for the Issue essay:

> You will be given a brief quotation that states or implies an issue of general interest and specific instructions on how to respond to that issue. You will have 30 minutes to plan and compose a response in which you develop a position on the issue according to the specific instructions. A response to any other issue will receive a score of zero.
>
> Make sure that you respond to the specific instructions and support your position on the issue with reasons and examples drawn from such areas as your reading, experience, observations, and/or academic studies.

Note how important it is to specifically address the assignment provided as part of the Issue prompt; not following ETS's directions will make your grader unhappy and result in a poor score on the essay.

The Argument Essay

The Argument essay requires a different type of response. Instead of presenting your own perspective, your job is to critique someone else's argument. You're supposed to address the logical flaws of the argument, not provide your personal opinion on the subject. The following is one example of the directions for the Argument essay:

> You will be given a short passage that presents an argument, or an argument to be completed, and specific instructions on how to respond to that passage. You will have 30 minutes to plan and compose a response in which you analyze the passage according to the specific instructions. A response to any other argument will receive a score of zero.
>
> Note that you are NOT being asked to present your own views on the subject. Make sure that you respond to the specific instructions and support your analysis with relevant reasons and/or examples.

In the Argument essay, the emphasis is on writing a logical analysis of the argument, not an opinion piece. It is absolutely essential that you don't confuse the two essay tasks on the GRE.

> ETS graders don't expect a perfect essay; occasional spelling, punctuation, and grammar errors won't kill your score.

HOW DOES THE WORD-PROCESSING PROGRAM WORK?

ETS has created a very simple program that allows students to compose their essays on the screen. Compared to any of the commercial word-processing programs, this one is extremely limited, but it does allow the basic functions. You can move the cursor with the arrow keys, and you can delete, copy, and paste. You don't have to use any of these functions. With just the backspace key and the mouse to change your point of insertion, you will be able to use the computer like a regular word-processing program.

Take a look at the image below to see what your screen will look like during the Analytical Writing section of the test:

The question will always appear at the top left of your screen. Beside it, in a box, will be your writing area (in the writing area above, you can see a partially completed sentence). When you click inside the box with your mouse, a winking cursor will appear, indicating that you can begin typing.

As we said above, the program supports the use of many of the normal computer keys.

- The "Backspace" key removes text to the left of the cursor.
- The "Delete" key removes text to the right of the cursor.
- The "Arrow" keys move the cursor up, down, left, or right.
- The "Home" key moves the cursor to the beginning of a line.
- The "End" key moves the cursor to the end of a line.
- The "Enter" key moves the cursor to the beginning of the next line.
- "Page up" moves the cursor up one page.
- "Page down" moves the cursor down one page.

You can also use the buttons above the writing area to copy and paste words, sentences, or paragraphs. To do this, you first have to highlight the desired text by clicking on the starting point with your mouse and holding down the mouse button while you drag it to the ending point. Then click on the "Cut" button. This deletes the text you've selected from the screen, but also stores it in the computer's memory. Next, just move the cursor to wherever you would like the selected text to reappear, and click on the "Paste" button. The selected text will appear in that spot.

If you make a mistake, simply click on the "Undo" button, which will undo whatever operation you have just done. You can undo a cut, a paste, or even the last set of words you've typed in. Unfortunately, unlike many word-processing programs, ETS's program does not have a "Redo" button, so be careful what you decide to undo.

Obviously, the small box on the screen is not big enough to contain your entire essay. However, by hitting the "Page up" and "Page down" keys on your keyboard, or by using the arrows on your keyboard, you will be able to go forward and backward to reread what you have written and make corrections.

Does Spelling Count?

Officially, no. The word-processing program doesn't have a spell checker, and ETS essay readers are supposed to ignore minor errors of spelling and grammar, but the readers wouldn't be human if they weren't influenced by an essay that had lots of spelling mistakes and improper grammar—it gives the impression that you just didn't care enough to proofread.

Because pervasive spelling errors will detract from your score, pick an easier word if you're really uncertain of how to spell a word.

Summary

o   Different programs value the essay section in different ways. Check with your program to see how important the essays are.

o   Understand the criteria ETS uses for judging your essay. Organization, examples, and language use are important. Perfect grammar and spelling less so.

o   On the GRE, longer essays tend to receive better scores, so strive to write as much as you can for each essay.

o   Make sure you understand the differences in the assignments for the Issue essay and the Argument essay.

o   Issue essays ask for your opinion on a topic, while Argument essays expect you to critique the logic of an argument. The ways in which you're asked to do each of these tasks will vary, so make sure you read each set of directions carefully.

o   The word processor ETS provides has only the most basic functions. You can delete, copy, and paste text, but not much more.

Chapter 18
The Issue Essay

The Issue essay of the GRE requires you to present your opinion on the provided topic. This chapter will show you the steps to take in order to write a clear, coherent essay in the limited time provided. You'll learn the key parts of a successful essay, and how to brainstorm ideas, combine them into a thesis, and then structure a cohesive essay that will get you the best possible result.

THREE BASIC STEPS

Because you don't have a lot of time to write the essays, you'll need to have a pretty good idea of how you're going to attack them as soon as you sit down at the computer on test day. Our approach to the essays involves three steps:

1. **Think.** Before you start writing, take a moment to brainstorm some thoughts about the topic.
2. **Organize.** Take the ideas you've come up with and fit them into the assignment for the prompt.
3. **Write.** Once you've completed the first two steps, the final step should be a snap.

Thirty minutes is not a lot of time to write an essay, so you have to get it right the first time out. While ETS advises you to leave enough time to proofread and edit your essay, it simply isn't feasible to expect to make any significant changes to your essay during the final minutes of the section. Furthermore, if you get halfway through your essay and realize you're stuck or you're not saying what you need to say, you'll be hard pressed to fix your essay in the time you have left.

You have to know what you want your essay to say before you can start writing.

It is essential, therefore, to make sure you spend time planning your essay before you start writing. You have to figure out what it is you want to say before you begin; otherwise, you run the risk of writing an incoherent, rambling essay. The first two steps are actually more important to a successful GRE essay than the final step; by spending a little time planning your essay, the actual writing part should be relatively painless.

> The keys to the essay: Think, Organize, Write

The basics parts of an essay include the introduction, body paragraphs, and conclusion.

Essay Essentials

As you learned in sixth-grade composition class, a basic essay has three parts: an introduction, some body paragraphs, and a conclusion. These three things are exactly what you should include in your Analysis of an Issue Essay. Each of these parts has a specific role to play.

1. The **introduction** should introduce the topic of the essay, discuss the issues surrounding it, and present the essay's thesis.
2. The **body paragraphs** should use examples to support the thesis of the essay.
3. The **conclusion** should summarize the major points of the issue, reiterate the thesis, and perhaps consider its implications.

Basically, if you try to think of each paragraph as having a specific job to do, you can pretty much preconstruct each type of paragraph and then fill in the specific details on test day.

Keys to a High-Scoring Essay

In order to write a high-scoring Issue essay, you should accomplish four key tasks. A high-scoring Issue essay

- considers the complexities of the issue
- supports the position with relevant examples
- is clear and well organized
- demonstrates superior facility with the conventions of standard written English

To put it more simply, your essay should be logically organized, include good examples to support whatever position you've taken, and demonstrate that you can use the English language reasonably well in writing.

Let's continue our discussion of the Issue essay by looking at a typical prompt.

The Prompt

> "True beauty is found not in the exceptional but in the commonplace."
>
> Write an essay in which you take a position on the statement above. In developing and supporting your essay, consider instances in which the statement does and does not hold true.

The prompts are supposed to get you thinking about areas of "general interest," whatever that means. A better way of thinking about the prompt is to look at it as an agree/disagree or pro/con statement. Your task in the essay will be to look at both sides of the issue, the pro and the con side, and take a position on the statement. Let's look at how to do that.

Step 1: Think

"Think" is a pretty broad command, so we need to clarify this step in order to make it more useful. Specifically, we want you to think about three things.

1. **Key Terms.** What are the key words or phrases in the prompt? Do the terms need clarifying before you can properly deal with them in the essay?
2. **Opposite Side.** What would the converse of the statement be?
3. **Examples.** What are some examples that would support the statement? What are some examples that would support the opposite statement?

Let's work through these steps with our sample prompt.

Key Terms

When preparing your essay, first look more closely at the key terms in the prompt. Do they need to be clarified? Are there multiple ways of interpreting the words? In order to make your essay as focused as possible, you might need to limit the key terms to a specific definition or interpretation. If the key terms in the prompt seem pretty straightforward, you still want to note them. By repeatedly returning to these terms in your essay, you'll convey the impression that your essay is strongly organized and on topic.

For the sample prompt above, write down the key terms:

_____

_____

_____

> Using key terms from the prompt throughout your essay contributes to its overall coherency.

For this prompt, the key terms are *beauty, true, exceptional,* and *commonplace*. We need to think about how we're going to use these terms in our essay. For example, what is *true beauty?* Do we want that to mean just natural beauty or can we consider man-made objects? As for the word *beauty,* do we want to limit our discussion to artistic beauty such as paintings and sculptures, or should we consider poems and literature as well? Should we discuss only natural beauty, such as stars and flowers, or should we consider personal beauty as well, such as models and GRE instructors? As you can see, we could write a lot on this topic, if we had the time. But we don't, so it's important to focus. By defining our key terms, we make the essay a lot more manageable and easier to write in a short amount of time. For this essay, let's include both natural objects and man-made artistic feats, but leave out personal beauty.

Opposite Side

In order to score well on the Issue essay, you'll have to consider both sides of the prompt. A simple "I agree, and here's why" essay won't be enough here; rather, you'll need to consider both sides of the issue and state a clear position that you can defend. Take a brief moment to look at the sample prompt again, and then write down the converse of the statement.

> "True beauty is found not in the exceptional but in the commonplace."

_____

For this prompt, the opposite side of the argument would be something along the lines of "True beauty is found not in the commonplace, but in the exceptional." Note that there is no right answer to the prompt; either side is valid. So if you find the opposite of the statement more convincing, that's fine. As long as you can support your position with some relevant examples, it doesn't matter what position you take on the prompt. This brings us to the final part of step one—brainstorming examples.

Examples

In many ways, the examples will be the most important part of your essay. Without strong, relevant examples, you cannot expect to achieve a high score on the Issue essay. As the instructions state, you should support your position with examples drawn from your reading, experience, observation, and academic studies. In general, the more specific your examples are, the better your essay score. And examples from history, literature, or current events are better than personal observations or experiences. Imagine that a friend asks you to read her essay and give feedback. Which sentence would you respond more favorably to?

"Few observers would doubt the awesome beauty of the ceiling of the Sistine Chapel in Rome, a work of art produced by the great Renaissance artist Michelangelo."

"Few observers would doubt the awesome beauty of the various paintings they see in museums, works of art produced by great artists."

Both sentences essentially say the same thing and use practically the same words. But you would probably respond more favorably to the first sentence because it contains a *specific* example.

Take a moment to jot down some examples for the previous prompt. Make sure you come up with examples for both the original statement and its opposite.

_____

_____

_____

Now take a moment to look over your examples. Are they specific? Are they relevant to the topic? Do they support a position on the topic? The strength of your examples will determine the strength of your argument. It's hard to write a convincing paper with weak examples. Here are some examples that might work for our sample topic, both weaker and stronger:

> Avoid hypothetical examples—the more specific your example is, the better.

Okay Example
paintings, artwork
buildings, churches
flowers, natural wonders

Better Example
Leonardo da Vinci's *Mona Lisa*
Notre Dame Cathedral in Paris
Niagara Falls

> Good examples are relevant to the topic and contain specific details.

In each case, the better example is the more specific, more detailed example. Also note that we've avoided any personal examples. While you certainly may feel that your boyfriend or girlfriend is the most beautiful person in the world, that sort of personal example won't be as effective as a more academic or global example. Use personal examples only when specifically instructed to by the prompt or as a last resort.

Step 2: Organize

Once you've identified the key terms, considered the opposite side of the issue, and generated some examples, it's time to organize your thoughts. Basically, you should do the following:

1. **Separate Your Examples**. How many of your examples support the pro side and how many support the con side? Divide your examples up and see which side has more support.
2. **Write Your Thesis Statement.** After evaluating the strength of your examples, decide what position you will take in your essay, and then write your thesis. Your thesis is the main point that you want your essay to express.

Let's continue the process on the sample prompt.

Separate Your Examples

Do this before you decide on your thesis statement. Even though you might have a strong preference for one position on the issue, you might notice that the examples you brainstormed tend to support the other side of the issue. Don't expend more time trying to think of examples to support your preconceptions; just write your essay supporting the other side! There is no right or wrong response. All that matters is being able to write a strong, coherent essay in a very limited time. Your personal views or beliefs are unimportant to the ETS graders. If we continue with the examples we used earlier, they would probably break down like this:

Pro	Con
natural wonders	*Mona Lisa*
	Notre Dame

> It doesn't matter what side of the issue you take on the GRE.

Based on some of the examples we've come up with, it looks like we'd be better off supporting the idea that "True beauty is found not in the commonplace, but in the exceptional." While natural wonders like sunsets and flowers are pretty commonplace, we've come up with a lot more exceptional examples. And it looks like we could even argue that it is the exceptional natural wonders, such as Niagara Falls, that are truly beautiful.

Write Your Thesis Statement

Now comes the culmination of all of our work. What point do we want to make about the topic? Write it down here:

_____

Our thesis should probably be something along the lines of this: "While certain commonplace natural objects are examples of beauty, true beauty is most often found in rare, exceptional cases."

Now that we have figured out what we want to say, we can focus on proving why we believe it. But remember: Only after working through these steps are we truly ready to write!

Practice: Steps 1 and 2

Work through steps one and two on the following Issue essay prompts below.

PROMPT 1

"Government funding should never be used to support art that the majority of the population finds distasteful or objectionable."

Write an essay in which you take a position on the statement above. In developing and supporting your position, you should consider whether the above statement is always true or whether there are exceptions to it.

On your scratch paper, write the (1) Key Terms, (2) Opposite Side, (3) Examples, and (4) Thesis.

PROMPT 2

"Oftentimes, the results of a particular action are not of consequence; rather, it is the way we go about the action that matters most."

Write an essay in which you take a position on the statement above. In developing and supporting your position, you should consider situations in which the ways matter most as well as situations in which the results matter most.

On your scratch paper, write the (1) Key Terms, (2) Opposite Side, (3) Examples, and (4) Thesis.

Practice: Sample Responses

Obviously, your examples and thesis statements will differ from those given below, but these sample responses will give you a good indication of what to aim for in your actual essay.

Prompt 1

Key Terms: What does *support* mean? Is that just giving money to the artist, or does the government have to commission the work or promote it? What population are we using to judge—the general population, the population of artists, or some other population? What do we mean when we say art is "objectionable" or "distasteful"? What standards are we using to determine that?

Opposite Side: "Government funding should be used to support art, even if the majority of the population finds the art distasteful."

Examples: Robert Mapplethorpe controversy; National Endowment for the Arts; Supreme Court rulings on obscenity; Government censorship

Thesis: "While artists have the right to create whatever objectionable art they wish, taxpayers should not have to pay for art they find offensive or obscene."

Prompt 2

Key Terms: What do we mean by *consequence*? Does this term refer to the results of the action, or the effects the action has on the person doing the action? Similarly, when we say the way we go about something "matters most," what criteria are we using?

Opposite Side: "The way we go about a certain action is not of consequence; the results we get are what matter most."

Examples: Rosa Parks, whose actions helped further the Civil Rights movement; Gandhi, whose methods of nonviolent resistance played a part in Indian independence; Revolutionary War, whose violent methods eventually led to independence for the United States

Thesis: "While people do note the ways in which people go about certain actions, it is usually the ultimate result that matters."

Step 3: Write

Now that we know how to prepare for our Issue essay, we can write it. In this section, we'll discuss various templates for essays and show you how you can pre-construct certain portions of your essay. Before we do that, though, let's revisit your goals for the essay.

Essay Essentials Review

Remember the format of your essay should include

- introduction
- body paragraphs
- conclusion

Another way to think about this structure is

- Say what you're going to say.
- Say it.
- Say what you said.

Preconstruction: The Introduction

For the Issue essay, a good introduction accomplishes the following tasks:

1. clearly establishes the topic of the paper
2. previews both sides of the issue at hand
3. presents a clear thesis

Let's look at each of these tasks in detail and discuss different ways to accomplish the goals of the introductory paragraph.

Establish the Topic

> Don't just restate the prompt! Come up with a strong "hook" for the beginning of your essay.

You want to make it clear what issue the essay is going to talk about. Even though the grader will see the prompt you're writing about, he or she should be able to figure out the prompt just from reading the introduction of your essay. There are a few different ways you can quickly establish the topic, so let's return to our original prompt and preconstruct some approaches.

Here, once again, is our prompt:

"True beauty is found not in the exceptional but in the commonplace."

Write an essay in which you take a position on the statement above. In developing and supporting your essay, consider instances in which the statement does and does not hold true.

One of the worst ways of establishing the topic is to merely quote the prompt, as that shows a lack of creativity and a potential lack of understanding of the prompt itself. So let's discuss some other ways to start our essay.

Approach 1: Rhetorical Questions

This approach is a tried-and-true way of introducing your topic. Instead of simply quoting or paraphrasing the prompt, turn it into a rhetorical question. Here are a few samples:

Where does true beauty lie, in the exceptional or in the commonplace?

Do we find the exceptional more beautiful or the commonplace?

Can we find beauty only in rare, exceptional instances or does it truly lie all around us?

It is immediately clear what topic the essay will explore, from each of these examples of introductory sentences. See if you can come up with a rhetorical question for either this topic or one from the previous drill.

Approach 2: Famous Quotations

Another classic approach to beginning an essay is to use either a well-known saying or a famous quote from someone. Many of the GRE topics are fairly bland, so even if you can't think of a famous quote, there are usually some classic aphorisms you use. Here's what we mean:

"Beauty is Truth, Truth Beauty," or so said the romantic poet John Keats.

A common saying is that beauty is in the eye of the beholder.

Obviously, this type of introduction can be tough to do if something doesn't pop into your head right away. Try to come up with a quote or common saying for this topic or one from the drill.

Approach 3: Anecdote

An anecdote is a brief story. Oftentimes you can grab your reader's attention and introduce the topic with a good anecdote. Consider this example:

| A good opening line is great to have, but if you're stuck, don't spend an excessive amount of time trying to come up with something clever. |

It is said that Cézanne, the famed French painter, was so concerned with the beauty of his paintings that he would destroy any of his works that he felt was flawed.

The Romantic poet John Keats was so struck by the beauty of Chapman's translation of Homer's work that he wrote a poem about it.

When using an anecdote, you might have to write a sentence or two explaining the relevance of your story. Try out an anecdote for this topic or one of the drill topics.

Approach 4: Fact/Statistic

For some topics, it might be appropriate to start your essay by stating a fact or statistic. Factual mistakes won't cost you any points, because this is an essay, not a book report. So don't be afraid if your fact isn't 100 percent accurate. Here's an illustration:

A recent scientific study showed that the faces that people find the most beautiful are those that are the most symmetrical.

Psychologists have demonstrated that people's responses to certain phenomena are based on certain innate mechanisms in the brain.

Give this approach a shot, using this topic or one from the drill.

Approach 5: Definition

One way you may wish to start your essay is by defining one of the key terms from the prompt:

Beauty, by definition, is that which moves us or impacts us significantly.

The "exceptional" typically refers to those things that stand out, which is also a plausible definition for beauty.

The advantage to this approach is that you already spent some time thinking along these lines when you were planning your essay. Come up with a sample introductory sentence for this topic or one of the drill topics.

Preview the Issue

Once you've told the reader what the topic is, your next task is to inform the reader of the issues at hand. You want to briefly touch on both sides of the debate, explaining the pros and cons of the prompt. A good way to accomplish this is to make use of strong transition words—words like *but, despite, while,* and *although.* Here are some examples.

While some people can find beauty in the most common of places, true beauty is found only in the exceptional.

Some would argue that beauty is found everywhere, from the flowers to the stars, but others would state that true beauty is found only in rare, special instances.

Despite the assertions of many that beauty is everywhere, true beauty is found only in exceptional cases.

Although one might argue that many commonplace things are beautiful, it is the exceptional things that possess true beauty.

There can be no doubt that some of the world's most common things are beautiful. And yet, it is often the exceptional objects that possess true beauty.

Practice writing sentences that address both sides of the issue. Use the sample topic or one from the drill.

Present the Thesis

Your final task in the introduction is to present the thesis. Some writers prefer to avoid the first person, refusing to use sentences such as "I believe..." or "I feel...." However, there is no penalty for use of the first person. A more important consideration when writing your thesis is giving some indication of why you hold your particular position. You should make it clear that you've thought about and analyzed the issue. Here are some examples of thesis statements.

> A good thesis tells the reader exactly what your position is and why.

I believe that beauty is truly found in the exceptional, not in the commonplace, because if common things were beautiful, the very word would lose its meaning.

In my view, beauty is found in the exceptional, not in the commonplace, because only exceptional things really stand out as special in our minds.

It is clear that true beauty is not to be found in the commonplace but in the exceptional. On closer inspection, even so-called common objects that people consider beautiful are actually exceptional.

After weighing the evidence, it is certain that beauty is the province of the exceptional, not the commonplace. People find true beauty in things that they rarely experience, not the things they experience every day.

For each thesis, you can see that the author is also giving some justification for the viewpoint. This justification will be of course explored more thoroughly in the body paragraphs, but it's good to give a preview of how your essay will take shape. Try writing thesis statements for some of the sample prompts.

Preconstruction: Body Paragraphs

A body paragraph should do the following:

1. use a good transition/topic sentence
2. present an example
3. explain how the example supports the thesis

Body paragraphs are a little harder to preconstruct because they are the most specific part of the essay. Still, there are some handy tips for creating body paragraphs that will make for a strong essay.

Transition/Topic Sentence

One attribute of the strongest essays is that they flow well. The best way to write an essay like this is to use strong topic sentences and good transitions for each of your body paragraphs. Your topic sentence should serve as a gentle reminder of what the thesis of the essay is. Here's an example:

One example of beauty found in the exceptional is Leonardo da Vinci's Mona Lisa.

A second instance in which true beauty lies not in the commonplace but in the exceptional is Notre Dame Cathedral in Paris.

Of course, you might want to avoid using simple transitions like "the first example" and "the second example." You can make your writing stronger by leading with the example and making the transition a little more subtle, like so:

Leonardo da Vinci's Mona Lisa *is surely one of the most exceptional, and beautiful, paintings ever created.*

Consider the beauty of Notre Dame Cathedral in Paris, a building that is in no way commonplace.

Or to get even fancier, refer to the previous example in your transition sentence:

Like da Vinci's Mona Lisa, *the cathedral of Notre Dame in Paris is an exceptional, and exceptionally beautiful, object.*

The important point is that each sentence introduces the example and reminds the reader of the purpose of the example, which in this case is to support the notion of beauty as exceptional. In the next few sentences, you'll provide details about your example. It's important that you remember to link the example to your thesis.

Explain How Your Example Supports Your Thesis

Don't just state the example; explain why the example is relevant to your thesis.

On the GRE essays, don't get so caught up in providing details for your example that you forget to explain how or why your example helps your thesis. The purpose of the Issue essay is not to just list some examples; the purpose is to develop and support a position on the issue. Here's an example of a body paragraph that doesn't quite fulfill that goal:

Like da Vinci's Mona Lisa, *the cathedral of Notre Dame in Paris is an exceptional, and exceptionally beautiful, object. Notre Dame is a stunning example of gothic architecture, famous for the flying buttresses that adorn the sides of the building. The cathedral also has rows and rows of beautiful sculptures recessed into the walls, as well as a gorgeous central stained-glass window. These features make Notre Dame one of the most beautiful cathedrals in the world.*

The writer here did a good job of providing specific details about the example, which definitely strengthens this paragraph. However, the writer failed to explain why Notre Dame supports the view that true beauty is exceptional, not commonplace. Let's fix that:

Like da Vinci's Mona Lisa, *the cathedral of Notre Dame in Paris is an exceptional, and exceptionally beautiful, object. Churches and cathedrals line the streets of most major cities in Western Europe, but few possess the renown of Notre Dame. Notre Dame is a stunning example of gothic architecture, famous for the flying buttresses that adorn the sides of the building. The cathedral also has rows and rows of beautiful sculptures recessed into the walls, as well as a gorgeous central stained-glass window. These features make Notre Dame one of the most beautiful cathedrals in the world. Compared to a common church or cathedral, Notre Dame is truly awe-inspiring; Victor Hugo used the building as the backdrop for his magnificent book* The Hunchback of Notre Dame *and thousands of tourists travel untold miles to view the cathedral. That sort of beauty is not possessed by just any church on the corner.*

This is a stronger body paragraph because it is more explicit in its discussion of the thesis. The author notes that churches and cathedrals are fairly common, but then argues that Notre Dame stands out as an exceptional cathedral. The author concludes the paragraph by showing how Notre Dame is more beautiful than any typical church. Just as the topic of the essay should be clear from the introduction, the thesis should be clear from each body paragraph.

Write a body paragraph for one of the examples for this sample topic, or one of your examples from the practice. Make sure you have a good topic/transition sentence, specific details for the example, and an explanation of how or why the example is relevant to the thesis.

Preconstruction: Conclusion Paragraphs

Your essay should always have a conclusion, for two reasons. First, a conclusion paragraph is evidence of good organization. It shows that you knew exactly what points you wanted to make, you made them, and now you're ending the essay. And second, an essay that lacks a conclusion seems incomplete, almost as if your writing abruptly ends before it should. This can give a negative impression of your essay. Fortunately, conclusion paragraphs are easy to write.

> Make sure your essay has a conclusion.

A good conclusion

1. alerts the reader that the essay is ending
2. summarizes the main points of the essay

Some test takers even prefer to write their introduction and conclusion first and then fill in the body paragraphs. This strategy has the advantage of making your essay seem complete even if you happen to run out of time writing the body paragraphs.

Alert the Reader

Conclusion paragraphs have their own topic/transition sentences, which generally should contain a word or phrase that signifies the end of the essay. Here are some examples:

In conclusion, it's clear that true beauty is found not in the commonplace, but in the exceptional.

Ultimately, beauty lies in the exceptional, not in the commonplace.

As the bulk of the evidence shows, the exceptional, not the commonplace, possesses true beauty.

Clearly, true beauty is found in exceptional things, not in commonplace ones.

The examples above all support the idea that we find true beauty in exceptional cases, not in commonplace ones.

Write some conclusion sentences for this topic or a sample topic from the sample prompts.

Summarize Main Points

Your conclusion should also summarize the main points of the essay, meaning that it should mention the thesis and how the examples support it. Additionally, you can briefly consider the implications of the thesis. Here are some sample conclusions:

In conclusion, it's clear that true beauty is found not in the commonplace, but in the exceptional. The Mona Lisa and Notre Dame Cathedral are both exceptional examples of fairly commonplace things and it is these exceptions that are noted as truly beautiful. If anything, the commonplace serves only as a contrast to what true beauty really is.

Ultimately, beauty lies in the exceptional, not the commonplace. While paintings and churches are fairly commonplace, only a small few of them, such as the Mona Lisa *or Notre Dame, truly reach the heights of beauty. It is in these exceptions that we find real beauty.*

The examples above all support the idea that we find true beauty in exceptional cases, not in commonplace ones. Common things may seem at first glance to be beautiful, but once we compare these commonplace examples to the truly exceptional ones, we see that the exceptional ones are truly beautiful.

Try your hand at constructing a conclusion paragraph, once again using this topic or one from the sample prompts.

Putting It All Together

Read through this sample essay that's based on the basic five-paragraph model. Then you'll have the chance to try writing a similar essay for a different prompt.

"True beauty is found not in the exceptional but in the commonplace."

Write an essay in which you take a position on the statement above. In developing and supporting your essay, consider instances in which the statement does and does not hold true.

Beauty, by definition, is that which moves us or impacts us significantly. Some would argue that beauty is found everywhere, from the flowers to the stars. But others would state that true beauty is found only in rare, special instances. After weighing the evidence, it is certain that beauty is the province of the exceptional, not the commonplace. People are moved most by things that they rarely experience, not the things they experience every day.

Those who would argue that true beauty is everywhere might point to the beauty of a flower, or the starlit night. These experiences are certainly common, but do they show that true beauty is commonplace? Flowers might be considered beautiful, but how often does a person stop to look at or appreciate every flower? Flowers are so common that in many cases, they are ignored or viewed as nothing special. However, on those rare occasions—exceptional occasions, one might say—when we want to commemorate an event or express emotion, we notice the beauty of flowers. Thus, it is not the commonplace flower that strikes us as beautiful, but the exceptional situations themselves that move us to appreciate the flower.

Now consider the exceptional. Leonardo da Vinci's Mona Lisa *is surely one of the most exceptional, and beautiful, paintings ever created. Few people who view the painting are not moved by the sheer beauty of it, and the* Mona Lisa *is instantly* recognized as a masterpiece of art. And yet, there have been literally millions of paintings produced in human history. Is every single one of them beautiful? Does every one of those paintings have the impact that da Vinci's does? Of course not. In order to find beauty, we must separate the exceptional cases from the common ones. True beauty is such because it stands out from the masses of the average and pedestrian.

Like da Vinci's Mona Lisa, the cathedral of Notre Dame in Paris is an exceptional, and exceptionally beautiful, object. Churches and cathedrals line the streets of most major cities in Western Europe, but few possess the renown of Notre Dame, one of the most beautiful cathedrals in the world. Compared to a common church or cathedral, Notre Dame is truly awe-inspiring; Victor Hugo used the building as the backdrop for his magnificent book The Hunchback of Notre Dame and thousands of tourists travel untold miles to view the cathedral. That sort of beauty is not possessed by just any church on the corner.

In conclusion, it's clear that true beauty is found not in the commonplace, but in the exceptional. The Mona Lisa and Notre Dame Cathedral are both exceptional examples of fairly commonplace things and it is these exceptions that are noted as truly beautiful. If anything, the commonplace serves only as a contrast so that we can understand what true beauty really is.

Your Turn

Try writing a similar essay for the prompt that follows this paragraph. Make sure you consider the opposing side of the argument. Devote a paragraph to looking at an example for the other side of the issue, but make sure you indicate that there is a flaw in the example or that the example is less than convincing. Set a timer for 30 minutes to practice GRE time constraints.

> "People most respect the powerful not when they exercise their power, but when they refrain from exercising it."
>
> Write an essay in which you develop and support a position on the statement above. In writing your essay, you should consider both when the statement may be true and when it may be false.

How to Score Your Essay

Now it's time to put on your essay-scoring hat and prepare to grade your own essay. If you're lucky enough to have a friend who is also preparing for the GRE, you could switch essays and grade each other's like you used to do in sixth grade. You'll need to be objective during this process. Remember, the only way to improve is to honestly assess your weaknesses and systematically eliminate them.

Set a timer for two minutes. Read the essay carefully but quickly, so that you do not exceed the two minutes on the timer.

Now ask yourself the following questions about the essay:

1. Overall, did it make sense?
2. Did you address the topic directly?
3. Did you address the topic thoroughly?
4. Did your introduction paragraph repeat the issue to establish the topic of the essay?
5. Did you consider both sides of the issue?
6. Did your examples make sense?
7. Did you flesh out your examples with details?
8. Did you explain how your examples supported your thesis?
9. Did your essay have a strong concluding paragraph?
10. Was your essay well organized, using transitions and topic sentences?
11. Did you use language that made the organization of the essay obvious?
12. Did you use correct grammar, spelling, and language, for the most part?

If you could answer "yes" to all or almost all of these questions, congratulations! Your essay would probably receive a score in the 5–6 range. If you continue to practice, and write an essay of similar quality on the real Analysis of an Issue section of the real test, you should score very well.

If you answered "yes" to fewer than 10 of the questions, you have room for improvement. Fortunately, you also know which areas you need to strengthen as you continue to practice.

If you answered "yes" to fewer than six of the questions, your essay would probably not score very well on a real GRE. An essay of this quality would not help you in the admissions process and could raise some red flags in the minds of the admissions people. You need to continue to practice, focusing on the areas of weakness that you discovered during this scoring process.

Another Sample Response
Take a look at a high-scoring response to the prompt you just practiced on. Your essay might look different and that's fine. This is just one of many ways to successfully complete the Issue essay assignment.

"The powerful are most respected not when they exercise their power, but when they refrain from exercising it."

Write an essay in which you develop and support a position on the statement above. In writing your essay, you should consider both when the statement may be true and when it may be false.

What aspect of power engenders the greatest respect? Some would argue that power inspires respect only by its ability to change things or bring about results. This camp respects the powerful only when they demonstrate their power by raising a massive army or bestowing charity on the less fortunate. Others believe that the true measure of power lies not in what it is used for, but in how it is restrained. These people believe that people most respect the powerful when they choose not to use their power, such as granting clemency to a criminal on death row or allowing critics of the government to speak out. However, even in these cases of restraint, it is clear that the exercise of power is more respected because of what that restraint implies about government power and control.

Consider first the respect people hold for the exercise of power. One of the mightiest displays of power is the ability to protect and safeguard people and property and this aspect of government is what many people respect. Indeed, in Hobbes's Leviathan, he argued that one of the reasons people sacrifice themselves for the good of the state is to preserve the power of the state to protect its members from outside attacks. And one of the stated goals of the United States massive military buildup was so that other countries would either "love us or fear us." Thus, it is clear that people have respect for displays of power. Similarly, the ability of the powerful to bestow gifts of charity on the less fortunate is also well respected. The names of philanthropists like Carnegie and Rockefeller are held in high esteem because they used their power to help those less fortunate than themselves.

On the other hand, the ability to show restraint can also engender respect. Recently, the governor of Illinois decided to commute the death sentences of all the prisoners on death row. Such an act of clemency brought high praise from human rights proponents around the world. Furthermore, the fact that democratic governments allow dissent when they could in many cases censor or squash unfavorable opinions also lends credence to the view that restraint of power is what people respect. For example, the arbitrary arrest and sentencing of political dissidents in Russia has brought much international criticism of the Kremlin, while countries that support freedom of speech and the press are widely respected in the world.

Ultimately, after considering both sides of the issue, it must be concluded that the exercise of power is most respected. This is because even in cases of restraint, the entity in power is still exercising its power. Granting clemency is possible only because the state holds the power of life and death. Allowing dissent is exceptional only because the government has the power to crush it. Thus, it is not the restraint of power that people most respect, it is the exercise of it.

FINAL THOUGHTS: WHAT TO DO WITH YOUR TIME

Now that you know how to construct your essay, you have to practice writing essays in a mere 30 minutes. Here's a guideline for how to use your time.

Your essay doesn't have to be perfect. Focus on the big picture.

- Find key terms, state the opposite side, brainstorm examples: 5–7 minutes
- Formulate a thesis: 2 minutes
- Write the essay: 18–20 minutes
- Proofread: 1–2 minutes

Notice that not a lot of time is allotted for proofreading. Remember that it's okay to have minor spelling and grammatical errors. Your time is better spent making sure you consider both sides of the issue completely and write an effective essay. For tons more practice, you can go to www.ets.org/gre for the complete list of essay topics.

Summary

o   Follow the three simple steps to essay success: Think, Organize, Write.

o   One of the keys to high-scoring essays is good examples. Make sure your examples are relevant to the topic and as specific as possible.

o   Try to use examples drawn from your readings, current events, literature, and history. Avoid personal examples.

o   Spice up your writing by employing an interesting "hook" to get your readers' attention. Consider using such hooks as rhetorical questions, quotes, anecdotes, facts and statistics, and other attention-getting devices.

o   A good GRE essay presents a smooth flow of ideas and examples. Make sure you use transitions to help show the progression of ideas in your essay.

o   Templates can be effective ways of organizing your essay, but don't feel restricted to them. Come up with your own template or modify the existing templates as you see fit.

Chapter 19
The Argument Essay

The Argument essay of the GRE asks you to examine and critique the logic of an argument. The arguments you will see in this chapter are similar to the ones you worked with in Chapter 7, and you will need to use the same approach to breaking these arguments down. This chapter will show you how to organize and write an essay once you've found the premises, conclusion, and assumptions of a GRE argument.

You'll be able to use all the skills we've discussed for the Analysis of an Issue essays on Argument essays as well, but in a slightly different way. Instead of asking for your opinion on a topic, the Analysis of an Argument essay asks you to critique someone else's argument. Before we jump into setting up templates and other preconstruction steps, let's take a look at how Analytical Writing arguments work.

THE PARTS OF AN ARGUMENT

As you read in Chapter 7 on Critical Reasoning, an argument, for GRE purposes, is a short paragraph in which an author introduces a topic and uses reasoning or factual evidence to back up his or her opinion about that topic.

The following statement is a really simplified example of an argument:

> My car broke down yesterday, and I need a car to get to work. Therefore, I should buy a new car.

The car argument above is composed of the following three parts:

- the conclusion—the author's opinion and recommendation for action
- the premises—the facts the author uses to back up his or her opinion
- the assumptions—unstated conditions that must be true in order for the argument to make sense

In this argument, the author's conclusion is "I should buy a new car."

The premises the author uses to support this conclusion are that his car broke down yesterday, and that he needs a car to get to work.

The premises must support the conclusion the way table legs support a tabletop. The tabletop is the most obvious and useful part of a table—you see more of it, and you can put things on it. But without the legs to hold it up, it's just a slab of wood on the floor. The same is true for the conclusion of an argument. The conclusion is the part that gets all the attention, since it recommends some course of action, but without the premises to support the conclusion, the conclusion won't hold up.

Conclusion Words

Certain words indicate a conclusion.

- so
- therefore
- thus
- hence
- showed that

- clearly
- then
- consequently
- as a result
- concluded that

When you see these words, you can be relatively sure that you've found the conclusion of the argument.

Premise Words

Certain words indicate premises.

- because
- since
- if
- given that

- in view of
- in light of
- assume

ASSUMPTIONS

An assumption is an unstated premise that supports the author's conclusion. It's the connection between the stated premises and the conclusion. In the example of the table, the assumption is that nails or glue hold the legs and the tabletop together. Without the glue or nails, the table will fall apart. Without the assumption, the argument will fall apart.

Sometimes the assumption is described as the gap between the facts that make up the premises and the conclusion. They don't always connect, so the assumption is the gap between them.

Let's take a look back at the car argument:

> *My car broke down yesterday, and I need a car to get to work. There-*
> *fore, I should buy a new car.*

The premises are that *my car broke down yesterday* and *I need a car to get to work.* The conclusion is that *I should buy a new car.*

When you first read this argument, you may have had some questions. These questions might have been along the lines of "Why can't the author just rent a car?" or "Why can't the author just fix the car?"

As you read an argument, identifying the premises and conclusion, questions may pop into your head. Those questions are pointing out the gap that leads to the assumption. Here, the gap is between having a broken car and still needing a car to get to work on the one side, and having to buy a new car on the other side.

Therefore, the assumption must be as follows:
There is no other way to have a car.

There are all sorts of smaller assumptions here—that the car can't be fixed, that a car can't be rented, that there's no other car the author can borrow—but those are all covered in the main assumption.

The assumption fills the gap between the premises and the conclusion, and, in fact, functions as an unstated premise:
My car broke down yesterday, and I need a car to get to work. There is no other way to have a car. Therefore, I should buy a new car.

Brainstorming for the Argument Essay consists primarily of coming up with a list of assumptions.

Three Common Types of Arguments and Their Assumptions

There are three types of arguments you are likely to see. They are Sampling, Analogy, and Causal. Becoming familiar with these three types will help you identify the assumptions in the argument more quickly when the clock is ticking on the real test.

1. The Sampling Assumption

A sampling argument assumes that a small group is representative of a much larger group to which it belongs. To attack a sampling argument, show that one cannot assume that the opinions or experiences of the smaller group are necessarily representative of the larger group.

2. The Analogy Assumption

An argument by analogy assumes that A = B or that what is true for one entity will be true for another. To attack an argument by analogy, simply show that the two groups or places or individuals are nothing like each other. What is true for one does not have to be true of the other.

3. The Causal Assumption

A causal argument assumes that A causes B, or that if you remove the cause, you will remove the effect. While there may be a strong correlation between A and B, it does not always follow that it is a causal relationship or that A is the cause of B. To attack a causal relationship, point out that there are other possible causes for B and brainstorm some possible examples.

Well, Great, But Why Do I Care?

You should care about taking apart the argument, and finding the assumptions in particular, because the key to writing a great Argument essay on the Analytical Writing section is ripping apart the argument.

Think about it. The official instructions on the test ask you to "critique" the author's argument. However, if you claim that everything the author says makes sense, you won't be able to write an essay that's more than a few sentences long. This means that in order to write a great essay, you'll need to tear the author's argument apart.

> **Danger:** The most common mistake people make in writing the Argument essay is expressing their own opinions. Don't do this! The Issue essay specifically asks you to give an opinion and then back it up. The Argument essay, on the other hand, wants a critique of someone else's opinion, not your own.

WRITING THE ARGUMENT ESSAY

Writing the Analysis of an Argument essay requires a series of steps.

Step 1: Read the topic and identify the conclusion and the premises.

Step 2: Since they're asking you to critique (that is, weaken) the argument, concentrate on identifying its assumptions. Look for gaps in the argument, weaknesses in the logic, and new information in the conclusion that wasn't present in the premises. Brainstorm as many different assumptions as you can think of. Write these out on your scratch paper or on the computer screen.

Step 3: Select three or four of the strongest assumptions around which to build your essay.

Step 4: Choose a template that allows you to attack the assumptions in an organized way.

Step 5: Write the essay, using all the tools and techniques that you'll be learning in this chapter.

Step 6: Read over the essay and edit it.

> You will have 30 minutes to plan and compose a response to the argument topic, so make sure to budget your time wisely.

KEYS TO A HIGH-SCORING ESSAY

In the Analysis of an Argument topic section, your job is to critique the argument's line of reasoning and the evidence supporting it, and to suggest ways in which the argument could be strengthened. Again, you aren't required to know any more about the subject than would any normal person—but you must be able to spot logical weaknesses. Make absolutely sure you have read and understood the previous section about taking apart the argument.

In order to write a high-scoring essay, you should accomplish four key tasks. According to a booklet prepared by ETS, "An outstanding argument essay...clearly identifies and insightfully analyzes important features of the argument; develops ideas cogently, organizes them logically, and connects them smoothly with clear transitions; effectively supports the main points of the critique; and demonstrates superior control of language, including diction, syntactic variety, and the conventions of standard written English. There may be minor flaws."

> Your opinion is not the point in an Analysis of an Argument essay.

To put it more simply, your essay should demonstrate all of the same things that you did for the Analysis of an Issue essay, plus one extra ingredient: a cursory knowledge of the rules of logic.

Doing the Actual Analysis of the Argument

In any Analytical Writing argument, the first thing you should do is separate the conclusion from the premises.

Let's see how this works with an actual essay topic.

Topic:

> The director of the International Health Foundation recently released this announcement:

> "A new medical test that allows the early detection of a particular disease will prevent the deaths of people all over the world who would otherwise die from the disease. The test has been extremely effective in allowing doctors to diagnose the disease six months to a year before it would have been spotted by conventional means. As soon as we can institute this test as routine procedure in hospitals around the world, the death rate from this disease will plummet."

> Save the fancy prose for English class! Your grader cares more that you can identify the parts of the argument than for a clever turn of phrase.

The conclusion in this argument comes in the first line:

> A new medical test that allows the early detection of a particular disease will prevent the deaths of people all over the world who would otherwise die from that disease.

The premises are the evidence in support of this conclusion.

> The test has been extremely effective in allowing doctors to diagnose the disease six months to a year before it would have been spotted by conventional means.

The assumptions are the unspoken premises of the argument—without which the argument would fall apart. Remember that assumptions are often causal, analogical, or statistical. What are some assumptions of this argument? Let's brainstorm.

Brainstorming for Assumptions

You can often find assumptions by looking for a gap in the reasoning. "Medical tests allow early detection": According to the conclusion, this medical test leads to the early detection of the disease. There doesn't seem to be a gap here.

Early detection allows patients to survive: In turn, the early detection of the disease allows patients to survive the disease. Well, hold on a minute. Is this necessarily true?

- First, do we know that early detection will *necessarily* lead to survival? We don't even know if this disease is curable. Early detection of an incurable disease is not going to help anyone survive it.
- Second, will the test be widely available and cheap enough for general use? If the test is expensive or available only in certain parts of the world, people will continue to die from the disease.
- Third, will doctors and patients interpret the tests correctly? The test may be fine, but if doctors misinterpret the results or if patients ignore the need for treatment, then the test will not save lives.

Death rate will plummet: There's a huge gap here in that there's absolutely no explanation of how merely detecting the disease will immediately cause the death rate from it to plummet. This area is ripe for exploration.

Organizing the Analysis of an Argument Essay

We're now ready to put this into a ready-made template. In any Analysis of an Argument essay, the template structure should be pretty straightforward. You're simply going to reiterate the argument, attack the argument in three different ways (each in a separate paragraph), summarize what you've said, and mention how the argument could be strengthened. From an organizational standpoint, this is pretty easy. Try to minimize your use of the word *I*. Your opinion is not the point in an Analysis of an Argument essay. To make your essay as reader-friendly as possible, be sure to indent each of the four or five paragraphs for clear breaks between your thoughts.

> The arguments provided for the writing assessment of the GRE typically contain more flaws than those you worked with in the multiple-choice section. The flaws are often easier to spot as well.

A Sample Template

Of course, you should develop your own template for the Analysis of an Argument essay, but to get you started, here's one possible structure:

The argument that (restatement of the conclusion) is not entirely logically convincing, since it ignores certain crucial assumptions.

First, the argument assumes that _____

_____ .

Second, the argument never addresses _____

_____.

Finally, the argument omits _____

_____.

Thus, the argument is not completely sound. The evidence in support of the conclusion is not sufficient to support the conclusion of the argument because

_____

*Ultimately, the argument might have been strengthened by*_____

_____.

The key to succeeding on an Analysis of an Argument essay is to critique the argument clearly.

How Would the Result of Our Brainstorming Fit into the Template?

Here's how the assumptions we came up with for this argument would fit into the template:

The argument that the new medical test will prevent deaths that would have occurred in the past is not entirely logically convincing since it ignores certain crucial assumptions.

First, the argument assumes that early detection of the disease will lead to an immediate drop in the mortality rate from this disease, yet it does nothing to explain how this will happen, and so on.

Second, the argument never addresses the point that the existence of this new test, even if totally effective, is not the same as the widespread use of the test, and so on.

Finally, even supposing the ability of early detection to save lives and the widespread use of the test, the argument still depends on the doctors' correct interpretation of the test and the patients' willingness to undergo treatment, and so on.

Thus, the argument is not completely sound. The evidence in support of the conclusion that the test will cause death rates to plummet does little to prove that conclusion, since it does not address the assumptions already raised. Ultimately, the argument might have been strengthened if the author could have shown that the disease responds to early treatment, which can be enacted immediately upon receipt of the test results, that the test will be widely available around the world, and that doctors and patients will make proper use of the test.

Customizing Your Analysis of an Argument Template

Your organizational structure may vary in some ways, but it will always include the following elements. The first paragraph should sum up the argument's conclusion. The second, third, and fourth paragraphs will attack the argument and the supporting evidence. The last paragraph should summarize what you've said and state how the argument could be strengthened. Here are some alternate ways of organizing your essay:

Variation 1

1st paragraph: Restate the argument.

2nd paragraph: Discuss the link (or lack thereof) between the conclusion and the evidence presented in support of it.

3rd paragraph: Show three holes in the reasoning of the argument.

4th paragraph: Show how each of the three holes could be plugged up by explicitly stating the missing assumptions.

5th paragraph: Summarize and conclude that because of these three holes, the argument is weak.

Variation 2

1st paragraph: Restate the argument and say it has three flaws.

2nd paragraph: Point out a flaw and show how it could be plugged up by explicitly stating the missing assumption.

3rd paragraph: Point out a second flaw and show how it could be plugged up by explicitly stating the missing assumption.

4th paragraph: Point out a third flaw and show how it could be plugged up by explicitly stating the missing assumption.

5th paragraph: Summarize and conclude that because of these three flaws, the argument is weak.

Write Your Own Template for the Argument Topic

1st paragraph:

2nd paragraph:

3rd paragraph:

4th paragraph:

5th paragraph:

You Are Ready to Write an Argument Essay

You've separated the conclusion from the premises. You've brainstormed for the gaps that weaken the argument. You've noted how the premises support (or don't support) the conclusion. Now it's time to write your essay. Start typing, indenting each of the four or five paragraphs. Use all the tools you've learned in this chapter. Remember to keep an eye on the time. Again, if you have a minute at the end, read over your essay and do any editing that's necessary.

What to Do with Your Time

Now that you know how to construct your essay, you have to practice writing essays in a mere 30 minutes. Here's a guideline for how to use your time.

- Break down the argument: 3–4 minutes
- Find 2–3 assumptions: 3–4 minutes
- Write the essay: 18–20 minutes
- Proofread: 1–2 minutes

As was the case with the Issue essay, not a lot of time is allotted for proofreading. Remember that it's okay to have minor spelling and grammatical errors. Your time is better spent making sure you consider both sides of the issue completely and write an effective essay.

Practice: Writing an Argument Essay

Practice on the following sample argument topic. If you have access to a computer, turn it on and start up a word-processing program (again, you may want to use a very rudimentary one like Notepad to simulate the ETS program you'll see on the real test). Then set a timer for 30 minutes. In that time, read the topic, brainstorm in the space provided in this book, and then type your essay into the computer.

A Sample Argument

The market for the luxury-goods industry is on the decline. Recent reports show that a higher unemployment rate, coupled with consumer fears, has decreased the amount of money the average household spends on both essential and nonessential items, but especially on nonessential items. Since luxury goods are, by nature, nonessential, this market will be the first to decrease in the present economic climate, and luxury retailers should refocus their attention to lower-priced markets.

Conclusion:

Why? (premises)

Assumptions:

Ways you can pull the argument apart:

Ways the argument could be made more compelling:

> When writing your essay, make sure to use terms like causal, analogy, sampling, and so forth. Nothing impresses an ETS grader more than a sentence like "The argument assumes the sample is representative."

Now use the template you developed earlier in this chapter to type your essay on a computer.

How to Score Your Essay

It's time to put on your essay-scoring hat and prepare to grade your own essay. (Again, if you're lucky enough to have a friend who is also preparing for the GRE, you could switch essays.) You'll need to be objective about the process. The only way to improve is to honestly assess your weaknesses and systematically eliminate them.

Set a timer for two minutes. Read the essay carefully but quickly, so that you do not exceed the two minutes on the timer.

Now ask yourself the following questions about the essay:

1. Overall, did it make sense?
2. Did you address the argument directly?
3. Did you critique the argument thoroughly?
4. Did your introduction paragraph repeat the argument to establish the topic of the essay?
5. Did you avoid injecting your own opinion into the essay?
6. Did your essay have three strong paragraphs critiquing the arguments?
7. Did your critiques make sense?
8. Did you flesh out your points to make the weaknesses of the argument explicit?
9. Did the examples apply directly to the topic?
10. Did the essay have a strong conclusion paragraph?
11. Was the essay well organized?
12. Did you use language that made the organization of the essay obvious?
13. Did you use correct grammar, spelling, and language, for the most part?
14. Was the essay of an appropriate length (four to five paragraphs of at least three sentences each)?

If you could answer "yes" to all or almost all of those questions, congratulations! Your essay would probably receive a score in the 5–6 range. If you continue to practice, and write an essay of similar quality on the Analysis of an Argument essay on the real test, you should score very well.

If you answered "yes" to fewer than 12 of the questions, you have room for improvement. Fortunately, you also know which areas you need to strengthen as you continue to practice.

If you answered "yes" to fewer than five of the questions, your essay would probably not score very well on a real GRE. You need to continue to practice, focusing on the areas of weakness that you discovered during this scoring process.

There are more Argument topics for you to get super familiar with that essay type found in the Practice Tests in the back of this book and online, but if you'd like to practice even more, go to www.ets.org/gre and view the list of real Argument topics. You cannot possibly practice writing essays on all of these real ETS topics, so don't even try. However, you should spend time reading through them to become familiar with the variety of topics that ETS may give you.

Just Keep Practicing

So now you've read everything you need to know about writing high-scoring essays on the GRE. With a little practice, writing these essays should become second nature, and you'll find yourself sitting at the word processor on test day confident and prepared. Keep it up!

Summary

- Always start by identifying the conclusion of the argument.

- Look for the common types of arguments: Sampling, Analogy, and Causal.

- Brainstorm all of the assumptions that attach the premises to the conclusion.

- Outline your essay on your scratch paper before you start writing.

- Leave yourself two minutes to proofread your essay once you've finished writing.

Part V
Answers and Explanations to Drills and Practice Sets

CHAPTER 4: TEXT COMPLETIONS

Practice: Finding the Clue (Page 47)

1. Your words: *harrowing, difficult, troubled*; Underline: *reflected in the harrowing nature…of his plays*

2. Your words: *tall, high, towering*; Underline: *second highest mountain in the world…reaching more than 28,000 feet high*

3. Your words: *negative, harmful, unhealthy*; Underline: *wind-chill warning is issued…minus 25 degrees Fahrenheit or lower*

4. Your words: *remnants, remains, artifacts* OR *devices, munitions, projectiles*; Underline: *unexploded shells… from World War II*

5. Your words: *non-interchangeable, distinct, different*; Underline: *use the terms interchangeably…mammoths were hairy with long tusks, while mastodons had low-slung bodies and fatter skulls*

6. Your words: *practical, pragmatic, apolitical*; Underline: *he crafted his policies not with an eye toward their political consequences but instead toward their practical effects*

7. Your words: *amount, volume, workload*; Underline: *he would have to read for hours and hours each day to finish it all*

8. Your words: *derived, descended, transcribed*; Underline: *word "ghoul"…from the Arabic word "Algol"*

Practice: Clues and Transitions (Page 50)

1. Your words: *bad, poor, uneven*; Underline: *top talents…performance as a rookie almost ended his career*; Circle: *but*

2. Your words: *praise, recognition, respect*; Underline: *she brokered a diplomatic solution to a potential crisis*; Circle: *work; she*

3. Your words: *beneficial, health-promoting, healthful*; Underline: *detrimental to one's health*; Circle: *While*

4. Your words: *disconnected, apart, isolated*; Underline: *increasing technological connectivity*; Circle: *Despite*

5. Your words: *attractive, graceful, charming*; Underline: *ugliness and clumsiness*; Circle: *Although*

6. Your words: *gauge, predictor, sign*; Underline: *use holiday sales to gauge future stock prices*; Circle: *prices; thus*

7.   Your words: *negativity, misgivings, doubts*; Underline: *it is somewhat ironic...negative view*; Circle: *while ... rarely display such*

8.   Your words: *(devastating) effects, harms, toxicity*; Underline: *devastating effects on insects*; Circle: *insects; however...the same*

Text Completions Drill (Page 54)

1. B sorrow

The blank is describing what *her eyes relayed* and the transition word *despite* indicates that what *her eyes relayed* must be the opposite *the smile that spread from ear to ear*. A good word for the blank is something like "sadness." Choice (A), *jubilance,* means something joyous, so eliminate it. Choice (B), *sorrow,* is a good match, so keep (B). *Lively* means energetic, so eliminate (C). *[V]ision* offers no contrast to "sadness," and *mischievousness* or naughtiness is closer to *smile* than to "sadness," so eliminate (D) and (E). The correct answer is (B).

2. D acute

The blank is describing *black bears...claws.* The transition word *[w]hile* indicates that the *claws of black bears* are different from those of *grizzly bears,* which are described as *long, flat, and somewhat blunt.* Black bears' claws are described in the sentence as *short* and *curved,* which are the opposite of *long* and *flat.* Therefore, a good word for the blank is the opposite of *somewhat blunt,* so use "sharp" and evaluate the answer choices. Choice (A) *obtuse* is a synonym for blunt, so eliminate (A). Choice (B), *abominable* may describe a bear, but the word doesn't mean "sharp" and so doesn't match the clue, so eliminate (B). Choice (C), *barren,* is not a match for "sharp" so eliminate it. Choice (D), *acute,* is a good match for "sharp," so keep (D). Choice (E), *fearful* does not match "sharp," so eliminate it. The correct answer is (D).

3. C static

The blank is describing *individual personalities.* The semicolon indicates that the clause before the semicolon should agree with the clause following it. Therefore, the duality of *stability versus change* must be matched in the second clause by the duality describing *personalities*—the word in the blank or *different.* The adjective *different* in the second clause corresponds to *change* in the first, so the word in the blank must be an adjective corresponding to *stability.* Recycle from the clue and use "stable." Choice (A) *transient,* means last for a short period of time, so eliminate (A). Choice (B), *maladjusted,* is not a match for "stable" so eliminate it. Choice (C), *static,* is a good match for the "stable" so keep (C). Choice (D), *disturbed,* and (E), *discreet,* are both poor matches for "stable," so eliminate (D) and (E). The correct answer is (C).

4. E prodigious

The blank is describing the kind of *economic ripples* caused by *[t]he Erie Canal's completion.* The clause after the semicolon provides further insight into the sentence: *property values and industrial output...rose exponentially.* Therefore, these ripples could thus be described as significant or "large," so use this word for the blank. Choice (A), *persistent,* is not a match for "large" so eliminate it. Choice (B), *invaluable,* doesn't quite mean "large," and (C), *incredulous,* is nothing like "large" so eliminate (B) and (C). *[S]evere* might describe a significant economic effect, but that effect would be negative, not positive as implied here, so eliminate (D). Choice (E), *prodigious,* meaning impressively great or large, is a good match for "large." The correct answer is (E).

5. **B   stolidity**

The blank is describing how *voters...respond to the levy of a new tax*. The clue in the sentence is the word *inured*, which means hardened to a negative situation. If *[v]oters* are *inured*, then their response *to the levy of a new tax* would not be strong. Thus, the word in the blank could be "resignation." Choice (A), *amazement*, is not a match for "resignation" so eliminate (A). Choice (B), *stolidity*, or lack of emotion, is a good match so keep (B). Choice (C), *exasperation*, may describe how voters feel generally toward politicians, but is not supported by the passage so eliminate (C). Choice (D), *alarm*, and (E), *perplexity*, are both poor matches for "resignation," so eliminate both answer choices. The correct answer is (B).

6. **B   commensurate**

The blank is describing *when...it is desirable to expand the yield of a harvest*. The sentence provides further insight into this by stating that *it is desirable to expand...yield*, but only if there aren't also certain *additions in time, exertion and other variable factors of production*. So, a word such as "similar" for the blank conveys the logic that expanded yield shouldn't require expanded additions in time and other factors. Choice (A), *predestined*, is not a match for "similar," so eliminate (A). Choice (B), *commensurate*, is a good match for the blank, so keep (B). Choice (D), *deliberate*, is not a match for the blank, so eliminate it. Choice (C), *analogous*, is close, but *commensurate* is more quantitative, so eliminate (C). While *indeterminate* or uncertain additions are certainly not desired, this choice doesn't match "similar," so eliminate (E). The correct answer is (B).

Text Completions Practice Set (Page 60)

1. **B   futile**

Begin by determining who/what the blank in the sentence is describing. The blank is describing *the conviction of the United States to remain neutral*. Now determine what else gives insight into the word for the blank. The sentence states that global interconnectedness is on the rise in the introductory phrase, which stands in contrast to *the conviction of the* United States *to remain neutral*. Therefore, in a climate of global interconnectedness, for a nation like the United States to remain neutral would be difficult to maintain, so use a word like "improbable" for the blank. Something *presumptuous* is not necessarily "improbable." *Futile* is a good match for "improbable" so keep (B). *Contemptuous* doesn't match "improbable," and both *pragmatic* and *admirable* are the opposite of "improbable."

2. **B   enamored of**

Begin by determining who/what the blank in the sentence is describing. The blank describes Flaubert's reaction to *belly dancing*. Now determine what else gives insight into the word for the blank. The sentence states that *the dancers alone made his trip worthwhile*. Therefore, he was undoubtedly "impressed by" the dancing, so use that phrase for the blank. *[O]verwhelmed by* is an extreme phrase implying that Flaubert was unsure what to make of the dancing, so eliminate (A). *[E]namored of* is a decent match for "impressed by," so keep (B). *[T]aken aback by* is a negative phrase, suggesting that Flaubert was surprised to the point of shock. This does not match "impressed by" so eliminate (C). The phrases *beseeched by* and *flustered by* are not good matches for "impressed by," so eliminate (D) and (E).

3. **A** *fragile* and **E** *vulnerability*

This is a two-blank Text Completion question, so determine which blank is easier. Try starting with the first blank. Determine who/what the blank in the sentence is describing. The blank is describing the kind of *species* that *the human race is*. Now determine what else gives insight into the word for the blank. The sentence states that *the façade of calm...is flimsy and effortlessly ruptured*. The same-direction transition word *as* indicates that the blank agrees with the clue, so the human species must be "easily broken" or "weak." *Fragile* is a good match for "broken," so keep (A). *Purposeful* and *daring* are not good matches for "broken," so eliminate (B) and (C). Begin work with the second blank by determining who/what the blank is describing. The blank is describing something that is *flimsy and easily ruptured*. The word *anxiety* gives further insight into the word for the blank as the transition word *and* indicates that the blank will match *anxiety*. Choice (D), *terror*, is extreme, so eliminate (D). Choice (E), *vulnerability*, is a good match for anxiety, so keep (E). Choice (F), *humor,* is the opposite of the expected word.

4. **B** *prerogative* and **F** *attainable by*

This is a two-blank Text Completion question, so determine which blank is easier. Work with the second blank first. Determine who/what the blank in the sentence is describing. The blank is describing something about *books* relationship to *the average man*. Now determine what else gives insight into the word for the blank. The statements that *the increased popularity of dime novels, the expansion of the number of bookstores, and the introduction of the paperback* in addition to time transition *until the late 1800s* indicate that books were more "affordable to" or "available to" the average man. *Dislikeable to* and *excitable to* do not make "affordable to" so eliminate (D) and (E). Choice (F), *attainable by,* is a good match for the blank, so keep (F). Now work with the first blank. The transition word *until* indicates that, before *the late 1800s*, the situation was different from the later attainability of books by the average man. The word in the first blank must therefore be a noun describing "something limited to" *the well-to-do. Conduit* is not a good match for "something limited to," so eliminate (A). Choice (B), *prerogative*, which means a right or privilege, is a good match, so keep this choice. Choice (C), *plight,* is also a poor match, so eliminate (C).

5. **A** *an ineluctable* and **F** *merely denouement*

This is a two-blank Text Completion question, so determine which blank is easier. Try starting with the first blank. Determine who/what the blank in the sentence is describing. The first blank describes the kind of *victory...those already in office can coast to*. Now determine what else gives insight into the word for the blank. The sentence states that *boundaries...are drawn in order to protect incumbents*, so a good word for the blank is something like "easy to get." Choice (A), *an ineluctable,* is a good match for the blank, while *an invidious,* which means inspiring ill will, and *a plangent,* which means reverberating, do not match the word for the blank. Keep (A) and eliminate (B) and (C). Now work with the second blank. Determine who/what the blank in the sentence is describing. The second blank describes *the general election*. Now determine what else gives insight into the blank. Though introduced by the same-direction transition *[o]f course*, the sentence actually sets up the possibility of a challenge to the incumbent, but the transition word *[n]evertheless* reverses this idea. Therefore, the word in the second blank describing *the general election* could be an adjective similar to "ineluctable." Try to rephrase the difficult answer choices. Both (D), *seldom nugatory,* meaning rarely trivial, and (E), *remarkably contentious,* go against the expected sense. *[M]erely denouement* suggests a simple outcome or mere formality, so this choice is a good match. Keep (F).

6. **A pedantic** and **D antediluvian**

This is a two-blank Text Completion question, so determine which blank is easier. Try starting with the first blank. Determine who/what the blank in the sentence is describing. The first blank describes certain *professors*. Now determine what else gives insight into the word for the blank. The passage states that the professors *insist that video games will never be a proper object of study*. The transition word *[w]hile* also indicates that these professors are different from *more heterodox academics*. The opposite of *heterodox academics* would be "orthodox," so that's a good word for the blank describing the professors. Choice (A), *pedantic*, meaning scholarly in a narrow-minded way, is a good match for the blank so keep (A). *Progressive* and *erudite* may describe professors generally, but do not match the word for the blank, so eliminate (B) and (C). Now work with the second blank. Determine who/what the blank in the sentence is describing. The second blank describes how *the rising generation* views the opinions of their pedantic colleagues. Now determine what else gives insight into the word for the blank. The sentence describes the *rising generation* as *more heterodox,* so they likely see these views as "overly conservative." Choice (D), *antediluvian*, which means old-fashioned, is a good match so keep (D). Choice (E), *pusillanimous*, and (F), *jejune*, are both poor matches for the blank, so eliminate (E) and (F).

7. **C fulfilled, F changes,** and **H perilously**

This is a three-blank Text Completion question, so determine which blank is easiest. The first sentence is self-contained so start with the first blank. Determine who/what the blank in the sentence is describing. The first blank describes the *presumption that the future will be similar to the past*. Now determine what else gives insight into the word for the blank. The sentence states that *predictions...prove...accurate*. The *presumption that the future will be similar to the past* leads to accurate predictions IF this presumption is "true," so use that word for the first blank. *[D]isproved* gives the opposite meaning, so eliminate (A). *[S]tipulated* implies that the truth of this presumption is somehow imposed, so eliminate (B). *[F]ulfilled* suggests that the presumption comes to pass. This is a good match, so keep (C). Now, work with the third blank and determine who/what the blank is describing. The third blank is describing how *wrong* the *predictions* can be. Determine what else gives insight into the word for the blank. The transition word *however* indicates that the meaning of the sentence switches direction, which means there is lack of predictability, so the third blank should emphasize the adjective *wrong*. *Thoughtfully* makes an assumption about those who are making the predictions, and does not address the predictions themselves, so eliminate (G). Choice (H), *perilously*, is a good fit for the blank as it describes *wrong*. Keep (H). *Carelessly* also makes an assumption about those who are making the predictions, and does not address the predictions themselves, so eliminate (I). Work with the second blank and determine who/what the blank is describing. The blank is describing the *periods*. Determine what else gives insight into the word for the blank. Wrong predictions will happen in different circumstances from those in the first sentence—that is, when the future and the past are not similar. So a word like "changes" is a good match for second blank. *Upswings* and *insurgencies* does not match "changes," so eliminate (D) and (E). *Changes* is the word in (F), so keep (F).

8. **B dense, F liquid,** and **G an illustration**

This is a three-blank Text Completion question, so determine which blank is easiest. Begin with the second blank and determine who/what the blank is describing. The blank is the second half of a comparison about *water*. Determine what else gives insight into the word for the blank. The first half of the comparison is water as a *solid*, so a good word for the blank will be something like "liquid." Choices (D) and (E) do not match "liquid," but (F) is an exact match, so keep (F). Now work with the first blank and determine who/what the blank is describing. The blank is describing what *water...as a solid*. Determine what else gives insight into the word for the blank. The sentence states that the blank will be a word for what water is *less of as a solid than as a liquid*. The sentence also states to *look at the floating ice in your water glass,* so water will float as a solid inside its liquid form. If something is lighter than the liquid it sits in, that thing will float, and because of the transition word *less,* the sentence is discussing the opposite of lighter, so use a word like "heavy" for the blank. Choice (A) is not a good match, so eliminate it. Choice (B), *dense,* is a match for "heavy," so keep (B). Choice (C) is not a match for "heavy," so despite that *aqueous* could be used to describe water, eliminate (C). Work with the third blank and determine who/what the blank is describing. The third blank describes something the reader might *need.* Determine what else gives insight into the word for the blank. The sentence states that what the reader might *need* is to *look at the floating ice in your water glass.* The semicolon is a transition that indicates the same direction, so the third blank is an "example" of the statements in the first part of the sentence. Choice (G), *an illustration,* is a good match for "example" so keep (G). Choices (H) and (I) are not matches for "example," so eliminate them both.

9. **C practicing, E articulate,** and **I unfamiliar**

This is a three-blank Text Completion question, so determine which blank is easiest. Begin with the first blank and determine who/what the blank is describing. The first blank describes something *Molly* was doing with *Spanish.* Determine what else gives insight into the word for the blank. The sentence states that she was going to take a *trip to Chile* and that she *could comprehend her friends,* so a good word for the blank is "studying." Choice (A), *mastering,* is too extreme and (B), *disregarding,* is the opposite of "studying," so eliminate (A) and (B). Choice (C), *practicing,* is a good match for the blank, so keep this choice. Now, work with the third blank and determine who/what the blank is describing. The blank describes *the... language.* The sentence gives further insight into the blank by stating that she was *practicing Spanish* and that *she could comprehend her friends.* Therefore, a good word for the blank is something like "new to her." Choices (G) and (H) do not match "new to her," so eliminate them both. Choice (I), *unfamiliar,* is a good match for "new to her," so keep (I). Determine who/what the second blank is describing. The blank is describing what Molly *could not* do with *her thoughts.* The opposite-direction transition word *although* indicates that her listening skills are good as *she could comprehend her friends,* but her speaking skills must be less solid because *she could not* "express" her thoughts. Choice (D), *acknowledge,* is not a good match for *express,* so eliminate (D). Choice (E), *articulate,* is a good match for "express," so keep (E). Choice (F) is also not a good match for the blank, so eliminate it.

10. **B demarcates, D apocryphal,** and **I senescence**

This is a three-blank Text Completion question, so determine which blank is easiest. Begin with the third blank and determine who/what the blank is describing. The third blank is describing a *phenomenon* in *turtles.* Determine what else gives insight into the word for the blank. The sentence states that turtles *showing no signs of aging* is a way to describe the phrase in quotes; thus, the phenomenon could be described as *negligible* "aging." Choice (G), *rejuvenation,* is the opposite of "aging" and (H), *superannuation,* means the state of being old. Choice (I), *senescence,* means the process of aging, so while (H) is a decent fit for the word in the blank, (I) is a better one, so eliminate (H) and keep (I). Work with the second blank and determine who/what the blank is describing. The blank is a descriptive word about the *stories* of *musket balls being found in the shells of living turtles.* Determine what else gives insight into the word for the blank. Using *while* as a transition, the second blank contrasts the *tales of musket balls...found in the shells of living turtles* with the known phenomenon of "negligible senescence." If "negligible senescence" is something legitimate and recognized, then the tales of musket balls in turtle shells *may be* "dubious" or "bogus." Choice (D), *apocryphal,* is a good fit for "dubious," while (E) is the opposite of "dubious," and (F) is extreme and implies a judgment. Keep (D). Determine who/what the first blank is describing. The blank is describing *the human lifespan.* Determine what else gives insight into the word for the blank. For the first blank, it can be inferred that the *[p]eople* who dismiss tales of musket balls in turtle shells think that the human lifespan "represents" *the outer bounds of animal longevity.* Choice (A), *belies,* is the opposite of "represents" so eliminate it. Choice (B), *demarcates,* is a good match for "represents," so keep (B). Choice (C), *antedates,* is also a poor match for "represents," so eliminate (C).

CHAPTER 5: SENTENCE EQUIVALENCE

Sentence Equivalence Drill (Page 69)

1. **C modern** and **E contemporary**

   The blank is describing the *observer*. The sentence gives further insight into the blank with the word *ancient* and the transition word *or*, which indicates that a good word for the blank is the opposite of *ancient*. Therefore, a good word for the blank could be "modern." Choice (A), *antiquated*, is the opposite of "modern" so eliminate (A). Choice (B), *perceptive*, is a poor match for "modern," so eliminate it. Choice (C), *modern*, is a perfect match, so keep (C). Choice (D), *astute*, is not a match for "modern," so eliminate it. Choice (E), *contemporary*, is a good match, so keep it. Choice (F), *archaic*, is the opposite of "modern," so eliminate it. The correct answer is (C) and (E).

2. **D innate** and **F inborn**

   The blank is describing *characteristics*. The passage gives further insight by stating that some *arise through experience* and that *[r]esearchers* are *interested in the nature versus nurture debate*. This duality is reflected later in the sentence when it's explained why these researchers *use identical twins…separated at birth* to *explore* this debate. Characteristics *which arise through experience* correspond to *nurture*, so the characteristics described by the blank should correspond to *nature*, so use "natural" as the word for the blank. *Intractable* is a poor match for "natural," so eliminate (A). Choice (B), *nascent*, means just coming into existence, which sounds like it could match "natural" but does not fit because something does not have to be "natural" to be called nascent. Eliminate (B). Choice (C), *erudite*, means scholarly, so eliminate it. Choice (D) is a good match for the blank, so keep it. Choice (E), *predilection*, means a preference, so eliminate it. Choice (F) is a good match for the blank, so keep it. The correct answer is (D) and (F).

3. **A capricious** and **D unconventional**

   The blank is describing the *behavior* and the sentence gives further insight into the clue by stating that the Canadian Prime Minister is *eccentric*. So, a good word for the blank is "eccentric." Choice (A), *capricious*, is a good match for "eccentric," so keep (A). Choice (B), *lackluster*, means not to standard, so eliminate it. Choice (C), *poised*, is the opposite of "eccentric," so eliminate (C). Choice (D), *unconventional*, is a good match for the blank, so keep (D). Choice (E), *repulsive*, could describe behavior in some, but is not a match for "eccentric," so eliminate (E). Choice (F), *decorous*, is also the opposite of "eccentric," so eliminate (F). The correct answer is (A) and (D).

4. **B dynamic** and **F oscillating**

   The blank is describing the *conditions of life*. The sentence gives further insight into the blank by listing examples of what the conditions of life could be, *such as…atmospheric pressure…physical activity, and diet*. These clues imply that the *conditions of life* are "varying." Choice (A), *inveterate*, means have a long-standing habit, so eliminate it. Choice (B) is a good match for the blank, so keep it. Choice (C), *timorous*, means nervousness, so eliminate it. Choice (D), *cowed*, means to pressure by intimidation, so eliminate it. Choice (E), *turgid*, means swollen, so eliminate (E). Choice (F) is a good match for the blank, so keep it. The correct answer is (B) and (F).

5. **B commandeer** and **F appropriate**

The blank is describing what the *armed forces* did to *any working form of transportation they could find*. The sentence gives further insight into the blank by stating the *armed forces* were *without an adequate number of vehicles of their own*, after *arriving…days after Hurricane Zelda*. So, the armed forces were "taking over" any form of transportation. Choice (A), *repatriate*, means to send someone back to their home country, so eliminate (A). Choice (B), *commandeer*, is a good match, so keep it. Choice (C), *extradite*, means to hand over someone to a judicial system, so eliminate (C). Choice (D), *interdict*, means to prohibit, so eliminate (D). Choice (E), *expurgate*, means to remove something questionable, so eliminate (E). Choice (F), *appropriate*, is a good match for the blank, so keep (F). The correct answer is (B) and (F).

Sentence Equivalence Practice Set (Page 78)

1. **B affinity** and **F predilection**

The word in the blank describes Jim's feelings *for gumdrops*. The clue is that he *enjoyed all kinds of candy*. There is an opposite-direction transition word, *but*, which in this case doesn't mean that his feelings for gumdrops contradict the clue, just that they are distinctive in some way. This is emphasized by the extra information that gumdrops were *his absolute favorite*. Thus, the word in the blank should be something like "preference." Both *affinity* and *predilection* mean "preference." *[O]dium* and *disregard* mean the opposite, and *nature* and *container* don't match at all.

2. **A fiasco** and **B debacle**

The blank is a noun describing the *Wright brothers' first attempted flight*. One clue is that *subsequent efforts similarly ended in failure*, where *similarly* is a same-direction transition word. Another clue is that *they… ultimately made the first successful…flight*, and the opposite-direction transition word *[a]lthough* indicates that the first flight was not successful. Thus, recycle the word "failure" for the blank. *[F]iasco* and *debacle* are the best matches as both are colorful words for "failure." Both *triumph* and *feat* have the opposite meaning. *[H]indrance* isn't strong enough to mean "failure," and *precedent* isn't a match at all.

3. **D diminishes** and **F wanes**

The clue *due to the increased aerodynamic drag* suggests a negative impact on *fuel efficiency…at speeds greater than 50 miles per hour*. Thus, the verb in the blank should be something like "decreases." Both *diminishes* and *wanes* work. The verbs *equalizes* and *stabilizes* imply that fuel efficiency simply levels off. However, if the negative factor of aerodynamic drag increases, then there must be a negative—not a neutral—impact on fuel efficiency. The word *increases* means the opposite of "decreases," and *adapts* isn't a match at all.

4. **B an inept** and **F a maladroit**

The clue is *the vast amount of time Francis dedicated to learning six…languages*. The opposite-direction transition word *[d]espite* indicates that the word in the blank describing Francis as a communicator is at odds with his dedication to learning languages. This idea is continued after the transitional semicolon with an additional clue regarding *his inability to construct cogent prose*. Thus, the word in the blank modifying *communicator* should be something like "poor" or "ineffective." *[I]nept* and *maladroit* are the correct answers. *[A]stute* has the opposite meaning of what's expected, and *morose* is out of place because it means gloomy. Though it's possible Francis is *florid* and *prolific*, the clues don't directly support these ideas.

5. **E temperament** and **F humor**

The transition word *yet* suggests that, despite being twins, the two sisters were very different. One is described as *sanguine*, which context implies is the ability to remain upbeat *even in times of stress*. The other is described as *choleric*, which context describes as *prone to angry outbursts*. The transition word *while* emphasizes the contrast between the sisters. What's being described here are personality traits, so the noun in the blank modified by *choleric* should be something like "personality" or "disposition." Eliminate *genotype*, referring to genetic makeup, and *environment*, referring to one's surroundings. *[P]hysiognomy*, referring to facial features, and *incarnation*, meaning embodiment, don't work either. The correct answer is *temperament* and *humor*.

CHAPTER 6: READING COMPREHENSION

Reading Comprehension Drill (Page 96)

For this drill, we will walk you through detailed explanations of every choice.

1. **A** The phrase *would most likely be* indicates that this is an inference question. The subject of the question is the intended audience. The task of the question is to find who this audience can be inferred to be. In order to answer the question, determine what the passage says about the subject and evaluate the answer choices, eliminating any choice which cannot be supported by the text. Look at each answer choice and try to find information in the passage that supports the choice.

    Choice (A): Correct. The passage contains information about the aye-aye's habitat (*Madagascar*), classification (*closely related to the lemur, a member of the primate order*), status (*listed as an engendered species*), and physical adaptations (*large, round eyes and long, extremely thin little middle*) that would be appropriate for visitors to a natural history museum.

    Choice (B): No. While the passage does mention evolution by citing the aye-aye's *large, round eyes and long, extremely thin middle finger* as *adaptations* that are *quite sensible*, this choice's reference to evolution is a memory trap. The remainder of the passage would not be relevant to *professors of evolutionary science*, who would want to know details of the aye-aye's evolutionary history.

    Choice (C): No. This choice is incorrect because the overview style of the passage is designed to describe the animal and its environment in a broad fashion that includes scientific details, but does not focus on them. This choice is a memory trap.

    Choice (D): No. The passage's only mention of religion is that the aye-aye is considered by the people of Madagascar as a *spirit animal* that is considered *an omen of death*. This does not necessarily indicate a religious belief, so this choice is a memory trap.

    Choice (E): No. While there are references to the culture of Madagascar, specifically in the people of Madagascar and their views on the aye-aye, the passage is more focused on the aye-aye itself than on the overall culture of Madagascar, so this choice is a memory trap.

    The correct answer is (A).

2. **A** The word *attitude* indicates that this is a tone question. The subject of the question is the author's attitude. The task of the question is to determine how this attitude can best be described. In order to answer the question, determine what the passage states about the subject and evaluate the answer choices, eliminating any choice which cannot be supported by the text. The highlighted text describes the aye-aye as *a superb example of life's variety*, which is a positive statement, so look at each answer choice and determine whether this information supports the choice.

    Choice (A): Correct. The passage states that the aye-aye is *a superb example of life's variety*, a positive statement that is matched by the positive word *admiring*.

    Choice (B): No. The word *mystified* means confused and does not match the positive attitude indicated by the phrase *a superb example of life's variety*.

    Choice (C): No. The word *reverent* is positive, and thus matches the general direction of the attitude indicated by the phrase *a superb example of life's variety*, but it is too extreme.

    Choice (D): No. The word *appalled* is negative and thus does not match the positive attitude indicated by the phrase *a superb example of life's variety*.

    Choice (E): No. The word *lachrymose* means sad and does not match the positive attitude indicated by the phrase *a superb example of life's variety*.

    The correct answer is (A).

3. **The aye-aye has been listed as an endangered species and, as a result, the government of Madagascar had designated an island off the northeastern coast of Madagascar as a protected reserve for aye-ayes and other wildlife.**

    The phrase *author's claim...is unlikely to happen* indicates that this is a Weaken question. The subject of the question is the author's claim. The task of the question is to find the sentence that suggests that this claim is unlikely to come true. To answer this question, determine the meaning of the author's claim and then identify the sentence that shows that this claim is unlikely to come true. The author's claim that *this practice may result in the loss of a superb example of life's variety* refers to the possible extinction of the aye-aye due to the practice by *the people of Madagascar* of any aye-aye that is *sighted* being *immediately killed*. The final sentence of the first paragraph, which mentions that *an island off the northeastern coast of Madagascar* has been *designated...as a protected reserve for aye-ayes*, would prevent this extinction and is thus the correct answer.

4. **B** The phrase *can be logically inferred* indicates that this is an Inference question. The task of the question is indicated by the word *inferred*. The subject of the question is *the aye-aye*. In order to answer the question, determine what the passage states about the subject and evaluate the answer choices, eliminating any choice which cannot be supported by the text. The entire passage is about the aye-aye, so look at the answer choices and try to find information in the passage that supports the choice.

    Choice (A): No. While the passage does mention that *the government of Madagascar has designated an island off the northeastern coast of Madagascar as a protected reserve for aye-ayes,* the phrase *only lives* in the answer choice is extreme language. The passage does not state the aye-aye *only lives* on the protected reserve, but rather states that the reserve exists and aye-ayes live there. It is possible that aye-ayes still live on the main island of Madagascar.

    Choice (B): Correct. The passage refers to the aye-aye as a *nocturnal denizen* and acknowledges the aye-aye's *large, round eyes,* which let the aye-aye *see well at night*.

Choice (C): No. The phrase *religion* in the answer choice is a memory trap that refers to the passage. The passage states that the people of Madagascar believe that the aye-aye is a type of spirit animal, but does not state that the spirit animal is a part of any practiced religion.

The correct answer is (B).

5. **A** The question asks what the author of the passage consider *to be most analogous*, which is an indication that this is a type of specific purpose question. The subject of the question is the highlighted passage, which states that *critics seem to presuppose that great literature must be somehow burdensome to the reader; it must be difficult for the uninitiated to understand*. The task of the question is to determine which of the answer choices is most analogous to this viewpoint. In order to answer this question, evaluate the answer choices individually, looking for viewpoints or situations that are similar to the highlighted text.

Choice (A): Correct. This choice mimics the viewpoint of the critics in the passage that they believe great literature must be burdensome to the uninitiated by drawing a comparison to how *avant-garde movies with complicated storylines* are seen in relationship to *Hollywood blockbusters with straightforward narrative*.

Choice (B): No. The choice contains the memory trap *inferior*, which is reminiscent of the passage's claims about the beliefs of critics of great literature. However, this choice does not consider the difficulty the uninitiated may face when considering the contents of the journal and documentaries, so it is out of scope.

Choice (C): No. This choice discusses that poetry *is considered superior to prose* not because it is burdensome, as is outlined in the passage, but because *it is shorter*. The critics from the passage make no mention of the length of the literature, so this choice is out of scope.

Choice (D): No. The choice uses the extreme language *too controversial* which is a comparison tool that is not employed by the passage, which instead uses as a comparison tool the difficulty the uninitiated have understanding the literature as a prerequisite for success.

Choice (E): No. The inclusion of the phrase *artistically superior* makes this choice out of scope. The passage is not concerned with artistic value.

The correct answer is (A).

6. **E** The phrase *can be inferred* indicates that this is an Inference question. The subject of the question is the passage. The task of the question is to determine what can be supported from the passage. In order to answer the question, evaluate the answer choices, eliminating any which cannot be supported by the text.

Choice (A): No. While the passage states that Allende's novel *draws deeply on the author's own family history*, it does not state that the novel is a retelling of her family's political struggles. This choice is a memory trap.

Choice (B): No. While the passage states that the critics' viewpoint prevented Allende's novel *from gaining the critical attention it deserves*, and discusses what critics expect from great literature, it does not indicate how critics treat great literature. This choice is too extreme to be supported.

Choice (C): No. While the passage states that Allende *borrows…from Gabriel Garcia Marquez* and that she is a power voice in *magical realism*, it does not indicate that Allende learned about magical realism from Marquez. This answer choice is too extreme to be supported.

Choice (D): No. The passage indicates that the *political message* of Allende's novel was included *subtly*, and that this was not *to-be-expected*, but it does not indicate that a clearer political message would have pleased critics. This choice is too extreme to be supported.

Choice (E): Correct. The passage states that, *rather than the to-be-expected socialist harangue, Allende subtly worked her political message within the fabric* of her narrative. This agrees with the idea that the novel's political message would have been expected to be stronger than it actually was.

The correct answer is (E).

7. **E** The phrase *author would agree* indicates that this is an Inference question. The subject of the question is the author. The task of the question is to determine which choice the author would not agree with. Note that this is an EXCEPT question, which means that the correct answer will be the choice that is NOT supported by the text. In order to answer the question, determine what the passage says about the subject and evaluate the answer choices, eliminating any choice which can be supported by the text.

Choice (A): No. The passages warns against overlooking *Alcott's importance...to the Transcendental Movement in particular*. This wording supports this choice, which means that the choice should be eliminated since the question asks for the answer choice that is not supported by the text.

Choice (B): No. The passage states that it is *in the text of his orations that one begins to appreciate* Alcott as a *visionary*. This wording supports this choice, which means that the choice should be eliminated since the question asks for the answer choice that is not supported by the text.

Choice (C): No. The passage states that Alcott *believed that...a student's intellectual growth was concomitant with his or her spiritual growth*. This wording supports this choice, which means that the choice should be eliminated since the question asks for the answer choice that is not supported by the text.

Choice (D): No. The passage states that *Alcott advocated what were at the time polemical ideas on education*. This wording supports this choice, which means that the choice should be eliminated since the question asks for the answer choice that is not supported by the text.

Choice (E): Correct. The passage states that Alcott was an erudite orator, which conflicts with this answer choice. Therefore, this answer choice cannot be supported by the text, which makes it the correct choice.

The correct answer is (E).

8. **B** The phrase *author would agree* indicates that this is an Inference question. The subject of the question is the author. The task of the question is to determine what can be inferred about the author's views. In order to answer the question, evaluate the answer choices, eliminating any choice which cannot be supported by the text.

Choice (A): No. The passage does criticize *Alcott's philosophical treatises* as *esoteric*, but it does not describe Transcendentalism in this way. This answer choice is recycled language and cannot be supported by the passage.

Choice (B): Correct. The passage states that *Alcott's gift was not as a writer*, which supports the answer choice.

Choice (C): No. The passage states that Alcott believed that *good teaching should be Socratic* and that *intellectual growth was concomitant with...spiritual growth*. This indicates that both factors can be part of good teaching. It is too extreme to assume that aligning these factors is *difficult*.

Choice (D): No. The passage states that *to remember the man [Alcott] solely by his associations is to miss his importance*. This contradicts the answer choice's assertion that Alcott should be chiefly known for the strengths of his associations. This answer choice is a reversal of the passage.

Choice (E): No. The passage states that, *in the text of his orations...Alcott advocated what were at the time polemical ideas*. This contradicts the answer choice's assertion that *Alcott's orations were widely accepted by his peers*. This answer choice is a reversal of the passage.

The correct answer is (B).

9. **B** The phrase *demonstrates the idea put forth* indicates that this is a Retrieval question. The subject of the question is the author's idea regarding animal classification. The task of the question is to find the choice or choices that demonstrate this idea. In order to answer the question, determine what the passage states about the subject and evaluate the answer choices, eliminating any choice which cannot be supported by the text.

Choice (A): No. The passage states that *taxonomic classification…is useful only when considered along with other information*, which is not consistent with *scientists rely*[ing] *solely on the traditional taxonomic designations*. This answer choice is a reversal of the information in the passage.

Choice (B): Correct. The example of *a team of researchers* that *monitors the actions of the animals* and *compares its findings with prevailing beliefs* is consistent with the passage's statement that *taxonomic classification…is useful only when considered along with other information*.

Choice (C): No. The passage states that t*axonomic classification…is useful only when considered along with other information*, which is not consistent with a zookeeper who *disregards taxonomic classifications and instead focuses on observational data*. This choice is a reversal of the information in the passage.

The correct answer is (B).

10. **B** The word *tone* indicates that this is a tone question. The subject of the question is the author's tone. The task of the question is to identify the word that describes this tone. In order to answer the question, determine what the passage indicates about the subject and evaluate the answer choices, eliminating any choice which cannot be supported by the text. The author focuses on scientific distinctions and uses words such as *actually*, *fascinating*, *ultimately*, and *likewise* to make specific observations. Thus, the author's tone is focused on clarifying scientific distinctions.

Choice (A): No. The author does not offer any strong negative opinion. This is not consistent with the answer choice *exasperated*.

Choice (B): Correct. The author's informational tone in the passage is consistent with this answer choice.

Choice (C): No. The author indicates detailed distinctions regarding animal classification. This position is not consistent with the answer choice *ambivalent*.

Choice (D): No. The author provides information regarding animal classification but does not offer any strong negative opinion. This is not consistent with the answer choice *morose*.

Choice (E): No. The author provides information regarding animal classification but does not offer any strong positive opinion. This is not consistent with the answer choice *laudatory*.

The correct answer is (B).

CHAPTER 7: CRITICAL REASONING
Practice: Identifying Conclusions (Page 104)

1.   "it is unlikely that the new defense bill will pass"

2.   "grass was not a significant part of the dinosaur diet"

3.   "automaker *X* will have no choice but to file for bankruptcy"

4.   "country *Y* will experience a decrease in obesity-related health problems"

5.   "machines will soon outnumber humans as the number-one users of the Internet"

Practice: Finding the Premise (Page 106)

1.   **Premise:** "A bipartisan group of 15 senators has announced that it does not support the legislation."

2.   **Premises:**

   (1) "The earliest known grass fossils date from approximately 55 million years ago."

   (2) "Dinosaurs most likely disappeared from the earth around 60 million years ago."

   (3) "fossilized remains of dinosaur teeth that indicate the creatures were more suited to eating ferns and palms"

3.   **Premises:**

   (1) "company's poor financial situation"

   (2) "the workers at automaker *X* are threatening to go on strike"

4.   **Premise:** "the leading members of the nation's food industry have agreed to provide healthier alternatives, reduce sugar and fat content, and reduce advertisements for unhealthy foods"

5.   **Premise:** "Recent advances in technology have led to a new wave of 'smart' appliances"

Practice: Locating Assumptions (Page 108)

1. **Conclusion:** There will be no decline in enrollment at the University.

   Why?

   Premise: The University plans to hire two highly credentialed biology professors to replace Professor Jones.

   Assumption: That the two new biology professors will be at least as attractive to prospective students as was Professor Jones.

2. **Conclusion:** "It is unjust to charge customers under the age of 25 more to rent a car than those over the age of 25."

   Why?

   Premise: "Most states allow people as young as 16 to have a driver's license and all states allow 18-year-olds the right to vote."

   Assumption: Because people under the age of 25 have the right to vote and drive, there is no reason to charge them more to rent a car.

3. **Conclusion:** "Roughly 12.5 percent of planets in the universe should have life on them."

   Why?

   Premise: "In our solar system, there are eight planets and at least one of them obviously has life on it."

   Assumption: All planetary systems in the universe have the same proportion of planets with life on them as does our solar system.

4. **Conclusion:** "The leaders of State A should institute the gas tax."

   Why?

   Premise: "58 percent of voters in Township B approve of a proposed 2-cent gasoline tax."

   Assumption: The opinion of Township B is representative of the opinion of all of State A.

Critical Reasoning Practice Set (Page 147)

1. **B** **Fact 1:** In 1989, corporate tax rates in some regions of the United States fell to their lowest level in 15 years, while rates in other regions reached new highs.

   Fact 2: In 1974, similar conditions led to a large flight of companies from regions with unfavorable corporate tax policies to regions with favorable policies.

   Fact 3: There was, however, considerably less corporate flight in 1989.

   The question asks *Which of the following, if true about 1989, most plausibly accounts for the finding that there was less corporate flight in 1989?*, which means this is a resolve/explain question. The correct answer will explain why there was less corporate flight in 1989.

Choice (A): No. The numbers of similar companies in regions with favorable tax policies in 1989 compared with 1974 does not explain why there was less corporate flight. This answer choice is out of scope.

Choice (B): Correct. This answer choice states that office rental costs in regions with the most favorable tax policies were significantly higher in 1989 than in 1974. This explains why corporate flight was less in 1989 than in 1974.

Choice (C): No. The benefits to areas with the most favorable tax policies and the difficulty of deciphering the tax codes does not explain why there was less corporate tax flight in 1989. This answer choice is out of scope.

Choice (D): No. Higher tax incentives offered by foreign countries make it harder to explain why there was less corporate flight in 1989.

Choice (E): No. The question makes no reference to individual tax incentives. This answer choice is out of scope.

2. **C** The question asks *Which of the following statements best describes Tello's response to Aramayo?*

Aramayo's premise is that *Our federal government seems to function most efficiently when decision-making responsibilities are handled by only a few individuals.* Aramayo's conclusion is that *Therefore, our government should consolidate its leadership and move away from a decentralized representative democracy.*

Tello responds by saying *But moving our government in this direction could violate our constitutional mission to provide government of, for, and by the people*, which means that Tello's response points out a negative consequence with the argument used by Aramayo. The correct answer identifies the reasoning Tello uses to respond to Aramayo.

Choice (A): No. Tello's response *But moving our government in this direction could violate our constitutional mission to provide government of, for, and by the people* does not contradict Aramayo's argument.

Choice (B): No. This answer choice is only partially correct. Tello's response is that there are negative consequences with the argument used by Aramayo.

Choice (C): Correct. Tello's response points out a negative consequence to Aramayo's argument.

Choice (D): No. Tello's response does not uncover any circular reasoning used by Aramayo.

Choice (E): No. Tello's response does not point out any overgeneralization used by Aramayo.

3. **B** The question states that *many businesses experience dramatic gains in productivity after installing a new computer system,* and that *a well-respected business journal recently stated that the person who serves as the Chief Information Officer is the consummate business computer system.* The premise is that installing a new computer system will lead to dramatic gains in productivity.

The question asks *By comparing a Chief Information Officer to business computer systems, the journal implicitly argues that...*, which means the correct answer shows why the journal made the comparison between a Chief Information Officer and a business computer system.

Choice (A): No. The journal made no reference to the actual function of a Chief Information Officer. This answer choice is out of scope.

Choice (B): Correct. The question states that installing a new computer system leads to dramatic gains in productivity. The journal stated that the person who serves as the Chief Information Officer is the consummate business computer system. So, installing a new computer system is like hiring a Chief Information Officer.

Choice (C): No. The journal made no reference to what many companies experience with new computer systems. This answer choice is out of scope.

Choice (D): No. The journal made no comparison between the relative effectiveness of a Chief Information Officer and a new computer system. This answer choice is out of scope.

Choice (E): No. The journal made no reference to the difficulty of measuring the impact of a Chief Information Officer on a company's productivity. This answer choice is out of scope.

4. **B** **Conclusion:** Laundry done at the Main Street Laundromat is cleaner than laundry done at the Elm Street Laundromat because the Main Street Laundromat uses more water per load.

Premise: Whenever Joe does his laundry at the Main Street Laundromat, the loads turn out cleaner than when he does his laundry at the Elm Street Laundromat.

Assumptions:

(1) It's not a coincidence. It's not a coincidence that laundry done at the Main Street Laundromat is cleaner than laundry done at the Elm Street Laundromat. (2) There's no other cause. Nothing else causes laundry done at the Main Street Laundromat to be cleaner than laundry done at the Elm Street Laundromat.

The question asks *Which of the following statements, if true, helps support the conclusion above?*, which means this is a Strengthen question. The assumption is that it is not a coincidence that laundry done at the Main Street Laundromat is cleaner than laundry done at the Elm Street Laundromat, and that there's no other cause than the Main Street Laundromat uses more water per load. In order to strengthen the argument, the correct answer shows how it is not a coincidence, or that other causes have been ruled out.

Choice (A): No. This is a restatement of the conclusion and does not rule out an alternate cause.

Choice (B): Correct. This choice rules out Joe using different detergents at both laundromats as a possible cause.

Choice (C): No. The question makes no reference to the Oak Street Laundromat. This answer choice is out of scope.

Choice (D): No. The question makes no reference to the amount of laundry Joe does at each laundromat. This answer choice is out of scope.

Choice (E): No. This answer choice states that *Joe tends to do his dirtier laundry at the Elm Street Laundromat*. The question states that *Whenever Joe does his laundry at the Main Street Laundromat, the loads turn out cleaner than when he does his laundry at the Elm Street Laundromat*. So, because Joe *tends* to do his dirtier laundry at the Elm Street Laundromat, it means that sometimes Joe does his dirtier laundry at the Main Street Laundromat. The question makes no exception for when Joe does dirtier laundry at the Main Street Laundromat. This answer choice is out of scope.

5. **A** **Conclusion:** The enormous increase in complaints must be a result of this systematic change.

Premises: According to the United States Postal Service bureau of information, the rate of complaints concerning late delivery was 30 times higher in 1991 than in 1964, and the United States Postal Service changed neighborhood routes from a multiple-truck delivery system to a single-truck delivery system between 1964 and 1991.

Assumptions:

It's not a coincidence. It's not a coincidence that the rate of complaints concerning late delivery was 30 times higher in 1991 than in 1964.

There's no other cause. There's no other cause that the rate of complaints concerning late delivery was 30 times higher in 1991 than in 1964.

The question asks *Which of the following, if true, weakens the conclusion drawn above?*, which means this is a Weaken question. The assumptions are that it is not a coincidence that the rate of complaints concerning late delivery was 30 times higher in 1991 than in 1964, and that there's no other cause than the United States Postal Service changed neighborhood routes from a multiple-truck delivery system between 1964 and 1991. In order to weaken the argument, the correct answer choice shows that it is a coincidence, or that there is another possible cause.

Choice (A): Correct. The answer choice states that *In 1991, most late-mail complaints were reported to the appropriate United States Postal Service office, whereas in 1964 most were not*. If true, this is another possible cause for the increase in complaints in 1991 than in 1964.

Choice (B): No. The question makes no reference to the number of late deliveries in a multiple-truck delivery system. This answer choice is out of scope.

Choice (C): No. The question makes no reference to registered mail. This answer choice is out of scope.

Choice (D): No. This answer choice rules out the amount of bulk mail being much larger in 1991 than in 1964 as a possible cause. This answer choice strengthens the argument.

Choice (E): No. The question makes no reference to the price of stamps. This answer choice is out of scope.

CHAPTER 9: VOCABULARY FOR THE GRE

Group 1 Exercises (Page 190)

1. **C**
2. **J**
3. **E**
4. **G**
5. **A**

6. **L**
7. **K**
8. **B**
9. **N**
10. **H**

11. **M**
12. **I**
13. **D**
14. **F**

Group 2 Exercises (Page 193)

1. **B**
2. **M**
3. **F**
4. **J**
5. **N**

6. **A**
7. **D**
8. **E**
9. **L**
10. **C**

11. **H**
12. **I**
13. **G**
14. **K**

Group 3 Exercises (Page 196)

1. **D**
2. **G**
3. **K**
4. **I**
5. **M**

6. **A**
7. **C**
8. **N**
9. **H**
10. **F**

11. **E**
12. **B**
13. **J**
14. **L**

Group 4 Exercises (Page 199)

1. **I**   6. **B**   11. **M**

2. **L**   7. **J**   12. **D**

3. **N**   8. **A**   13. **H**

4. **C**   9. **G**   14. **F**

5. **K**   10. **E**

CHAPTER 11: MATH FUNDAMENTALS

Math Fundamentals Drill (Page 245)

1. **C**, **D**, and **F**

   To solve this problem, try writing out the possibilities. The least prime number is 2. $(2 \times 2) + 3 = 7$; so (C) is correct. The next prime number is 3: $(3 \times 3) + 5 = 14$, so (D) is correct. The next prime number is 5: $(5 \times 5) + 7 = 32$, which is not an answer choice. The next prime number is 7: $(7 \times 7) + 11 = 60$, so (F) is correct. The next prime number is 11: $(11 \times 11) + 13 = 134$, which is a greater value than the answer choice possibilities. The correct answer is (C), (D), and (F).

2. **C** To answer this question, first write an equation with the information given. So, *number of cases ordered* $\times$ *$1,757 = total amount of money spent*. Now begin figuring out the answer to Quantity A and the answer to Quantity B. The number of books is equal to *number of cases* $\times$ *150*, so it is possible to figure out how many cases were sold. Set up the equation and solve. *Cases* $\times$ *$1,757 = $10,550*, so *Cases* $= \dfrac{\$10,550}{\$1,757} = 6.004$ cases. Since it is not possible to order a partial case, only 6 cases can be ordered for $10,550. This results in $6 \times 150 = 900$ books. Solve for Quantity B in the same way. *Cases* $\times$ *$1,757 = $12,290*, so *Cases* $= \dfrac{\$12,290}{\$1,757} = 6.99$ cases. Since it is not possible to order a partial case, once again, only 6 cases can be ordered and Quantity B equals 6×150, or 900. The quantities are equal, and the correct answer is (C).

3. **A** and **E**

   To begin, find the factors of 91: 1 and 91 or 7 and 13. Remember that the product of two negative numbers is positive, so the integers could also be negative factors. The question asks for the sum of the two integers. Choice (A) is the sum of –91 and –1. Choice (E) is the sum of 7 and 13. None of the other answer choices are possible, so the correct answer is (A) and (E).

4. **D** List all of the distinct prime integers less than 20. The prime integers are 2, 3, 5, 7, 11, 13, 17, and 19. The problem asks for the sum, so add all of the values up to yield 2 + 3 + 5 + 7 + 11 + 13 + 17 + 19 = 77. The ones digit is a 7, so the correct answer is (D).

5. **B, C,** and **D**

   A $20 scarf can be discounted as much as 50 percent, and 50 percent of 20 is $20 \times \dfrac{50}{100} = \$10$, so the minimum sale price of a scarf is $20 – $10 = $10. The least discount is 25 percent, and 25 percent of 20 is $20 \times \dfrac{25}{100} = \$5$, so the maximum sale price of a scarf is $20 – $5 = $15. Therefore, the range of possible sale prices for scarves is $10 to $15. Now, eliminate choices that fall outside of that range. Choice (A) is less than $10, and (E) is greater than $15, so eliminate both of them. The correct answer is (B), (C), and (D).

6. **300**

   There are 3 terms in the sequence and they repeat. The question asks about the product of the 81st, 82nd, 83rd, 84th, and 85th term. Use the fact that the values of the terms in the sequence repeat after every third term to determine the value of the 81st term. Divide 81 by 3 to find that there are 27 complete iterations of the sequence. The 81st term is at the end of one of these repetitions, so its value is –5. Therefore, the 82nd term is –2, the 83rd is 3, the 84th is –5, and the 85th is –2. Therefore, the product is $(–5) \times (–2) \times 3 \times (–5) \times (–2) = 300$. The correct answer is 300.

7. **C** Recognize the Distributive Law at work here. If the expression in Quantity A is distributed, the resulting expression is $2x + 8y$, which is the same as Quantity B. Therefore, the two quantities are equal, and the correct answer is (C).

8. **A** Quantity A is the greatest number of consecutive nonnegative integers whose sum is less than 22, so start adding the numbers with the least value. However, Quantity A contains an important clue with the word *nonnegative*. This means that the number 0 could be a value. Start with 0 and add until the sum is the greatest it could be without exceeding 22. So 0 + 1 + 2 = 3; 3 + 3 = 6; 6 + 4 = 10; 10 + 5 = 15; and 15 + 6 = 21. Therefore, the consecutive nonnegative integers whose sum is less than 22 are 0, 1, 2, 3, 4, 5, and 6. That is 7 values. Quantity A is greater than Quantity B, and the correct answer is (A).

9. **D** The question asks for the greatest possible value of $x + y$. Therefore, find the greatest values of x and y. The greatest value of x is when 4 is divided by 6, which produces a remainder of 4. The greatest value of y is when 2 is divided by 3, which produces a remainder of 2. Therefore, the greatest value of $x + y$ is 6, and the correct answer is (D).

10. **E** Follow the order of operations. Start with the parentheses first and do the division and multiplication, so $12 - \left(\dfrac{6}{3} - 4 \times 3 \right) - 8 \times 3 = 12 - (2 - 12) - 8 \times 3$. Now finish the parentheses to find that the expression is $12 - (-10) - 8 \times 3$. Now multiply so that the expression is $12 - (-10) - 24$. Now work the rest of the problem to find that $22 - 24 = -2$, and the correct answer is (E).

CHAPTER 12: ALGEBRA (AND WHEN TO USE IT)

Algebra (And When to Use It) Drill (Page 284)

1. **19** Plug In $100 for the cost of the item to the retailer. Therefore, the original selling price is $140, or 40 percent more than the retail price. To find the reduced price, subtract 15 percent of $140 from $140 to get $119. The difference between the reduced price and the cost of the item to the retailer is then $119 – $100 = $19. Therefore, the question is asking what percent of 100 is 19. The correct answer is 19 percent.

2. **B** First, put the equation in standard form: $x^2 + 8x + 7 = 0$. Now factor: $(x + 7)(x + 1) = 0$. Solve: $x = -7$ or -1. Both of the possible values for x are negative, so Quantity B is always greater than Quantity A.

3. **27** Because $9 = 3^2$; the original equation becomes $3^3 \times (3^2)^{12} = 3^x$; or, $3^3 \times 3^{24} = 3^x$; or, $3^{3 + 24} = 3^x$. Therefore, $x = 27$.

4. **E** Because there are variables in the answers, Plug In. Let's make $x = 10$, $y = 7$, and $c = 3$. Then $A = 2 \times 10 - (7 - 2 \times 3)$. Solve for the numbers in the parentheses before subtracting: $A = 20 - (7 - 6)$. Therefore, $A = 19$. $B = (2 \times 10 - 7) - 2 \times 3$. Again, solve for the numbers in the parentheses before subtracting: $B = (20 - 7) - 6$. Therefore, $B = 7$. Be careful, the question is asking for $A - B = 19 - 7 = 12$. Plug $y = 7$ and $c = 3$ into the answers. Only (E) yields the target, 12. Choice (C) is a trap designed to catch test takers who subtracted before simplifying the numbers in the parentheses.

5. **A** While the relationship among the can prices is provided, no actual numbers are supplied, so try plugging in some numbers for can prices. A good number to choose for the cost of the large cans is the value of the small can multiplied by the value of the medium can, or $5 \times $7 = $35. This means the medium can costs $\dfrac{\$35}{\$5} = \$7$, and the small can costs $\dfrac{\$35}{\$7} = \$5$. The amount of money needed to buy 200 medium cans is $200 \times $7 = $1,400. Now PITA. Start with (C). If the customer purchases 72 small cans, that will cost her $72 \times $5 = $360. If she purchases 72 small cans, she also purchases 72 large cans so $72 \times $35 = $2,520, which is more than the $1,400 spent on medium cans. This number is too great, so eliminate (C), (D), and (E). Choice (B) also works out to be too great, which leaves (A). 35 small cans × $5 a can = $175. 35 large cans × $35 = $1,225. $1,225 + $175 = $1,400, the same price as the medium cans. Choice (A) is correct.

6. **25** Stack and add the first two equations. Multiply the second equation by –1.

$$6k - 5l = 27$$
$$+ \underline{2k - 3l = 13}$$
$$8k - 8l = 40$$

Divide by 8 to yield $k - l = 5$. Multiply by 5 to yield the final answer of $5k - 5l = 25$.

7. **B** This problem has a relationship between variables, so Plug In. Let $a = 2$, so $3a = 6$. 6 is 4 less than 10, which equals $6b$. $6b = 10$ yields that $b = \dfrac{10}{6}$. $a - 2b$ yields $2 - 2\left(\dfrac{10}{6}\right) = -\dfrac{8}{6}$, or $-\dfrac{4}{3}$.

8. **A** Work with one quantity at a time to compare them. Quantity A is $\dfrac{2^{-4}}{4^{-2}}$, which can be rewritten as $\dfrac{2^{-4}}{4^{-2}} = \dfrac{\frac{1}{2^4}}{\frac{1}{4^2}} = \dfrac{\frac{1}{16}}{\frac{1}{16}}$. This fraction can be manipulated by moving the fraction out of the denominator; however, that is unnecessary as the numerator and denominator are the same thing. So $\dfrac{\frac{1}{16}}{\frac{1}{16}} = 1$, which is the value of Quantity A. Quantity B can be simplified to $\dfrac{\sqrt{64}}{-2^3} = \dfrac{8}{-8} = -1$. Therefore, Quantity A is greater, and the answer is (A).

9. **B** This is a simultaneous equation question. Both quantities ask for the value of $x + y$, so try to combine the equations to find that value. If you multiply $3x + 4y = 12$ by 3, the result is $9x + 12y = 36$. This can be subtracted from the other equation to find that $2x + 2y = -6$. Divide both sides of the equation by 2 to find that $x + y = -3$. Quantity A, then, is equal to –3. Quantity B is now $(-3)^{-2}$, which can be rewritten as $\dfrac{1}{(-3)^2} = \dfrac{1}{9}$. Therefore, Quantity B is greater than Quantity A, and the correct answer is (B).

10. **E** Since there are variables in the answers, Plug In. If $a = 3$ and $b = 2$, then $x = 9$ and $y = 18$. So, $2(x + y) = 2(9 + 18) = 54$. So, 54 is the target. Now, evaluate each answer choice. Choices (A), (B), (C), and (D) all evaluate to 54 and match the target. Choice (E), however, equals 36. Since the question uses the word EXCEPT, choose the answer that doesn't match the target. Choice (E) is the correct answer.

CHAPTER 13: REAL-WORLD MATH

Real-World Math Drill (Page 308)

1. $\dfrac{1}{6}$ Plug In to solve this problem. When working with fractions, a good number to Plug In is the product of the denominators. The fractions used in the problem are $\dfrac{1}{3}$ and $\dfrac{1}{2}$, so Plug In $3 \times 2 = 6$ for the number of paintings Sadie started with. Sadie started with 6 paintings and gave away one-third of them: $6 \times \dfrac{1}{3} = 2$. She has 4 paintings left. She then sold another half of the original 6: $6 \times \dfrac{1}{2} = 3$. So, she has 1 painting left, or $\dfrac{1}{6}$ of the total.

2. **D** When there are variables in the question stem, it's time to Plug In. For this problem, it's easier to Plug In if you simplify the equation first. Rearrange the equation to put the variables on opposite sides of the equal sign. $8x = 4y$. Then divide both sides by 4 to get that $2x = y$. Now, choose some easy numbers such as $x = 2$ and $y = 4$. In this case, Quantity B is greater, so eliminate (A) and (C). Next, try something like $x = 0$ and $y = 0$. In this case, the two quantities are equal. Eliminate (B), and the correct answer is (D).

3. **D** The population rankings for Year X are as follows: (1) Massachusetts, (2) Connecticut, (3) Maine, (4) Rhode Island, (5) New Hampshire, (6) Vermont. The rankings for Year Y are as follows: (1) Massachusetts; (2) Connecticut; (3) Rhode Island; (4) New Hampshire; (5) Maine; (6) Vermont. Maine, Rhode Island, and New Hampshire have different rankings from Year X to Year Y.

4. **D** In Year X, Vermont's population is 5 percent of 15 million (or 0.75 million), and the population of Massachusetts is 40 percent of 15 million (or approximately 6 million). 6 million is what percent of 0.75 million? Now translate: 6 million $= \dfrac{x}{100} \times 0.75$ million: $x = 800$.

5. **D** In Year X, the population of Rhode Island was 10 percent of 15 million, or 1.5 million. In Year Y, the population of Rhode Island was 15 percent of 25 million, or 3.75 million. The increase was 2.25 million, or 2,250,000.

6. **C** This question asks for a specific number and the answer choices are integers in order from least to greatest, which means that Plug In the Answers might be a good approach. However, that would mean constructing a rather involved equation. A better approach might be to construct a short 3 column table (see below), with headings for *Days*, (Amount to) *Add*, and *Gallons* (in the jug).

Days	Add (50% of current)	Gallons
0	—	4 (20% of × 20 gal.)
3	50% × 4 = 2	6
6	50% × 6 = 3	9
9	50% × 9 = 4.5	13.5
⑫	50% × 13.5 = 6.75	20.25 ≥ ⑰

The question states that the 20-gallon jug is 20% full to start. So enter "0" in the *Days* column and 20% × 20 = 4 in the *Gallons* column. The question states that every 3 *Days*, an amount of water equal to 50% of the amount already in the jug is added to the jug. So in the next line enter "3" in the *Days* column, 50% × 4 = 2 in the *Add* column, and 4 + 2 = 6 in the *Gallons* column. In the next line, enter "6" in the *Days* column, 50% × 6 = 3 in the *Add* column, and 6 + 3 = 9 in the *Gallons* column. The question asks how many *Days* until the jug is at least 85% full. 85% × 20 = 17, so continue filling in the table until the number of gallons in the jug is greater than or equal to 17. The correct answer is (C). Note that (A) is a trap answer that represents the number of *times* (4) water needs to be added to the jug so the total gallons in the jug is greater than or equal to 17.

7. **A** This is an average question, so make an Average Pie any time the word *average* is used. Begin by figuring out how many supporters of the referendum are in each town. The question states that there is an average of 3,500 supporters in Towns *B* and *D*, so there is a total of 3,500 × 2 = 7,000 supporters in these towns. The question also states that Town *B* has 3,000 supporters, so the number of supporters in Town *D* is 7,000 − 3,000 = 4,000. Additionally, the question states that there is an average of 5,000 supporters in Towns *A* and *C*, so there is a total of 5,000 × 2 = 10,000 supporters in these towns. It's also stated that Town *A* has 3,000 supporters, so the number of supporters in Town *C* is 10,000 − 3,000 = 7,000. Now, compare the quantities. Quantity A is the average number of supporters for Towns *C* and *D*, and Quantity B is the average number of supporters for Towns *B* and *C*. Because both quantities use Town *C*, and both quantities ask for an average, those values cancel out and all that remains is to compare the number of supporters in Towns *B* and *D*. There are 3,000 supporters in Town *B* and 4,000 in Town *D*, so Quantity A is greater, and the correct answer is (A). Alternatively, solve for the average given in both quantities. However, the result is the same; the correct answer is (A).

8. **E** The question states that $500,000 was given to employees rated *A*, *B* or *C* as follows: *A* employees received twice the amount that *C* employees received, and *B* employees received one and a half the amount that *C* employees received. There were 50 *A* employees, 100 *B* employees and 150 *C* employees. The question asks how much was paid to each *A* employee. The answers are in order from least to greatest, so Plug In the Answers. Begin with (C). If $740 was paid to each *A* employee, then $\frac{\$740}{2} = \$370$ was paid to each *C* employee, and 1.5 × $370 = $555 was paid to each *B* employee, which means that the total amount paid to all employees would be equal to $(50 \times \$740) + (100 \times \$555) + (150 \times \$370) = \$148,000$. This is quite short of $500,000, so eliminate (A), (B), and (C). Try (D). If $1,250 was paid to each *A* employee, then $\frac{\$1,250}{2} = \$625$ was paid to each *C* employee, and 1.5 × $625 = $937.50 was paid to each *B* employee, which means that the total amount paid to all employees would be equal to $(50 \times \$1,250) + (100 \times \$937.50) + (150 \times \$625) = \$250,000$. Eliminate (D). The correct answer is (E). Note that $250,000 is one-half of $500,000, and $1,250, (D), is one-half of $2,500, (E).

9. **B** The question asks what the median reading test score was for ninth grade students in 2013. The median is the middle score, or the 50th percentile. The distribution of scores for ninth grade students is shown in the first pie chart. The chart shows that 16% of ninth grade students had scores below 65. The chart shows that 37% of ninth grade students scored in the 65–69 point range. 16% + 37% = 53%, which means that the 50th percentile is in the 65–69 point range. The correct answer is (B).

10. **A** The question states that the number of students in grades 9 through 12 represents 35% of the total students at School District X in 1995 and asks how many total students were in School District X in 1995. Information about 1995 is found on the first chart. Looking at the solid line data, in 1995 there were 1,350 students in 9th grade, 950 students in 10th grade, 625 students in 11th grade, and 500 students in 12th grade. $1,350 + 950 + 625 + 500 = 3,425$ students in grades 9 through 12. If T represents the total number of students in 1995, then $3,425 = 0.35 \times T$, which means that $\frac{3,425}{0.35} = T = 9,785 \approx 9,700$. The correct answer is (A).

11. **E** There were 1,200 ninth-graders in 2013. 25 percent of them, or 300, scored in the 70–79 point range. 14 percent, or 168, scored in the 80–89 point range. The difference between 300 and 168 is 132. The correct answer is (E).

12. **D** This is a question about ratios, so draw ratio boxes for each ratio. The question states that one ounce of Solution X contains ingredients a and b in the ratio of 2:3, which means that for every 2 parts of a there are 3 parts of b. That makes 5 parts in total. So, enter 2, 3 and 5 in the top row of a ratio box marked Solution X. One ounce of Solution Y contains ingredients a and b in the ratio of 1:2, which means that for every 1 part of a there are 2 parts of b. That makes 3 parts in total. So, enter 1, 2, and 3 in the top row of a ratio box marked Solution Y. The combined solution of 630 ounces contains Solution X and Solution Y in the ratio of 3:11, which means that for every 3 ounces of Solution X there are 11 ounces of Solution Y. That makes 14 ounces in total. So, enter 3, 11, and 14 in the top row of a ratio box marked Combined, and enter 630 in the last row under the Total column in the Combined ratio box. Divide 630 by 14 to get 45 as the multiplier in the Combined ratio box. Multiply 45 times 3 to get 135 ounces of Solution X, and multiply 45 times 11 to get 495 ounces of Solution Y. Enter 135 in the last row under the Total column in the Solution X ratio box and enter 495 in the last row under the Total column in the Solution Y ratio box. Now divide 135 by 5 to get 27 as the multiplier in the Solution X ratio box and divide 495 by 3 to get 165 as the multiplier in the Solution Y ratio box. The question asks how many ounces of ingredient a are in the combined solution. Multiply 27 times 2 to get 54 ounces of ingredient a from Solution X and multiply 165 times 1 to get 165 ounces of ingredient a from Solution Y. Add 54 plus 165 to get 219 ounces of ingredient a. The correct answer is (D).

Solution X			
	a	b	Total
Ratio	2	3	5
Multiplier	27	27	27
Totals	(54)	81	135

Solution Y			
	a	b	Total
Ratio	1	2	3
Multiplier	165	165	165
Totals	(165)	330	495

Combined			
	Sol. X	Sol. Y	Total
Ratio	3	11	14
Multiplier	45	45	45
Totals	135	495	630

CHAPTER 14: GEOMETRY BASICS

Degrees, Lines, and Angles Drill (Page 317)

1. **No.** The degrees that are formed when two lines intersect have to add up to 360 and abide by the vertical angles rule, which dictates that the angles opposite each other have to be the same measure. These four angles add up to 360, but the opposite angles cannot be equal because there are not two pairs.

2. **Yes.** The angles add up to 360 degrees and there are two pairs of angles.

3. **No.** The angles do not add up to 360 degrees.

4. **Yes.** The angles add up to 360 degrees and there are two pairs of angles.

5. **Yes.** The angles add up to 360 degrees and there are two pairs of angles.

6. a. **75**
   b. **75**
   c. **105**
   d. **105**
   e. **75**
   f. **75**
   g. **105**

Triangles Drill (Page 320)

1. **Angles; isosceles**

2. **12** $18 = \frac{1}{2}(3)\left(height\right)$ and $height = 12$.

3. **4; 8** The third side is greater than the difference, but less than the sum of the other two sides. The difference is $6 - 2 = 4$ and the sum is $6 + 2 = 8$.

4. **140** $180 - 20 - 20 = 140$

5. **15** This is an equilateral triangle, so all the side lengths are equal.

Pythagorean Theorem and Area of a Triangle Drill (Page 321)

1. **Missing side:** $a^2 + 7^2 = 8^2$; $a^2 + 49 = 64$; $a^2 = 15$; $a = \sqrt{15}$

   Area: $\dfrac{1}{2}(7)(\sqrt{15}) = \dfrac{7\sqrt{15}}{2}$

2. **Missing side:** $2^2 + 1^2 = c^2$; $4 + 1 = c^2$; $5 = c^2$; $\sqrt{5} = c$

   Area: $\dfrac{1}{2}(2)(1) = 1$

3. **Missing side:** $a^2 + \left(\sqrt{10}\right)^2 = \left(\sqrt{15}\right)^2$; $a^2 + 10 = 15$; $a^2 = 5$; $a = \sqrt{5}$

   Area: $\dfrac{1}{2}\left(\sqrt{5}\right)\left(\sqrt{10}\right) = \dfrac{1}{2}\left(\sqrt{50}\right) = \dfrac{\sqrt{50}}{2} = \dfrac{5\sqrt{2}}{2}$

4. **Missing side:** $3^2 + 3^2 = c^2$; $9 + 9 = c^2$; $18 = c^2$; $c = \sqrt{18} = 3\sqrt{2}$

   Area: $\dfrac{1}{2}(3)(3) = \dfrac{1}{2}(9) = \dfrac{9}{2}$

Special Right Triangles Drill (Page 324)

1. B
2. H
3. C
4. A
5. F
6. E
7. J
8. I
9. G
10. D

Rectangles Drill (Page 325)

1. The area of a rectangle is found by the expression *base × height*. The number of perimeters is equal to the number of unique perimeters possible based on the measurements for the base and height. The factors of 24 are 1 × 24, 2 × 12, 3 × 8, and 4 × 6. The possible perimeters are 1 + 1 + 24 + 24 = 50, 2 + 2 + 12 + 12 = 28, 3 + 3 + 8 + 8 = 22, and 4 + 4 + 6 + 6 = 20. There are four different possible perimeters.

2. Perimeter = 3 + 3 + 7 + 7 = 20

   Area = 7 × 3 = 21

3. This figure looks like a diamond, but it is just a rectangle turned onto its side.

   Perimeter: 4 + 4 + 9 + 9 = 26

   Area: 4 × 9 = 36

4.   The sum of the interior angles of any rectangle, regardless of its perimeter or area, is always 360 degrees.

5. a. Area (36 > 24)

    b. Perimeter (28 > 24)

    c. Perimeter (14 > 12)

    d. Perimeter (4 > 1)

Squares Drill (Page 327)

1. **False.** The perimeter of a square with side length 2 is 4(2) = 8.

2. **True.** The area of a square with side length 4 is 4^2 = 16 and the perimeter of a square with side length 4 is 4(4) = 16.

3. **False.** The diagonal of a square with side length 3 is $3\sqrt{2}$.

4. **True.** The diagonal of a square is the expression $x\sqrt{2}$, where x is the length of a side of the square. So, solve for x to find that $7 = x\sqrt{2}$ and $x = \dfrac{7}{\sqrt{2}}$.

5. **False.** The interior angles of a square have a sum of 360 degrees.

Circles Drill (Page 330)

Radius	Diameter	Circumference	Area
4	8	8π	16π
8	16	16π	64π
1	2	2π	π
7	14	14π	49π
6	12	12π	36π
$\dfrac{4}{\pi}$	$\dfrac{8}{\pi}$	8	$\dfrac{16}{\pi}$
$\sqrt{3}$	$2\sqrt{3}$	$2\pi\sqrt{3}$	3π
$\dfrac{3}{\sqrt{\pi}}$	$\dfrac{6}{\sqrt{\pi}}$	$\dfrac{6\pi}{\sqrt{\pi}}$	9
$\dfrac{3}{\pi^2}$	$\dfrac{6}{\pi^2}$	$\dfrac{6}{\pi}$	$\dfrac{9}{\pi^3}$
$\dfrac{8}{\pi}$	$\dfrac{16}{\pi}$	16	$\dfrac{64}{\pi}$

Other Figures—Polygons Drill (Page 333)

1. Total Angle: $180(5 - 2) = 180(3) = 540°$

    Single Angle: $\dfrac{180(5-2)}{5} = \dfrac{540}{5} = 108°$

2. Total Angle: $180(6 - 2) = 180(4) = 720°$

    Single Angle: $\dfrac{180(6-2)}{6} = \dfrac{720}{6} = 120°$

3. Total Angle: $180(8 - 2) = 180(6) = 1{,}080°$

    Single Angle: $\dfrac{180(8-2)}{8} = \dfrac{1{,}080}{8} = 135°$

Parallelograms and Trapezoids Drill (Page 335)

1. This is a parallelogram. The area of a parallelogram is found by the expression *base* × *height*. The base is 20. The height is the length of the dotted line. The dotted line is one of the sides of a right triangle with a hypotenuse of 13 and a short side of 20 − 15 = 5. Use the Pythagorean Theorem, or recognize the special right triangle, to determine that the height is 12. The area of the parallelogram is 20 × 12 = 240.

2. This is a trapezoid. Find the area by splitting the figure into 3 smaller figures—two identical triangles and a rectangle. The base of the triangles are a combined length of 11 − 5 = 6. Because the diagonal lengths of the trapezoids are equal, the lengths of the base of eawch triangle are equal. So each has a length of 3. The hypotenuse of the triangle is 5, so use the Pythagorean Theorem, or recognize the special right triangle, to determine that the height is 4. The area of a single triangle is 6, so the area of both triangles is 12. The area of the rectangle is 4 × 5 = 20. The area of the trapezoid is 12 + 20 = 32.

Coordinate Geometry Drill (Pages 338-339)

1. **False.** A point with two positive values is in Quadrant I. A point with a negative *x* and positive *y* is in Quadrant II. A point with two negative values is in Quadrant III. A point with a positive *x* and a negative *y* is in Quadrant IV.

2. **True.** This point is in Quadrant III, and points in this quadrant have negative values for *x* and *y*.

3. **True.** Perpendicular lines have slopes that are negative reciprocals of each other. The slope of this line is 2, so the slope of a line perpendicular to it is $-\dfrac{1}{2}$.

4. **False.** The slope of this line is $\dfrac{0-(-1)}{0-(-2)} = \dfrac{1}{2}$, which is a positive slope. The point $(-2, -1)$ is in Quadrant III and the line crosses the origin with a positive slope. The point $(-1, 2)$ is in Quadrant II. This line cannot intersect point $(-1, 2)$ because that point is behind both the x- and y-intercept in a quadrant that is adjacent to the line's path. Draw the points and line to visualize this better.

5. **False.** The slope of the line is $\dfrac{6-2}{-1-1} = \dfrac{4}{-2} = -2$.

6. **False.** Convert the equation to the equation of a line. Subtract $3x$ from both sides and divide both sides by 2 to find that the equation is $y = -\dfrac{3}{2}x + 3$. The slope is negative.

7. **True.** Use the points to find the slope of the line is $\dfrac{6-0}{2-0} = \dfrac{6}{2} = 3$. Use one of the points to determine the equation of the line. So if $x = 2$ and $y = 6$, then the equation of the line is $6 = 3(2) + b$. Solve to get that $b = 0$. The equation of this line is $y = 3x$.

8. **True.** Use the two points to find that the slope is $\dfrac{9-1}{-1-3} = \dfrac{8}{-4} = -2$. Now use one of the points in addition to the slope to determine the y-intercept, so $1 = -2(3) + b$ and $b = 7$. So, the y-intercept is 7. Now use this to determine the x-intercept, which is $0 = -2x + 7$ and $x = \dfrac{7}{2}$.

3D Figures – Cylinders Drill (Page 341-342)

1. Area of the body of the figure: 20π

   Area of the top of the figure: 4π

   Surface area of the figure: 28π

   The body of the figure is the rectangle created by cutting one rounded side of the figure and laying it flat. The area is the height of the figure multiplied by the circumference of the top of the figure. The height is 5 and the circumference is 4π, so the area is 20π. The area of the top of the figure is πr^2 and $r = 2$, so the area of the top is 4π. The surface area of the figure is the area of the body plus twice the area of the top, so $20\pi + 2(4\pi) = 28\pi$.

2. The formula for volume is $Volume = \pi r^2(height)$. The volume is 18π and the radius is 3, so the height is 2 $(18\pi = \pi(3^2)(height) = 9\pi(height) = 2)$.

3.   a radius of 3: 36π

an area of the top of 4π: 16π

a diameter of 8: 64π

The formula for volume is *Volume* $= \pi r^2(height)$. The height is 4, so all that is needed to solve for the volume is a value of r or πr^2. If the radius is 3, then the volume is $\pi(3^2)(4) = 36\pi$. If the area of the base is 4π, then $\pi r^2 = 4\pi$ and the volume is $4\pi(4) = 16\pi$. If the diameter is 8, then the radius is 4 and the volume is $\pi(4^2)(4) = 64\pi$.

4.   Surface area 30π

Surface area 20π

Surface area 12π

Surface area 24π

The formula for surface area is *Surface Area* $= 2\pi r(height) + 2(\pi r^2)$. If the height is 2 and the radius is 3, then the formula is $(2\pi(3))(2) + 2(\pi 3^2)$ and the surface area is $12\pi + 18\pi = 30\pi$. If the height is 3 and the radius is 2, then the formula is $(2\pi(2))(3) + 2(\pi 2^2)$ and the surface area is $12\pi + 8\pi = 20\pi$. If the height is 5 and the radius is 1, then the formula is $(2\pi(1))(5) + 2(\pi 1^2)$ and the surface area is $10\pi + 2\pi = 12\pi$. If the height is 1 and the radius is 3, then the formula is $(2\pi(3))(1) + 2(\pi 3^2)$ and the surface area is $6\pi + 18\pi = 24\pi$.

3D Figures – Rectangular Solids Drill (Page 345)

1.   Surface Area: $6(1^2) = 6$

Volume: $1 \times 1 \times 1 = 1$

Diagonal Length: $1^2 + 1^2 + 1^2 = 3$, so $d^2 = 3$ and $d = \sqrt{3}$

2.   Surface Area: $2(3 \times 4) + 2(3 \times 5) + 2(4 \times 5) = 24 + 30 + 40 = 94$

Volume: $3 \times 4 \times 5 = 60$

Diagonal Length: $3^2 + 4^2 + 5^2 = 50$, so $d^2 = 50$ and $d = \sqrt{50} = 5\sqrt{2}$

3.   Surface Area: $2(2 \times 2) + 2(2 \times 6) + 2(6 \times 2) = 8 + 24 + 24 = 56$

Volume: $2 \times 2 \times 6 = 24$

Diagonal Length: $2^2 + 2^2 + 6^2 = 44$, so $d^2 = 44$ and $d = \sqrt{44} = 2\sqrt{11}$

4.   Surface Area: $2(5 \times 4) + 2(5 \times 3) + 2(4 \times 3) = 40 + 30 + 24 = 94$

Volume: $5 \times 4 \times 3 = 60$

Diagonal Length: $5^2 + 4^2 + 3^2 = 50$, so $d^2 = 50$ and $d = \sqrt{50} = 5\sqrt{2}$

CHAPTER 15: GRE GEOMETRY

Geometry Drill (Page 386)

1. **A, B,** and **C**

   The three interior angles of a triangle add up to 180°. A right triangle has one 90° angle, which means the remaining two angles in a right triangle must add up to 180° − 90° = 90°. So, look for answer choices where the angles add up to 90°. The correct answers are (A), (20° + 70° = 90°), (B), (30° + 60° = 90°), and (C), (45° + 45° = 90°).

2. **B** Redraw the figure. The perimeter is the sum of all sides of the figure. This is a pentagon with three right angles, which means that the figure is the combining of a right triangle and a rectangle, as shown by the dotted line in the figure below. The unknown side of the figure is equal to the hypotenuse of the right triangle. The right triangle has legs of 5 and 12, which means the hypotenuse is equal to $\sqrt{5^2 + 12^2} = 13$. Add all the sides to get 17 + 5 + 12 + 17 + 13 = 64. The correct answer is (B).

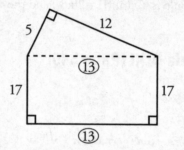

3. **A** The question states that $AB = BC = EG$. The three angles of the triangle are equal, which means that the triangle is equilateral, and that $EG = FG = 8$. The side of the square is equal to $FG = 8$, which means the area of the square is equal to $8^2 = 64$. The correct answer is (A).

4. **D** Draw the XY coordinate plane and attempt to plot the two points in the question. The first point $(a, 6)$ is in Quadrant I, which means that a is any positive number. The second point $(−6, b)$ is in Quadrant II, which means that b is also any positive number. So, a could be 1 and b could be 2, or a could be 2 and b could be 1. The correct answer is (D).

5. **E** There is a variable in the question and in the answer choices, so Plug In. The question states that the

   longer piece is 2 yards longer than 3 times the shorter piece. If the shorter piece is 2 yards, then the

   longer piece is 3 × 2 + 2 = 8 yards, which means that the total length t of twine is 2 + 8 = 10 yards.

   The question asks what is the length of the longer piece in terms of t. The length of the longer piece

   is 8, so the target is 8. Plug In $t = 10$ in the answer choices. Choice (A) is $\frac{10+3}{3} = \frac{13}{3}$. Eliminate (A).

   Choice (B) is $\frac{3 \times 10 + 2}{3} = \frac{32}{3}$. Eliminate (B). Choice (C) is $\frac{10-2}{4} = 2$. Eliminate (C). Note that (C) is equal to the length of the shorter piece. Choice (D) is $\dfrac{3 \times 10 + 4}{4} = \dfrac{34}{4}$. Eliminate (D). Choice (E) is

$\dfrac{3 \times 10 + 2}{4} = 8$, which is equal to the length of the longer piece, the target answer. The correct answer

is (E).

6. **D** The question asks for the area of semicircle *EAB*. The questions states that the circle with center *D* has a radius of 3 because *CD* = 3, which means that the diameter of the smaller circle is equal to 2 × 3 = 6. The radius of the larger circle with center *C* is the diameter of the smaller circle, which is equal to 6. So, the area of the larger circle is $\pi 6^2 = 36\pi$. The area of semicircle *EAB* is equal to one half the area of the larger circle, so one half of 36π is 18π. The correct answer is (D).

7. **2** Draw a diagram. The question states that Karl started *x* meters below the boat and then swam 8 meters straight down, which puts Karl *x* + 8 meters below the boat. Karl makes a right turn and swims parallel to the water 24 meters. He then swims 26 meters directly back to the boat. This completes a right triangle with a hypotenuse of 26 meters and legs of 24 and *x* + 8 meters. Use the Pythagorean Theorem to show that 10^2 meters + 24^2 meters = 26^2 meters. So, this is a 10-24-26 triangle, which is twice the sides of a familiar 5-12-13 triangle. The question asks for the value of *x*, the number of meters below the boat that Karl began his dive from, which is found by the equation *x* + 8 = 10, so *x* = 2.

8. **A** There is a variable in both quantities, so Plug In. Try *r* = 2. The circumference of a circle with radius 2 equals $4\pi \approx 12$, and the perimeter of a square with side 2 equals 4 × 2 = 8. Try *r* = 10. The circumference of a circle with radius 10 equals $20\pi \approx 60$, and the perimeter of a square with side 10 equals 4 × 10 = 40. Quantity A is greater than Quantity B, so the correct answer is (A).

9. **C** Draw a circle with center *C* and points *A* and *B* on the circumference of the circle and draw triangle *ABC*. The question states that the area of the circle is $25\pi = \pi r^2$, which means that the radius of the circle is 5. Because sides *AC* and *BC* of triangle *ABC* are equal to the radius of the circle, they are each equal to 5. The question states that angle *ACB* = 60°, which means that angles *CAB* and *CBA* are also equal to 60°, and that triangle *ABC* is equilateral. So, *AB* = *AC* = *BC* = 5. The correct answer is (C).

10. **A** The question asks if the length of the third side of a triangle, *x*, is greater than or less than 5.9. The third side of a triangle is greater than the difference and less than the sum of the other two sides. The other two sides of the triangle are 9 and 3, which means that the difference is 9 − 3 = 6, and the sum is 9 + 3 = 12. So, *x* is greater than 6 and less than 12, which means that *x* is greater than 5.9. The correct answer is (A).

11. **A** This is a Quant Comp geometry question, so redraw the figures and label any information from the problem in the figures. The question states that *AB* = *BC*. This means that angle *BCA* is also equal to *x* because *AB* = *BC*. Similarly, because *EF* and *FG* are equal side lengths, angle *FGE* is equal to *y*. There is no further information provided by the problem, so work with the quantities. Quantity A is the value of *x*, which is the value of angle *BAC*. There may not appear to be a way to solve for *x* at first, but work with the figure. Line *BD* splits angle *B* directly down the middle and is a right angle, so line segments *AD* and *DC* are equal. *AD* is equal to $\dfrac{10}{2} = 5$, which means that triangle *ABD* is an isosceles right triangle

because *AD* and *BD* are equal. Isosceles right triangles have interior angle measurements of 45 : 45: 90 degrees. Thus, angle *BAC* is equal to 45° and $x = 45$. Now work with Quantity B. Triangle *EFH* is a right triangle isosceles with two sides equal to 6 and 12. If the hypotenuse of a right triangle is double one of the legs of the triangle, that triangle is a 30 : 60 : 90 right triangle because the side lengths of a 30 : 60 : 90 triangle are in the relationship $x : x\sqrt{3} : 2x$. In this case, $x = 6$ and $2x = 12$. The angle that is opposite the side length of x is 30 degrees, because it is the smallest. Therefore, angle y is 30 degrees and $y = 30$. Quantity A is greater than Quantity B. The correct answer is choice (A).

12. **B** If $y = 4.2$, then the line includes points $(2, 3)$, $(x, 4.2)$, and the origin $(0, 0)$. The slope of the line is equal to $\dfrac{y_2 - y_1}{x_2 - x_1}$. Using points $(0, 0)$ and $(2, 3)$, the slope equals $\dfrac{3 - 0}{2 - 0} = \dfrac{3}{2}$, which means that using points $(0, 0)$ and $(x, 4.2)$, the slope needs to be $\dfrac{3}{2}$. So, $\dfrac{4.2 - 0}{x - 0} = \dfrac{4.2}{x} = \dfrac{3}{2}$. So $x = \dfrac{4.2 \times 2}{3} = 2.8$. The correct answer is (B).

13. **A** The question asks for the area of triangle *ABD*, which is a right triangle with a hypotenuse of 5 and a leg of 3 and an unknown leg x. Using the Pythagorean Theorem, $3^2 + x^2 = 5^2$, and $x^2 = 25 - 9 = 16$, which means that $x = 4$. Triangle *ABD* is a familiar 3-4-5 right triangle, and the area equals $\dfrac{3 \times 4}{2} = 6$. The correct answer is (A).

14. **B** Angle *AOB* = angle *BOC*, which means that the area of sector *AOB* is equal to the area of sector *BOC*. The area of triangle *AOB* is less than the area of sector *AOB*, which means that the area of triangle *AOB* is less than the area of sector *BOC*. The correct answer is (B).

15. **C** The interior angles of a parallelogram add up to 360°, and two adjacent angles of a parallelogram add up to 180°. Angle *OLM* = 108°, which means that angle *AOB* = 180° − 108° = 72°. The ratio of a central angle to 360° is equal to the ratio of the arc defined by the central angle to the circumference, which is 15π. So, $\dfrac{72°}{360°} = \dfrac{\text{minor arc } AB}{15\pi}$, which means that minor arc $AB = \dfrac{72° \times 15\pi}{360°} = 3\pi$. The correct answer is (C).

CHAPTER 16: MATH ET CETERA

Et Cetera Drill (Page 407)

1. **C** The question states that there is a total of 15 marbles and that the number of red marbles r is one more than the number of blue marbles b. Use $r + b = 15$ and $r = b + 1$ to find that there are 8 red marbles and 7 blue marbles in the bowl. The question asks for the probability of randomly selecting a blue marble. Using $\dfrac{\textit{number of blue marbles}}{\textit{total number of marbles}}$, the probability of randomly selecting a blue marble is $\dfrac{7}{15}$. The correct answer is (C).

2. **D** Plug In the value of x in the expression into the corresponding value of x in the definition of the function $¥(x)$. Use $¥(x) = 10x - 1$ to find that $¥(5) = 10 \times 5 - 1 = 49$, and that $¥(3) = 10 \times 3 - 1 = 29$. So, $¥(5) - ¥(3) = 49 - 29 = 20$. The correct answer is (D).

3. **B** Plug In the value of x for each of the quantities using the definition of the function $\#x$. Use $\#x = 2^{-x}$ to find that $\#8 = 2^{-8} = \dfrac{1}{2^8} = \dfrac{1}{256}$, and that $\#4 = 2^{-4} = \dfrac{1}{2^4} = \dfrac{1}{16}$. So, Quantity A is $\dfrac{1}{256}$ and Quantity B is $\dfrac{1}{16}$. Quantity B is greater than Quantity A. The correct answer is (B).

4. **20** The question asks, out of 5 finalists, how many ways two of them could be awarded "Best in Show" and "Honorable Mention." Order matters, which means this is a permutation question. There are five finalists who can be awarded "Best in Show," which means there are four remaining finalists who can be awarded "Honorable Mention." So, $5 \times 4 = 20$. The correct answer is 20.

5. **A** The question states that, out of a total advertising budget of $90,000, $40,000 is budgeted for product A, $30,000 is budgeted for product B, and $15,000 is budgeted for products A and B combined. Use the group equation Group 1 + Group 2 − Both + Neither = Total to find that $40,000 + $30,000 − $15,000 + Neither = $90,000. So, Neither is equal to $90,000 − $55,000 = $35,000, which means the amount of advertising spent on products other than product A and product B is $35,000. Quantity A is $35,000 and Quantity B is $20,000. Quantity A is greater than Quantity B. The correct answer is (A).

6. **B** List the two-digit primes less than 50. They are 11, 13, 17, 19, 23, 29, 31, 37, 41, 43, and 47. There are 11 total two-digit primes less than 50. Because the question asks for probability, the number 11 is the denominator of the probability fraction. Because 11 is a prime number, it cannot be reduced. Therefore, eliminate (A), (C), and (D) because they do not have 11 in the denominator of the fraction. The question asks for the probability that, out of those primes, the tens digit is greater than the units digit. The two-digit primes less than 50 where the tens digit is greater than the units digit are 31, 41, and 43. Use

probability = $\dfrac{\text{want}}{\text{total}}$ to find that the probability that the tens digit is greater than the units digit is $\dfrac{3}{11}$. The correct answer is (B).

7. **A** The question asks for the minimum number of staff members needed so that there are at least 20 different groups of five that could be taken to the location. The answers are all integers, so Plug In the Answers beginning with the least number, in this case 7. If there are 7 staff members, then there are $7 \times 6 \times 5 \times 4 \times 3$ different ways five members could be selected. Order doesn't matter, so divide by the number of ways five members could be arranged, or $5 \times 4 \times 3 \times 2 \times 1$. So, $\dfrac{7 \times 6 \times 5 \times 4 \times 3}{5 \times 4 \times 3 \times 2 \times 1} = 21$ different groups of five members. Because all of the remaining answer choices are greater than 7, none of them can be the minimum number of staff members. The correct answer is (A).

8. **E** There are variables in the question and in the answer choices, so Plug In. Try $x = 2$ and $y = 3$. Use $x \# y = x(x - y)$ to find that $2 \# (2 \# 3)$ is equal to $2 \# (2 \times (2 - 3)) = 2 \# -2$. Use the definition of the function again to find that $2 \# -2 = 2 \times (2 - (-2)) = 8$, which is the target answer. Plug In $x = 2$ and $y = 3$ in the answer choices. Choice (A) is $2^2 - 2 \times 3 = -2$. Eliminate (A). Choice (B) is $2^2 - 2 \times 2 \times 3 = -8$. Eliminate (B). Choice (C) is $2^3 - 2^2 - 2 \times 3 = -2$. Eliminate (C). Choice (D) is $2^3 - (2 \times 3)^2 = 8 - 36 = -28$. Eliminate (D). Choice (E) is $2^2 - 2^3 + 2^2 \times 3 = 4 - 8 + 12 = 8$, which matches the target answer. The correct answer is (E).

9. **B** The question states that there are a total of 12 marbles, and that the number of yellow marbles, y, is twice the number of green marbles, g. Use $y + g = 12$ and $y = 2g$ to find that there are 8 yellow marbles and 4 green marbles in the jar. The question asks what the probability of one marble being yellow and one being green would be if two marbles are randomly selected from the jar. There are two ways one yellow marble and one green marble can be selected. Either yellow first and then green, or green first and then yellow. The probability of selecting a yellow marble first and a green marble second is $\dfrac{8}{12} \times \dfrac{4}{11} = \dfrac{32}{132} = \dfrac{8}{33}$. The probability of selecting a green marble first and a yellow marble second is $\dfrac{4}{12} \times \dfrac{8}{11} = \dfrac{32}{132} = \dfrac{8}{33}$. Add the two probabilities together to get $\dfrac{8}{33} + \dfrac{8}{33} = \dfrac{16}{33}$. The correct answer is (B).

10. **B** The question states that there are 10 points on a plane, and that no three points are collinear, which means that any three points can form a triangle, and any four points can form a quadrilateral. The number of

distinct triangles that can be formed is equal to the number of distinct combinations of three points that can be selected from a group of 10 points. There are $10 \times 9 \times 8$ ways three points can be selected from a group of 10. Order doesn't matter, so divide by the number of ways three points can be arranged, or $3 \times 2 \times 1$. So, $\frac{10 \times 9 \times 8}{3 \times 2 \times 1} = 120$, which means that there are 120 distinct triangles that can be created. The number of distinct quadrilaterals that can be formed is equal to the number of distinct combinations of four points that can be selected from a group of 10 points. There are $10 \times 9 \times 8 \times 7$ ways four points can be selected from a group of 10. Order doesn't matter, so divide by the number of ways four points can be arranged, or $4 \times 3 \times 2 \times 1$. So, $\frac{10 \times 9 \times 8 \times 7}{4 \times 3 \times 2 \times 1} = 210$, which means that there are 210 distinct quadrilaterals that can be created. Quantity A is 120 and Quantity B is 210. Quantity B is greater than Quantity A. The correct answer is (B).

Comprehensive Math Drill (Page 409)

1. **B** The question states that the radius of the circle with center C is 5, which means that $AC = 5$. A line tangent to a circle is perpendicular to the radius of the circle, which means that AC and AB are perpendicular, and that triangle ABC is a right triangle with hypotenuse $BC = \frac{10\sqrt{3}}{3}$. Use the Pythagorean Theorem to find that $5^2 + (AB)^2 = \left(\frac{10\sqrt{3}}{3} \right)^2$, which means that $(AB)^2 = \frac{100 \times 3}{9} - 25 = \frac{100 - 75}{3} = \frac{25}{3}$, and that $AB = \frac{5}{\sqrt{3}} = \frac{5\sqrt{3}}{3}$. Another approach is to recognize that triangle ABC is a familiar 30-60-90 triangle with sides in the ratio of $s : s\sqrt{3} : 2s$. The shorter leg is opposite the 30° angle and is one-half times the hypotenuse. So, $AB = \frac{1}{2} \times \frac{10\sqrt{3}}{3} = \frac{5\sqrt{3}}{3}$, and the longer leg $AC = \frac{5\sqrt{3} \times \sqrt{3}}{3} = 5$, which is opposite the 60° angle. Quantity B is greater than Quantity A. The correct answer is (B).

2. **C** There are variables in the question, so Plug In. Try $x = 10$. Quantity A is $\frac{10}{10} = 1$, and Quantity B is $\frac{\frac{10}{5}}{2} = \frac{2}{2} = 1$. The two quantities are equal, so eliminate (A) and (B). Try $x = 50$. Quantity A is $\frac{50}{10} = 5$, and Quantity B is $\frac{\frac{50}{5}}{2} = \frac{10}{2} = 5$. The quantities are equal again. The correct answer is (C).

3. **C** The standard deviation of a set of numbers is based on the distance of each number in the set from the mean. The mean of the set {1,3,5} is 3, and the distance from the mean of each number in the set is 2, 0, and 2, respectively. The mean of the set {8,10,12} is 10, and the distance from the mean of each number in the set is 2, 0, and 2, respectively. The distances from the means are the same, which means that Quantity A is equal to Quantity B. The correct answer is (C).

4. **A** The slope-intercept form of a linear equation is $y = mx + b$, where m is the slope and b is the y-intercept, which is the point where x is equal to zero and the line crosses the y-axis. The question states that $y = -\frac{5}{6}x + 1$, which means that the line crosses the y-axis at $y = 1$, and that point P is $(0, 1)$. Point O is $(0, 0)$, which means that OP is equal to the distance from $(0, 0)$ to $(0, 1)$, which is equal to 1. Point Q is the point where the line crosses the x-axis, which is the point where y is equal to zero. Use $y = -\frac{5}{6}x + 1$ and set $y = 0$ to find that $0 = -\frac{5}{6}x + 1$, which means that $-\frac{5}{6}x = -1$ and $x = \frac{6}{5}$. So, point Q is $\left(\frac{6}{5}, 0\right)$. OQ is equal to the distance from $(0, 0)$ to $\left(\frac{6}{5}, 0\right)$, which is equal to $\frac{6}{5}$. Quantity A is $OQ = \frac{6}{5}$, which is greater than Quantity B, which is $OP = 1$. The correct answer is (A).

5. **B** The question states that there are 20 judges. Quantity A is the number of distinct pairs of judges, which means that order does not matter. Therefore, Quantity A is a combination. Use

$$\frac{\text{number judges for each of 2 slots}}{\text{factorial of the number of slots}}$$

to find that the number of distinct pairs of judges is equal to

$\frac{20 \times 19}{2 \times 1} = 190$. The question states that there are 10 dogs. Quantity B is the number of possible rankings of dogs from first to third place, which means that order matters and that Quantity B is a permutation.

So, the number of possible rankings of dogs from first to third place is $10 \times 9 \times 8 = 720$. Quantity A is 190 and Quantity B is 720. Quantity B is greater than Quantity A. The correct answer is (B).

6. **D** There are variables in Quantity A and in Quantity B, so Plug In. The question states that $k > 0$ and $l > 1$.

Try $k = \dfrac{1}{2}$ and $l = 2$. Quantity A is $\dfrac{1}{\frac{1}{\frac{1}{2}} + \frac{1}{2}} = \dfrac{1}{\frac{5}{2}} = \dfrac{2}{5}$, and Quantity B is $\dfrac{\frac{1}{2} \times 2}{\frac{1}{\frac{1}{2}} + \frac{1}{2}} = \dfrac{1}{\frac{5}{2}} = \dfrac{2}{5}$. Quantity A is

equal to Quantity B, so eliminate (A) and (B). Try $k = 1$ and $l = 2$. Quantity A is $\dfrac{1}{\frac{1}{1} + \frac{1}{2}} = \dfrac{1}{\frac{3}{2}} = \dfrac{2}{3}$, and

Quantity B is $\dfrac{1 \times 2}{\frac{1}{1} + \frac{1}{2}} = \dfrac{2}{\frac{3}{2}} = \dfrac{4}{3}$. Quantity A is less than Quantity B, so eliminate (C). The correct answer

is (D).

7. **A** The factors of 78 are 1, 2, 3, 6, 13, 26, and 39. Of these, 39 is the greatest odd factor, and 13 is the greatest prime factor. Quantity A is greater than Quantity B. The correct answer is (A).

8. **4** The question states that Joe has $200 and spends $150 for a DVD player, which means that Joe has $50 to spend on DVDs. DVDs cost $12 each, so divide $50 by $12 to get $4\dfrac{1}{6}$, which means that Joe can purchase 4 DVDs. The correct answer is 4.

9. **A** The area of a triangle is equal to $\dfrac{b \times h}{2}$, where b is the base and h is the height. The question asks for the

area of triangle ABC. AC is the base b, which is equal to the distance from $(0, 3)$ to $(0, 4)$, or 1. The height

h is equal to the distance from the top of the triangle on a line perpendicular to a line equal to the base

of the triangle. Therefore, h is equal to the distance from point B, which is $(0, 4)$, to $(0, 0)$. So, $h = 4$ and

$b = 1$, which means that the area of triangle $ABC = \dfrac{1 \times 4}{2} = 2$. The correct answer is (A).

10. **A** Factor $10(9^6)$ into its prime factors to find that $10(9^6) = 2 \times 5 \times (3^2)^6 = 2 \times 5 \times 3^{12}$. This means that any factor of $10(9^6)$ has no more than one factor of 2, one factor of 5, and twelve factors of 3, and has no other prime factors. Factor each of the answer choices into prime factors. Choice (A) is 90, which is equal to $2 \times 5 \times 3^2$, or one factor of 2, one factor of 5, and two factors of 3. Keep (A). Choice (B) is 100, which is equal to $2^2 \times 5^2$, or two factors of 2 and two factors of 5. Eliminate (B). Choice (C) is 330, which is equal to $2 \times 5 \times 3 \times 11$. There are no factors of 11 in $10(9^6)$. Eliminate (C). Choice (D) is 540, which is equal to $2^2 \times 5 \times 3^3$, or two factors of 2, one factor of 5, and three factors of 3. Eliminate (D). Choice (E) is 720, which is equal to $2^4 \times 5 \times 3^2$, or four factors of 2, one factor of 5, and two factors of 3. Eliminate (E). The correct answer is (A).

11. **B** and **C**

   The question states that Roberta drove 50 miles in 2 hours, which is equivalent to $\dfrac{50}{2} = 25$ miles per hour.

   The question asks which proportions are equivalent to 25. Evaluate each of the answer choices. Choice (A) is equivalent to $\dfrac{5}{20} = \dfrac{1}{4}$. Eliminate (A). Choice (B) is equivalent to $\dfrac{100}{4} = 25$. Keep (B). Choice (C) is equivalent to $\dfrac{400}{16} = 25$. Keep (C). Choice (D) is equivalent to $\dfrac{20}{500} = \dfrac{1}{25}$. Eliminate (D). Choice (E) is equivalent to $\dfrac{520}{20} = 26$. Eliminate (E). The correct answers are (B) and (C).

12. **C** Use the chart to find that the temperature highs for each city for Year Y is shown by the dashed line, and the temperature highs for each city for Year X is shown by the solid line. The question asks how many of the cities shown had a highest temperature in Year Y that was greater than or equal to the highest temperature in Year X. The dashed line is higher than or equal to the solid line for Baltimore, Detroit, Las Vegas, Minneapolis, New York, Phoenix, and San Francisco, or 7 cities. The correct answer is (C).

13. **C** Use the chart to find that the average temperature for years X and Y for each city are shown by the heavy bars. The question asks for the approximate percent increase from the lowest average temperature for Years X and Y to the highest average temperature for Years X and Y. The lowest average temperature for Years X and Y is 34° in Anchorage, Alaska, and the highest average temperature for Years X and Y is 83° in Las Vegas, Nevada. Use the percentage change formula, which is $\dfrac{difference}{original} \times 100$, to find that the percent increase is $\dfrac{83° - 34°}{34°} \times 100 \approx 144\% \approx 140\%$. The correct answer is (C).

14. **C** Use the chart to find that the temperature highs for each city for Year Y is shown by the dashed line and the temperature highs for each city for Year X is shown by the solid line. The heavy bars are the average temperatures for Years X and Y, which are equal to the average high temperatures for Years X and Y plus the average low temperatures for Years X and Y, divided by 2. For Baltimore, the average high temperature for Years X and Y is $\dfrac{103° + 97°}{2} = 100°$, and the average temperature for Years X and Y is 60°. So, $60° = \dfrac{100° + average\ low\ temperature}{2}$, which means that the average low temperature for Baltimore is equal to $60° \times 2 - 100° = 20°$. The correct answer is (C).

15. **A, B,** and **C**

   Simplify the inequality. Subtract 2 from both sides to get $|2x - 3| > 5$. The question asks for values that satisfy the inequality, and the answer choices are integers, so Plug In the Answers. Plug In (A) to find that $|(2x - 4) - 3| = 11$. Keep (A). Plug In (B), which yields $|(2x - 3) - 3| = 9$. Keep (B). Plug In (C), which is $|(2x - 2) - 3| = 7$. Keep (C). Plug In (D) to find that $|(2x - 1) - 3| = 5$. Eliminate (D). Plug In (E), which yields $|(2 \times 0) - 3| = 3$. Eliminate (E). Plug In (F) to show that $|(2 \times 1) - 3| = 1$. Eliminate (F). Plug In (G) to find $|(2 \times 2 - 3| = 1$. Eliminate (G). Plug In (H), which yields $|(2 \times 3) - 3| = 3$. Eliminate (H). The answer is (A), (B), and (C).

16. **A** The question asks for values of x that satisfy the inequality $x + y + z < z$, where x, y, and z are consecutive odd integers and $x < y < z$. Simplify the inequality $x + y + z < z$. Subtract z from both sides to get $x + y < 0$, which means that $x + y$ is negative. There are variables in the answer choices, so Plug In the Answers. Plug In (A) to find that $x = -3$ and $y = -1$, and that $-3 + -1 = -4$. Keep (A). Plug In (B) to find that $x = -1$ and $y = 1$, and that $-1 + 1 = 0$. Eliminate (B). Choice (C) is 0, and the question states that x is an odd integer. Eliminate (C). Plug In (D) to find that $x = 1$ and $y = 3$, and that $1 + 3 = 4$. Eliminate (D). Plug In (E) to find that $x = 3$ and $y = 5$, and that $3 + 5 = 8$. Eliminate (E). The correct answer is (A).

17. **E** The question states that $4^x = 1,024$, which means that $x = 5$, and that $(4^{x+1})(5^{x-1}) = 4^6 \times 5^4$. The answer choices are in terms of 4^n, 5^n, and 10^n. Recognize that $4^6 \times 5^4 = (4^4 \times 4^2) \times 5^4 = (4^4 \times 2^4) \times 5^4 = 4^4 \times 10^4$. The correct answer is (E).

18. **D** Use the volume of a rectangular solid, $V = l \times w \times h$, to find that $780 = 12 \times w \times 5$, and that $w = \dfrac{780}{12 \times 5} = 13$. So, the dimensions of the rectangular solid are 12, 5, and 13. The greatest distance between vertices in a rectangular solid is the distance between opposite corners. Use the formula for the diagonal of a rectangular solid $l^2 + w^2 + h^2 = d^2$ to find that $12^2 + 5^2 + 13^2 = 144 + 25 + 169 = 338 = d^2$, which means that $d = \sqrt{338} = \sqrt{169 \times 2} = 13\sqrt{2}$. The correct answer is (D).

19. **D** The question asks how many arrangements are possible for a group of three boys and three girls to sit on a park bench, where no boy can sit on either end of the bench. Order matters, so this is a permutation question. There are six slots, and the end slots can only be filled by girls, which means that in the first slot there are three choices, and in the last slot there are two choices. So, fill in the remaining slots to get $3 \times 4 \times 3 \times 2 \times 1 \times 2 = 144$. The correct answer is (D).

20. **C** Use the Average Pie to find that the number of items 3 times the average 16 is equal to the total 48, which means that $48 = 24 + p + q$, and that $p + q = 48 - 24 = 24$. So, $16(p + q) = 16 \times 24 = 384$. The correct answer is (C).

Part VI
Practice Tests

TEST INSTRUCTIONS

It's important to become familiar with the instructions for the test now, so that you don't waste time figuring them out on test day.

General Instructions

Each exam consists of six sections—two Analytical Writing sections, two Verbal Reasoning sections, and two Quantitative Reasoning sections. The Analytical Writing sections will always be first. The Verbal and Quantitative Reasoning sections may appear in any order. You will have 30 minutes for each Analytic Writing section, 30 minutes for each Verbal, and 35 minutes for each Quantitative Reasoning section. If desired, you may take a 10-minute break after Section 4. Remember that during the actual test, there may be an additional verbal or quantitative experimental section.

Need More Practice?
The Princeton Review's *1,027 GRE Practice Questions* offers drills for every question type, along with detailed, comprehensive explanations.

Section 1	30 minutes	Analytical Writing
Section 2	30 minutes	Analytical Writing
Section 3	30/35 minutes	Verbal or Quantitative Reasoning
Section 4	30/35 minutes	Verbal or Quantitative Reasoning
Section 5	30/35 minutes	Verbal or Quantitative Reasoning
Section 6	30/35 minutes	Verbal or Quantitative Reasoning

When taking a Verbal or Quantitative Reasoning section, you are free to skip questions that you might have difficulty answering and come back to them later during the time allotted for that section. You may also change your response to any question in a section during the time allotted to work on that section. You may not go back to an earlier section of the test after time for that section runs out.

Analytical Writing Instructions

Issue Topic

You will be given a brief statement on an issue of general interest and specific instructions on how to respond to that issue. You will have 30 minutes to plan and write a response in which you develop a position on the issue. Make sure that you respond to the specific instructions and support your position on the issue with reasons and examples drawn from such areas as your reading, experience, observations, and/or academic studies.

Before you begin writing, you may want to think for a few minutes about the passage and the instructions and then outline your response. Be sure to develop your analysis fully and organize it coherently. Leave a minute or two at the end to reread what you have written and make any revisions you think are necessary.

Argument Topic

You will be given a short passage that presents an argument, or an argument to be completed, and specific instructions on how to respond to that passage. You will have 30 minutes to plan and write a response in which you analyze the passage. Note that you are NOT being asked to present your own views on the subject. Make sure that you respond to the specific instructions and support your analysis with relevant reasons and/or examples.

Before you begin writing, you may want to think for a few minutes about the passage and the instructions and then outline your response. Be sure to develop your analysis fully and organize it coherently. Leave a minute or two at the end to reread what you have written and make any revisions you think are necessary.

Verbal Reasoning Instructions

Each Verbal Reasoning section is 30 minutes long and has 20 questions. For some questions, you will be instructed to choose one or more answer choices. The instructions may or may not specify the number of answers you must choose. If the number of answers is specified, you must choose all of the correct answers in order to have your response counted as correct. If the number is not specified, choose all that correctly answer the question. No credit will be given if fewer or more than all of the correct answers are chosen.

Quantitative Reasoning Instructions

Each Quantitative Reasoning section is 35 minutes long and has 20 questions. You will be provided with a five-function calculator—one with addition, subtraction, multiplication, division, and square-root features—during Quantitative Reasoning sections.

For some questions, you will be instructed to choose one or more answer choices. The instructions may or may not specify the number of answers you must choose. If the number of answers is specified, you must choose all of the correct answers in order to have your response counted as correct. If the number is not specified, choose all that correctly answer the question. No credit will be given if fewer or more than all of the correct answers are chosen.

Some questions will require you to enter your own answer. If the question provides a single response space, enter a single number. You may enter negative signs and decimal points. If the question tells you to round your answer, do so. Otherwise, enter the entire answer. If the question provides two response spaces, you must enter your answer in the form of a fraction. You are not required to enter fractions in their most reduced form. If you are aware of more than one correct response, you should enter only one of them.

Some questions will ask you to fill blanks in the text by clicking to select from a list of choices. Sometimes all of the choices will be used, and sometimes only some of the choices will be used. The correct answer always requires you to put a different choice in every blank.

Note on Numbers and Figures

Numbers: All numbers used are real numbers.

Figures: The position of points, angles, regions, and so on can be assumed to be in the order shown, and angle measures can be assumed to be positive. Lines shown as straight can be assumed to be straight. Figures can be assumed to lie in a plane unless otherwise indicated. Any other figures are not necessarily drawn to scale, unless a note states that a figure is drawn to scale.

Practice Test 1

SECTION 1: ISSUE TOPIC

Directions:

You will be given a brief quotation that states or implies an issue of general interest and specific instructions on how to respond to that issue. You will have 30 minutes to plan and compose a response in which you develop a position on the issue according to the specific instructions. A response to any other issue will receive a score of zero.

"Governments are justified in circumventing civil laws when doing so is vital to the protection of national security."

Write an essay in which you take a position on the statement above. In developing and supporting your position, you should consider ways in which the statement might or might not hold true.

SECTION 2: ARGUMENT TOPIC

Directions:

You will be given a short passage that presents an argument, or an argument to be completed, and specific instructions on how to respond to that passage. You will have 30 minutes to plan and compose a response in which you analyze the passage according to the specific instructions. A response to any other argument will receive a score of zero.

Note that you are NOT being asked to present your own views on the subject. Make sure that you respond to the specific instructions and support your analysis with relevant reasons and/or examples.

The following is from a recent email from the Diord Corp. Human Resources Manager: "Tobor Technologies found that mental health problems and mental illness were responsible for about 15 percent of employee sick days. Tobor amended its employee insurance plan so that workers receive the same coverage for mental illness as they do for physical illness. In addition, the company hired an on-site psychologist and created a system that allows workers to schedule confidential counseling appointments. After one year, the number of sick days used by employees declined by 10 percent. Diord Corp. has had an increase in employee sick days over the past two years, so we should introduce a similar insurance plan and counseling program. These measures will surely reduce employee absenteeism and cause an increase in productivity."

Write a response in which you examine the argument's unstated assumptions, making sure to explain how the argument depends on the assumptions and what the implications are if the assumptions prove unwarranted.

SECTION 3: QUANTITATIVE REASONING

For each of Questions 1 to 7, compare Quantity A and Quantity B, using additional information centered above the two quantities if such information is given. Select one of the four answer choices below each question and fill in the circle to the left of that answer choice.

(A) Quantity A is greater.

(B) Quantity B is greater.

(C) The two quantities are equal.

(D) The relationship cannot be determined from the information given.

A symbol that appears more than once in a question has the same meaning throughout the question.

1 of 20

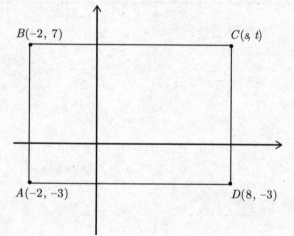

AB is parallel to CD.

BC is parallel to AD.

Quantity A	Quantity B
s	t

○ Quantity A is greater.

○ Quantity B is greater.

○ The two quantities are equal.

○ The relationship cannot be determined from the information given.

A certain punch is created by mixing two parts soda and three parts ice cream. The soda is 4 parts sugar, 5 parts citric acid, and 11 parts other ingredients. The ice cream is 3 parts sugar, 2 parts citric acid, and 15 parts other ingredients.

Quantity A	Quantity B
Parts sugar in the punch	Parts citric acid in the punch

○ Quantity A is greater.

○ Quantity B is greater.

○ The two quantities are equal.

○ The relationship cannot be determined from the information given.

3 of 20

The average (arithmetic mean) high temperature for x days is 70 degrees. The addition of one day with a high temperature of 75 degrees increases the average to 71 degrees.

Quantity A	Quantity B
x	5

○ Quantity A is greater.

○ Quantity B is greater.

○ The two quantities are equal.

○ The relationship cannot be determined from the information given.

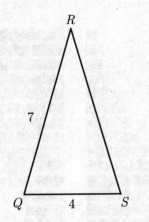

Each angle in $\triangle QRS$ has a degree measurement of either x or y and $2x + y = 180$.

Quantity A	Quantity B
Perimeter of QRS	17

○ Quantity A is greater.

○ Quantity B is greater.

○ The two quantities are equal.

○ The relationship cannot be determined from the information given.

Set A consists of the elements $\{1,3,5,7\}$. If Set B consists of the elements $\{12,14,16,x\}$, and the standard deviation of Set B is higher than that of Set A, then which of the following is a possible value of x?

Indicate <u>all</u> such values.

☐ 15

☐ 16

☐ 17

☐ 18

☐ 19

☐ 20

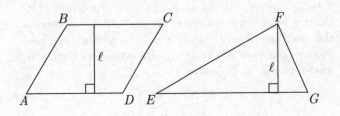

AB is parallel to CD.

AD is parallel to BC.

$$2AD = EG$$

Quantity A	Quantity B
The area of $ABCD$	The area of EFG

○ Quantity A is greater.

○ Quantity B is greater.

○ The two quantities are equal.

○ The relationship cannot be determined from the information given.

$$(3x - 4y)(3x + 4y) = 2$$

Quantity A	Quantity B
$9x^2 - 16y^2$	4

○ Quantity A is greater.

○ Quantity B is greater.

○ The two quantities are equal.

○ The relationship cannot be determined from the information given.

If $8a - 2 = 22$, then $4a - 1 =$

○ 2

○ $\frac{11}{4}$

○ 11

○ 12

○ 44

SECTION 3: QUANTITATIVE REASONING

Twenty percent of the sweaters in a store are white. Of the remaining sweaters, 40 percent are brown, and the rest are blue. If there are 200 sweaters in the store, then how many more blue sweaters than white sweaters are in the store?

Click on the answer box and type in a number.
Backspace to erase.

$$\frac{4^{13} - 4^{12}}{4^{11}} =$$

- ○ 0
- ○ 1
- ○ 4
- ○ 12
- ○ 16

Questions 11 through 14 refer to the following graph.

SUBSCRIPTIONS TO NEWSMAGAZINE x, 1995–2010

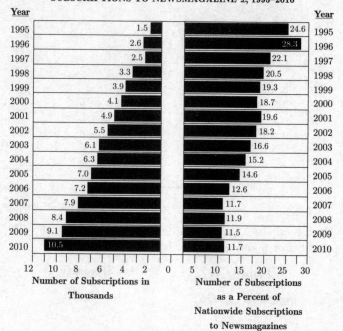

Year	Number of Subscriptions in Thousands	Number of Subscriptions as a Percent of Nationwide Subscriptions to Newsmagazines	Year
1995	1.5	24.6	1995
1996	2.6	28.3	1996
1997	2.5	22.1	1997
1998	3.3	20.5	1998
1999	3.9	19.3	1999
2000	4.1	18.7	2000
2001	4.9	19.6	2001
2002	5.5	18.2	2002
2003	6.1	16.6	2003
2004	6.3	15.2	2004
2005	7.0	14.6	2005
2006	7.2	12.6	2006
2007	7.9	11.7	2007
2008	8.4	11.9	2008
2009	9.1	11.5	2009
2010	10.5	11.7	2010

NATIONWIDE NEWSMAGAZINE SUBSCRIPTIONS: 1997 TO 2009

Newsmagazine	1997	2000	2003	2006	2009
x	2,500	4,100	6,100	7,200	9,100
y	1,700	3,100	4,600	5,700	7,200
z	3,600	5,800	7,600	9,400	11,400
Others	3,500	8,900	18,500	34,700	51,300

The total number of nationwide newsmagazine subscriptions in 1995 is approximately what percent less than of the total number of nationwide newsmagazine subscriptions in 2010?

- ○ 93%
- ○ 94%
- ○ 95%
- ○ 96%
- ○ 97%

SECTION 3: QUANTITATIVE REASONING

In which of the following years did subscriptions to Newsmagazine z account for approximately $\frac{1}{6}$ of the total nationwide magazine subscriptions?

- ○ 2009
- ○ 2006
- ○ 2003
- ○ 2000
- ○ 1997

What was the approximate percent increase in nationwide subscriptions to newsmagazines between 1995 and 1996 ?

- ○ 4%
- ○ 11%
- ○ 26%
- ○ 51%
- ○ 73%

In 1998, what was the approximate number of subscriptions to newsmagazines nationwide?

- ○ 3,000
- ○ 13,000
- ○ 16,000
- ○ 20,000
- ○ 67,000

If $a = (27)(3^{-2})$ and $x = (6)(3^{-1})$, then which of the following is equivalent to $(12)(3^{-x}) \times (15)(2^{-a})$?

- ○ $5(-2245)(320)$
- ○ $\frac{2}{5}$
- ○ $\frac{5}{2}$
- ○ $5(24)(38)$
- ○ $5(2245)(320)$

Jill has received 8 of her 12 evaluation scores. So far, Jill's average (arithmetic mean) is 3.75 out of a possible 5. If Jill needs an average of 4.0 points to get a promotion, which list of scores qualifies Jill to receive her promotion?

Indicate all such lists.

- ☐ 3.0, 3.5, 4.75, 4.75
- ☐ 3.5, 4.75, 4.75, 5.0
- ☐ 3.25, 4.5, 4.75, 5.0
- ☐ 3.75, 4.5, 4.75, 5.0

SECTION 3: QUANTITATIVE REASONING

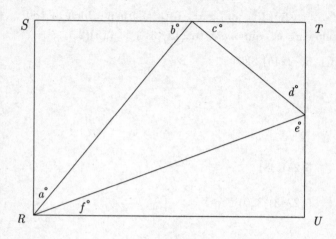

In the figure above, if $RSTU$ is a rectangle, what is the value of $a + b + c + d + e + f$?

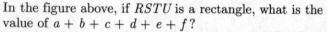

Click on the answer box and type in a number.
Backspace to erase.

If the probability of selecting, without replacement, 2 red marbles from a bag containing only red and blue marbles is $\frac{3}{55}$ and there are 3 red marbles in the bag, what is the total number of marbles in the bag?

- ○ 10
- ○ 11
- ○ 55
- ○ 110
- ○ 165

All first-year students at Blue State University must take calculus, English composition, or both. If half of the 2,400 first-year students at Blue State University take calculus and half do not, and one-third of those who take calculus also take English composition, how many students take English composition?

- ○ 400
- ○ 800
- ○ 1,200
- ○ 1,600
- ○ 2,000

If $\frac{13!}{2^x}$ is an integer, which of the following represents all possible values of x ?

- ○ $0 \le x \le 10$
- ○ $0 < x < 9$
- ○ $0 \le x < 10$
- ○ $1 \le x \le 10$
- ○ $1 < x < 10$

NO TEST MATERIAL ON THIS PAGE

SECTION 4: VERBAL REASONING

For questions 1 through 6, select one entry for each blank from the corresponding column of choices. Fill all blanks in the way that best completes the text.

The professor is a noteworthy intellect, and as a teacher she shows more (i)_____ than her colleagues, whose teaching skills are (ii)_____.

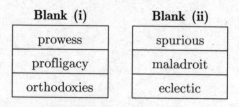

Blank (i)	Blank (ii)
prowess	spurious
profligacy	maladroit
orthodoxies	eclectic

It would be (i)_____ for our leaders, given their responsibilities as democratically elected officials, to neglect to do everything they could to (ii)_____ an entirely (iii)_____ problem.

Blank (i)	Blank (ii)	Blank (iii)
irresponsible	forestall	benign
necessary	sustain	unimportant
frivolous	cultivate	avoidable

Despite her mentor's advice that she attempt to sound consistently _____ , the graduate student often resorted to using slang when presenting significant parts of her thesis, her habitual speech patterns overriding her years of learning.

lucid
didactic
panegyrical
erudite
rational

Although she felt Steve (i)_____ the subtlety of the delicious stew recipe with his addition of the sweet potato, she thought the pungent onion (ii)_____ the otherwise (iii)_____ taste combination.

Blank (i)	Blank (ii)	Blank (iii)
depleted	exaggerated	delicate
permeated	overwhelmed	zesty
augmented	satiated	detestable

SECTION 4: VERBAL REASONING

At first, a still-life painting can appear quite (i)_____ , its focus on such everyday objects as flowers or fruits apparently uninspired. In the hands of (ii)_____ painter, however, careful attention to slight shifts of color and texture can lead to a truly (iii)_____ and exemplary painting.

Blank (i)	Blank (ii)	Blank (iii)
vital	a gauche	unstinting
luxuriant	an adept	sublime
banal	an ascetic	prosaic

The leaders of Ukraine's "Orange Revolution" were a study in contrasts. At the center of the political storm stood Viktor Yushchenko, his once (i)_____ face transformed into a monstrous mask by dioxin poisoning; but, at his side, no one could miss the (ii)_____ Yulia Tymoshenko, soon to become the world's only prime minister to adorn the covers of fashion magazines.

Blank (i)	Blank (ii)
quiescent	prepossessing
fatuous	decorous
comely	felicitous

SECTION 4: VERBAL REASONING

For each of Questions 7 to 11, select one answer choice unless otherwise instructed.

Questions 7 through 9 are based on the following reading passage.

In analyzing the poetry of Mona Feather, we are confronted with three different yardsticks by which to measure her work. We could consider her poems as the product of a twentieth-century artist in the tradition of James Joyce, T.S. Eliot, and Wallace Stevens. However, to do so would be to ignore a facet that informs every word she writes and that stems from her identity as a woman. Yet, to characterize her solely as a woman poet is to deny her cultural heritage, for Mona Feather is also the first modern poet of stature who is also an American Indian.

Stanley Wilson has argued compellingly that the huge popularity Feather enjoys among the Indian reservation school population of the United States is creating a whole new generation of poetry enthusiasts in an age when the reading of poetry is on the wane. While this is undoubtedly true, Mr. Wilson's praise gives the impression that Feather's readership is limited to her own culture—an impression which hints that Mr. Wilson is himself measuring her by only one criterion. Radical feminist writers have long found in Feather's poetry a sense of self-pride which strikes a chord with their own more political philosophies. Her imagery, which always made use of the early Native American traditions in which the woman had an important role, was seen as the awakened sensibility of a kindred spirit.

Yet for all the "feminist" touches in her writing, it would be a disservice to consign Feather to the ranks of politicized writers, for her message is deeper than that. The despair that characterized twentieth-century modern poets is to be found in Mona Feather's work as well; she writes of the American Indians of the 1930s confined to ever-shrinking reservations and finds in that a metaphor for all of modern mankind trapped on a shrinking earth of limited resources.

The primary purpose of the passage is to

○ describe the work of Mona Feather

○ compare Feather with Joyce, Eliot, and Stevens

○ show Feather's roots in her Native American heritage

○ argue that Mona Feather's work can be looked at in several different ways

○ discuss the women's movement in America

The passage implies that the author believes Stanley Wilson's view of Feather is

○ a compelling and complete assessment of her work

○ focused too much on her status as a Native American poet

○ meant to disguise his opinion of Feather as a poet lacking in talent

○ critical of Native American children's literary judgment

○ based on all major themes and images in her poetry

The author mentions James Joyce, T.S. Eliot, and Wallace Stevens in order to

○ compare the political messages in Feather's work to those in the work of other authors

○ highlight the radical differences between male and female poets in the twentieth century

○ contrast Feather's thematic choices with those of her contemporaries

○ enumerate a list of artists whose sensibilities made them Feather's kindred spirits

○ describe a critical context in which Feather's work can be analyzed

SECTION 4: VERBAL REASONING

Questions 10 through 11 are based on the following reading passage.

Among the more interesting elements of etymology is the attempt to derive the meaning of seemingly nonsensical expressions. Take, for instance, the increasingly archaic rural phrase "to buy a pig in a poke." For centuries, the expression has been used to signify the purchase of an item without full knowledge of its condition. It relates to the common Renaissance practice of securing suckling pigs for transport to market in a poke, or drawstring bag. Unscrupulous sellers would sometimes attempt to dupe purchasers by replacing the suckling pig with a cat, considered worthless at market. An unsuspecting or naïve buyer might fail to confirm the bag's contents; a more urbane buyer, though, would be sure to check and—should the seller be dishonest—"let the cat out of the bag."

Consider each of the choices separately and select all that apply.

Which of the following phrases from the passage would help the reader infer the meaning of the word urbane as used in context?

- ☐ "increasingly archaic rural phrase"
- ☐ "without full knowledge"
- ☐ "unsuspecting or naïve buyer"

Select the sentence in which the author provides a definition for an antiquated term that may be unfamiliar to the reader.

For questions 12 through 15, select the two answer choices that, when used to complete the sentence, fit the meaning of the sentence as a whole and produce completed sentences that are alike in meaning.

Although she was such a bad-mannered child that she was sent to a boarding school, as an adult she is the very model of _____ .

- ☐ friendliness
- ☐ diffidence
- ☐ propriety
- ☐ reticence
- ☐ decorum
- ☐ brashness

Politicians sometimes appear to act in a manner that is almost _____ ; however, when all the information is released after the fact, it is apparent that they were acting according to a deliberate plan.

- ☐ pithy
- ☐ conventional
- ☐ conformist
- ☐ whimsical
- ☐ flawless
- ☐ capricious

SECTION 4: VERBAL REASONING

Forced to take an alternate road when a massive oil spill closed the highway, the two-hour detour made their already arduous trip even more _____ .

- ☐ irksome
- ☐ onerous
- ☐ facile
- ☐ glib
- ☐ implacable
- ☐ immutable

Though many of her contemporaries found her odd, Ella Wilkins is now much admired for her _____ spirit, especially her willingness to reject prevailing feminine roles and to travel to foreign lands alone.

- ☐ forlorn
- ☐ magnanimous
- ☐ adventurous
- ☐ bellicose
- ☐ desolate
- ☐ doughty

For each of Questions 16 to 20, select one answer choice unless otherwise instructed.

Microfiber synthetics have been taking the place of natural fibers in an ever-increasing number of clothes because they provide the same durability and deplete fewer natural resources. A shirt made of microfiber synthetics is, however, three times as expensive to produce as a natural-fiber shirt. It follows that the substitution of microfiber synthetic clothes for natural-fiber clothes is, at this time, not recommended from a financial standpoint.

Which of the following statements, if true, most seriously weakens the argument?

- ○ A microfiber synthetic shirt costs one-half the price of a natural-fiber shirt to maintain.

- ○ The production of microfiber synthetic clothes necessitates garment factories to renovate obsolete machinery and to hire extra workers to operate the new machines.

- ○ The upkeep of natural-fiber shirts is far less expensive than the upkeep of any other natural-fiber garment in current production.

- ○ While producers anticipate that the cost of microfiber synthetics will remain stable, they recognize that the advent of recycling programs for natural fibers should bring down the costs of natural fibers.

- ○ The cost of providing stain guards for microfiber synthetic shirts would probably be greater than what garment producers now spend on stain guards for natural-fiber shirts.

SECTION 4: VERBAL REASONING

Questions 17 through 18 are based on the following reading passage.

Scholars of early Buddhist art agree that Buddha images in human form emerged around the first century A.D. in the regions of Mathura, located in central India, and Gandhara, now part of Pakistan and Afghanistan. Uncertainty exists, however, about whether Mathura or Gandhara has the stronger claim to primacy. Those who believe that anthropomorphic sculptures of the Buddha first appeared in Gandhara point out that earlier Buddhist art was largely aniconic and that *bas relief* was far more common than sculpture. They argue that Greek influence in Gandhara promoted the development of the new style and form of representation of the divine. Other scholars make the case for indigenous development of such representations in Mathura, citing a centuries-long record of iconic art in pre-Buddhist traditions. They do not reject all foreign influence, but they argue that local traditions provided a strong foundation for the development of Buddhist sculpture.

Art historians bolster their arguments by highlighting distinctive features of the sculptures from each region. For example, the artists of Gandhara sculpted their Buddhas in heavy, pleated drapery, similar to that of Greek statues. Wavy lines indicating hair also reflect Greek influence. Mathura Buddhas, on the other hand, are portrayed wearing lighter robes draped in a monastic style, often with part of the shoulder and chest left bare. Elongated earlobes and strong facial features characterize Mathura images of the Buddha, whereas Gandhara images possess more angular features. Sorting out dates and directions of influence has proven difficult, but the totality of evidence suggests that the Buddha image evolved simultaneously in both regions and was shaped by the predominant cultural influences in each region.

Which of the following, if true, would those who believe that anthropomorphic images of Buddha originated in Gandhara be likely to cite as evidence for their viewpoint?

○ Pre-Buddhist subcultures in the Gandhara region created representations of their deities in human form.

○ Mathuran Buddhas' lightweight robes appear to have been modeled on the real robes of people who lived in a warm climate.

○ Gandharan artists were isolated from the larger society and not exposed to influences from outside the region.

○ Rulers from the Mathura region had political ties to Greek rulers and frequently exchanged gifts with them.

○ The hairstyles worn by Gandharan Buddhas are similar to those depicted on Greek pottery from the same period.

According to the passage, Buddhist art

○ first appeared in regions that are now part of India, Pakistan, and Afghanistan

○ experienced a period during which human representations of the Buddha were not common

○ characteristically portrayed figures with elongated earlobes and strong facial features

○ began to appear in the medium of *bas relief* as a result of Greek influence

○ was more influenced by foreign artworks than by indigenous artistic traditions

SECTION 4: VERBAL REASONING

Questions 19 through 20 are based on the following reading passage.

In 1887, Eugene Dubois began his search in Sumatra for the "missing link"—the being that would fill the evolutionary gap between ape and man. He discovered a fossilized human-like thighbone and a section of skull. He confirmed that these fossils were of significant age by examining other fossils in the same area. The thighbone's shape indicated that it belonged to a creature that walked upright. Dubois estimated the size of the creature's skull from the skull fragment and concluded that this creature's brain volume was between that of the higher primates and that of current humans. Although the concept of "missing link" has changed dramatically and a recent analysis showed Dubois's fossils to be far too recent for humans to have evolved from this "missing link," the value of his discovery and the debate it generated is unquestionable.

Consider each of the choices separately and select all that apply.

The passage supplies information to answer which of the following questions?

☐ What was the approximate age of the fossils found by Dubois?

☐ Does Dubois's find meet current definitions of the "missing link"?

☐ Do the flaws in Dubois's conclusions invalidate his work?

Select a sentence in which the author reaches a conclusion.

NO TEST MATERIAL ON THIS PAGE

SECTION 5: QUANTITATIVE REASONING

For each of Questions 1 to 8, compare Quantity A and Quantity B, using additional information centered above the two quantities if such information is given. Select one of the four answer choices below each question and fill in the circle to the left of that answer choice.

(A) Quantity A is greater.
(B) Quantity B is greater.
(C) The two quantities are equal.
(D) The relationship cannot be determined from the information given.

A symbol that appears more than once in a question has the same meaning throughout the question.

A circle with center R has a radius of 6 and is inscribed in square $ABCD$.

Quantity A	Quantity B
The area of the largest triangle that can be drawn inside square $ABCD$	The area of the circle with center R

○ Quantity A is greater.
○ Quantity B is greater.
○ The two quantities are equal.
○ The relationship cannot be determined from the information given.

$$xy \neq 0$$

$$\frac{a}{xs} = 632 \text{ and } \frac{a}{ys} = 158$$

Quantity A	Quantity B
x	y

○ Quantity A is greater.
○ Quantity B is greater.
○ The two quantities are equal.
○ The relationship cannot be determined from the information given.

Quantity A	Quantity B
The remainder when 135 is divided by 7	The remainder when 135 is divided by 19

○ Quantity A is greater.
○ Quantity B is greater.
○ The two quantities are equal.
○ The relationship cannot be determined from the information given.

a and b are integers.

$$a^2 = b^3$$

Quantity A	Quantity B
a	b

○ Quantity A is greater.
○ Quantity B is greater.
○ The two quantities are equal.
○ The relationship cannot be determined from the information given.

$$ab < 0$$

$$bc > 0$$

Quantity A	Quantity B
ac	0

○ Quantity A is greater.
○ Quantity B is greater.
○ The two quantities are equal.
○ The relationship cannot be determined from the information given.

$$|x| = 6$$
$$y = x + 4$$

Quantity A

y

Quantity B

10

○ Quantity A is greater.

○ Quantity B is greater.

○ The two quantities are equal.

○ The relationship cannot be determined from the information given.

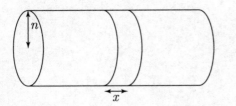

A rectangular ribbon of width x is wrapped around the circumference of a right circular cylinder of radius n, encircling the cylinder without overlap as shown in the figure above. The area of the ribbon is equal to the area of the base of the cylinder.

Quantity A

x

Quantity B

n

○ Quantity A is greater.

○ Quantity B is greater.

○ The two quantities are equal.

○ The relationship cannot be determined from the information given.

List A: 1, 2, 7, 8, 15, 2, 3, 5, 6, 13

x is the median of the even numbers in List A.

y is the median of the prime numbers in List A.

z is the median of the least and greatest numbers in List A.

Quantity A

The median of $2x$, y, and z

Quantity B

z

○ Quantity A is greater.

○ Quantity B is greater.

○ The two quantities are equal.

○ The relationship cannot be determined from the information given.

Oil is pumped from a well at a rate of 500 gallons per hour. How many gallons of oil are pumped from the well in 3 hours and 15 minutes?

 gallons

Click on the answer box and type in a number. Backspace to erase.

A certain pet store sells only dogs and cats. In March, the store sold twice as many dogs as cats. In April, the store sold twice the number of dogs that it sold in March, and three times the number of cats that it sold in March. If the total number of pets the store sold in March and April combined was 500, how many dogs did the store sell in March?

○ 80

○ 100

○ 120

○ 160

○ 180

In the xy-plane, rectangle $WXYZ$ has vertices at $(-2, -1)$, $(-2, y)$, $(4, y)$, and $(4, -1)$. If the area of $WXYZ$ is 18, what is the length of its diagonal?

○ $3\sqrt{2}$

○ $3\sqrt{3}$

○ $3\sqrt{5}$

○ $3\sqrt{6}$

○ $3\sqrt{7}$

How many three-digit integers can be created using only 5 distinct digits?

○ 10

○ 15

○ 20

○ 30

○ 60

At Megalomania Industries, factory workers were paid $20 per hour in 1990 and $10 per hour in 2000. The CEO of Megalomania Industries was paid $5 million in 1990 and $50 million in 2000. The percent increase in the pay of Megalomania's CEO from 1990 to 2000 was what percent greater than the percent decrease in the hourly pay of Megalomania's factory workers over the same period?

○ 850%

○ 900%

○ 950%

○ 1,700%

○ 1,900%

Questions 14 through 16 refer to the following graph.

PRIVATE DONATIONS TO CHARITABLE
CAUSES IN COUNTRY *X*. JAN. 1971–DEC. 1989

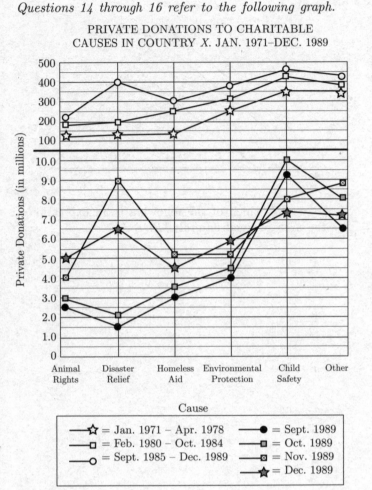

Cause

```
☆ = Jan. 1971 – Apr. 1978      ● = Sept. 1989
□ = Feb. 1980 – Oct. 1984      ■ = Oct. 1989
○ = Sept. 1985 – Dec. 1989     ⊠ = Nov. 1989
                               ★ = Dec. 1989
```

If there were 38 child safety organizations and the funds contributed to these organizations in September 1989 were evenly distributed, how much did each charity receive?

○ $12,000,000

○ $9,400,000

○ $2,500,000

○ $250,000

○ $38,000

From September 1985 to December 1989, what was the approximate ratio of private donations for homeless aid to private donations for animal rights?

○ 20 : 9

○ 3 : 2

○ 4 : 3

○ 5 : 4

○ 6 : 5

Which of the following charitable causes received the least percent increase in private donations from September 1989 to October 1989 ?

○ Animal Rights

○ Disaster Relief

○ Homeless Aid

○ Environmental Protection

○ Child Safety

In the repeating decimal 0.0653906539..., the 34th digit to the right of the decimal point is

○ 9

○ 6

○ 5

○ 3

○ 0

If $3x + 2y = 24$, and $\dfrac{7y}{2x} = 7$, then $y =$

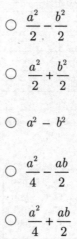

Click on each box and type in a number.
Backspace to erase.

If the average (arithmetic mean) of 6, 8, 10, and x is between 6 and 12, what is the greatest possible integer value of x ?

○   8

○ 11

○ 23

○ 28

○ 44

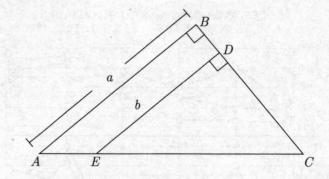

If $AB = BC$, which of the following is an expression for the area of quadrilateral $ABDE$?

○ $\dfrac{a^2}{2} - \dfrac{b^2}{2}$

○ $\dfrac{a^2}{2} + \dfrac{b^2}{2}$

○ $a^2 - b^2$

○ $\dfrac{a^2}{4} - \dfrac{ab}{2}$

○ $\dfrac{a^2}{4} + \dfrac{ab}{2}$

NO TEST MATERIAL ON THIS PAGE

SECTION 6: VERBAL REASONING

For questions 1 through 6, select one entry for each blank from the corresponding column of choices. Fill all blanks in the way that best completes the text.

Many fashions that were considered daring in their time have been so widely worn and imitated that the (i)_____ style is no longer seen as (ii)_____ .

Blank (i)	Blank (ii)
proposed	outlandish
original	commonplace
revealing	copied

Western culture has so influenced Middle Eastern music that even the latter's roles of composer and performer, at one time inseparable, have now begun to _____ .

divulge
retreat
retrench
diverge
fuse

Kazan was quickly (i)_____ by many of his contemporaries for his transgression, who saw his testimony as treachery, an act of (ii)_____ that stained how they viewed him both as an artist and as a man. It was only by continually making films that he was able to (iii)_____ his perceived sins and achieve some measure of atonement.

Blank (i)	Blank (ii)	Blank (iii)
rebuked	perfidy	exacerbate
lauded	sophistry	deviate
mitigated	redemption	expiate

Although tranquilizers usually have a _____ effect, this is not always the case, especially when the abuse of these drugs results in a failure to induce the much-desired sleep.

soporific
sedulous
coruscating
debilitating
penetrating

As a rule, (i)_____ interpretations of events are rejected by modern scientists in their attempts to find secular insights into the matrix of causes and effects in our modern world. Paradoxically, this fact does not (ii)_____ the existence of individual scientists who possess views that may be (iii)_____ with a belief in supernatural causes.

Blank (i)	Blank (ii)	Blank (iii)
falsifiable	countenance	at variance
preternatural	enhance	consonant
teleological	preclude	discrepant

The Johnsons were not known for their (i)_____ ; at the very least, none of the family members was fearful of (ii)_____ , of appearing or acting differently from other people.

Blank (i)	Blank (ii)
candor	pettiness
vulgarity	eccentricity
conformity	complaisance

SECTION 6: VERBAL REASONING

For each of Questions 7 to 12, select one answer choice unless otherwise instructed.

Questions 7 through 10 are based on the following reading passage.

According to most scientists, the universe began approximately 10 to 15 billion years ago and has been expanding ever since. This theory, known as the Big Bang theory, is the fairly direct result of Hubble's law, which states that objects farther away from Earth are receding faster than those closer. This expansion implies a singular point which all matter is expanding from.

Complicating the scientific explanation is that the Big Bang cannot be thought of as an explosion from some identifiable source—rather, space and time were created in the Big Bang. Furthermore, the relationship between distance and speed is not precisely linear. So, if one were to think of galaxies as particles created in a big bang, these galaxies have both a local component of motion, as well as playing a role in the overall expansion of the universe.

A further complication is that galactic distances are so great that galactic motion, even if the galaxies are moving at incredible speeds, is difficult to observe. Scientists must therefore rely on a "standard candle," an object of known brightness within the galaxy they wish to observe. Using the inverse square law, scientists can then measure how far that galaxy is away from our own. For instance, suppose a supernova in galaxy A appears one hundred times as bright as one in galaxy B. By the inverse square law, galaxy B is ten times farther away than galaxy A, assuming, of course, that distance is the only factor affecting brightness.

7 of 20

It can be inferred from the sentence highlighted in the passage that a standard candle is useful to scientists for which of the following reasons?

- ○ Standard candles do not have their own locus of motion.

- ○ Standard candles more reliably adhere to the law of inverse squares than do other supernovas.

- ○ Only standard candles provide a known measure of brightness.

- ○ Knowledge of an object's brightness allows scientists to measure the speed at which the object is moving toward Earth.

- ○ Knowledge of an object's brightness allows scientists to accurately measure its distance from Earth.

Consider each of the choices separately and select all that apply.

According to the passage, if two astronomical objects of differing distances from Earth were observed, which of the following would be true of the object closer to Earth?

- ☐ It would not be as bright as the object farther from Earth.

- ☐ It would be younger than the object farther from Earth.

- ☐ It would be traveling away from the Earth more slowly than the farther object.

9 of 20

It can be inferred from the passage that a standard candle may not provide an accurate measure of distance if

- ○ the galaxy being measured is moving too quickly

- ○ interstellar dust makes the object measured appear dimmer than it really is

- ○ the galaxy being measured has a local component of measurement

- ○ the particles being measured do not completely accord with a linear motion

- ○ the galaxies being measured move at different speeds

10 of 20

According to the passage, if two supernovas are observed and one of those supernovas is brighter than the other, scientists can conclude that

- ○ the brighter supernova is moving closer to our galaxy at a higher speed

- ○ the precise location of the supernova is measurable

- ○ the brighter supernova may be closer to our own galaxy

- ○ the brighter supernova is farther away from Earth by a distance that is roughly inversely proportional to the dim supernova

- ○ the distance between the supernovas and our own galaxy is inversely proportional

SECTION 6: VERBAL REASONING

Questions 11 through 12 are based on the following reading passage.

Throughout the twentieth century, it was accepted as fact that cells in our brains, called neurons, do not regenerate. Research by neurologist Elizabeth Gould overturned this core doctrine within the span of a few years. Her experiments on rats showed that even after suffering severe trauma, their brains were able to heal themselves by regenerating neurons. Gould's findings have incited a flood of new research into applications that may take advantage of neurogenesis.

One such study examines the role of reduced neurogenesis among individuals suffering from depression. It is speculated that neurogenesis may contribute to an explanation for the so called "Prozac lag." As an antidepressant, the immediate boost of serotonin caused by Prozac should have had instantaneous mood elevating effects. However, patients suffering from depression only begin to experience mood elevation weeks after beginning treatment. The study speculates that during this period, the brain may be regenerating neurons.

The author mentions the "Prozac lag" primarily in order to

○ raise a possible objection to a newly proposed theory

○ present a situation for which a new theory may serve an explanatory role

○ offer evidence that runs counter to a previously held belief

○ suggest a counterexample that undermines a newly proposed theory

○ provide supporting evidence that a newly discovered phenomenon may have unforeseen effects

In the second paragraph, select the sentence in which the author describes an unexpected observation.

SECTION 6: VERBAL REASONING

For questions 13 through 16, select the two answer choices that, when used to complete the sentence, fit the meaning of the sentence as a whole and produce completed sentences that are alike in meaning.

Plato, an important philosopher, is primarily known because he wrote down Socrates's _____ conversations. It is through Plato's record of these dialogues that Socrates's teachings have survived and continue to enlighten seekers of wisdom.

- ☐ inspiring
- ☐ edifying
- ☐ tedious
- ☐ grating
- ☐ rousing
- ☐ didactic

Even the colossal meal failed to _____ her voracious appetite.

- ☐ cadge
- ☐ exacerbate
- ☐ provoke
- ☐ satiate
- ☐ mendicate
- ☐ allay

Slicks of oil on a rain-soaked street are _____ and beautiful, but the lovely rainbows they produce on the asphalt can seem rather ugly when one reflects upon the road hazards they create and the environmental damage they entail.

- ☐ anodyne
- ☐ iridescent
- ☐ monocoque
- ☐ pavonine
- ☐ parietal
- ☐ saturnine

He had not always been so callous, but with time he became _____ to the violence around him.

- ☐ adorned
- ☐ cauterized
- ☐ sensitized
- ☐ ostracized
- ☐ inured
- ☐ attuned

SECTION 6: VERBAL REASONING

For each of Questions 17 to 20, select one answer choice unless otherwise instructed.

When the maker of Megapower, a vitamin supplement, modified its formula two years ago, Tasmania, an island off the coast of New Zealand, suffered a decrease in its export earnings. Tasmania's only export, kiwi fruit, constitutes a substantial portion of the world supply of that fruit. Researchers concluded that the old Megapower formula contained natural kiwi extract, but the new formula does not.

Which of the following, if true, gives the strongest support for the researchers' claim?

○ Some South American countries have begun to grow kiwi fruit successfully.

○ United States chemists have started development of a synthetic kiwi extract.

○ The manufacturers of Megapower chose not to renew their contract with the Tasmanian kiwi growers.

○ Imports of kiwi fruit have fallen in the country where Megapower is manufactured.

○ There was a marked drop in sales of a number of formerly profitable items that used kiwi as an ingredient.

Questions 18 through 20 are based on the following reading passage.

While art historians do not necessarily agree on the date of the birth of modern art, they do agree that mid-nineteenth century French art shows a clear and distinct break from tradition. Pressed to point to a single picture that represents the vanguard of the modern art movement, art historians will often point to Courbet's *The Painter's Studio*.

The peculiar subtitle of Courbet's work, "Real allegory summing up a seven-year period of my life" confirms that Courbet was striving to do something strikingly original with his work. The argument has been made that the painting struck a blow for the independence of the artist, and that since Courbet's work, artists have felt freed from the societal demands placed upon their work. Paintings prior to Courbet's time were most often focused on depicting events from the Bible, history, or literature. With his singular painting, Courbet promulgated the idea that an artist is capable of representing only that which he can experience through his senses of sight and touch; the true artist will then be compelled to make his representation as simply and directly as possible.

Which of the following would most effectively replace the word promulgated as it is used in the context of the passage?

○ Displayed

○ Disseminated

○ Proclaimed

○ Concealed

○ Secreted

SECTION 6: VERBAL REASONING

Select the sentence in the passage that best explains the effect of Courbet's work on other artists.

The effect that Courbet had on painting is most analogous to which situation?

- ○ An avant-garde writer who subverts novelistic conventions

- ○ A machinist who tinkers and improves his invention

- ○ A watercolor painter who paints in the same style as his peers

- ○ A scientist who comes up with a unified theory of several discordant scientific ideas

- ○ A seamstress who makes a ball gown using several different types of fabric

Practice Test 1:
Answers and
Explanations

PRACTICE TEST 1: ANSWER KEY

Section 3: Quantitative Reasoning

1. A
2. A
3. B
4. D
5. E and F
6. C
7. B
8. C
9. 56
10. D
11. A
12. B
13. D
14. C
15. C
16. B and D
17. 270
18. B
19. E
20. A

Section 4: Verbal Reasoning

1. prowess and maladroit
2. irresponsible, forestall, and avoidable
3. erudite
4. augmented, overwhelmed, and delicate
5. banal, an adept, and sublime
6. comely and prepossessing
7. D
8. B
9. E
10. C
11. It relates to the common Renaissance practice of securing suckling pigs for transport to market in a poke, or drawstring bag.
12. propriety and decorum
13. whimsical and capricious
14. irksome and onerous
15. adventurous and doughty
16. A
17. E
18. B
19. B and C
20. Although the concept of "missing link" has changed dramatically and a recent analysis showed Dubois's fossils to be far too recent for humans to have evolved from this "missing link," the value of his discovery and the debate it generated is unquestionable.

Section 5: Quantitative Reasoning

1. B
2. D
3. C
4. D
5. B
6. D
7. B
8. C
9. 1,625
10. B
11. C
12. E
13. D
14. D
15. C
16. E
17. D
18. $\dfrac{48}{7}$
19. C
20. A

Section 6: Verbal Reasoning

1. original and outlandish
2. diverge
3. rebuked, perfidy, and expiate
4. soporific
5. preternatural, preclude, and consonant
6. conformity and eccentricity
7. E
8. C
9. B
10. C
11. B
12. However, patients suffering from depression only begin to experience mood elevation weeks after beginning treatment.
13. edifying and didactic
14. satiate and allay
15. iridescent and pavonine
16. cauterized and inured
17. D
18. C
19. The argument has been made that the painting struck a blow for the independence of the artist, and that since Courbet's work, artists have felt freed from the societal demands placed upon their work.
20. A

INTERPRETING YOUR RESULTS

After you check your answers on the following pages, fill out this sheet to interpret your results.

Analytical Writing

To evaluate your performance on the Analytical Writing sections, compare your response to the advice and samples in the Analytical Writing chapter.

Verbal Reasoning

Refer to the explanations to check your answers. Count the number of questions you got correct in each Verbal Reasoning section, and calculate the total number correct. Find the section of the Interpretive Guide (below) that corresponds to your total to get an idea of how your performance compares to that of other test takers.

Test 1	# Correct
Section 4	
Section 6	
Total	

Quantitative Reasoning

Refer to the explanations to check your answers. Count the number of questions you got correct in each Quantitative Reasoning section, and calculate the total number correct. Find the section of the Interpretive Guide (below) that corresponds to your total to get an idea of how your performance compares to that of other test takers.

Test 1	# Correct
Section 3	
Section 5	
Total	

Interpretive Guide

The table below provides a guide for interpreting your performance based on the number of questions you got correct in each subject.

Subject	Above Average	Average	Below Average
Verbal Reasoning	30–40	22–29	1–21
Quantitative Reasoning	33–40	24–32	1–23

Section 3

1. **A** Point *C* has the same *x*–coordinate as point *D*, so *s* = 8. Point *C* also has the same *y*-coordinate as point *B*, so *t* = 7. That means that Quantity A is greater.

2. **A** The punch is made with two parts soda and three parts ice cream. This means that in one mixture if you added two parts of soda, then that's $4 \times 2 = 8$ parts sugar and $5 \times 2 = 10$ parts citric acid. If you added three parts ice cream, then that's $3 \times 3 = 9$ parts sugar and $2 \times 3 = 6$ parts citric acid. There's $8 + 9 = 17$ total parts sugar and $10 + 6 = 16$ total parts citric acid. There's more sugar than citric acid. Choice (A) is correct.

3. **B** This is a Quant Comp question with variables, so Plug In more than once. To easily compare the two quantities, recycle the number in the problems by Plugging In *x* = 5. This problem involves averages, so draw an Average Pie. If *x* = 5, and the average high temperature over the course of 5 days is 70 degrees, then the total temperature for the 5 days is $5 \times 70 = 350$. The problem states that one additional day has a high temperature of 75 degrees, so draw another average pie. There are now six days and the total high temperature is $350 + 75 = 425$ and the average high temperature for the six days is $\frac{425}{6} = 70\frac{5}{6}$. This is less than the 71 degree average specified in the problem. Because the two quantities cannot both equal 5, eliminate (C). If it is unclear whether the value for *x* needs to be greater or less than 5 to make the average high temperature at the end of the problem equal to 71 degrees, Plug In again. This time, try a number less than 5, such as *x* = 4. If *x* = 4, then the total temperature for 4 days with an average of 70 degrees is $4 \times 70 = 280$. The addition of one day with a high temperature of 75 degrees means that the total high temperature is $280 + 75 = 355$ over the course of 5 days. Therefore, the average is $\frac{355}{5} = 71$. Therefore, the correct value of *x* is 4 and so the value of Quantity A is 4. This is less than the value of Quantity B, so the correct answer is (B).

4. **D** Because $\triangle QRS$ is isosceles, side *RS* must be equal to one of the other sides, and *x* could measure 4 or 7. Thus, the perimeter could be $4 + 4 + 7 = 15$, or the perimeter could be $4 + 7 + 7 = 18$. You can't tell if the perimeter is greater or less than 17, so the answer is (D). Remember, you cannot trust the figure to be drawn to scale!

5. **E and F** Start by finding the mean for Set A—this can be done by calculating the sum of the set divided by 4, or by observing that the numbers are evenly spaced, so the sum must be the average of the two middle numbers. The total variance of the set (the total distance of the members from the mean) is 8. Therefore, the possible values of *x* must create a total variance for Set B of equal to or greater than 8. Since the values of Set A are evenly spaced with a difference of 2 between each value, look for the answer choice that creates the same condition for Set B. The value 18 creates the set {12, 14, 16, 18}, which has a mean of 15 and a total variance from the mean of 8. This set would thus have the same standard deviation as that of Set A. Since the question asks for the values of *x* that would create a Set B with a higher standard deviation than that of Set A, *x* must be greater than 18. The correct answers are (E) and (F).

6. **C** Plug In numbers for the sides. Let *AD* = 4, so *EG* = 8. Let *l* = 3. The area of *ABCD* = $3 \times 4 = 12$, and the area of *EFG* = $\frac{1}{2}(3 \times 8) = 12$. The two quantities can be equal, so eliminate (A) and (B). Try changing your numbers, and you will see that the two quantities will always be equal.

7. **B** FOIL out the equation given, and you'll get $(3x - 4y)(3x + 4y) = 9x^2 - 16y^2$, so Quantity A is 2. Quantity B is therefore bigger, and the answer is (B).

8. **C** Solve for a by adding 2 to each side to get $8a = 24$. Divide by 8 to find $a = 3$. Plug $a = 3$ into the second equation to find $4(3) - 1 = 12 - 1 = 11$. Alternatively, you could save yourself some time by noticing that $8a - 2$ is $2(4a - 1)$. If $2(4a - 1) = 22$, divide by 2 to get $4a - 1 = 11$.

9. **56** Twenty percent of the sweaters in the store are white, so there are $200 \times \dfrac{20}{100} = 40$ white sweaters. There are $200 - 40 = 160$ sweaters remaining. Of the remaining sweaters, $160 \times \dfrac{40}{100} = 64$ are brown. That means that $160 - 64 = 96$ are blue. There are $96 - 40 = 56$ more blue sweaters than white sweaters.

10. **D** Because 4^{12} is a common factor of both 4^{13} and 4^{12}, you can rewrite the numerator as $4^{12}(4 - 1)$. Now look at the whole fraction: $\dfrac{4^{12}(4-1)}{4^{11}}$. You can divide 4^{12} by 4^{11}, leaving you with $4^1(4 - 1)$. Now the calculation should be much easier: $4 \times 3 = 12$, (D).

11. **A** The question deals with the total number of nationwide newsmagazine subscriptions in 1995 and 2010. These years are only present in the top chart, so use this chart to determine the total number of nationwide newsmagazine subscriptions in these years. In 1995, newsmagazine x represented 24.6% of total nationwide newsmagazine subscriptions and there were 1.5 thousand subscriptions. Set up an equation to find that $1.5 = 24.6 / 100$ (total) and the total is 6.09 thousand subscriptions in 1995. In 2010, newsmagazine x represented 11.7% of total nationwide newsmagazine subscriptions and there were 10.5 thousand subscriptions. Set up an equation to find that $10.5 = 11.7 / 100$ (total) and the total is 89.74 thousand subscriptions. The question asks what percent less the total number nationwide newsmagazine subscriptions is from the total number of nationwide newsmagazine subscriptions in 2010. Use the percent change formula to find that $89.74 - 6.09 / 89.74 = 93.2\%$.

The correct answer is choice (A).

12. **B** In 2006, Newsmagazine z accounted for 9,400 out of 57,000 newsmagazine subscriptions. Therefore, Newsmagazine z accounted for approximately 9,000 out of 57,000, or $\dfrac{1}{6}$, of the nationwide newsmagazine subscriptions.

13. **D** In 1995, there were 1,500 subscriptions to Newsmagazine x, which accounted for approximately 25 percent of total nationwide subscriptions. Total nationwide subscriptions in 1995, then, were equal to about 6,000 (25 percent of total nationwide subscriptions = 1,500). Using the same process, total nationwide subscriptions in 1996 were equal to about 9,000 (30 percent of total nationwide subscriptions = 2,600). The percent increase between 1995 and 1996 is $\dfrac{difference}{original}$ or $\dfrac{9,000 - 6,000}{6,000} = \dfrac{3,000}{6,000} = \dfrac{1}{2}$, or 50 percent.

14. **C** In 1998, Newsmagazine x had 3,300 subscriptions, or 20.5 percent of the total number of newsmagazine subscriptions. Set up the calculation to find the total: $3,300 = \dfrac{20.5}{100}x$. Solve it to find that $x = 16,000$.

15. **C** $a = 27 \times \dfrac{1}{3^2} = 3$, and $x = 6 \times \dfrac{1}{3} = 2$. Find $(12)(3^{-x})(15)(2^{-4}) = (12)(3^{-2})(15)(2^{-3}) = \dfrac{(12)(15)}{(3^2)(2^3)}$. Now, reduce: $\dfrac{(2 \times 2 \times 3)(3 \times 5)}{(3 \times 3)(2 \times 2 \times 2)} = \dfrac{5}{2}$.

16. **B and D**   Use the Average Pie to find that Jill's mean of 3.75 for 8 evaluations gives her a current total of $3.75 \times 8 = 30$ points. Use the Average Pie to find that if she needs an average of 4.0 for 12 scores, she needs $4.0 \times 12 = 48$ total points. Jill still needs $48 - 30 = 18$ points. Her four remaining scores must total 18 or greater. Only (B) and (D) have a total of at least 18.

17. **270**   To answer this question remember that each angle in a rectangle is 90 degrees and there are 180 degrees in a triangle. Look at the figure. When presented with a shape like this, look for shapes that are familiar. The rectangle has been divided into 4 separate triangles. Three of the triangles have one side of the triangle that is represented by the angle of the original rectangle. For example, a triangle is represented by the angles of a and b as well as the 90 degree angle that is represented by point S. Since there are 180 degrees in a triangle, and 90 of those degrees are found at point S, the sum of angles a and b is 90. The same principle can be applied to the triangle that is created by angles c, d, and point T, as well as the triangle created by angles e, f, and point U. Since this is true, $c + d = 90$ and $e + f = 90$. Therefore, the sum of all the angles is 270.

18. **B**   Plug In the Answers, starting with (C). If the total is 55, then the probability would be $\left(\dfrac{3}{55}\right)\left(\dfrac{2}{54}\right)$, which does not equal $\dfrac{3}{55}$. The denominator is too large, so try (B). If the total is 11, then the probability is $\left(\dfrac{3}{11}\right)\left(\dfrac{2}{10}\right)$, which reduces to $\dfrac{3}{55}$.

19. **E**   Use the group formula to solve this problem, which is Total = Group 1 + Group 2 − Both + Neither. Because the question states that all the students have to take calculus, English composition, or both there is no Neither group. So, Neither = 0. The question states the half the students take calculus and half to do not so 1,200 students take calculus and 1,200 do not. The question then states that one-third of the students who take calculus also take English composition. This means that one-third of 1,200 students take both calculus and English composition, so Both = 400. Because 400 of the 1,200 students who take calculus also take English composition, then the number of students who take only calculus is $1,200 - 400 = 800$. Make Group 1 the number of students who only take calculus. The question states that there are 2,400 students, so the formula is now $2,400 = 800 + \text{Group 2} - 400$. Group 2 is the number of students who take only English composition. Find the value of Group 2, which is 2,000. The correct answer is choice (E).

20. **A**   To solve this expression you need to break apart the factorial of 13 to the common prime number in the denominator, in this case the number 2. 13! can be expressed as $13 \times 12 \times 11 \times 10 \times 9 \times 8 \times 7 \times 6 \times 5 \times 4 \times 3 \times 2 \times 1$. When you break apart this factorial into its prime numbers, you are left with $13 \times 11 \times 7 \times 5^2 \times 3^5 \times 2^{10}$. For a fraction to result in an integer, the denominator of the fraction must share at least one prime factor with the numerator. The greatest number of 2s that can be found in the prime factorization of 13! is 10, so $x \leq 10$. Eliminate (B), (C), and (E). Now for the tricky part! Any nonzero number raised to the power 0 is 1. Since the result when any integer is divided by 1 is also an integer, 0 must be included in the range of possible x values. The answer is (A).

Section 4

1. **prowess** and **maladroit**

   The first blank has a strong clue, so begin there. The blank is describing the *professor...as a teacher* and gives further insight that *she shows more...teaching skills* than her colleagues. The transition word *and* indicates that there is consistency between her description as a *noteworthy intellect* and her skills as a teacher. Therefore, a good word for the first blank is "skills." Choice (A), *prowess*, is a good match for "skills" so keep (A). Choice (B), *profligacy*, means reckless extravagance and (C), *orthodoxies*, means beliefs. Eliminate (B) and (C). The second blank is describing the professor's *colleagues...teaching skills*. The sentence gives further insight by stating that the professor shows more skills than her colleagues. Therefore, a good word for the blank is "unskilled" or "not good." Choice (D), *spurious*, means fake which is not a match for "unskilled" so eliminate (D). Choice (E), *maladroit*, is a good match for the blank, so keep (E). Choice (F), *eclectic*, means from different sources, so eliminate (F). The correct answer is (A) and (E).

2. **irresponsible, forestall,** and **avoidable**

   The keys to the first blank are the clues "given their responsibilities as democratically elected officials" and "neglect to do everything they could." These clues indicate that the first blank should have a negative connotation; a word that means something as simple as *bad* would eliminate *thoughtful* and *intuitive*, leaving *irresponsible*. Blanks (ii) and (iii) build on the idea set up in the first half of the sentence. The second blank describes the action that would be bad, so use something that means solve. *Sustain* and *cultivate* are the opposites of what's needed for the second blank, leaving *forestall*. The last blank describes the type of problem, and entirely suggests it's a solvable problem. *Avoidable* is close, and it helps the whole sentence make sense.

3. **erudite**

   Despite is a transition word that implies a contrast between the student's actual behavior when presenting her thesis and her mentor's advice. The student resorted to using slang, language that is informal and unscholarly. Therefore, the word in the blank must mean *formal* or *scholarly*. The only word that fits that description is *erudite*, which is the best choice. The other answer choices can be used to describe speech, but none of these words contrast the mentor's advice with the student's use of slang.

4. **augmented, overwhelmed,** and **delicate**

   Start with the second blank. The clue *pungent* tells you this onion did something bad to the delicious stew. *Exaggerated* and *satiated* are positive; *overwhelmed* is the only fit. The transition *otherwise* tells you to change direction from the third blank's clue of *pungent*. Look for a word that means *subtle* or *soft*. Only *delicate* fits. For the first blank, the clue is that Steve's stinky onion hurt the delicate stew. The transition *although* tells you to change direction. So, this addition of the sweet potato was good. Only *augmented* fits.

5. **banal, an adept,** and **sublime**

   The first clue is *its focus on such everyday objects as flowers or fruits apparently uninspired,* so the first blank has to mean something such as "uninspired." *Banal,* which means predictable, matches this. For the second blank, the painter must pay *careful attention,* so the second blank must mean "careful" or "talented," which matches *an adept*. Since the painting is *exemplary,* the third blank must be *sublime*.

6. **comely** and **prepossessing**

The first blank describes Viktor Yuschenko's face. The clue is that his face was *transformed into a monstrous mask by dioxin poisoning* and the transition word *once* tells us an appropriate word for the blank would be the opposite of monstrous; something like attractive would work nicely. *Quiescent* means calm, and *fatuous* means foolish, so those words don't work. *Comely*, which means attractive, is the only word that works. The second blank is describing Yulia Tymoshenko. Both the transition phrase *a study in contrasts* and the clue about *fashion magazines* suggest that a word that means beautiful is appropriate. Though it might not sound like it, *prepossessing* does, in fact, mean beautiful. *Felicitous* means well-expressed, and *decorous* means full of propriety, so although they are both positive words, they aren't as fitting here as the credited response is.

7. **D** According to the first sentence, her work can be viewed three different ways. The rest of the passage describes those ways: as the work of a modern poet, of a woman, and of a Native American. Choice (A) is too vague, and the passage doesn't so much describe her work as how it should be viewed. Choices (B) and (C) are too narrow and don't describe the overall purpose. Choice (E) doesn't match the passage.

8. **B** In the second paragraph the author states, "Mr. Wilson's praise gives the impression that Feather's readership is limited to her own culture—an impression which hints that Mr. Wilson is himself measuring her by only one criterion," which best fits (B). Choices (A) and (E) contradict the passage and are too broad and extreme. Choice (C) contradicts the passage, and (D) is not supported.

9. **E** The second sentence of the passage claims, "We could consider her poems as the product of a twentieth-century artist in the tradition of James Joyce, T.S. Eliot, and Wallace Stevens." Thus, the author mentions Joyce, Eliot, and Stevens in order to describe one context—twentieth-century poetry—in which Feather's work can be analyzed. Eliminate (A) because the author doesn't compare Feather's political messages to those of these authors. Eliminate (B) because the author doesn't use these authors to discuss differences between male and female poets. Eliminate (C) because the author doesn't contrast Feather's themes with those of these authors. Although Joyce, Eliot, and Stevens were, like Feather, twentieth-century artists, the passage doesn't say that they shared sensibilities, which eliminates (D). Choice (E) is the answer.

10. **C** Only (C) provides a clue to the meaning of *urbane* as used here: the urbane buyer is contrasted with the "unsuspecting or naïve buyer," so it must mean "not unsuspecting" or "not naïve." Choice (A) tantalizingly dangles the word "rural" before our eyes, trying to take advantage of that word's well-known association with the word *urban*. *Urbane*, though, means *sophisticated*. Moreover, if (A) were accepted, the strangely illogical proposition that city-dwellers knew best how to buy animals at market would have to be accepted as well. Choice (B), thankfully, presents no such difficulties of interpretation and appears in the definition of the obscure expression itself, not in the comparison between unsuspecting and urbane.

11. **It relates to the common Renaissance practice of securing suckling pigs for transport to market in a poke, or drawstring bag.**

In this sentence the author defines the term "poke" as a drawstring bag. This is the only instance in which the author gives a definition for a word that the reader may not be familiar with because the word "poke" is not a common term used to describe a drawstring bag.

12. **propriety** and **decorum**

The clue is "was such a bad-mannered child." Time acts as a change-of-direction transition ("as an adult") that indicates the blank should mean something like well-mannered. Only *propriety* and *decorum* mean well-mannered. *Diffidence*, *reticence*, and *brashness* are all traits that would be considered bad-mannered. *Friendliness* does not necessarily mean well-mannered.

13. **whimsical** and **capricious**

    The blank describes how politicians act. The clue is "acting according to a deliberate plan." The change-of-direction transition *however* tells you that they appear not to have a plan. Words that mean unplanned or random should be in the blank. Both *whimsical* and *capricious* fit this meaning. *Conventional* and *conformist* have the opposite meaning. The other two words are unrelated to the blank.

14. **irksome** and **onerous**

    The transition *even more* tells you to stay in the same direction as the clue. "Forced to take an alternate road," "two-hour detour," and "arduous trip" tell you that the journey was difficult. Put a word that means hard or tiring in the blank. Only *irksome* and *onerous* fit this meaning. *Facile* and *glib* describe something easy, and *implacable* and *immutable* describe something that doesn't change.

15. **adventurous** and **doughty**

    The transition *especially* tells you to stay in the same direction as the clue "willingness to reject prevailing feminine roles and to travel to foreign lands alone." Thus, she has a bold spirit. Only *adventurous* and *doughty* mean bold. Although she is traveling alone, there is nothing to support that she is lonely, as *forlorn* and *desolate* suggest. *Magnanimous* and *bellicose* do not fit.

16. **A** The argument concludes that the substitution of microfiber clothes for those made from natural fabrics is not financially sound. The premise is that microfiber clothes last as long as natural fabric clothes but are three times as expensive to produce. The argument assumes that there are no other factors that need to be considered to evaluate the cost effectiveness of switching. Choice (A) points out another factor that would affect the overall costs and so weakens the argument. Choice (B) helps to explain why the microfiber synthetic shirt is more expensive to produce than a natural fiber shirt, but it does not weaken the argument. In (C), comparing natural fiber shirts and other fiber garments is not relevant. Choice (D) strengthens the argument. Choice (E), by pointing out additional costs associated with microfibers, also strengthens the argument.

17. **E** The first paragraph presents the Gandhara-first view that "Greek influence in Gandhara promoted the development of the new style and form of representation of the divine." The second paragraph provides evidence Gandharan Buddhas shared certain features with Greek art. Choice (E) provides additional information about those similarities and is the best choice. Choices (A) and (C) undermine the idea that Gandharan artists were responding to outside influences. Choice (B) is irrelevant, and (D) provides evidence for outside influences in Mathura.

18. **B** The first sentence says that "images in human form emerged around the first century A.D.," and the middle of the first paragraph states that "earlier Buddhist art was largely aniconic." You can conclude from these statements that the earliest Buddhist art didn't usually depict the Buddha in human form. Eliminate (A); although human representations first appeared in these regions, the passage doesn't say that the first Buddhist art appeared in the same places. The passage doesn't support (C), (D), and (E).

19. **B** and **C**

    For (A), the passage says only that the age of these fossils was "far too recent for humans to have evolved" from them. This does not give an age for the fossils. The last sentence says that "the concept of 'missing link' has changed dramatically," which answers the question in (B). The last sentence also answers the question in (C) because it says, "the value of his discovery and the debate it generated is unquestionable."

20. **Although the concept of "missing link" has changed dramatically and a recent analysis showed Dubois's fossils to be far too recent for humans to have evolved from this "missing link," the value of his discovery and the debate it generated is unquestionable.**

    In the last sentence, the author states that the value of Dubois's fossils is "unquestionable." This statement represents the author's conclusion.

Section 5

1. **B** Draw the figure. You have a square with a circle inside of it that has a radius of 6. Therefore, the length of one side of the square is 12. Quantity A asks for the area of the largest triangle that can be drawn inside the square. The largest triangle cuts the square in half diagonally (subsequently creating a 45:45:90 triangle) and has a height and base of length 12. So the area of the triangle is $\frac{1}{2}$ (12)(12) = 72. Quantity B is asking for the area of the circle with center R. So the area of the circle is $6^2\pi$, or 36π. π is approximately 3, so you know that 36 times 3 is greater than 72. Quantity B is greater.

2. **D** There are a lot of variables in this problem, so start thinking about Plugging In. The variable a has to be the same for each equation. You cannot pick just any number, however, because you must satisfy the equations. When you feel stuck on a problem, start looking at the numbers; remember the math will always work out nicely. Examining the two equations, you realize that $158 \times 4 = 632$, so these two numbers are related. So the easiest number to Plug In for a is 632. Now you know that $xs = 1$, and $ys = 4$. Since the variable s is the same in both equations, they cancel each other out and you are left with $x = 1$ and $y = 4$. Eliminate (A) and (C). Next, try a FROZEN number such as $a = -632$. In this case, $xs = -1$ and $ys = -4$ or $x = -1$ and $y = -4$. Eliminate (B). The correct answer is (D).

3. **C** $135 \div 7 = 19$, remainder 2. $135 \div 19 = 7$, remainder 2. Both Quantity A and Quantity B equal 2.

4. **D** Plug In. Let $a = 8$ and $b = 4$. Quantity A can be greater than Quantity B, so eliminate (B) and (C). Now let $a = b = 1$. Quantity A can be equal to Quantity B, so eliminate (A).

5. **B** Plug In numbers for a, b, and c. If $a = -2$, $b = 3$, and $c = 4$, then $ac = -8$. Quantity B is greater; eliminate (A) and (C). If $a = 2$, $b = -3$, and $c = -4$, then ac is still negative. Quickly consider different numbers, but realize that Quantity A will always be negative.

6. **D** If $|x| = 6$, then $x = 6$, or $x = -6$. If $x = 6$, then $y = 6 + 4 = 10$. The quantities are equal, so you can eliminate (A) and (B). If $x = -6$, then $y = -6 + 4 = -2$, and Quantity B is greater. Eliminate (C), and select (D).

7. **B** Plug In for the radius, n, and solve for x. Let's make $n = 3$: The area of the base of the cylinder is now 9π, and the circumference of the base is 6π. The ribbon itself is a rectangle, and we now know both its area, which is the same as the area of the base, and its length, which is the same as the circumference of the base. Now we can solve for x, which is the other side of the rectangle: $6\pi x = 9\pi$, so $x = \dfrac{9\pi}{6\pi}$, or $\dfrac{3}{2}$. Our value for n is greater than our value for x, so Quantity B is greater.

8. **C** Remember that median is the number that ends up in the middle of the list when you rewrite the list in numerical order. Find x: the even numbers are 2, 2, 6, 8. Because 2 and 6 are in the middle, find their

mean: $\frac{2+6}{2}$ = 4. So, x = 4. Find y: the prime numbers are 2, 2, 3, 5, 7, 13. Remember: 1 is not prime. Because 3 and 5 are in the middle, find their mean: $\frac{3+5}{2}$ = 4. So, y = 4. Find z: the least is 1, and the greatest is 15. The median of 1 and 15 is $\frac{1+15}{2}$ = 8. So, z = 8. For Quantity A, find the median of 2(4), 4, and 8. So, the median of 4, 8, 8 is 8. Quantity B is also 8.

9. **1,625**

Set up a proportion: $\frac{1 \text{ hour}}{500 \text{ gallons}} = \frac{3.25 \text{ hours}}{x \text{ gallons}}$. Cross multiply to find that x = 500 × 3.25 = 1,625 gallons.

10. **B** Plug In the Answers, starting with the middle choice. If 120 dogs were sold in March, then 60 cats were sold that month. In April, 240 dogs were sold, along with 180 cats. The total number of dogs and cats sold during those two months is 600, which is too large, so eliminate (C), (D), and (E). Try (B). If there were 100 dogs sold in March, then 50 cats were sold; in April, 200 dogs were sold along with 150 cats. The correct answer is (B) because 100 + 50 + 200 + 150 = 500.

11. **C**

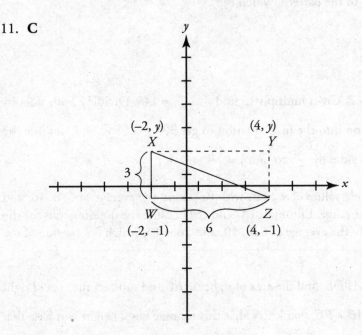

Notice that the length of WZ is 4 – (–2) = 6. If the area is 18 = 6 × w, then w is equal to 3. Now you have a right triangle with legs of 3 and 6. Use the Pythagorean Theorem: $3^2 + 6^2 = c^2$, or 9 + 36 = c^2. So, $c = \sqrt{45} = \sqrt{9 \times 5} = 3\sqrt{5}$.

12. **E** Order matters in this problem, so remember you do not divide; you multiply! For the first integer, you have 5 options. For the second, you have 4. For the third, you have 3; 5 × 4 × 3 is 60, which is (E).

13. **D** The percent increase in the CEO's pay was $\frac{\$50 - \$5}{5} \times 100\%$ = 900 percent. The percent decrease in the factory workers' pay was $\frac{\$20 - \$10}{20} \times 100\%$ = 50 percent. To find what percent greater 900 percent is than 50 percent, do the following: $\frac{900\% - 50\%}{50\%} \times 100\%$ = 1,700 percent, or (D).

14. **D** Divide the $9.4 million in private donations received by child safety organizations in September 1989 by the 38 organizations operating at the time. The amount is approximately $250,000.

15. **C** From the line graph, you see that homeless aid groups took in about $300 million in private donations, and animal rights groups about $225 million. The ratio of $300 million to $225 million is 4 to 3.

16. **E** Identify the markers for September 1989 and October 1989 on the chart. The question is asking about the least percent increase between these two data points. So, begin by evaluating the data points. All of the differences between the data points for these two months are very similar; they all seem to have a difference of approximately 0.5. Because 0.5 is a lesser percent of a greater number, the least percent increase corresponds to the data point with the greatest numbers. Therefore, the correct answer is (E), *child safety*. Alternatively, find the percent increase for each of the answer choices by dividing the difference between the two points by the original, which in this case is the number for September 1989. The least percent increase is still (E), *child safety*, which is the correct answer.

17. **D** This is a pattern problem. The pattern has five digits: 06539. Divide 34 by 5, which gives you a remainder of 4. So the 34th digit will be the fourth in the pattern, which is 3.

18. $\dfrac{48}{7}$

First, solve for x using the equation $\dfrac{7y}{2x} = 7$. Cross multiply to find that $7y = 14x$. Dividing both sides by 14 yields $\dfrac{1}{2}y = x$. Substitute this expression into the first equation to get $3(\dfrac{1}{2}y) + 2y = 24$. Combine the like terms to get $\dfrac{7}{2}y = 24$; multiply both sides by $\dfrac{2}{7}$ to find $y = \dfrac{48}{7}$.

19. **C** Plug In the Answers, which are the possible values of x. Start with (C). Find the average of 6, 8, 10, and 23, which is 11.75, which is in the correct range. Eliminate (A) and (B) because the question asks for the greatest possible value of x. Next, try (D). The average of 6, 8, 10, and 28 is 13, which lies outside of the range. The correct answer is (C).

20. **A** Plug In! To find the area of quadrilateral $ABDE$, find the area of right $\triangle ABC$ and subtract the area of right $\triangle EDC$. Make $a = 4$ and $b = 2$. Because $AB = BC$, you know that this triangle has a height and base that are both equal to 4. The area of ABC is $4 \times 4 \times \dfrac{1}{2} = 8$. The area of EDC is $2 \times 2 \times \dfrac{1}{2} = 2$. The area of $ABDE$ is $8 - 2 = 6$. Plug In for a and b and find that (A) is the only one that works. Alternatively, to find the area of quadrilateral $ABDE$, find the area of right $\triangle ABC$ and subtract the area of right $\triangle EDC$. Both the base and the height of $\triangle ABC$ are a, so the area equals $\dfrac{1}{2} \times a \times a$, or $\dfrac{a^2}{2}$. Both the base and the height of $\triangle EDC$ are b, so the area equals $\dfrac{1}{2} \times b \times b$, or $\dfrac{b^2}{2}$. Therefore, the area of quadrilateral $ABDE$ is $\dfrac{a^2}{2} - \dfrac{b^2}{2}$.

Section 6

1. **original** and **outlandish**

   Try working with the second blank first. The clues are that the fashions were "considered daring" and then "imitated." Starting with the second blank, the sentence suggests that the fashions have changed from what they once were—in other words, daring. *Outlandish* is a good synonym for daring and it makes sense that, in the first blank, the fashions were *original* and then lost their impact because of excess imitation.

2. **diverge**

   Take note of the time transition *at one time inseparable...now*, which indicates that the combined roles in Middle Eastern music are now not inseparable. You need a word that means divide or separate. *Divulge* starts with the proper root, but its meaning is way off. Meanwhile, neither *retreat* nor *retrench* means divide, while *fuse* is the opposite of what you want. *Diverge* is the correct answer.

3. **rebuked, perfidy,** and **expiate**

   Start with the second blank, which must mean something close to an act of "treachery." *Perfidy* means this. Since his contemporaries believed Kazan had committed treachery, they would have "harshly criticized" him, so the first blank means *rebuked*. For the last blank, he was able to achieve *atonement*, which is what *expiate* means.

4. **soporific**

   The sentence requires you to figure out the effect that "tranquilizers usually have," and this is provided by the clue in the later part of the sentence, when you read that the "abuse of these drugs results in a failure to induce the much-desired sleep." You can infer that the usual effect of tranquilizers is to produce sleep. *Soporific*, which means sleep-inducing, is the correct answer choice. While *sedulous* might remind you of "sedative," it actually means hardworking.

5. **preternatural, preclude,** and **consonant**

   The clue for the first blank is "are rejected by modern science in its attempts to find secular insights." Otherworldly interpretations contrast the secular, and the best choice for the first blank is *preternatural*. There would be a paradox only if scientists could hold non-secular beliefs. Therefore, a good word for the second blank is *prevent*, and a good phrase for the last blank would be *in agreement*. *Preclude* is synonymous with *prevent*, and *consonant* is synonymous with *in agreement*, making these the correct answers.

6. **conformity** and **eccentricity**

   Try working with the second blank first. The clue is "none of the family members were fearful...of appearing or acting differently from other people." Therefore, find a word for the second blank that means uniqueness. *Eccentricity* fits the bill. Considering the clue, "The Johnsons were not known for their," the two blanks must be opposites. Eliminate *candor* and *vulgarity* based on the clue and the word choice for the second blank, and choose *conformity*.

7. **E** In the last paragraph, the author discusses the difficulties inherent in measuring intergalactic distances. He notes that scientists use a standard candle in combination with the inverse square law to measure those distances.

8. **C** The passage states in the third paragraph that brighter objects are closer than dim objects, so eliminate (A). The passage never specifies what scientists know about the age of astronomical objects, so eliminate (B). The first paragraph says that, according to Hubble's law, "objects farther away from Earth are receding faster than those closer." This means that the farther object will travel faster, so (C) is correct.

9. **B** According to the last line in the paragraph, "By the inverse square law, galaxy B is ten times farther away than galaxy A, assuming, of course, that distance is the only factor affecting brightness." Therefore, if interstellar dust affects the brightness of an object, the brightness of the object is affected, and the distance scientists measure may be inaccurate.

10. **C** According to the passage, "By the inverse square law, galaxy B is ten times farther away than galaxy A, assuming, of course, that distance is the only factor affecting brightness." Therefore, assuming that all other factors affecting brightness can be known, we can conclude that the brighter of the supernovas will be closer to Earth.

11. **B** "Prozac lag" is a phenomenon for which there is currently no explanation, but neurogenesis may offer a solution. Choice (A) contradicts this. The passage offers "Prozac lag" as supporting evidence of a new theory, not disproving an old one, as (C) suggests, or disproving a new one, as (D) states. Choice (E) goes too far by discussing "unforeseen effects." Choice (B) is the best option.

12. **However, patients suffering from depression only begin to experience mood elevation weeks after beginning treatment.**

    The second paragraph has five sentences, so this question has five answer choices. For an "unexpected observation," a good place to start would be to check the transition words. The fourth sentence starts with the word "however." While the effects should occur immediately, these don't occur until weeks after starting treatment. The answer is the fourth sentence.

13. **edifying** and **didactic**

    The blank describes Socrates's conversations. The clue is "Socrates's teachings have survived and continue to enlighten seekers of wisdom," so the blank must mean instructional. *Edifying* and *didactic* are the closest in meaning. *Tedious, grating, inspiring,* and *rousing* could all be used to describe Socrates's conversations, but they do not match the clue.

14. **satiate** and **allay**

    You would expect "the colossal meal" to fill someone up, but the sentence says that "failed to…her voracious appetite." Thus, she was not full, and the meal failed to satisfy. *Satiate* and *allay* are the best match. *Cadge* and *mendicate* mean the meal begged her hunger. *Exacerbate* and *provoke* go in the wrong direction.

15. **iridescent** and **pavonine**

    The clue for this sentence is "the lovely rainbows they produce," which suggests that the blank should be filled by a word meaning colorful. Both *iridescent* and *pavonine* mean exactly that. Even if you don't agree that the blank necessarily refers to rainbows of color, the missing word does have to agree with *beautiful* due to the transition word *and*, and none of the other four options does: *anodyne* means eliminating physical pain, *monocoque* means constructed in one piece, *parietal* mean college-related, and *saturnine* means gloomy.

16. **cauterized** and **inured**

   The clue for this sentence is *callous,* so the blank must mean "used to," or "didn't notice." Choices (B), *cauterized,* and (E), *inured,* mean this. Choice (F) is incorrect because he didn't notice the violence more, but rather noticed it less.

17. **D** The conclusion of the argument is that the old formula for Megapower contained natural kiwi extract, while the new formula does not. The evidence is that Tasmania suffered a decrease in its kiwi exports. The assumption is that Megapower is not getting kiwi fruit from Tasmania. Choice (D) strengthens the argument by pointing out that kiwi imports have fallen in the country that produces Megapower, which would reinforce that assumption that the manufacturer is not getting kiwis from Tasmania. Choice (A) would weaken the argument by providing a potential alternate source for kiwi fruit. Choice (C) weakens the argument by providing evidence that the manufacturer of Megapower could be getting kiwi fruit from another source. Choices (B) and (E) are not relevant to the conclusion.

18. **C** While the word *promulgated* can take on the meanings given in (A), (B), or (C), within the context of the sentence it is clear that Courbet is taking a stand on what he believes art should be. Therefore, (C) is closest to the correct meaning.

19. **The argument has been made that the painting struck a blow for the independence of the artist, and that since Courbet's work, artists have felt freed from the societal demands placed upon their work.**

   While the rest of the passage enumerates Courbet's ideas on painting, only this sentence points to the effect that Courbet's work may have had on other artists when it states that "since Courbet's work artists have felt freed from the societal demands placed on their work."

20. **A** According to the passage, Courbet broke with convention by "striving to do something strikingly original." Only (A) provides that sense of defying a convention to do something original.

Practice Test 2

SECTION 1: ISSUE TOPIC

Directions:

You will be given a brief quotation that states or implies an issue of general interest and specific instructions on how to respond to that issue. You will have 30 minutes to plan and compose a response in which you develop a position on the issue according to the specific instructions. A response to any other issue will receive a score of zero.

"Studying foodways—what foods people eat and how they produce, acquire, prepare, and consume them—is the best way to gain deep understanding of a culture."

Write an essay in which you take a position on the statement above. In developing and supporting your position, you should consider ways in which the statement might or might not hold true.

SECTION 2: ARGUMENT TOPIC

Directions:

You will be given a short passage that presents an argument, or an argument to be completed, and specific instructions on how to respond to that passage. You will have 30 minutes to plan and compose a response in which you analyze the passage according to the specific instructions. A response to any other argument will receive a score of zero.

Note that you are NOT being asked to present your own views on the subject. Make sure that you respond to the specific instructions and support your analysis with relevant reasons and/or examples.

Fossil evidence indicates that the blompus—an extremely large, carnivorous land mammal—inhabited the continent of Pentagoria for tens of thousands of years until its sudden decline and ultimate extinction about twelve thousand years ago. Scientists have determined that the extinction coincided with a period of significant climate change and with the arrival of the first humans. Some scholars theorize that the climate change so altered the distribution of plants and animals in the environment that the food chain upon which the blompus depended was irretrievably disrupted. Others contend that predation by humans is the more plausible explanation for the rapid population decline.

Write a response in which you discuss specific evidence that could be used to decide between the proposed explanations above.

SECTION 3: VERBAL REASONING

For questions 1 through 6, select one entry for each blank from the corresponding column of choices. Fill all blanks in the way that best completes the text.

The (i)_____ with which a statement is conveyed is frequently more important to the listener in determining the intended meaning than the actual words (ii)_____ . For example, a compliment, when delivered sarcastically, will be perceived by the receiver as fairly insulting.

Blank (i)	Blank (ii)
inflection	implied
pitch	repudiated
accuracy	utilized

Though a film studio produces works that are (i)_____ and artistic, its priorities often dictate that creativity be (ii)_____ to a secondary position since the creative process can (iii)_____ the organization and hierarchy necessary to running a large company.

Blank (i)	Blank (ii)	Blank (iii)
expressive	compared	respond to
tedious	uplifted	conflict with
tiresome	relegated	coexist with

Science and religion each have core tenets that are considered _____ ; however, because some scientific tenets are in conflict with some religious ones, these tenets cannot all be correct.

historic
axiomatic
disputable
ubiquitous
empirical

Although most preventative medical ointments commonly in use would have (i)_____ an infection, the particular one Helen applied to her sores actually, much to her dismay, (ii)_____ her (iii)_____ .

Blank (i)	Blank (ii)	Blank (iii)
surrendered to	contributed to	medicine
exacerbated	detracted from	salve
staved off	disbursed with	affliction

A single (i)_____ remark can easily ruin the career of a politician, so most are trained to avoid such offhand remarks and instead stick to prepared talking points. This training can result in a lack of (ii)_____, however, and elicit merely (iii)_____ , lukewarm responses from crowds.

Blank (i)	Blank (ii)	Blank (iii)
elated	spontaneity	ardent
glib	equanimity	tepid
pedantic	rigidity	morose

Oscar Wilde's *The Importance of Being Earnest* satirizes the _____ nature of upper crust British society; its characters take trivial concerns seriously while thoughtlessly dismissing important ones.

maladaptive
insincere
unusual
insignificant
shallow

SECTION 3: VERBAL REASONING

For each of Questions 7 to 12, select one answer choice unless otherwise instructed.

Questions 7 through 10 are based on the following reading passage.

In 1798, economist Thomas Robert Malthus stated in his "Essay on the Principle of Population" that "population increases in a geometric ratio, while the means of subsistence increases in an arithmetic ratio." However, Malthus's dire prediction of a precipitous decline in the world's population has not come to pass. The miscalculations in what has come to be known as the Malthus Doctrine are partly due to Malthus's inability to foresee the innovations that allowed vast increases in worldwide wheat production.

In the late nineteenth century, the invention of the tractor staved off a Malthusian disaster. While the first tractors were not particularly powerful, the replacement of animals by machinery meant that land that had been devoted to hay and oats could now be reclaimed for growth of crops for human consumption. Nevertheless, the Malthusian limit might still have been reached if crop yield had not been increased.

A natural way to increase crop yield is to supply the soil with additional nitrogen. In 1909, chemist Fritz Haber succeeded in combining nitrogen and hydrogen to make ammonia, the white powder version of which, when added to the soil, improves wheat production. Haber nitrogen, however, was not widely used until later in the twentieth century, largely due to farmers' resistance to spreading an unnatural substance on their crops. Haber's invention had a further drawback: If applied in incorrect quantities, the wheat crop would grow taller and thicker, eventually toppling over and rotting.

Interestingly, in the late twentieth century the discovery of genetic engineering, which provides a means of increasing rice and maize production, met with equal resistance, this time from the environmental movement. Even without direct genetic engineering, it is likely that science will discover new methods to improve agricultural production.

According to the passage, which of the following is true about Haber nitrogen?

○ Haber nitrogen is more effective at increasing the yield of wheat crops than that of maize or oat crops.

○ Undesired effects can result from the application of surplus quantities of Haber nitrogen.

○ Haber nitrogen was the first non-naturally occurring substance to be applied to crops as fertilizer.

○ Haber nitrogen may not be effective if applied at an improper time in wheat's growth cycle.

○ Farmers were quick to adopt Haber nitrogen because it made their crops grow taller and thicker.

The passage implies all of the following EXCEPT

○ world food production has kept pace with world population growth

○ technological innovation is one factor that allowed for an increase in crop production

○ farmers are not the only group that has opposed artificial efforts to increase crop yield.

○ the Malthusian limit might well have been reached if new methods to increase crop production had not been found

○ a Malthusian disaster would have been ensured if it were not for the invention of genetic engineering

SECTION 3: VERBAL REASONING

Which of the following, if true, would best represent Malthus' contention in the first paragraph?

○ By 2040 the world's population increases marginally, and food production keeps pace with demand.

○ By 2040 the world's population decreases marginally, and food production outstrips demand.

○ By 2040 the world's population remains unchanged, and food production declines slightly.

○ By 2040 the world's population has significantly increased, and food production has increased slightly.

○ By 2040 the world's population has significantly decreased, and food production has decreased slightly.

Which of the following most nearly means the word precipitous, as used in context?

○ anticipated

○ deliberate

○ gradual

○ risky

○ sharp

Questions 11 through 12 are based on the following reading passage.

The dearth of natural resources on the Australian continent is a problem with which government officials there have long struggled. As long distance travel has become less of an obstacle, the tourism industry has become ever more important to the national economy. Tourism represents more than 10 percent of national export earnings annually, and in less developed regions such as the Western Territory, the percentage is much higher.

Unfortunately, this otherwise rosy prospect has one significant cloud on the horizon. In recent years, there has been a move towards returning some of the land to the Aboriginal people. As Western society and culture have flourished on Australian soil, tribal people have been forced ever farther inland in an attempt to maintain their traditional ways of living, a desire that the government has striven to respect.

One of the central beliefs of the Aboriginal religion is that certain natural formations have spiritual significance and must be treated accordingly. Strict guidelines determine who may visit these sites and at what times. Unfortunately, many of these sites are the very natural wonders tourists flock to see. If non-Aboriginal people are forbidden to visit these natural wonders, many may choose not to vacation in a region that sorely needs the income generated by tourism.

The Australian government has dealt with this dilemma thus far by trying to support both sides. The Aboriginal council is still trying to put an end to such use of certain sites, however, and it remains to be seen whether respect for tradition or economic desires will ultimately triumph.

In the context of the passage, which of the following most closely matches the meaning of the phrase "otherwise rosy prospect has one significant cloud on the horizon"?

○ A colorful sunset is marred by a dark storm cloud.

○ A generally promising future has a potential problem.

○ The view is beautiful but partially blocked.

○ The future of the Aboriginal people is doubtful.

○ Although the situation looks good, in reality it is hopeless.

Consider each of the choices separately and select all that apply.

According to the passage, which of the following is a cause of the current dispute between the Aborigines and the Australian government?

☐ economic hardships in certain regions of the country

☐ increasing dominance by European norms and lifestyles

☐ limited natural resources in most of Australia

SECTION 3: VERBAL REASONING

George was a mercurial character; one moment he was optimistic about his prospects, and the next he was _____ .

- ☐ immoral
- ☐ hopeful
- ☐ witty
- ☐ morose
- ☐ dour
- ☐ buoyant

Growing up in a wealthy suburb, she felt quite the _____ as she began her first job as a llama caretaker on a rural farm.

- ☐ tyro
- ☐ concierge
- ☐ agronomist
- ☐ cultivator
- ☐ neophyte
- ☐ curator

William Shakespeare's *Macbeth* was based upon a highly _____ version of events that the playwright wrought from Raphael Holinshed's *Chronicles of England, Scotland, and Ireland*; King Duncan's death at the hand of Macbeth comprises the play's only historical truth.

- ☐ anachronistic
- ☐ effusive
- ☐ embellished
- ☐ prosaic
- ☐ serpentine
- ☐ colored

While comic book artists such as Neal Adams demonstrated a more thorough mastery of human anatomy than did the generation that preceded them, some readers wondered whether the superheroes they drew were really supposed to be so _____ that every detail of their musculatures would be visible through their clothing.

- ☐ thewy
- ☐ sinewy
- ☐ superfluous
- ☐ pneumatic
- ☐ flocculent
- ☐ atrophied

SECTION 3: VERBAL REASONING

For each of Questions 17 to 20, select one answer choice unless otherwise instructed.

Questions 17 through 18 are based on the following reading passage.

One of the most curious structures in cellular biology is the telomere, a length of repeated bases located at the end of every chromosome that, unlike the rest of the DNA strand, carries no useful genetic information. While the telomere seems on the surface to be nothing more than a useless afterthought of DNA, a closer look proves that it is not only important, but also crucial to the functioning of any organism. Indeed, without this mundane structure, every cell division would be a step into senescence, and the onset of old age would begin at birth.

Scientists have found that during cell division not every base of the DNA strand can be replicated, and many, especially those near the end, are lost. If, instead of telomeres, our chromosomes stored valuable genetic information at the end of the DNA strand, then cell division would cause our cells to lose the ability to code for certain information. In fact, many ailments associated with normal old age begin only after the telomere buffer has been exhausted through years of cell division.

Consider each of the choices separately and select all that apply.

Which of the following can reasonably be inferred based on the passage?

- [ ] An individual who aged faster than the average person may have had a shorter telomere buffer than the average person.

- [ ] Scientists once believed that telomeres served no useful purpose.

- [ ] If DNA degradation were absent, then telomeres would be less important to human health.

The passage suggests that if telomere buffers did not exist

- ○ problems associated with aging would begin earlier in life

- ○ people would age so rapidly that almost no one would live past childhood

- ○ cellular senescence would probably be prevented by DNA bases

- ○ chromosomes would lose the ability to store genetic codes

- ○ DNA strands would contain only useful genetic information

SECTION 3: VERBAL REASONING

Questions 19 through 20 are based on the following reading passage.

Music education in America emerged in the early eighteenth century out of a desire to ensure that church goers could sing the weekly hymns in tune. In 1721, John Tufts, a minister, penned the first textbook for musical education entitled *An Introduction to the Singing of Psalm Tunes.* Tufts's pedagogical technique relied primarily on rote learning, omitting the reading of music until a student's singing abilities had improved.

In the same year that Tufts's publication emerged, Reverend Thomas Walter published *The Ground and Rules of Music Explained,* which, while also focusing on preparing students to sing religious music, took a note-based approach by teaching students the rudiments of note reading from the onset. The "note versus rote" controversy in music education continued well into the mid-nineteenth century. With no curriculum to guide them, singing school teachers focused on either the rote or note method with little consistency.

The author discusses Walter's pedagogical technique in order to

○ suggest that rote learning is superior to note learning

○ present a contrast with Tufts's educational technique

○ argue that rote learning improves a student's singing ability

○ show the origin of Tufts's educational techniques

○ show that rote learning was inconsistently practiced

Select the sentence in the passage that best describes the endurance of the tension between pedagogical techniques.

SECTION 4: QUANTITATIVE REASONING

For each of Questions 1 to 8, compare Quantity A and Quantity B, using additional information centered above the two quantities if such information is given. Select one of the four answer choices below each question and fill in the circle to the left of that answer choice.

(A) *Quantity A is greater.*

(B) *Quantity B is greater.*

(C) *The two quantities are equal.*

(D) *The relationship cannot be determined from the information given.*

A symbol that appears more than once in a question has the same meaning throughout the question.

Quantity A	Quantity B
$\dfrac{98^7}{7^{63}}$	$\dfrac{2^7}{7^{49}}$

○ Quantity A is greater.

○ Quantity B is greater.

○ The two quantities are equal.

○ The relationship cannot be determined from the information given.

2 of 20

5 is r percent of 25.

s is 25 percent of 60.

Quantity A	Quantity B
r	s

○ Quantity A is greater.

○ Quantity B is greater.

○ The two quantities are equal.

○ The relationship cannot be determined from the information given.

3 of 20

g and h are positive integers such that the value of g is twice the value of h.

Quantity A	Quantity B
The ratio of g to 1	The ratio of 1 to h

○ Quantity A is greater.

○ Quantity B is greater.

○ The two quantities are equal.

○ The relationship cannot be determined from the information given.

4 of 20

Quantity A	Quantity B
The average (arithmetic mean) of 67, 78, x, and 101	The average (arithmetic mean) of 66, 79, x, and 102

○ Quantity A is greater.

○ Quantity B is greater.

○ The two quantities are equal.

○ The relationship cannot be determined from the information given.

5 of 20

In a certain country, the total weight of recycled newspapers increases annually by 0.79 million tons.

Quantity A	Quantity B
The percent increase in the weight of recycled newspapers in 1989 over 1988	The percent increase in the weight of recycled newspapers in 1990 over 1989

○ Quantity A is greater.

○ Quantity B is greater.

○ The two quantities are equal.

○ The relationship cannot be determined from the information given.

SECTION 4: QUANTITATIVE REASONING

Quantity A	**Quantity B**
The total weight of m peanuts with a weight of $n + 3$ mg each	The total weight of n almonds with a weight of $m + 3$ mg each

○ Quantity A is greater.

○ Quantity B is greater.

○ The two quantities are equal.

○ The relationship cannot be determined from the information given.

Quantity A	**Quantity B**
$5^{27}(575)$	$5^{28}(115)$

○ Quantity A is greater.

○ Quantity B is greater.

○ The two quantities are equal.

○ The relationship cannot be determined from the information given.

Alejandro has a six-sided die with faces numbered 1 through 6. He rolls the die twice.

Quantity A	**Quantity B**
The probability that he rolls two even numbers	The probability that neither number rolled is a multiple of 3

○ Quantity A is greater.

○ Quantity B is greater.

○ The two quantities are equal.

○ The relationship cannot be determined from the information given.

If $4(r - s) = -2$, then what is r, in terms of s ?

○ $\dfrac{-s}{2}$

○ $s - \dfrac{1}{2}$

○ $s - \dfrac{3}{2}$

○ $s + 2$

○ $2s$

At Tenderloin Pharmaceuticals, 25 percent of the employees take the subway to work. Among those who ride the subway, 42 percent transfer from one subway line to another during their commutes, and the rest do not transfer. What percent of all employees transfer lines?

[   ] percent

Click on the answer box and type in a number. Backspace to erase.

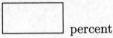

If the value of the expression above is to be halved by doubling exactly one of a, b, c, d, or e, which should be doubled?

○ a

○ b

○ c

○ d

○ e

SECTION 4: QUANTITATIVE REASONING

$$\left(\sqrt{5} - \sqrt{3}\right)^2 =$$

○ $2 - 2\sqrt{15}$

○ $2 - \sqrt{15}$

○ $8 - 2\sqrt{15}$

○ 2

○ $8 - 2\sqrt{5}$

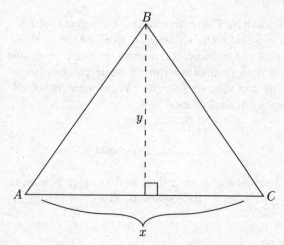

ΔABC has an area of 108 cm². If both x and y are integers, which of the following could be the value of x ?

Indicate all such values.

☐ 4

☐ 5

☐ 6

☐ 8

☐ 9

Questions 14 through 16 refer to the following graphs.

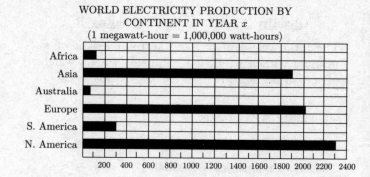

WORLD ELECTRICITY PRODUCTION BY CONTINENT IN YEAR x
(1 megawatt-hour = 1,000,000 watt-hours)

Electricity Production in Megawatt - hours

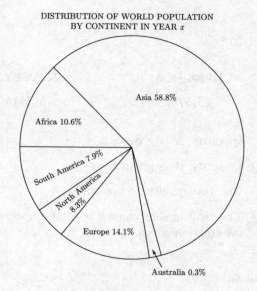

DISTRIBUTION OF WORLD POPULATION BY CONTINENT IN YEAR x

In Year x, on which other continent did electricity production most closely equal electricity production in Europe?

○ Africa

○ Asia

○ Australia

○ South America

○ North America

SECTION 4: QUANTITATIVE REASONING

In Year x, for which continent was the ratio of electricity production to percent of population the greatest?

○ Africa

○ Asia

○ South America

○ Europe

○ North America

In Year x, if South America had a population of approximately 368 million, what was the approximate population, in millions, of Africa?

○ 494

○ 470

○ 274

○ 150

○ 39

The average (arithmetic mean) weight of 5 crates is 250 pounds. The 2 lightest crates weigh between 200 and 205 pounds each, inclusive, and the 2 heaviest crates weigh between 300 and 310 pounds each, inclusive. If the weight of the fifth crate is x pounds, then x is expressed by which of the following?

○ $220 \leq x \leq 250$

○ $230 \leq x \leq 260$

○ $240 \leq x \leq 270$

○ $250 \leq x \leq 270$

○ $260 \leq x \leq 280$

In a certain sequence, $s_1, s_2 \ldots s_x$ if $s_1 = 2$, $s_2 = 2$, $s_3 = 2$, and for $x \geq 4$, $s_x = 2s_{x-1} + s_{x-2}$, what is the value of s_6?

○ 30

○ 34

○ 37

○ 38

○ 40

Y is a point on line segment XZ such that $XY = \frac{1}{2} XZ$. If the length of YZ is $4a + 6$, and the length of XZ is 68, then $a =$

[ ]

Click on the answer box and type in a number. Backspace to erase.

Talk show host Ralph Burke has exactly one guest on his show each day, and Burke's show airs every Monday through Friday. Burke always schedules politicians on Mondays and Wednesdays, actors on Tuesdays and athletes on Thursdays, but can have a guest of any one of these three kinds on Friday. No guest appears more than once per week on Burke's show. If Burke has five politicians, three actors and six athletes he could invite, and if no politician is also an actor or an athlete and no actor is also an athlete, how many different schedules of guests from Monday to Friday could Burke create?

○ 30

○ 1,200

○ 3,600

○ 4,500

○ 6,300

SECTION 5: VERBAL REASONING

For questions 1 through 6, select one entry for each blank from the corresponding column of choices. Fill all blanks in the way that best completes the text.

Despite what _____ philosophies of child-rearing suggest, there is no imperative that the day-to-day action of raising a child be simple, unambiguous, and unchanging—no requirement, in other words, ensures that life follows philosophy.

inexact
aggressive
random
shameless
systematic

All the greatest chess players in the world know that it is folly to be (i) _____ when facing a formidable opponent, as stubbornness will almost surely lead to mistakes that force a player to (ii) _____ to the prevailing strategy of his or her opponent.

Blank (i)	Blank (ii)
finicky	capitulate
obdurate	dissent
vituperative	repudiate

The novel emphasizes the innate (i)_____ of all humans, showing how each and every character within the narrative is, ultimately, (ii)_____ . This motif becomes tiresome due to its (iii)_____, however, as character after character is bribed, either explicitly or implicitly, into giving up his or her supposedly cherished beliefs.

Blank (i)	Blank (ii)	Blank (iii)
zealousness	adroit	redundancy
corruptibility	cunning	triviality
optimism	venal	subtlety

Although pirating software, such as borrowing a friend's copy of an installation CD or downloading software from unapproved sources is (i)_____ , many people continue to do so (ii)_____ , almost as if they were unaware that such acts amount to theft.

Blank (i)	Blank (ii)
uncommon	savagely
illegal	sensibly
difficult	unabashedly

Having squandered his life's savings on unprofitable business ventures, the _____ entrepreneur was forced to live in squalor.

former
unlikely
insolvent
perturbed
eccentric

Teachers of composition urge their students to (i)_____ in their writing and instead use clear, simple language. Why use a (ii)_____ vocabulary when (iii)_____ phrasing conveys one's meaning so much more effectively?

Blank (i)	Blank (ii)	Blank (iii)
exscind obloquy	recreant	an arcane
eschew obfuscation	redolent	a limpid
evince ossification	recondite	a droll

SECTION 5: VERBAL REASONING

For each of Questions 7 to 11, select one answer choice unless otherwise instructed.

Questions 7 through 8 are based on the following reading passage.

Neurobiologists have never questioned that axon malfunction plays a role in neurological disorders, but the nature of the relationship has been a matter of speculation. George Bartzokis's neurological research at UCLA suggests that many previously poorly understood disorders such as Alzheimer's disease may be explained by examining the role of the chemical compound myelin.

Myelin is produced by oligodendrocyte cells as a protective sheathing for axons within the nervous system. As humans mature and their neurochemistries grow more complex, oligodendrocyte cells produce increasing amounts of myelin to protect the byzantine circuitry inside our nervous systems. An apt comparison may be to the plastic insulation around copper wires. Bereft of myelin, certain areas of the brain may be left vulnerable to short circuiting, resulting in such disorders as ADHD, schizophrenia, and autism.

Consider each of the choices separately and select all that apply.

It can be inferred from the passage that the author would be most likely to agree with which of the following statements regarding the role of myelin?

- ☐ The levels of myelin in the brain can contribute to the neurological health of individuals.
- ☐ Increasing the levels of myelin in the brain can reverse the effects of neurological damage.
- ☐ The levels of myelin in the brain are not fixed throughout the lifetime of an individual.

In the context in which it appears, byzantine most nearly means

- ○ devious
- ○ intricate
- ○ mature
- ○ beautiful
- ○ electronic

The cost of operating many small college administrative offices is significantly reduced when the college replaces its heavily compensated administrative assistants with part-time work-study students whose earnings are partially subsidized by the government. Therefore, large universities should follow suit, as they will see greater financial benefits than do small colleges.

In the above argument it is assumed that

- ○ replacing administrative assistants with work-study students is more cost-effective for small colleges than for large universities
- ○ large universities usually depend upon small colleges for development of money-saving strategies
- ○ the financial gains realized by large universities would not be as great were they to use non-work-study students in place of the administrative assistants
- ○ work-study students at large universities could feasibly fulfill a similar or greater proportion of administrative assistant jobs than what they could at small colleges
- ○ the smaller the college or university, the easier it is for that college or university to control costs

SECTION 5: VERBAL REASONING

Questions 10 through 11 are based on the following reading passage.

The nineteenth century marked a revolutionary change in the way wealth was perceived in England. As landed wealth gave way to monied wealth, investments became increasingly speculative.

A popular investment vehicle was the three-percent consol which took its name from the fact that it paid three pounds on a hundred pound investment. The drawback to the consol was that once issued, there was no easy way for the government to buy back the debt. To address the problem, the British government instituted a sinking fund, using tax revenue to buy back the bonds in the open market. The fact that the consol had no fixed maturity date ensured that any change in interest rate was fully reflected in the capital value of the bond. The often wild fluctuation of interest rates ensured the consol's popularity with speculative traders.

Which of the following best describes the relationship of the first paragraph of the passage to the passage as a whole?

○ It provides a generalization which is later supported in the passage.

○ It provides an antithesis to the author's main argument.

○ It briefly compares two different investment strategies.

○ It explains an investment vehicle that is later examined in greater detail.

○ It provides a historical framework by which the nature of the nineteenth-century investor can more easily be understood.

In the second paragraph, select the sentence that describes a solution to a problem.

For questions 12 through 15, select the two answer choices that, when used to complete the sentence, fit the meaning of the sentence as a whole and produce completed sentences that are alike in meaning.

Owing to a combination of its proximity and _____ atmosphere, Mars is the only planet in our solar system whose surface details can be discerned from Earth.

☐ viscous

☐ ossified

☐ rarefied

☐ estimable

☐ copious

☐ meager

Using the hardships of the Joad family as a model, John Steinbeck's *The Grapes of Wrath* effectively demonstrated how one clan's struggles epitomized the _____ experienced by an entire country.

☐ reticence

☐ adversity

☐ repudiation

☐ quiescence

☐ verisimilitude

☐ tribulation

SECTION 5: VERBAL REASONING

The Mayan pyramid of Kukulkan is more than just _____ edifice; this imposing structure was built to create a chirping echo whenever people clap their hands on the staircase. This echo sounds just like the chirp of the Quetzal, a bird which is sacred in the Mayan culture.

- ☐ a venerable
- ☐ a humble
- ☐ a beguiling
- ☐ an august
- ☐ a specious
- ☐ a prosaic

Some wealthy city-dwellers become enchanted with the prospect of trading their hectic schedules for a bucolic life in the countryside, and they buy property with a pleasant view of farmland—only to find the stench of the livestock so _____ that they move back to the city.

- ☐ bovine
- ☐ pastoral
- ☐ noisome
- ☐ atavistic
- ☐ olfactory
- ☐ mephitic

For each of Questions 16 to 20, select one answer choice unless otherwise instructed.
Questions 16 through 18 are based on the following reading passage.

Often the most influential developments initially appear to be of minor significance. Consider the development of the basic stirrup for example. Without stirrups horse and rider are, in terms of force, separate entities; lances can be used from horseback, but only by throwing or stabbing, and mounted warriors gain only height and mobility. In medieval times, a lance couched under the rider's arm, unifying the force of rider and weapon, would throw its wielder backwards off the horse at impact. Stirrups unify lance, rider, and horse into a force capable of unprecedented violence. This development left unusually clear archaeological markers: With lethality assured, lances evolved barbs meant to slow progress after impact, lest the weight of body pull rider from horse. The change presaged the dominance of mounted combat, and increasingly expensive equipment destroyed the venerable ideal of freeman warriors. New technology demanded military aristocracy, and chivalric culture bore its marks for a millennium.

The primary purpose of the passage is to

- ○ discuss the influence of a recent archeological discovery
- ○ explore the societal significance of a technological innovation
- ○ assess the state of research in a given field
- ○ lament the destruction of certain social ideals
- ○ explicate the physics of combat artillery

SECTION 5: VERBAL REASONING

It can be inferred from the passage that the author believes which of the following about innovations in military technology?

○ Their study merits additional research.

○ They had more lasting influence than did those of the ancient world.

○ Most of them had equally far-reaching repercussions.

○ Prior to their application, the military value of horses was considered insignificant.

○ Many of them are archaeologically ambiguous.

Select the sentence in the passage in which the author cites the physical effects of a technological innovation being discussed as an example of a previous generalization.

Questions 19 through 20 are based on the following reading passage.

Few mathematical constructs seem as conceptually simple as that of randomness. According to the traditional definition, a number is random if it is chosen purely as the result of a probabilistic mechanism such as the roll of a fair die. In their groundbreaking work regarding complexity and the limitations of formal systems, mathematicians Gregory Chaitin and A.N. Kolmogorov force us to consider this last claim more closely.

Consider two possible outcomes of throwing a fair die three times: first, 1, 6, and 2; second 3, 3, and 3. Now let us construct two three-member sets based on the results. Though the first set—{1,6,2}—intuitively seems more random than the second—{3,3,3}, they are each as likely to occur, and thus according to the accepted definition, must be considered equally random. This unwelcome result prompts Chaitin and Kolmogorov to suggest the need for a new standard of randomness, one that relies on the internal coherence of the set as opposed to its origin.

Which of the following best describes the organization of the passage as whole?

○ A concept is introduced; a traditional definition is put forward; a thought experiment is described; a new definition is proposed; the traditional definition is amended as a result.

○ A concept is introduced; a traditional definition is supported by authorities; a thought experiment is described; the implications of the experiment are discussed.

○ A concept is introduced; a traditional definition is considered and rejected; a thought experiment is described; a new definition is proposed.

○ A concept is introduced; a traditional definition is called into question; a thought experiment is described; the implications of the experiment are discussed.

○ A concept is introduced; authorities are called in to reevaluate a definition; a thought experiment is described; the implications of the experiment are considered and rejected.

Consider each of the choices separately and select all that apply.

Which of the following is an inference made in the passage above?

☐ The results of the same probabilistic mechanism will each be as likely as the other to occur.

☐ According to the traditional definition of randomness, two numbers should be considered equally random if they result from the same probabilistic mechanism.

☐ Different probabilistic mechanisms are likely to result in similar outcomes.

NO TEST MATERIAL ON THIS PAGE

SECTION 6: QUANTITATIVE REASONING

For each of Questions 1 to 7, compare Quantity A and Quantity B, using additional information centered above the two quantities if such information is given. Select one of the four answer choices below each question and fill in the circle to the left of that answer choice.

(A) *Quantity A is greater.*
(B) *Quantity B is greater.*
(C) *The two quantities are equal.*
(D) *The relationship cannot be determined from the information given.*

A symbol that appears more than once in a question has the same meaning throughout the question.

$$\frac{x}{6} + 2 = \frac{6}{2}$$

$$\frac{y}{3} + 2 = \frac{9}{3}$$

Quantity A	**Quantity B**
$\dfrac{(x-1)}{y}$	$\dfrac{(y-1)}{x}$

○ Quantity A is greater.

○ Quantity B is greater.

○ The two quantities are equal.

○ The relationship cannot be determined from the information given.

Quantity A	**Quantity B**
The distance that Bob drives in 3 hours at an average speed of 44 miles per hour	The distance that Inez drives in 2 hours and 30 minutes at an average speed of 50 miles per hour

○ Quantity A is greater.

○ Quantity B is greater.

○ The two quantities are equal.

○ The relationship cannot be determined from the information given.

The height of a rectangular solid is increased by p percent, its depth is decreased by p percent and its width is unchanged.

Quantity A	**Quantity B**
The volume of the new rectangular solid if $p = 20$	The volume of the new rectangular solid if $p = 40$

○ Quantity A is greater.

○ Quantity B is greater.

○ The two quantities are equal.

○ The relationship cannot be determined from the information given.

In $\triangle ABC$, $AB = AC$

Quantity A	**Quantity B**
The sum of the degree measures of angle B and angle C	90

○ Quantity A is greater.

○ Quantity B is greater.

○ The two quantities are equal.

○ The relationship cannot be determined from the information given.

12.5 percent of k is 80.
k is y percent of 80.

Quantity A	**Quantity B**
y	650

○ Quantity A is greater.

○ Quantity B is greater.

○ The two quantities are equal.

○ The relationship cannot be determined from the information given.

SECTION 6: QUANTITATIVE REASONING

Set $P = \{a, b, c, d, e, f, g\}$

Set $Q = \{a, b, c, d, e, f\}$

$a, b, c, d, e, f,$ and g are distinct integers

Quantity A	Quantity B
Range of Set P	Range of Set Q

○ Quantity A is greater.

○ Quantity B is greater.

○ The two quantities are equal.

○ The relationship cannot be determined from the information given.

Sequence F is defined as $F_n = F_{(n-1)} + 3$ and $F_1 = 10$.

Quantity A	Quantity B
The sum of F_4 through F_{10}	The sum of F_6 through F_{11}

○ Quantity A is greater.

○ Quantity B is greater.

○ The two quantities are equal.

○ The relationship cannot be determined from the information given.

A number, n, is multiplied by 6 and the product is increased by 24. Finally, the entire quantity is divided by 3. Which of the following is an expression for these operations, in terms of n ?

○ $\dfrac{n}{3} + 8$

○ $\dfrac{n + 24}{2}$

○ $2n + 8$

○ $3n + 24$

○ $16n$

The average (arithmetic mean) of a and b is 10, and the average of c and d is 7. If the average of a, b, and c is 8, what is the value of d ?

Click on the answer box and type in a number. Backspace to erase.

In the xy-plane, square $ABCD$ has vertices at A (3, 7), B (3, 12), C (8, x), D (8, y). What is the area of $ABCD$?

○ 16

○ 20

○ 25

○ 30

○ 36

Houses Sold in July		
Week	Peter	Dylan
Week 1	4	9
Week 2	6	3
Week 3	10	10
Week 4	4	2

The table above shows the number of houses sold per week for the month of July by two real estate agents, Peter and Dylan. What is the difference between the median number of houses sold per week by Dylan and the median number of houses sold per week by Peter?

○ 0

○ 1

○ 2

○ 5

○ 6

SECTION 6: QUANTITATIVE REASONING

At Flo's Pancake House, pancakes can be ordered with any of six possible toppings. If no toppings are repeated, how many different ways are there to order pancakes with three toppings?

○ 20

○ 40

○ 54

○ 120

○ 720

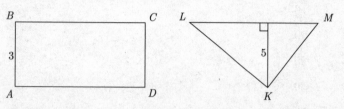

The area of triangle *KLM* is equal to the area of rectangle *ABCD*. If the perimeter of *ABCD* is 16, what is the length of *LM* ?

○ $\dfrac{3}{2}$

○ 3

○ $\dfrac{16}{5}$

○ 5

○ 6

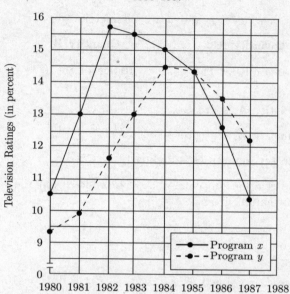

TELEVISION RATINGS* IN THE UNITED STATES
1980–1987

*Ratings equal the percent of television households in the United States that viewed the program.

For how many of the years shown did the ratings for Program *y* increase over the ratings for Program *y* in the previous year?

○ Two

○ Three

○ Four

○ Five

○ Six

SECTION 6: QUANTITATIVE REASONING

In 1995, there were 95 million television households in the United States. In 1983, if the number of television households was 80 percent of the number of television households in 1995, then approximately how many television households, in millions, viewed Program y in 1983 ?

○ 80

○ 76

○ 15

○ 12

○ 10

In 1984, there were 80 million television households in the United States. If 65 million television households viewed neither Program x nor Program y, then approximately how many of the television households, in millions, in the United States viewed both Program x and Program y ?

○ 8.6

○ 11.9

○ 16.5

○ 23.2

○ 23.6

Each of the 576 houses in Tenantville is owned by one of the following landlords: Matt, Gavin, Angela, or Susan. Matt and Angela together own twice as many houses as Gavin and Susan own. If Gavin owns 100 more houses than Susan owns, and Matt owns 100 more houses than Angela owns, how many houses does Susan own?

○ 46

○ 142

○ 146

○ 192

○ 242

One-fourth of the cars that an automobile manufacturer produces are sports cars, and the rest are sedans. If one-fifth of the cars that the manufacturer produces are red and one-third of the sports cars are red, then what fraction of the sedans is red?

Click on each box and type in a number.
Backspace to erase.

A candy jar has 4 lime, 10 cherry, 8 orange, and x grape candies. If Tom selects a candy from the jar at random and the probability that he selects an orange candy is greater than 20 percent, which of the following could be the value of x ?

Indicate all such values.

☐ 10

☐ 14

☐ 18

☐ 22

☐ 24

☐ 28

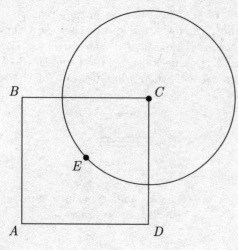

Square $ABCD$ and a circle with center C intersect as shown. If point E is the center of $ABCD$ and if the radius of circle C is k, then what is the area of $ABCD$, in terms of k ?

○ $\dfrac{k^2}{2\pi}$

○ $\dfrac{\pi k^2}{2}$

○ πk^2

○ k^2

○ $2k^2$

Practice Test 2:
Answers and
Explanations

PRACTICE TEST 2: ANSWER KEY

Section 3: Verbal Reasoning

1. inflection and utilized
2. expressive, relegated, and conflict with
3. axiomatic
4. staved off, contributed to, and affliction
5. glib, spontaneity, and tepid
6. shallow
7. B
8. E
9. D
10. E
11. B
12. A, B, and C
13. morose and dour
14. tyro and neophyte
15. embellished and colored
16. thewy and sinewy
17. A and C
18. A
19. B
20. The "note versus rote" controversy in music education continued well into the mid-nineteenth century.

Section 4: Quantitative Reasoning

1. C
2. A
3. A
4. B
5. A
6. D
7. C
8. B
9. B
10. 10.5
11. D
12. C
13. A, C, D, and E
14. B
15. E
16. A
17. A
18. B
19. 7
20. C

Section 5: Verbal Reasoning

1. systematic
2. obdurate and capitulate
3. corruptibility, venal, and redundancy
4. illegal and unabashedly
5. insolvent
6. eschew obfuscation, recondite, and a limpid
7. A and C
8. B
9. D
10. A
11. To address the problem, the British government instituted a sinking fund, using tax revenue to buy back the bonds in the open market.
12. rarefied and meager
13. adversity and tribulation
14. a venerable and an august
15. noisome and mephitic
16. B
17. E
18. Stirrups unify lance, rider, and horse into a force capable of unprecedented violence.
19. D
20. A and B

Section 6: Quantitative Reasoning

1. A
2. A
3. A
4. D
5. A
6. D
7. A
8. C
9. 10
10. C
11. B
12. A
13. E
14. C
15. E
16. A
17. A
18. $\dfrac{7}{45}$
19. A and B
20. E

INTERPRETING YOUR RESULTS

After you check your answers on the following pages, fill out this sheet to interpret your results.

Analytical Writing

To evaluate your performance on the Analytical Writing sections, compare your response to the advice and samples in the Analytical Writing chapter.

Verbal Reasoning

Refer to the explanations to check your answers. Count the number of questions you got correct in each Verbal Reasoning section, and calculate the total number correct. Find the section of the Interpretive Guide (below) that corresponds to your total to get an idea of how your performance compares to that of other test takers.

Test 2	# Correct
Section 3	
Section 5	
Total	

Quantitative Reasoning

Refer to the explanations to check your answers. Count the number of questions you got correct in each Quantitative Reasoning section, and calculate the total number correct. Find the section of the Interpretive Guide (below) that corresponds to your total to get an idea of how your performance compares to that of other test takers.

Test 2	# Correct
Section 4	
Section 6	
Total	

Interpretive Guide

The table below provides a guide for interpreting your performance based on the number of questions you got correct in each subject.

Subject	Above Average	Average	Below Average
Verbal Reasoning	30–40	22–29	1–21
Quantitative Reasoning	33–40	24–32	1–23

Section 3

1. **inflection** and **utilized**

   For the first blank, the transition "more important" tells you to change direction from "actual words." Also, *sarcastically* is an example of tone. Look for a choice that means tone. *Inflection* fits tone. *Pitch* is nonverbal, but it does not match the example of sarcastically. *Accuracy* does not fit. For the second blank, look for a word that means *conveyed* or *spoken. Utilized* is the best match. *Implied* and *repudiated* don't fit.

2. **expressive**, **relegated**, and **conflict with**

   Try working with the first blank first. The clue is *artistic*, and the transition *and* indicates the first blank should be a word that is the same as artistic. *Expressive* is the best choice; neither *tedious* nor *tiresome* works. *Though* changes the direction of the sentence—though the studio likes the creative/artistic aspect, something negative must be happening to creativity—it's brought down to a secondary position. Eliminate *uplifted* and *compared* for blank (ii) because they are not negative, and choose *relegated*. Turning to the third blank, "organization and hierarchy" are in opposition to *creativity*, so *conflict with* makes the most sense.

3. **axiomatic**

   You are given the clue that the beliefs "are in conflict" and "cannot all be correct." Therefore, whatever goes into the blank must be synonymous with *correct* or something we can infer correctness from. The correct answer is *axiomatic*, which means self-evident or universally true. *Disputable* is the opposite of what the sentence requires, and *ubiquitous* and *historic* are not synonymous with self-evident. Although *empirical*, meaning derived from observation, might fit science, it is not a good fit for religion.

4. **staved off**, **contributed to,** and **affliction**

   The clue "Although most preventative medical ointments commonly in use" tells you that most ointments would prevent an infection, the one Helen used did not. Recycle the clue, and put a word that means prevent in the first blank; *staved off* is the best match. Work with the second and third blanks together. The ointment did not prevent an infection, and the clue "much to her dismay" tells you that something bad happened. The only pair that makes sense together is *contributed to* and *affliction* because they tell you that the ointment made her problem worse.

5. **glib, spontaneity,** and **tepid**

   For the first blank, the clue is *offhand remarks,* so the blank means something like "offhand." *Glib,* which means "superficial or showing a lack of concern," is the closest match for this. Sticking to *prepared talking points* can result in a lack of "excitement" or "naturalness," which *spontaneity* matches. For the last blank, you know the crowd's responses are *lukewarm,* so the answer for that blank is *tepid.*

6. **shallow**

   The clue is the entire clause that follows the semicolon: "its characters take trivial concerns seriously while thoughtlessly dismissing important ones." Look for a word that means superficial or petty to go in the blank. The only one that fits is *shallow.*

7. **B** The third paragraph states that if incorrect quantities of Haber nitrogen were applied, "the wheat crop would grow taller and thicker, eventually toppling over and rotting." Losing a crop would be an undesirable effect, making (B) the correct answer. Eliminate (A) because the passage doesn't compare the effects of Haber nitrogen on different kinds of crops. The passage doesn't provide any information to support (C) and (D). Choice (E) contradicts the passage, which says the farmers were wary of the substance.

8. **E** According to the first paragraph, there has been no sharp decline in the world's population and, therefore, we can surmise that food production has been sufficient to allow for the existing population growth, as in (A). In the second paragraph, the author mentions the invention of the tractor as one of the factors that allowed more crops to be grown for human consumption. This reflects the technological innovation in (B). In the last paragraph, the author notes that the environmental movement has opposed efforts at genetic engineering. Thus, (C) is implied as well. The author notes that increases in crop production through the invention of the tractor and ammonia prevented Malthus's predictions from being realized, and this rules out (D). The extent of the impact of genetic engineering is not clear. We don't know that a Malthusian disaster would have been a *certainty* without genetic engineering. Therefore, the correct answer is (E) because it is not implied.

9. **D** The first paragraph states that Malthus believed that "population increases in a geometric ratio, while the means of subsistence increases in an arithmetic ratio." More simply put, Malthus argued that population growth happens at a significantly faster rate than food production. Only (D) demonstrates this.

10. **E** The first paragraph presents Malthus's prediction about what would happen if population growth were to outstrip food production. If there were too many people and not enough food, you would expect a significant or rapid population decline. Look for a word to replace *precipitous* that is similar to *significant* or *rapid*. *Sharp*, (E), is the best word.

11. **B** The "rosy prospect" refers to the previous paragraph's discussion of the booming tourism industry in Australia, which implies a positive future, and the "cloud on the horizon" refers to the conflict between the rights of the Aborigines and the need for the money from tourism, a potential problem. Choice (A) incorrectly interprets the quote as referring to a literal *horizon and prospect.* Choice (C) is also too literal, taking *prospect* to mean view. Choice (D) is incorrect because, although this may be true based on later information in the passage, it is not an accurate interpretation of this phrase. Choice (E) is too strong because the future is described as generally good, not hopeless.

12. **A, B,** and **C**

All three statements are given as sources of the conflict. Choice (A), *economic hardships*, is mentioned in the third paragraph. Due to financial difficulties, many regions are unwilling to give up the income derived from tourists visiting Aboriginal lands. Choice (B) is discussed in the second paragraph. The expansion of Western culture is the reason that the Aborigines have moved inland and abandoned other sacred sites. Choice (C) is mentioned in the first sentence. Tourism is described as particularly important due to the "dearth of natural resources."

13. **morose** and **dour**

The first part of the clue is "mercurial character," which means George's moods change frequently. The second part of the clue is "one moment he was optimistic about his prospects," and the transition is *the next he was*. Thus, the blank should be the opposite of optimistic; look for words that mean pessimistic. Both *morose* and *dour* are similar to pessimistic. *Hopeful* and *buoyant* have the opposite meaning, and *witty* and *immoral* are not related.

14. **tyro** and **neophyte**

The clue is that she "began her first job." Also, the contrast of "wealthy suburb" and "llama caretaker on a rural farm" suggests that she'd feel out of place or lacking in experience at her first job. Look for words that mean beginner. *Tyro* and *neophyte* are the only words that mean beginner. *Agronomist* and *cultivator* are traps for people who focused too heavily on the farm. *Concierge* and *curator* are traps for people who focused too heavily on *caretaker*.

15. **embellished** and **colored**

The clue "King Duncan's death at the hand of Macbeth comprises the play's only historical truth" tells you that the version of events related in Macbeth was not very accurate. Does *anachronistic* mean inaccurate? No; cross it out. What about *effusive*? No. In contrast, *embellished* works well, but *prosaic* and *serpentine* do not. Finally, *colored*—which, like embellished, means *misrepresented* or *distorted*—fits the blank nicely.

16. **thewy** and **sinewy**

The word that goes into the blank describes superheroes, of whom the clue phrase states that "every detail of their musculatures would be visible through their clothing." Clearly, something like *muscular* is called for, and both *thewy* and *sinewy* fit the bill. The other four words don't fit: *superfluous* means unnecessary, *pneumatic* means full of air, *flocculent* means covered in wool, and *atrophied* means shriveled due to disuse.

17. **A** and **C**

Choice (A) is correct because the passage states that "...without this mundane structure, every cell division would be a step into senescence, and the onset of old age would begin at birth." Choice (B) is not correct because there is no information about what scientists used to think about telomeres. Choice (C) is correct because you are told that one function of telomeres is to mitigate the loss of DNA bases. If no bases are lost, then this role is not important anymore.

18. **A** The first paragraph says that without telomere buffers "every cell division would be a step into senescence, and the onset of old age would begin at birth," and the last sentence of the passage states that "many ailments associated with normal old age begin only after the telomere buffer has been exhausted through years of cell division." If the protection offered by the buffers didn't exist, you could expect problems related to aging to start sooner, as (A) suggests. Choice (B) goes too far; though the passage speaks on the onset of old age at birth, there is no certainty that almost no one would live past childhood. The passage provides no support for (C), (D), or (E).

19. **B** The passage as a whole provides a short history of two types of early musical education, the rote method and the note method. Nowhere in the passage does the author come out in favor of either method, thereby ruling out (A) and (C). Given that Reverend Walter taught music by the note method he developed, (D) doesn't make sense. While it is true that rote learning was inconsistently practiced, as (E) states, this does not answer the question.

20. **The "note versus rote" controversy in music education continued well into the mid-nineteenth century.**

    The use of the word "controversy" in the final paragraph is the only indication the author gives that the decision between "note" or "rote" as a musical learning technique was in any way contentious.

Section 4

1. **C** The quantities have numbers with great exponents and none of the exponent rules can be applied, so look for a way to factor. In Quantity A, factor 98^7 into its prime factors. The prime factors of 98 are $2 \times 7 \times 7$, so 98^7 can be rewritten as $(2 \times 7^2)^7$. Use the Power-Multiply rule to combine the exponents and simplify to $2^7 \times 7^{14}$. Quantity A can be rewritten as $\dfrac{2^7 \times 7^{14}}{7^{63}}$. Use the Divide-Subtract rule to combine the exponents with base 7 to find that $\dfrac{2^7 \times 7^{14}}{7^{63}} = \dfrac{2^7}{7^{49}}$. Therefore, the quantities are equal. The correct answer is (C).

2. **A** Translate and solve each expression. The expression "5 is r percent of 25" becomes $5 = \dfrac{r}{100} \times 25$. So, $r = 20$. The expression "s is 25 percent of 60" becomes $s = \dfrac{25}{100} \times 60$. So, $s = 15$, and Quantity A is greater.

3. **A** Plug In for this question. Let $h = 3$, which makes $g = 6$. Quantity A equals $\dfrac{6}{1} = 6$ and Quantity B equals $\dfrac{1}{3}$. Quantity A can be greater than Quantity B, so eliminate (B) and (C). Because g and h are positive integers, Quantity A will always be greater than 1 and Quantity B will always be less than or equal to 1. Quantity A will always be greater than Quantity B.

4. **B** The average is the sum divided by the number of elements. Because three elements make up both averages, you can simply compare the sum of each set. $67 + 78 + 101 + x = 246 + x$, and $66 + 79 + 102 + x = 247 + x$. Thus, Quantity B is greater.

5. **A** Plug In! Say there were 10 million tons in 1988. The percent increase was $\dfrac{0.79}{10}$. Then in 1989 there were 10.79 tons, so the percent increase from 1989 to 1990 was $\dfrac{0.79}{10.79}$. Quantity A must be greater.

6. **D** Plug In. Make $m = 2$ and $n = 3$. For Quantity A, the weight of 2 peanuts at $3 + 3$ mg each is $2 \times 6 = 12$ mg. For Quantity B, the weight of 3 almonds at $2 + 3$ mg each is $3 \times 5 = 15$ mg. Eliminate (A) and (C). Plug In again to see if you can get a different result. Keep $m = 2$, and change n to 2. For Quantity A, the weight of two peanuts at $2 + 3$ mg each is $2 \times 5 = 10$ mg. For Quantity B, the weight of two almonds at $2 + 3$ mg each is $2 \times 5 = 10$ mg. Eliminate (B), and choose (D).

7. **C** Remember, when you have large exponents, try to break them down into their prime factors. You can rewrite Quantity A as $5^{27}(5)(115)$, or $5^{28}(115)$. The quantities are equal.

8. **B** For Quantity A, there are three ways to get an even number (these are 2, 4, 6). So, the probability of "rolling an even" and then "rolling an even" is $\dfrac{3}{6} \times \dfrac{3}{6} = \dfrac{1}{4}$. For multiple independent events, multiply the probabilities. For Quantity B, there are four ways to not get a multiple of 3 (these are 1, 2, 4, 5). The probability of "not rolling a multiple of 3" and then "not rolling a multiple of 3" is $\dfrac{4}{6} \times \dfrac{4}{6} = \dfrac{4}{9}$. Quantity B is greater than Quantity A.

9. **B** There are variables in the answer choices, so Plug In. If $r = 2$, then $4((2) - s) = -2$. Divide both sides by 4 to find $2 - s = -0.5$. So, $s = 2.5$. The target answer is r, which is 2. Go to the answer choices and Plug In 2.5 for s. Choice (B) is the only answer choice that matches your target of 2.

10. **10.5**

    Plug In! Let's say there are 100 employees. 25 percent of the employees take the subway to work, so $\dfrac{25}{100} \times 100 = 25$. Of the 25 employees who ride the subway, 42 percent of them transfer during the commute, so $\dfrac{42}{100} \times 25 = 10.5$. Therefore, 10.5 out of 100 employees transfer lines. This is 10.5 percent.

11. **D** Plug In. If $a = 3$, $b = 6$, $c = 3$, $d = 5$, and $e = 10$, the value of the equation is $\dfrac{10\left(3 + \dfrac{6}{3}\right)}{5} = 10$. Half of 10 is your target of 5. Try doubling each variable to find the one that yields 5. The only one that works is doubling d to 10 so that the equation is $\dfrac{(10)\left(3 + \dfrac{6}{3}\right)}{10} = 5$.

12. **C** For this question, you can FOIL: $(\sqrt{5})^2 - (\sqrt{3})(\sqrt{5}) - (\sqrt{5})(\sqrt{3}) + (\sqrt{3})^2$. This simplifies to $5 - 2\sqrt{15} + 3$, or $8 - 2\sqrt{15}$.

13. **A, C, D, and E**

Plug the information given into the formula for the area of a triangle to learn more about the relationship between x and y: $A = \dfrac{bh}{2} = \dfrac{xy}{2} = 108$. The product of x and y is 216, so x needs to be a factor of 216. The only number in the answer choices that is not a factor of 216 is 5. The remaining choices are possible values of x.

14. **B** Europe's electricity production (2,000 megawatt-hours) most closely matches that of Asia (1,900 megawatt-hours).

15. **E** The ratio for North America is 2,300 to 0.083 or, $\dfrac{2,300}{0.083} = 27,710$. This is the greatest ratio of any of the continents.

16. **A** Africa's population is 10.6 percent on the pie chart; South America's is 7.9 percent. Right away, you can eliminate all of the answer choices that are smaller than 368. Now you are left with (A) and (B). Because the question gives you South America's population (368 million), you can use a proportion to find the population of Africa. The proportion would look like this: $\dfrac{0.079}{368} = \dfrac{0.106}{x}$, where x is equal to the population of Africa. Cross multiplying gives you $0.079x = 0.106 \times 368$, so $x = 493.7$.

17. **A** If the average of 5 crates is 250, then their total = $5 \times 250 = 1,250$. To find the high end of the range for the fifth crate, make the other crates as light as possible: Make the two lightest crates 200 each, for a total of 400, and the two heaviest crates 300 each, for a total of 600; together, those four crates weigh 1,000 pounds, leaving 250 pounds for x. Because only (A) sets 250 pounds as the high end, you can eliminate (B), (C), (D), and (E).

18. **B** Substitute 6 for x in the equation, $s_x = 2s_{x-1} + s_{x-2}$ and work carefully from there. $s_6 = 2s_{6-1} + s_{6-2}$, which simplifies to $s_6 = 2s_5 + s_4$. However, you don't know s_5 or s_4. Use the equation to find these missing terms. $s_4 = 2s_3 + s_2$ and the problem tells you s_2 and s_3 are equal to 2. $s_4 = (2 \times 2) + 2$, which is 6. Now you need to find s_5. Using the equation, you get $s_5 = (2 \times 6) + 2$, which is 14. Now that you know s_5 and s_4, go back to your original equation, $s_6 = 2s_5 + s_4$, and $s_6 = (2 \times 14) + 6$, which is 34.

19. **7** Always draw a figure when one is not provided. In this case, line segment XZ has a length of 68. Point Y is the midpoint of the segment, because $2XY = XZ$. To find the lengths of these segments, divide 68 by 2. Segment $YZ = 34$. Because $YZ = 4a + 6$, you know that $34 = 4a + 6$, so $a = 7$.

20. **C** Make a spot for each day and fill in the number of guests who could occupy that spot. Burke has 5 choices for Monday, 3 choices for Tuesday, 4 choices for Wednesday (because one politician was chosen on Monday), 6 choices for Thursday, and 10 choices for Friday (because 4 of the 14 potential guests have already been chosen). Multiply these to arrive at 3,600 different schedules.

Section 5

1. **systematic**

   The clue is "simple, unambiguous, and unchanging." The transition phrase is *in other words*. The transition maintains the direction of the clue. Therefore, find a word that means regimented. *Systematic* is the best match.

2. **obdurate** and **capitulate**

   Try working with the second blank first. The second blank is talking about what a player will be forced to do if he's stubborn. The clue is that the "mistakes" the player makes will lead to the "prevailing strategy of his or her opponent." Because of these clues, we know that a word that means "to give in" would be a good match. *Capitulate* is the only word that works, as *dissent* means to disagree and *repudiate* means to reject. Now look at the first blank. The first blank is referring to something all great chess players know. The clue tells us that they know *stubbornness will almost surely lead to mistakes that force a player to capitulate to the prevailing strategy of his or her opponent.* As you can see, we needed to solve for the second blank first, as we would not have known what *stubbornness* would lead to without doing so. Recycle the word *stubbornness* as your word for the blank. *Obdurate* is the only word that works for the first blank. *Finicky* means to be overly particular, and *vituperative* means to be combative.

3. **corruptibility, venal**, and **redundancy**

   The first two blanks are related, but there isn't a strong clue for either one in the first part, so start with the third blank. Since the motif is *tiresome,* the third blank must mean something close to "repetitive." *Redundancy* matches this. At the end of the paragraph, each character is *bribed...into giving up...beliefs.* So the first two blanks must mean "bribable." *Corruptibility* in the first blank and *venal* in the second both match this.

4. **illegal** and **unabashedly**

   For the first blank, the clues "pirating software" and "downloading software from unapproved sources" describe unauthorized activities, so *illegal* is the best fit. *Uncommon* and *difficult* are incorrect because the sentence says that "many people continue to do so." If people are doing something despite its illegality and "almost as if they were unaware that such acts amount to theft," you could describe them as acting *brashly. Unabashedly* is the best fit.

5. **insolvent**

   The phrase "squandered his life's savings on unprofitable business ventures" tells you that the entrepreneur had no money left. The blank needs a word that means broke. *Former* and *unlikely* are tempting choices, but they don't match broke. Eliminate them. *Eccentric* also doesn't match, while *perturbed* only describes the entrepreneur's possible feelings. *Insolvent* agrees with the clue, so keep it.

6. **eschew obfuscation**, **recondite**, and **a limpid**

   The key clue is that the teachers urge students to "use clear, simple language." The transition *instead* indicates that the phrase that goes into the blank will present an alternative to using clear, simple language, while the *and* indicates that the phrase will nevertheless agree with the clue. Something like "avoid difficult language" would be best. Difficult language is the alternative to clear, simple language, but the two phrases still agree because the difficult language is something to avoid. Thus, *eschew obfuscation* is best. *Eschew* means avoid, while *obfuscation* means the act of hiding the meaning of something. *Exscind obloquy* means to cut out critical language, while *evince ossification* means to show excessive rigidity, neither of which is appropriate here. The second blank needs a word that means difficult or obscure because teachers call into question the use of difficult vocabulary; *recondite* means obscure and hard to understand. *Recreant* means cowardly; *redolent* means fragrant. The final blank requires a word like *clear* because that is the type of language that "conveys one's meaning so much more effectively." *Limpid* means easily understood, so it is correct.

7. **A** and **C**

   Choice (A) is supported because the passage says that myelin protects the brain's circuitry. Choice (C) is supported by the fact that "as humans mature" increasing levels of myelin need to be produced. While the passage suggests that a lack of myelin leaves the brain vulnerable, that doesn't mean that increasing the levels of myelin will reverse damage.

8. **B** In the passage, *byzantine* refers to the "circuitry inside our nervous systems." Previously, the circuitry is described as growing more complex, so you need to find a word with a similar meaning. Choice (A) is an alternate meaning for byzantine, but it is not supported by the passage. Choices (C), (D), and (E) do not have meanings similar to complex.

9. **D** The argument concludes that large universities should utilize work-study students rather than administrative assistants. The premise is that a similar strategy realizes a cost savings at small colleges. This is an argument by analogy. Hence, the argument assumes that there are similar conditions at small colleges and at large universities. Choice (D) says that students at universities are just as qualified to take over the administrative roles as they are in small colleges. In other words, the administrative jobs at universities are not appreciably different than those at colleges. For (A), whether the practice would be of greater benefit to the small colleges is out of scope. For (B), whether large universities usually depend on small colleges for ideas is out of scope. For (C), the issue of non-work-study students is out of scope. For (E), whether anyone has an easier ride than anyone else is out of scope.

10. **A** The first paragraph acts as an introduction to the rest of the passage. The author notes that in the nineteenth century "investments became increasingly speculative." In the last paragraph, the author explains that due to fluctuating interest rates, the consol was popular with speculative investors. There is no support in the passage for (B), (C), or (D). Although the first paragraph provides a historical framework, as suggested in (E), it does not provide a way "by which the nature of the nineteenth-century investor" could be understood.

11. **To address the problem, the British government instituted a sinking fund, using tax revenue to buy back the bonds in the open market.**

    The second paragraph has five sentences, so this question has five answer choices. The third sentence begins, "To address the problem...." This is a clear indication that the sentence describes a solution to a problem. The correct answer is the third sentence.

12. **rarefied** and **meager**

What sort of atmosphere would make Mars the only planet "whose surface details can be discerned from Earth?" You need a word that means transparent or thin for the blank. *Viscous* takes you in the wrong direction, so toss it. The next choice, *ossified*, makes no sense; toss that one too. In contrast, *rarefied* works well, so hang onto it. Meanwhile, a *copious* atmosphere would definitely not be easy to see through, so cross out that choice. *Meager* fits nicely and agrees with *rarefied*, making those two the correct answers.

13. **adversity** and **tribulation**

The clue is "Using the hardships of the Joad family as a model." Recycle *hardships* and use POE. Does *reticence* mean *hardships*? No; cross it out. *Adversity* works, so leave it. Do the same for the remaining choices. Only *tribulation* agrees with *hardships,* so that's the other correct answer.

14. **a venerable** and **an august**

The blank is a description of the pyramid. The clue is "imposing structure" because this is the only other description of the pyramid. *Venerable* and *august* are the only words that match *imposing*.

15. **noisome** and **mephitic**

The word that fills the blank must describe "the stench of the livestock," which is so malodorous that it drives the newcomers back to the city; it must mean something like, well, "stinky." Both *noisome* and *mephitic* are appropriate choices. The other words don't work; if you were tempted by *olfactory*, realize that it simply means "related to the sense of smell" and does not actually describe a particular scent.

16. **B** Choice (B) correctly sums up the purpose of the passage. It explores the significance—the creation of a military aristocracy and chivalric culture—of a technological innovation—the stirrup. Choice (A) is incorrect because nothing in the passage suggests that this discussion has a basis in recent discovery. Choice (C) is too broad for the limited subject matter discussed. Choice (D) is too extreme. Choice (E) is incorrect because the physics, while important in connecting the stirrup to its social effects, isn't really the point of the passage—and, in any event, the physics relates to cavalry, not artillery.

17. **E** Choice (E) is supported by the passage because the sixth sentence suggests that the development of the barbed lance serves as an "unusually clear" marker. Choice (A) is incorrect because no additional subjects for research are brought up in the passage. Choices (B) and (C) require comparisons beyond the scope of the information in the passage. No other technology, ancient or medieval, was discussed. Choice (D), finally, is an extreme overstatement. Although the stirrup increased the military value of the horse, nowhere is it suggested that it had previously been considered militarily insignificant.

18. **Stirrups unify lance, rider, and horse into a force capable of unprecedented violence.**

In this sentence, the author says that stirrups improve the ability of a lance and rider. This is an improvement on the issues discussed earlier when the author states that a "lance couched under the rider's arm, unifying the force of rider and weapon, would throw its wielder backwards off the horse at impact."

19. **D** Choice (D) describes the organization of the passage. Choice (A) can be eliminated because the traditional definition is never amended. Choice (B) can be eliminated because the authorities do not support the traditional theory. Choice (C) can be eliminated because no new definition is proposed. Choice (E) can be eliminated because the "implications of the experiment" are not rejected.

20. **A and B**

    The author's dismissal of the traditional definition of randomness rests upon the premises that the results of the same probabilistic mechanism will all have the same likelihood of occurring and, as such, should be considered equally probable. The passage never mentions how the results of different probabilistic mechanisms relate to each other, so eliminate (C).

Section 6

1. **A** Solve for x in the top equation, $\frac{x}{6} + 2 = \frac{6}{2}$, by reducing the right side: $\frac{x}{6} + 2 = 3$. Subtract 2 from both sides, and multiply both sides by 6 to find that $x = 6$. Solve for y in the second equation, $\frac{y}{3} + 2 = \frac{9}{3}$, by reducing the right side: $\frac{y}{3} + 2 = 3$. Subtract 2 from both sides, and multiply both sides by 3 to find that $y = 3$. If $x = 6$ and $y = 3$, Quantity A becomes $\frac{5}{3}$, and Quantity B becomes $\frac{2}{6} = \frac{1}{3}$.

2. **A** Use the equation *distance = rate × time*. Bob's time is 3 hours, and his rate is 44 miles per hour, so his distance is $3 \times 44 = 132$ miles. Inez's time is 2.5 hours, and her rate is 50 miles per hour, so her distance is $2.5 \times 50 = 125$ miles.

3. **A** Plug In! Let's say that the height is 10, the depth is 20, and the width is 20. If the height is increased by 20%, the new height is 12. If the depth is decreased by 20%, the new depth is 16 and the width remains 20. The new volume is $12 \times 16 \times 20 = 3,840$. If you use those same numbers but make the changes by 40%, the new volume is $14 \times 12 \times 20 = 3,360$. Quantity A is greater. However, make sure you switch the numbers to check all possibilities. Make the height 20, the depth 10 and the width 20. If p is 20, the volume of the new 3D figure is $24 \times 8 \times 20 = 3,840$. If p is 40, the volume of the new 3D figure is $28 \times 6 \times 20 = 3,360$. The quantities are the same regardless of what numbers you Plug In. The answer is (A).

4. **D** Draw the figure. Triangle ABC has two adjacent sides, AB and AC, that are equal in length. The angles that are opposite these sides, angles B and C, are also equal. One common triangle that has two equal sides is the 45 : 45 : 90 triangle. If angles B and C were both 45 degrees, then their sum would be 90 and the answer would be (C). However, you know nothing about the third side of the triangle, so it is possible that this is equal as well, which creates an equilateral triangle with angles of 60. The sum of the angles in Quantity A is now 120. You cannot determine which is greater, so the answer is (D).

5. **A** Translate: $\frac{12.5}{100}k = 80$, so $\frac{1}{8}k = 80$, and $k = 640$. Use this information in the other equation:

$k = 640 = \frac{y}{100} \times 80$, and solve for y: $y = \frac{10}{8} \times 640 = 800$. Quantity A is greater than Quantity B.

6. **D** Plug In values for each set. If $P = \{1, 2, 3, 4, 5, 6, 7\}$ and $Q = \{1, 2, 3, 4, 5, 6\}$, the range of Q is smaller. Eliminate (B) and (C). If you change P to $\{1, 2, 3, 4, 5, 7, 6\}$, and Q to $\{1, 2, 3, 4, 5, 7\}$, the range of Q is equal to that of P. Eliminate (A), and select (D).

7. **A** One way to attack this problem is to list F_1 to F_{11}: 10, 13, 16, 19, 22, 25, 28, 31, 34, 37, 40. Notice that F_6 through F_{10} are included in both quantities, so focus on what's different. Quantity A is $F_4 + F_5$ and Quantity B is F_{11}. Quantity A is $19 + 22 = 41$, and Quantity B is 40. Alternatively, you know that F_4 has had 3 changes from F_1. So, $F_4 = F_1 + 3(3) = 10 + 9 = 19$. F_5 has had 4 changes from F_1, so $F_5 = F_1 + 3(4) = 10 + 12 = 22$. F_{11} has had 10 changes from F_1, so $F_{11} = F_1 + 3(10) = 10 + 30 = 40$.

8. **C** Plug In a number for n. Let $n = 5$. Because $5 \times 6 = 30$, the product is 30. Add 24 to get 54. Divide by 3 to get 18 as your target. If you Plug In 5 for n in each answer choice, only (C) matches the target: $2n + 8 = 2(5) + 8 = 18$.

9. **10** If the average of a and b is 10, then $a + b = 20$. Likewise, if the average of c and d is 7, then $c + d = 14$. If the average of a, b, and c is 8, then $a + b + c = 24$. Because $a + b = 20$, $c = 4$. If $c = 4$, then $d = 10$.

10. **C** To find the area of a square, you need the length of a side. To find a side, find the distance between two vertices. If A is at $(3, 7)$ and B is at $(3, 12)$, then the length of a side is equivalent to the difference in the y-coordinates: $12 - 7 = 5$. So, side AB has a length of 5. Square this to find the area: $5^2 = 25$. The fact that there are variables for the y-value of points C and D is irrelevant to solving this problem.

11. **B** Get Dylan's median by putting his weekly sales into increasing order and finding the middle value. Dylan's set is $\{2, 3, 9, 10\}$, and his median is the average of 3 and 9, or 6. Next, do the same thing for Peter's sales numbers. Peter's set is $\{4, 4, 6, 10\}$, so his median is the average of 4 and 6, which is 5. The difference between the medians is $6 - 5 = 1$.

12. **A** Order doesn't matter, so remember you must divide by the factorial of the number of decisions made. For the first topping, you have 6 options. For the second topping, you have 5 options. For the third topping, you have 4 options. $\frac{6 \times 5 \times 4}{3 \times 2 \times 1} = 20$, (A).

13. **E** Because you know the perimeter of the rectangle, you can figure out that both BC and $AD = 5$. Thus, the area of the rectangle is $3 \times 5 = 15$. The area of the triangle is therefore also 15. Because the area of a triangle $= \frac{1}{2}bh$, you can put in the values you know to find $15 = \frac{1}{2}(b \times 5)$ and solve for the base, which is 6. LM is the base of the triangle, so $LM = 6$.

14. **C** From 1981 through 1984, the ratings for Program *y* were higher than they were in the previous year.

15. **E** There were 95 million times 80 percent, or 76 million, television households in 1983. Thirteen percent of them viewed Program *y*. 76 million times 13 percent (0.13) is 9.88 million, or approximately 10.

16. **A** The problem asks for the number of households that viewed both Program *x* and Program *y*, so this is a group problem. Use the group formula, which is Total = Group 1 + Group 2 – Both + Neither. Evaluate the information in the graph and the question stem to determine the values for the variables in the formula. The total is provided by the question stem, which states there were 80 million television households, so Total is equal to 80. Because this problem asks for approximates, choose numbers that are easy to work with. In 1984, approximately 15% of television households viewed Program *x*, so there were 0.15× 80 = 12 million households who viewed Program *x*. Therefore, Group 1 is 12. In 1984, approximately 14.5% of television households viewed program *y*. This is close to 15%, so use 15% again to determine that approximately 0.15 × 80 = 12 million households who viewed Program *y*. Therefore, Group 2 is 12. The problem states that 65 million television households viewed neither Program *x* nor Program *y*, so Neither is 65. Now insert all of these numbers into the group formula and solve for the value of Both. So, 80 = 12 + 12 – Both + 65 and 80 = 89 – Both, which means that –9 = – Both and Both = 9. Because the value for Program *y* was rounded up from 14.5% to 15%, this number is greater than the actual number. The only number less than 9 is 8.6. The correct answer is (A).

17. **A** Plug In the Answers, starting with (C). If Susan owns 146, Gavin owns 246, and together they own 392. Matt and Angela together would own 784, and the total number of houses would be 1,176. Choice (C) is too large, so also cross off (D) and (E). Try a smaller number. For (A), if Susan owns 46, Gavin owns 146, and together they own 192. Matt and Angela together would own 384, and the total number of houses would be 576.

18. $\dfrac{7}{45}$

Plugging In is a great way to tackle this question. Multiply the denominators of $\dfrac{1}{4}$, $\dfrac{1}{5}$, and $\dfrac{1}{3}$ together to get 60, which will be an easy number with which to work. Make the total number of cars 60. $60 \times \dfrac{1}{4}$ = 15 sports cars, and 60 – 15 = 45 sedans. The number of red cars is $60 \times \dfrac{1}{5}$ = 12. The number of red sports cars is $15 \times \dfrac{1}{3}$ = 5, which means that there are 12 – 5 = 7 red sedans. The fraction of the sedans that are red is $\dfrac{7}{45}$.

19. **A** and **B**

Plug In the Answers. Start with one of the middle values, such as (C). If there are 18 grape candies, then there are 40 total candies in the jar. The probability of selecting an orange candy is $\dfrac{8}{40}$, or 20 percent. The question states that the probability of selecting an orange candy is greater than 20 percent, so (C) cannot work. Values larger than 18 also do not work because when the denominator becomes larger than 40, the probability becomes less than 20 percent. The only choices that could work are (A) and (B).

20. **E** Plug In for k, and let $k = 3$. CE is a radius and also half of the square's diagonal. If k is 3, then CE is 3, and the diagonal is 6. The diagonal of a square is also the hypotenuse of a 45:45:90 triangle. To get the hypotenuse from a side, multiply by $\sqrt{2}$; so, to get a side from the hypotenuse, divide by $\sqrt{2}$. The sides of the square are each $\dfrac{6}{\sqrt{2}}$. To find the area, square the side to find $\left(\dfrac{6}{\sqrt{2}}\right)^2 = \dfrac{6^2}{\sqrt{2}^2} = \dfrac{36}{2} = 18$. Plug $k = 3$ into the answers to find one that yields your target of 18. Choice (E) yields the target of 18.

Appendix: Accommodated Testing

If you plan to request accommodations, you need a copy of the Testing Accommodations Request Form, which is part of the Bulletin Supplement for Test Takers with Disabilities or Health-Related Needs. The Bulletin Supplement is at www.ets.org/s/disabilities/pdf/bulletin_supplement_test_takers_with_disabilities_health_needs.pdf, or you can request it by phone at 866-387-8602 (toll-free for test takers in the United States, American Samoa, Guam, Puerto Rico, U.S. Virgin Islands and Canada) or 609-771-7780. You can also contact ETS teh following ways:

General Email Inquiries: stassd@ets.org

Requests for Testing Accomodations: disability.reg@ets.org

Mail:

ETS Disability Services
P.O. Box 6054
Princeton, NJ
08541-6054

Available accommodations include the following:

- extended testing time (There are no untimed tests.)
- additional rest breaks
- test reader
- scribe
- sign language interpreter for spoken directions only
- screen magnification
- large print
- trackball
- audio recording
- braille

This is not an exhaustive list. ETS will consider any accommodation requested for a disability or medical condition.

Processing a request for accommodations takes time, so you should submit your request as early as possible (at least six weeks before you intend to take the test). The request must include the following:

- a completed Computer-Based Test (CBT) Authorization Voucher Request form and the proper test fee
- a completed Testing Accommodations Request Form
- a Certification of Eligibility: Accommodations History (COE), which verifies your use of accommodations at your college, university, or place of employment. In some cases, the COE is sufficient to document a disability and can be used in place of sending full documentation to ETS. If you are eligible to use the COE in this way, the documentation on file with the college, university, or employer must meet all ETS documentation criteria. Please see the Bulletin Supplement for details.

- documentation (unless you are using the COE as described above)

  ○ If you have a psychiatric disability, physical disability or health-related need, traumatic brain injury, or autism spectrum disorder, you must submit documentation.

  ○ Documentation must also be submitted if your disability has been diagnosed within the last 12 months, regardless of the accommodations you are requesting.

The documentation you submit must meet the following criteria:

- clearly state the diagnosed disability

- describe the functional limitations resulting from the disability

- Be current: within the last five years for a learning disability or autism spectrum disorder, last six months for a psychiatric or physical disability or a health-related need, or last three years for other disabilities. Documentation of physical or sensory disabilities of a permanent or unchanging nature may be older if it provides all of the pertinent information.

- include complete educational, developmental, and medical history relevant to the disability

- include a list of all test instruments used in the evaluation report and all subtest, composite, and/or index scores used to document the stated disability

- describe the specific accommodations requested

- state why the disability qualifies you for the requested accommodations

- Be typed or printed on official letterhead and be signed and dated by an evaluator qualified to make the diagnosis. The report should include information about the evaluator's license or certification and area of specialization.

If you have a learning disability, ADHD, a physical disability, a psychiatric disability, a hearing loss or visual impairment, a traumatic brain injury, or an autism spectrum disorder, refer to the ETS website at www.ets.org/disabilities for specific documentation.

ETS will send you an approval letter confirming the accommodations that have been approved for you.

- **National Paper-Based Testing (PBT)**
  When you receive your approval letter, you are registered. The approval letter will identify the testing location and test administrator. If the testing center cannot accommodate your request on the scheduled testing date, you will be contacted by the test administrator to arrange an alternate test date.

- **Computer-Administered Testing (CBT)**
  The approval letter will include instructions that you must follow to schedule your test. **Do not schedule a CBT test until you receive your approval letter.** When scheduling your test, be prepared to provide the authorization/voucher number and the information contained in the letter.

- **Alternate-Format Testing**
  A representative from ETS Disability Services will contact you to confirm the accommodations approved for you and to schedule your test.

NOTES